Nature–Inspired Algorithms for Big Data Frameworks

Hema Banati
Dyal Singh College, India

Shikha Mehta
Jaypee Institute of Information Technology, India

Parmeet Kaur
Jaypee Institute of Information Technology, India

A volume in the Advances in Computational
Intelligence and Robotics (ACIR) Book Series

Published in the United States of America by
IGI Global
Engineering Science Reference (an imprint of IGI Global)
701 E. Chocolate Avenue
Hershey PA, USA 17033
Tel: 717-533-8845
Fax: 717-533-8661
E-mail: cust@igi-global.com
Web site: http://www.igi-global.com

Library of Congress Cataloging-in-Publication Data

Names: Banati, Hema, 1970- editor. | Mehta, Shikha, editor. | Kaur, Parmeet,
    1976- editor.
Title: Nature-inspired algorithms for big data frameworks / Hema Banati,
    Shikha Mehta, and Parmeet Kaur, editors.
Description: Hershey, PA : Engineering Science Reference, 2018. | Includes
    bibliographical references.
Identifiers: LCCN 2017059210| ISBN 9781522558521 (hardcover) | ISBN
    9781522558538 (ebook)
Subjects: LCSH: Evolutionary programming (Computer science) | Evolutionary
    computation. | Computer algorithms. | Big data.
Classification: LCC QA76.618 .N376 2018 | DDC 006.3/823--dc23 LC record available at https://lccn.loc.gov/2017059210

This book is published in the IGI Global book series Advances in Computational Intelligence and Robotics (ACIR) (ISSN: 2327-0411; eISSN: 2327-042X)

Advances in Computational Intelligence and Robotics (ACIR) Book Series

Ivan Giannoccaro
University of Salento, Italy

ISSN:2327-0411
EISSN:2327-042X

MISSION

While intelligence is traditionally a term applied to humans and human cognition, technology has progressed in such a way to allow for the development of intelligent systems able to simulate many human traits. With this new era of simulated and artificial intelligence, much research is needed in order to continue to advance the field and also to evaluate the ethical and societal concerns of the existence of artificial life and machine learning.

The **Advances in Computational Intelligence and Robotics (ACIR) Book Series** encourages scholarly discourse on all topics pertaining to evolutionary computing, artificial life, computational intelligence, machine learning, and robotics. ACIR presents the latest research being conducted on diverse topics in intelligence technologies with the goal of advancing knowledge and applications in this rapidly evolving field.

COVERAGE

- Computational Logic
- Artificial Intelligence
- Synthetic Emotions
- Adaptive and Complex Systems
- Fuzzy systems
- Natural Language Processing
- Agent technologies
- Heuristics
- Algorithmic Learning
- Machine Learning

IGI Global is currently accepting manuscripts for publication within this series. To submit a proposal for a volume in this series, please contact our Acquisition Editors at Acquisitions@igi-global.com or visit: http://www.igi-global.com/publish/.

Titles in this Series

For a list of additional titles in this series, please visit: www.igi-global.com/book-series

701 East Chocolate Avenue, Hershey, PA 17033, USA
Tel: 717-533-8845 x100 • Fax: 717-533-8661
E-Mail: cust@igi-global.com • www.igi-global.com

I dedicate this book to my parents for being my inspiration, my guiding light, my pillars of strength,and for being there always for me!

Hema Banati

To Teana, Ayush, and my better half for their illimitable love, support, and patience.

Shikha Mehta

To Jaskaran, Jasjit, and my parents for their love and encouragement.

Parmeet Kaur

Editorial Advisory Board

Shantanu Sharma, *Ben-Gurion University of the Negev, Israel*
Seema Shukla, *JSS Academy of Technical Education, India*
R. Sireesha, *GITAM University, India*
Rachna Soni, *Kurukshetra University, India*
Abhishek Swaroop, *Galgotia University, India*
Siba Udgata, *University of Hyderabad, India*
P. Raghu Vamsi, *Jaypee Institute of Information Technology, India*
Ankita Wadhwa, *Jaypee Institute of Information Technology, India*

Table of Contents

Section 1
Nature-Inspired Algorithms for High Dimensions

Section 2
Nature-Inspired Approaches for Complex Optimizations

Detailed Table of Contents

Section 1
Nature-Inspired Algorithms for High Dimensions

Priti Srinivas Sajja, Sardar Patel University, India
Rajendra Akerkar, Western Norway Research Institute, Norway

Traditional approaches like artificial neural networks, in spite of their intelligent support such as learning from large amount of data, are not useful for big data analytics for many reasons. The chapter discusses the difficulties while analyzing big data and introduces deep learning as a solution. This chapter discusses various deep learning techniques and models for big data analytics. The chapter presents necessary fundamentals of an artificial neural network, deep learning, and big data analytics. Different deep models such as autoencoders, deep belief nets, convolutional neural networks, recurrent neural networks, reinforcement learning neural networks, multi model approach, parallelization, and cognitive computing are discussed here, with the latest research and applications. The chapter concludes with discussion on future research and application areas.

Deepak Singh, National Institute of Technology Raipur, India
Dilip Singh Sisodia, National Institute of Technology Raipur, India
Pradeep Singh, National Institute of Technology Raipur, India

Discretization is one of the popular pre-processing techniques that helps a learner overcome the difficulty in handling the wide range of continuous-valued attributes. The objective of this chapter is to explore the possibilities of performance improvement in large dimensional biomedical data with the alliance of machine learning and evolutionary algorithms to design effective healthcare systems. To accomplish the goal, the model targets the preprocessing phase and developed framework based on a Fisher Markov feature selection and evolutionary based binary discretization (EBD) for a microarray gene expression classification. Several experiments were conducted on publicly available microarray gene expression datasets, including colon tumors, and lung and prostate cancer. The performance is evaluated for accuracy and standard deviations, and is also compared with the other state-of-the-art techniques. The experimental results show that the EBD algorithm performs better when compared to other contemporary discretization techniques.

Chapter 3

Parul Agarwal, Jaypee Institute of Information Technology, India
Shikha Mehta, Jaypee Institute of Information Technology, India

Subspace clustering approaches cluster high dimensional data in different subspaces. It means grouping the data with different relevant subsets of dimensions. This technique has become very effective as a distance measure becomes ineffective in a high dimensional space. This chapter presents a novel evolutionary approach to a bottom up subspace clustering SUBSPACE_DE which is scalable to high dimensional data. SUBSPACE_DE uses a self-adaptive DBSCAN algorithm to perform clustering in data instances of each attribute and maximal subspaces. Self-adaptive DBSCAN clustering algorithms accept input from differential evolution algorithms. The proposed SUBSPACE_DE algorithm is tested on 14 datasets, both real and synthetic. It is compared with 11 existing subspace clustering algorithms. Evaluation metrics such as F1_Measure and accuracy are used. Performance analysis of the proposed algorithms is considerably better on a success rate ratio ranking in both accuracy and F1_Measure. SUBSPACE_DE also has potential scalability on high dimensional datasets.

Chapter 4

Appavu Alias Balamurugan Subramanian, K.L.N. College of Information Technology, India

In high dimensional space finding clusters of data objects is challenging due to the curse of dimensionality. When the dimensionality increases, data in the irrelevant dimensions may produce much noise. And also, time complexity is the major issues in existing approach. In order to rectify these issues our proposed method made use of efficient feature subset selection in high dimensional data. We are considering the input dataset is the high dimensional micro array dataset. Initially, we have to select the optimal features so that our proposed technique employed Social Spider Optimization (SSO) algorithm. Here the traditional Social Spider Optimization is modified with the help of fruit fly optimization algorithm. Next the selected features are the input for the classifier. The classification is performed using optimized radial basis function based neural network (ORBFNN) technique to classify the micro array data as normal or abnormal data. The effectiveness of RBFNN is optimized by means of artificial bee colony algorithm (ABC).

Section 2
Nature-Inspired Approaches for Complex Optimizations

Chapter 5

Abhishek Ghosh Roy, IIT Kharagpur, India
Pratyusha Rakshit, Jadavpur University, India

The chapter proposes a novel optimization framework to solve the motion planning problem of non-holonomic wheeled mobile robots using swarm algorithms. The specific robotic system considered is a vehicle with approximate kinematics of a car. The configuration of this robot is represented by position and orientation of its main body in the plane and by angles of the steering wheels. Two control inputs are available for motion control including the velocity and the steering angle command. Moreover, the car-like robot is one of the simplest non-holonomic vehicles that displays the general characteristics and constrained maneuverability of systems with non-holonomicity. The control methods proposed in this chapter do not require precise mathematical modeling of every aspect a car-like system. The swarm algorithm-based motion planner determines the optimal trajectory of multiple car-like non-holonomic robots in a given arena avoiding collision with obstacles and teammates. The motion planning task has been taken care of by an adaptive bio-inspired strategy commonly known as Bat Algorithm.

Chapter 6

Sumitra Mukhopadhyay, University of Calcutta, India
Soumyadip Das, University of Calcutta, India

Spectrum sensing errors in cognitive radio may occur due to constant changes in the environment like changes in background noise, movements of the users, temperature variations, etc. It leads to under usage of available spectrum bands or may cause interference to the primary user transmission. So, sensing parameters like detection threshold are required to adapt dynamically to the changing environment to minimise sensing errors. Correct sensing requires processing huge data sets just like Big Data. This chapter investigates sensing in light of Big Data and presents the study of the nature inspired algorithms in sensing error minimisation by dynamic adaptation of the threshold value. Death penalty constrained handing techniques are integrated to the genetic algorithm, particle swarm optimisation, the firefly algorithm and the bat algorithm. Based on them, four algorithms are developed for minimizing sensing errors. The reported algorithms are found to be faster and more accurate when compared with previously proposed threshold adaptation algorithms based on a gradient descend.

Chapter 7

Prativa Agarwalla, Heritage Institute of Technology, Kolkata, India
Sumitra Mukhopadhyay, Institute of Radio Physics & Electronics, India

Microarray study has a huge impact on the proper detection and classification of cancer, as it analyzes the changes in expression level of genes which are strongly associated with cancer. In this chapter, a new weighted objective wolf-swarm colony optimization (WOWSC) technique is proposed for the selection of significant and informative genes from the cancer dataset. To extract the relevant genes from datasets, WOWSC utilizes four different objective functions in a weighted manner. Experimental analysis shows that the proposed methodology is very efficient in obtaining differential and biologically relevant genes which are effective for the classification of disease. The technique is able to generate a good subset of genes which offers more useful insight to the gene-disease association.

Chapter 8

Shikha Mehta, Jaypee Institute of Information Technology, India
Parmeet Kaur, Jaypee Institute of Information Technology, India

Workflows are a commonly used model to describe applications consisting of computational tasks with data or control flow dependencies. They are used in domains of bioinformatics, astronomy, physics, etc., for data-driven scientific applications. Execution of data-intensive workflow applications in a reasonable amount of time demands a high-performance computing environment. Cloud computing is a way of purchasing computing resources on demand through virtualization technologies. It provides the infrastructure to build and run workflow applications, which is called 'Infrastructure as a Service.' However, it is necessary to schedule workflows on cloud in a way that reduces the cost of leasing resources. Scheduling tasks on resources is a NP hard problem and using meta-heuristic algorithms is an obvious choice for the same. This chapter presents application of nature-inspired algorithms: particle swarm optimization, shuffled frog leaping algorithm and grey wolf optimization algorithm to the workflow scheduling problem on the cloud. Simulation results prove the efficacy of the suggested algorithms.

Chapter 9

Rathindra Nath Biswas, Acharya Jagadish Chandra Bose Polytechnic, India
Anurup Saha, Jadavpur University, India
Swarup Kumar Mitra, MCKV Institute of Engineering, India
Mrinal Kanti Naskar, Jadavpur University, India

An antenna pattern synthesis scheme based on particle swarm optimization (PSO) technique is proposed. Synthesized patterns always contain narrower beamwidth and minimum side-lobes level reducing coverage areas towards the attackers in wireless networks. On such patterns, deep nulls are also steered at various interfering directions as to provide a second layer of protection. Using selective patterns at each point-to-point link, data privacy is ensured throughout entire route from source to sink. This approach is simple enough to be commensurate with flexible design methods on a real-time platform. Thus, an FSM (finite state machine) rule-based digital system model is further developed and tested on Xilinx Virtex4 FPGA (field programmable gate array) board. Its performance under harsh radio environmental conditions is also verified with several fixed-point simulations in terms of pattern synthesis accuracy and computational overheads. These results corroborate such system integration onto wireless infrastructures for the secured data communication services.

Chapter 10

Ajay Kaushik, Delhi Technological University, India
S. Indu, Delhi Technological University, India
Daya Gupta, Delhi Technological University, India

Wireless sensor networks (WSNs) are becoming increasingly popular due to their applications in a wide variety of areas. Sensor nodes in a WSN are battery operated which outlines the need of some novel protocols that allows the limited sensor node battery to be used in an efficient way. The authors propose the use of nature-inspired algorithms to achieve energy efficient and long-lasting WSN. Multiple nature-inspired techniques like BBO, EBBO, and PSO are proposed in this chapter to minimize the energy consumption in a WSN. A large amount of data is generated from WSNs in the form of sensed information which encourage the use of big data tools in WSN domain. WSN and big data are closely connected since the large amount of data emerging from sensors can only be handled using big data tools. The authors describe how the big data can be framed as an optimization problem and the optimization problem can be effectively solved using nature-inspired algorithms.

Chapter 11
    Abhishek Ghosh Roy, IIT Kharagpur, India
    Naba Kumar Peyada, IIT Kharagpur, India

Application of adaptive neuro fuzzy inference system (ANFIS)-based particle swarm optimization (PSO) algorithm to the problem of aerodynamic modeling and optimal parameter estimation for aircraft has been addressed in this chapter. The ANFIS-based PSO optimizer constitutes the aircraft model in restricted sense capable of predicting generalized force and moment coefficients employing measured motion and control variables only, without formal requirement of conventional variables or their time derivatives. It has been shown that such an approximate model can be used to extract equivalent stability and control derivatives of a rigid aircraft.

Section 3
Nature-Inspired Solutions for Web Analytics

Chapter 12
    Ruchi Mittal, Netaji Subhas Institute of Technology, India
    M. P. S. Bhatia, Netaji Subhas Institute of Technology, India

Many real-life social networks are having multiple types of interaction among entities; thus, this organization in networks builds a new scenario called multiplex networks. Community detection, centrality measurements are the trendy area of research in multiplex networks. Community detection means identifying the highly connected groups of nodes in the network. Centrality measures indicate evaluating the importance of a node in a given network. Here, the authors propose their methodologies to compute the eigenvector centrality of nodes to find out the most influential nodes in the network and present their study on finding communities from multiplex networks. They combine a few popular nature-inspired algorithms with multiplex social networks to do the above tasks. The authors' experiments provide a deep insight into the various properties of the multiplex network. They compare the proposed methodologies with several alternative methods and get encouraging and comparable results.

Chapter 13
    Mukta Goyal, Jaypee Institute of Information Technology, India
    Rajalakshmi Krishnamurthi, Jaypee Institute of Information Technology, India

Due to the emerging e-learning scenario, there is a need for software agents to teach individual users according to their skill. This chapter introduces software agents for intelligent tutors for personalized learning of English. Software agents teach a user English on the aspects of reading, translation, and writing. Software agents help user to learn English through recognition and synthesis of human voice and helps users to improve on handwriting. Its main objective is to understand what aspect of the language users wants to learn. It deals with the intuitive nature of users' learning styles. To enable this feature, intelligent soft computing techniques have been used.

Chapter 14

Anuja Arora, Jaypee Institute of Information Technology, India
Aman Srivastava, Haptik Inc., India
Shivam Bansal, Exzeo Software Private Limited, India

The conventional approach to build a chatbot system uses the sequence of complex algorithms and productivity of these systems depends on order and coherence of algorithms. This research work introduces and showcases a deep learning-based conversation system approach. The proposed approach is an intelligent conversation model approach which conceptually uses graph model and neural conversational model. The proposed deep learning-based conversation system uses neural conversational model over knowledge graph model in a hybrid manner. Graph-based model answers questions written in natural language using its intent in the knowledge graph and neural conversational model converses answer based on conversation content and conversation sequence order. NLP is used in graph model and neural conversational model uses natural language understanding and machine intelligence. The neural conversational model uses seq2seq framework as it requires less feature engineering and lacks domain knowledge. The results achieved through the authors' approach are competitive with solely used graph model results.

Chapter 15

Pavani Konagala, Vaagdevi College of Engineering, India

A large volume of data is stored electronically. It is very difficult to measure the total volume of that data. This large amount of data is coming from various sources such as stock exchange, which may generate terabytes of data every day, Facebook, which may take about one petabyte of storage, and internet archives, which may store up to two petabytes of data, etc. So, it is very difficult to manage that data using relational database management systems. With the massive data, reading and writing from and into the drive takes more time. So, the storage and analysis of this massive data has become a big problem. Big data gives the solution for these problems. It specifies the methods to store and analyze the large data sets. This chapter specifies a brief study of big data techniques to analyze these types of data. It includes a wide study of Hadoop characteristics, Hadoop architecture, advantages of big data and big data eco system. Further, this chapter includes a comprehensive study of Apache Hive for executing health-related data and deaths data of U.S. government.

Preface

The spread of digital revolution has brought a deluge of data in almost every domain, be it; ecommerce, social networks, gaming, stock markets or mobile wearable sensors, to name a few. Also referred to as Information era, this era is witnessing generation of large volume of data which needs to be processed and further analyzed for filtering domain-specific information critical for business decisions. Conventional approaches to data analytics and computing are insufficient in handling the volume and complexity of data generated by the present day pervasive and ubiquitous applications. Extraction of meaningful information from data requires algorithms that are capable of handling the constraints of processing time, memory usage, dynamic and unstructured nature of data.

Nature-inspired algorithms provide a potential efficient solution for addressing the challenges of processing and analyzing high volumes of data. Techniques such as particle swarm optimization, ant colony optimization, bat algorithm etc., which take inspiration from real life behaviour of natural phenomenon or living beings have effectively provided near optimal solutions for a number of large-scale, dynamic and multi-objective problems. These algorithms can be used for mining complex patterns from data, dealing with heterogeneous or high dimensional data, handling the high dynamicity of real-time data. The significance of the work in this direction increases where raw data is largely unlabeled and un-categorized. Role of nature-inspired machine learning techniques for optimization and learning involving data intensive applications are interesting areas of study.

This book focuses on application of nature-inspired algorithms for handling issues and challenges posed by big data in diverse environments. The objective is to highlight the usability and performance measures of these techniques in dealing with data related problems of emerging areas. The book presents innovative techniques, cutting-edge systems and novel applications supported by experimental results that reflect the current advances in these domains.

The book is intended as a research guide for graduate students as well as researchers in this field. The issue will benefit practitioners to understand and disseminate the current state of art and advances in the field to the interested readers and researchers. The theme of the book is in synch with the latest technologies, systems and applications which can be of immense benefit to solve research problems in diverse domains.

The work presented in the book is divided in three main sections. Handling high dimensional data forms the thrust area of the chapters in Section 1. This section, Chapters 1-4, presents nature-inspired solutions for clustering, classification and analysis of high dimensional data. Chapters in Section 2, Chapters 5-11, provide an insight as to how natural inspired techniques can be optimally applied for complex optimizations in varied domains such as gene selection, workflow handling, error optimisation, etc. Section 3, Chapters 12-15, looks into the nature-inspired solutions for web analytics. The chapters in this section tap nature-inspired algorithms for analyzing the massive amount of data available in varied domains such as e-learning, or online social interaction

Chapter 1, "Deep Learning for Big Data Analytics," discusses the difficulties while analyzing big data and introduces deep learning as a solution. This chapter discusses various deep learning techniques and models for big data analytics. The chapter presents necessary fundamentals on artificial neural network, deep learning and big data analytics. Different deep models such as autoencoders, deep belief nets, convolutional neural networks, recurrent neural networks, reinforcement learning neural networks, multi model approach, parallelization, and cognitive computing are discussed comprehensively with latest research and applications.

Discretization is one of the popular pre-processing techniques that helps a learner overcome the difficulty of handling wide range of continuous-valued attributes. The chapter "Genetic Algorithm-Based Pre-Processing Strategy for High Dimensional Micro-Array Gene Classification: Application of Nature-Inspired Intelligence" explores the possibilities of performance improvement for large dimensional biomedical data. To accomplish the goal, the model targeted the preprocessing phase and developed framework based on Fisher Markov feature selection and evolutionary based binary discretization (EBD) for microarray gene expression classification. The experimental results indicate that EBD algorithm performs better compared to other contemporary discretization technique.

Subspace clustering approach clusters high dimensional data in different subspaces. This technique is more effective than distance measure in high dimensional space. Chapter 3, "Subspace Clustering of High Dimensional Data Using Differential Evolution," presents a novel evolutionary approach to bottom up subspace clustering SUBSPACE_DE which is scalable to high dimensional data. SUBSPACE_DE uses self-adaptive DBSCAN algorithm to perform clustering in data instances of each attribute and maximal subspaces. Self-adaptive DBSCAN clustering algorithm accepts its input from differential evolution algorithm. Performance analysis of presented algorithm established its supremacy over the contemporary algorithms and potential scalability on high dimensional datasets.

In high dimensional space, finding clusters of data objects is challenging due to the curse of dimensionality. When the dimensionality increases, data in the irrelevant dimensions may produce much noise. Time complexity is another related and significant issue. Chapter 4, "Nature-Inspired Feature Selector for Effective Data Classification in Big Data Frameworks," proposes to address these issues by making use of efficient feature subset selection in high dimensional data. The approach employs a modification of Social Spider Optimization (SSO) algorithm with the help of fruit fly optimization algorithm, to select the optimal features. The selected features form the input for the classifier. The classification is performed using optimized radial basis function based neural network (ORBFNN) technique to classify the micro array data as normal or abnormal data. The effectiveness of RBFNN is optimized by means of artificial bee colony algorithm (ABC).

Section 2 provides an interesting insight into the diverse ways in which Nature-inspired techniques can be employed for solving problems in varied domains. One such interesting application is the focus of Chapter 5. The chapter, "Motion Planning of Non-Holonomic Wheeled Robots Using Modified Bat Algorithm," proposes a novel optimization framework to solve the motion planning problem of non-holonomic wheeled mobile robots using swarm algorithms. The specific robotic system considered is a vehicle with approximate kinematics of a car. The configuration of this robot is represented by position and orientation of its main body in the plane and by angles of the steering wheels. Two control inputs are available for motion control including the velocity and the steering angle command. The control methods proposed in this chapter do not require precise mathematical modelling of every aspect a car-like system. The swarm algorithm-based motion planner determines the optimal trajectory of multiple car-like non-holonomic robots in a given arena avoiding collision with obstacles and teammates. The motion planning task has been taken care of by an adaptive bio-inspired strategy commonly known as Bat Algorithm.

Another interesting application of nature-inspired algorithm is presented in Chapter 6, applying nature-inspired algorithm for spectrum sensing. Spectrum sensing error in cognitive radio may occur due to constant changes in the environment like changes in background noise, movements of the users, temperature variations, etc. It leads to under usage of available spectrum bands or may cause interference to the primary user transmission. Hence, the sensing parameters like detection threshold are required to be changed dynamically to adapt to the changing environment to minimise sensing error. Correct sensing requires processing huge data sets, in other words, Big Data. Chapter 6, "Application of Nature-Inspired Algorithms for Sensing Error Optimization in Dynamic Environment," investigates sensing in the light of Big Data and presents the study of the nature-inspired algorithms in sensing error minimisation by dynamic adaptation of threshold value. Death penalty constrained handing technique is integrated to genetic algorithm, particle swarm optimisation, firefly algorithm and bat algorithm. Based on them, four algorithms are developed for sensing error minimisation. The reported algorithms are found to be faster and more accurate when compared with the previously proposed threshold adaptation algorithm based on gradient descent.

Yet another significant domain where applicability of nature-inspired algorithms is being explored is the medical domain. Chapter 7 explores wolf-swarm colony algorithm for the same. The chapter, "Wolf-Swarm Colony for Signature Gene Selection Using Weighted Objective Method," proposes a new weighted objective wolf-swarm colony optimization (WOWSC) technique for the selection of significant and informative genes from the cancer dataset. To extract the relevant genes from datasets, WOWSC utilizes four different objective functions in a weighted manner. Experimental analysis revealed that the proposed methodology can efficiently obtain differential and biologically relevant genes, effective for the classification of disease. The technique is able to generate a good subset of genes which offers more useful insight to the gene-disease association.

Workflows are a commonly used model to describe applications consisting of computational tasks with data or control flow dependencies. They are used in domains as Bioinformatics, astronomy, Physics etc., for data driven scientific applications. Execution of data intensive workflow applications in a reasonable amount of time demands a high-performance computing environment. Cloud computing provides the infrastructure to build and run workflow applications; called 'Infrastructure as a Service'.

However, it is necessary to schedule workflows on cloud in a way that reduces the cost of leasing resources. Scheduling tasks on resources is a NP hard problem and using meta-heuristic algorithms is an obvious choice for the same. Chapter 8, "Scheduling Data Intensive Scientific Workflows in Cloud Environment Using Nature-Inspired Algorithms," presents application of nature-inspired algorithms: particle swarm optimization, shuffled frog leaping algorithm and grey wolf optimization algorithm to the workflow scheduling problem on cloud.

Chapter 9 presents an antenna pattern synthesis scheme based on particle swarm optimization (PSO) technique. The chapter, "PSO-Based Antenna Pattern Synthesis: A Paradigm for Secured Data Communications," works on the issue of data privacy. Synthesized patterns always contain narrower beam width and minimum side-lobes level reducing coverage areas towards the attackers in wireless networks. On such patterns, deep nulls are also steered at various interfering directions as to provide a second layer of protection. Using selective patterns at each point-to-point link, data privacy is ensured throughout entire route from source to sink. A FSM (finite state machine) rule based digital system model is developed and tested on Xilinx Virtex4 FPGA (field programmable gate array) board.

Wireless sensor networks (WSNs) are becoming increasingly popular and a large amount of data is generated from wireless sensor networks in the form of sensed information which encourages the use of big data tools in WSN domain. WSN and Big data are closely connected since the large amount of data emerging from sensors can only be handled using big data tools. Chapter 10, "Nature-Inspired Algorithms in Wireless Sensor Networks," proposes the use of nature-inspired algorithms to achieve energy efficient and long lasting WSN. Multiple nature-inspired techniques like BBO, EBBO and PSO are proposed in this chapter to minimize the energy consumption in a WSN. The chapter describes how handling of big data can be framed as an optimization problem and the optimization problem can be effectively solved using nature-inspired algorithms.

Chapter 11, "Aircraft Aerodynamic Parameter Estimation Using Intelligent Estimation Algorithms," presents an application of Adaptive Neuro Fuzzy Inference System ANFIS based particle swarm optimization PSO algorithm to the problem of aerodynamic modelling and optimal parameter estimation for aircraft. The ANFIS based PSO optimizer constitutes the aircraft model in restricted sense capable of predicting generalized force and moment coefficients employing measured motion and control variables only, without formal requirement of conventional variables or their time derivatives. The work indicates that such an approximate model can be used to extract equivalent stability and control derivatives of a rigid aircraft.

Social networks form the backbone of all online social interactions. Many real-life social networks have multiple types of interaction among entities; leading to a new scenario in networks called multiplex networks. Chapter 12, "Analysis of Multiplex Social Networks Using Nature-Inspired Algorithms," employs few popular nature-inspired algorithms to explore multiplex social networks. The work computes the eigenvector centrality of nodes to find out the most influential nodes in the network and present a study on finding communities from multiplex networks.

The emerging e-learning scenario recognizes need of software agents to teach individual user according to their skill. Chapter 13, "Pedagogical Software Agents for Personalized E-Learning Using Soft Computing Techniques," introduces software agent for intelligent tutor towards personalised learning of English. It deals with the intuitive nature of user's learning style. The software agents teach, a user, English on the aspects of reading, translation and writing. The objective is to understand the aspect of the language a user wants to learn. To enable this feature the chapter employs intelligent soft computing techniques.

Chapter 14 introduces and showcases a deep learning-based conversation system approach. The chapter, "An Intelligent Graph and Neural Network-Based Intelligent Conversation System," presents an intelligent conversation model approach which conceptually uses graph model and neural conversational model. The proposed deep learning-based conversation system uses neural conversational model over knowledge graph model in a hybrid manner. Graph based model answers questions written in natural language using its intent in the knowledge graph and neural conversational model converses answer based on conversation content and conversation sequence order. NLP is used in graph model and neural conversational model uses natural language understanding and machine intelligence. The neural conversational model uses seq2seq framework as it requires less feature engineering and lacks domain knowledge. The results achieved are competitive with solely used graph model results.

The last chapter of the book presents a brief study of big data techniques. Chapter 15, "Big Data Analytics Using Apache Hive to Analyze Health Data," includes a wide study of Hadoop characteristics, Hadoop architecture, advantages of Big Data and Big Data Eco system. Further, this chapter includes the comprehensive study of Apache Hive for executing health-related data and Deaths data of U.S. government.

Acknowledgment

The editors wish to acknowledge the support of everyone involved in this book's journey from a vision to reality. This book could not have been completed timely without their encouragement and valuable assistance.

The editors would like to express their gratitude to all authors for their contributions. This book is a combined effort of various experts in the field of nature inspired computing. Knowledge is not accumulated in a single day. We acknowledge that the chapters which have been provided to us by our expert authors are not the output of a single frame of time. It is the result of the various years of their effort in the respective domain. We acknowledge their expertise as well as time and effort contributed towards this book.

Our sincere thanks are also for the reviewers who made immensely constructive and effective efforts with regard to quality, readability and content of the book's chapters. Some of our authors also reviewed others' chapters and we thank them for their valuable time and efforts. Words cannot express our sincere thanks to all of them without whose timely comments, this book would have not have taken its current shape.

We would also like to thank the development editors and their team from IGI Global for their kind help and prompt responses throughout the book's publishing. In particular our journey as editors of this book would not have been possible without the valuable inputs and guidance from (Ms) Jan Travers, Director of Intellectual Property and Contract, and Ms. Jordan Tepper, Assistant Development Editor, IGI Global.

We are also thankful to our organizations – Dyal Singh College, University of Delhi, Delhi and Jaypee Institute of Information Technology, Noida; for providing us the logistics required to complete this project.

Last but not the least; we are thankful to our family members for their boundless love, support and motivation during the whole journey of this project.

Hema Banati
University of Delhi, India

Shikha Mehta
Jaypee Institute of Information Technology, India

Parmeet Kaur
Jaypee Institute of Information Technology, India

Section 1
Nature–Inspired Algorithms for High Dimensions

Chapter 1
Deep Learning for Big Data Analytics

Priti Srinivas Sajja
Sardar Patel University, India

Rajendra Akerkar
Western Norway Research Institute, Norway

ABSTRACT

Traditional approaches like artificial neural networks, in spite of their intelligent support such as learning from large amount of data, are not useful for big data analytics for many reasons. The chapter discusses the difficulties while analyzing big data and introduces deep learning as a solution. This chapter discusses various deep learning techniques and models for big data analytics. The chapter presents necessary fundamentals of an artificial neural network, deep learning, and big data analytics. Different deep models such as autoencoders, deep belief nets, convolutional neural networks, recurrent neural networks, reinforcement learning neural networks, multi model approach, parallelization, and cognitive computing are discussed here, with the latest research and applications. The chapter concludes with discussion on future research and application areas.

INTRODUCTION

Deep learning refers to a kind of machine learning techniques in which several stages of non-linear information processing in hierarchical architectures are utilized for pattern classification and for feature learning. Recently, it also involves a hierarchy of features or concepts where higher-level concepts are defined from lower-level ones and where the same lower-level concepts help to define higher-level ones. With the enormous amount of data available today, big data brings new opportunities for various sectors; in contrast, it also presents exceptional challenges to utilize data. Here deep learning plays a key role in providing big data analytics solutions. The chapter discusses in brief fundamentals of big data analytics, neural network, deep learning. Further, models of deep learning are analyzed with their issues and limitations along with possible applications. Summary of the literature review is also provided in this chapter. Further, future possible enhancements are also listed in the domain. This chapter is organized as follows.

DOI: 10.4018/978-1-5225-5852-1.ch001

Section 1 introduces various fundamental topics such as big data analytics, artificial neural network, and deep learning. Section 2 highlights big data analytics by discussing large scale optimization, high dimensional data handling, and handling dynamic data. Section 3 discusses different deep models such as autoencoders, deep belief nets, deep convolutional neural networks, recurrent neural networks, reinforcement learning neural networks, multi model approach, parallelization, and cognitive computing with latest research and applications. Section 4 discusses some successful applications of deep learning for big data analytics. Section 5 discusses the issues and problems with the deep learning. Section 6 concludes the paper with summary and provides discussion on the work done so far and future research and application areas in the domain.

Big Data Analytics

Data word came from 'Datumn' which means 'thing given'. It has been used since early 1500 i.e. since beginning of computing. With the evolution of computing technology, the word has become more popular. Data are raw observations from domain of interest. It can be collection of numbers, words, measurements, or textual description of things. Obviously, data is everywhere and serves as an important base for business related decision making. It is also said that data is currency of knowledge as it provides basis of reasoning and analysis. Every business generates lots of data, which further act as a good resource to analyze, understand and improve the business. It is really an irony that the data which can help in improving quality of business makes the life miserable just because of our limitations to understand and use it properly. Such data creates a big problem due to its size, unstructuredness and redundancy. Some researchers identify the parameters like volume, velocity and variety as main reasons of the problem to handle data. According to Eric Horvitz and Tom Mitchell (2010) and James Manyika et al., (2011) such data when analyzed and used properly, offers a chance to solve problems, accelerates economic growth, and improve quality of life.

Big data is also a kind of data but big enough to handle. For example, consider a medical store having cough syrup bottles on shelves. The labels on the bottles show medicine name, type, components, batch number and expiry date. These data are very structured, small in amount (even for thousands of bottles in many batches, and such many medicines in the store) and homogeneous in nature. On the other hand, why the particular medicine expires so early requires really a big amount of data (and big amount of time and effort also). Such big data can act as a good resource to increase productivity and hence improves businesses in terms of quality, brand image and customer surplus. Effective use of big data can be one of the key factors of competition and growth for individual firm. It is predicted that by 2018, the United States alone could face a shortage of 140,000 to 190,000 people with deep analytical skills as well as 1.5 million managers and analysts with the know-how to use the analysis of big data to make effective decisions (Manyika, et al., 2011).

Big data handling encompasses activities in five dimensions. The first step is the data procurement, where data are identified and procured as per the requirement and available sources. Prior to the data collection, it is required to have proper vision and plan to make sure that how these data will be handled and what are the expectations. The volume, velocity and variety of the data make these procedures more challenging. Since the data is big, procurement would not be an easy job. It may leave some gap and results in missing data. To compensate the gap, data processing is needed, which is the second step. One may use soft computing techniques (such as fuzzy logic) to predict the missing data and fill in the gap. Next step is to find out a proper representation scheme so that the complete set of data can be presented and preserved in a suitable format. This phase is known as data curation. The word curation comes from the concept that valuable artifacts are preserved in a museum and the museum curator preserves and facilitates artifact for further use such as analysis. Here, data curators do this job. Most of the time, the data are represented into electronic form to facilitate efficient analysis. Otherwise, due to volume of data, it is very difficult to analyze them manually. After proper representation of data, the data are ready to be analyzed. Further, the data and the analysis made can be presented in visual forms. Figure 1 represents the four dimensional activities to manage big data.

For different activities in these five dimensions, many tools are used. Statistical tools, mathematical tools, soft computing and machine learning tools, etc. can be used to manage different activities related to the big data.

Artificial Neural Network

Artificial Neural Network (ANN) is a methodology that mimics the working of nervous system in a narrow domain. Basic component of a neural network is neuron. ANN generally have many neurons connected with each other in a predefined order and are capable of learning (from the data or without data) using various paradigms. Hopfield model with parallel relaxation learning, perceptron with fixed increment learning, multi-layer perceptron with back propagation learning and Kohenon with unsupervised learning are a few popular models with the respective learning algorithm. There are many situations where data is available but it is really difficult to derive generalize logic from the data. In this case, ANNs help most.

The typical multiplayer neural networks, particularly multi-layer perceptron, consist of one (or at most two) hidden layer(s) with input and output layer. If there is no hidden layer, it can solve only linearly

Figure 1. Five dimensional activities in big data management

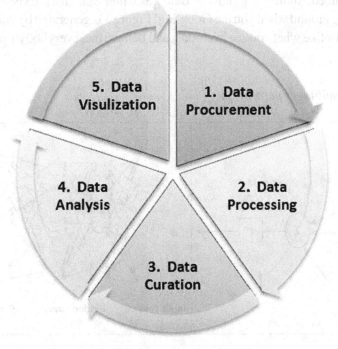

separable problems as illustrated in first part of the Figure 2. If there is one hidden layer, the ANN can approximate a function that having a continuous mapping from one finite space to another. If there are two hidden layers it can approximate any smooth mapping to any accuracy. The hidden layers do not interact with the external interface, but they can influence the working of ANN. Rather, introduction of the hidden layer helps the network to exhibit non-linear behavior. Figure 2 illustrates structure of multiplayer perceptron with one hidden layer.

Such typical (or shallow) neural network works well and remarkably useful for standard applications. Adding more hidden layers can help learning in perfect non-linear manner, but simultaneously it over fits the network and increase the issues related to efficiency. That is, the earlier layers can learn better, but learning later layer may get stuck.

Deep Learning

Deep Learning is a technique of machine learning that consists of many hierarchical layers to process the information in'non-linear manner, where some lower level concepts help to define the higher level concepts. Deep learning is defined as "Deep neural networks contain multiple non-linear hidden layers and this makes them very expressive models that can learn very complicated relationships between their inputs and outputs…" by Nitish Srivastava et al., (2014). The shallow artificial neural network, as stated above are not capable of handling big amount of complex data, which are obvious in many mundane applications such as natural speech, images, information retrieval and other human like information processing applications. Deep learning is suggested for such applications. With deep learning, it is possible to recognize, classify and categorize patterns in data for a machine with comparatively less efforts. A word 'less engineering labor' is used by Mark Bergen (2015) to mention less effort by machines. He further stated at the same source that the deep learning enables the process to unfold huge reams of previously unmanageable data. Google is pioneer to experiment deep learning, which is initiated by the Stanford Computer Scientist named Andrew Ng (now at Baidu as Chief Scientist). Experiment Google's "deep dream" images floating around when you are Googling! Figure 3 is generated by Google (On Circulation, n.d.). The concept is just like what you see in clouds; and believe me, everybody's perception is different.

Figure 2. Single and multilayer perceptron

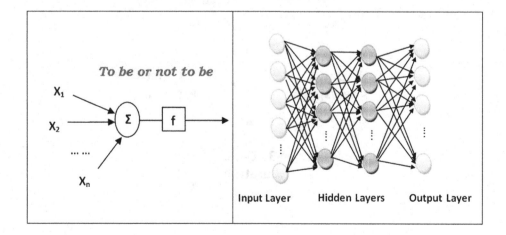

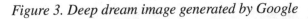

Figure 3. Deep dream image generated by Google

Deep learning offers human like multi layered processing in comparison with the shallow architecture. The basic idea of deep learning is to employ hierarchical processing using many layers of architecture. The layers of the architecture are arranged hierarchically. Each layer's input is provided to its adjacent layer after some pre-training. Most of the time, such pre-training of a selected layer is done in unsupervised manner. Deep learning follows distributed approach to manage big data. The approach assumes that the data are generated considering various factors, different time and various levels. Deep learning facilitates arrangement and processing of the data into different layers according to its time (occurrence), its level, or nature. Deep learning is often associated with artificial neural network.

There are three categories of deep learning architectures namely (i) generative, (ii) discriminative, and (iii) hybrid deep learning architectures (Deng, 2014). Architectures belong to the generative category focus on pre-training of a layer in unsupervised manner. This approach eliminates the difficulty of training the lower level architectures, which relay on the previous layers. Each layer can be pre-trained and later included into the model for further general tuning and learning. Doing this resolves the problem of training neural network architecture with multiple layers and enables deep learning. Neural network architecture may have discriminative processing ability by stacking output of each layer with the original data or by various information combinations and thus forming deep learning architecture. According to Li Deng (2014) the descriptive model often considers the neural network outputs as conditional distribution over all possible label sequences for the given input sequence, which will be optimized further through an objective function. The hybrid architecture combines the properties of the generative and discriminative architecture. The typical structure and mechanism of deep learning ANN is shown in Figure 4. The typical deep learning can be done as follows.

- Construct a network consisting of an input layer and a hidden layer with necessary nodes.
- Train the network.
- Add another hidden layer on the top of the previously learned network to generate a new network.

Figure 4. ANN for deep learning

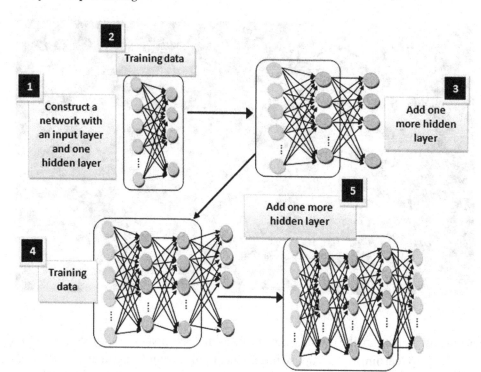

- Re-train the network.
- Repeat adding more layers and after every addition, retrain the network.

ANALYZING BIG DATA

The big data analytics is required to manage huge amounts of data efficiently. The major aspects that can be considered while dealing with big data are large scale optimization, high dimensional data handling and dynamical data handling.

Large Scale Optimization

Optimization deals with finding the most effective solution to the problems using well defined procedures and models. Everybody deals with the problem of optimization either in direct (systematic) way or indirect (informal) way. The problems which need optimization include travelling salesperson problem, selecting a course from available courses under given stream (say science stream) and level (12th grade), e-commerce activities (selection of best mobile through various online shopping sites), etc.

Optimization helps in finding the cost-effective alternatives to perform the task. Commonly, it is considered as maximization or minimization of a function of resources. Some examples are maximization of profit, minimization of cost and errors. For domains with finite dimension, various models for such problem are available; however, when it comes to the big data, task of optimization becomes challenging. In case of the big data, not only the size of transactions is voluminous, but the number of variables and number of constraints are also high. On the contrary, sometime data and constraints are moderate but their structure is complex. Such complexity in the structure increases difficulty of applying current methods on them. For example, feature learning from the large repository of medical images in optimum manner will be difficult with support of the traditional method. Further, it would require manual tuning of some parameters. Besides traditional approaches, machine learning and parallel optimization methods are also becoming popular. Some traditional methods for the optimization methods are Newton-Raphson's method, Broyden–Fletcher–Goldfarb–Shanno (BFGS) method, conjugate gradient method and stochastic gradient descent method and stochastic gradient descent method (SGD). Many researchers have worked in this domain (Dean & Ghemawat, 2008), (Chu, et al., 2007), (Teo, Le, Smola, & Vishwanathan, 2007), (Mann, McDonald, Mohri, Silberman, & Walker, 2009), (Zinkevich, Weimer, Smola, & Li, 2010). In the work of Jeffrey Dean, et al., (2012), a problem of training a deep network with billions of parameters using tens of thousands of CPU cores is discussed. The model is successfully tested on large repository of image and then on speech recognition application. Experiments on Speech recognition was also carried out using the deep learning approachfor large scale optimization by George Dahl, et al., (2012) and Geoffrey Hinton, et al., (2012). Yann Dauphin, et al., (2014) have also used deep learning for efficient optimization.

High Dimensional Data Handling

Complexity increases when the problem has more dimensions. Limited dimension of the problem makes the problem easy to solve, however, the solution is not powerful and does not provide any high-level knowledge. Increased number of dimensions results in tremendous growth of data which are difficult to handle, visualize and solve. It is said that due to exponential growth of number of possible values with each dimension, complete enumeration of all subspaces becomes intractable with increased dimensionality, which is known as the curse of dimensionality. Deep learning will be helpful in managing such high dimensional data and help in clustering, processing and visualizing such data. Bio informatics, sensor web, vision and speech recognition are fields where one can find such high dimensional data. Deep learning models are used for managing such high dimensional data (Krizhevsky, Sutskever, & Hinton, 2012), (Hinton, et al., 2012). Deep learning technique is also useful in extracting meaningful representations besides dimensionality reduction (Bengio, Courville, & Vincent, 2013). Yann Le Cun, et al., (2015) have also documented and proved the utility of deep learning technology to handle high dimensional data in various fields such as industry, business and research.

Handling Dynamical Data

Besides the volume and structure, time is another major factor that increases the complexity in the data and hence makes the job of managing data more difficult. Dynamic data are varying in terms of size, volume, and underlying structure. Large scale and dynamic data are generated and manipulated in many areas such as fluid dynamics, material science, modular dynamics and bio-inspired systems. An example domain is human speech generation. Human speech generation follows hierarchical structure. Deep learning would be useful in modeling structured speech. Researchers like Li Deng, et al., (2013) and Sabato Marco Siniscalchi, et al., (2013) have claimed that such models are really deeper and effective than the existing solutions. Deep learning is also useful in managing hidden dynamic models as well as network also (Carneiro & Nascimento, 2013). While creating a neural network with an aim to learn deep, a node of the network can also be created dynamically. This approach can handle the afore-mentioned aspect of the dynamic input data. Such approach is experimented long back by Timur Ash (1989). Deep neural network approach is also used by Itamar Arel, et al., (2009) for dynamic pattern representation in combining various concepts in unsupervised manner. Researchers have used the deep learning approach to handle log time gaps between events using the non-linear and adaptive extensions (Mozer, 1989), (Hihi & Bengio, 1996).

DIFFERENT DEEP MODELS

This section introduces various models of deep learning.

Autoencoders

An autoencoder is an artificial neural network capable of learning various coding patterns. The simple form of the autoencoder is just like the multilayer perceptron containing an input layer, one or more hidden layers, and an output layer. The major difference between the typical multilayer perceptron and feed forward neural network and autoencoder is in the number of nodes at the output layer. In case of the autoencoder, the output layer contains same number of nodes as in the input layer. Instead of predicting target values as per the output vector, the autoencoder has to predict its own inputs. The broad outline of the learning mechanism is as follows.

For each input x,

- Do a feed-forward pass to compute activation functions provided at all the hidden layers and output layers.
- Find the deviation between the calculated values with the inputs using appropriate error function.
- Back propagate the error in order to update weights.

Repeat the task till satisfactory output.

If the number of nodes in the hidden layers is fewer than the input/output nodes, then the activations of the last hidden layer are considered as a compressed representation of the inputs. When the hidden layer nodes are more than the input layer, an autoencoder can potentially learn the identity function and become useless in majority of the cases. The classic use of the autoencoder is described by Li Deng, et al., (2010).

Deep Belief Net

Deep belief network is a solution to the problem of handling non-convex objective functions and local minima while using the typical multilayer perceptron. The concept of the deep belief network was first suggested by Geoffrey Hinton, et al., (2006). This is an alternative type of deep learning consisting of multiple layers of latent variables with connection between the layers. The deep belief network can be viewed as Restricted Boltzmann Machines (RBM) where each sub-network's hidden layer acts as the visible input layer for the adjacent layer of the network. It makes the lowest visible layer training set for the adjacent layer of the network. This way, each layer of the network is trained independently and greedily. The hidden variables are used as the observed variables to train each layer of the deep structure. The training algorithm for such deep belief network is provided as follows.

- Consider a vector of inputs.
- Train a restricted Boltzmann machine using the input vector and obtain the weight matrix.
- Train the lower two layers of the network using this weight matrix.
- Generate new input vector by using the network (RBM) through sampling or mean activation of the hidden units.
- Repeat the procedure till the top two layers of the network are reached.

The fine tuning of the deep belief network is very similar to the multilayer perceptron. Such deep belief networks are useful in acoustic modeling (Mohamed, Dahl, & Hinton, 2012), speech recognition (Mohamed, Yu, & Deng, 2010), phone recognition (Mohamed, Dahl, & Hinton, 2009) and other hierarchical process requiring deep learning.

Convolutional Neural Networks

Convolutional neural network is another variant of the feed forward multilayer perceptron. It is a type of feed forward neural network, where the individual neurons are arranged in such a way that they respond to overlapping regions in the visual field. Such network follows the visual mechanism of the living organisms. The cells in the visual cortex are sensitive to small sub-regions of the visual field, called a receptive field. The sub-regions are arranged to cover the entire visual field and the cells act as local filters over the input space. According to David Hubel and Torsten Wiesel (1968) such cells are well-suited to exploit the strong spatially local correlation present in natural images. Earlier, similar approach had been used for recognition of hand written characters called neocognitron. According to Yann Le Cun, et al., (2015), the neocognitron is considered as a predecessor of the convolutional networks. Back-propagation algorithm is used to train the parameters of each convolution kernel. Further, each kernel is replicated over the entire image with the same parameters. There are convolutional operators which extract different features of the input. Besides the convolutional layer, the network contains rectified linear unit layer, pooling layers to compute the max or average value of a particular feature over a region of the image, and a loss layer consisting of application specific loss functions. Image recognition and video analysis and natural language processing are major applications of such neural network. Some of the latest work in the area is discussed below.

Ranking convolutional neural network for the age estimation is experimented by Shixing Chen, et al., (2017). ResNet-101 deep network model for 3DMM regression is proposed by Anh Tuan Tran, et al., (2017) which uses deep learning and available for download with the network technical details and values of the chosen parameters.

Deep convolutional neural networks are also used in work of Hueu-Fang Yang, et al., (2018). The paper highlights use of the deep learning model for construction of binary hash codes from labeled data in order to search large scale images. Deep neural networks have been used for unlabeled or poorly labeled data also. Oscar Keller, et al., (2016) discusses convolutional network, its training and its performance for 1 billion hand images, where data are continuous and poorly labelled.

Deep networks have also been used for geographic information analysis such as analysis of images of earth (Audebert, Saux, & Lefevre, 2016). Recently, a very effective deep learning algorithm is introduced for channel pruning without degradation and efficiently accelerates learning of very deep network. Work of Yihui He, et al., (2017) explains it in detail.

Recurrent Neural Networks

The convolutional model works on fixed number of inputs, generates a fix sized vector as output with predefined number of steps. The recurrent networks allow us to operate over sequences of vectors in input and in output. In case of recurrent neural network, the connection between units forms a directed cycle. Unlike the traditional neural network, the recurrent neural network input and output are not independent, but related. Further, the recurrent neural network shares the common parameters at every layer. One can train the recurrent network in a way which is similar to the traditional neural network using back-propagation method. Here, calculation of gradient depends not on the current step, but on previous steps also. A variant called bidirectional recurrent neural network is also used for many applications. The bidirectional neural network not only considers the previous but also the expected future output. In bidirectional and simple recurrent neural networks, deep learning can be achieved by introducing multiple hidden layers. Such deep networks provide higher learning capacity with lots of learning data. Speech, image processing and natural language processing are some of the candidate areas where recurrent neural networks can be used. Applications of the recurrent neural network are described in various papers (Mikolov, Karafiat, Burget, Cernocky, & Khudanpur, 2010), (Mikolov, Kombrink, Burget, Cernocky, & Khudanpur, 2011), (Sutskever, Martens, & Hinton, 2011), (Graves & Jaitly, 2014).

Reinforcement Learning to Neural Networks

Reinforcement learning is a kind of hybridization of dynamic programming and supervised learning (Bertsekas & Tsitsiklis, 1996). Typical components of the approach are environment, agent, actions, policy and cost functions. The agent acts as a controller of the system; policy determines the actions to be taken; and the reward function specifies the overall objective of the reinforcement learning problem. In Reinforcement Learning, an agent plays a key role learning next course of action through trial and error-based experiments. The overall idea of the reinforcement learning is as follows.

"An agent iteratively interacts with an environment by carrying out an action u_t based on its observed state information x_t, which can be smaller (partially observable) or equal (fully observable) to the environmental state s_t. In return it retrieves a feedback in form of a reward R_{t+1}, which it uses to improve its policy and thereby increase its future sum of rewards ($t = 1, \ldots\ldots, \infty$)" (Sutton & Barto, 1998).

Application of this approach can be found in robotics, games, swarm intelligence, multi agent systems and control theory.

Multi-Modalities for Deep Learning

So far, we have seen the approaches, models and applications for single modalities of the neural network, specifically deep neural networks. However, the deep neural networks can also be applied to learn features over multi modalities. Multi-model learning involves relating information from multiple sources. For example, manipulating audio and visual sources at a time falls into this category. This can be done in two ways. First way is to consider data from all modalities and make them available at every phase. Such work is demonstrated in work of Garasimos Potamianos, et al., (2004) regarding audiovisual speech recognition. Another way follows cross modality learning. Here data from multiple modalities is available for feature learning phase only. Typically, supervised training and testing phases deal with the data from a single modality; however, Jiquan Ngiam, et al., (2011) describe a work on cross modality and present a series of tasks for multi model learning and shows training of deep networks that learn features to address these tasks. Many applications (Huang & Kingsbury, 2013), (Kim, Lee, & Provost, 2013), (Ngiam, et al., 2011) employ the approach in the field of audio visual data. Other applications of the approach include work of many researchers (Lai, Bo, Ren, & Fox, 2013), (Lenz, Lee, & Saxena, 2013) in the field of robotics with visual and depth data; and medical applications with visual and temporal data (Shin, Orton, Collins, Doran, & Leach, 2013).

Parallelization

To reduce the time of training, parallelization of the learning processes is essential. By this way, training of deep neural network becomes fast and efficient. Parallelization is done via distributing the model and applying same data sets for learning. For example, the 1000 * 1000 weight matrix can be divided into two processing units with effective size of 1000*500. Such data parallelism is fast for small network and slow for big network. Parallelism can be applied on model as well as data. In case of model parallelism, different parts of models are trained in parallel. In case of the data parallelism, data are distributed on models. In case of later choice, the model parameters must be synchronized.

Cognitive Computing

Cognitive computing is defined as a simulation of human thinking process with the help of machine learning algorithms and other areas of artificial intelligence. As stated earlier, deep learning is suitable of simulation of many human dominated processes such as perception, natural language processing, etc. helping in general thinking, and decision making. Such processes are hierarchical in nature; hence it is suitable for deep learning technique. Cognitive computing facilitated via deep learning techniques is also used for analyzing the so called dark data, which are yet to be analyzed. Dark data are generally data which are in bulk, unstructured in nature and difficult to analyze and visualize. Another aspect of the dark data is concerned with its location. They are stored generally in locations which are difficult and challenging to explore. To identify, process, analyze and visualize such dark and big data, deep learning can be utilized. IBM and other companies have started employing deep learning techniques for understanding, speech, vision, language translation, dialog and other tasks. An application for healthcare is also developed by IBM Research and Memorial Sloan Kettering Cancer Center for detecting skin cancer using smart phones and could computing platform. The application works in conjunction with deep learning to flag cancer images and analyze them on demand.

SUCCESSFUL APPLICATIONS OF DEEP LEARNING

The generative deep model using unsupervised manner was introduced by work of Geoffrey Hinton, et al., (2006), which was named as Deep Belief Network (DBN). The network learns with the help of a greedy learning algorithm in order to optimize the weights. These weights are provided later to a multi layered network as an initial weight set. Work done by Abdel Mohamed, et al., (2010), Geoffrey Hinton et al., (2012) and Abdel Mohamed, et al.,(2012) also fall in the category of pre-trained back-propagation learning. A real-world application of prelearning is discussed by Veselin Stoyanov et al., (2011) using deep generative graphical models. Work of Ray Kurzweil (2012) also illustrates a generative deep learning model. A deep learning architecture is designed by Graham Taylor et al., (2006) for human motion modeling. For natural language processing and natural scene parsing, a deep learning model is proposed by Richard Socher, et al., (2011). Mohammad Havaei et al., (2015) used deep learning concept for large data set containing medical imaging.

Spoken language identification and phone recognition is done through deep discriminative learning by Dong Yu et al., (2010) and Dong Yu and Li Deng (2010) respectively. Later Dong Yu, et al., (2010) suggested an improved model for natural language processing. Nelson Morgan (2012) has also proposed a deep learning approach for automatic speech recognition. He has used discriminatively trained, feed forward neural networks for automatic speech recognition involving large and complex data.

The hybrid deep learning refers to the utilization of generative and discriminative deep learning concept in architecture. The generative concept and discriminative concept may work in cooperative or concurrent manner with the ultimate aim of getting dual advantages from both the concepts. Such hybridization is experimented in the work of Tara Sainath, et al., (2013) managing deep convolutional neural network for managing vocabulary for continuous speech recognition, which is practically very large and complex to handle with typical approaches. Similar work is presented by George Dahl, et al., (2012) while the latest work in this category is the work of Cha Zhang and Zhengyou Zhang (2014) with the basic objective to improve the multi-view face detection.

There are some other noticeable works on big data manipulation using the deep learning approach. A survey is presented in the work of Yann Le Cun, et al., (2015) as well as Maryam Najafabadi, et al., (2015). As discussed, the deep learning networks are slow and difficult to train. Further, they have tendency to over-fit themselves. To solve these problems, residual framing deep learning network is proposed by Kaiming He, et al., (2016). As per the claims of the authors, the network layers are reformulated using residual functions. The above-mentioned paper uses 152 layers and proposes really very deep learning.

Table 1 enlists some applications in various domains with reference.

Those who want to experiment ready models of the big data for various domains, pre-trained models are available at model zoo (Hasanpour, 2018). These models can be used to experiment deep learning in selected domains. The models available in this repository are ready to use, pre-learned, and can be downloaded by running following script.

```
scripts/download_model_binary.py<dirname>
```

where <dirname> is a name of directory associated with concern model in the zoo repository.

ISSUES AND LIMITATIONS OF DEEP LEARNING

Deep learning has started late in comparison with other machine learning techniques. A few of the many reasons can be lack of data and lack of able infrastructure, particularly slow processors in comparison with the modern era. It is said by Yann Lecun, et al., (2015) that the data set were approximately 1,000

Table 1. Latest work done in the area of big data manipulation using deep learning

Reference	Domain	Year
Cireşan, D., Meler, U., Cambardella, L. & Schmidhuber, J. (2010). Deep, big, simple neural nets for handwritten digit recognition. *Neural Computation, 22*(12), 3207-3220.	Handwritten digit recognition	2010
Seide, F., Li, G. &Yu, D. (2011). Conversational speech transcription using context-dependent deep neural networks. In *Proceedings of Interspeech*, Florence, Italy (pp. 437-440).	Conversational speech transcription	2011
Collobert, R., Weston, J., Bottou, L., Karlen, M., Kavukcuoglu, K. & Kuksa, P. (2011). Natural language processing almost from scratch. *Journal of Machine Learning & Research, 12*, 2493–2537.	Natural language processing	2011
Gantz, J. & Reinsel, D. (2011). *Extracting value from chaos*. Hopkinton, MA: EMC.	Chaos Management	2011
Lin, J. & Kolcz, A. (2012). Large-scale machine learning at twitter. In *Proceeding of ACM SIGMOD*, Scottsdale, Arizona (pp. 793-804).	Twitter data handling	2012
Hinton, G., Deng, L., Yu, D., Dahl, G., Mohamed, A., Jaitly, N., … Kingsbury, B. (2012). Deep neural networks for acoustic modeling in speech recognition. *IEEE Signal Processing Magazine, 29*(6), 82-97.	Speech Recognition	2012
Panda, B., Herbach, J., Basu, S. & Bayardo, R. (2012). *MapReduce and its application to massively parallel learning of decision tree ensembles. Scaling Up Machine Learning: Parallel and Distributed Approaches*. Cambridge, UK: Cambridge University.	Parallel learning of decision tree	2012
Srivastava, N. & Salakhutdinov, R. (2012). Multimodal learning with deep Boltzmann machines. In *Proceedings of Neural Information Processing Systems*, Lake Tahoe, Nevada.	Multi model learning	2012
Crego, Muñoz, & Islam, (2013). Big data and deep learning: Big deals or big delusions?	Comments on big data	2013
Mikolov, T., Le, QV, Sutskever, I. (2013). Exploiting similarities among languages for machine translation. Computation and Language. arXiv:1309.4168	Machine translation	2013
Zhang, K. &Chen, X. (2014). Large-scale deep belief nets with MapReduce. *IEEE Access, 2*, 395-403.	Deep belief network using MapReduce	2014
Jones, N. (2014). Computer science: The learning machines. *Nature, 505*(7482), 146-148.	Learning machines	2014
Fei-Fei, L., Karpathy, A., Leung, T., Shetty, S., Sukthankar, R., & Toderici, G. (2014). Large-scale video classification with convolutional neural networks. In *IEEE Conference on Computer Vision and Pattern Recognition*, Columbus, Ohio.	Large scale video classification	2014
Lapedriza, À., Oliva, A., Torralba, A., Xiao, J., & Zhou, B. (2014). Learning deep features for scene recognition using places database. In *Conference on Neural Information Processing Systems*, Montreal, Canada.	Scene learning	2014
He, K., Zhang, X., Ren, S. & Sun, J. (2015). Delving deep into rectifiers: Surpassing human-level performance on image net classification. In *International Conference on Computer Vision*, Santiago, Chile.	Image classifiers from very large set of images	2015
He, K., Zhang, X., Ren, S., & Sun, J. (2014). Spatial pyramid pooling in deep convolutional networks for visual recognition. In *European Conference on Computer Vision*, Zurich. and He, K., Zhang, X., Ren, S., & Sun, J. (2016). Deep Residual Learning for Image Recognition. IEEE Conference on Computer Vision and Pattern Recognition, (pp. 770-778). Las Vegas, USA.	Image recognizer, and uses more than 150 layers	2014, 2016
Larsson, G., Maire, M., Shakhnarovich, G. (2016). Learning representations for automatic colorization. In *European Conference on Computer Vision*, Amsterdam.	Recolouring black and white images	2016
Koller, O., Ney, H., & Bowden, R. (2016). Deep Hand: How to Train a CNN on 1 Million Hand Images. In *IEEE International Conference on Computer Vision and Pattern Recognition*, Las Vegas, NV.	Convolutional network, its training and its performance for 1 billion hand images, where data are continuous and poorly labelled	2016

continued on following page

Table 1. Continued

Reference	Domain	Year
Audebert, N., Saux, B., & Lefevre, S. (2016). Semantic Segmentation of Earth Observation Data Using Multimodal and Multi-scale Deep Networks. In *Asian Conference on Computer Vision*, Taipei, Taiwan.	Geographic information analysis such as analysis of images of earth	2016
He, K., Zhang, X., Ren, S., & Sun, J. (2016). Deep Residual Learning for Image Recognition. In *IEEE Conference on Computer Vision and Pattern Recognition*, Las Vegas, NV (pp. 770-778).	Channel pruning without degradation and efficiently accelerates learning of very deep network	2016
Chen, S., Caojin, Z., Ming, D., Jialiang, L., & Mike, R. (2017). Using ranking-CNN for age estimation. Honolulu, Hawaii.	Ranking convolutional neural network for the age estimation	2017
Anh Tuan, T., Tal, H., Iacopo, M., & Gerard, M. (2017). Regressing robust and discriminative 3D morphable models with a very deep neural network. In *IEEE Conference on Computer Vision and Pattern Recognition*, Honolulu, HI.	ResNet-101 deep network model for 3DMM regression	2017
Huei-Fang, Y., Kevin, L., & Chu-Song, C. (2018). Supervised learning of semantics-Preserving hash via deep convolutional neural networks. In IEEE Transactions on Pattern Analysis and Machine Intelligence (pp. 437-451).	Construction of binary hash codes from labeled data in order to search large scale images	2017
Aksan, E., Pece, F. & Hilliges, O. (2018). Deep Writing: Making digital ink editable via deep generative modeling. In *SIGCHI Conference on Human Factors in Computing Systems*, Montréal, Canada.	Deep Generative Modeling	2018
Wang, H., Zhang, F., Xie, X. & Guo, M. (2018). DKN: Deep knowledge-aware network for news recommendation. In *The Web Conference*, Lyon, France.	Online news recommender systems	2018
Lee, J., Park, J., Kim, K.L. & Nam, J. (2018). Sample CNN: End-to-end deep convolutional neural networks using very small filters for music classification. *Applied Sciences*, 8(150).	Music classification	2018

times smaller and computing infrastructure were approximately 1,000,000 times slower in comparison with today's volume of data sets and computing infrastructure. Further, no proper consideration was given to the domain of deep learning. It was believed that adding many layers to an artificial neural network, that is increasing dimensionality of the neural network, over-fits the network and also degrades its performance. Due to really big data overflow in various domains led experts and researchers to think about the deep leaning.

Deep learning can be put in category of empirical success, just "simple parametric models trained with gradient descent" as mentioned by Francois Chollet (2017) and many real-life applications still can be solved with the deep learning techniques. However, because of simplicity and its belongingness in the category of the simple parametric and empirical model, many researchers consider it is not suitable for the real life complex problem solving. There are some other limitations of deep learning in general, which are discussed below.

- Deep neural networks are hard to train as each layer is learning at vastly different rate. Many a times the later layers learn at fast rate and starting layers still busy in learning. Reverse situation may also occur surprisingly, in which the initial layers learn in fast manner and later layers are still struggling for the same.

- Applications that require reasoning and explanation are not the candidate applications for deep learning technologies. The main reason of this is the knowledge of any neural network-based system is stored in its connection in indirect form, which is not easy to be converted in verbal form. Here one can think for neuro-fuzzy system to get dual advantages of fuzzy logic-based systems such as uncertainty and explanation; besides advantages of neural network based systems. Some example applications are planning, scheduling, automatic programming, advisory systems, etc. are the example of the same. Further, such hybridization can incorporate advance fuzzy technology such as type 2 fuzzy inference system.

- Often deep learning models misclassify the inputs to some absurd classes. This can be made possible through some tricky training sets called "adversarial examples". Such examples are designed to confuse the model and trickedly lead the model to understand them in other way and classify into different than intended category.

- It should be noted that the deep leaning models cannot understand the inputs, hence human like understanding is bit far to achieve. By providing them validated big training data sets, one can only make the deep leaning models to learn geometric transformation from input to output without any human like understanding of the images.

- Deep models are generally experimented on narrow domains, for the concepts they are taught for; rather than the concepts they are not aware of. Humans can handle with partial, incompetent and ambiguous data also.

- The deep learning requires lots of data. Human beings are having capabilities to learn required knowledge from the very small amount of data and can come up with a physical model for problem solving. Deep learning models cannot do this. They require large amount of data. Further, in case of deep learning, even if it is trained with a sufficiently large amount of data, it may fail if it sees slightly different data.

CONCLUSION

From the discussion and aforementioned references, it is clear that deep learning might be helpful to effectively manage the great volume of complex data in a business. Many different models and algorithms have made it practically possible to implement deep learning in various domains. Some of the possible applications of deep learning to manage big data are mentioned below which can be developed with the help of tools such as MatLab using Octave toolbox for deep learning or dedicated software such as cuda-convnet[1] offering a fast C++ implementation of convolutional neural networks.

- Natural language processing and natural query.
- Film industry where dubbing of film, re-colouring film prints and adding sounds to the silent films.
- News aggregators.
- Machine Translation in partly or fully automatic manner; also sentence corrections.
- Classification, abstraction and identification of multimedia objects.
- Automatic prescription of handwriting production and understanding.
- Managing knowledge wallet.
- Chatting agents.

- Intelligent games.
- Google's automatic statistician project.
- Intelligent web applications including searching and intelligent crawling.
- Image, speech and multimedia mining.
- Utilization of social network platform for various activities.
- Development for resources and sustainable development, population information, governance (weather forecasting, infrastructural development, natural resources).
- Sensor web, agricultural information, decision support systems in domains like forestry and fisheries.

The above-mentioned domains have possibility to generate and deal with lot many data, which are big in terms of volume, velocity and variety. Typical approach may not solve the problem with the desired effectiveness. Further, from the literature survey, it is observed that only a few of them are traversed. There is a good research opportunity in the above-mentioned applications and domains. One can also consider exploring the area such as privacy, security and intellectual copy rights of the big data and its analyzed results. Beside the above-mentioned applications, the generalized deep network that are self-evolutionary in nature can also be considered as a major future enhancement. In future, models of deep learning may be more generic in nature. The generated solutions need to be not only generic, but reusable too. As stated, deep learning requires lots of data and human control when data feeding and data interpreting is concerned. So, in the future, hybrid deep learning-based systems will become more popular. The key technologies that can be used for hybridization is fuzzy logic, genetic algorithms, rough sets and other modern artificial intelligent techniques. The results also lead to general and broader Artificial Intelligence techniques. Automatic machine learning and growing reusable generic systems are the future of deep learning.

REFERENCES

Anh Tuan, T., Tal, H., Iacopo, M., & Gerard, M. (2017). Regressing robust and discriminative 3D morphable models with a very deep neural network. In *IEEE Conference on Computer Vision and Pattern Recognition*. Honolulu, HI.

Arel, I., Rose, D., & Coop, R. (2009). DeSTIN: A scalable deep learning architecture with application to high-dimensional robust pattern recognition. In *AAAI Fall Symposium* (pp. 11-15).

Ash, T. (1989). Dynamic node creation in backpropagation neural networks. *Connection Science*, *1*(4), 365–375. doi:10.1080/09540098908915647

Audebert, N., Saux, B., & Lefevre, S. (2016). Semantic segmentation of earth observation data using multimodal and multi-scale deep networks. In *Asian Conference on Computer Vision*, Taipei, Taiwan.

Bengio, Y., Courville, A., & Vincent, P. (2013). Representation learning: A review and new perspectives. *IEEE Transactions on Pattern Analysis and Machine Intelligence*, *35*(8), 1798–1828. doi:10.1109/TPAMI.2013.50 PMID:23787338

Bergen, M. (2015, July 15). Deep learning AI is taking over tech what is it? *Recode.net*. Retrieved from http://recode.net/2015/07/15/deep-learning-ai-is-taking-over-tech-what-is-it/

Bertsekas, D., & Tsitsiklis, J. (1996). *Neuro-dynamic programming*. Belmont, MA: Athena Scientific.

Carneiro, G., & Nascimento, J. C. (2013). Combining multiple dynamic models and deep learning architectures for tracking the left ventricle endocardium in ultrasound data. *IEEE Transactions on Pattern Analysis and Machine Intelligence, 35*(11), 2592–2607. doi:10.1109/TPAMI.2013.96 PMID:24051722

Chen, S., Caojin, Z., Ming, D., Jialiang, L., & Mike, R. (2017). *Using ranking-CNN for age estimation*. doi:10.1109/CVPR.2017.86

Chollet, F. (2017). *Deep Learning with Python*. New York, USA: Manning Publications.

Chu, C. T., Kim, S. K., Lin, Y. A., Yu, Y., Bradski, G., Ng, A. Y., & Olukotun, K. (2007). *Map reduce for machine learning on multicore* (pp. 281–288). Advances in Neural Information Processing Systems Vancouver.

Crego, E., Muñoz, G., & Islam, F. (2013, May 26). Big Data and Deep Learning: Big Deals or Big Delusions? *Huffington Post*. Retrieved from https://www.huffingtonpost.com/george-munoz-frank-islam-and-ed-crego/big-data-and-deep-learnin_b_3325352.html

Dahl, G. E., Yu, D., Deng, L., & Acero, A. (2012). Context-dependent pre-trained deep neural networks for large-vocabulary speech recognition. *IEEE Transactions on Audio, Speech, and Language Processing, 20*(1), 30–42. doi:10.1109/TASL.2011.2134090

Dauphin, Y., Pascanu, R., Gulcehre, C., Cho, K., Ganguly, S., & Bengio, Y. (2014). Identifying and attacking the saddle point problem in high-dimensional non-convex optimization. In *27th International Conference on Neural Information Processing Systems*, Montreal, Canada (pp. 2933-2941).

Dean, J., Corrado, G. S., Monga, R., Chen, K., Devin, M., Le, Q. V., ... Ng, A. Y. (2012). Large scale distributed deep networks. In *Conference on Neural Information Processing Systems*, Lake Tahoe, NV.

Dean, J., & Ghemawat, S. (2008). Mapreduce: Simplified data processing on large clusters. *Communications of the ACM, 51*(1), 107–113. doi:10.1145/1327452.1327492

Deng, L. (2014). *A tutorial survey of architectures, algorithms, and applications for deep learning*. In *APSIPA Transactions on Signal and Information Processing*.

Deng, L., Hinton, G., & Kingsbury, B. (2013). New types of deep neural network learning for speech recognition and related applications: An overview. *International Conference on Acoustics, Speech and Signal Processing*. Vancouver, Canada. 10.1109/ICASSP.2013.6639344

Deng, L., Seltzer, M., Yu, D., Acero, A., Mohamed, A., & Hinton, G. (2010). Binary coding of speech spectrograms using a deep auto-encoder. In INTERSPEECH 2010,Makuhari, Chiba.

Graves, A., & Jaitly, N. (2014). Towards end-to-end speech recognition with recurrent neural networks. In *31st International Conference on Machine Learning*. Beijing, China.

Hasanpour, S. H. (2018). Model Zoo. Retrieved from https://github.com/BVLC/caffe/wiki/Model-Zoo

Havaei, M., Davy, A., Farley, D., Biard, A., Courville, A., Bengio, Y., . . . Larochelle, H. (2015). *Brain tumor segmentation with deep neural networks*. Retrieved from http://arxiv.org/abs/1505.03540

He, K., Zhang, X., Ren, S., & Sun, J. (2016). Deep residual learning for image recognition. In *IEEE Conference on Computer Vision and Pattern Recognition*, Las Vegas, NV (pp. 770-778).

Hihi, S. E., & Bengio, Y. (1996). Hierarchical recurrent neural networks for long-term dependencies. In D. S. Touretzky, M. C. Mozer, & M. E. Hasselmo (Eds.), (pp. 493–499). Advances in Neural Information Processing Systems. MIT Press.

Hinton, G., Deng, L., Yu, D., Dahl, G., Mohamed, A., Jaitly, N., ... Kingsbury, B. (2012). Deep neural networks for acoustic modeling in speech recognition. *IEEE Signal Processing Magazine*, *29*(6), 82–97. doi:10.1109/MSP.2012.2205597

Hinton, G., Osidero, S., & Teh, Y. (2006). A fast learning algorithm for deep belief nets. *Neural Computation*, *18*(7), 1527–1554. doi:10.1162/neco.2006.18.7.1527 PMID:16764513

Horvitz, E., & Mitchell, T. (2010). *From data to knowledge to action: A global enabler for the 21st century* (White Paper). A Computing Community Consortium.

Huang, J., & Kingsbury, B. (2013). Audio-visual deep learning for noise robust speech recognition. In *IEEE International Conference on Acoustics, Speech and Signal Processing*, Vancouver, Canada. 10.1109/ICASSP.2013.6639140

Hubel, D., & Wiesel, T. (1968). Receptive fields and functional architecture of monkey striate cortex. *The Journal of Physiology*, *195*(1), 215–243. doi:10.1113/jphysiol.1968.sp008455 PMID:4966457

Huei-Fang, Y., Kevin, L., & Chu-Song, C. (2018). Supervised Learning of Semantics-Preserving Hash via Deep Convolutional Neural Networks. *IEEE Transactions on Pattern Analysis and Machine Intelligence*, 437–451. PMID:28207384

Kim, Y., Lee, H., & Provost, E. (2013). Deep learning for robust feature generation in audiovisual emotion recognition. In *IEEE International Conference on Acoustics, Speech and Signal Processing*. Vancouver, Canada. 10.1109/ICASSP.2013.6638346

Koller, O., Ney, H., & Bowden, R. (2016). Deep hand: how to train a CNN on 1 million hand images. *IEEE International Conference on Computer Vision and Pattern Recognition*, Las Vegas, NV.

Krizhevsky, A., Sutskever, I., & Hinton, G. (2012). Imagenet classification with deep convolutional neural networks. *Advances in Neural Information Processing Systems*, *25*, 1106–1114.

Kurzweil, R. (2012). *How to create a mind: The secret of human thought revealed*. Audio Book.

Lai, K., Bo, L., Ren, X., & Fox, D. (2013). RGB-D object recognition: Features, algorithms, and a large scale benchmark. In A. Fossati, J. Gall, H. Grabner, X. Ren, & K. Konolige (Eds.), *Consumer depth cameras for computer vision* (pp. 167–192). London: Springer-Verlag. doi:10.1007/978-1-4471-4640-7_9

LeCun, Y., Bengio, Y., & Hinton, G. (2015). Deep Learning. *Nature*, *521*(7553), 436–444. doi:10.1038/nature14539 PMID:26017442

Lenz, I., Lee, H., & Saxena, A. (2013). Deep learning for detecting robotic grasps. *International Conference on Learning Representations*. Scottsdale, Arizona.

Mann, G., McDonald, R., Mohri, M., Silberman, N., & Walker, D. D. (2009). *Efficient large-scale distributed training of conditional maximum entropy models*. In Advances in Neural Information Processing Systems.

Manyika, J., Chui, M., Brad, B., Bughin, J., Dobbs, R., Roxburgh, C., & Hung Byers, A. (2011, May). Big data: The next frontier for innovation, competition, and productivity. *McKinsey*. Retrieved March 4, 2015, from http://www.mckinsey.com/insights/business_technology/big_data_the_next_frontier_for_innovation

Mikolov, T., Karafiat, M., Burget, L., Cernocky, J., & Khudanpur, S. (2010). Recurrent neural network based language model. In *11th Annual Conference of the International Speech Communication Association*, Chiba, Japan (pp. 1045-1048).

Mikolov, T., Kombrink, S., Burget, L., Cernocky, J., & Khudanpur, S. (2011). Extensions of recurrent neural network language model. In *36th International Conference on Acoustics, Speech and Signal Processing*, Prague, Czech Republic (pp. 5528-5531). 10.1109/ICASSP.2011.5947611

Mohamed, A., Dahl, G., & Hinton, G. (2009). Deep belief networks for phone recognition. In *NIPS Workshop*. Vancouver, Canada.

Mohamed, A., Dahl, G., & Hinton, G. (2012). Acoustic Modeling using Deep Belief Networks. *IEEE Transactions on Audio, Speech, and Language Processing, 20*(1), 14–22. doi:10.1109/TASL.2011.2109382

Mohamed, A., Yu, D., & Deng, L. (2010). *Investigation of full-sequence training of deep belief networks for speech recognition*. Makuhari, Japan: Interspeech.

Morgan, N. (2012). Deep and wide: Multiple layers in automatic speech recognition. *IEEE Transactions on Audio, Speech, and Language Processing, 20*(1), 7–13. doi:10.1109/TASL.2011.2116010

Mozer, M. C. (1989). A focused back-propagation algorithm for temporal sequence recognition. *Complex Systems, 3*, 349–381.

Najafabadi, M., Villanustre, F., Khoshgoftaar, T., Seliya, N., Wald, R., & Muharemagic, E. (2015). Deep learning applications and challenges in big data analytics. *Journal of Big Data, 2*.

Ngiam, J., Khosla, A., Kim, M., Nam, J., Lee, H., & Ng, A. (2011). Multimodal deep learning. In *28th International Conference on Machine Learning*, Bellevue.

On Circulation. (n.d.). Deep Dreaming with Google. Retrieved from https://oncirculation.com/2015/07/14/deep-dreaming-with-google/

Potamianos, G., Neti, C., Luettin, J., & Matthews, I. (2004). Audio-visual automatic speech recognition: An overview. In G. Potamianos, C. Neti, J. Luettin, & I. Matthews (Eds.), *Issues in visual and audio-visual speech processing* (pp. 356–396). Cambridge: MIT Press.

Sainath, T., Mohamed, A., Kingsbury, B., & Ramabhadran, B. (2013). Deep convolutional neural networks for LVCSR. In *IEEE International Conference on Acoustics, Speech and Signal Processing*. Vancouver, Canada.

Shin, H., Orton, M., Collins, D., Doran, S., & Leach, M. (2013). Stacked autoencoders for unsupervised feature learning and multiple organ detection in a pilot study using 4D patient data. *IEEE Transactions on Pattern Analysis and Machine Intelligence, 35*(8), 1930–1943. doi:10.1109/TPAMI.2012.277 PMID:23787345

Siniscalchi, S. M., Yu, D., Deng, L., & Lee, C. (2013). Exploiting deep neural networks for detection-based speech recognition. *Neurocomputing, 106*, 148–157. doi:10.1016/j.neucom.2012.11.008

Socher, R., Lin, C., Ng, A., & Manning, C. (2011). Learning continuous phrase representations and syntactic parsing with recursive neural networks. In *International Conference on Machine Learning*. Bellevue, Washington, USA.

Srivastava, N., Hinton, G., Krizhevsky, A., Sutskever, I., & Salakhtdinov, R. (2014). Dropout: A simple way to prevent neural networks from overfitting. *Journal of Machine Learning Research, 15*, 1929–1958.

Stoyanov, V., Ropson, A., & Eisner, J. (2011). Empirical risk minimization of graphical model parameters given approximate inference, decoding, and model structure. In 14th International Conference on Artificial Intelligence and Statistics, Fort Lauderdale, FL (pp. 725-733). .

Sutskever, I., Martens, J., & Hinton, G. (2011). Generating text with recurrent neural networks. In *28th International Conference on Machine Learning*. Bellevue, USA.

Sutton, R., & Barto, A. (1998). *Reinforcement learning: An introduction (Adaptive computation and machine learning)*. Cambridge, MA: MIT Press.

Taylor, G., Hinton, G., & Roweis, S. (2006). Modeling human motion using binary latent variables. In *Annual Conference on Neural Information Processing Systems*, Vancouver, Canada (pp. 1345-1352).

Teo, C. H., Le, Q., Smola, A., & Vishwanathan, S. V. (2007). A scalabe modular convex solver for regularized risk minimization. In *Conference on Knowledge Discovery and Data Mining*, San Francisco, CA.

Yann, L., Yoshua, B., & Geoffrey, H. (2015). Deep learning. *Nature, 521*(7553), 436–444. doi:10.1038/nature14539 PMID:26017442

Yihui, H., Xiangyu, Z., & Sun, J. (2017). Channel Pruning for Accelerating Very Deep Neural. In *IEEE International Conference on Computer Vision*, Venice, Italy (pp. 1389-1397).

Yu, D., & Deng, L. (2010). Deep-structured hidden conditional random fields for phonetic recognition. In Eleventh Annual Conference of the International Speech Communication Association. Makuhari, Japan: Interspeech.

Yu, D., Wang, S., & Deng, L. (2010). Sequential labeling using deep structured conditional random fields. *IEEE Journal of Selected Topics in Signal Processing, 4*(6), 965–973. doi:10.1109/JSTSP.2010.2075990

Yu, D., Wang, S., Karam, Z., & Deng, L. (2010). Language recognition using deep-structured conditional random fields. In *IEEE International Conference on Acoustics Speech and Signal Processing*, Dallas, TX (pp. 5030-5033). 10.1109/ICASSP.2010.5495072

Zhang, C., & Zhang, Z. (2014). Improving multiview face detection with multi-task deep convolutional neural networks. In *IEEE Winter Conference on Applications of Computer Vision*, Steamboat Springs, CO (pp. 1036-1041). 10.1109/WACV.2014.6835990

Zinkevich, M., Weimer, M., Smola, A., & Li, L. (2010). Parallelized stocastic gradient descent. In *Conference on Neural Information Processing Systems*, Vancouver, Canada.

ENDNOTES

[1]   https://code.google.com/p/cuda-convnet/

Chapter 2
Genetic Algorithm Based Pre-Processing Strategy for High Dimensional Micro-Array Gene Classification:
Application of Nature Inspired Intelligence

Deepak Singh
National Institute of Technology Raipur, India

Dilip Singh Sisodia
National Institute of Technology Raipur, India

Pradeep Singh
National Institute of Technology Raipur, India

ABSTRACT

Discretization is one of the popular pre-processing techniques that helps a learner overcome the difficulty in handling the wide range of continuous-valued attributes. The objective of this chapter is to explore the possibilities of performance improvement in large dimensional biomedical data with the alliance of machine learning and evolutionary algorithms to design effective healthcare systems. To accomplish the goal, the model targets the preprocessing phase and developed framework based on a Fisher Markov feature selection and evolutionary based binary discretization (EBD) for a microarray gene expression classification. Several experiments were conducted on publicly available microarray gene expression datasets, including colon tumors, and lung and prostate cancer. The performance is evaluated for accuracy and standard deviations, and is also compared with the other state-of-the-art techniques. The experimental results show that the EBD algorithm performs better when compared to other contemporary discretization techniques.

DOI: 10.4018/978-1-5225-5852-1.ch002

INTRODUCTION

Advancement in healthcare technology enabled a revolution in health research that could expedite endurance of the leaving being (Acharya & Dua, 2014). Early diagnosis with higher accuracy that provides the faster treatment conditions is feasible due to the enormous findings in technology. The approach to the study of the biological data had a significant contribution in discovering medical illness. However, the challenges associated with biomedical problem solving is handling and management of complex data sets. Here we consider one such example is DNA microarray gene dataset (Statnikov, Tsamardinos, Dosbayev, & Aliferis, 2005) where thousands of gene expressions measured for each biological sample using microarray and used for the diagnosis of cancer and its classification. The heterogeneity, ambiguity and inconsistencies persist with microarray data sets are biggest hurdle to tackle. Mostly these data are inconsistent because of noise, missing values, outliers, redundant values and data imbalance. Computational approaches can provide the means to resolve these challenges (Le, Paul, & Ong, 2010). Decision making, knowledge extraction, data management and data transmissions are the complex tasks that were effectively performed by the computational models. The recent trend in the computational methods evolves opportunities to disseminate the newly efficient techniques that can be helpful in designing prominent health care systems (Tsai, Chiang, Ksentini, & Chen, 2016). With the advent of nature inspired intelligence technique and the current paradigm of machine learning together can accelerate the current biomedical computational models.

The foundation of Machine learning is laid around the Knowledge discovery in database principle, consists of three basic steps namely the data preprocessing, learning phase, and validation phase (García, Luengo, & Herrera, 2015). The pre-processing phase has the objective of transforming data and discovering patterns by removing redundant features. Moreover, the pre-processing data phase is helpful in identifying the influential factors that contribute towards the classification. These techniques play a vital role in machine learning for improving the system performance. Various pre-processing (García et al., 2015) techniques are used for handling data inconsistencies which in turn help learner for efficient classification of the data. The performance of a learner is heavily relied on the class-attribute dependency of the training data. Dealing with a large number of instances or attributes in heterogeneous data could agitate the dependency (class-attribute) and hence requires preprocessing strategies (Liu, Motoda, Setiono, & Zhao, 2010; Molano, Cobos, Mendoza, & Herrera-viedma, 2014; Houari, Bounceur, Kechadi, Tari, & Euler, 2016) which is an essential step for eliminating lesser informative features and instances. Reduction of inconsistencies varies according to the preprocessing strategies considered. Feature selection (Diao & Shen, 2015) and Discretization (García et al., 2013) are the most popular measures for reduction of unnecessary information in data mining. Feature selection is the process of selecting the subset of the most relevant features from the set of features whereas discretization achieves the reduction by (Maimon, Oded, and Rokach, 2002) converting continuous values into discrete values with fixed interval span.

Feature selection has numerous methods which can be grouped into two categories: filters and wrappers (Liu et al., 2010). Filter method searches and evaluates either each gene individually (univariate filters) or the subset of genes (multivariate filters) by measuring their intrinsic properties related to class discrimination, independent of a learning method. Wrapper method encapsulates a global search method and the classifier in a single approach. The search method explores the gene space for all possible gene subsets, and the goodness of each subsets evaluated by a specific classifier for sample classification. In discretization, data partition is done through cut-point selection by applying different types of heuristics including Equal-interval-width (Chan, 1991), Equal-frequency-per-interval, minimal-class-entropy (Arbor, 1992) and cluster-based methods (Chmielewski & Grzymala-Busse, 1996). Recent trend suggests (Tahan & Asadi, 2017) that discretization is a promising technique to solve the complexities associated with the large volume of continuous value datasets. In microarray gene classification problem, there are large volume of continuous value data which is to be classified into certain countable classes thus discretization is useful for the effective dimensionality reduction. The advantages of discretization are to narrow down the range occupied by the continuous attribute. Study shows (Ramírez-Gallego et al., 2016) that the performance of learners including Decision tree and Bayesian rule-based learning on biomedical data is improved when data is discretized. For example in the case of decision tree learners it helps (Wu, Xiang, David Bell, Martin McGinnity, Girijesh Prasad, Guilin Qi, 2006) to form a smaller and simpler tree compared to large and complex tree formed due to the real-valued attribute.

It is evident from the existing work on feature selection and discretization (Garcia, Luengo, Sáez, Lopez & Herrera, 2013) that using these techniques as a preprocessing step for refinement of dataset improves the performance and efficiency. These techniques, however, have challenges:

- Selection between filter based or wrapper based amongst the feature selection algorithms.
- Limited number of cut points as a parameter, criteria for the selection of optimum clusters and use of exhaustive search methods in discretization.
- How to exploit relations among data instances to validate the class-attribute dependency.
- Large number literature found on the feature selection (Li & Yin, 2013) in biomedical gene expression data but on the contrary very few literature (Ramírez-Gallego et al., 2016) (Tahan & Asadi, 2017) found on the discretization.
- Absence of a unified framework that can have both feature selection and discretization in the single framework for the classification of microarray gene data.

Therefore, these motivate to explore the capability of combined approach using feature selection and discretization techniques in single framework for microarray gene data with an objective to improve the classification rate.

Due to the limitations of slow computation and greater search complexity required for high dimensionality dataset in wrapper-based approach, filters have the advantages of less computational complexity and faster execution time over wrappers (Lazar et al., 2012). The problem of exhaustive search and desired number cut point can be solved by employing search strategy. Evolutionary algorithm (Holland, 1962) is one of the search strategy for solving complex problems. It works on the principle of simple natural evolution but this simple evolution process has solved complex problems of the real world. Its application on various areas gives it a certificate of prominence. Data processing problems are also in the list of areas where application of evolutionary algorithm has performed to a great extent (Garcia, Fernandez, Luengo, Herrera, 2009). Another issue of class-attribute dependency can be exploited effectively by the use of heuristics-based knowledge.

This chapter proposes a framework that amalgamate filter based feature selection, entropy-based heuristics for cut point selection and evolutionary algorithm for search strategy in high dimensional gene data classification problem. To be precise framework is bi-level feature reduction scheme, where in the first level Fisher Markov feature selection (Cheng, Zhou, & Cheng, 2011) is used to select the highly informative features. Low computational load and univariate feature evaluation are the benefits that enforce Fisher-Markov feature selector for the feature selection technique. In the second level, high informative selected features are further selectively reduced by applying evolutionary based discretization technique. Evolutionary algorithm's heuristic search approach efficiently looks for the optimal cut point for discretization. The proposed method makes discretization very easy and simple by evaluating only one cut point in the attributes of data set to have high class-attribute dependency. The attributes of data sets are divided into two classes. This division is achieved through the entropy heuristics-based fitness function is deployed in genetic algorithm. This proposed integrated framework overcomes the limitation of the existing techniques.

To validate the proposed framework, we conduct an experiment on publicly available microarray gene expression dataset comprises of 10 data including colon tumor, lung and prostate cancer for the classification of samples (Statnikov et al., 2005). These data are of high dimensional size thus proposed framework is incorporated to reduce the dimensionality for improved diagnosis. The performance of complete model is evaluated using average accuracy and standard deviations and compared with the four state of art techniques. To test the significance of result, Wilcoxon and Friedman statistical significant test are also conducted and the results show that proposed framework performs better than the other contemporary discretization technique.

The rest of chapter is organized as follows, literature work is illustrated in section 2, discretization of the features is presented in section 3, working principle of Evolutionary Algorithm is discussed in section 4. The fifth section describes the proposed framework; section 6 shows the feasibility study of the proposed system based on the various analysis parameters and the last section 7 is making a concluding remark on the overall performance of the system.

RELATED WORK

This section briefly discusses the study of discretization and the heuristics which were used for the selection of cut point. A review of literature helps to identify the gap and limitations in the current scenario. Most existing solutions use heuristics based cutpoint selection criterion. To start with Chi-square, it is a parameter used to determine the similarity between intervals. This statistic is used in ChiMerge, for the partitioning the continuous attributes (Kerber, 1992). This technique does not consider the class information for interval formation. A parallel distance-based measure was demonstrated in the other work which has an adverse effect on time complexity (Method, Cerquides, & Mantaras, 1992). In another work, the author addresses the utilization of the entropy minimization heuristics for discretizing the range of continuous attribute into numeric interims (Fayyad, 1993).

Maximum class-attribute interdependence redundancy is another heuristic for the desired goal. The algorithm attempts to maximize the mutual dependence of class labels and attribute intervals (Chan & Ching, 1995). Cluster-based discretization method was another prominent contribution where the use of clustering method is employed and compared the performance with three known local methods (Chmielewski & Grzymala-Busse, 1996). The Bayesian rule for the discretization is yet another heuristic, where real-valued discretizes before the induction takes place (Wu, 1996). A new technique based on zeta for discretization of continuous variables were introduced, where Zeta is defined as the maximal accuracy achievable if each value of an independent variable must predict a different value of a dependent variable (Ho & Scott, 1997). The work of feature selection via discretization is accomplished in (Liu & Setiono, 1997). It can handle mixed attributes along with multi-class data and remove irrelevant and redundant attributes. FUSINTER is a new method which is based on the size of the sample, measures that were computed are very much sensitive to the instance size (Zighed, Rabaséda, & Rakotomalala, 1998).

USD (Unparametrized Supervised Discretization), is another approach which uses the idea of transforming the continuous attributes in a finite group of intervals and utilizing it in the generation of decision rules, without compromising accuracy or goodness (Giráldez, Aguilar-Ruiz, Riquelme, Ferrer-Troyano, & Rodriguez, 2002). An abstract description and systematic study with their history of development, the effect on classification, and the trade-off between speed and accuracy, were discussed in (Liu, Hussain, Tan, & Dash, 2002). Khiops based discretization method was introduced with an objective of solving the problem in a global manner that too without the need of stopping criterion (Boulle, 2004). CAIM (class-attribute interdependence maximization) is yet another technique to work in supervised data. The objective of the algorithm is to get a minimum number of a cut point while maximizing the class-attribute interdependence (Kurgan & Cios, 2004). The correlation structure of the attributes is utilized for the interval generation in the PCA based discretization algorithm proposed in (Mehta, Parthasarathy, & Yang, 2005). MODL1 discretization method laid the foundation on a Bayesian approach and introduced Bayes optimal evaluation criterion of discretization. Further, the author also proposes a new super-linear optimization algorithm that manages to find near-optimal discretization's (Boullé, 2006).

A different way of discretizing numeric values using information theory is described in (Lee, 2007). Hellinger divergence is used for measurement of the amount of information with a constraint of an equal amount of information in each interval after discretization. A dichotomic entropy based novel distribution-index-based discretizer is proposed for achieving the objective in (Wu, Bell, Prasad, & Mcginnity, 2007). Another technique for supervised discretization based on the interval distances by utilizing a novel idea of the neighborhood in the search space is discussed in (Ruiz, Angulo, & Agell, 2008). The concept of greedy method and class attribute contingency coefficient for raising the quality of discretized data is discussed, and the idea of contingency coefficient is further extended in the proposed model of (Tsai, Lee, & Yang, 2008). Ameva is a discretization algorithm which generates a potentially minimal number of discrete intervals by maximizing a contingency coefficient based on Chi-square statistics. It does not need the user to explicitly mention the number of intervals (Gonzalez-Abril, Cuberos, Velasco, & Ortega, 2009). The two efficient unsupervised, proportional discretization and fixed frequency discretization methods that can effectively manage discretization bias and variance were presented in (Yang & Webb, 2009).

The author introduces a new hypercube division-based (HDD) algorithm for supervised discretization. It tries to find a minimal set of cut points, which splits the continuous attributes into a finite number of hypercube, and the objects within each hypercube belong to the same decision class (Ping Yang, Li, & Huang, 2011). A new algorithm, named as an extended Chi2 algorithm, which has characteristics to come out of the drawbacks of Variable Precision Rough Sets (VPRS) model and the variance of the merged intervals is proposed in (Chao- Ton & Jyh-Hwa, 2005). A subset selection of cut points from the attributes with the utilization of evolutionary algorithm for defining the best criterion of splitting using a wrapper fitness function was proposed as EMD algorithm (Ramírez-Gallego et al., 2016). Multi-objective evolutionary algorithm approach with the goal of minimizing classification error (the first objective function) and a number of cut points (the second objective function) are simultaneously performed in (Tahan & Asadi, 2017). The additional objective function involves selecting low-frequency cut points so that a smaller degree of information is lost during this conversion (from continuous to discrete).

Gene Annotation Based Discretization (GABD) is proposed where the discretization width is determined by maximizing the positive predictive value (PPV), computed using gene annotations, for top 20,000 gene pairs (Misra & Ray, 2017). This was the first attempt of discretizing the high dimensional gene data. A method combining discretization and Feature Selection in a single stage using BBPSO for high-dimensional continuous data is proposed in (Tran, Xue, & Zhang, 2016). The author also presents a new representation for particles in BBPSO to achieve this goal. Recently a new evolutionary multi-objective discretization algorithm for imbalanced datasets (EMDID) is proposed which optimizes three objective functions simultaneously: number of cut points, AUC, and the total frequency of the selected cut points (Tahan & Asadi, 2018). Prediction of the presence of various bird species in Andalusia from land use data is considered in (Ropero, Renooij, & van der Gaag, 2018) where three species with different prevalence rates are classified. Further they indicate that the Chi-Merge is the preferred method for discretizing the continuous variables, since with this method the best averaged performance results in terms of both sensitivity and specificity were found.

Feature Selection

Feature section problem can be well understood by the mathematical model of maximizing the classification evaluation functions while keeping the minimum number of a feature from the feature set (Kira & Rendell, 1994). To simplify, Let $f(c)$ is classification evaluation function with a characteristic of maxima and its values $f(c) \in [0,1]$ where 1 yields the ideal best performance. Data of size $N*M$ matrix denotes the N number of instances and M number of features. The objective of feature selection is to obtain the data of size $N*M'$ such that $M' < M$ and the value of $f(c)$ being the maximum. There are no constraints put on the data type of feature, it can be discrete, real or nominal. There is the probability of the presence of more than one subset solution whose function value $f(c)$ being optimal or same.

Several strategies have been offered over the recent years for feature/gene selection: filter (Li, Li, & Zhang, 2016), wrapper (Huang, Cai, & Xu, 2007), embedded (Liu et al., 2010), and more recently ensemble techniques (Yang, Yang, Zhou, & Zomaya, 2010; Oliveira, Morita, & Sabourin, n.d.).

Filter techniques evaluate the discriminative power of features based only on inherent properties of the data. As a general rule, these methods estimate a relevance score and a threshold scheme is used to select the best-scoring features/ genes. Filter techniques are not necessarily used to build predictors. This group of techniques is independent of any classification scheme but under particular conditions they could give the optimal set of features for a given classifier. The practical advantages of these methods stating that "even when the subset of features is not optimal, they may be preferable due to their computational and statistical scalability."

Wrapper techniques select the most discriminant subset of features by minimizing the prediction error of a particular classifier. These methods are dependent on the classifier being used and they are mainly criticized because of their huge computational demands. More than that, there is no guarantee that the solution provided will be optimal if another classifier is used for prediction. Embedded techniques represent a different class of methods in the sense that they still allow interactions with the learning algorithm, but the computational time is smaller than wrapper methods. Ensemble techniques represent a relatively new class of methods for FS. They have been proposed to cope with the instability issues observed in many techniques for FS when small perturbations in the training set occur. These methods are based on different subsampling strategies. A particular FS method is run on a number of subsamples and the obtained features/genes are merged into a more stable subset.

Compared to the wrapper and embedded models, algorithms of the filter model are independent of any learning model, therefore do not have bias associated with any learning models, one advantage of the filter model. Another advantage of the filter model is that it allows the algorithms to have very simple structure, which usually employs a straightforward search strategy, such as backward elimination or forward selection, and a feature evaluation criterion designed according to certain criterion. Therefore, in this work filter-based technique is preferred over wrapper based approach.

Fisher-Markov feature selector discriminates the classes by projecting high-dimensional input data onto low-dimensional subspaces with linear transformations, with the goal of maximizing inter-class variations while minimizing intra-class variations. Fisher-Markov selector identify those features that are the most useful in describing essential differences among the possible groups. The detailed description of the Fisher-Markov selector is shown in Even though Fisher's discriminant analysis performs no feature selection but projection onto subspaces through linear transformations, the spirit of maximizing the class separations can be exploited for the purpose of feature selection. This spirit induces the Fisher-Markov selector's class separability measure.

DISCRETIZATION

The most trivial problem with many classification algorithms is that they perform well with categorical variables (Yang & Webb, 2009). In most cases data sets do not have categories and have attributes with heterogeneous values. Discretization is a process through which classification of data sets can be handled easily. Discretization is a process through which continuous functions, models, equations and data are

Figure 1. Flow chart of discretization process

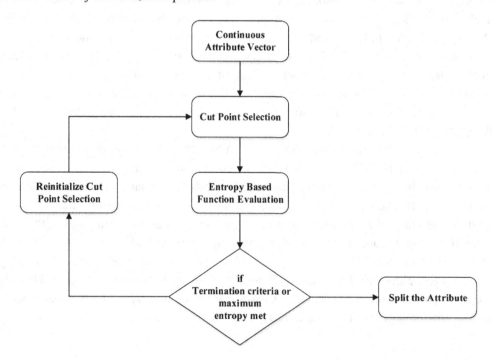

transferred into discrete value. The process is useful for numerical evaluation and reducing complexities. To define it formally, Let A be a vector of the numeric attribute, and the domain of A be in the interval of [lb, ub]. Let the domain of A is divided into k subinterval and denoted by P_a.

$$P_a = \{[I_1, I_2, I_{3,} \ldots\ldots\ldots I_k]\} \; k >= 2$$

where $I_1 = [d_0, d_1]$, $I_j = [d_{j-1}, d_j]$, $I_k = [d_{k-1}, d_k]$

d0 = lb, dj-1 < dj and dk = ub, Ij is the interval within the range dj-1…j. These ranges are the interval bound values of the continuous attribute which will be used for the conversion into the discrete form.

if $d_{j-1} \leq A(i) < d_j$ then A(i) = Ij

Binary discretization is the process where the partition ranges into two intervals. A threshold value t_h is determined which partitioned the data into two by

if A(i) <= t_h then A'(i) = 1

else A'(i) = 0

As seen above, there are several intervals between the upper and lower bound of domain for an attribute to be discretized and to select an optimal cut point from the intervals Entropy value is used. The cut point which has the minimum entropy value is selected as the cut point.

A dataset has many instances with large number of attributes and to select optimal cut point from attributes, domain entropy based selection process applied recursively until the desired stopping criteria. Dataset has a label class vector C which is associated with each attributes of dataset. Label class vector describes the class in a dataset. To understand, let's suppose that there are n numbers of classes in the vector C and an instance set S portioned into subsets S_1 and S_2. Then the class entropy for instance S without partition is calculated by

$$Ent(S) = -\sum_{k=0}^{n} P(C_k, S) \log P(C_k, S) \tag{1}$$

where $P(C_k, S)$ is a probability function which denotes the number of attributes lying in class C_k.

When instance S is partitioned into two subset S_1 and S_2 then the resulting entropy for set S is calculated by adding the weighted average entropy of partitioned subsets. For calculating weighted average, first individual entropy of each subset needs to be calculated. Individual entropy is calculated by

$$Ent(S_i) = -\sum_{k=0}^{n} P(C_k, S_i) \log P(C_k, S_i) \tag{2}$$

Here in equation 2 all variables are same as equation 1 except subscript 'i' which denotes the subset number. In above case 'i' takes only two value because only two subsets are present.

After calculation of individual entropy for subsets, entropy for set S is calculated by addition of weighted average of individual subset entropy as shown in equation 3.

$$Ent\left(S,T\right) = \frac{\left|S_1\right|}{\left|S\right|} Ent\left(S_1\right) + \frac{\left|S_2\right|}{\left|S\right|} Ent\left(S_2\right) \qquad (3)$$

Where T is cut point selected from the domain interval.

To access whether the selected cut point is optimal cut point or not Gain value is calculated by

$$Gain = Ent\left(S\right) - Ent\left(S,T\right) \qquad (4)$$

$Ent(S)$ is the entropy of class label C. The gain value is the difference between the class entropy and the weighted partition entropy. For the best partition value T this gain value should be maxima and can be achieved through the iterative procedure.

The flow chart in Figure 1 shows the process; here the iterative statement of finding the cut-point is based on the maxima gain. The drawback of cut-point selection is the runtime complexity because data consist of N * M matrices value and the N and M are large.

METHODOLOGY

Evolutionary Computation is a general framework for problem-solving, specifically solving a difficult optimization problem with mimicking the natural process of evolution. It basically comprises of the three approaches, genetic algorithm (GA), evolutionary strategies (ES) and evolutionary programming (EP). They all work on the same principle and differences can only be visualized through the individual representation, update operators, and the selection procedure.

Figure 2. Work flow diagram of proposed framework

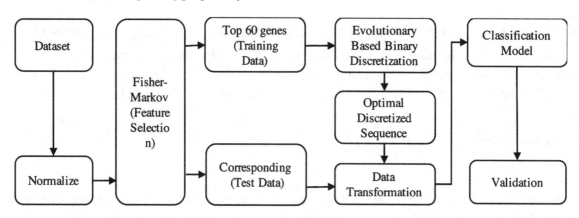

In this framework, the gene data is normalized in the first step, further this normalized data is passed through the Fisher-Markov feature selection algorithm to reduce the higher gene dimensionality. Fisher Markov is the filter-based feature selection algorithm that ranks the attributes according to the inter and intra class variations. Based on these ranking top 60 genes are considered for the participation in EBD phase. The role of EBD phase is to discretize some selected genes from the top 60 genes in such a way that the classification rate should be improved. The optimal sequence and cut value is produced by genetic algorithm (EBD). This sequence then used to transform the train and test data into the discretized data and will be used for the validation of classifiers. Figure 3 depicts the whole process flow.

Genetic algorithm (Goldberg & Holland, 1988) is preferred over the other two approaches because of wide applicability and success ratio. It is an evolutionary based algorithm where the set of chromosomes formed by the genes are trying to produce a better solution with the help of some genetic operators in an iterative way. Some random solutions are formulated as chromosomes and genes at an initialization step, and the process of crossover and mutation takes place in a certain way to improve the potential solution. A genetic algorithm has the two classical variant binary coded genetic algorithm (Holland, 1973) and real-coded genetic algorithm (Goldberg, 1991). The binary coded genetic algorithm solves the discrete optimization problem whereas the real coded can be applied to the real problems Individuals are represented as a string of binary in the binary coded genetic algorithm and in the case of real coded individuals are coded in the form of real numbers lying in the problem defined range. The proposed work uses both binary and real coded genetic algorithm (Goldberg, 1991) for solving the optimal cut point selection problem.

EVOLUTIONARY BASED BINARY DISCRETIZATION

This section describes the evolutionary based discretization technique; genetic algorithm is applied and formulated for solving the problem. The difference between class entropy and the weighted partition entropy used as a fitness function depicted in the equation 4.

Individual Representation

In the real coded genetic algorithm, the individual is assigned by the real numbers. It is an array of real numbers. The search space of the problem is the range of attribute values which are to be discretized. For the initialization of the chromosomes or individual, the minimum and maximum domain value of each attribute is calculated; these minimum and maximum values are the boundary points and are considered as lower bound (lb) and upper bound (ub). The random initialization of the initial population uses these lb and ub vectors. In this way, the chromosomes consist of random value lying in the domain [lb, ub] of attributes. Not all the attributes required discretization thus in addition to it, each gene has associated binary value that represents the presence and absence of corresponding attribute in discretization. This will produce the optimum sequence of discretized attributes and also save the computational effort required for each attributes.

Fitness Function

For the optimum discretization, it is mandatory to have the best fitness function that has the potential to evaluate the competency of each individual. Entropy-based criterion (Fayyad, 1993; Rebelo, Sá, Soares, & Knobbe, 2016) explained in section 3 is formulated for the fitness evaluation.

$$fit\left(x\right) = \max \sum_{j=1}^{n} Gain_j \tag{5}$$

To simplify the concept let us take an example of Prostate Tumor database present in GEMS where the dataset has 10501 attributes and all are continuous value. As Fisher-Markov selector will select the top 60 genes from total of 12601 genes. Thus the objective of the best 60 features is to classify into prostate tumor and normal tissues (two class). In order to apply the proposed technique, initial population will be randomly initialized form the lower and upper bound. The length of both the vector will be 60 in this case and shown below:

lb = [-20.0, -12.0, -32.0, ..., -71.0, -65.0]

ub = [51.0, 18.0, 96.0,..., 73, 61]

The initial population is initialized randomly between the values of lb and ub. For an example pop_i

$$pop_i = [17.34\ -23.056\ -17.78\ ....\ 4.79\ 10.69]$$

and for each population pop_i there is population participation vector is associated which will decide whether the corresponding index attribute will participate in discretized or not

$$pop\_part_i = [1\ 0\ 1\ ....\ 0\ 0]$$

if $pop\_part_i = 1$ *then* discretize i^{th} attribute *else* do nothing

Now from the class label given in the dataset we can calculate the class entropy, as the class label present in database is binary so entropy can be calculated by using equation 1, here 102 are the total instances given out of 102 data 52 data are normal tissues and 50 data are 'prostate tumor', so class entropy:

Ent_{cl} = - ((52 / 102) * log (52 / 102) + (50 / 102) * log (50 / 102))

Ent_{cl} = 0.9917

For the population pop_i shown above has cut value 17.34 for the first attribute and also its participation vector has value 1 depicts the first attribute will participate in discretization, so splitting the first input attribute with values greater than 17.34 into one and value lesser than 17.34 into the other. This will result into two new subset S_1 and S_2, further the entropy of S_1, S_2 splitting attribute is calculated

$$Ent_{S1} = - ((50 / 90) * \log (50 / 90) + (40 / 90) * \log (40 / 90))$$

$$Ent_{S1} = 0.9911$$

$$Ent_{S2} = ((10 / 12) * \log (10 / 12)) + ((2 / 12) * \log (2 / 12))$$

$$Ent_{S2} = 0.65$$

After partition the class entropy is calculated by adding the average entropy of subset S1 and S2

$$Ent_S = (90 / 102) * 0.9911 + (12 / 102) * 0.65$$

$$Ent_S = 0.9510$$

Next the gain value is computed for the attribute by subtracting the weighted splitting entropy with class label entropy without partition.

$$gain_{i,j} = 0.9917 - 0.9510 = 0.0407$$

Finally the fitness value is obtained by adding the gain values calculated using algorithm's individual population generated cut-point of the attributes.

$$fit_i = \sum_{j=1}^{n} gain$$

Algorithm 1 does the discretization with maxima gain achievable using fitness function designed.

The algorithm for the proposed system is shown above. Three pseudo codes named Evolutionary based Binary Discretization (EBD), Calculate Entropy Fitness (CEF) and Calculate Entropy (CE) were designed to achieve the objective of binary discretization.

EXPERIMENTAL SETUP AND RESULT

To prove the proclaimed efficiency of the proposed algorithm an exhaustive experiment is performed on 10 benchmark micro array gene dataset using the proposed methodology and four other discretization algorithms are considered for the sake of comparison. This section shows the experimental results and provides the sufficient evidence of competency of proposed algorithm. This section categorizes into three subsections, Experimental setup, Empirical results and Statistical test.

Algorithm 1. Calculate Entropy Fitness (CEF)

```
Procedure CEF

1. input data X and label Y

2. while length of the individual chromosome do

3. split the attribute by the chromosome value

4. Compute the indices of the splitting S₁, S₂ attribute

5. Calculate the entropy of the S₁ and S₂ by calling procedure CE

6. Compute Sᵢ the weighted average entropy of S₁ and S₂

7. Gainᵢ = Ent_cl - Sᵢ

8. end while
```

$$9.\ \text{fit} = \sum_{i=1}^{n} Gain_i$$

return fit

Experimental Setup

Algorithm performance is analyzed on 10 benchmark gene dataset referred from GEMS (Statnikov et al., 2005) dataset. Table 1 gives dataset summary, second column of table shows the data name, the third column titled with Number of samples enlists the number of instances, fourth column titled with Number of classes enlists the number of classes present in the dataset and the fifth column titled with Number of Genes represents the number of attributes in the dataset.

To prove the proposed system's efficiency, its performance has been compared with some of the prominent contemporary discretization algorithms. Four popular algorithms are chosen for performance comparison. These are Ameva (Gonzalez-Abril et al., 2009), class attribute interdependence maximization (CAIM) (Kurgan & Cios, 2004), ChiMerge (Kerber, 1992) and evolutionary multivariate discretizer (EMD) (Ramírez-Gallego et al., 2016). The proposed and other algorithms are mainly data preprocessing techniques which are used to process and remove the redundancy exist in data. The performance is validated on two classifiers decision tree (Quinlan, 2014) and naïve bayes (Yang & Webb, 2009). Each algorithm has its own set of standard parameters which need to be set before the experiment. Table 2 presents the parameters that were set during the experimentation. CAIM and AMEVA were run on the default values. Genetic algorithm parameter are the empirically set by the best value selected based on many runs.

Empirical Result

This subsection shows the performance of proposed system through experimental results. Exhaustive experiments were conducted and to list the results, this section is further organized into three subsections. These three subsections show significant portion of experiment. First section shows the effect on

Algorithm 2. Evolutionary based Binary Discretization (EBD)

```
Procedure EBD

1. Input Dataset X_{m*n}

2. Calculate LB and UB from each column of X

3. Initialize the parameter npop, ntime, cr, mu

4. Randomly initialize the population

5. Evaluate the initial population with entropy-based fitness call procedure
CEF

6. While termination criteria met do

7. if cr < threshold value then \\ crossover rate = 0.7

8. Apply the selection operator for parent selection

9. Initialize crossover parameter

10. Applying crossover

11. end if

12. if mu < threshold value then \\ Mutation rate = 0.8

13. Apply the selection operator for individual selection

14. Initialize mutation parameter

15. Applying Mutation

16. end if

17. Evaluate the updated population

18. Replace the worst solution

19. end while

20. end
```

classifier when used with proposed system. Second section illustrate the performance comparison of classifier when used with proposed system and four state-of art techniques AMEVA, CAIM, ChiMerge and EMD discretization algorithms. Third part shows the statistical test performed on the obtained results to show the significance improvement achieved by the proposed framework. Wilcoxon, Friedman and post hoc Holms test were conducted to validate the performance improvement over the other contemporary techniques.

Table 3 depicts the first part of the result. It shows the comparative analysis of accuracy obtained by classifier algorithm when used alone and when used along with EBD. Table has been divided into two parts, first column lists the data name. Second and third column of both the part of table belong to Naïve Bayes and C4.5 experimental results. Second column w/o EBD shows the Naïve Bayes accuracy

Algorithm 3. Calculate Entropy (CE)

```
Procedure CE

1. Input the class label L

2. for each unique label in class label L do

3. Find the length of indices of label i

4. Calculate the entropy of label i by using equation 1

5. S = S + entropy of label i

6. end for

7. return S
```

Table 1. Summary description of microarray dataset

Dataset Number	Dataset Name	Number of Samples	Number of Classes	Number of Genes
1	11-tumors	60	9	5726
2	9-tumors	174	11	12533
3	Brain-Tumors1	90	5	5920
4	Brain-Tumors2	50	4	10367
5	Leukemia1	72	3	5327
6	Leukemia2	72	3	11225
7	Lung-Cancer	203	5	12600
8	SRBCT	83	4	2308
9	Prostate-Tumor	102	2	10509
10	DLBCL	77	2	5469

when used without EDB algorithm. Fourth column shows the accuracy of Naïve Bayes when used on data preprocessed by EBD algorithm. Third column of the table show the accuracy of C4.5 when used without EBD. Fifth column represents accuracy value of C4.5 classifier when used over the preprocessed data by EBD. Some elements of the table are shown in bold. This bold value represents the instances when classifier along with Proposed EBD outperforms the classifier not used with EBD. From the table 3, we can infer that the performance of decision tree with EBD is producing better results in 9 datasets out of the 10 considered dataset while the performance of naïve Bayes is better in 7 out of 10 datasets. From the table it can be concluded that performance of classifier algorithm is improved by utilizing the proposed framework.

Table 2. Parameters of the classifier and discretizer

Method	Parameters
C4.5	Pruned tree, confidence = 0.25, 2 items per leaf
Naïve Bayes	Distribution = 'kernel'
Validation	10 – Fold Cross validation
ChiMerge	Confidence threshold = 0.05
Genetic Algorithm	Population = 50, crossover rate = 0.8, tolerance = 1e-6 Mutation rate = 0.6 Crossover = 'Scattered', Mutation = 'Gaussian'

Table 3. Average accuracy obtained naïve Bayes and C4.5 with EBD and without EBD

Data Name	Naïve Bayes		C4.5		Naïve Bayes+EBD		C4.5+EBD	
	Avg. Accuracy	STD	Avg. Accuracy	STD	Avg. Accuracy	STD	Avg. Accuracy	STD
11-tumors	92.380	0.916	91.975	0.701	**92.719**	0.765	**92.436**	0.824
9-tumors	79.483	1.468	78.405	1.330	**80.515**	1.871	**80.210**	1.811
Brain-Tumors1	96.460	1.038	96.394	0.805	**96.791**	0.783	96.369	0.828
Brain-Tumors2	99.155	0.564	98.870	0.726	98.687	0.553	**98.926**	0.459
Leukemia1	99.613	0.252	99.631	0.325	99.530	0.260	**99.824**	0.263
Leukemia2	99.466	0.319	99.402	0.321	99.431	0.278	**99.586**	0.206
Lung-Cancer	98.796	0.684	98.890	0.591	**98.996**	0.632	**99.080**	0.515
SRBCT	97.659	0.869	97.825	0.894	**98.506**	0.814	**98.341**	0.932
Prostate-Tumor	99.489	0.252	99.389	0.260	**99.462**	0.135	**99.562**	0.296
DLBCL	98.679	0.541	98.898	0.591	**98.953**	0.667	**99.104**	0.426

Table 4 represents the second sub section of the result discussion. This table shows the comparative performance for Naïve Bayes classifier when used with EBD and four other discretization algorithms individually. The column of the table represents the average accuracy and standard deviation of the discretizers computed during the experimentation. Best values have been highlighted in bold face. From the table it is clear that more than half of the considered dataset are classified more accurately then the other three algorithms.

Table 5 shows the comparative analysis of Decision tree C4.5 classifier when used with EBD, CAIM, ChiMerge and EMD individually. The performance of classifier is measured in terms of average accuracy and standard deviation. The best performances have been highlighted in bold face. By analyzing table, it could be said that decision tree when used with EBD outperforms the other discretization algorithms and are competent enough by producing the higher accuracies in nine datasets.

The final and third part of the result is represented in table 6 where characteristics of the two classification algorithms with EBD is represented. Both the algorithms C45 and Naïve Bayes use the data discretized by evolutionary based binary Discretization. The comparison of performance is based on

Table 4. Naive Bayes accuracy performance with EBD

Data Name	Ameva		CAIM		ChiMerge		EMD		EBD	
	Avg.	Std-Dev	Avg.	Std-Dev	Avg.	Std-Dev	Avg.	Std-Dev	Avg.	Std-Dev
11-tumors	92.335	0.986	92.148	0.884	92.572	1.016	92.239	0.657	**92.719**	0.765
9-tumors	79.855	2.086	79.657	1.488	79.511	1.408	80.255	1.781	**80.515**	1.871
Brain-Tumors1	96.198	1.022	94.716	0.680	94.442	0.727	96.751	1.638	**96.791**	0.783
Brain-Tumors2	99.225	0.519	99.214	0.604	99.254	0.662	99.787	1.535	98.687	0.553
Leukemia1	99.179	0.237	99.419	0.222	99.275	0.270	98.305	1.602	**99.530**	0.260
Leukemia2	99.481	0.285	99.146	0.288	99.105	0.297	99.891	1.728	99.431	0.278
Lung-Cancer	99.176	0.656	99.102	0.637	99.460	0.451	99.023	0.312	98.996	0.632
SRBCT	97.564	0.844	97.504	0.945	97.763	0.835	97.506	0.414	**98.506**	0.814
Prostate-Tumor	99.344	0.311	99.298	0.232	99.235	0.280	98.462	0.325	**99.462**	0.135
DLBCL	98.726	0.522	99.086	0.646	99.205	0.460	99.253	0.367	98.953	0.667

Table 5. Decision tree accuracy performance with EBD

Data Name	Ameva		CAIM		ChiMerge		EMD		EBD	
	Avg.	Std-Dev	Avg.	Std-Dev	Avg.	Std-Dev	Avg.	Std-Dev	Avg.	Std-Dev
11-tumors	92.085	0.786	92.167	0.809	92.019	0.888	92.145	0.879	**92.436**	0.824
9-tumors	78.952	1.973	79.746	1.774	79.060	2.045	79.924	2.064	**80.210**	1.811
Brain-Tumors1	96.531	1.091	96.549	0.904	96.925	0.773	97.021	1.654	96.369	0.828
Brain-Tumors2	96.052	0.509	94.009	0.595	98.311	0.517	97.845	0.894	**98.926**	0.459
Leukemia1	99.584	0.209	99.502	0.294	99.496	0.294	99.245	0.324	**99.824**	0.263
Leukemia2	99.452	0.230	99.556	0.309	99.389	0.265	99.103	0.248	**99.586**	0.206
Lung-Cancer	98.643	0.388	99.031	0.590	98.975	0.603	98.901	0.617	**99.080**	0.515
SRBCT	96.697	0.688	97.260	0.771	97.857	0.641	98.254	0.964	**98.341**	0.932
Prostate-Tumor	99.462	0.286	99.487	0.298	99.532	0.297	99.127	1.024	**99.562**	0.296
DLBCL	98.900	0.750	99.037	0.575	98.589	0.623	99.012	2.244	**99.104**	0.426

dimensionality reduction achieved by the EBD. First discretization of dataset and classification is performed on Decision tree and then C45 separately. Table 6 divided into two parts first part represents decision tree's performance when used with EBD. Second part shows the Naïve Bayes classifiers' performance when used with EBD. The results shown in table are in terms of number of genes considered for discretizing and its percentage of the discretization. From the table it is depicted that proposed EBD outperformed in the dimensionality reduction and simultaneously delivering the improved accuracy. However, the performance in of C45 is observed better than the Naïve Bayes algorithm.

Table 6. Characteristics of proposed framework

Dataset	Total Number of Genes	Decision Tree		Naïve Bayes	
		No. of Genes Discretized	Percentage of Genes Discretized	No. of Genes Discretized	Percentage of Genes Discretized
11-tumors	5726	28.2	0.0049	34.7	0.0061
9-tumors	12533	27.3	0.0022	28.9	0.0023
Brain-Tumors1	5920	20.6	0.0035	36.4	0.0061
Brain-Tumors2	10367	15.3	0.0015	21.5	0.0021
Leukemia1	5327	8.4	0.0016	13.8	0.0026
Leukemia2	11225	12.6	0.0011	27.9	0.0025
Lung-Cancer	12600	24.6	0.0020	23.7	0.0019
SRBCT	2308	28.9	0.0125	42.6	0.0185
Prostate-Tumor	10509	25.6	0.0024	35.9	0.0034
DLBCL	5469	34.2	0.0063	43.8	0.0080

Statistical Test

The nonparametric statistical test is considered for carrying the statistical test. Wilcoxon signed rank test (Demšar, 2006), and the Friedman test (Benavoli, Corani, & Mangili, 2016) results are computed on the fold wise accuracy of each dataset.

Table 7 summarizes the result obtained by Wilcoxon test at $\alpha = 0.05$ level of significance. The table is divided into two sections: C4.5 and Naïve Bayes,

The measure of the average accuracy of these classifiers were used. The + symbol lists the number of best readings of the all discretization algorithms, and ± symbol indicates the number of best and identical best results for all the discretization algorithms. The numbers which are highlighted in bold are maximum number of best result given by an algorithm. From the table 7 it is clear that proposed EBD algorithm shows the significant difference.

Figure 3 and Figure 4 are the interactive graphs generated for the multiple comparisons using Friedman ranking test. This figure has the four horizontal lines with a center mark representing the mean value of the ranking; the Friedman rank test is performed on Matlab which produces the mean rank of four methods with the largest value being the best ranking.

Table 8 presents the statistical analysis observed by the Friedman test for C4.5 and Naïve Bayes classification accuracy. The ranking is generated based on the performance of the various discretizer on the benchmark data; Second column of the table shows the ranking where higher value is the better.

Table 7. Wilcoxon test results for accuracy

Algorithms	α = 0.9		α = 0.95	
	+	±	+	±
Ameva	0	2	0	2
CAIM	0	2	0	2
ChiMerge	0	2	0	2
EMD	0	2	0	2
EBD	**3**	**3**	**3**	**3**

Figure 3. Estimates of mean with comparison for C4.5

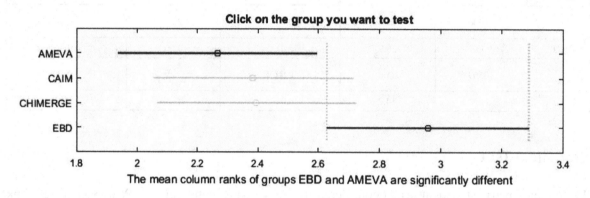

Figure 4. Estimates of mean with comparison for Naive Bayes

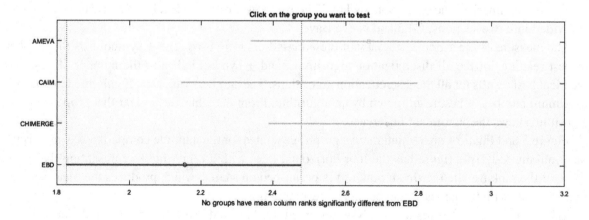

Table 8. Friedman procedure and adjusted p-value with Holm's test

Algorithms	C4.5		Naïve Bayes	
	Ranking	P_{holm}	Ranking	P_{holm}
Ameva	2.266	0.036	2.663	0.185
CAIM	2.383	0.114	2.469	0.598
ChiMerge	2.394	0.125	**2.714**	0.121
EBD	**2.957**	-	2.153	-

EBD in the case of C4.5 has the first ranking while in the case of Naïve Bayes its ranking is third. The third column shows the post hoc Holm's test (Holm, 1979) adjusted P-value. EBD proves it's significant by being better than the other with a level of significance $\alpha = 0.1$ in the case of C4.5 whereas Naïve Bayes is not significantly different amongst the group.

Table 9 assembles the result gathered by Wilcoxon test on the evolutionary based discretization algorithms EMD and EBD; the table is showing both the classifier performance on the test with a considering the values of $\alpha = 0.05$.

CONCLUSION

In this paper, a framework for micro array gene data classification based on Evolutionary based Binary Discretization (EBD) technique is proposed to discretize continuous attribute present in datasets so that the performance can be improved. Proposed technique uses the Fisher Markov selector and selects the top 60 attributes. From this 60 attributes EBD discretizes some selected attributes by partitioning it into binary classes that is in two separate classes. A class entropy-based fitness function is used to evaluate the cut points generated by proposed EBD. 10 benchmark datasets are taken from the GEMS repository for experimental purposes. To check the effectiveness of the proposed framework decision tree (C4.5) and naïve Bayes classifiers are used in this study. The competitiveness of the proposed method with three other prominent algorithms are evaluated and compared. The four algorithms are Ameva, CAIM, Chimerge and EMD. The experiment performed were exhaustive and time consuming. From the experimental results, it can be said that the proposed EBD method improved the performance of classifier algorithms slightly compared to other discretization algorithms in the gene classification. The proposed method could be used as feasible option for preprocessing of large biomedical datasets as it shows the

Table 9. Wilcoxon Test Result between EBD and without EBD

Algorithm	C4.5		Naïve Bayes	
	+	±	+	±
EBD	1	1	**1**	**1**
Without EBD	0	0	1	1

equal potential present in existing preprocessing algorithms. As the experiment of the proposed system is on the higher dimensional data that various dimension of improvement remain untouched. For future, the limitations associated with the proposed algorithm will be handled few of them could be the, tuning of parameters could generate more improved result because the proposed system was tested with the standard set of parameters which was remained constant throughout experiment. Results could be more improved by increasing the number of partition using the evolutionary model. The purpose of the experiment is to show that by using simple binary classification entangled with the features of evolutionary algorithm could result into higher predictive capability.

REFERENCES

Acharya, U. R., & Dua, P. (2014). *Machine Learning in Healthcare Informatics* (Vol. 56). Springer Berlin Heidelberg. doi:10.1007/978-3-642-40017-9

Su, C. T., & Hsu, J. H. (2005). An Extended Chi2 algorithm for discretization of real value attributes. *IEEE Transactions on Knowledge and Data Engineering*, 17(3), 437–441. doi:10.1109/TKDE.2005.39

Arbor, A. (1992). On the Handling of Continuous-Valued Attributes in Decision Tree Generation. *Machine Learning*, 8(1), 87–102. doi:10.1007/BF00994007

Benavoli, A., Corani, G., & Mangili, F. (2016). Should we really use post-hoc tests based on mean-ranks? *Journal of Machine Learning Research*, 17, 1–10.

Boulle, M. (2004). Khiops: A Statistical Discretization Method of Continuous Attributes. *Machine Learning*, 55(1), 53–69. doi:10.1023/B:MACH.0000019804.29836.05

Boullé, M. (2006). MODL: A Bayes optimal discretization method for continuous attributes. *Machine Learning*, 65(1), 131–165. doi:10.100710994-006-8364-x

Chan, C. (1991). Determination of quantization intervals in rule based. In *Decision Aiding for Complex Systems* (pp. 1719–1723). Conference.

Chan, K. C. C., & Ching, J. Y. (1995). Class-Dependent Discretization for Inductive Learning from Continuous and Mixed-Mode Data. *IEEE Transactions on Pattern Analysis and Machine Intelligence*. doi:10.1109/34.391407

Cheng, Q., Zhou, H., & Cheng, J. (2011). The Fisher-Markov Selector. *Fast Selecting Maximally Separable Feature Subset for Multiclass Classification with Applications to High-Dimensional Data*, 33(6), 1217–1233. PMID:21493968

Chmielewski, M. R., & Grzymala-Busse, J. W. (1996). Global discretization of continuous attributes as preprocessing for machine learning. *International Journal of Approximate Reasoning*, 15(4), 319–331. doi:10.1016/S0888-613X(96)00074-6

Demšar, J. (2006). Statistical Comparisons of Classifiers over Multiple Data Sets. *Journal of Machine Learning Research*, 7, 1–30. doi:10.1016/j.jecp.2010.03.005

Diao, R., & Shen, Q. (2015). Nature inspired feature selection meta-heuristics. *Artificial Intelligence Review, 44*(3), 311–340. doi:10.100710462-015-9428-8

Fayyad, U., & Irani, K. (1993). Multi-interval discretization of continuous-valued attributes for classification learning. In Machine Learning (pp. 1022-1027).

Garcia, S., Fernandez, A., Luengo, J., & Herrera, F. (2009). A study of statistical techniques and performance measures for genetics-based machine learning: Accuracy and interpretability. *Soft Computing, 13*(10), 959–977. doi:10.100700500-008-0392-y

García, S., Luengo, J., & Herrera, F. (2015). *Data Preprocessing in Data Mining* (Vol. 72). Intelligent Systems Reference Library; doi:10.1007/978-3-319-10247-4

Garcia, S., Luengo, J., Sáez, J. A., Lopez, V., & Herrera, F. (2013). A Survey of Discretization Techniques: Taxonomy and Empirical Analysis in Supervised Learning. *IEEE Transactions on Knowledge and Data Engineering, 25*(4), 734–750. doi:10.1109/TKDE.2012.35

García, S., Luengo, J., Sáez, J. A., López, V., Herrera, F., Garcia, S., ... Herrera, F. (2013). A survey of discretization techniques: Taxonomy and empirical analysis in supervised learning. *IEEE Transactions on Knowledge and Data Engineering, 25*(4), 734–750. doi:10.1109/TKDE.2012.35

Giráldez, R., Aguilar-Ruiz, J. S., Riquelme, J. C., Ferrer-Troyano, F., & Rodr'iguez, D. (2002). Discretization Oriented to Decision Rules Generation. *Frontiers in Artificial Intelligence and Applications, 82,* 275–279.

Goldberg, D. (1991). Real-coded genetic algorithms, virtual alphabets, and blocking. *Complex Systems, 5(2),* 139–167.

Goldberg, D. E., & Holland, J. H. (1988). Genetic Algorithms and Machine Learning. *Machine Learning, 3*(2), 95–99. doi:10.1023/A:1022602019183

Gonzalez-Abril, L., Cuberos, F. J., Velasco, F., & Ortega, J. A. (2009). Ameva: An autonomous discretization algorithm. *Expert Systems with Applications, 36*(3 PART 1), 5327–5332. doi:10.1016/j.eswa.2008.06.063

Ho, K., & Scott, P. (1997). Zeta: A global method for discretization of continuous variables. In Proceedings of the 3rd International Conference on Knowledge Discovery and Data Mining (pp. 191-194). Retrieved from http://www.aaai.org/Papers/KDD/1997/KDD97-037.pdf

Holland, J. H. (1962). Outline for a Logical Theory of Adaptive Systems. *Journal of the Association for Computing Machinery, 9*(3), 297–314. doi:10.1145/321127.321128

Holland, J. H. (1973). Genetic algorithms and the optimal allocation of trials. *SIAM Journal on Computing, 2*(2), 88–105. doi:10.1137/0202009

Holm, S. (1979). A Simple Sequentially Rejective Multiple Test Procedure. *Scandinavian Journal of Statistics, 6*(2), 65–70.

Houari, R., Bounceur, A., Kechadi, M., Tari, A., & Euler, R. (2016). Dimensionality reduction in data mining: A Copula approach. *Expert Systems with Applications, 64,* 247–260. doi:10.1016/j.eswa.2016.07.041

Huang, J., Cai, Y., & Xu, X. (2007). A hybrid genetic algorithm for feature selection wrapper based on mutual information. *Pattern Recognition Letters*, *28*(13), 1825–1844. doi:10.1016/j.patrec.2007.05.011

Kerber, R. (1992). Chimerge: Discretization of numeric attributes. In *Proceedings of the Tenth National Conference on Artificial Intelligence* (pp. 123–128). Retrieved from http://dl.acm.org/citation.cfm?id=1867154%5Cnpapers2://publication/uuid/F1C11C06-12F0-4A83-82D3-CC62A52FBE75

Kira, K., & Rendell, L. (1994). A practical approach to feature selection. In *Proceedings of the Ninth International Conference on Machine Learning*.

Kurgan, L. A., & Cios, K. J. (2004). CAIM Discretization Algorithm. *IEEE Transactions on Knowledge and Data Engineering*, *16*(2), 145–153. doi:10.1109/TKDE.2004.1269594

Lazar, C., Taminau, J., Meganck, S., Steenhoff, D., Coletta, A., Molter, C., ... Nowe, A. (2012). A Survey on Filter Techniques for Feature Selection in Gene Expression Microarray Analysis. *IEEE/ACM Transactions on Computational Biology and Bioinformatics*, *9*(4), 1106–1119. doi:10.1109/TCBB.2012.33 PMID:22350210

Le, T. M., Paul, J. S., & Ong, S. H. (2010). Computational Biology. *Applied Bioinformatics*, *673*(1), 243–271. doi:10.1007/978-1-4419-0811-7

Lee, C. H. (2007). A Hellinger-based discretization method for numeric attributes in classification learning. *Knowledge-Based Systems*, *20*(4), 419–425. doi:10.1016/j.knosys.2006.06.005

Li, J., Li, X., & Zhang, W. (2016). A Filter Feature Selection Method Based LLRFC and Redundancy Analysis for Tumor Classification Using Gene Expression Data. In *2016 12th World Congress on Intelligent Control and Automation (WCICA)* (pp. 2861-2867). IEEE.

Li, X., & Yin, M. (2013). Multiobjective binary biogeography based optimization for feature selection using gene expression data. *IEEE Transactions on Nanobioscience*, *12*(4), 343–353. Retrieved from http://www.ncbi.nlm.nih.gov/pubmed/25003163 doi:10.1109/TNB.2013.2294716 PMID:25003163

Liu, H., Hussain, F., Tan, C. L., & Dash, M. (2002). Discretization: An enabling technique. *Data Mining and Knowledge Discovery*, *6*(4), 393–423. doi:10.1023/A:1016304305535

Liu, H., Motoda, H., Setiono, R., & Zhao, Z. (2010). Feature Selection: An Ever Evolving Frontier in Data Mining. In *The Fourth Workshop on Feature Selection in Data Mining* (pp. 4–13).

Liu, H., & Setiono, R. (1997). Feature selection via discretization. *IEEE Transactions on Knowledge and Data Engineering*, *9*(4), 642–645. doi:10.1109/69.617056

Maimon, O., & Rokach, L. E. (2002). Handbook of Data Mining and Knowledge Discovery. Oxford University Press.

Mehta, S., Parthasarathy, S., & Yang, H. (2005). Toward Unsupervised Correlation Preserving Discretization. *IEEE Transactions on Knowledge and Data Engineering*, *17*(9), 1174–1185. doi:10.1109/TKDE.2005.153

Method, D. D., Cerquides, J., & De Mantaras, R. L. (1992). Proposal and Empirical Comparison of a Parallelizable. In *KDD: Proceedings / International Conference on Knowledge Discovery & Data Mining. International Conference on Knowledge Discovery & Data Mining* (pp. 139–142). Retrieved from http://citeseerx.ist.psu.edu/viewdoc/summary?doi=10.1.1.109.7428

Misra, S., & Ray, S. S. (2017). Finding optimum width of discretization for gene expressions using functional annotations. *Computers in Biology and Medicine, 90*, 59–67. doi:10.1016/j.compbiomed.2017.09.010 PMID:28941844

Molano, V., Cobos, C., Mendoza, M., & Herrera-viedma, E. (2014). Feature Selection Based on Sampling and C4. 5 Algorithm to Improve the Quality of Text Classification Using Naïve Bayes. In *Mexican International Conference on Artificial Intelligence* (pp. 80–91). Springer.

Oliveira, L. S., Morita, M., & Sabourin, R. (2006). (n.d.). *Feature Selection for Ensembles Using the Multi-Objective Optimization Approach, 74*, 49–74.

Quinlan, J. R. (2014). *C4. 5: programs for machine learning*. Elsevier.

Ramírez-Gallego, S., García, S., Benítez, J. M., & Herrera, F. (2016). Multivariate Discretization Based on Evolutionary Cut Points Selection for Classification. *IEEE Transactions on Cybernetics, 46*(3), 595–608. doi:10.1109/TCYB.2015.2410143 PMID:25794409

Rebelo, C., Sá, D., Soares, C., & Knobbe, A. (2016). Entropy-based discretization methods for ranking data. *Information Sciences, 329*, 921–936. doi:10.1016/j.ins.2015.04.022

Ropero, R. F., Renooij, S., & van der Gaag, L. C. (2018). Discretizing environmental data for learning Bayesian-network classifiers. *Ecological Modelling, 368*, 391–403. doi:10.1016/j.ecolmodel.2017.12.015

Ruiz, F. J., Angulo, C., & Agell, N. (2008). IDD: A supervised interval distance-based method for discretization. *IEEE Transactions on Knowledge and Data Engineering, 20*(9), 1230–1238. doi:10.1109/TKDE.2008.66

Statnikov, A., Tsamardinos, I., Dosbayev, Y., & Aliferis, C. F. (2005). GEMS: A system for automated cancer diagnosis and biomarker discovery from microarray gene expression data. *International Journal of Medical Informatics, 74*(7-8), 491–503. doi:10.1016/j.ijmedinf.2005.05.002 PMID:15967710

Tahan, M. H., & Asadi, S. (2017). MEMOD: A novel multivariate evolutionary multi-objective discretization. *Soft Computing*. doi:10.100700500-016-2475-5

Tahan, M. H., & Asadi, S. (2018). EMDID: Evolutionary multi-objective discretization for imbalanced datasets. *Information Sciences, 432*, 442–461. doi:10.1016/j.ins.2017.12.023

Tran, B., Xue, B., & Zhang, M. (2016). A New Representation in PSO for Discretisation-Based Feature Selection. Retrieved from http://homepages.ecs.vuw.ac.nz/~xuebing/Papers/tran_Cybernetics2017.pdf

Tsai, C. J., Lee, C. I., & Yang, W. P. (2008). A discretization algorithm based on Class-Attribute Contingency Coefficient. *Information Sciences, 178*(3), 714–731. doi:10.1016/j.ins.2007.09.004

Tsai, C. W., Chiang, M. C., Ksentini, A., & Chen, M. (2016). Metaheuristic Algorithms for Healthcare: Open Issues and Challenges. *Computers & Electrical Engineering*, *53*, 421–434. doi:10.1016/j.compeleceng.2016.03.005

Wu, Q., Bell, D., McGinnity, M., Prasad, G., Qi, G., & Huang, X. (2006). Improvement of decision accuracy using discretization of continuous attributes. In *International Conference on Fuzzy Systems and Knowledge Discovery* (pp. 674–683).

Wu, Q., Bell, D. A., Prasad, G., & Mcginnity, T. M. (2007). A distribution-index-based discretizer for decision-making with symbolic AI approaches. *IEEE Transactions on Knowledge and Data Engineering*, *19*(1), 17–28. doi:10.1109/TKDE.2007.250582

Wu, X. (1996). A Bayesian Discretizer for real-valued attributes. *The Computer Journal*, *39*(8), 688–691. doi:10.1093/comjnl/39.8.688

Yang, P., Li, J.-S., & Huang, Y.-X. (2011). HDD: A hypercube division-based algorithm for discretisation. *International Journal of Systems Science*, *42*(4), 557–566. doi:10.1080/00207720903572455

Yang, P., & Yang, Hwa, Y., Zhou, B.B., & Zomaya, A.Y. (2010). A review of ensemble methods in bioinformatics. *Current Bioinformatics*, *5*(4), 296–308. doi:10.2174/157489310794072508

Yang, Y., & Webb, G. I. (2009). Discretization for naive-Bayes learning: Managing discretization bias and variance. *Machine Learning*, *74*(1), 39–74. doi:10.100710994-008-5083-5

Zighed, D. A., Rabaséda, S., & Rakotomalala, R. (1998). Fusinter: A method for discretization of continuous attributes. *International Journal of Uncertainty, Fuzziness and Knowledge-based Systems*. doi:10.1142/S0218488598000264

Chapter 3
Subspace Clustering of High Dimensional Data Using Differential Evolution

Parul Agarwal
Jaypee Institute of Information Technology, India

Shikha Mehta
Jaypee Institute of Information Technology, India

ABSTRACT

Subspace clustering approaches cluster high dimensional data in different subspaces. It means grouping the data with different relevant subsets of dimensions. This technique has become very effective as a distance measure becomes ineffective in a high dimensional space. This chapter presents a novel evolutionary approach to a bottom up subspace clustering SUBSPACE_DE which is scalable to high dimensional data. SUBSPACE_DE uses a self-adaptive DBSCAN algorithm to perform clustering in data instances of each attribute and maximal subspaces. Self-adaptive DBSCAN clustering algorithms accept input from differential evolution algorithms. The proposed SUBSPACE_DE algorithm is tested on 14 datasets, both real and synthetic. It is compared with 11 existing subspace clustering algorithms. Evaluation metrics such as F1_Measure and accuracy are used. Performance analysis of the proposed algorithms is considerably better on a success rate ratio ranking in both accuracy and F1_Measure. SUBSPACE_DE also has potential scalability on high dimensional datasets.

1. INTRODUCTION

Clustering is one of the vital approaches in the field of data mining. It forms the groups of similar data on basis of certain properties. The most common property is distance measure. The criteria for assembling the similar datasets into one group and dissimilar in other groups vary from algorithm to algorithm. In today's world clustering is being used in number of fields like engineering, medicines, marketing, economics etc. In engineering field (Hans-Peter Kriegel, Kröger, & Zimek, 2009), clustering plays an important role in artificial intelligence, spatial database analysis, web mining, computer vision, pattern

DOI: 10.4018/978-1-5225-5852-1.ch003

recognition, face recognition, machine learning (Ira Assent, 2012) and many more. It also has its application in mechanical engineering, electrical engineering, medical sciences like microbiology, genetics, pathology etc. There are variety of clustering algorithms (Fahad et al., 2014) like partition based (K-Means, K-Mediods, K-Modes, CLARA, PAM, fuzzy c means), density based (DBSCAN, OPTICS, DENCLUE), hierarchical based (BIRCH, CURE, ROCK), grid based (STING, OPTIGRID, CLIQUE) and model based (EM, COBWEB).

The traditional clustering algorithms clusters data in full dimensional space i.e. considering all attributes while clustering. However, when number of attributes increases i.e. dimensions of data are amplified then traditional algorithms fails to give meaningful clusters. The reason behind this failure is that data becomes sparse in high dimensional space and distance measure becomes meaningless. This problem is coined as curse of dimensionality (Ira Assent, 2012). Traditional clustering algorithm breakdown when implemented on high dimensions. In high dimensional data, it is possible that there exists number of clusters for which only few dimensions are relevant instead of all dimensions. The subsets of dimensions are called subspaces. Clustering in high dimension is possible through subspaces and is called subspace clustering. However, there are number of challenges in subspace clustering (Parsons et al., 2004) like huge combinations of dimensions, overlapping subspaces etc. Due to these challenges, there has been scope of improvement in these algorithms. Subspace clustering not only determines the clusters in dataset but also the subspaces in which these clusters are present. There are two main search methods of subspace clustering: top down and bottom up search methods (Parsons et al., 2004).

Top down approach of subspace clustering method searches the subspaces and clusters in descending fashion. It follows three phases of clustering i.e. initialization phase, iteration phase and refinement of clusters formed in iterations. The input parameter for this approach is size of subspace and number of clusters. Algorithms of top down approach start from initializing all dimensions with same weight. Clustering in initialization phase is performed in full dimensional space. When clusters are formed, each dimension is assigned new weights for each cluster. The next iteration starts by considering the new weights of dimensions for clustering. This is an exhaustive process as it requires multiple iterations for best results. The one way to implement this approach is use of sampling. Sampling can improve the performance of top down subspace clustering algorithms. However, there are number of drawbacks in this approach. Top down approach is based on only partitioning of dataset that means each instance will belong to only one cluster. Overlapping subspaces could not be determined. The input parameters requires in top down approach are hard to determine prior of clustering. For unlabelled dataset or for unknown number of clusters, this approach is not suitable. Additionally, determining size of subspace priory is an intricate problem. If sampling strategy is used, then size of sample is also a critical parameter that should be known before clustering. Some algorithms of top down approach are PROCLUS, ORCLUS, FINDIT and COSA (Parsons et al., 2004).

Bottom up approach of subspace search method finds the subspaces and clusters in ascending fashion of dimensions. It uses APRORI principle to reduce the search space for subspace clustering. The algorithm starts clustering at lower dimensions. It determines the dense points at small dimensions and then move towards larger subspaces. The downward closure property is followed. If the point is dense at D dimensions that it is dense at (D-1) projections of dimensions. The algorithm based on bottom up approach terminates unless no dense unit is discovered. The advantage of bottom up approach is that it is capable of detecting overlapping subspaces. This implies that a data point or instance can be a part of more than one subspace or cluster. The input parameters of this approach are the grid size and density threshold. Efficacy of bottom up subspace clustering algorithms is largely dependent on input parameters. These control parameters are quite difficult to determine where data distribution is not known. Hence, algorithm would work efficiently if parameters are well defined. Grid size of input parameter can be either static (e.g. CLIQUE, ENCLUS) or data driven (e.g. MAFIA, DOC, etc.) (Parsons et al., 2004).

Algorithms of subspace clustering are characterized under 3 categories (Emmanuel Müller, Günnemann, Assent, & Seidl, 2009) namely: cell based, density based and clustering oriented approaches. Cell based approach describes the minimum number of objects in a fixed or variable grid size. Subspaces formed are restricted to cells. Dimensions that could not get an opportunity to be part of subspace are spanned by cells individually. Examples of cell-based algorithms are CLIQUE (Road & Jose, 1998), DOC (Procopiuc, 2002), MINECLUS (Yiu & Mamoulis, 2003) AND SCHISM (Sequeira & Zaki., 2004). The second strategy is density-based clustering approach. It differentiates dense region by sparse region. Cluster exists only in dense region. The density in dataset could be determined by computing distance between instances. This distance computation is done in relevant subset of dimensions instead of complete attribute set. However, varying input parameters could determine clusters of varying density. Examples of density-based subspace algorithms are SUBCLU (Kailing, Kriegel, & Oger, 2004), FIRES (Kriegel, Kroger, Renz, & Wurst., 2005) AND INSCY (Assent, Krieger, Müller, & Seidl, 2008). The third category i.e. clustering oriented approach of subspace clustering do not depends on density or number of objects. It clusters the datasets considering number of clusters, number of subspaces, average number of dimensions in each subspace where clusters are formed etc. This approach does not depend on parameters of each cluster rather total number of clusters as whole. Algorithms belonging to this category are PROCLUS (Aggarwal, Wolf, Yu, Procopiuc, & Park., 1999), P3C (Moise, Sander, & Ester, 2006) and STATPC (Moise & Sander., 2008).

A novel subspace clustering algorithm has been proposed in this work. This algorithm follows bottom up approach of subspace clustering. The algorithm starts by grouping the datasets of single dimension. While clustering each attribute of dataset, DBSCAN algorithm is employed and parameters of DBSCAN are self-adapted by an evolutionary approach called differential evolution. Differential evolution is a powerful evolutionary algorithm (Storn & Price, 1997) which defines candidate solutions to optimize objective function. It initializes candidate solutions according to population size and then improves the solution according to the objective function through mutation, crossover and selection methods. Optimized parameters of DBSCAN algorithm are obtained through differential evolution depending upon the data provided. All data points participating in one dimension clustering could be a part of subspace clustering. Concept of hashing is introduced where each data point is assigned a large random integer to avoid collision. This integer is termed as signature. Dense units are entered in hash table that contain sum of signatures of data points belonging to particular dense unit. Maximal subspaces are obtained by combining the dimensions of same signatures. Again, clustering through self-adaptive DBSCAN is performed. This approach of novel subspace clustering algorithm overcomes short coming of bottom up approach by determining parameters according to dataset through differential evolution. Additionally, it does not need to normalize the original dataset for clustering as done by many of existing algorithms (Kaur & Datta, 2015). Normalization may reduce the originality of dataset and hence proposed technique is better than existing one. The proposed subspace clustering algorithm is compared against existing subspace algorithms on synthetic and real datasets up to 500 dimensions on basis of accuracy and F1_Measure. Performance analysis is made on following criteria:

- Success Rate Ratio Ranking
- Scalability on Dimensions

Rest of the chapter is organized as follows:

Section 2 describes related work, section 3 presents algorithm concepts along with pseudocode, section 4 illustrate experimental set up. Experimental results and performance analysis along with discussion is depicted in section 5. Section 6 concludes the chapter with future work.

2. LITERATURE REVIEW

Bottom up approach of subspace clustering is one of the efficient methods of clustering in high dimensional data. Various related studies of high dimensional subspace clustering have been shown in Table 1. Bradley et. al. (Bradley, Fayyad, & Reina, 1998) introduced an approach of scalable clustering in large datasets. This approach mainly reduces the multiple scanning of complete dataset for clustering. The algorithm finds dense and sparse regions and store only dense data points in memory. Evaluation of algorithm is mainly performed on basis of log liklihood, average information gain and standard deviation on 100 dimensional dataset. The algorithm could not find clusters in different subspaces. A genetic based high dimensional clustering algorithm is given by Sun and Xiong (Sun & Xiong, 2009). The algorithm finds the relevant dimensions for subspace clustering. The optimized cluster centers are determined and clustering is performed on basis of error rate on 10 dimensional data. Lu et al. (Lu, Wang, Li, & Zhou, 2011) proposed a solution for variable weighting problem using particle swarm optimization for projected high dimensional clustering. The technique mainly employs soft projected clustering. A minimization type of objective function with bounded constraint through k-means is designed and optimized through PSO. The algorithm is evaluated against existing subspace algorithms on real and synthetic datasets. Nourashrafeddin et. al. (Nourashrafeddin, Arnold, & Milios, 2012) presented an evolutionary approach of determining effective attributes in lower dimension data for clustering in high dimensional dataset. These relevant attributes are represented by centroids. Thereafter the centroids are used to cluster the datasets. Evolutionary subspace algorithm removes irrelevant attributes and cluster up to 500 dimensional spaces. Conversely, outliers and overlapping clusters are not detected through this approach. Projected clustering through particle swarm optimization was given by Gajawada and Toshniwal (2012). Optimized subspace cluster center is determined by PSO; k-means is used to find neighborhood cluster centers. However, this approach determines spherical and non-overlapping clusters only. The algorithm is evaluated on 126-dimensional dataset. Vijendra and Laxman (2013) presented a multi-objective evolutionary algorithm for high dimensional clustering. The algorithm works in two phases. In first phase, all data points are categorized in dense and sparse region depending upon their location in dataset. The second phase of algorithm proceeds by removing outliers and finding subspace clusters in dense region. The algorithm was investigated against PROCLUS on basis of clustering error. The dataset included is upto 250 dimensions only. Timmerman et al. (2013) introduced a variant of k-means algorithm called subspace k-means for determining true clusters across all dimensions. The algorithm was compared with k-means, reduced k-means, factorial k-means and mixture factor analysis on basis of error variance, in cluster variance and adjusted rand index. The maximum dimension evaluated is 9 only. Kothari et. al. (2014) presented an extended version of fuzzy c means clustering to cluster the big data. The algorithm was based on random sampling; however highest dimension datasets used for testing the efficacy was 54 only.

A new subspace algorithm named subscale is given by Kaur and Datta (2014). Subscale was evaluated against existing subspace algorithms like INCY, SUBCLU and CLIQUE. The maximum dimensional dataset considered for evaluation is Madelon which has 500 attributes. Normalized datasets are only used in algorithm. Lin et. al. (2014) proposed an evolutionary approach for better clustering quality in subsets of dimensions i.e. subspaces. The evolutionary approach uses particle swarm optimizer (PSO) as local search strategy in genetic algorithm (GA) and evaluates up to 13 dimensions only on bases of error rate. Fahad et. al. (2014) presented a survey paper on state of art clustering algorithms on big data on various evaluation metrics. However, maximum number of dimensions evaluated on big data is 149 only. None of the algorithms are related to subspace clustering.

Goebl et al. (2014) developed the algorithm for finding optimal subspaces for clustering (FOSSCLU). The motive of developing FOSSCLU is to define the relationship between inter clusters, intra cluster and the subspaces in lower dimension. The algorithm was compared to various existing clustering algorithm with maximum 16 attributes only. These dimensions are relative very few in terms of high dimensions. Kaur and Datta (2015) presented their novel clustering algorithm SUBSCALE to cluster high dimensional datasets. The algorithm was compared with INCY, SUBCLU and CLIQUE algorithms on basis of time and F1_measure. The maximum dimension defined in work is 6144, though no result is depicted for that dataset. The datasets used for evaluation are adopted from Emmanuel Müller et al. (2009). Kumar et.al. (2016) proposed a clustering algorithm named clusiVat for big data clustering. clusiVat was compared with 4 clustering algorithms and proved to be fastest algorithm than CURE (clustering using representative), SKM (single pass k-means), OKM (online k-means) and k-means. Maximum dimension considered for comparison is 500 and evaluation metrics are accuracy and time. However, clusiVAT algorithm is applicable only in few cases for big data. Also, the algorithm is unable to exclude outliers while clustering.

Thus, existing subspace clustering algorithms are either evaluated on small dimensions only or they are unable to detect outliers or overlapping clusters. Some of them are fitted to specific class of problems only or some may not use input data in original form. It was observed from Table 1 that subscale algorithm given by Kaur and Datta (2015) performs effective clustering on dataset of highest dimension i.e. 6144. However, no results are shown on 6144 dimensional dataset. The original datasets are normalized before feeding into the algorithm. This might lose the originality of dataset.

Nature inspired algorithms are the techniques inspired from nature. Classification of algorithms along with applications are defined in Agarwal & Mehta (2014). It has been used in context aware filtering Mehta & Banati (2014). Empirical analysis of five nature inspired algorithms are defined Agarwal & Mehta (2017). Differential evolution is an evolutionary algorithm applied in various applications of diverse field. A survey on differential evolution including all its variants are described in Das & Suganthan (2011). Automatic clustering is performed using improved differential evolution in Das, Abraham, & Konar (2008). Clustering is also performed using flower pollination algorithm Agarwal & Mehta (2015). Improved flower pollination algorithm is also applied on clustering application in Agarwal & Mehta (2016).

Although there exist number of subspace algorithms; there is no algorithm that perfectly combines nature inspired algorithm with subspace clustering to yield effective results. In this chapter, one of the efficient evolutionary algorithms named differential evolution (DE) is used to determine parameters of DBSCAN algorithm i.e. tau (minimum number of points to form cluster) and epsilon (distance between the points for cluster formation). Similar type of technique is proposed by Karami & Johansson (2014). The DBSCAN algorithm is used to cluster the dataset of each attribute independently with parameters

Table 1. Literature review on subspace clustering algorithms

S. No.	Paper Reference, Year	Algorithms Developed	Performance With Other Algorithms (Best to Worst)	Evaluation Parameter	Max. Number of Attributes/ Dimensions	Max. Size of Dataset
1.	(Kumar et al., 2016), 2016	clusiVAT algorithm	clusiVAT, single pass K-Means, CURE, Online K-Means, K-Means	Accuracy, Time	500	500,000
2.	(Kaur & Datta, 2015), 2015	Subscale algorithm	Subscale, INSCY, SUBCLU, CLIQUE	F1 Measure	6144	3661
3.	(Goebl, Xiao, Plant, & Bohm, 2014),2014	FOSSCLU (Finding the Optimal SubSpace for CLUstering),	FOSSCLU, LDA-K-Means, EM after PCA, EM after ICA, ORCLUS, 4C	Normalized Mutual Information (NMI)	16	10,992
4.	(Fahad et al., 2014), 2014	Survey	EM, Optigrid, Birch, FCM, Denclue	Runtime, stability, internal validity	149	377,526
5.	(Lin et al., 2014), 2014	GA-PSO clustering algorithm	GA-PSO, ESC (Evolutionary Subspace Clustering)	Error rate	13	187
6.	(Kaur & Datta, 2014), 2014	Subscale	Subscale, INCY, Subclu, Clique	F1 Measure, running time	500	4400
7.	(Kothari et al., 2014), 2014	Systematic Random Sampling based extended FCM algorithm	Systematic Random Sampling based extended FCM algorithm, Multistage random sampling, Simple random sampling, literal FCM	Run time	54	581012
8.	(Timmerman et al., 2013), 2013	Subspace K-Means	Subspace K-Means, mixtures of factor analyzers (MFA), reduced K-Means (RKM), factorial K-Means (FKM), MCLUST	Between-cluster variance, and the error variance, Adjusted Rand Index	9	600
9.	(Vijendra & Laxman, 2013), 2013	multi objective subspace clustering (MOSCL) algorithm	MOSCL, PROCLUS	Clustering Error	250	50000
10.	(Gajawada & Toshniwal, 2012), 2012	Projected Clustering Particle Swarm Optimization (PCPSO) algorithm	-	Number of matching points and mismatched dimensions between input and output cluster	126	300
11.	(Nourashrafeddin et al., 2012), 2012	EsubClus (evolutionary subspace clustering)	EsubClus, Mineclus, EM, Proclus	F1 Score, running time	500	2500
12.	(Lu et al., 2011), 2011	PSO for variable weighting (PSOVW) algorithm	PSOVW, EWKM (Entropy weighting K-means algorithm), LAC (Locally adaptive metrics for clustering), W-K-means (weighted K-Means)	FSCORE, Average run time	2000	500
13.	(Sun & Xiong, 2009), 2009	GA-HD clustering algorithm (genetic based high dimensional)	GA-HD, K-Means	Error rate	10	150
14.	(Bradley et al., 1998), 1998	Scale K-Means(SKM)	SKM, Online K-Means (OKM), sampler K-means (SampKM)	Log Liklihood, Average Information Gain, Standard deviation	100	50,000

obtained from DE. Thereafter, subspaces are formed by combining the relevant dimensions of datasets with same data points and same signatures. The proposed algorithm is able to determine overlapping subspace clusters of arbitrary shape and size. The approach proposed in this work yields results of clustering in form of F1_measure and accuracy up to 500 dimensions. The next section discusses details of proposed algorithm along with pseudocode.

3. PROPOSED ALGORITHM (SUBSPACE_DE)

In this chapter, a novel subspace clustering algorithm is proposed. In this algorithm differential evolution algorithm is inculcated in subspace clustering algorithm in order to achieve valuable outcome. This algorithm does not make use of k-means algorithm and is independent of determining centroids which is used in most of the evolutionary based subspace clustering algorithms in literature. However, proposed technique makes use of DBSCAN algorithm which is much efficient in determining outliers and clusters of arbitrary shape. The proposed technique could also determine clusters existing in overlapping subspaces. The proposed algorithm works in 3 phases. The first phase is finding clusters in all single dimension of dataset. Second phase is determining the subspaces where clusters exists using hash table and third phase is clustering with self-adaptive DBSCAN algorithm in each subspace obtained from second phase. Detailed explanation of all phases along with pseudocode is described in first subsection. In second subsection, self-adaptive DBSCAN algorithm is presented which is used in first and third phase of proposed algorithm. In third subsection binary differential evolution algorithm is illustrated which is used in determining optimal parameters values of self-adaptive DBSCAN algorithm.

3.1 Subspace Differential Evolution (SUBSPACE_DE) Clustering Algorithm

The proposed algorithm SUBSPACE_DE follows bottom up approach of subspace clustering. It starts clustering from small dimensions and proceeds to cluster in higher dimension subspaces. The strategy employs Apriori principle. According to this principle if the data points are dense in high dimension say h subspace, then these data points are also dense in lower dimensional projection of these subspace Agrawal, Gehrke, Gunopulos, & Raghavan (1998). It can be also said that data points that are found dense in one dimensional subspace will participate in high dimensional subspace. Common points in 1 dimensional data will form dense points in higher subspaces. This approach leads to create maximal subspaces. Once maximal subspaces are formed, clustering can be performed to obtain overlapping as well as non-overlapping clusters in difference subspaces. It will result into clustering in high dimensional data.

Proposed SUBSPACE_DE algorithm works in 3 phases. Initially each data point is assigned a large random integer called signature. The reason of choosing large random integer is to minimize collision in hash table. An empty hash table is also initialized. Working of each phase is defined as follows:

Phase 1: (Clustering in 1 dimension data) This phase starts from clustering each dimension of dataset by applying self-adaptive DBSCAN algorithm. The algorithm clusters dataset in each attribute with different parameter values depending upon the dataset. The parameter values are adopted from binary differential evolution algorithm. Self-adaptive DBSCAN algorithm and differential evolution are described in subsections. After clustering each dimension of dataset, the clustered data points and their respective sum of signatures of each cluster are stored in a table. Now, the clustered datasets, sum of signatures and dimensions are entered into hash table. Key to the hash table is sum of signatures. If any of the entries is having same signatures already present in hash table then dimensions and data points are merged into single entry. The dimensions belong to same subspace.

Phase 2: (Managing hash table) In previous phase all the duplicate keys in hash table are removed and their subspaces and data points are merged into single entry. In this phase hash table is analyzed for subspaces. If any of the entries are having same subspaces, then data points are merged into single entry and duplicate entries are removed. In this way, maximal subspaces are formed. These subspaces can be single dimensions or combination of any dimensions depending upon the dataset.

Phase 3: (Clustering in maximal subspaces) In each entry of hash table which is refined after phase 2, self-adaptive DBSCAN algorithm is executed to determine the clusters existing in subspaces. Self-adaptive DBSCAN algorithm takes the input parameters tau and epsilon from binary differential evolution algorithm depending upon dataset to be clustered. In this way the ultimate goal of clustering in high dimensional data can be achieved.

Pseudocode of SUBSPACE_DE is given in Algorithm 1.

Algorithm 1.

```
1. For each data point in dataset, generate a large random integer 'n' random-
ly. This large number is termed as signature for each data point.

2. An empty hash table is initialized possessing following parameters:

Hash = {Sum, Data, Sub}

where Sum is the sum of signatures of each clustered data point, Sub is the
set of dimension or dimensions and Data is the data points that form clusters.

3. For each dimension i of dataset Z

4. Apply self adaptive DBSCAN algorithm shown in Algorithm 2. The parameters
of algorithm are extracted from binary differential evolution described in Al-
gorithm 3.

5. Clusters formed in step 4 are added into table T. Two attributes for each
cluster i.e. sum of signatures and data points are added in table T.

T = {sum(Data), Data}

6. For each entry of T

7. if some signatures (key) of hash table are same i.e. Hash.h_x==sum

8. append i dimension to subspace Sub of hash table in entry h_x.Sum

9. else
```

continued on following page

Algorithm 1. Continued

10. add new entry in hash table *Hash* as{ *Sum, Data, i*}

11. end if (step 7)

12. end for (step 6)

13. end for (step 3)

14. for each row of hash table *Hash* as {h_x, h_y, h_z,...}

15. if there exists duplicate entries of subspaces in hash table i.e.

h_x.Sum== h_y.Sum== h_z.Sum==...

16. Concatenate dense points *Data* of h_y.*Data, h_z.Data*... to h_x.*Data* and remove duplicate entries.

17. end if (step 15)
18. end for (step14)

19. for each entry h_x of hash table *Hash*

20. Perform clustering in each maximal subspace using self-adaptive DBSCAN algorithm defined in Algorithm 2.

21. End for (step 19)

22. Output clusters in each maximal subspace of high dimensional data.

3.2 Self Adapting DBSCAN

DBSCAN stands for density based spatial clustering of applications with noise. It is the most common density-based clustering algorithm which clusters the high density data i.e. minimum number of points within certain threshold distance. Sparse points i.e. points in low density region and are not within threshold distance to any other points are termed as noise. These are also called outliers i.e. the points that are not part of any cluster. The major advantages of DBSCAN algorithm over k-means algorithm is the detection of outliers. DBSCAN algorithm cluster the datasets based on concepts of density reachability and density connectivity. Hence it is able to find clusters of arbitrary shape and size. Additionally, it requires no information about number of clusters. Thus, it is suitable for unlabelled datasets. DBSCAN algorithm uses only two input parameters. These are *minpts* i.e. minimum number of points required to form cluster and *epsilon* i.e. maximum threshold distance between the points to achieve density reachability. The point 'x' is said to be density connected to 's' if there is set of points between 'x' and 's' that form chain of density reachability. Let 'x' is density reachable from 'y', 'y' is density reachable from 'z' and 'z' is density reachable from 's' then 'x' and 's' are said to be density connected points. All the data points in dataset are marked as core point or border point or outlier.

A point is a core point if it has atleast *minpts* data points in its neighborhood within epsilon distance. Points that do not have *minpts* data point within epsilon distance but are density reachable from certain core points. Such data points are termed as border point. Points that are not even density reachable from any core point or border point are called outliers. They lie in least density region. A cluster is formed from atleast one core point including all data points that are density connected from core points. Hence, input parameters used in algorithm are *minpts* and *epsilon*. The performance of DBSCAN algorithm is greatly affected by values of control (input) parameters.

The algorithm proposed in this chapter makes use of DBSCAN algorithm which extracts its parameter values from binary differential evolution algorithm according to the dataset. This version of DBSCAN algorithm is called self-adaptive DBSCAN as it takes best parameter values automatically from evolutionary strategy. The evolutionary strategy used is binary differential evolution algorithm. The next subsection answers how to obtain optimal parameter values from differential evolution algorithm.

3.3 Binary Differential Evolution

Differential evolution (DE) is introduced by Storn and Price in 1997 (Storn & Price, 1997). It is an evolutionary algorithm used for global optimization of continuous objective functions. Performance of DE largely depends on three operators i.e. mutation, crossover and selection. These operators are important because it generate new chromosomes in population for achieving optimized results. The binary differential evolution algorithm is used for the optimization of discrete problems. In self adaptive DBSCAN algorithm binary DE is employed (Karami & Johansson, 2014). Initial population is encoded with binary coding scheme where individuals/chromosomes are represented by bit string. Each individual depict *minpts* and assigned bit string randomly. The fitness/objective function is considered as purity metric. Higher the purity better is the solution. Hence purity metrics is maximized in this algorithm. The next

Algorithm 2.

```
1. Initially all points are marked unvisited.

2. Obtain parameters minpts and epsilon from Algorithm 3.

3. Select any arbitrary point that is unvisited.

4. Find all the neighbors which are density reachable from arbitrary point.

5. If number of neighborhood points >= τ

6. Mark it as core point and assign all points including core point to a cluster.

7. Mark the core point visited.

8. Find other density connected points from each neighborhood point and repeat from step 3.

9. Else the point is marked noise.

10. If cluster is completely formed the algorithm will repeat from step 2 (for unvisited points).
```

step is mutation. In mutation, mutant individual is generated from each individual of population using Equation 1.

$$m_i = x_a + SF \cdot \left(x_b - x_c \right) \tag{1}$$

where m_i is the mutant vector, x_a, x_b and x_c are the individuals of population called target vectors and are different from each other. Also, i, a, b and c is an index of population such that i~=a~=b~=c. SF is a scaling factor which controls the mutation rate. In the proposed algorithm SF takes any number randomly between the range of Bmin and Bmax.

After obtaining the mutant vector, crossover is applied over target vector and mutant vector using Equation 2. The resultant vector after mutation and crossover is called trial vector.

$$t_{ij} = \begin{cases} m_{ij}, & if\, rand[0,1] \leq CR\, or\, j == j_{rand} \\ x_{ij}, & otherwise \end{cases} \tag{2}$$

Where j is the dimension index in an individual. j_{rand} is index chosen randomly between 1 to D. This ensures that trial vector t_{ij} will contain atleast one mutant vector m_{ij}. CR is the crossover rate which regulates the selection of target and mutant vector.

Mutation operator of differential evolution could generate real number, however binary DE requires vector in bit string form. In order to obtain binary string repair function given in Equation 3 is applied on trial vector.

$$new\_t_{ij} = min\left(max\left(t_{ij}, 0 \right), 1 \right) \tag{3}$$

According to repair function negative value is coded to 0 and positive value is coded to 1. Thereafter fitness value is computed for trial vector and target vector. Tournament selection is applied between fitness of target and trial vector. Higher fitness value vector is selected for next generation. In order to define fitness function, firstly epsilon value is generated by from *minpts*. *minpts* is obtained by decimal conversion of selected trial or target vector. Epsilon is generated by analytical formula (Daszykowski, Walczak, & Massart, 2001) using Equation 4.

$$Epsilon = \left(\frac{\left(\prod_{i=1}^{max(x)-min(x)} i \right) * k * \gamma \left(0.5n + 1 \right)}{m\sqrt{\pi^n}} \right)^{1/n} \tag{4}$$

Let the dataset is matrix X of size m×n, where m is number of rows and n is number of attributes. k is the *minpts* obtained target or trial vector. A gamma function γ is used to interpolate factorial of given number defined in Equation 5.

$$\gamma\left(n+1\right) = factorial\left(n\right) \tag{5}$$

Epsilon value obtained is stored in every iteration. Tournament selection is employed in each iteration to select best epsilon value based on purity metric. Epsilon with high purity is selected to be used in DBSCAN algorithm. Fitness value is obtained from purity metric which is obtained after executing DBSCAN algorithm defined in Algorithm 2. DBSCAN takes its input parameter as *minpts* which is decimal number representation of target or trial vector and selected epsilon value. After executing DBSCAN algorithm clusters are formed. Supervised learning is used to measure the goodness of clusters. Counting the number of points assigned to correct cluster divided by total number of points give purity metric.

$$purity = \frac{\sum_{j=1}^{k} \max_{1<i<l}\left(class_i \cap cluster_j\right)}{N} \tag{6}$$

Where i is the total number of classes, k is the number of clusters, $\max_i$ means that class i is assigned to cluster j as cluster j has maximum data points of class i.

High purity value is always favorable to good clustering algorithm. Psuedocode is given in Algorithm 3. Fitness function

1. Calculate epsilon from *minpts* using Equation 4 and 5.
2. Use tournament selection to obtain best *epsilon* value from stored *epsilon* values based on purity metric.
3. Execute DBSCAN using *minpts* and *epsilon*.
4. Apply purity metric using Equation 6 on cluster obtained from DBSCAN algorithm.
5. Return *purity, minpts, epsilon*

4. EXPERIMENTAL SETUP

In order to test the efficacy of SUBSPACE_DE, it is compared with existing subspace clustering algorithms (Müller et al., 2009). Subspace algorithm mainly belongs to three categories namely: cell based, density based and clustering oriented based. Cell based algorithm include CLIQUE, DOC, MINECLUS and SCHISM. Some density-based algorithms are SUBCLU, FIRES and INCY. Clustering oriented based algorithms include PROCLUS, P3C and STATPC. SUBSPACE_DE is also compared with SUBSCALE algorithm (Kaur & Datta, 2015) which belongs to density-based algorithm. The comparison between algorithms is made on basis of F1_Measure and accuracy. Existing subspace algorithms except SUBSCALE are executed on WEKA tool of subspace clustering provided by (Müller, Günnemann, Assent, Seidl, & Färber, 2009). The parameters of algorithms for repeatability of experiments are also given in (Müller et al., 2009).

Execution of SUBSPACE_DE and SUBSCALE algorithms are made on MATLAB 2013a. Hardware configurations include Intel Core i5 processor with 16.0GB RAM, 64 bit Windows7 operating system. Subsections illustrate evaluation measures, parameter setting and dataset descriptions.

Algorithm 3.

1. Input dataset.

2. Initialize parameters of differential evolution algorithm i.e. Maximum iterations *MaxIt*, population size *pop*, number of variables used to represent bit string (*minpts*) D.

3. Initialize global solution *globalsol* to 0. Store the best values of *minpts, epsilon* and *purity*.

4. Initialize each individual (*minpts*) of population (target vector) randomly with bit string of size D.

5. For it=1 to *MaxIt*

6. For j=1 to *pop*

7. Apply mutation operator on each individual using Equation 1 to obtain mutated vector.

8. Apply crossover operator on mutated and target vector using Equation 2 to achieve trial vector.

9. Call repair function on trial vector using Equation 3.

10. Apply fitness function (given below) on trial and target vector

11. Perform selection over fitness values of target and trial vector

12. If *target.purity > trial.purity*

13. *globalsol.minpts=target*

14. Else

15. *globalsol.minpts=trial*

16. End if

17. Save the best values of *minpts, epsilon* and *purity* to *globalsol*.

18. End for step 6

19. End for step 5

4.1 Evaluation Measures

For the sake of testing the performance of SUBSPACE_DE and comparing against various existing subspace clustering algorithms, certain evaluation measures are needed. The technique proposed in this chapter uses an approach of clustering through classification. In case of labeled dataset, true cluster labels (TR) are available for each data points in the dataset. For example, let there are m true clusters, cluster labels are *TR= {TR1, TR2, ..., TRm}*. The subspace clustering algorithm predicts the clusters of dataset. Let these clusters be k and it is called predicted cluster (PR). PR and TR labels forms the confusion matrix through which it is possible determine evaluation measures. The most common evaluation measures are F1_Measure and accuracy.

- **F1_Measure:** F1_measure is obtained from harmonic mean of recall and precision values. Higher the F1_measure, better is the clustering quality and algorithm. It defines the maximum match of predicted label with true label. In other words, clusters formed by algorithm should carry maximum data points from actual cluster (TR) and minimum data points from other cluster. Formulation of F1_Measure is given below in Equation 7.

$$F1\_Measure = \frac{1}{m} \sum_{i=1}^{m} \frac{2 * recall(T_i) * precision(T_i)}{recall(T_i) + precision(T_i)} \tag{7}$$

Where m is the number of actual clusters (TR). High recall value denotes that predicted cluster covers maximum items from true cluster and high precision signifies minimum data points from other clusters.

- **Accuracy:** accuracy is a measure that is also computed from confusion matrix. It signifies the goodness of clusters formed from algorithm. Accuracy is defined as ratio of data points correctly labeled by algorithm to the total number of data points in the algorithm. Higher the accuracy better is the clusters formed. Hence a good clustering algorithm possesses high accuracy with respective dataset.

- **Success Rate Ratios Ranking (SRR) of Algorithms:** SRR i.e. success rate ratio ranking is computed over both F1_Measure and accuracy. It is an approach of ranking classification algorithms. In this method ratio of success rates is calculated for every pair of algorithms. For determining significant differences between algorithms, SRR proves to be highly efficient. Success rate ratio ranking is applied on synthetic and real datasets on basis of accuracy and F1_measure independently. For every dataset SRR table is created on basis of accuracy of algorithms. Ratio of accuracy of algorithm for which success rate is created to the accuracy of rest of the algorithms is computed. Computation of success rate ratio is performed using Equation 8.

$$SRR^x_{i,j,i\neq j} = \frac{Accuracy^x_i}{Accuracy^x_j} \tag{8}$$

Where x is the dataset on which success rate is computed, i and j are the pair of algorithms. $SRR_{i,j}$ is perceived as success rate ratio of algorithm i with respect to algorithm j. In the similar way, SRR can be computed for all datasets. Let the number of datasets be d. For given pair of algorithms, SRR can be obtained for all datasets using Equation 9.

$$SRR_{i,j,i\neq j} = \frac{\sum_{x=1}^{d} SRR^x_{i,j,i\neq j}}{d} \tag{9}$$

Hence, success rate ratio of an algorithm with respect to another algorithm on all datasets can be computed using Equation 9. SRR of an algorithm can be calculated in an identical way with respect to all the rest of the algorithms on all datasets. Thereafter, SRR of an algorithm with respect to all other algorithms are added and mean SRR of an algorithm i is computed using Equation 10.

$$SRR_i = \frac{\sum_j SRR_{i,j,i \neq j}}{t-1} \tag{10}$$

where t is the total count of subspace clustering algorithms used for ranking. Thus, SRR for each algorithm on all dataset with respect to rest of the algorithms is computed. This SRR is ranked in descending order and final ranks of each algorithm are obtained. Similar method is followed for computing success rate ratio ranks of algorithm on F1_measure.

4.2 Parameter Tuning

Parameter settings of existing subspace clustering algorithms i.e. CLIQUE, DOC, MINECLUS, SCHISM, SUBCLU, FIRES, INCY, PROCLUS, P3C and STATPC are defined in (E Müller et al., 2009) and same has been used in this work. The best values are taken after executing all algorithms with given set of parameter values. Approximately, 1100 experiments on synthetic datasets are performed to obtain best results. Parameters of SUBSCALE algorithm are defined in (Kaur & Datta, 2015). The parameter values of proposed algorithm (SUBSPACE_DE) are given in Table 2.

Parameters of SUBSPACE_DE are adopted after repeating the number of experiments. The values shown in Table 2 are taken on basis of algorithm's best accuracy and F1_Measure.

4.3 Dataset Description

The efficacy of SUBSPACE_DE is assessed on basis of F1_measure and accuracy on synthetic and real datasets. All the existing subspace clustering algorithm, subscale algorithm and proposed SUBSPACE_DE are evaluated on six synthetic and eight real datasets. Additionally, SUBSPACE_DE is also evaluated on Madelon high dimensional real dataset. Description of synthetic datasets is given in Table 3. These datasets are formed from 10, 15, 25, 50 and 75 dimensions. The same datasets has been used in (Müller et al., 2009).

Real datasets (Bache & Lichman, 2006) used for assessing the performance of algorithms are described in Table 4. These datasets are standard dataset for evaluation of subspace algorithms and has been used in various studies (Assent et al., 2008; Moise & Sander, 2008; Sequeira & Zaki, 2004). For each dataset, parameter values are taken corresponding to best accuracy and F1_Measure.

Table 2. Parameters and their values for SUBSPACE_DE

Parameter	Values
Population Size	20
Iterations	50
Crossover(cr)	0.25
[betamin, betamax]	[0.2,0.8]
D	7

Table 3. Synthetic datasets description

Name of Dataset	No. of Tuples	No. of Attributes (Dimensions)
D10	1596	10
D15	1596	15
D20	1596	20
D25	1596	25
D50	1596	50
D75	1596	75

Table 4. Real datasets description

Name of Dataset	No. of Attributes (Dimensions)	No. of Tuples
LIVER DISORDER	6	345
DIABETES	8	768
GLASS	9	214
VOWEL	10	990
PENDIGITS	16	7494
SHAPE	17	160
BREAST	33	198
MADELON	500	4400

5. EXPERIMENTAL RESULTS AND STUDY

Meticulous experiments are performed for examining and analyzing the efficacy and accuracy of SUBSPACE_DE on high dimensional datasets. These datasets are inclusive of synthetic and real. Real datasets include liver disorder, diabetes, vowel, glass, breast, shape and pendigits. SUBSPACE_DE is executed 30 times independently on each real and synthetic datasets. One more dataset is included i.e. madelon which consists of 500 dimensions. Best values of F1_Measure and accuracy out of 30 runs are considered for comparison. Accuracy and F1_Measure values of existing subspace clustering algorithms like Clique, Doc, Mineclus, Schism, SubClu, Fires, Incy, Proclus, P3C and StatPC on real datasets are available in (Müller et al., 2009). On the other hand, results of existing subspace algorithms on synthetic datasets are not available. Thus, all these algorithms are executed on extended WEKA framework for subspace clustering (Müller et al., 2009). During the time of execution, it was observed that CLIQUE and SUBCLU could not cope up for more than 10 dimensions. Hence, these algorithms are not incorporated in comparison with SUBSPACE_DE. Additionally, SCHISM and INCY are not able to find solutions for more than 25 dimensional dataset.

There are mainly two subsections in this section. The first section 5.1 depicts the assessment of SUBSPACE_DE with state of art subspace algorithms. The second section 5.2 shows the result of SUBSPACE_DE on real high dimensional Madelon dataset.

5.1 Assessment of Proposed Algorithm (SUBSPACE_ DE) With Existing Subspace Algorithms

This section illustrates the evaluation of SUBSPACE_DE algorithm with other subspace clustering algorithms on various synthetic and real datasets. Evaluation measures for comparison are accuracy and F1_Measure. In order to present fair comparison between the algorithms, success rank ratio method (Brazdil & Soares, 2000) is employed. Algorithms are ranked on basis of this ranking. For testing the scalability of SUBSPACE_DE against existing subspace clustering algorithm, scalability graphs are presented on basis of data dimensionality. The best values of 30 independent runs are considered for comparison in SUBSPACE_DE. While for existing subspace algorithms best values of accuracy and F1_measure are used after repeating various experiments on different parameter settings.

There are two subsections of this section: section 5.1.1 defines success rate ratio along with rank of algorithms on synthetic and real datasets. Section 5.1.2 portrays scalability of algorithms on basis of data dimensionality in terms of0 accuracy and F1_Measure.

5.1.1 Success Rate Ratios Ranking (SRR) of Algorithms

Accuracy and F1_Measure of SUBSPACE_DE, SUBSCALE and all other subspace clustering algorithms on synthetic and real datasets are described in this section. SRR ranking is also shown independently for both types of datasets in following subsections.

5.1.1.1 Synthetic Datasets

Synthetic datasets include D10, D15, D20, D25, D50 and D75 described in Table 3. Table 5 depicts actual accuracy values of all algorithms for synthetic datasets. It has been analyzed from accuracy values that proposed algorithm SUBSPACE_DE perform better than SUBSCALE, DOC, MINECLUS, FIRES, PROCLUS, STATPC and P3C algorithms. It achieves more than 80% accuracy on all datasets. However, the performance of SUBSPACE_DE with respect to INCY and SCHISM is noticeable. Though

Table 5. Accuracy of algorithms on synthetic datasets

	D10	**D15**	**D20**	**D25**	**D50**	**D75**
SUBSPACE_DE	0.85	0.9	0.82	0.86	0.92	0.96
SUBSCALE	0.81	0.78	0.81	0.73	0.82	0.9
DOC	0.72	0.99	0.63	0.85	0.79	0.74
MINECLUS	0.94	0.43	0.62	0.99	0.62	0.78
SCHISM	0.97	0.97	0.81	0.93	-	-
FIRES	0.83	0.75	0.79	0.91	0.86	0.88
INCY	0.91	0.88	0.95	0.93	-	-
PROCLUS	0.67	0.59	0.76	0.67	0.65	0.6
STATPC	0.16	0.17	0.33	0.29	0.1	0.09
P3C	0.86	0.65	0.65	0.73	0.65	0.68

INCY and SCHISM gives good accuracy on small dimensions (10-25 dimensions) but fails to achieve any result after 25 dimensions. SUBSPACE_DE achieves more than 90% accuracy on high dimensions (D50 and D75).

Table 6 illustrates F1_Measure values of subspace clustering algorithms on synthetic datasets. It is observed that SUBSPACE_DE gives superior performance on high dimensions (D50 and D75) when compared with existing subspace clustering algorithm. However, on small dimensions (D10-D25), F1_measure of SUBSPACE_DE is average to the rest of the algorithms.

Table 7 portrays the SRR ranking of all subspace clustering algorithms for comparison on basis of accuracy and F1_Measure. SRR ranking measures the actual difference in values which is not considered in average ranking. Ranking in both accuracy and F1_Measure for all algorithms are identical. SUB-SPACE_DE come up with the first rank on accuracy and F1_Measure. The second and third rank is of DOC and MINECLUS respectively which belongs to cell based approach. The last ranks are occupied by

Table 6. F1_Measure of algorithms on synthetic datasets

	D10	D15	D20	D25	D50	D75
SUBSPACE_DE	0.55	0.62	0.59	0.6	0.71	0.82
SUBSCALE	0.48	0.47	0.5	0.42	0.51	0.66
DOC	0.56	0.83	0.91	0.5	0.57	0.56
MINECLUS	0.98	0.21	0.38	0.91	0.35	0.55
SCHISM	0.71	0.5	0.55	0.59	-	-
FIRES	0.57	0.5	0.68	0.63	0.51	0.44
INCY	0.78	0.59	0.58	0.73	-	-
PROCLUS	0.69	0.39	0.59	0.67	0.42	0.5
STATPC	0.02	0.02	0.27	0.21	0.06	0.05
P3C	0.52	0.34	0.28	0.32	0.3	0.33

Table 7. Success rate ratios rank of algorithms on synthetic datasets

	Accuracy	F1_Measure
SUBSPACE_DE	1	1
SUBSCALE	6	6
DOC	2	2
MINECLUS	3	3
SCHISM	8	8
FIRES	4	4
INCY	7	7
PROCLUS	5	5
STATPC	10	10
P3C	9	9

STATPC and P3C which are under clustering oriented based approach. Thus, it can be concluded from above investigation that SUBSPACE_DE is the best performer on synthetic datasets. The next comes cell based algorithms and thereafter density based algorithms and clustering oriented based algorithms.

5.1.1.2 Real Datasets

Table 8 and table 9 depicts actual values of accuracy and F1_measure respectively on real datasets including glass, diabetes, liver disorder, breast, vowel, pendigit and shape. It also shows comparison of SUBSPACE_DE against SUBSCALE and various subspace clustering algorithms. Analysis of table 8 and table 9 reveals that SUBSPACE_DE gives approximately or better performance on real datasets.

Table 8. Accuracy of algorithms on real datasets

	GLASS	DIABETES	LIVER DIS.	BREAST	VOWEL	PENDIGITS	SHAPE
SUBSPACE_DE	0.62	0.68	0.69	0.78	0.52	0.69	0.71
SUBSCALE	0.4766	0.6563	0.7217	0.7626	0.399	0.334935	0.125
CLIQUE	0.67	0.72	0.67	0.71	0.64	0.96	0.76
DOC	0.63	0.72	0.68	0.81	0.44	0.54	0.79
MINECLUS	0.52	0.71	0.65	0.78	0.37	0.86	0.79
SCHISM	0.63	0.73	0.68	0.75	0.62	0.93	0.74
SUBCLU	0.65	0.71	0.64	0.77	0.58	--	0.7
FIRES	0.49	0.65	0.58	0.76	0.13	0.73	0.51
INCY	0.65	0.7	0.62	0.77	0.61	0.78	0.76
PROCLUS	0.6	0.72	0.63	0.8	0.44	0.74	0.72
P3C	0.47	0.66	0.58	0.77	0.17	0.72	0.61
STATPC	0.49	0.7	0.65	0.78	0.56	0.92	0.74

Table 9. F1_Measure of algorithms on real datasets

	GLASS	DIABETES	LIVER DIS.	BREAST	VOWEL	PENDIGITS	SHAPE
SUBSPACE_DE	0.7	0.79	0.8	0.87	0.3	0.39	0.51
Subscale	0.54	0.77	0.74	0.78	0.23	0.24	0.22
CLIQUE	0.51	0.7	0.68	0.67	0.23	0.3	0.31
DOC	0.74	0.71	0.67	0.73	0.49	0.52	0.9
MINECLUS	0.76	0.72	0.73	0.78	0.48	0.87	0.94
SCHISM	0.46	0.7	0.69	0.67	0.37	0.45	0.51
SUBCLU	0.5	0.74	0.68	0.68	0.24	--	0.36
FIRES	0.3	0.52	0.58	0.49	0.16	0.45	0.36
INCY	0.57	0.65	0.66	0.74	0.82	0.65	0.84
PROCLUS	0.6	0.67	0.53	0.57	0.49	0.78	0.84
P3C	0.28	0.39	0.36	0.63	0.08	0.74	0.51
STATPC	0.75	0.73	0.69	0.41	0.22	0.91	0.43

It is also noticeable that SUBCLU algorithm could not give results for large dataset like pendigit with 7494 instances.

Success rate ratio ranking of SUBSPACE_DE, SUBSCALE and various other subspace clustering on real datasets on basis of accuracy and F1_measure are shown are in Table 10. SUBSPACE_DE maintains its consistent performance and obtains fifth position on both evaluation measures. CLIQUE and SCHISM stands on first and second position respectively in terms of accuracy while it is at ninth and seventh position on the basis of F1_Measure. Other cell-based algorithms i.e. DOC and MINECLUS are at sixth and eight position in terms of accuracy and third and second position in terms of F1_measure. Density based algorithms i.e. FIRES, INCY, SUBCLU are at eleventh, third and ninth position respectively in terms of accuracy. On basis of F1_Measure INCY wins over all algorithms and is at first position while FIRES and SUBCLU are at twelfth and tenth position respectively. Clustering oriented based approach algorithms i.e. PROCLUS, P3C and STATPC are at seventh, tenth and fourth position respectively on basis of accuracy. While on F1_Measure, these algorithms are at fourth, eleventh and sixth position. Thus, it can be concluded that on real datasets cell-based algorithms are top performer, thereafter density based and clustering oriented based algorithms give similar kind of performances. SUBSPACE_DE is an average performer but gives good results on high dimensional dataset.

Therefore, it has been observed from analysis of success rate ratio ranking that SUBSPACE_DE gives good efficacy when executed on high dimensional dataset in terms of consistency and reliability. The next section proves the scalability of SUBSPACE_DE algorithm in terms data dimensionality.

5.1.2 Scalability of Algorithms

This section illustrates the scalability of SUBSPACE_DE, SUBSCALE and various other subspace clustering algorithms in terms of data dimensionality. The efficacy of subspace clustering algorithms in depicted with increase in dimensionality of data. Scalability of data dimensions is shown on synthetic datasets. This is because these datasets are artificially created and have same number of instances

Table 10. Success rate ratios rank of algorithms on real datasets

	Accuracy	F1_Measure
SUBSPACE_DE	5	5
SUBSCALE	12	8
CLIQUE	1	9
DOC	6	3
MINECLUS	8	2
SCHISM	2	7
SUBCLU	9	10
FIRES	11	12
INCY	3	1
PROCLUS	7	4
P3C	10	11
STATPC	4	6

with varying attributes. Hence, in order to present fair scalability of algorithms on data dimensionality, selection of synthetic datasets is a good choice. This section is divided into two subsections. Section 5.1.2.1 shows the scalability of algorithms on basis of accuracy and sections 5.1.2.2 portrays scalability on F1_measure.

5.1.2.1 On Basis of Accuracy

Figure 1, figure 2 and figure 3 demonstrate scalability in dimensionality of data of proposed algorithm SUBSPACE_DE against cell based, density based and clustering oriented based algorithms respectively. Graphs shown in figures are drawn in X axis and Y axis. X axis represent data dimensionality from 10 to 75 dimensions. Y axis represents accuracy. It is examined that SUBSPACE_DE gives uniform consistent behavior. Its efficiency increases with increase in dimensions. Cell based algorithm DOC and MINECLUS shows random behavior on data dimensionality while SCHISM could not evaluate dataset with more than 25 dimensions. Density based algorithms like FIRES shows increase in accuracy with increase in dimensions initially but depreciates afterwards at high dimensions. INCY gives good efficiency on data dimensionality but could not perform at higher dimensions. SUBSCALE also shows increase in efficacy with increase in dimensions but could not reach to SUBSPACE_DE. Clustering oriented based algorithms P3C, STATPC and PROCLUS lags behind SUBSPACE_DE in terms of accuracy. Hence, SUBSPACE_DE wins over clustering oriented based algorithm. Though SUBSPACE_DE does not show highest accuracy on small dimensions (D10-D25) but it gives excellent performance on high dimensions (D50 and D75).

Figure 1. Scalability of SUBSPACE_DE vs. Cell based

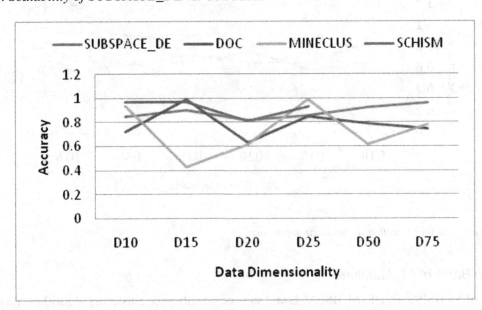

For a more accurate representation see the electronic version.

Figure 2. Scalability of SUBSPACE_DE vs. Density based

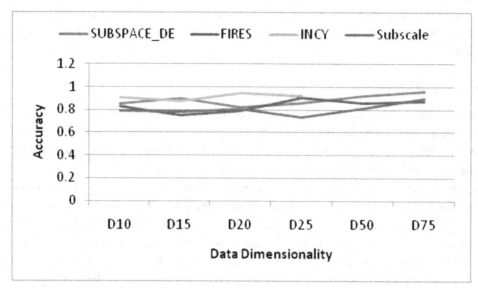

*For a more accurate representation see the electronic version.

Figure 3. Scalability of SUBSPACE_DE vs. Clustering Oriented

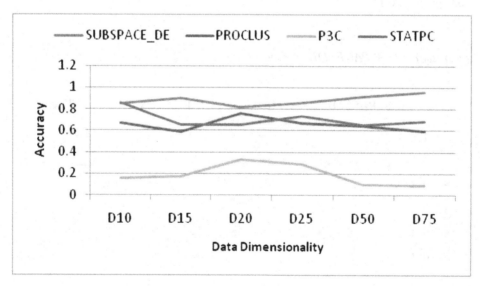

*For a more accurate representation see the electronic version.

5.1.2.2 On Basis of F1_Measure

Scalability of SUBSPACE_DE, SUBSPACE and state of art subspace clustering algorithms on basis of F1_measure are shown in form of graphs. Figure 4, figure 5 and figure 6 depicts scalability in terms of data dimensionality of proposed SUBSPACE_DE versus cell based, density based and clustering oriented based respectively. The x axis of graph depicts data dimensionality and Y axis represents F1_Measure. It has been observed that SUBSPACE_DE depicts high F1 score with increase in dimensions. At high

Figure 4. Scalability of SUBSPACE_DE vs. Cell based

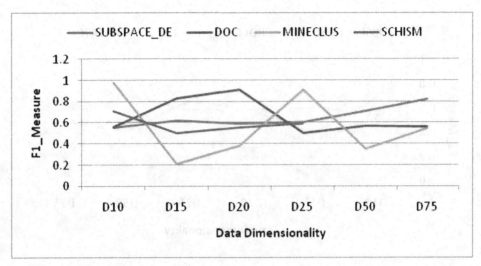

For a more accurate representation see the electronic version.

Figure 5. Scalability of SUBSPACE_DE vs. Density based

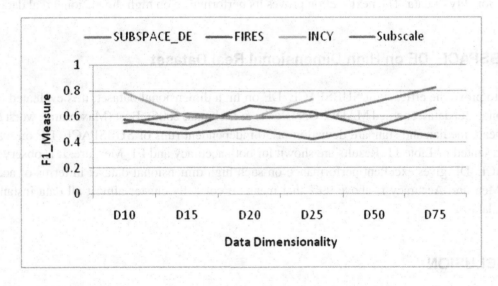

For a more accurate representation see the electronic version.

dimensions (D50 and D75), it outperforms all competitor algorithms and gives superior performance. Additionally, SUBSPACE_DE performance is consistent throughout all dimensions. MINECLUS and DOC show random behavior on data dimensionality while INCY and SCHISM depicts good efficiency but breaks down after 25 dimensions. FIRES performance gets degrade after 20-dimensional dataset. SUBSCALE graph matches with SUBSPACE_DE but could not reach its score. PROCLUS and P3C show random behavior while STATPC shows approximately static performance throughout data dimensionality. SUBSPACE_DE outperform all these algorithms on high dimensional dataset.

Figure 6. Scalability of SUBSPACE_DE vs. Clustering Oriented

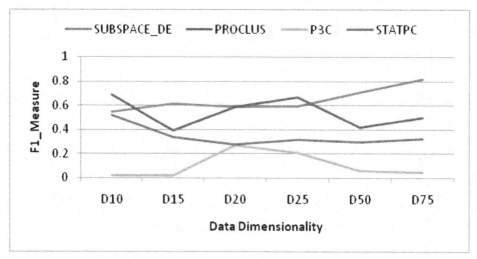

*For a more accurate representation see the electronic version.

Hence, SUBSPACE_DE confirms good efficiency in terms of F1_measure and accuracy with increase in dimensionality of data. The next section proves its performance on high dimensional real dataset i.e. Madelon.

5.2 SUBSPACE_DE on High Dimensional Real Dataset

In order to prove the efficacy of SUBSPACE_DE on high dimensional dataset, it is evaluated on 500 dimensional real dataset named MADELON (Bache & Lichman, 2006). Best (Maximum), worst (Minimum), mean, median and standard deviation of 30 independent runs of SUBSPACE_DE on madelon data is presented in Table 11. Results are shown for both accuracy and F1_Measure. It is observed that SUBSPACE_DE gives excellent performance on such high dimensional dataset in terms of accuracy and F1_Measure. Accuracy is above 99% that means it correctly cluster almost all data instances of madelon dataset.

6. CONCLUSION

Subspace clustering is an extended version of tradition clustering techniques. The subsets of dimensions are called subspaces. In high dimensional data, clusters may exist in different subspaces. However,

Table 11. F1_Measure of SUBSPACE_DE on Madelon dataset

	Best	Worst	Mean	Median	Std. Deviation
Accuracy	0.9961	0.9928	0.99404	0.9945	0.001873
F1_Measure	0.99541	0.99012	0.992832	0.99253	0.002155

subspace clustering poses number of challenges such as number of subspaces and number of hidden clusters are not known in prior. In case of large number of attributes, number of subspaces may increase exponentially. Such a large number of subspaces give computational challenge in field of data mining. This derives a need for good subspace clustering algorithm. The "good subspace clustering algorithm" refers to the algorithm that could take original dataset without any normalization and could determine overlapping subspace clusters as well as outliers. The good subspace clustering algorithm should be scalable to high dimensional datasets.

A novel SUBSPACE_DE clustering algorithm is introduced in this chapter. The algorithm works in three phases of determining clusters in single dimension, managing hash table to create maximal subspaces and clustering data instances in maximal subspaces. Clustering in SUBSPACE_DE is performed through self-adaptive DBSCAN algorithm. Parameters of DBSCAN algorithm are determined automatically from differential evolution algorithm according to the dataset employed. The algorithm was compared with 11 existing subspace clustering algorithms on 14 datasets. These datasets include synthetic and real data. Standard evaluation measures considered for experimentation are accuracy and F1_measure. Experimental comparison and analysis is made on success rate ratio ranking and scalability in dimensionality. Proposed algorithm (SUBSPACE_DE) outperforms on most of the datasets against various algorithms. It is also potentially scalable to high dimensional dataset. The proposed algorithm can be used in any high dimensional clustering applications such as customer recommended system, market segmentation problem, face recognition in computer vision, movie rating system etc.

REFERENCES

Agarwal, P., & Mehta, S. (2014). Nature-Inspired Algorithms: State-of-Art, Problems and Prospects. *International Journal of Computers and Applications, 100*(14), 14–21. doi:10.5120/17593-8331

Agarwal, P., & Mehta, S. (2015). Comparative Analysis of Nature Inspired Algorithms on Data Clustering. In *IEEE International Conference on Research in Computational Intelligence and Communication Networks (ICRCICN)* (pp. 119–124). 10.1109/ICRCICN.2015.7434221

Agarwal, P., & Mehta, S. (2016). Enhanced flower pollination algorithm on data clustering. *International Journals of Computers and Applications, Taylor and Francis, 7074*(August), 1–12. doi:10.1080/1206 212X.2016.1224401

Agarwal, P., & Mehta, S. (2017). Empirical analysis of five nature-inspired algorithms on real parameter optimization problems. *Artificial Intelligence Review*, 1–57. doi:10.100710462-017-9547-5

Aggarwal, C., Wolf, J., Yu, P., C. Procopiuc, & Park., J. (1999). Fast Algorithm for Projected Clustering. *CM SIGMoD Record, 28*(2), 61-72.

Agrawal, R., Gehrke, J., Gunopulos, D., & Raghavan, P. (1998). *Automatic subspace clustering of high dimensional data for data mining applications. In 1998 ACM SIGMOD international conference on Management of data* (pp. 94–105).

Assent, I. (2012). Clustering high dimensional data. *Wiley Interdisciplinary Reviews. Data Mining and Knowledge Discovery, 2*(4), 340–350. doi:10.1002/widm.1062

Assent, I., Krieger, R., Müller, E., & Seidl, T. (2008). INSCY: Indexing subspace clusters with in-process-removal of redundancy. In *Eighth IEEE International Conference on Data Mining ICDM'08. (pp. 719-724). IEEE.*

Bache, K., & Lichman, M. (2006). UCI machine learning repository. Retrieved from http://archive.ics.uci.edu/ml

Bradley, P. S., Fayyad, U., & Reina, C. (1998). Scaling Clustering Algorithms to Large Databases. In KDD-98 (pp. 1–7).

Brazdil, P., & Soares, C. (2000). A Comparison of Ranking Methods for Classification Algorithm Selection. *Machine Learning: ECML, 1810,* 63–75. doi:10.1007/3-540-45164-1_8

Das, S., Abraham, A., & Konar, A. (2008). Automatic Clustering Using an Improved Differential Evolution Algorithm. *IEEE Transactions on Systems, Man, and Cybernetics. Part A, Systems and Humans, 38*(1), 218–237.

Das, S., & Suganthan, P. N. (2011). Differential Evolution: A Survey of the. *IEEE Transactions on Evolutionary Computation, 15*(1), 4–31. doi:10.1109/TEVC.2010.2059031

Daszykowski, M., Walczak, B., & Massart, D. L. (2001). Looking for natural patterns in data: Part 1. density-based approach. *Chemometrics and Intelligent Laboratory Systems, 56*(2), 83–92. doi:10.1016/S0169-7439(01)00111-3

Fahad, A., Alshatri, N., Tari, Z., Alamri, A., Khalil, I., Zomaya, A. Y., ... Bouras, A. (2014). A survey of clustering algorithms for big data: Taxonomy and empirical analysis. *IEEE Transactions on Emerging Topics in Computing, 2*(3), 267–279. doi:10.1109/TETC.2014.2330519

Gajawada, S., & Toshniwal, D. (2012). Projected Clustering Using Particle Swarm Optimization. *Procedia Technology, 4,* 360–364. doi:10.1016/j.protcy.2012.05.055

Goebl, S., Xiao, H., Plant, C., & Bohm, C. (2014). Finding the Optimal Subspace for Clustering. In *2014 IEEE International Conference on Data Mining* (pp. 130–139). 10.1109/ICDM.2014.34

Kailing, K., Kriegel, H.-P., & Oger, P. K. (2004). Density-connected subspace clustering for high-dimensional data. In *Proceedings of the 2004 SIAM International Conference on Data Mining* (pp. 246-256). Society for Industrial and Applied Mathematics.

Karami, A., & Johansson, R. (2014). Choosing DBSCAN Parameters Automatically using Differential Evolution. *International Journal of Computers and Applications, 91*(7), 1–11. doi:10.5120/15890-5059

Kaur, A., & Datta, A. (2014). {SUBSCALE:} Fast and Scalable Subspace Clustering for High Dimensional Data. In *2014 IEEE International Conference on Data Mining Workshops, ICDM Workshops 2014, Shenzhen, China, December 14* (pp. 621-628). doi:10.1109/ICDMW.2014.100

Kaur, A., & Datta, A. (2015). A novel algorithm for fast and scalable subspace clustering of high-dimensional data. *Journal of Big Data, 2*(1), 17. doi:10.118640537-015-0027-y

Kothari, D., Narayanan, S. T., & Devi, K. K. (2014). Extended Fuzzy C-Means with Random Sampling Techniques for Clustering Large Data. *International Journal of Innovative Research in Advanced Engineering*, *1*(1), 1–4.

Kriegel, H.-P., Kroger, P., & Renz, M., & Wurst., S. (2005). A generic framework for efficient subspace clustering of high-dimensional data. In *Proceedings of the Fifth IEEE International Conference on Data Mining* (pp. 250-257). 10.1109/ICDM.2005.5

Kriegel, H.-P., Kröger, P., & Zimek, A. (2009). Clustering high-dimensional data: a survey on subspace clustering, pattern-based clustering, and correlation clustering. *ACM Transactions on Knowledge Discovery from Data*, *3*(1), 1–58. doi:10.1145/1497577.1497578

Kumar, D., Bezdek, J. C., Palaniswami, M., Rajasegarar, S., Leckie, C., & Havens, T. C. (2016). A Hybrid Approach to Clustering in Big Data. *IEEE Transactions on Cybernetics*, *46*(10), 2372–2385. doi:10.1109/TCYB.2015.2477416 PMID:26441434

Lin, L., Gen, M., & Liang, Y. (2014). A hybrid EA for high-dimensional subspace clustering problem. In *Proceedings of the 2014 IEEE Congress on Evolutionary Computation, CEC 2014* (pp. 2855–2860). 10.1109/CEC.2014.6900313

Lu, Y., Wang, S., Li, S., & Zhou, C. (2011). Particle swarm optimizer for variable weighting in clustering high-dimensional data. *Machine Learning*, *82*(1), 43–70. doi:10.100710994-009-5154-2

Mehta, S., & Banati, H. (2014). Context aware filtering using social behavior of frogs. *Swarm and Evolutionary Computation*, *17*, 25–36. doi:10.1016/j.swevo.2014.02.003

Moise, G., & Sander, J. (2008). Finding non-redundant, statistically significant regions in high dimensional data: a novel approach to projected and subspace clustering. In *Proceedings of the 14th ACM SIGKDD international conference on Knowledge discovery and data mining* (pp. 533–541). 10.1145/1401890.1401956

Moise, G., Sander, J., & Ester, M. (2006). P3C: A robust projected clustering algorithm. In *Proceedings of the Sixth International Conference on Data Mining* (pp. 414–425).

Müller, E., Günnemann, S., Assent, I., & Seidl, T. (2009). Evaluating clustering in subspace projections of high dimensional data. *Proceedings of the VLDB Endowment International Conference on Very Large Data Bases*, *2*(1), 1270–1281. doi:10.14778/1687627.1687770

Müller, E., Günnemann, S., Assent, I., Seidl, T., & Färber, I. (2009). Evaluating Clustering in Subspace Projections of High Dimensional Data. Retrieved from http://dme.rwth-aachen.de/en/OpenSubspace/evaluation

Nourashrafeddin, S., Arnold, D., & Milios, E. (2012). An evolutionary subspace clustering algorithm for high-dimensional data. In *Proceedings of the Fourteenth International Conference on Genetic and Evolutionary Computation Conference Companion* (pp. 1497–1498). 10.1145/2330784.2331011

Parsons, L., Parsons, L., Haque, E., Haque, E., Liu, H., & Liu, H. (2004). Subspace Clustering for High Dimensional Data: A Review. *ACM SIGKDD Explorations Newsletter*, *6*(1), 90–105. doi:10.1145/1007730.1007731

Procopiuc, C. M., Jones, M., Agarwal, P. K., & Murali, T. M. (2002, June). A Monte Carlo algorithm for fast projective clustering. In *Proceedings of the 2002 ACM SIGMOD international conference on Management of data* (pp. 418-427). ACM.

Road, H., & Jose, S. (1998). Automatic Subspace Clustering Mining of High Dimensional Applications for Data. In *Proceedings of the 1998 ACM SIGMOD International Conference on Management of Data* (pp. 94-105). doi:10.1145/276305.276314

Sequeira, K., & Zaki, M. (2004). SCHISM: A new approach for interesting subspace mining. In *Proceedings of the Fourth IEEE International Conference on Data Mining* (pp. 186–193).

Storn, R., & Price, K. (1997). Differential evolution – a simple and efficient heuristic for global optimization over continuous spaces. *Journal of Global Optimization*, *11*(4), 341–359. doi:10.1023/A:1008202821328

Sun, H., & Xiong, L. (2009). Genetic Algorithm-Based High-dimensional Data Clustering Technique. In *2009 Sixth International Conference on Fuzzy Systems and Knowledge Discovery* (pp. 485–489). 10.1109/FSKD.2009.215

Timmerman, M. E., Ceulemans, E., De Roover, K., & Van Leeuwen, K. (2013). Subspace K-means clustering. *Behavior Research Methods*, *45*(4), 1011–1023. doi:10.375813428-013-0329-y PMID:23526258

Vijendra, S., & Laxman, S. (2013). Subspace Clustering of High-Dimensional Data: An Evolutionary Approach. *Applied Computational Intelligence and Soft Computing*, *2013*(1), 1–13. doi:10.1155/2013/863146

Yiu, M. L., & Mamoulis, N. (2003). Frequent-pattern based iterative projected clustering. In *Proceedings of the Third IEEE International Conference on Data Mining* (pp. 689–692).

Chapter 4
Nature Inspired Feature Selector for Effective Data Classification in Big Data Frameworks

Appavu Alias Balamurugan Subramanian
K.L.N. College of Information Technology, India

ABSTRACT

In high dimensional space finding clusters of data objects is challenging due to the curse of dimensionality. When the dimensionality increases, data in the irrelevant dimensions may produce much noise. And also, time complexity is the major issues in existing approach. In order to rectify these issues our proposed method made use of efficient feature subset selection in high dimensional data. We are considering the input dataset is the high dimensional micro array dataset. Initially, we have to select the optimal features so that our proposed technique employed Social Spider Optimization (SSO) algorithm. Here the traditional Social Spider Optimization is modified with the help of fruit fly optimization algorithm. Next the selected features are the input for the classifier. The classification is performed using optimized radial basis function based neural network (ORBFNN) technique to classify the micro array data as normal or abnormal data. The effectiveness of RBFNN is optimized by means of artificial bee colony algorithm (ABC).

1. INTRODUCTION

The profound increase in the technologies and their usage has led to the huge amount of data in terms of both number of attributes or features as well as records. Hypothetically, it appears to be coherent that more number of features means more precise information, nevertheless increase in number of features has created the curse of dimensionality problem. This implies that with the escalation in the number of dimensions, the performance of conventional algorithms begins to degrade. The nearness of pertinent and unessential features in the data can impede the working of classifier. They can make the classifier computationally more expensive and can also generate overfitted data model. In order to solve this problem, dimensionality reduction via feature selection is an appropriate strategy. Feature selection comprises of

DOI: 10.4018/978-1-5225-5852-1.ch004

choosing the pertinent features and disposing the insignificant ones to get a subset of features that best represent the data without losing any information. In addition, reduction in number of features helps in reducing the computational cost. Feature selection is an active area of research most applied in pattern recognition, information mining, genomics, bioinformatics, and computational science due to its added advantages.

These feature selection techniques are also known as feature subset selection strategies or feature ranking strategies. Feature Ranking (FR) strategies positions the features as indicated by their value in the classification problem. The Feature Subset Selection (FSS) strategies focus on providing the set of most important features for the classification model. Feature selection procedures are also classified as filters, wrappers, and embedded strategies. In wrapper techniques a subset of features is used to train the model iteratively. Subsequently, based on the performance of the model, features are added or removed features from the subsets. On the other hand, filter methods are commonly used as a preprocessing step. It is independent of the classification algorithm where features are chosen on the basis of their correlation with the outcome variable obtained by performing varied statistical tests. A hybrid feature selection technique known as embedded methods combines the qualities' of both the filter and wrapper techniques. These methods are implemented using the algorithms having their feature selection methods like LASSO and RIDGE regression which have inbuilt mechanism to control overfitting.

Researchers have characterized feature subset selection (FSS) as a search problem. In order to obtain the ideal subset of features, the most mainstream variable selection techniques for the most part incorporate forward, in reverse and floating successive strategies, which dependably utilize heuristic ways to deal with given an imperfect arrangement. The chosen ideal subsets of features produce higher classification precisions as compared to original set of features. After feature selection, two-stage classification procedure is applied to training and test data to compute the classification accuracy of the proposed approach. Rest of the chapter is organized as follows: Section 2 presents literature survey followed by proposed methodology in section 3. Experiments and results are discussed in Section 4 followed by conclusion.

2. LITERATURE SURVEY

Suhail Khokhar et al. (2016) proposed a novel method of programmed classification of single and cross breed PQDs. The proposed algorithm comprised of the Discrete Wavelet Transform (DWT) and Probabilistic Neural Network based Artificial Bee Colony (PNN-ABC) ideal feature selection of PQDs. DWT with Multi-Resolution Analysis (MRA) was utilized for the feature extraction of the noise. The PNN classifier was utilized as a successful classifier for the classification of the PQDs. It was observed that the new PNN-ABC based feature selection approach was more efficient for classification of PQDs.

Qi *et al.* (2016) emphasized that feature selection and classification have an important role in the field of Hyper Spectral Image (HSI) investigation They addressed the issue of HSI classification from the three perspectives. Primarily, they exhibited a novel basis by standard deviation, Kullback–Leibler separation and connection coefficient for feature selection. Subsequently they improved the SVM classifier by exploring the e most proper estimation of the parameters utilizing particle swarm optimization (PSO) with transformation instrument. At long last, they proposed a group learning system, which applied the boosting strategy to take in various kernel classifiers for classification issues. Trials were led on benchmark HSI classification information sets. The assessment comes about demonstrated that the proposed strategy could accomplish preferred precision and proficiency over best in class strategies.

Even though feature selection techniques have accomplished promising advancement, human variables have at times been considered. To handle such an issue, Xuan Zhoua et al. (2016) conveyed a novel two-step feature selection strategy for picture classification by considering human components and utilizing the estimation of eye tracking information. In the coarse selection step, with the assistance of eye following information, Regions of Interests (ROIs) from the human point of view were initially distinguished to characterize a picture with visual features. At that point, with an improved quantum genetic algorithm (IQGA) that joined a novel mutation technique for easing the untimely merging, a subset of features was perceived for the resulting fine selection. In the fine selection arrange, a crossover strategy was proposed to coordinate the proficiency of the minimal-Redundancy Maximal-Relevance (mRMR) and the viability of the Support Vector Machine-oriented Recursive Feature Elimination (SVM-RFE). Specifically, the positioning standard of the SVM-RFE was enhanced by joining the positioning data acquired from the mRMR.

High-dimensional shape descriptors (HDSD) are valuable for demonstrating sub cortical cerebrum surface morphometry. In spite of the fact that HDSD is a valuable reason for illness biomarkers, its high dimensionality needs cautious therapy in its usage to machine figuring to alleviate the scourge of dimensionality. Wade et al. (2015) investigated the utilization of HDSD feature sets by looking at the execution of two feature selection methodologies, Regularized Random Forest (RRF) and LASSO, to no feature selection (NFS). Every list of features was connected to three classifiers: Random Forest (RF), Support Vector Machines (SVM) and Naïve Bayes (NB). Combined feature-selection-classifier methodologies were 10-overlay cross-approved on two indicative differences: Alzheimer's ailment and mellow psychological weakness, both with respect to controls crosswise over fluctuating example sizes to assess their power. LASSO helped classification effectiveness, notwithstanding, RRF and NFS managed more hearty exhibitions. Execution fluctuated significantly by classifier with RF being generally steady. They educated cautious thought with respect to execution effectiveness tradeoffs in picking feature selection techniques for HDSD.

Relevance Sample-Feature Machine (RSFM) performs joint feature selection and classification with best in class execution as far as exactness and sparsity. In any case, it experiences high computational cost for substantial preparing sets. To quicken that's preparation strategy, Yalda Mohsenzadeha et al. (2016) presented another variation of that algorithm named Incremental Relevance Sample-Feature Machine (IRSFM). In IRSFM, the peripheral probability expansion strategy was altered to such an extent that the model learning followed a valuable technique (beginning with an unfilled design that iteratively added or overlooked premise capacities to develop the scholarly model). Their broad examinations on different information sets and correlation with different contending algorithms exhibited the viability of the proposed IRSFM with respect to precision, sparsity and run-time. While the IRSFM accomplished practically an indistinguishable classification precision from the RSFM that profited by sparser educated model both in test and feature spaces and considerably lessened preparing time than RSFM particularly for substantial information sets.

The conventional feature selection strategies utilized in brain-computer interface (BCI) field (e.g. Mutual Information-based Best Individual Feature (MIBIF), Mutual Information-based Rough Set Reduction (MIRSR) and cross approval) concentrate on the general execution on every one of the trials in the preparation set, and along these lines may have exceptionally poor execution on some particular examples, which is not satisfactory. To address that issue, Luo et al. (2016) anticipated a novel successive forward feature selection strategy called Dynamic Frequency Feature Selection (DFFS). The DFFS technique underscored the significance of the examples that got misclassified while just seeking high general classification execution. In the DFFS based classification plan, the EEG information was initially changed to recurrence space utilizing Wavelet Packet Decomposition (WPD), which was then utilized as the applicant set for further oppressive feature selection. The chosen features were then nourished to a classifier prepared by arbitrary forest algorithm.

A standout amongst the most mainstream picture representations for picture classification depends on the bag of-words (BoW) features. In any case, the quantity of key indicates that need to be distinguished from pictures to produce the BoW features is normally vast, which causes two issues. Initially, the computational cost amid the vector quantization step is high. Second, a portion of the distinguished key focuses are not useful for acknowledgment. To determine those confinements, Lin et al. (2016) put forth a method called iterative key point selection (IKS), with which to choose agent key focused for quickening the computational duration to produce the BoW features, prompting to more discriminative feature representation. Every emphasis in IKS included two stages. In the initial step some illustrative key point(s) were recognized from every picture. At that point, the key focuses were sifted through if the separations amongst them and the distinguished agent key point(s) were not exactly a pre-characterized remove. The cycle procedure proceeded until no unrepresentative key focused could be detected.

3. PROPOSED METHOD

Feature selection is the process of identifying and removing many irrelevant and redundant features. Irrelevant features, along with redundant features, severely affect the accuracy of the learning algorithms. Therefore, the proposed feature selection method selects optimal features for classification. In high dimensional space, finding clusters of data objects is challenging due to the curse of dimensionality. When the dimensionality increases, data in the irrelevant dimensions may produce much noise. Also, another significant challenge presented by the classification methods is related to time complexity issues. In order to handle these issues, the proposed method makes use of efficient feature subset selection for high dimensional data. Here we are considering the high dimensional micro array dataset as the input dataset. Initially, in order to select the optimal features, the proposed technique employs Modified Social Spider Optimization (SSO) algorithm. Here the traditional Social Spider Optimization is modified with the help of fruit fly optimization algorithm. Next the selected features form the input for the classifier. Here the classification is performed using Optimized Radial basis Function based neural network (RBFNN) technique to classify the micro array data as normal or abnormal data. The effectiveness of RBFNN is optimized by means of artificial bee colony algorithm (ABC). The overall structure of the recommended technique is shown in Figure 1.

The overall process of the proposed methodology is divided into three stages, as follows 1) Preprocessing, 2) Optimal feature selection and 3) Classification. The detailed explanation of each stage is described in next section.

3.1. Preprocessing

Unfavorable results may be achieved when partially filtered data is evaluated. Therefore, it is essential to properly characterize data prior to its evaluation. Identification of knowledge in the training method becomes difficult due to the presence of unwanted or irrelevant data. Irrelevant data may be in the form

Figure 1. The structure of recommended technique

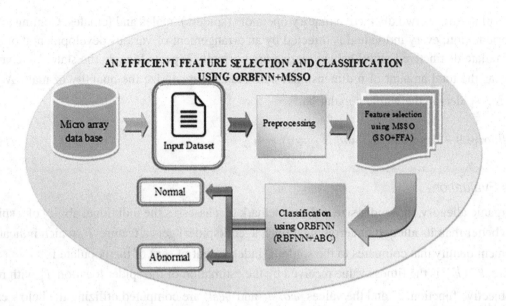

of noise, discrepancy and mislaid values. The duration for processing increases for both data preparation as well as the filtering stages. Further, if the input dataset containing irrelevant data is fed to preprocessing task, the presence of irrelevant information makes the output worse. In order to overcome those issues preprocessing is preferred to achieve effective results. Data preprocessing plays a vital role in data mining task for processing as well as conversion of original dataset. In our proposed method data preprocessing separates the categorical and non-categorical data. The non-categorical data are eliminated and subsequent steps proceed using only the categorical data.

3.2. Feature Selection

Feature selection, otherwise called variable selection, characteristic selection or variable subset selection, is the technique of selecting a subset of redundant features (factors, indicators) for utilization in the proposed model. Here optimal features are selected using Social Spider Optimization (SSO) algorithm, where the traditional Social Spider Optimization is modified with the help of fruit fly optimization algorithm.

3.2.1 Modified Social Spider Optimization (SSO) Algorithm

The SSO expects that the whole inquiry space is a communal web, where all the social-spiders communicate with each other. In the proposed approach, every arrangement inside the inquiry space characterizes a specific location in the communal web. All spiders get features as per the fitness estimation of the arrangement that is represented by the social-spider. In order to improve the feature selection, the spiders are once again updated with the help of fruit fly optimization algorithm.

Update of Population

The algorithm utilizes two distinctive inquiry operators (spiders): males and females. Contingent upon sexual orientation, every individual is directed by an arrangement of various developmental operators which emulate distinctive helpful behaviors that are normally expected inside the state. By characterizing N as the total amount of n-dimensional individual, characterize the quantity of male N_{ms} and female N_{fs} spiders in the whole population F.

$$N_{fs} = floor[0.9 - rand.025).N] \; and \; N_{ms} = N - N_{fs}$$

Fitness Evaluation

In the organic allegory, the spider size is the trademark that assesses the individual ability of a spider to perform better than its allotted undertakings. Each agent (spider) gets a feature F_i which indicates the arrangement quality that compares to the spider i (independent of sex) of the populate F.

Where $Fit(F_i)$ is the fitness value received by the estimation of the spider location F_i with respect to the objective function F and the values $worst_t$ and $best_t$ are computed utilizing the below expression.

Modeling of the Vibrations Through the Communal Web

The communal web is used as a mechanism to transmit information among the colony members. This information is encoded as small vibrations that are critical for the collective coordination of all individuals in the population. The vibrations depend on the weight and distance of the spider which has generated them. Since the distance is relative to the individual that provokes the vibrations and the member who detects them, members located near the individual that provokes the vibrations, perceive stronger vibrations in comparison with members located in distant positions. In order to reproduce this process, the vibrations perceived by the individual i as a result of the information transmitted by the member j are modeled according to the following equation:

$$Vibr_{ij} = w_i f^{-d_{ij}^2}$$

Where, d_{ij} is the Euclidian distance between the spiders i and j, such that $d_{ij} = \left\| F_i - F_j \right\|$;

Initializing the Population Based on Fitness Value

The algorithm starts by instating the set F of N spider locations, where every spider location is $f_{si} \, and \, m_{si}$ is a dimensional vector consisting of the parameter qualities to be improved. Such values are arbitrarily and consistently dispersed between the pre-indicated low beginning parameter limit p_j^{low} and the higher introductory value limit p_j^{high} similarly as it conveyed by utilizing equation given below

$$f_{si,j}^0 = p_j^{low} + rand(0,1).(p_j - p_j^{low}), i = 1,2,..N \; and \; j = 1,2,...n$$

where i, j *and* k represents the limitation and individual indexes correspondingly while zero signals are the original populations. Hence $f_{si,j}$ is the *jth* value of the *ith* female spider location.

Cooperative Operators

1. Female Cooperative Operator

Female spiders show a fascination or repulsion over others regardless of sexual orientation. For a specific female spider, such fascination or repulsion is normally created over different spiders as indicated by their vibrations which are discharged over the collective web. Since vibrations rely upon the weight and separation of the individuals which have begun them, solid vibrations are delivered either by big spiders or other neighboring individuals locating adjacent to the individual seeing them. The initiator includes the adjustment with respect to the closest part to i that holds a high weight and creates vibration $Vibrc_i$.

The Vibration $Vibrd_i$ is received by the identity $i(F_i)$ as an aftereffect of the data transmitted by the spider $c(F_c)$ who is a member that contains two essential qualities: it is the closest part to i and has a higher weight in contrast with $i(w_c > w_i)$. The Vibration $Vibrb_i$ are seen by the spider i as a consequence of the data transmitted by the individual $b(F_b)$ with b being the individual holding the best weight that its fitness of the whole populace F to such an extent that $w_b = \max_{k \in \{1,2,...N\}}(w_k)$.

Since the final movement of attraction or repulsion depends on several random phenomena, the selection is modeled as a stochastic decision. For this operation, a uniform random number is generated within the range [0,1]. If the random number is less than threshold T_h an attraction motion is produced; or else a revulsion motion is produced. Hence the operator is represented as follows:

$$f_{si}^{k+1} = \begin{cases} f_{si}^k + vibrc_i.(F_c - f_{si}^k) + \gamma.vibrb_i.(F_b - f_{si}^k) + \lambda.(rand - \frac{1}{2}) \, with \, probability \, T_h \\ f_{si}^k - vibrc_i.(F_c - f_{si}^k) - \gamma.vibrb_i.(F_b - f_{si}^k) + \lambda.(rand - \frac{1}{2}) \, with \, probability \, 1 - T_h \end{cases}$$

Where γ *and* λ are arbitrary values between [0, 1] whereas 1 indicates the iteration value. The individual F_c *and* F_b indicate the adjacent member to i that contains a high weight and the best individual of the whole population F.

2. Male Cooperative Operator

Male individuals, with weight esteem over the middle esteem inside the male populace, are viewed as the predominant people D. Then again, those under the middle esteem are named as non-dominant ND males. With a specific end goal to actualize such calculation, the male populace $mP\left(mP = \left\{mP_1, mP_2, ...mP_{n_m}\right\}\right)$ is orchestrated by weight esteem in diminishing request. Accordingly, the person whose weight w_{Nf+m} is situated in the center is viewed as the middle male part the vibration of the male $Vibrf_i$ computed by utilizing underneath condition. The Vibration $Vibrf_i$ saw by the person $i(F_i)$ as a consequence of the data transmitted by the part $f(F_j)$ with g being the closest female individual to i.

$$Vibrf_i = w_f . e^{-d_{i,f}^2}$$

Since files of the male populace S with respect to the whole populace F are expanded by the quantity of female individuals N_f, the middle weight is ordered by $N_f + mP$. As per this, alteration of locations for the male spider can be demonstrated as follows.

By utilizing this operator, two distinct practices are created. To start with, the arrangement D of particles is pulled in to others keeping in mind the end goal to incite mating. Such conduct permits consolidating differing qualities into the populace. Second, the arrangement ND of particles is pulled in to the weighted mean of the male populace mP. This reality is utilized to mostly control the pursuit procedure as per the normal execution of a subgroup of the populace.

- **Mating Procedure:** Mating in a social- spider state is done by dominant males and the female individuals. Under such conditions, when a dominant male m_s spider finds an arrangement f_s of female individuals inside a particular limit R (range of mating), it mates, framing another brood F_{new}. The range R is characterized as a span which relies upon the measure of the pursuit space. Initialize arbitrarily the female $\left(f_s = \left\{ fs_1, fs_2, ... fs_{N_f} \right\} \right)$ and male $\left(m_s = \left\{ ms_1, ms_2, ... ms_{N_m} \right\} \right)$ then compute the radius mating.

$$R = \frac{\sum_{j=1}^{n} \left(p_j^{high} - p_j^{low} \right)}{2.n}$$

In the mating procedure, the weight of all included spider characterizes the likelihood of impact for every person into the new brood. The spiders holding a heavier weight will probably impact the new item, while components with lighter weight have a less likelihood.

Once mating procedure is completed, the new spiders are fed to the fruit fly optimization algorithm. The step by step procedure of spider updation using fruit fly optimization algorithm is described next.

- **Fruit Fly Updation:** The random location of a fruit fly or spider is initialized as $\left(SU_{axis}, SV_{axis} \right)$ and then exploration is performed using arbitrary path and detachment to the olfactory organ.

$$SU_m = SU_{axis} + Rand$$

$$SV_m = SV_{axis} + Rand$$

Since food's location is unfamiliar, the distance (D) from the beginning is evaluated initially, and the computed value of smell concentration (S_c), known as the reverse of distance, is computed next.

$$D_m = \sqrt{U_m^2} + SV$$

$$S_{Cm} = 1 / D_m$$

Based on the above procedure, the solutions are updated and then the updated solution is further processed with SSO algorithm. Once the new spider is framed, it is contrasted with the new spider member F_{new} containing the most exceedingly bad spider of the state, as per their weight values. In the event that the new spider is superior to the most noticeably awful spider, the latter spider is supplanted by the new one. Or else, the new spider is disposed of and the populace does not endure modifications. In the event of substitution, the new spiders expect the sexual orientation and list from the supplanted spider. Such certainty guarantees that the whole populace F keeps up the first rate amongst female and male individuals. These procedures locate the ideal hidden layer and neuron of the neural system procedure. In light of above, the said procedure accomplishes the optimal feature value selection. The resultant output is fed to the classification process.

3.3. Classification

Once we select the optimal features from the input dataset, the classification is performed by Optimized Radial basis Function based neural network (ORBFNN) technique. ORBFNN is utilized to classify the micro array data as normal or abnormal data. The detailed explanation of ORBFNN technique is shown next

3.3.1. Optimal Radial Basis Function Based Neural Network (ORBFNN) Technique

In this section, we explain the efficient data classification based on optimal radial basis function neural network (ORBFNN). The parameter used in the RBFNN (number of neurons, their respective centers, radii and weight) is optimized with the help of artificial bee colony algorithm. Radial basis function (RBF) networks were introduced into the neural network literature with the help of Broom head and Lowe. In contrast to classical models, it is a network with local units that was interested with the help of the occurrence of numerous local response components in human brain. Neurons with a close by tuned response feature can be established in numerous portions of the nervous scheme, for instance cells in the auditory scheme discerning to small bands of incidences or cells in the visual cortex sensitive to bars concerned with in a convinced direction or additional visual characteristics inside a minor region of the visual field. The RBFNN is the kind of NN, which has three layers, such as input layer, hidden layer and output layer. The RBFNN is employed to categorize the data as normal or abnormal. The optimal selected features of the data are used to the input of the RBFNN, which is indicated as. After that the neurons are coached with the different operating conditions drive at the particular target.

The output of the RBF-NN is calculated according to,

$$O = \sum_{i=1} W_i\left(f, c_i\right) = \sum_{i=1}^{N} W\left(\left\|f - c_i\right\|_2\right)$$

Where,

$\left\|.\right\|_2$ signifies the Euclidean norm

W are the weights of the links that attaches unseen neuron number i and output neuron number O in the output layer

N is the sum of neurons in the unseen layer

$c_i \in R^{n\times1}$ are the RBF centers in the input vector space.

The input layer is poised of input information. The unseen layer alters the information from the input space to the unseen space with the help of a non-linear function. The output layer is linear and revenues the response of the network. A standardized Gaussian function typically is utilized as the radial basis function as below:

$$\zeta_i\left(f, c_i\right) = \left(\frac{-\left\|f - c_i\right\|_2}{r_i^2}\right)$$

where r_i signify the radius of the ith node. It has been verified that if enough units are delivered, a RBFNN can imprecise any multivariate continuous function as anticipated. The effectiveness of RBFNN is optimized by means of artificial bee colony algorithm (ABC).

Artificial Bee Colony Algorithm (ABC)

In the ABC algorithm, the province of artificial bees consists of three gatherings of honey bees: employed bees, onlookers and scouts. A honey bee attending to the move zone for settling decision to pick a food source is known as an onlooker and a honey bee heading off to the food source visited by it beforehand is named an employed bee. A honey bee doing arbitrary search is known as a scout. In the ABC algorithm, first 50% of the province comprises of employed artificial bees and the second half comprises the onlookers. For each food source, there is just a single employed bee. As such, the quantity of employed bees is equivalent to the quantity of food sources around the hive. The employed bee whose food source is depleted by the employed and onlooker bees turns into a scout.

- Employed honey bees decide a nourishment source inside the area of the sustenance source in their memory.
- Employed honey bees impart their data to onlookers inside the hive and after that the onlookers choose one of the sustenance sources.
- Onlookers choose a sustenance source inside the area of the nourishment sources picked by their selves.
- An employed bee of which the source has been deserted turns into a scout and begins to look for another nourishment source arbitrarily.

The fundamental strides of the algorithm are explained below:

- Initialization
- Repetition
  - Locate the employed bees on the nourishment sources in the memory;
  - Put the onlooker bees on the nourishment sources in the memory;
  - Transfer the scouts to the look zone for finding new sustenance sources.
- UNTIL (effectiveness of RBFNN is optimized).

The different steps concerned in executing ABC algorithm are elucidated below,

Step 1: Initialize the Food Source

The algorithm is established by arbitrarily generating food source location that corresponds to the result in the search space. Produce the initial food source Pi (i=1,2,3..n) where n indicates the number of food source. This procedure is called initialization process.

Step 2: Fitness Evaluation

Using fitness function, the fitness value of the food resource is calculated to get the finest food resource. It's revealed in below,

$$fit_i = Max\,Accuracy$$

Step 3: Employed Bee Phase

In the employed bee's stage, every employed bee discovers a fresh food resource P_{ij}^{new} in the locality of its existing resource P_i. The fresh food resource is intended by using equation given below.

$$P_{ij}^{new} = (P_{ij} - P_{kj})$$

where P_{ij} is the jth parameter of the ith employed bee; P_{ij}^{new} is a new solution for P_{ij} in the jth dimension; P_{kj} is the neighbor bee of P_{ij} in employed bee population; ξ is a number arbitrarily chosen in the range of [-1, 1].

Step 4: Fitness Evaluation for New Food Source

Fitness values are established for each fresh food resource to decide the best food resource.

Step 5: Greedy Selection Process

After deciding the best food resources, greedy selection method is subsequently utilized. The probability of the selected food resource is calculated using the following equation

$$\text{Pr}_i = \frac{fi_i}{\sum\limits_{i=1}^{n} fit_i}$$

where, fit_i is a fitness value of ith employed bee.

Step 6: Onlooker Bee Stage

After computing the probability of the selected food resource quantity of onlooker bee is created. At the similar time, original result is formed for the onlooker bee and fitness task are calculated for the original result. Subsequently, greedy selection method is utilized in order to discover the outstanding food resource.

Step 7: Scout Bee Stage

In a cycle, after all employed bees and onlooker bees complete their searches, the algorithm checks to see if there is any exhausted source to be abandoned. In order to decide if a source is to be abandoned, the counters which have been updated during search are used. If the value of the counter is greater than the control parameter of the ABC algorithm, known as the ''limit'', then the source associated with this counter is assumed to be exhausted and is abandoned. The food source abandoned by its bee is replaced with a new food source discovered by the scout.

Step 8: Stop Criteria

Repeat from step 2, until a better fitness or maximum number of iterations are met and the solution which is holding the best fitness value is selected and it is specified as best parameters for prediction. Once the best fitness is attained by means of ABC algorithm, selected solution is allocated for RBF neural network. Based on the optimal parameters the RBFNN classifier is used to effectively classify the data. Once the training process is completed, the network is trained well to provide the target output. This neural network can classifythe data as normal data or abnormal data.

Testing Phase

In training phase, the RBFNN is provided only with inputs for which there are no known answers. RBFNN must develop its own representation of the input stimuli by calculating the acceptable connection weights. Based on these we classify the data and the efficiency of the proposed method is evaluated and analyzed in section.4.

4. RESULTS AND DISCUSSIONS

The experimental results obtained for the proposed method are explained clearly in this section. In our proposed method, modified Social Spider Optimization (SSO) algorithm is used for optimal feature selection and optimized radial basis function based neural network (RBFNN) technique is utilized to classify the micro array data as normal or abnormal data. The effectiveness of RBFNN is optimized by means of artificial bee colony algorithm (ABC). The proposed method is implemented using MATLAB. Our proposed method is performed in windows machine containing Intel Core i5 processor with speed 1.6 GHz and 4 GB RAM. The proposed system is experimented with the five datasets such as Breast cancer, leukemia, Lung cancer, Lymphoma and Ovarian.

Evaluation Metrics

The performance of our proposed data classification method is evaluated utilizing the sensitivity, specificity and accuracy metrics. The metrics are explained using the equations given below,

$$S_t = \frac{T_P}{T_P + F_N}$$

$$S_p = \frac{T_N}{T_N + F_P}$$

$$A = \frac{T_P + T_N}{T_P + F_P + T_N + F_N}$$

where,

$S_t \rightarrow$ Specified as sensitivity

$S_p \rightarrow$ Specified as specificity

$A \rightarrow$ Specified as accuracy

$T_P \rightarrow$ Specified as true positive

$T_N \rightarrow$ Specified as True negative

$F_P \rightarrow$ Specified as False positive

$F_N \rightarrow$ Specified as False negative

Performance Analysis

The results of proposed work help to analyze the efficiency of the classification process. Here classification of data is performed using Optimized Radial basis Function based neural network (RBFNN) and the effectiveness of RBFNN is optimized by means of artificial bee colony algorithm (ABC). The results are given below in the following table,

Table 1. Performance analysis of the proposed method

Dataset	Accuracy	Sensitivity	Specificity
Breast	93.66	0.880	0.974
Leukemia	97.09	0.977	0.982
Lung	98.66	0.939	1
Lymphoma	98.28	1	0.871
Ovarian	98.93	0.988	0.989

For breast cancer dataset the accuracy value is 93.66%, sensitivity value is 0.880% and the specificity value is 0.974% using the proposed method. The value of accuracy, sensitivity and specificity using the proposed method for Leukemia dataset is 97.09%, 0.977% and 0.982%. 98.66%, 0.939% and 1% of accuracy, sensitivity and specificity are obtained for lung dataset. For lymphoma dataset the accuracy value is 98.28%, sensitivity value is 1% and the specificity value is 0.871%. The value of accuracy obtained for ovarian dataset using the proposed method is 98.93%, sensitivity value is 0.988% and the specificity value is 0.989% respectively.

Comparison Analysis

For comparison analysis our proposed method is compared with other existing methods. In our proposed method effective classification is done by ORBFNN, in order to select the optimal features SSO algorithm is utilized along with FFA algorithm whereas in existing methods RBFNN+SSO, RBFNN+FFA, CG-ANN [23] algorithms were used for efficient classification. The effectiveness of the proposed method is proved using comparison analysis in the form of accuracy, sensitivity and specificity and are as follows,

From the graph it is clear that the value of accuracy for breast data set is 93.66% using ORBFNN+SSO while the accuracy values obtained using RBFNN+FFA, RBFNN+SSO, CGA-NN is 83.33%, 85%, 91.66% respectively. The accuracy value obtained using the proposed method is 97.09% and 78.38%, 82.25% and 96.77% of accuracy value is obtained using traditional RBFNN+FFA, RBFNN+SSO, CGA-NN methods for leukemia dataset. The value of accuracy using ORBFNN+SSO is 98.66% for lung dataset while the accuracy value for existing methods are lower than the proposed method and are 87.22%, 90.55% and 98.88% respectively for RBFNN+FFA, RBFNN+SSO and CGA-NN respectively. For lymphoma dataset the accuracy value using the proposed method is 98.28% using the proposed method and 90%, 82.85% and 97.14% of accuracy value is obtained using RBFNN+FFA, RBFNN+SSO and CGA-NN. The accuracy value of ovarian dataset is 90.80% using RBFNN+FFA, 77% using RBFNN+SSO and 97.14% using CGA-NN while 98.93% of accuracy value is obtained using the proposed method.

From the above figure it is clear that the sensitivity value of proposed method for breast dataset is 0.880%, while the sensitivity value using RBFNN+FFA, RBFNN+SSO and CGA-NN is 0.952%, 0.714% and 0.857% respectively. The sensitivity value for leukemia dataset using the proposed method is 0.977%, the sensitivity value using RBFNN+FFA is 0.95%, for RBFNN+SSO the sensitivity value is 0.77% and sensitivity value using CGA-NN is 0.95%. The sensitivity value for lung dataset using ORBFNN+SSO is 0.93%, 0.85% of sensitivity value is obtained using RBFNN+FFA, sensitivity value using RBFNN+SSO is 0.39% and 0.91% of sensitivity value is obtained using CG-ANN. For lymphoma data set the sensitivity value for ORBFNN+SSO, RBFNN+FFA, RBFNN+SSO and CG-ANN are 1%,

Figure 2. Sensitivity comparison

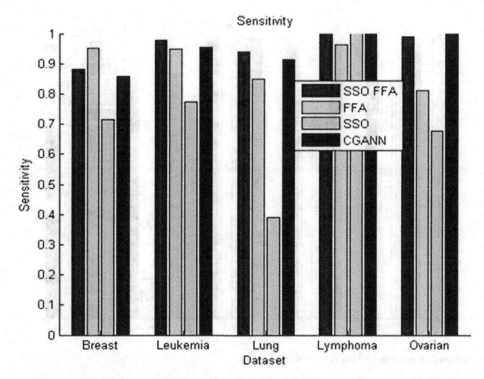

For a more accurate representation see the electronic version.

0.96%, 1% and 1% respectively. The sensitivity value for ovarian dataset is 0.98% using ORBFNN+SSO, 0.811% using FFA, 0.677% using SSO and 1% using CG-ANN.

For breast dataset the specificity value using the proposed method is 0.97% and the specificity value using RBFNN+FFA, RBFNN+SSO and CG-ANN is 0.85%, 0.92% and 0.94% respectively. The specificity value obtained using ORBFNN+SSO is 0.98%, specificity value using RBFNN+FFA is 0.75%, value of specificity using RBFNN+SSO is 0.85%, 0.975% of specificity value using CG-ANN for leukemia dataset. 1%, 1%, 0.98% and 1% of specificity value is obtained using RBFNN+SSO, RBFNN+FFA, RBFNN+SSO and CG-ANN for lung dataset. For lymphoma dataset the value of specificity using ORBFNN+SSO, RBFNN+FFA, RBFNN+SSO, and CG-ANN is 0.87%, 0.81%, 0.14% and 0.85% respectively. 0.98%, 0.96%, 0.85% and 0.97% of specificity value is obtained for ovarian dataset using ORBFNN+SSO, RBFNN+FFA, RBFNN+SSO and CG-ANN respectively. In order to prove the efficiency of the feature selection method, our proposed technique is compared with an existing method. Here the existing technique is to select the input attributes without any feature selection method, and the input attributes are directly given to the classification technique. But in our proposed technique, SSO algorithm is used for feature selection and only the selected features are given to the classification (ORBFNN) technique. Table appearing below shows the comparison result for accuracy value for various dataset with and without feature selection method.

From the result, we understand our proposed approach of ORBFNN+SSO classifier based high dimensional data classification outperforms other existing approaches. The proposed feature selection method attained maximum classification accuracy value when compared to the existing techniques. Hence from the above discussion, it is clear that our proposed method has higher accuracy value, higher

Figure 3. Specificity comparison

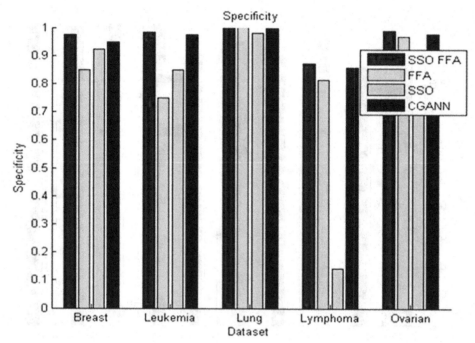

For a more accurate representation see the electronic version.

Table 2. Comparison result for accuracy value with and without feature selection method

Datasets	Accuracy Value of Proposed Technique With Feature Selection	Accuracy Value of Proposed Technique Without Feature Selection	Accuracy Value of the Multiple Kernel Fuzzy C-Means Clustering With Rough Set Theory RS-MKFCM Based Feature Selector
Breast	99	85	95.666
Leukemia	96	75.13	93.774
Lung	97	89.452	92.888
Lymphoma	98.93	89. 8	92.142
Ovarian	96.93	87.71	93.930

sensitivity value and higher specificity value than the existing methods. Hence our method serves as the better data classification technique.

CONCLUSION

An efficient feature selection and classification technique is proposed in thischapter. Here modified social spider optimization algorithm is applied on the high dimensional micro array dataset to select the optimal features. After that, the classification is done through ORBFNN classifier. The performance of the proposed approach was evaluated by sensitivity, specificity, and accuracy on the five benchmarks datasets such as Breast cancer, Leukemia, Lung cancer, Lymphoma and ovarian cancer datasets. The results verify that our proposed approach of ORBFNN classifier-based prediction has higher accuracy value, higher sensitivity value and higher specificity value than the existing methods. Hence our method serves as the better data classification technique. In future, the researchers can explore various feature selection techniques and produce newer heights of excellence in performance.

REFERENCES

Khokhar, S., Zina, A. A. M., Memon, A. P., & Mokhtar, A. S. (2016). A new optimal feature selection algorithm for classification of power quality disturbances using discrete wavelet transform and probabilistic neural network. *Measurement*, *95*, 246–259. doi:10.1016/j.measurement.2016.10.013

Lin, W., Tsai, C., Chen, Z., & Ke, S. (2016). Keypoint selection for efficient bag-of-words feature generation and effective image classification. *Information Sciences*, *329*, 33–51. doi:10.1016/j.ins.2015.08.021

Luo, J., Feng, Z., Zhang, J., & Lu, N. (2016, August). approach for classification of motor imageries. *Computers in Biology and Medicine*, *75*, 45–53. doi:10.1016/j.compbiomed.2016.03.004 PMID:27253616

Mohsenzadeha, Y., Sheikhzadehb, H., & Nazari, S. (2016). Incremental relevancesample-feature machine: a fast marginal likelihood maximization approach for jointfeature selection and classification. *Pattern Recognition*, *60*, 835–848. doi:10.1016/j.patcog.2016.06.028

Qi, C., Zhou, Z., Sun, Y., Song, H., Hu, L., & Wang, Q. (2016). Feature selection and multiple kernel boosting framework based on PSO with mutation mechanism for hyperspectral classification. *Neurocomputing*, *220*, 181–190. doi:10.1016/j.neucom.2016.05.103

Wade, B. S. C., Joshi, S. H., Gutman, B. A., & Thompson, P. M. (2015). Machine Learning on High Dimensional Shape Data from Subcortical Brain Surfaces: A Comparison of Feature Selection and Classification Methods. *Pattern Recognition*, *63*, 731–739. doi:10.1016/j.patcog.2016.09.034

Zhoua, X., Gaob, X., Wanga, J., Yua, H., Wangc, Z., & Chid, Z. (2016). Eye Tracking Data Guided Feature Selection for Image Classification. *Pattern Recognition*, *63*, 56–70. doi:10.1016/j.patcog.2016.09.007

ADDITIONAL READING

Al-Angari, H. M., Kanitz, G., Tarantino, S., & Cipriani, C. (2016). Distance and mutual information methods for EMG feature and channel subset selection for classification of hand movements. *Biomedical Signal Processing and Control*, *27*, 24–31. doi:10.1016/j.bspc.2016.01.011

Bolon-Canedo, V., Fernández-Francos, D., Peteiro-Barral, D., Alonso-Betanzos, A., Guijarro-Berdiñas, B., & Sánchez-Maroño, N. (2016). A unified pipeline for online feature selection and classification. *Expert Systems with Applications*, *55*, 532–545. doi:10.1016/j.eswa.2016.02.035

Fahad, A., Tari, Z., Khalil, I., Habib, I., & Alnuweiri, H. (2013). Toward an efficient and scalable feature selection approach for internet traffic classification. *Computer Networks*, *57*(9), 2040–2057. doi:10.1016/j.comnet.2013.04.005

Hernández-Pereira, E., Bolón-Canedo, V., Sánchez-Maroño, N., Álvarez-Estévez, D., Moret-Bonillo, V., & Alonso-Betanzos, A. (2016). A comparison of performance of K-complex classification methods using feature selection. *Information Sciences*, *328*, 1–14. doi:10.1016/j.ins.2015.08.022

Javed, K., Maruf, S., & Babri, H. A. (2015). A two-stage Markov blanket based feature selection algorithm for text classification. *Neurocomputing*, *157*(1), 91–104. doi:10.1016/j.neucom.2015.01.031

Jothi, G. (2016). Hybrid Tolerance Rough Set–Firefly based supervised feature selection for MRI brain tumor image classification. *Applied Soft Computing*, *46*, 639–651.

Lian, C., Ruan, S., & Denœux, T. (2015). An evidential classifier based on feature selection and two-step classification strategy. *Pattern Recognition*, *48*(7), 2318–2327. doi:10.1016/j.patcog.2015.01.019

Marafino, B. J., Boscardin, W. J., & Dudley, R. A. (2015). Efficient and sparse feature selection for biomedical text classification via the elastic net: Application to ICU risk stratification from nursing notes. *Journal of Biomedical Informatics*, *54*, 114–120. doi:10.1016/j.jbi.2015.02.003 PMID:25700665

Nalband, S., Sundar, A., Prince, A. A., & Agarwal, A. (2016). Feature selection and classification methodology for the detection of knee-joint disorders. *Computer Methods and Programs in Biomedicine*, *127*, 94–104. doi:10.1016/j.cmpb.2016.01.020 PMID:27000292

Nancy, S. G., & Appavu, S. (2016). Optimal feature selection for classification using rough set-based CGA-NN classifier. *International Journal of Business Intelligence and Data Mining*, *11*(4), 357–378. doi:10.1504/IJBIDM.2016.082212

Sasikala, S., Balamurugan, S. A. A., & Geetha, S. (2016). A novel adaptive feature selector for supervised classification. *Information Processing Letters*, *117*, 25–34. doi:10.1016/j.ipl.2016.08.003

Singh, R. K., & Sivabalakrishnan, M. (2012). Feature Selection of Gene Expression Data for Cancer Classification: A Review. *Procedia Computer Science*, *50*, 52–57. doi:10.1016/j.procs.2015.04.060

Uysal, A. K. (2016). An improved global feature selection scheme for text classification. *Expert Systems with Applications*, *43*, 82–92. doi:10.1016/j.eswa.2015.08.050

Yanli, D., & Jin, W. (2015). Feature selection based on sparse representation with the measures of classification error rate and complexity of boundary. *Optik International Journal for Light and Electron Optics*, *126*(20), 2634–2639. doi:10.1016/j.ijleo.2015.06.057

Zhang, Y., Yang, C., Yang, A., Xiong, C., Zhou, X., & Zhang, Z. (2015). Feature selection for classification with class-separability strategy and data envelopment analysis. *Neurocomputing*, *166*, 172–184. doi:10.1016/j.neucom.2015.03.081

Zhao, G., Wu, Y., Chen, F., Zhang, J., & Bai, J. (2015). Effective feature selection using feature vector graph for classification. *Neurocomputing*, *151*, 376–389. doi:10.1016/j.neucom.2014.09.027

Section 2
Nature-Inspired Approaches for Complex Optimizations

Chapter 5
Motion Planning of Non-Holonomic Wheeled Robots Using Modified Bat Algorithm

Abhishek Ghosh Roy
IIT Kharagpur, India

Pratyusha Rakshit
Jadavpur University, India

ABSTRACT

The chapter proposes a novel optimization framework to solve the motion planning problem of non-holonomic wheeled mobile robots using swarm algorithms. The specific robotic system considered is a vehicle with approximate kinematics of a car. The configuration of this robot is represented by position and orientation of its main body in the plane and by angles of the steering wheels. Two control inputs are available for motion control including the velocity and the steering angle command. Moreover, the car-like robot is one of the simplest non-holonomic vehicles that displays the general characteristics and constrained maneuverability of systems with non-holonomicity. The control methods proposed in this chapter do not require precise mathematical modeling of every aspect a car-like system. The swarm algorithm-based motion planner determines the optimal trajectory of multiple car-like non-holonomic robots in a given arena avoiding collision with obstacles and teammates. The motion planning task has been taken care of by an adaptive bio-inspired strategy commonly known as Bat Algorithm.

INTRODUCTION

Population increase in large cities results an increase in the number of vehicles used by the community which causes an increased demand for autonomous motion planning for commuter vehicles. Complications like closed parking bays, dense traffic, and driving fatigue are very common in city life. Parking of a car in a parking lot may be agreed to be one of the most complex parts of the driving action. By the help of the improvements in computer technology, automatic control of local vehicle maneuvers to obtain a self-parking action is no more a fantasy. Most of the research about this subject is done to develop a

DOI: 10.4018/978-1-5225-5852-1.ch005

self-parking strategy and some to develop driver aid systems. The studies about self-navigating cars and mobile robots are also important because of the similar control techniques that are used.

The motion planning problem considered here aims at determining a continuous collision-free path for transportation of n car-like robots from their given starting positions to fixed goal positions in an arbitrary rigid polyhedral environment by application of appropriate steering angles (Daxwanger & Schmidt, 1996; Miyata et al., 1996; Motoji & Akira, 1995; Moran & Nagai, 1995; Kong & Kosko; Laugier et al., 1999; Roy et al., 2013). The paths of the car-like robots can be determined globally or locally. The local planning is more flexible to its global counterpart because of its capability to take care of dynamic obstacles. Moreover, small time is required in local planning to identify the next position of the car-like robots only, rather than deriving the entire trajectory of their motion. Consequently, in this chapter, the local planning is addressed to solve the motion planning problem.

The kinematics of non-holonomic car-like systems are represented by constraint equations concerned with the time derivatives of the system configuration variables. Unfortunately, such systems suffer from the difficulty of non-integrability of the constraint equations when the number of control inputs is less than the configuration variables (De Luca et al., 1998). It thus restricts the application of the classical geometric techniques for motion planning for non-holonomic car-like systems. Moreover, till today, there is no general motion-planning algorithm for any non-holonomic system to ensure their successful arrival at given goal configurations. The existing approximate methods (Dubins, 1957; Laumond et al., 1998) guarantee only the system reaches a neighborhood of the goal. It thus paves the way for applying evolutionary and swarm optimization techniques together with geometric methods to address the motion planning of the non-holonomic car-like.

This chapter considers a swarm optimization framework for motion planning of non-holonomic car like systems of definite size. The starting and the goal positions of each car-like robot on the grid map are given, and a swarm algorithm is used to locally plan their trajectory of motion with an aim to minimize the total path traversed without collision with obstacles and teammates. Constraints due to obstacles are expressed directly in the manifold of configurations. The non-holonomic constraints in the tangent space linking the parameter derivatives (Laumond et al., 1998) are also considered during development of the optimization framework of the present motion planning problem.

Any traditional swarm algorithm can be selected to solve the problem. We have here selected *bat algorithm* (BA) (Yang, 2010; Yang & Gandomi, 2012; Yang & He, 2013; Chowdhury et al., 2014) in the present context for its proven merits in global optimization. Some of the attractive features of BA, justifying its selection in the design of motion planning algorithm for car-like robots, include its structural simplicity with ease of coding and faster convergence with respect to other swarm/evolutionary algorithms. Recently, BA (Yang, 2010; Yang & Gandomi, 2012; Yang & He, 2013; Chowdhury et al., 2014) has gained immense popularity in the domain of population-based metaheuristic search algorithms by effectively employing the swarm behavior of bats to solve complex multi-modal real-world optimization problems. However, there exists literature indicating that BA may often get trapped at the local optima primarily due to its fixed step-size control parameter (Chowdhury et al., 2014). On the other hand, accurate tuning of the step-size over its possible span [0, 1] by trial and error process may improve the performance of the BA, however, at the computational cost. Therefore, it is desirable to adapt the values of these parameters over generations. In this chapter, we propose a modified BA (MBA) to gradually self-adapt the values of step-size over generations by learning from their previous experiences in generating quality solutions (locations of bats). Consequently, a more suitable value of step-size can be determined adaptively to match different search phases.

Performance analysis of the proposed MBA is studied using a set of 28 CEC'2013 recommended benchmark functions (Liang et al., 2013) and compared with the optimization efficiency of the traditional BA, artificial bee colony (ABC) (Karaboga & Basturk, 2008), ant colony optimization (ACO) (Dorigo & Birattari, 2011) and cuckoo search (CS) (Yang & Deb, 2009) algorithms. Experiments undertaken reveal that the proposed MBA outperforms other competitors in a statistically significant manner. Experiments undertaken on simulation platform of motion planning of multiple car-like non-holonomic robots also substantiate the statistically significant superiority of the MBA-based motion planner over its contenders with respect to the performance metrics used in the existing literature (Roy et al., 2013). The Wilcoxon rank-sum test (Garcia et al., 2009), the Friedman test (Garcia et al., 2009), the Iman-Davenport test (Garcia et al., 2009) and the Bonferroni-Dunn post-hoc analysis (Garcia et al., 2009) are undertaken here to arrive at the above-mentioned conclusion.

LITERATURE REVIEW

One of the studies about this subject is done in the München Technical University of Germany by Daxwanger and Schmidt (Daxwanger & Schmidt, 1996). In this study the acquisition and transfer of an experienced driver's skills to an automatic parking controller is performed. The interesting part of this study is the way of taking input information and approaches to cloning the skills of an expert driver. A CCD video image sensor is employed to collect data from the environment. The image sensor is composed of a gray-scale CCD camera, which is combined with an aspheric mirror to perform an inverse perspective mapping of the scene in front of the vehicle. By the help of this set-up a 4 m × 4 m field of view is obtained. An integrated sensor-processing unit is also utilized to generate a gradient image of the view to process data. No other information, such as the vehicle position relative to the goal location, is needed as extra input. In this study two approaches clone the skills of an expert driver are proposed and compared. A human driver is able to demonstrate his skills by parking a car in the parking bay instead of explicitly describing his information processing while generating an adequate steering action from visual information for parking. Imitating this "black-box" behavior and using the same obvious inputs and outputs leads to direct neural control architecture as the first approach. On the other hand, the expert driver may be able to describe his parking strategy roughly in terms of linguistic rules, which leads to a parking strategy that can be implemented by means of a fuzzy network as the second approach. A robot vehicle, which has car-like kinematics with one steering wheel and a driven rigid axle, is employed to get the experimental performance of the control architectures. The results are satisfactory with a cost of high signal processing requirements of the input data.

Another interesting study about this subject is performed in Tottori University of Japan by Ohkita (Miyata et al., 1996). In this study fuzzy control theory is used for controlling an autonomous mobile robot with four wheels for parallel parking and fuzzy rules are derived by modeling driving actions of the conventional car. Six supersonic transducers are used for recognizing the position and attitude of the robot. A stepper motor is also employed to control and move the sensors to keep the suitable angle to the wall for preventing the occurrence of dead angles. In the study of Ohkita, three microprocessors are used for calculations and peripheral access. This kind of architecture seems bulky when combined with the number of the sensors. But using so many sensors has an advantage of an increase in the sampling rate of the input data when compared to a positioned single sensor system. The fuzzy reasoning of the system is composed of three fuzzy rule groups each with three, five and seven rules respectively. The active rule group is determined according to the current state of the mobile robot. The performance of this system is satisfactory except the behaviors of the system during the absence of the walls. To overcome this problem, utilization of gyro-sensors and a CCD camera is recommended by the authors.

Parking motion control of a car-like robot is discussed in the study of Motoji and Akira (1995). The constraints of steering operation and obstacle avoidance with a garage and walls are also considered and a motion planning and control method that is using a fuzzy neural network is presented. The fuzzy neural network system for parking motion is made to learn good motions by human operations to generate motion control strategy of parking and the system is used for parking motion planning and control.

A similar study is performed by Moran and Nagai (1995). A new design method for autonomous parking systems by integrating fuzzy systems and neural networks is presented. In this study, a fuzzy driver is designed that is based on the experience of a human driver and it is refined by designing a fuzzy-neuro driver. Then the performance of both the fuzzy driver and fuzzy-neuro driver are analyzed and compared.

Another study about this subject is performed by Kong and Kosko (1990). In this study, a fuzzy and a neural truck backer-upper control system are designed and compared. Vertical parking at the middle of one of the walls of a parking bay is performed by using a fuzzy control system with just 25 rules. The results are satisfactory except some dead points.

In the study of Fraichard and Garnier (Laugier et al., 1999), motion control architecture for a car-like vehicle intended to move in dynamic and partially known environments is presented. A fuzzy controller is designed to solve the motion planning problem and it is implemented and tested on a real computer-controlled car, equipped with sensors of limited precision and reliability. In addition, there exists plethora of literature on large scale mapping and path planning algorithms employing a large variety of different sensors by different open source community (Haehnel et al., 2003; Dolgov et al., 2010; Martinez-Cantin et al., 2007; Nguyen et al., 2007; Pfaff et al., 2007; Davison et al., 2007).

It is however noteworthy that the existing stratagems for motion planning still suffer from the lack of autonomy. The existing strategies still rely on capability of human observer in the feedback loop of the path planning and control algorithms. For a single map of the environment there exist multiple possible trajectories that provide a complete exploration of the environment but only few of them are acceptable because point turns are prohibited for a non-holonomic robot. Desirable characteristics for an exploration strategy would be to cover the space optimally and collect necessary environment data. In essence it should maximize environmental coverage while minimizing the probability of revisiting the previous positions. The motion planning strategy proposed in this chapter would fill this void by employing swarm optimization technique.

FORMULATION OF MOTION PLANNING PROBLEM OF NON-HOLONOMIC WHEELED ROBOTS

The motion planning problem here is formulated in the optimization framework with an aim to determine the optimal path of traversal of n car-like robots from their predefined starting positions to their fixed goal positions in a given parking area amidst a set of static obstacles, however, avoiding collision with obstacles and teammates. The state space modeling of a car-like robot with front wheel steering and rear wheel drive is considered here to devise the mathematical model of the objective function of the present optimization problem. The steering arrangement conforms to the Ackerman steering constraint, satisfying the concurrency of the normal to the car tire tracks for any nonzero steering angle. The assumptions made in order to derive the state space mathematical model of the car-like robot are as follows.

- The current configuration and goal configuration of each car-like robot are known with respect to a given inertial frame of reference.
- The motion planning problem of each robot is executed in steps until all the robots reach their respective goals.
- There is no tire slipping motion involved during the traversal of derived trajectory.
- The vehicle does not collide with the obstacles and teammates if a safe distance is maintained between their centers of mass.
- The trajectory executed by the center of mass of a vehicle is circular for a constant non-zero steering angle.
- The vehicle chassis approximates a rigid body to a considerable degree of accuracy.
- For the specific case of front wheel steered vehicle (car-like robot) with Ackerman steering constraint, the kinematics of the vehicle must satisfy certain conditions in order to be able to turn sleep free. The constraint equation is given in (1).

$$\cot \varphi_o - \cot \varphi_i = W / L$$

Here φ_i and φ_o respectively denote the inner and outer steering angles of the vehicle. The mass center of the vehicle of length L and width W executes a circular trajectory of radius R, given by

$$R = \sqrt{a_2^2 + L^2 \cot^2 \varphi} \tag{2}$$

where a_2 represents the distance between rear wheel axle center and the center of mass of the vehicle. The steering angle φ of the equivalent bicycle model (will be discussed shortly) is given by

$$\varphi = \cot^{-1}(\cot \varphi_i + \cot \varphi_0) \tag{3}$$

Let us now consider a wheel as shown in Figure 1 that rolls on a plane while keeping its body vertical to the plane. The system is commonly referred to as a *unicycle system*. The configuration of a unicycle system is described by a vector $\vec{\psi}$ of three generalized coordinates, including the Cartesian coordinates x and y, and the angle θ capturing the orientation of the wheel with respect to the x-axis. It is noteworthy that the values of the generalized coordinates of such system are constrained by

$$[\sin \theta \quad -\cos \theta \quad 0][\dot{x} \quad \dot{y} \quad \dot{\theta}]^T = 0 \tag{4}$$

The kinematics of the car-like robot considered in this work are derived from the kinematics of an automobile. For the sake of simplicity, let us assume that two wheels on each axle collapse into a single wheel located at the midpoint of the axle. The front wheel can be steered with the orientation of the rear

Figure 1. Configuration of unicycle system

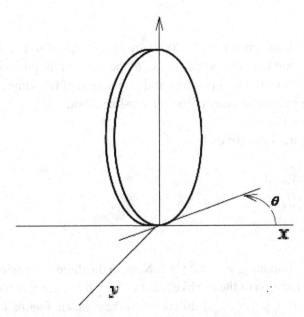

wheel being fixed. This arrangement is referred to as the equivalent *bicycle model* of a car-like robot. In such system, the generalized coordinates are given by

$$\vec{\psi} = [x \quad y \quad \theta \quad \varphi]^T \tag{5}$$

where *x* and *y* denote the Cartesian coordinates of the rear wheel, θ denotes the orientation of the car body with respect to the positive direction of the x-axis and φ represents the steering angle. The kinematic of the car with a rear-wheel driving is given by

$$[\dot{x} \quad \dot{y} \quad \dot{\theta} \quad \dot{\varphi}]^T = [\cos\theta \quad \sin\theta \quad \tan(\varphi/L) \quad 0]^T u_1 + [0 \quad 0 \quad 0 \quad 1]^T u_2 \tag{6}$$

where u_1 symbolizes the input velocity and u_2 represents the steering input. It is to be noted from (6) that there is a model singularity at $\varphi = \pm\pi/2$, where the first vector field has a discontinuity corresponding to the car becoming jammed when the front wheel is normal to the longitudinal axis of the body. It is, however, worth mentioning taht in our case the importance of this singularity is limited due to the re-stricted range of steering angle φ in $[-\pi/5, +\pi/5]$.

The kinematic steering condition thus derived can be used to evaluate the space requirement of a vehicle during a turning maneuver. Let consider the front wheel of a two-wheel vehicle, steered in ac-cordance with Ackerman geometry as pictorially represented in Figure 2. The outer point of a vehicle executes a trajectory of maximum radius R^{max}, whereas a point on the inner side of the vehicle executes a trajectory of minimum radius R^{min}. The front outer point has an overhang distance *g* from the axle. The width of the ring-shaped area, as shown in Figure 2, occupied by the vehicle while executing a turning maneuver is then given by

$$\Delta R = \sqrt{(L / \tan \varphi + 2W)^2 + (L + g)^2} - L / \tan \varphi \tag{7}$$

The principles used in (Chakraborty et al., 2009) are also followed so that the car-like robot is able to approximate an automobile kinematics. Let (x_i, y_i, θ_i) be the current position and orientation of the i-th car at time t, (x'_i, y'_i, θ'_i) be the next position and orientation of the same robot at time $(t + \Delta t)$ for small Δt. Let $u_1 = v_i$ be the current velocity of the i-th car-like robot, and $(x_{ig}, y_{ig}, \theta_{ig})$ be the goal position and orientation of the robot Figure 3.

It is apparent from Figure 3 and (6) that

$$\theta'_i(t) = \theta_i(t) + v_i \Delta t / L * \tan(\varphi_i(t))$$
$$x'_i(t) = x_i(t) + v_i \Delta t \cos(\theta_i(t)) \tag{8}$$
$$y'_i(t) = y_i(t) + v_i \Delta t \sin(\theta_i(t))$$

For convenience in programming, we set $\Delta t = 1$. Now, in the three-dimensional configuration space, we need to select the next location of the car-like robot (x'_i, y'_i, θ'_i), such that the line joining $\{(x_i, y_i, \theta_i),$ $(x'_i, y'_i, \theta'_i)\}$ and $\{(x'_i, y'_i, \theta'_i), (x_{ig}, y_{ig}, \theta_{ig})\}$ do not touch the obstacle Figure 4.

Now, the automatic car parking problem can be formulated as a constrained optimization problem in the present context. The objective function for the proposed optimization problem is given by

$$J = C_1 J_1 + C_2 J_2 + C_3 J_3 + C_4 J_4 \tag{9}$$

Figure 2. Space requirement for turning maneuver

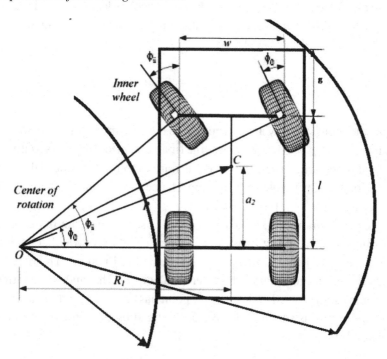

Figure 3. Current and next position of the i-th car

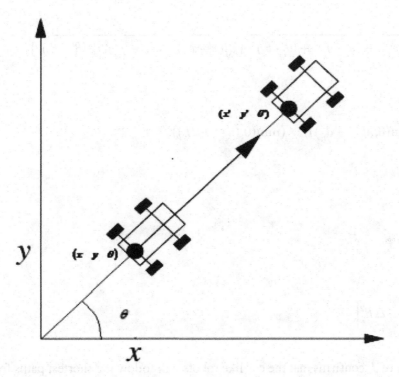

Figure 4. Selection of (x'ᵢ, y'ᵢ, θ'ᵢ) from (xᵢ, yᵢ, θᵢ) to avoid collision with obstacle

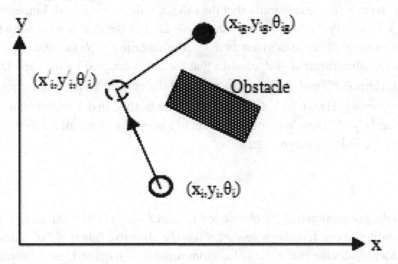

where

$$J_1 = \sum_{i=1}^{n} \{ \sqrt{(x_i - x_i')^2 + (y_i - y_i')^2 + (\theta_i - \theta_i')^2} + \sqrt{(x_i' - x_{ig})^2 + (y_i' - y_{ig})^2 + (\theta_i' - \theta_{ig})^2} \} \tag{10}$$

$$J_2 = \sum_{\substack{i',j'=1 \\ i' \neq j'}}^{n(n-1)/2} \left[(\min(0, (d_{i'j'} - d_{ij})))^2 \times (\min(0, (d_{i'j'} - 2L)))^2 \right] \tag{11}$$

$$J_3 = \sum_{i=1}^{n} 1/dist_{i-obst} \tag{12}$$

$$J_4 = \sum_{i=1}^{n} \left| \Delta R_i'^2 - \Delta R_i^2 \right| \tag{13}$$

Minimization of J_1 confirms that the car-like robots will follow the shortest paths from their current configuration (x_i, y_i, θ_i) to their respective goal configuration $(x_{ig}, y_{ig}, \theta_{ig})$ for $i = 1, 2, ..., n$. Let d_{ij} and $d_{i'j'}$ respectively be the distance between the centres of mass of the i-th and the j-th cars' current and next positions. Then J_2 represents the constraint that the i-th car will not hit its j-th kin, approaching the i-th car (i.e., $d_{i'j'} < d_{ij}$), by satisfying both $d_{i'j'} \geq d_{ij}$ and $d_{i'j'} \geq 2L$. Let the distance between the next position of the i-th car and a static obstacle is given as d_{i-obs}. Minimization of J_3 facilitates collision avoidance with static obstacles. Minimization of J_4 ensures that the area occupied by the vehicle in maneuvering is also optimized. Here $\Delta R_i'$ and ΔR_i are the next and the current width of the ring occupied by the i-th vehicle during turning. Here C_1, C_2, C_3, and C_4 are scale factors. In our experiments, we used $C_1 = 10$, $C_2 = 50$, $C_3 = 100$ and $C_4 = 5$. These parameters are set in a manner to have all the terms on the right hand side of (9) in the same order of magnitude.

Algorithm

It is evident from the last section that the objective function J needs to be minimized for optimal motion planning of the car-like robots. It is also noteworthy that the objective function J is multi-modal in nature, even comprising local discontinuities at finite locations in the search space. Hence, the traditional calculus based optimization technique, utilizing gradient information, is incompetent to handle such multi-modal optimization problem. It calls for a meta-heuristic algorithm to optimize the above-mentioned objective function. It is also worth mentioning that among existing plethora of meta-heuristic algorithms capable to address the optimization problem, very few of them can effectively locate the global optimum as the fitness landscape consists of multiple rough local optima. The proficiency of the meta-heuristic search algorithms to track the global optimum in a multi-modal fitness landscape greatly depends on the appropriate selection of its control parameters.

We here propose a solution to solve the robot motion planning problem by first selecting a meta-heuristic algorithm to serve the optimization task. Then, we adapt the control parameters of the algorithm according to the objective function values of its candidate solutions. It essentially helps in learning and thus capturing the objective surface model at the location of the trial solutions. The knowledge of parametric selection, acquired through previous generations of evolution, is used to guide the parametric choice of candidate solutions of the current generation. The bat algorithm (BA) (Yang, 2010; Yang & Gandomi, 2012; Yang & He, 2013) here has been used as the basic optimization algorithm and we propose a novel learning methodology as the parameter-tuning algorithm. The synergistic effect of both improves the solutions for the given robot motion planning problem.

We first present the BA, and then propose a new algorithm to improve the BA to judiciously select its parameters for selected candidate solutions. This in turn improves the accuracy of BA in the context of multi-modal single objective optimization.

Bat Algorithm

BA (Yang, 2010; Yang & Gandomi, 2012; Yang & He, 2013) is in principle a multi-agent parallel search technique. Bats are conceptual entities which fly through the multi-dimensional search space. At any particular instant each bat has a position and a velocity. The position vector of a bat with respect to the origin of the search space represents a potential solution of the search problem.

1. **Initialization:** BA commences from an initial population

$$\mathbf{P}_G = \left\{ \left(\vec{X}_1(G), \vec{V}_1(G) \right), \left(\vec{X}_2(G), \vec{V}_2(G) \right), \cdots, \left(\vec{X}_{NP}(G), \vec{V}_{NP}(G) \right) \right\}$$

of *NP*, *D*-dimensional bat position

$$\vec{X}_i(G) = \left\{ x_{i,1}(G), x_{i,2}(G), ..., x_{i,D}(G) \right\}$$

and the corresponding velocity vector

$$\vec{V}_i(G) = \left\{ v_1(G), v_2(G), ..., v_D(G) \right\}$$

at generation $G = 0$, uniformly randomized within the range $\left[\vec{X}^{\min}, \vec{X}^{\max} \right]$ and $\left[\vec{V}^{\min}, \vec{V}^{\max} \right]$ respectively, where

$$\vec{X}^{\min} = \left\{ x_1^{\min}, x_2^{\min}, ..., x_D^{\min} \right\},$$

$$\vec{X}^{\max} = \left\{ x_1^{\max}, x_2^{\max}, ..., x_D^{\max} \right\},$$

$$\vec{V}^{\min} = \left\{ v_1^{\min}, v_2^{\min}, \ldots, v_D^{\min} \right\}$$

and

$$\vec{V}^{\max} = \left\{ v_1^{\max}, v_2^{\max}, \ldots, v_D^{\max} \right\}$$

by setting

$$x_{i,j}(0) = x_j^{\min} + \text{rand} \times (x_j^{\max} - x_j^{\min}) \tag{14}$$

$$v_{i,j}(0) = v_j^{\min} + \text{rand} \times (v_j^{\max} - v_j^{\min}) \tag{15}$$

for $i = 1, 2, \ldots, NP$ and $j = 1, 2, \ldots, D$. Here rand $\text{rand}(0,1)$ $\text{rand}(0,1)$ is a uniformly distributed random number in (0, 1). The loudness $A_i(G)$ and the pulse emission rate $r_i(G)$ (used by the i-th bat for echolocation) at $G = 0$ are also initialized for $i = 1, 2, \ldots, NP$.

2. **Evaluating the Global Best Position:** The objective function $J(\vec{X}_i(G))$ is evaluated for $i = 1, 2, \ldots, NP$. The position of a bat with the minimum objective function value (for minimization problem) is selected as the global best position $\vec{X}^{best}(G)$ at generation G. Mathematically,

$$\vec{X}^{best}(G) \leftarrow \arg\left(\min_{i=1}^{NP}(J(\vec{X}_i(G))) \right) \tag{16}$$

3. **Frequency Selection:** The frequency f_i of the pulse emitted by the i-th bat is randomly selected from the pre-defined range $[f^{\min}, f^{\max}]$ as follows for $i = 1, 2, \ldots, NP$.

$$f_i = f^{\min} + \text{rand} \times \left(f^{\max} - f^{\min} \right) \tag{17}$$

4. **Velocity Update:** The frequency f_i dtermined in (17) is used to control the pace and range of movement of the bats for $i = 1, 2, \ldots, NP$. The frequency modulated velocity uodate of the i-th bat for $i = 1, 2, \ldots, NP$ is given below.

$$\vec{V}_i(G+1) = \vec{V}_i(G) + f_i \times (\vec{X}_i(G) - \vec{X}^{best}(G)) \tag{18}$$

5. **Position Update:** The position of the i-th bat for $i = 1, 2, \ldots, NP$ is then updated as follows.

$$\vec{X}_i(G+1) = \vec{X}_i(G) + \vec{V}_i(G+1) \tag{19}$$

The frequency modulated velocity and position updates help the candidate solutions (i.e., bats) to globally explore the search space.

6. **Generating Local Position:** BA is also equipped with the local exploitation capability of bats. Every population member locally searches the area around its own position $\vec{X}_i(G+1)$ and thus discovers a new position $\vec{X}_i' = \{x_{i,1}', x_{i,2}', \cdots, x_{i,D}'\}$ for $i = 1, 2, \ldots, NP$ with a probability $(1-r_i)$ using

$$x_{i,j}' = x_{i,j}(G+1) + \varepsilon \times A_{avg}(G) \tag{20}$$

for $j = 1, 2, \ldots, D$. Here the step size ε is selected randomly from $[-1, 1]$. $A_{avg}(G)$ denotes the average loudness of all NP bats in the current population P_G.

$$A_{avg}(G) = \frac{\sum_{i=1}^{NP} A_i(G)}{NP} \tag{21}$$

7. **Update Loudness and Pulse Emission Rate:** The current updated position $\vec{X}_i(G+1)$ is replaced with the newly discovered neighborhood position $\vec{X}_i'$ with a probability A_i provided that $J(\vec{X}_i') < J(\vec{X}_i(G+1))$ (for minimization problem). On successful substitution of $\vec{X}_i(G+1)$ by better position $\vec{X}_i'$, the loudness is reduced and pulse emission rate is increased following (22) and (23).

$$A_i(G+1) \leftarrow \alpha \times A_i(G) \tag{22}$$

$$r_i(G+1) \leftarrow r_i(G) \times (1 - \exp(-\gamma \times G)) \tag{23}$$

Here α and γ are constant parameters in $(0, 1)$. This is repeated for $i = 1, 2, \ldots, NP$.

8. **Convergence:** This process is iterated from step 3 for a certain number of time steps, or until some acceptable solution has been found by the algorithm or until an upper limit of CPU usage has been reached.

Modified Bat Algorithm

The local search capability of the traditional BA is a crucial deterministic factor of its optimization performance. The step size ε in (20) is the control parameter governing the effective balance between exploitation and exploration. In the traditional BA, the value of ε remains constant throughout the evolutionary generations of the algorithm and is selected randomly from the range [–1, 1]. It is noteworthy that a lower value of ε influences the exploitation in the local neighborhood of the current solution, with an aim to restrict the search process in the promising area using small steps, resulting in a slow convergence. Contrarily, a larger setting of ε accelerates the global search at a cost of reduced exploitation capability of the perturbation process. For enhancing the optimization performance of the BA in multi-modal fitness landscape, we propose a novel method of adapting the step size parameter ε within the range $\left[\varepsilon^{\min}, \varepsilon^{\max}\right]$ with $\varepsilon^{\min} = -1$ and $\varepsilon^{\max} = 1$. The self-adaptation of ε helps BA to automatically balance the trade-off between the computational accuracy and run-time complexity.

In the proposed amended version of BA, referred to as modified bat algorithm (MBA), a pool of n discrete values of step sizes, denoted by $\left\{\varepsilon_1, \varepsilon_2, \cdots, \varepsilon_n\right\}$ is maintained. Here $\left\{\varepsilon_1, \varepsilon_2, \cdots, \varepsilon_n\right\}$ represents the n possible values of step size to be used by the bats of the population for their local search operation. Apparently, $\varepsilon_1 = \varepsilon^{\min} = -1$ and $\varepsilon_n = \varepsilon^{\max} = 1$. In each generation, prior to the local exploitation (as in (20)) by each candidate solution (i.e., bat), a step size ε_j is selected from the pool $\left\{\varepsilon_1, \varepsilon_2, \cdots, \varepsilon_n\right\}$. The selection of ε_j from $\left\{\varepsilon_1, \varepsilon_2, \cdots, \varepsilon_n\right\}$ by each bat in the population depends on the success history of ε_j gradually learned from experiences over the past generations to discover improved promising locations around the best solution. The more successfully ε_j has performed in the previous generations to produce quality bat positions, the more probably ε_j will be selected for local exploitation operation in the current generation. Over the past generations, the number of neighborhood locations generated by ε_j, with better (or worse) objective function value than the best solution of the corresponding generation, represent the success (or failure) history of ε_j for $j = 1, 2, \ldots, n$. This information is stored in the success (or failure) memory, which guide the judicious selection of step size in the future generations.

The contents of success and failure memory, built using the knowledge acquired over last few generations, are used to evaluate the probability $p_{j,G}$ of selecting the step size ε_j from the pool $\left\{\varepsilon_1, \varepsilon_2, \cdots, \varepsilon_n\right\}$ at generation G by the members of population P_G. Evidently, the selecton probabilities help in the right selection of step size $\varepsilon_j \in \left\{\varepsilon_1, \varepsilon_2, \cdots, \varepsilon_n\right\}$ for the candidate solutions of the population. For example, a candidate solution has a high probability of selecting $\varepsilon = \varepsilon_j$ at generation G, if $p_{j,G}$ is the largest among $p_{l,G}$ for $l = 1, 2, , n$. It is apparent that if $p_{l,G} > p_{j,G}$, $\forall$ for all l, then selection of $\varepsilon = \varepsilon_j$ by the population members over the last few generations have resulted in discovery of promising solutions in the search space. Naturally, the learning experience will guide the candidate solution at generation G to select $\varepsilon = \varepsilon_j$ with a high probability.

To maintain population diversity (by overcoming the premature convergence), in addition to the action probabilities, Roulette-wheel selection strategy is employed for selection of potentially useful step sizes. The Roulette-wheel selection of step size $\varepsilon = \varepsilon_j$ for a candidate solution of generation G (being governed by the selection probabilities $p_{l,G}$ for $l = 1, 2, ., n$), is realized by the following strategy. First, a random number r is generated between (0, 1). Then we determine ε_j, such that the cumulative probability of $\varepsilon = \varepsilon_1$ through $\varepsilon = \varepsilon_{j-1}$ is less than r, and the cumulative probability for $\varepsilon = \varepsilon_1$ through $\varepsilon = \varepsilon_j$ is greater than r. Symbolically, we need to hold

$$\sum_{l=1}^{j-1} p_{l,G} \leq r \leq \sum_{l=1}^{j} p_{l,G} \tag{24}$$

The learning based autonomous adaptation of step size is realized in BA as follows.

1. At $G = 0$, $p_{j,G}$ for $j = 1, 2, ..., n$ is initialized with $1/n$ signifying that all n discrete values of the step size in the pool $\{\varepsilon_1, \varepsilon_2, \cdots, \varepsilon_n\}$ are equally likely to be selected.

2. At generation G, each candidate solution (i.e., bat) of population P_G selects a step size from $\{\varepsilon_1, \varepsilon_2, \cdots, \varepsilon_n\}$ before participation in the local exploitation process based on the selection probability induced Roulette-wheel selection strategy, as given by (24).

3. At generation G, the number of neighborhood locations, discovered by local exploitation using ε_j, which successfully replace the bat position is recorded as $s_{j,G}$ for $j = 1, 2, ..., n$. The value is stored in a success memory (SM).

4. At generation G, the number of neighborhood locations, discovered by local exploitation using ε_j, which are discarded with respect to the current bat position is recorded as $f_{j,G}$ for $j = 1, 2, ..., n$. The value is stored in a failure memory (FM).

5. Steps 3 and 4 are repeated for a fixed number of generations, known as *learning period* (*LP*). The *SM* and *FM*, each of dimension *LP*×*n*, developed after *LP* generations are pictorially represented in Boxes 1 and 2. In other words, the first *LP* generations are used to form the success and failure history of $\{\varepsilon_1, \varepsilon_2, \cdots, \varepsilon_n\}$ and thus capture their individual capability to generate promising solutions. This information is used in subsequent generations to guide the search process.

6. When $G > LP$, steps 3 and 4 are also performed. However, the rows $s_{j,G-LP}$ and $f_{j,G-LP}$ are respectively removed from the *SM* and *FM* leaving room for the newly available $s_{j,G}$ and $f_{j,G}$ for $j = 1, 2, ..., n$. The update of *SM* is elaborated in Figure 5. The same procedure is followed to update *FM* for $G > LP$.

7. For each generation G after *LP* ($G > LP$), the success rate $SR_{j,G}$ of $\varepsilon_j \in \{\varepsilon_1, \varepsilon_2, \cdots, \varepsilon_n\}$ is identified based on its success history $s_{j,g}$ and failure history $f_{j,g}$, acquired over the last *LP* generations for $g = G - LP, G - LP + 1, ..., G - 1$. The $SR_{j,G}$ for $j = 1, 2, ..., n$ is evaluated by the following expression.

$$SR_{j,G} = \frac{\sum\limits_{g=G-LP}^{G-1} s_{j,g}}{\sum\limits_{g=G-LP}^{G-1} s_{j,g} + \sum\limits_{g=G-LP}^{G-1} f_{j,g}} + \varepsilon \qquad (25)$$

It is evident from (25) that the success rate $SR_{j,G}$ attains its ideal (highest) value 1 for $f_{j,g} = 0$ for $g = G - LP, G - LP + 1, ..., G - 1$. The success rates $SR_{j,G}$ at generation G are evaluated for all discrete values of step size $\{\varepsilon_1, \varepsilon_2, \cdots, \varepsilon_n\}$ for $j = 1, 2, ..., n$. The small constant value $\varepsilon = 0.01$ is used to avoid the possible null success rates.

8. Intuitively, higher the value of $SR_{j,G}$, higher is the probability of selecting $\varepsilon_j \in \{\varepsilon_1, \varepsilon_2, \cdots, \varepsilon_n\}$ at generation G by the candidate solutions (i.e., bats) of the current population P_G. The probability $p_{j,G}$ of selecting ε_j from $\{\varepsilon_1, \varepsilon_2, \cdots, \varepsilon_n\}$ is now determined based on its success rate $SR_{j,G}$ as follows

$$p_{j,G} = \frac{s_{j,G}}{\sum\limits_{l=1}^{n} s_{l,G}}, \quad j = [1, n], \quad G > LP \qquad (26)$$

for $j = 1, 2, ..., n$. The updated probabilities are now used by the population members of subsequent generations to take part in the local search operation around the best solution and the cycle is repeated from step 2. The pseudo code of MBA is given below.

Procedure MBA

Input: Population size NP, search space dimension D, search range $\left[\vec{X}^{\min}, \vec{X}^{\max}\right]$, velocity range $\left[\vec{V}^{\min}, \vec{V}^{\max}\right]$, frequency range $[f^{\min}, f^{\max}]$, initial loudness $A_i(0)$ and initial emission rate $r_i(0)$ for $i = 1, 2, ..., NP$, step size range $\left[\varepsilon^{\min}, \varepsilon^{\max}\right]$, number of discrete possible values n of step size.

Output: The optimal solution $\vec{X}^{best}$.

Box 1. Success memory (SM) built over LP generations (SS: step size)

G	SS			
	ε_1	ε_2	$\cdots$	ε_n
1	$s_{1,1}$	$s_{2,1}$	$\cdots$	$s_{n,1}$
2	$s_{1,2}$	$s_{2,2}$	$\cdots$	$s_{n,2}$
$\vdots$	$\vdots$	$\vdots$	$\cdots$	$\vdots$
LP	$s_{1,LP}$	$s_{2,LP}$	$\cdots$	$s_{n,LP}$

Box 2. Failure memory (FM) built over LP generations (SS: step size)

	SS			
G	ε_1	ε_2	...	ε_n
1	$f_{1,1}$	$f_{2,1}$	...	$f_{n,1}$
2	$f_{1,2}$	$f_{2,2}$	...	$f_{n,2}$
:	:	:	...	:
LP	$f_{1,LP}$	$f_{2,LP}$	...	$f_{n,LP}$

Figure 5. Update of SM with success history of step sizes at generation G after learning period LP

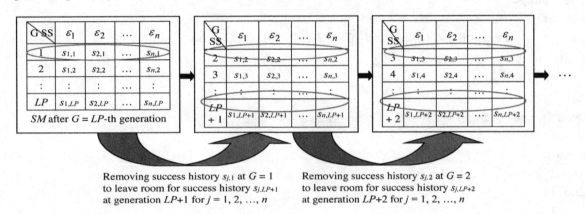

Removing success history $s_{j,1}$ at $G = 1$ to leave room for success history $s_{j,LP+1}$ at generation $LP+1$ for $j = 1, 2, ..., n$

Removing success history $s_{j,2}$ at $G = 2$ to leave room for success history $s_{j,LP+2}$ at generation $LP+2$ for $j = 1, 2, ..., n$

```
Begin
1.          Initialize NP, D-dimensional bat-position X⃗ᵢ(G), corresponding ve-
locity V⃗ᵢ(G), the loudness Aᵢ(G) and pulse emission rate rᵢ(G) at generation G =
0 using (14) and (15) respectively for i= 1, 2, …, NP.
2.          Evaluate the objective function value   J(X⃗ᵢ(G)) for i= 1, 2, …, NP.
3.          Identify the best bat position X⃗ᵇᵉˢᵗ(G) satisfying (16).
4.          Select frequency of pulse emission fᵢ using (17) for i= 1, 2, …, NP.
5.          While termination condition is not reached do
Begin
5.1.        Set s_{j,G} ← 0 and f_{j,G} ← 0 for j = 1, 2, …, n.
5.2.        If G > LP then do
Begin
Calculate SR_{j,G} and p_{j,G} using (25) and (26) respectively for j = 1, 2, …, n.
Remove s_{j,G-LP} and f_{j,G-LP} from success and failure memories respectively for j =
1, 2, …, n.
Else
Set p_{j,G} ← 1/n for j = 1, 2, …, n. /*before exhaustion of learning period LP all
possible step sizes are equally probably to be selected*/
```

```
End If
5.3.           For i= 1 to NP do
Begin
a.             Update the velocity  $\vec{V}_i(G+1)$  using (18).
b.             Update the position  $\vec{X}_i(G+1)$  using (19).
c.             If rand > $r_i(t)$ then do /*local search around individual bat posi-
tion*/
Begin
Select  $\varepsilon_j \in \{\varepsilon_1, \varepsilon_2, \cdots, \varepsilon_n\}$  using (24) for local search operation by i-th bat.
Produce  $\vec{X}_i'$  following (20) and (21) using the  $\varepsilon_j \in \{\varepsilon_1, \varepsilon_2, \cdots, \varepsilon_n\}$  selected in the
last step.
End If
d.             If rand< $A_i(G)$  and  $J(\vec{X}_i') < J(\vec{X}_i(G+1))$  then do
Begin
Set  $\vec{X}_i(G+1) \leftarrow \vec{X}_i'$ ;
Set  $s_{j,G} \leftarrow s_{j,G} + 1$ .
Update the loudness  $A_i(G+1)$  using (22).
Update the pulse emission rate  $r_i(G+1)$  using (23).
Else
Set  $f_{j,G} \leftarrow f_{j,G} + 1$ .
End If
End For
5.4.           Set G ← G+1.
End While
6.             Identify the best bat position  $\vec{X}^{best}(G)$  satisfying (16).
7.             Return  $\vec{X}^{best}(G)$ .
End
```

EXPERIMENTS AND RESULTS

Simulation Results

The performance of the proposed MBA is studied here with respect to minimizing 28 CEC'2013 recommended benchmark functions (Liang et al., 2013) of 50 dimensions each. In this work, the comparative framework includes the proposed MBA, its traditional counterpart BA (Yang, 2010), artificial bee colony (ABC) (Karaboga & Basturk, 2008), ant colony optimization (ACO) (Dorigo & Birattari, 2011) and cuckoo search (CS) (Yang & Deb, 2009) algorithms. For all competitor algorithms, uniform initialization, uniform population size, and the same terminating condition are maintained for pair comparison. The population of each contender algorithm is initialized with the same random seed to ascertain uniform initialization. The population size NP is set after a few trials of adapting NP between 10 and 60 with an incremental step of 5. Experiments undertaken reveal no significant improvement in optimization performance of all algorithms beyond $NP = 50$. Hence, the population size is thus fixed at 50. The best parametric set-up for all these four competitor algorithms are employed here as prescribed in their respective sources. For the proposed MBA, we have set $A_i(0) = 1$, $r_i(0) = 0.5$, $f_{min} = 1$, $f_{max} = 2$, $n = 10$ and $LP = 50$.

The median and inter-quartile range *IQR* of the 50 independent runs for each of the seven competitor algorithms are presented in Table 1. The best metric value in each case has been set in bold. The statistical significance level of the difference of the 50 *FEV* metric sample values of any two competitive algorithms is judged by the Wilcoxon rank sum test (Garcia et al., 2009) with a significance level $\alpha = 0.05$. The p-values obtained through the rank sum test between the best algorithm and each of the remaining algorithms over the benchmark functions are also reported in Table 1. Here NA stands for not applicable representing the case of comparing the best algorithm with itself. The null hypothesis here considers that the performances of any two competitor algorithms are statistically equivalent. If the p-value, associated with the comparative performance analysis of the i-th and j-th algorithms, is less than α, then the null hypothesis is rejected.

It is evident that for a few comparatively simpler benchmark instances including f01–f07, most of the algorithms wind up with almost equal accuracy. Statistically significant performance differences, however, are detected for the remaining more challenging benchmark functions. It is apparent from Table 1 that MBA outperforms its contenders in 25 out of 28 benchmark instances. In addition, for f09 and f16, MBA is respectively outperformed by BA and ABC. MBA yields statistically equivalent results to BA for benchmark function f27. However, it is noteworthy that MBA achieves the lowest IQR for f27.

Table 1a. Comparison of algorithms with respect to FEV for f01 to f16

Functions	Metric	MBA	BA	ABC	ACO	CS
f01	Median FEV	**0.00e+00**	1.49e-08	2.15e-08	1.80e-07	2.07e-07
	IQR	**0.00e+00**	6.77e-09	7.03e-09	1.36e-08	3.61e-08
	p value	**NA**	3.86e-05	4.16e-05	1.68e-05	2.66e-06
f02	Median FEV	**0.00e+00**	2.17e-05	4.41e-05	9.78e-04	1.13e-03
	IQR	**6.76e-05**	1.29e-02	5.44e+00	1.34e+02	9.13e+02
	p value	**NA**	4.12e-02	4.14e-02	9.32e-05	5.30e-06
f03	Median FEV	**2.97e-03**	5.58e-03	6.83e-03	4.04e-02	6.30e-02
	IQR	**3.51e-03**	5.65e+00	6.89e+01	2.28e+02	2.45e+02
	p value	**NA**	3.20e-01	2.06e-01	4.47e-02	1.66e-02
f04	Median FEV	**6.03e-05**	8.77e-05	9.76e-04	4.73e-03	6.48e-03
	IQR	**1.19e-05**	3.02e-04	4.73e-04	1.04e-03	6.91e-02
	p value	**NA**	3.17e-03	2.61e-03	3.13e-04	2.39e-04
f05	Median FEV	**0.00e+00**	9.39e-09	3.11e-08	1.51e-06	3.28e-05
	IQR	**5.48e-05**	7.63e-04	1.69e-03	4.19e-03	4.87e-03
	p value	**NA**	6.00e-05	5.18e-06	4.49e-07	4.83e-07
f06	Median FEV	**3.16e+00**	3.00e+01	3.03e+01	4.04e+01	4.18e+01
	IQR	**6.60e-16**	8.00e-02	2.65e+00	3.43e+00	4.01e+00
	p value	**NA**	1.46e-04	2.57e-05	3.23e-06	2.29e-06

continued on following page

Table 1a. Continued

Functions	Metric	MBA	BA	ABC	ACO	CS
f07	Median FEV	**1.25e+01**	2.94e+01	3.57e+01	4.10e+01	4.25e+01
	IQR	**5.20e+00**	5.90e+00	7.37e+00	9.20e+00	1.06e+01
	p value	**NA**	1.68e-03	3.29e-05	1.84e-07	2.09e-07
f08	Median FEV	**2.09e+01**	2.09e+01	2.10e+01	2.11e+01	2.11e+01
	IQR	**3.31e-02**	3.96e-02	4.28e-02	4.64e-02	5.03e-02
	p value	**NA**	4.14e-02	3.44e-02	5.42e-03	5.16e-03
f09	Median FEV	1.98e+01	**1.04e+01**	3.71e+01	4.90e+01	5.02e+01
	IQR	1.72e+00	**1.70e+00**	2.46e+00	2.92e+00	3.49e+00
	p value	3.58e-02	**NA**	6.12e-02	5.38e-02	5.09e-02
f10	Median FEV	**1.43e-07**	2.67e-04	4.22e-04	1.15e-02	2.23e-02
	IQR	**4.02e-05**	1.58e-03	1.14e-03	6.69e-03	9.08e-03
	p value	**NA**	3.76e-04	1.36e-06	2.85e-09	2.62e-09
f11	Median FEV	**4.88e-01**	3.35e+00	7.55e+00	1.21e+01	1.48e+01
	IQR	**9.97e-04**	2.49e-02	3.29e-01	8.70e-01	1.80e+00
	p value	**NA**	2.52e-03	1.46e-05	1.40e-05	4.33e-08
f12	Median FEV	**6.22e+00**	2.73e+01	4.27e+01	8.61e+01	1.01e+02
	IQR	**1.77e+00**	6.09e+00	8.08e+00	2.06e+01	2.23e+01
	p value	**NA**	3.49e-04	1.85e-04	2.51e-07	3.21e-09
f13	Median FEV	**6.22e+01**	8.01e+01	8.89e+01	1.65e+02	1.68e+02
	IQR	**4.58e+00**	8.09e+00	1.43e+01	2.07e+01	3.22e+01
	p value	**NA**	4.96e-06	3.14e-06	3.17e-07	2.65e-07
f14	Median FEV	**1.72e+01**	1.98e+01	4.76e+01	4.94e+02	7.52e+02
	IQR	**1.41e+00**	8.65e+00	2.88e+01	1.27e+02	2.53e+02
	p value	**NA**	3.42e-03	6.20e-08	2.42e-11	2.35e-11
f15	Median FEV	**9.23e+02**	2.20e+03	3.74e+03	6.38e+03	7.01e+03
	IQR	**2.85e+02**	3.55e+02	4.27e+02	5.03e+02	5.55e+02
	p value	**NA**	4.95e-03	5.10e-03	1.74e-05	5.11e-06
f16	Median FEV	1.39e+00	8.07e-01	**7.84e-02**	1.62e+00	1.73e+00
	IQR	1.41e-01	4.37e-02	**2.73e-02**	2.02e-01	2.36e-01
	p value	5.06e-04	1.49e-03	**NA**	1.60e-04	5.04e-05

The Friedman and the Iman-Davenport non-parametric statistical tests (Garcia et al., 2009) are undertaken to validate the superiority of the proposed MBA over its contenders based on the results reported in Table 1. Table 2 summarizes the Friedman rankings of the seven algorithms. The null hypotheses are concerned with the equivalent performance of all algorithms. It is evident from Table 2 that the null hypotheses are rejected with the level of significance $\alpha=0.05$, as the respective statistics exceed their corresponding critical values (in parenthesis). The results in Table 2 emphasize MBA as the best

Table 1b. Comparison of algorithms with respect to FEV for f17 to f28

Functions	Metric	MBA	BA	ABC	ACO	CS
f17	Median FEV	**4.88e+01**	5.07e+01	5.22e+01	5.68e+01	5.86e+01
	IQR	**9.32e-03**	1.74e-02	3.37e-01	1.68e+00	2.06e+00
	p value	**NA**	3.14e-07	1.40e-07	8.07e-09	3.70e-15
f18	Median FEV	**6.33e+01**	1.14e+02	1.27e+02	1.41e+02	1.61e+02
	IQR	**1.00e+01**	1.27e+01	1.55e+01	3.44e+01	3.65e+01
	p value	**NA**	2.97e-06	1.46e-06	1.27e-08	2.93e-09
f19	Median FEV	**2.26e+00**	3.25e+00	3.33e+00	3.60e+00	3.92e+00
	IQR	**2.79e-01**	2.99e-01	4.49e-01	5.70e-01	7.33e-01
	p value	**NA**	3.59e-04	2.46e-04	7.92e-13	8.20e-16
f20	Median FEV	**1.48e+01**	1.91e+01	1.92e+01	1.94e+01	2.03e+01
	IQR	**3.86e-01**	4.60e-01	5.14e-01	6.48e-01	7.81e-01
	p value	**7.85e-06**	2.91e-05	5.70e-06	2.65e-06	2.03e-06
f21	Median FEV	**2.24e+02**	2.40e+02	2.49e+02	3.26e+02	5.14e+02
	IQR	**1.38e+01**	7.96e+01	1.80e+02	2.67e+02	2.92e+02
	p value	**NA**	6.01e-04	8.18e-05	2.84e-06	6.74e-10
f22	Median FEV	**2.62e+01**	2.29e+01	1.74e+02	3.46e+02	7.33e+02
	IQR	**1.35e+01**	2.52e+01	3.91e+01	2.55e+02	3.02e+02
	p value	**NA**	6.77e-04	6.41e-04	3.03e-07	2.31e-07
f23	Median FEV	**7.13e+02**	1.18e+03	3.83e+03	7.61e+03	8.25e+03
	IQR	**3.28e+02**	4.46e+02	5.30e+02	6.36e+02	7.03e+02
	p value	**NA**	3.36e-07	9.98e-09	1.02e-10	1.36e-14
f24	Median FEV	**2.18e+02**	2.31e+02	2.37e+02	2.81e+02	2.87e+02
	IQR	**4.49e+00**	6.56e+00	1.03e+01	1.39e+01	1.54e+01
	p value	**NA**	3.18e-03	1.50e-03	9.18e-06	4.96e-07
f25	Median FEV	**2.59e+02**	2.83e+02	3.13e+02	3.31e+02	3.57e+02
	IQR	**4.11e+00**	7.67e+00	1.04e+01	1.31e+01	1.45e+01
	p value	**NA**	1.51e-05	3.56e-05	1.22e-11	2.98e-12
f26	Median FEV	**1.95e+02**	1.13e+02	2.09e+02	2.49e+02	2.83e+02
	IQR	**3.81e-01**	1.80e+01	2.45e+01	5.64e+01	7.89e+01
	p value	**NA**	6.69e-03	2.65e-05	2.85e-07	9.50e-09
f27	Median FEV	**3.40e+02**	**3.40e+02**	9.22e+02	1.05e+03	1.21e+03
	IQR	**4.67e+01**	**8.09e+01**	1.18e+02	1.47e+02	1.64e+02
	p value	**NA**	**NA**	2.36e-07	6.31e-08	7.36e-10
f28	Median FEV	**3.40e+02**	4.06e+02	4.29e+02	4.41e+02	4.59e+02
	IQR	**2.83e-04**	1.87e-01	2.47e+01	3.08e+02	4.19e+02
	p value	**NA**	3.58e-05	1.52e-05	1.35e-09	9.77e-11

Table 2. Friedman ranks with α=0. 05

Algorithms	MBA	BA	ABC	ACO	CS
Friedman Rank	**1.089**	1.946	2.928	4.000	5.000
Rank Difference	**NA**	0.857	1.839	2.911	3.911
Friedman Statistics	106.9154 (Critical Value: 9.488)				
Iman-Davenport Statistics	567.7412 (Critical Value: 2.46)				
Bonferroni-Dunn Statistics	1.0556				

algorithm, so the Bonferroni-Dunn post-hoc analysis is undertaken with MBA as the control method (Garcia et al., 2009). The critical difference value of the Bonferroni-Dunn test in the present context comes out as 1.0556 with α=0.05. If the average Friedman ranks of any two algorithms differ at least by the critical difference, we infer a statistically significant difference in their respective performance measures. Table 2 shows that MBA outperforms all its competitors in a statistically significant fashion except for BA with $\alpha = 0.05$.

Experiments on Motion Planning of Non-Holonomic Car-Like Robots

The motion planning problem is implemented in C on a Pentium processor with $n \in \{4, 6, 8, 10\}$ similar car-like robots. Experiments are undertaken in different world maps by adding new obstacles, however, retaining the old ones. The maximum number of obstacles in a world map is considered here to be 10. In a specific run of the motion planning program, the velocities of all n car-like robots are set equal. To assess the performance of the proposed motion-planning problem of n car-like robots in different world maps, three performance metrics are used, including i) total number of steps required by robots to reach their respective goals, ii) average total path traversed (*ATPT*) and iii) average total path deviation (*ATPD*). *ATPD* and *ATPT* are defined below.

Let the total distance traversed by the i-th robot from its given starting position S_i to the given goal position G_i in a specific world map in the k-th run of the program be denoted by $L_{i,k}$. Then the average total path traversed (ATPT) by the i-th robot over M runs of the program in the same environment is given by

$$ATPT_i = \sum_{k=1}^{M} L_{i,k} \Big/ M \tag{27}$$

The average path deviation for the i-th robot is then measured by taking the difference between $ATPT_i$ and the shortest ideal path length $L_{i\text{-}ideal}$ possible from S_i to G_i. In other words, the average path deviation is given by

$$ATPD_i = L_{i-ideal} - ATPT_i \tag{28}$$

Therefore, for n robots in the given world map, $ATPD$ is given by

$$ATPD = \sum_{i=1}^{n} ATPD_i \tag{29}$$

Figure 6 shows the paths traversed by $n = 6$ car-like robots from their fixed starting to goal positions in a given world map with 4 static obstacles as obtained by different contender algorithms. Figure 6 clearly reveals that the proposed MBA-based path-planner provides the shortest paths for all $n = 6$ car-like robots with minimal path deviation from the ideal paths (shown by bold lines) avoiding collision with obstacles and teammates.

Tables 3–6 report the median and IQR values of the *ATPT* and *ATPD* metrics obtained over $M = 25$ runs of each algorithm for world maps with number of obstacles varying from 4 to 10. Tables 3–6 also report the p-value obtained by Wilcoxon rank-sum test between the best algorithm and each of the remaining competitors with a significance level $\alpha = 0.05$. It is evident from Tables 3–6 that the proposed MBA consistently outperforms its contenders in a statistically significant fashion irrespective of the number of obstacles and the number of robots.

Figure 6a. Final configuration of the world map after execution of the MBA based simulations with 6 car-like robots and 4 obstacles requiring 25 steps

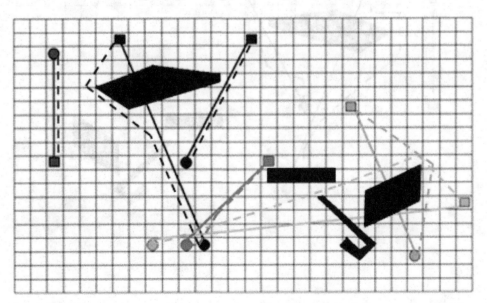

Figure 6b. Final configuration of the world map after execution of the BA based simulations with 6 car-like robots and 4 obstacles requiring 27steps

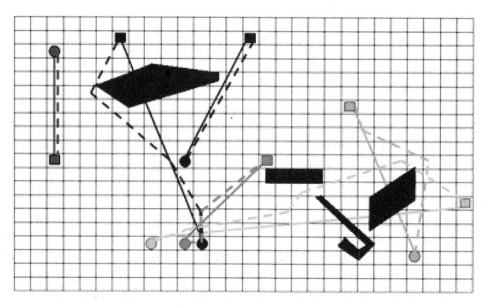

Figure 6c. Final configuration of the world map after execution of the ABC based simulations with 6 car-like robots and 4 obstacles requiring 30 steps

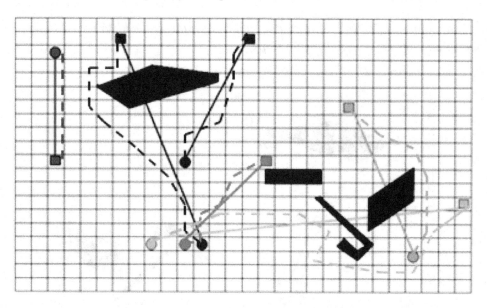

Figure 6d. Final configuration of the world map after execution of the ACO based simulations with 6 car-like robots and 4 obstacles requiring 33 steps

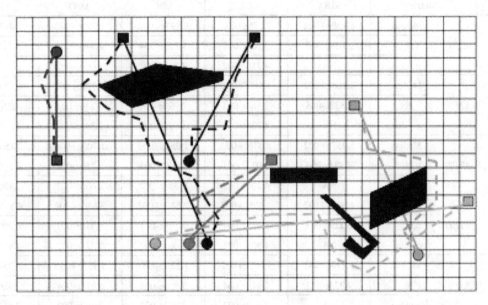

Figure 6e. Final configuration of the world map after execution of the CS based simulations with 6 car-like robots and 2 obstacles requiring 36 steps

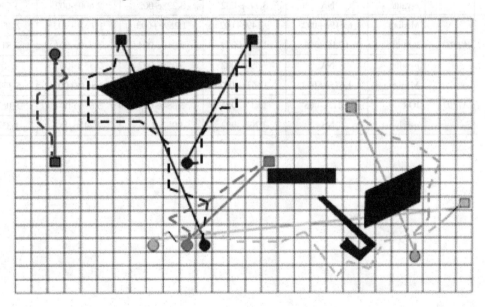

Table 3. Comparison of algorithms for path planning in presence of 4 obstacles

Robots	Metric		MBA	BA	ABC	ACO	CS
4	ATPT	Median	**5.139e+002**	7.276e+002	8.897e+002	1.699e+003	2.040e+003
		IQR	**3.839e-005**	9.264e-005	1.157e-004	4.940e-004	6.215e-004
		p-value	NA	4.718e-002	3.903e-002	3.609e-002	2.733e-002
	ATPD	Median	**1.108e+002**	1.568e+002	2.285e+002	3.579e+002	4.156e+002
		IQR	**2.533e-005**	1.367e-004	1.990e-004	4.236e-004	4.310e-004
		p-value	NA	4.726e-002	3.682e-002	3.395e-002	1.829e-002
6	ATPT	Median	**5.357e+002**	8.336e+002	1.052e+003	1.705e+003	2.150e+003
		IQR	**3.893e-005**	1.077e-004	2.449e-004	5.259e-004	6.829e-004
		p-value	NA	4.100e-002	3.359e-002	2.636e-002	2.129e-002
	ATPD	Median	**1.301e+002**	2.195e+002	2.643e+002	3.650e+002	4.575e+002
		IQR	**3.229e-005**	1.755e-004	2.593e-004	4.340e-004	6.209e-004
		p-value	NA	4.306e-002	3.605e-002	2.724e-002	1.654e-002
8	ATPT	Median	**6.490e+002**	9.082e+002	1.220e+003	1.752e+003	2.206e+003
		IQR	**4.024e-005**	1.418e-004	3.408e-004	5.513e-004	7.466e-004
		p-value	NA	3.828e-002	3.222e-002	2.367e-002	2.117e-002
	ATPD	Median	**1.418e+002**	2.294e+002	2.835e+002	3.827e+002	4.829e+002
		IQR	**4.227e-005**	1.794e-004	2.726e-004	4.661e-004	6.317e-004
		p-value	NA	3.775e-002	3.228e-002	2.600e-002	1.590e-002
10	ATPT	Median	**6.619e+002**	9.349e+002	1.289e+003	1.794e+003	2.256e+003
		IQR	**4.736e-005**	1.452e-004	4.016e-004	5.810e-004	7.813e-004
		p-value	NA	3.499e-002	3.055e-002	2.355e-002	1.706e-002
	ATPD	Median	**1.675e+002**	2.363e+002	3.074e+002	3.861e+002	5.379e+002
		IQR	**6.215e-005**	1.817e-004	3.084e-004	5.656e-004	8.053e-004
		p-value	NA	3.706e-002	3.067e-002	2.242e-002	1.351e-002

Table 4. Comparison of algorithms for path planning in presence of 6 obstacles

Robots	Metric		MBA	BA	ABC	ACO	CS
4	ATPT	Median	**7.279e+002**	9.366e+002	1.358e+003	1.852e+003	2.761e+003
		IQR	**5.201e-005**	1.584e-004	4.381e-004	5.827e-004	7.982e-004
		p-value	**NA**	3.480e-002	2.881e-002	2.200e-002	1.214e-002
	ATPD	Median	**1.778e+002**	2.594e+002	3.144e+002	4.127e+002	5.534e+002
		IQR	**6.987e-005**	1.864e-004	3.752e-004	5.882e-004	8.196e-004
		p-value	**NA**	3.357e-002	2.930e-002	2.212e-002	1.214e-002
6	ATPT	Median	**7.345e+002**	9.571e+002	1.434e+003	1.973e+003	2.772e+003
		IQR	**6.902e-005**	2.058e-004	4.851e-004	6.572e-004	8.074e-004
		p-value	**NA**	3.381e-002	2.657e-002	2.122e-002	1.120e-002
	ATPD	Median	**1.822e+002**	2.613e+002	3.231e+002	4.560e+002	5.807e+002
		IQR	**1.152e-004**	1.870e-004	3.787e-004	5.984e-004	8.261e-004
		p-value	**NA**	3.310e-002	2.719e-002	2.212e-002	1.045e-002
8	ATPT	Median	**7.515e+002**	9.969e+002	1.555e+003	2.086e+003	2.825e+003
		IQR	**8.073e-005**	2.475e-004	5.055e-004	6.823e-004	8.200e-004
		p-value	**NA**	3.377e-002	2.590e-002	2.114e-002	8.794e-003
	ATPD	Median	**1.924e+002**	2.692e+002	3.455e+002	4.730e+002	5.979e+002
		IQR	**1.167e-004**	1.985e-004	3.825e-004	6.603e-004	8.331e-004
		p-value	**NA**	3.310e-002	2.652e-002	1.967e-002	9.853e-003
10	ATPT	Median	**7.533e+002**	1.046e+003	1.608e+003	2.115e+003	3.059e+003
		IQR	**9.466e-005**	2.699e-004	5.234e-004	7.018e-004	8.271e-004
		p-value	**NA**	3.272e-002	2.357e-002	1.722e-002	5.281e-003
	ATPD	Median	**2.183e+002**	2.806e+002	4.011e+002	4.851e+002	6.430e+002
		IQR	**1.294e-004**	2.681e-004	4.053e-004	6.697e-004	8.809e-004
		p-value	**NA**	3.238e-002	2.627e-002	1.796e-002	7.500e-003

Table 5. Comparison of algorithms for path planning in presence of 8 obstacles

Robots	Metric		MBA	BA	ABC	ACO	CS
4	ATPT	Median	**8.200e+002**	1.280e+003	1.641e+003	2.462e+003	3.200e+003
		IQR	**1.058e-004**	3.738e-004	5.264e-004	7.156e-004	8.608e-004
		p-value	**NA**	3.193e-002	2.312e-002	1.626e-002	4.711e-003
	ATPD	Median	**2.323e+002**	3.109e+002	4.050e+002	5.510e+002	6.681e+002
		IQR	**1.648e-004**	2.764e-004	4.226e-004	6.699e-004	8.830e-004
		p-value	**NA**	3.237e-002	2.612e-002	1.751e-002	6.944e-003
6	ATPT	Median	**8.700e+002**	1.291e+003	1.828e+003	2.883e+003	3.208e+003
		IQR	**1.762e-004**	4.643e-004	6.278e-004	7.240e-004	8.863e-004
		p-value	**NA**	3.037e-002	2.305e-002	1.445e-002	4.556e-003
	ATPD	Median	**2.454e+002**	3.178e+002	4.072e+002	6.122e+002	6.748e+002
		IQR	**1.699e-004**	3.196e-004	4.286e-004	6.725e-004	9.211e-004
		p-value	**NA**	3.197e-002	2.397e-002	1.739e-002	5.961e-003
8	ATPT	Median	**9.865e+002**	1.511e+003	1.968e+003	2.952e+003	3.232e+003
		IQR	**1.911e-004**	4.764e-004	6.525e-004	7.330e-004	9.057e-004
		p-value	**NA**	3.011e-002	2.038e-002	1.405e-002	4.541e-003
	ATPD	Median	**2.552e+002**	3.472e+002	4.296e+002	6.462e+002	7.334e+002
		IQR	**2.061e-004**	3.504e-004	5.316e-004	7.041e-004	9.433e-004
		p-value	**NA**	3.179e-002	2.294e-002	1.311e-002	5.485e-003
10	ATPT	Median	**1.187e+003**	1.553e+003	2.149e+003	2.977e+003	3.240e+003
		IQR	**2.393e-004**	4.950e-004	6.630e-004	8.023e-004	9.142e-004
		p-value	**NA**	2.993e-002	1.934e-002	1.345e-002	3.440e-003
	ATPD	Median	**2.581e+002**	3.969e+002	4.555e+002	6.462e+002	7.506e+002
		IQR	**2.339e-004**	3.908e-004	5.437e-004	7.329e-004	9.521e-004
		p-value	**NA**	3.139e-002	2.251e-002	1.282e-002	5.290e-003

Table 6. Comparison of algorithms for path planning in presence of 10 obstacles

Robots	Metric		MBA	BA	ABC	ACO	CS
4	ATPT	Median	**1.220e+003**	1.908e+003	2.306e+003	2.992e+003	3.252e+003
		IQR	**2.693e-004**	4.992e-004	6.852e-004	8.030e-004	9.296e-004
		p-value	**NA**	2.654e-002	1.437e-002	9.587e-003	1.788e-003
	ATPD	Median	**3.077e+002**	4.051e+002	5.109e+002	6.564e+002	7.573e+002
		IQR	**2.975e-004**	3.970e-004	5.524e-004	7.405e-004	9.818e-004
		p-value	**NA**	3.037e-002	2.122e-002	1.181e-002	4.691e-003
6	ATPT	Median	**1.513e+003**	2.092e+003	2.568e+003	3.106e+003	3.302e+003
		IQR	**3.420e-004**	5.050e-004	7.179e-004	8.920e-004	9.635e-004
		p-value	**NA**	2.287e-002	1.332e-002	7.683e-003	1.680e-003
	ATPD	Median	**3.728e+002**	5.026e+002	5.220e+002	6.910e+002	7.594e+002
		IQR	**2.991e-004**	4.373e-004	5.872e-004	8.570e-004	9.828e-004
		p-value	**NA**	2.911e-002	2.081e-002	1.093e-002	3.180e-003
8	ATPT	Median	**2.203e+003**	2.239e+003	2.838e+003	3.108e+003	3.386e+003
		IQR	**4.593e-004**	6.138e-004	8.194e-004	9.047e-004	9.789e-004
		p-value	**NA**	1.598e-002	1.204e-002	7.636e-003	3.358e-004
	ATPD	Median	**4.408e+002**	5.357e+002	5.544e+002	7.132e+002	7.693e+002
		IQR	**3.461e-004**	4.872e-004	5.936e-004	9.072e-004	9.842e-004
		p-value	**NA**	2.704e-002	2.023e-002	9.601e-003	2.223e-003
10	ATPT	Median	**2.366e+003**	2.744e+003	2.900e+003	3.334e+003	3.488e+003
		IQR	**4.937e-004**	7.252e-004	8.876e-004	9.732e-004	9.881e-004
		p-value	**NA**	1.274e-002	9.433e-003	3.400e-003	5.755e-005
	ATPD	Median	**5.164e+002**	6.213e+002	6.723e+002	7.464e+002	7.858e+002
		IQR	**4.948e-004**	6.483e-004	7.011e-004	9.832e-004	9.991e-004
		p-value	**NA**	1.974e-002	1.324e-002	5.970e-003	9.789e-004

CONCLUSION

Successful demonstration on multiple car-like robots and results obtained by the simulation show that proposed planner can generate nice paths satisfying the non-holonomic problem of car-like mobile robots. Experiments undertaken in different world maps reveal the robustness of this planner. Modified Bat Algorithm (MBA) has been proposed by utilizing combined benefit of Bat Algorithm (BA) for global exploration and self-adaptation of step size for local exploitation. In MBA, the step size parameter is probabilistically assigned to each bat for their movement according to the probabilities gradually learned from the experience to generate improved solutions.

REFERENCES

Chakraborty, J., Konar, A., Jain, L. C., & Chakraborty, U. K. (2009). Cooperative multi-robot path planning using differential evolution. *Journal of Intelligent & Fuzzy Systems, 20*(1, 2), 13-27.

Chowdhury, A., Rakshit, P., Konar, A., & Nagar, A. K. (2014, July). A modified bat algorithm to predict Protein-Protein Interaction network. In *2014 IEEE Congress on Evolutionary Computation (CEC)* (pp. 1046-1053). IEEE. 10.1109/CEC.2014.6900518

Davison, A. J., Reid, I. D., Molton, N. D., & Stasse, O. (2007). MonoSLAM: Real-time single camera SLAM. *IEEE Transactions on Pattern Analysis and Machine Intelligence, 29*(6), 1052–1067. doi:10.1109/TPAMI.2007.1049 PMID:17431302

Daxwanger, W. A., & Schmidt, G. (1996). Neural and fuzzy approaches to vision-based parking control. *Control Engineering Practice, 4*(11), 1607–1614. doi:10.1016/0967-0661(96)00176-1

De Luca, A., Oriolo, G., & Samson, C. (1998). Feedback control of a nonholonomic car-like robot. In *Robot motion planning and control* (pp. 171–253). Berlin: Springer. doi:10.1007/BFb0036073

Dolgov, D., Thrun, S., Montemerlo, M., & Diebel, J. (2010). Path planning for autonomous vehicles in unknown semi-structured environments. *The International Journal of Robotics Research, 29*(5), 485–501. doi:10.1177/0278364909359210

Dorigo, M., & Birattari, M. (2011). Ant colony optimization. In *Encyclopedia of machine learning* (pp. 36–39). Boston, MA: Springer.

Dubins, L. E. (1957). On curves of minimal length with a constraint on average curvature, and with prescribed initial and terminal positions and tangents. *American Journal of Mathematics, 79*(3), 497–516. doi:10.2307/2372560

García, S., Molina, D., Lozano, M., & Herrera, F. (2009). A study on the use of non-parametric tests for analyzing the evolutionary algorithms' behaviour: A case study on the CEC'2005 special session on real parameter optimization. *Journal of Heuristics, 15*(6), 617.

Haehnel, D., Thrun, S., & Burgard, W. (2003, August). An extension of the ICP algorithm for modeling nonrigid objects with mobile robots. In *IJCAI'03 Proceedings of the 18th international joint conference on Artificial intelligence* (pp. 915–920).

Karaboga, D., & Basturk, B. (2008). On the performance of artificial bee colony (ABC) algorithm. *Applied Soft Computing, 8*(1), 687–697. doi:10.1016/j.asoc.2007.05.007

Kong, S. G., & Kosko, B. (1990). Comparison of fuzzy and neural truck backer-upper control systems. In *1990 IJCNN International Joint Conference on Neural Networks* (pp. 349-358). IEEE.

Laugier, C., Fraichard, T. H., Garnier, P., Paromtchik, I. E., & Scheuer, A. (1999). Sensor-based control architecture for a car-like vehicle. *Autonomous Robots*, *6*(2), 165–185. doi:10.1023/A:1008835527875

Laumond, J. P., Sekhavat, S., & Lamiraux, F. (1998). Guidelines in nonholonomic motion planning for mobile robots. In *Robot motion planning and control* (pp. 1–53). Berlin, Heidelberg: Springer. doi:10.1007/BFb0036070

Liang, J. J., Qu, B. Y., Suganthan, P. N., & Hernández-Díaz, A. G. (2013). Problem definitions and evaluation criteria for the CEC 2013 special session on real-parameter optimization (Technical Report). Computational Intelligence Laboratory, Zhengzhou University, Zhengzhou, China and Nanyang Technological University, Singapore.

Martinez-Cantin, R., Castellanos, J. A., & de Freitas, N. (2007). Multi-robot marginal-slam. In Workshop On Multirobotic Systems For Societal (p. 52).

Miyata, H., Ohki, M., Yokouchi, Y., & Ohkita, M. (1996). Control of the autonomous mobile robot DREAM-1 for a parallel parking. *Mathematics and Computers in Simulation*, *41*(1-2), 129–138. doi:10.1016/0378-4754(95)00065-8

Moran, A., & Nagai, M. (1995). Autonomous parking of vehicles with intelligent fuzzy-neural networks. *JSAE Review*, *2*(16), 216.

Motoji, Y., & Akira, M. (1995). Automatic Parking Motion Control for a Car-Like Robot Using a Fuzzy Neural Network. *JSAE Review*, *1*(16), 98. doi:10.1016/0389-4304(95)94722-Y

Nguyen, V., Gächter, S., Martinelli, A., Tomatis, N., & Siegwart, R. (2007). A comparison of line extraction algorithms using 2D range data for indoor mobile robotics. *Autonomous Robots*, *23*(2), 97–111. doi:10.100710514-007-9034-y

Pfaff, P., Triebel, R., & Burgard, W. (2007). An efficient extension to elevation maps for outdoor terrain mapping and loop closing. *The International Journal of Robotics Research*, *26*(2), 217–230. doi:10.1177/0278364906075165

Roy, A. G., Rakshit, P., Konar, A., Bhattacharya, S., Kim, E., & Nagar, A. K. (2013, June). Adaptive firefly algorithm for nonholonomic motion planning of car-like system. In *2013 IEEE Congress on Evolutionary Computation (CEC)* (pp. 2162-2169). IEEE. 10.1109/CEC.2013.6557825

Yang, X. S. (2010). A new metaheuristic bat-inspired algorithm. In *Nature inspired cooperative strategies for optimization (NICSO 2010)* (pp. 65–74). Berlin: Springer. doi:10.1007/978-3-642-12538-6_6

Yang, X. S., & Deb, S. (2009, December). Cuckoo search via Lévy flights. In *World Congress on Nature & Biologically Inspired Computing NaBIC '09* (pp. 210-214). IEEE.

Yang, X. S., & He, X. (2013). Bat algorithm: Literature review and applications. *International Journal of Bio-inspired Computation*, *5*(3), 141–149. doi:10.1504/IJBIC.2013.055093

Yang, X. S., & Hossein Gandomi, A. (2012). Bat algorithm: A novel approach for global engineering optimization. *Engineering Computations*, *29*(5), 464–483. doi:10.1108/02644401211235834

Chapter 6
Application of Nature-Inspired Algorithms for Sensing Error Optimisation in Dynamic Environment

Sumitra Mukhopadhyay
University of Calcutta, India

Soumyadip Das
University of Calcutta, India

ABSTRACT

Spectrum sensing errors in cognitive radio may occur due to constant changes in the environment like changes in background noise, movements of the users, temperature variations, etc. It leads to under usage of available spectrum bands or may cause interference to the primary user transmission. So, sensing parameters like detection threshold are required to adapt dynamically to the changing environment to minimise sensing errors. Correct sensing requires processing huge data sets just like Big Data. This chapter investigates sensing in light of Big Data and presents the study of the nature inspired algorithms in sensing error minimisation by dynamic adaptation of the threshold value. Death penalty constrained handing techniques are integrated to the genetic algorithm, particle swarm optimisation, the firefly algorithm and the bat algorithm. Based on them, four algorithms are developed for minimizing sensing errors. The reported algorithms are found to be faster and more accurate when compared with previously proposed threshold adaptation algorithms based on a gradient descend.

INTRODUCTION

The present age is the age of information. Huge volumes of data are being generated at an unprecedented speed from different applications of social media, internet, search engine, space, communication etc. This has given rise to multiple major concerns in the domain of information processing and regarding the factors related to providing QoS to the users. Efficient techniques are required to be developed for

DOI: 10.4018/978-1-5225-5852-1.ch006

managing, handling, processing and extracting important information from this ever-increasing dataset. This gives rise to the concept of Big Data analysis and the requirement of tools for its management. In today's world if we look around ourselves, there are ample sources of enormous amount of data and in recent advancement majority of the data sources are from different communication-oriented applications. Number of mobile users is increasing every day with a requirement of ultra-reliable and massive bandwidth. Also, with wide implementation of Internet-of-Things (IoT), huge bandwidth requirement is coming into play. Static Spectrum Allocation policy which is presently used in different countries, leads to inefficient use of spectrum, where some of the bands are over utilized and most of the bands remain under-utilized (Letaief & Zhang, 2009). Now to resolve such a scenario, people are working on cognitive radio (CR) technology where spectrum bands are dynamically sensed, shared and recycled. The implementation of CR technology requires prediction of optimized parameter set in real time environment. The prediction techniques always work on historical analysis of spectrum which involves huge processing of data. The conventional technique may not be adequate to handle the complexity and enormity of the spectrum data set. On the other hand, bio-inspired optimizations are widely and successfully used for feature extraction of Big Data set under uncertainty and noise. Therefore, in this chapter, we have tried to define the equivalence of spectrum data set and Big Data set. Once the equivalence is established, then the bio-inspired techniques may be applied for parameter prediction for different spectrum related analysis of CR technology. In this chapter, we have worked on parameter prediction for dynamic spectrum sensing.

Big Data refers to high volumes of varied types of data, structured and un-structured, streaming at exponentially increasing speed, inconsistent and of varied quality. So, Big Data is described by characteristics like volume, velocity, variety, variability and veracity (Schroeck, Shockley, Smart, Romero-Morales & Tufano, 2012). These make the conventional data processing techniques inadequate to manage and analyze to extract required information accurately. Mathematical optimization has immense applications in various fields of engineering like electronic design automation, VLSI, machine learning, signal processing, Big Data, communication, etc. Nature inspired optimization algorithms are used to efficiently analyze Big Data (Hajeer & Dasgupta, 2016).

In CR technology, the spectrum bands are allotted to the users who are not licensed, i.e., secondary users (SU) when the bands remain unused by the licensed users known as Primary Users (PU), without causing any harmful interference to the PU transmission. The SU senses the available spectrum holes (vacant spectrum band) and transmits, until PU again starts to transmit via the allotted band. Thus, spectrum sensing becomes a key issue in CR technology. A number of different spectrum sensing algorithms are described in the literatures (Letaief & Zhang, 2009; Liang, Zeng, Peh & Hoang, 2008; Zhang, Mallik & Letaief, 2008; Zhang, Jia & Zhang, 2009; Joshi, Popescu & Dobre, 2011; Li, Hei & Qiu, 2017). The energy detection method (Letaief & Zhang, 2009), multitaper method, pilot signals and matched filtering methods (Letaief & Zhang, 2009), cyclo-stationary based methods (Letaief & Zhang, 2009), and poly phase filter bank methods (Letaief & Zhang, 2009), etc., are some of the widely known methods of spectrum sensing. The techniques mentioned above are generally tested under static environment. However, practical systems are subjected to change in background noises due to temperature change, ambient interference, etc. and the spectrum usage changes as the number of active users and transmission parameter changes. Other challenges, like reliability issues, uncertainty in the performance and parameter detection in real time degrades the sensing performance and causes sensing failure problem. Also, according to IEEE 802.22 standard, any spectrum sensing technique must detect the presence of the licensed user within 2 seconds from the appearance of the user (Shellhammer, 2008). Therefore, the problem of spectrum sensing in dynamic environment is an important aspect of CR and the proper parameter adjustment of such technique leads to a challenging task. It requires huge amount of historical spectrum processing for efficient prediction of parameters under constrained environment. Just like Big Data, spectrum data is continuous, massive, and can be characterized by large volume, velocity and variability (Ding, Wu, Wang & Yao, 2014). Larger volume of sample increases sensing accuracy. Again, in the dynamic radio environment, spectrum data arrive at high velocity and signal samples are required to be processed in real time. Movement of the transmitters and receivers, changes in noise variance, fading etc. degrades signal quality that accounts for variability of the sample data. So correct spectrum sensing is a big challenge in real time scenario.

Here in this chapter, the authors discuss the application methodology and significance of nature inspired optimization techniques for dynamic parameter adjustment in cognitive radio (CR) environment. This requires large data samples to be processed in real time for correct sensing. The energy detection technique is considered as the spectrum sensing technique for analysis in this chapter.

The classical energy detection technique is one of the simplest and most popular techniques of spectrum sensing which works without having any dependency on the information from the primary user and the sensing aspect depends on the threshold parameter detection. Selecting a proper decision threshold is thus important in energy-based spectrum sensing and wrong selection gives rise to erroneous decision about the presence of PU. If threshold is very high, a Primary User's (PU's) signal of low signal-to-noise ratio (SNR) may not be detected, which is called miss detection and the secondary user (SU) may start transmitting thereby interfering the PU transmission. Again, if the threshold is too low, a noise may be detected as a PU signal, which is called false alarm, and thus SU will miss a transmitting opportunity. Thus, it is required to find out the optimized threshold in a dynamic environment within limited time constraint and the problem may be formulated as a constrained optimization problem.

The task of finding the optimal solution is to determine a better solution among all available feasible solutions. Each feasible solution has a fitness value for the problem at hand and all such feasible solutions constitute the search space. Thus, the optimum point in the search space that represents a better solution to the problem is searched. There are a number of classical searching algorithms; however, the worst case time complexity of those algorithms for Big Data handling becomes higher order polynomial or exponential in nature. Still a numerical solution can be possible, but run time of such algorithms become overwhelmingly large as the instance size of the algorithm increases.

In case of dynamic spectrum sensing problems, as the environment is dynamic in nature, therefore such a scenario leads to a requirement of dynamic adjustment of threshold and other parameters. This causes a huge resource involvement, and therefore, instead of deterministic algorithms, usages of nature inspired algorithms are of great interest. These will demonstrate the revolutionary effect in the real-time prediction of parameters for spectrum sensing in the cognitive radio environment.

Natural phenomenon like evolution, intelligence, etc. have inspired the development of stochastic algorithms called bio-inspired algorithms. They include evolutionary algorithms (EA) like genetic algorithm (GA) (Holland, 1992; Goldberg, 1989), differential evolution (DE) (Storn & Price, 1997), etc., and swarm based algorithms like particle swarm optimization (PSO) (Shi, 2001; Kennedy, 2011), ant colony optimization algorithm (Dorigo & Di Caro, 1999), firefly algorithm (Yang, 2008; Fister, Yang & Brest, 2013), bat optimization algorithm (BA) (Yang, 2010), grey wolf optimization algorithm (Mirjalili, Mirjalili & Lewis, 2014), cuckoo search algorithm (Yang & Deb, 2009), etc. In this chapter the authors work with two classes of nature inspired algorithms, namely evolutionary algorithm and swarm-based algorithm for parameter adaptation. Five well known nature inspired algorithms like genetic algorithm, differential evolution, firefly algorithm, particle swarm optimization, and bat algorithms are considered and individually, they have been used for the solution of the constrained sensing error minimization problem. The algorithms are modified according to the requirement for parameter adaptation in real time environment.

Evolutionary algorithm works primarily based on natural biological evolution, EAs optimize a problem by iteratively searching for better solutions utilizing natural phenomena like growth, development, reproduction, selection, survival of the fittest of a population of possible solutions, etc. Genetic algorithm was first proposed by Holland (Holland, 1992) and it is a robust evolutionary algorithm for finding optimized solutions (Goldberg, 1989). Constrained optimization problems, like traveling salesman problem (Dorigo & Gambardella, 1997), circuit partitioning problem (Manikas & Cain, 1996), the Hamiltonian circuit problem (Johnson & Tarjan, 1976), etc. have been solved using genetic algorithm successfully. GA is applied across many disciplines to find acceptable solutions to complex problems in a finite amount of time and that is why the importance and application of GA is increasing with time. However, along with its advantages some shades of disadvantages are there in its feather. Improper choice of fitness function may lead the searching towards the local optima of the solution where other simpler algorithm may find the best solution. Also, GA may fail to produce promising results with dynamic dataset.

Another equally important and comparatively newer bio-inspired optimization algorithm is Differential Evolution. DE was proposed by Price and Storn et al. (Storn & Price, 1997; Price, Storn & Lampinen, 2006) and it is a simple yet powerful stochastic search method for global optimization problems in a continuous search domain. It also constitutes the steps like mutation, crossover and selection. Here, the trial vectors are generated using mutation and crossover operators and selection operator is used to determine the vectors that form the next generation of solution. Though DE is widely and successfully used as a population-based algorithm in different engineering problems, in some of the cases, it may also lead to unstable convergence in the advanced stage of solution and gets confined into local optima. This is primarily due to the factor that the performance of DE is mostly guided by its control parameter, crossover and mutation operator. Therefore, the initial selection of such parameters has a profound effect on final convergence to global optima.

Swarm intelligence, on the other hand, is the demonstration of collective behaviour of decentralized and self-organized swarm. Here in this chapter, we consider three swarm-based technique like particle swarm optimization (PSO), firefly algorithm and bat algorithm for proper selection of threshold parameters in spectrum sensing problems.

Particle Swarm Optimization algorithm (PSO), proposed by Eberhart and Kennedy in 1995 (Eberhart & Kennedy, 1995), is one of the efficient global optimization technique and it is inspired by the social behaviour of a bird flock. In the PSO algorithm, swarms of particles are considered to locate the possible solution for the problem in the multi-dimensional problem space. The velocity of each particle in each dimension of the problem space is altered with each generation of movement. Subsequently the positions of the particles are also altered based on the updated velocity.

Firefly algorithm (FA) (Yang, 2008; Fister, Yang & Brest, 2013) is another member of swarm-based algorithms. The researchers are extensively working on this algorithm with different modifications and improvements and they are also reported in the literature. FA is a population-based method and it simulates the flashing and communication behaviour of fireflies. The brightness of a firefly indicates about the improvement of the objective function in obtaining the solution. Brighter firefly is more promising in finding the solution and it attracts other fireflies. As the distance between fireflies increases, the attractiveness decreases exponentially because of the light absorption of the medium.

The third algorithm in the series, which is discussed in this chapter for parameter identification, is the bat optimization algorithm. It is a new heuristic optimization algorithm and was proposed by Yang (Yang, 2009). The echolocation behaviour of bats is modelled here for searching the optimum solution. Bats according to its biological behaviour takes help of different methods to detect theirs preys or other shapes around them in the dark places. They emit a sound pulse to the air and sense the presence of prey by listening for the echoes reflect back from them. Generally, echolocation calls are modelled by three important parameters like the pulse emission rate, the frequency and the loudness. Once the information is received, the virtual image of the surrounding is deduced and the prey in the vicinity of the bat is identified. The modelling of this unique feature of echolocation helps in better understanding of the surrounding environment in darkness and the optimal solution is identified.

Therefore, it is evident that these classes of algorithms are very effective in searching optimal solution due to their inherent biological nature and they may be modelled in several ways to increase the convergence speed, accuracy, etc. Subsequently, the problem of sensing error minimization through threshold adaptation will be formulated as a constrained optimization problem and the nature inspired algorithms may be applied for parameter identification in a dynamic environment. The above targets will be achieved by properly balancing the exploration and exploitation capabilities of an algorithm.

The remaining section of the chapter is organized as follows: First the equivalence of Big Data and spectrum data will be established and thus the justification for the usage of nature inspired algorithm for parameter prediction in the domain of spectrum sensing will come up as an obvious choice. An overview of the sensing error minimization problem will be provided and its importance will be highlighted in cognitive radio environment. Also sensing error minimization problem will be formulated as a constrained optimization problem. Next, a brief review of the nature inspired algorithms and related work is presented, followed by the proposal of the above mentioned five bio-inspired and swarm-based techniques for real time parameter identification in spectrum sensing problem. After that, the results of the above-mentioned techniques will be demonstrated as well as comparative results are given and the significance of the work will be highlighted. Finally, the work has been concluded.

BACKGROUND AND REVIEW WORK

Scarcity of the available spectrum band is a major issue nowadays in modern applications with a requirement of high speed communications (Haykin, Thomson & Reed, 2009; Yucek & Arslan, 2009; Cabric, Mishra & Brodersen, 2004). Different spectrum sensing algorithms include energy detection (Letaief & Zhang, 2009), cyclo-stationary feature detection (Letaief & Zhang, 2009; Zhang, Mallik & Letaief, 2008), matched filtering (Zhang, Mallik & Letaief, 2008), poly phase filter banks (Farhang-Boroujeny, 2008), etc. They sense the presence of unused spectrum and allow the SU to use those bands. However, it is mandatory for SU to sense the presence of PU and instantly vacate the band. According to IEEE 802.22 standard (Shellhammer, 2008), any spectrum sensing technique must detect the presence of the licensed user within two seconds. In practical situations, the factors like background noise, interference, etc. hinders the sensing process and it requires the sensing parameters to be dynamically changed for more accurate spectrum sensing.

Big Data and Spectrum Sensing

The volume of data and the variants of data are continuously increasing in real world application. The storage and management of such distributed and huge data in a structured format is becoming a challenging task. In today's scenario, we name that enormous amount of data as Big Data and when they are processed successfully useful content may be accessed from them. However most of the time maximum of those data remains unattended and unutilized. These data may be produced by different devices and applications like social media applications, stock exchange, mobile, search engine, communication applications, etc. The characteristics of Big Data are as follows (Schroeck et al., 2012):

- **Volume:** Large volumes of data are collected from a variety of sources like social media, sensors, business transactions, etc.
- **Velocity:** Data size increases at an overwhelming speed.
- **Variability:** The data is highly inconsistent.
- **Variety:** The data is available in various kinds of formats like numeric, text, video, audio, etc.
- **Veracity:** The quality of the data varies widely.

It may be observed that handling and feature extraction from Big Data is a challenge for conventional techniques in acceptable time. Hence, data mining tools are equipped with nature inspired algorithms like EAs to handle Big Data efficiently (Hajeer et al., 2016).

Here, we focus on Cognitive radio related applications and primarily on real time parameter prediction of spectrum sensing algorithm in dynamic environment. Cognitive radio technology is playing an important role in today's communication application where scarcity of spectrum is a major issue in high bandwidth applications. In CR the spectrum bands are allotted to secondary users (SU) when the bands remain unused by the licensed users known as Primary Users (PU), without causing any harmful interference to the PU transmission.

Spectrum data samples that are processed for sensing can also be characterized to have the above properties in common to Big Data (Ding et al., 2014). They are as follows:

- **Volume of Spectrum Data:** Massive quantities of spectrum data are being generated from a massive number of SUs, which must be processed for spectrum detection and sensing and prediction of parameters. Also, huge volumes of spectrum occupancy data are stored for prediction.
- **Velocity of Spectrum Data:** Huge volumes of spectrum data are being generated at high speed making it difficult for traditional systems to analyse it.
- **Variety of Spectrum Data:** Spectrum data comes from different spectrum sensors like mobile devices or spectrum measurement equipment.
- **Veracity of Spectrum Data:** Veracity means quality of spectrum data. Noise, fading, shadowing, movement of SUs, changing weather conditions, etc. degrades quality of received signal.

In order to utilize spectrum efficiently, this huge volume of spectrum data samples having varied quality must be accurately analyzed at a very high speed. Now it has been observed from different literature that nature inspired algorithms are quite good and successful for exploration and exploitation of large dataset having immense uncertainty and noise. They extract the non-redundant features from the high dimensional dataset for proper parameter prediction, clustering and classification. As spectrum data are massive and continuous in nature, all these above observations lead to the conclusion that nature inspired algorithms may be a viable alternative for efficient spectrum sensing in real time. In Table 1, the list of symbols and variables used in this chapter is provided.

Table 1. Symbols and variables and their notations

n	Time instant
$y(n)$	Signal received by secondary user
$u(n)$	independent identically distributed (iid) additive white Gaussian noise (AWGN)
σ_u^2	Noise variance
$s(n)$	Primary user signal
σ_s^2	Signal variance
ϵ	Sensing threshold
T	test statistic of the energy detector
M	Number of signal samples
P_{fa}	probability of false alarm
P_m	probability of missed detection
σ^2	variance of the received signal
γ	Signal to noise ratio
e	sensing error
e^*	Minimum sensing error attainable at an environmental scenario
$e_{\min}$	Minimum sensing error obtained by an algorithm in an environmental scenario
α	maximum allowable value of P_m
β	maximum allowable value of $P_{(fa)}$
δ	weighting parameter, which determines the relative contribution of P_{fa} and P_m to e
μ	step size of gradient descent algorithm

continued on following page

Table 1. Continued

G	The generation number in an algorithm
x_i^G	i^{th} member of the Gth generation in an optimization algorithm
N	The population size in an algorithm
m_i^G	mutant vector for i^{th} member of the Gth generation of DE
$trial_i^{G+1}$	trial vector for i^{th} member of the $(G+1)^{th}$ generation of DE
F	Amplification factor of DE
CR	the crossover probability of DE
D	number of optimization parameters/dimension of a problem
p_{best}^i	best position i^{th} particle has ever encountered in PSO
g_{best}	Best particle of the whole population in PSO
v^i	Velocity of the ith particle in PSO
x^i	Position of the ith particle in PSO
c_1	The cognitive learning factor in PSO
c_2	Social learning factor in PSO
$B\left(r_{ij}\right)$	attractiveness between two fireflies X_i and X_j at a distance r_{ij} in FA
A_c	Light absorption coefficient of Firefly algorithm
St	Step factor of Firefly algorithm
f_i	Frequency of the ith bat in BA
x_i^t	Position
v_i^t	Velocity of ith bat in t^{th} step in BA
A^t	Average loudness of all the bats in t^{th} step in BA
η	Difference between e* and e_min
η'	Average η obtained by an algorithm in a dynamic environment
p	penalty value
R	Feasible region

Spectrum Sensing by Energy Detection

Spectrum sensing is done to determine whether the primary user (PU) is using the spectrum or not at a particular time instant. In case the PU is absent, a secondary user is allowed to opportunistically use the spectrum and thus enhance the spectrum utilization. Spectrum sensing can thus be modeled as a binary hypothesis problem where the null hypothesis (H$_0$) and the alternative hypothesis (H$_1$) are given as follows:

H$_0$: PU is absent
H$_1$: PU is in operation

Let at the nth time instant, $y(n)$ be the signal received by the Secondary User (SU) system; $u(n)$ be an independent identically distributed (iid) additive white Gaussian noise (AWGN) with mean zero and variance σ_u^2; $s(n)$ be the PU signal which is an iid random signal with mean zero and variance σ_s^2.

When PU is not transmitting signal, only the AWGN noise is present in the channel. So the signal received at the secondary receiver for H$_0$ is given as

$$y(n) = u(n) \tag{1}$$

Again, when PU is transmitting signal through the channel, both AWGN noise and PU signal are present. Hence, the signal received at the secondary receiver for H$_1$ is given as

$$y(n) = s(n) + u(n) \tag{2}$$

In such hypothesis testing problems, a test-statistic is first calculated from finite set of received signal samples. This test statistic is then compared with a suitably chosen threshold to make a decision in favour of any of the two hypotheses. The key design issues are therefore to select a suitable test statistic and to set a proper detection threshold.

In energy-based spectrum sensing, the test statistics T is calculated by measuring the total energy of the M samples of the received signal y(n). The decision rule can then be stated as

$$\text{decide for} \begin{cases} H_0, & \text{if } T < \epsilon \\ H_1, & \text{if } T \geq \epsilon \end{cases} \tag{3}$$

where, ϵ is the sensing threshold which can be determined based on performance criteria and T is the test statistic of the energy detector as mentioned before and is calculated as

$$T(y) = \sum_{n=1}^{M} |y(n)|^2 \tag{4}$$

To measure the performance of any spectrum sensing technique, two important metrics are used which measure the probabilities of two different kinds of sensing error, namely the probability of false alarm (P_{fa}) and probability of missed detection (P_m). Probability of false alarm is the probability of declaring H_1 when H_0 is true i.e. $P_{(fa)} = P(T \geq \varepsilon \mid H_0)$ and probability of miss detection is the probability of declaring H_0 when H_1 is true i.e. $P_m = P\left(T \langle \varepsilon \mid H_1\right)$. In other words, the probability that the presence of primary signal is detected when PU is actually absent is called probability of false alarm (P_{fa}) and the probability that primary signal is not detected when PU is actually present is called probability of missed detection (P_m). In terms of the complementary error function, erfc(.) the above probabilities can be analytically calculated as (Joshi, Popescu & Dobre, 2011)

$$P_{(fa)}\left[\varepsilon(n)\right] = \Pr\left[\left(T(y) > \varepsilon(n)\right) \mid H_0\right] = \frac{1}{2} erfc\left[\frac{(\varepsilon(n) - M\sigma_u^2)}{(2\sigma^2 \sqrt{m})}\right] \tag{5}$$

$$P_m = 1 - \frac{1}{2} erfc\left[\frac{\varepsilon(n) - M\sigma^2}{2\sigma^2 \sqrt{M}}\right] \tag{6}$$

$$\sigma^2 = \sigma_s^2 + \sigma_u^2 \tag{7}$$

where, σ^2 is the variance of the received signal $y(n)$.

To calculate P_{fa} and P_m signal to noise ratio (SNR) is required which is given by $\gamma = \sigma_s^2 / \sigma_u^2$. The noise variance σ_u^2 is assumed to be known beforehand (Shellhammer, 2008), may be determined experimentally (Wellens & Mähönen, 2010) or can be estimated by modelling uncontaminated PU signal as p-th order AR model along with Yule-Walker equation (Joshi, Popescu & Dobre, 2011; Paliwal, 1988). The PU power can be calculated by subtracting the noise power from the received signal power or the same can be known by the IEEE 802.22 standard (Shellhammer, 2008) and thus SNR can be calculated.

Sensing Error Minimization as a Constrained Optimization Problem

Dynamic environment arises due to background noise and interference, movements of the transmitters and users, etc. False alarm and miss-detection are functions of the detection threshold $\varepsilon(n)$. So, with changes in the environment, it is required to optimize $\varepsilon(n)$ to minimize the sensing error probabilities. For a high value of P_{fa}, the secondary user misses an opportunity to use the vacant spectrum. Again, higher the value of $\varepsilon(n)$, lesser is the P_{fa} (5). So, the high value of $\varepsilon(n)$ is ideal for the interest of the SU. But, from equation (6), if the $\varepsilon(n)$ is too high, P_m increases, that is, for high sensing threshold,

Figure 1. Generalized schematic of sensing error minimization

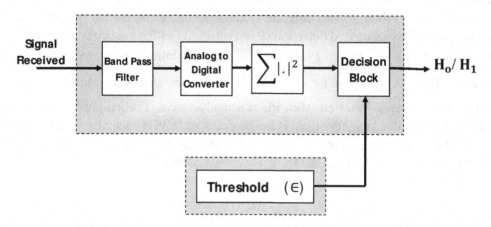

signal with low SNR cannot be detected. Thus, the optimal value of threshold $\varepsilon(n)$ must be chosen with two goals, namely,

1.   Increasing $\varepsilon(n)$ to minimize the probability of false alarm and
2.   Decreasing $\varepsilon(n)$ to minimize the probability of missed detection

The total sensing error (e) is contributed by P_{fa} and P_{m} and is given as follows

$$e\big[\varepsilon(n)\big] = (1-\delta)P_{m} + \delta P_{fa} \tag{8}$$

where, δ is defined as a weighting parameter, which determines the relative contribution of P_{fa} and P_{m} to the spectrum sensing error $e\big[\varepsilon(n)\big]$. δ is supplied by the designer.

Thus, spectrum sensing error minimization by dynamic threshold adaptation can be formulated as a constrained optimization problem, formally defined as follows

$$\underset{\varepsilon(n)}{\text{minimize}} \; e\big[\varepsilon(n)\big]$$

$$\text{subject to } P_{m}\big[\varepsilon(n)\big] \le \alpha \text{ and } P_{fa}\big[\varepsilon(n)\big] \le \beta \tag{9}$$

where α and β are maximum allowable values of P_{m} and P_{fa}, respectively.

Joshi et al. (2011) considered the sensing error minimization problem in a dynamic environment and proposed gradient descent optimization-based sensing threshold adaptation (GTA). However, the speed and accuracy of the gradient descent algorithm is highly dependent on the initial assumption of trial value of threshold and the step size μ. Repeated trial experimentations are required to find the correct values of the parameters for efficient functioning of the algorithm. Now a day, for further efficient identification of threshold parameters and to overcome the above-mentioned drawbacks, the bio-inspired and swarm-based algorithms may be applied. In Das et al. (2016), DE algorithm has been used for threshold parameter adaptation in a dynamic environment and promising result has been reported within given time constraints. With an inspiration, from that work, this chapter is a humble effort on application and analysis of the number of nature inspired algorithm to cater the need of parameter identification of dynamic, time critical sensing error minimization problem.

Brief Description on Nature Inspired Optimization Technique

The increasing complexity of the real-world problems leads to a known fact that these problems cannot be solved optimally due to some inherent constraints of the classical optimization problem. Above all multi-modality, differentiability, hybridization and high dimensionality are the generic characteristics of such problems which makes it difficult to locate the precise solution. These have motivated the researchers to focus on mainly two main important aspects of computation: The first one is based on Darwin's principle of survivor. Genetic Algorithm (Holland, 1975; Goldberg, 1989), and Differential Evolution (Storn et al., 1995) are the two important members of this class of algorithm. The common features of these algorithms are crossover, mutation and selection operations. The second class of computation is based on swarm-based computation where a swarm of particles or entities search for the optimal solutions simultaneously. Among many widely used members of this family, here we will present a brief review on particle swarm optimization (PSO), firefly and bat algorithm. In recent years, many modifications of these algorithms are pursued in search of betterment of finding a more optimistic solution. They can be equally applied to any problem from any domain to find the solution with varied complexities. However, in this chapter, we have only considered five fundamental representative algorithms combining both the classes to provide a proof of the fact that bio-inspired and swarm-based algorithms provides promising results with dynamic constrained real time spectrum sensing problem. As an extension of the work the modified algorithms may be developed and applied at any phase of the application. The brief description of each of this algorithm will be discussed below.

Genetic Algorithm

Genetic algorithm (Holland, 1992; Goldberg, 1989) is based on the natural principle of "survival of the fittest". It constitutes of a number of steps like initial population generation, fitness evaluation, parent selection, crossover, and, mutation. In genetic algorithm, solutions are generated iteratively with an expectation that successive iteration will produce better solutions to the problem.

The search process starts with the generation of a set of initial population of solutions, each entitled as a chromosome. Each chromosome represents some characteristics of the solution to the problem. In the next step called fitness evolution or fitness assessment, the characteristics of the solutions are evaluated. In parent selection step, the set of chromosomes having promising fitness value is selected to form a set called mating pool for subsequent genetic operations to create new solutions. There are a number of alternative processes to carry out parent selection. This may be done either by Roulette Wheel selection or Tournament selection strategy. The genetic operation consists of two steps, called crossover and mutation. The crossover operation mimics the genetic crossover process that occurs during the formation of new individual called offspring in living beings and the mutation operation mimics the mutation process. Now the fitness values of these new chromosomes developed from the genetic operations are evaluated. The best solutions are selected to form a new set of parents and they will participate in the parent selection to form the mating pool for the next iteration of genetic operation. Successive generations consist of improved solutions. In Figure 2 the block diagram of the genetic algorithm cycle is illustrated.

Differential Evolution

DE (Storn & Price, 1997) is a comparatively newer bio-inspired optimization algorithm. It constitutes the steps like mutation, crossover and selection. In Figure 3, the block diagram of the differential evolution cycle is illustrated. Here, trial vectors are generated using mutation and crossover operators and selection operator is used to determine the vectors that form the next generation. The D numbers of optimization parameters are encoded to form a D-dimensional solution called an individual. The search process starts with the formation of the initial population consisting of individuals chosen randomly with uniform distribution in the search space denoted by x_i^G, $i = 1, 2, 3, .., N$. where N is the population size and G denotes the generation number. Mutation operator is used to generate a mutant vector for each individual as follows

Figure 2. Block Diagram of Genetic Algorithm Cycle

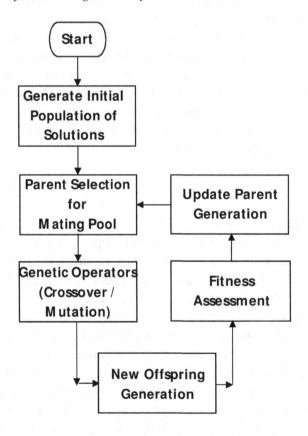

$$m_i^G = x_{r_1}^G + F * \left(x_{r_2}^G - x_{r_3}^G \right) \tag{10}$$

where $x_{r_1}^G, x_{r_2}^G$ and $x_{r_3}^G$ are different, $F \in [0,2]$ is the amplification factor.

In crossover step, the trial vector is generated as follows,

$$trial_{ij}^{G+1} = \begin{cases} x_{ij}^G, & rand(j) \le CR \, or \, j = randn(i) \\ m_{ij}^G, & rand(j) > CR \, and \, j \ne randn(i) \end{cases} \tag{11}$$

where $j = 1,2,\dots D$, $randn(i) \in \{1,2,\dots D\}$ is a random integer, $rand(j) \in [0,1]$ is a random number and $CR \in [0,1]$ is the crossover probability. Finally, the selection operator compares the fitness values of the target vector and the trial vector and selects one of them into the next generation as follows (for a minimization problem)

$$x_i^{G+1} = \begin{cases} trial_i^{G+1}, & f\left(trial_i^{G+1}\right) < f\left(x_i^G\right) \\ x_i^G, & f\left(trial_i^{G+1}\right) \ge f\left(x_i^G\right) \end{cases} \tag{12}$$

Among the N solutions of the new generation, the one having the best fitness value is the output of that generation. This process repeats iteratively in search of a better solution considering this new generation as the parent generation on which the mutation, crossover and selection operators act again in the same way.

Particle Swarm Optimization

Particle swarm optimization (Shi, 2001; Kennedy, 2011) is one of the popular swarm intelligence-based algorithm which is inspired by social cognizance and the collective behaviour of colonies. The algorithm exploits the behaviour of particles present in the population and search for the solution within the decision space. Each particle updates its velocity based on its own experience and knowledge of the best individuals in the group. Each particle also remembers the best position it has ever encountered $\left(p_{best}^i \right)$.

Figure 3. Block Diagram of Differential Evolution Algorithm Cycle

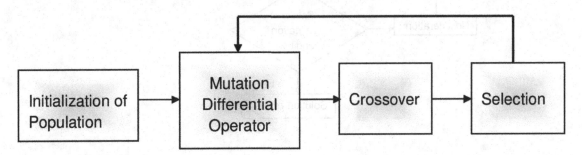

and also all the individual in the population keep track of the position of the best performer in the whole population $\left(g_{best}\right)$. Subsequently the position of each of the particles is updated. In initial stage, the position of the ith particle is randomly updated and subsequently the velocity $\left(v^i\right)$ and position $\left(x^i\right)$ are updated according to rules given for i[th] particle in G[th] generation

$$v^i\left(t\right) = w \times v^i\left(t-1\right) + c_1 \times rand \times \left(p^i_{best} - x^i\right) + c_2 \times rand \times \left(g_{best} - x^i\right) \tag{13}$$

$$x^i\left(t\right) = x^i\left(t-1\right) + v^i\left(t\right) \tag{14}$$

where c_1, the cognitive learning factor, represents the attraction of a particle toward its own success $\left(p^i_{best}\right)$ and c_2, social learning factor, represents the attraction of a particle toward the swarm's best position $\left(g_{best}\right)$, and w is the inertia weight.

The optimal solution is identified when the convergence criterion is reached. In Figure 4 the block diagram of PSO cycle is illustrated.

Figure 4. Block Diagram of Particle Swarm Optimization Algorithm Cycle

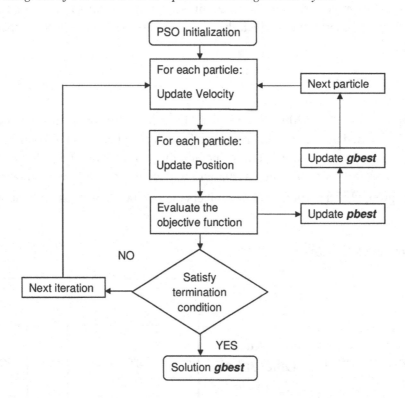

Firefly Algorithm

The firefly algorithm (Yang, 2008; Fister, Yang & Brest, 2013) is also a promising population-based stochastic search algorithm which simulates the flashing and communication behaviour of fireflies. Each member of the population is a firefly in the search space which controls its improvement in terms of its brightness. Brighter firefly is more promising in finding the solution and it attracts other fireflies, which are measured in terms of their fitness values. As the distance between fireflies increases, the attractiveness decreases exponentially because of the light absorption of the medium.

Let X_i be the ith firefly in the population, where i = 1, 2, . . ., N and N is the population size. The attractiveness between two fireflies X_i and X_j can be calculated as follows

$$B\left(r_{ij}\right) = B_0 e^{-A_c r_{ij}^2} \tag{15}$$

$$r_{ij} = \left\|X_i - X_j\right\| = \sqrt{\sum_{d=1}^{D}\left(x_{id} - x_{jd}\right)^2} \tag{16}$$

where d = 1, 2, ..., D, D is the problem dimension; r_{ij} is the distance between X_i and X_j; x_{id} and x_{jd} are the dth dimension of X_i and X_j, respectively. Further, the parameter B_0 denotes the attractiveness at the distance r = 0, and A_c is the light absorption coefficient.

Each firefly X_i is compared with all other fireflies X_j where j = 1, 2, ..., N and $j \neq i$. If X_j is brighter (better) than X_i, X_i will be attracted to and move toward X_j. The movement of X_i .can be defined by

$$x_{id}\left(t+1\right) = x_{id}\left(t\right) + B_0 e^{-A_c r_{ij}^2}\left(x_{jd}\left(t\right) - x_{jd}\left(t\right)\right) + St * r_i \tag{17}$$

where r_i is a random value uniformly distributed in the range[-0.5,0.5] and $St \in \left[0,1\right]$ is the step factor. In Figure 5 the block diagram of firefly algorithm cycle is represented.

Bat Algorithm

Bat Algorithm (Yang, 2010) is another popular and recently proposed algorithm in the family of meta-heuristic algorithms and was proposed by Yang. The echolocation behaviour of microbat is simulated in this algorithm to search the optimal solution. The echolocation, in the real world, exists only a few thousandths of a second (up to about 8–10 ms) and a frequency is in the region of 25–150 kHz, corresponding to the wavelengths of 2–14 mm in the air. The echolocation is the natural property of microbats, used to search its prey. In the search period, the bats emit short pulses and as and when the presence of prey is sensed, the pulse emission rate is increased and the frequency is tuned up.

Figure 5. Block Diagram of Firefly Algorithm Cycle

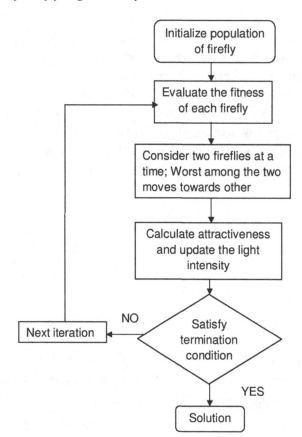

In the process of frequency tuning the wavelength of echolocation gets changed and accuracy of search increases. This property of echolocation is simulated in bat algorithm as follows,

1.   The echolocation in the bat algorithm is used to sense the distance between the food source and background barriers.
2.   The random fly of bat is simulated with velocity v_i at position x_i with a fixed frequency f_{min} varying wavelength λ and loudness A_0. The wavelength of the emitted pulse and the rate of pulse emission $r\epsilon[0,1]$ can be automatically adjusted, depending on the proximity of their target.
3.   The loudness is also varied in many ways starting from a large (positive) constant A_0 to a minimum constant value A_{min}.

Based on the above properties, the basic bat algorithm is described as follows:

The position of each bat corresponds to a predicted solution. At t^{th} step, the position x_i^t and velocity v_i^t of ith bat is updated in subsequent iterations and they are calculated using the following equations,

$$f_i = f_{min} + \left(f_{max} - f_{min}\right)r \qquad (18)$$

$$v_i^t = v_i^{t-1} + \left(x_i^{t-1} - x^*\right)f_i \tag{19}$$

$$x_i^t = x_i^{t-1} + v_i^t \tag{19a}$$

where $r\varepsilon[0,1]$ is a random vector drawn from a uniform distribution and x* is the current global best location(solution) found so far, which is located after comparing all the solutions among all the n bats at the current iteration.

It is also observed that bat performs both local and global search by switching from one search domain to other and vice-versa. The local search is a random walk and it is given as

$$x_{new}^t = x_{old}^{t-1} + rA^t \tag{20}$$

Where, the random number r is drawn from $[-1, 1]$, and A^t is the average loudness of all the bats in this step. The block diagram of bat algorithm cycle is illustrated in Figure 6.

Figure 6. Block Diagram of Bat Algorithm Cycle

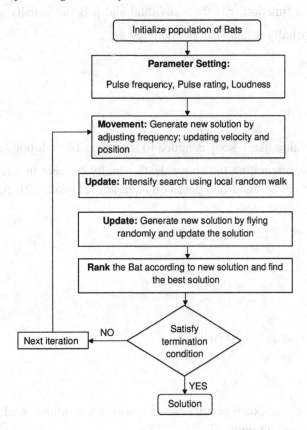

PROPOSED THRESHOLD ADAPTATION FOR SENSING ERROR MINIMIZATION: APPLICATION OF NATURE INSPIRED OPTIMIZATION TECHNIQUE

Spectrum sensing is an important aspect of the cognitive radio environment where the presence of licensed user (PU) is to be determined by the secondary at a particular time instant. In the previous few sections the importance of sensing error minimization problem has been established and also the problem has been formulated as a constrained optimization problem. In this section, we develop a generic method and stepwise apply the bio-inspired and swarm-based optimization algorithm for sensing error minimization and threshold adaptation.

Generic Approach for Integration of Death Penalty Concept With Optimization Algorithms for Constrained Handling

The death penalty is a simple constraint handling method (Yeniay, 2005). This approach is integrated with the existing five optimization methods separately for constraint handling and we propose death penalty based nature inspired optimization methods. Here, an evaluation function is defined as

$$eval(x) = f(x) + p \tag{21}$$

where, $f(x)$ is the fitness function, x is the individual and p is the penalty value. If R denotes the feasible region, then the penalty value p can be modeled as,

$$p = \begin{cases} 0 & if\ x \in R \\ +\infty & otherwise \end{cases} \tag{22}$$

Thus, a large penalty value like $(+\infty)$ is added to the infeasible solutions so that they are rejected during the selection. Now, integrating the above death penalty concept in sensing error minimization problem, equation (8) and (9) are modified based on equation (21) and (22) and the final equations are given as,

$$eval(\varepsilon(n)) = e[\varepsilon(n)] + p \tag{23}$$

where

$$p = \begin{cases} 0 & if\ P_m[\epsilon(n)] \leq \alpha\ and\ P_{fa}[\varepsilon(n)] \leq \beta \\ +\infty & otherwise \end{cases} \tag{24}$$

The generic approach of the death penalty-based constraint handling mechanism for sensing error minimization problem is given in Figure 7.

Figure 7. Schematic of constrained sensing error minimization using threshold adaptation

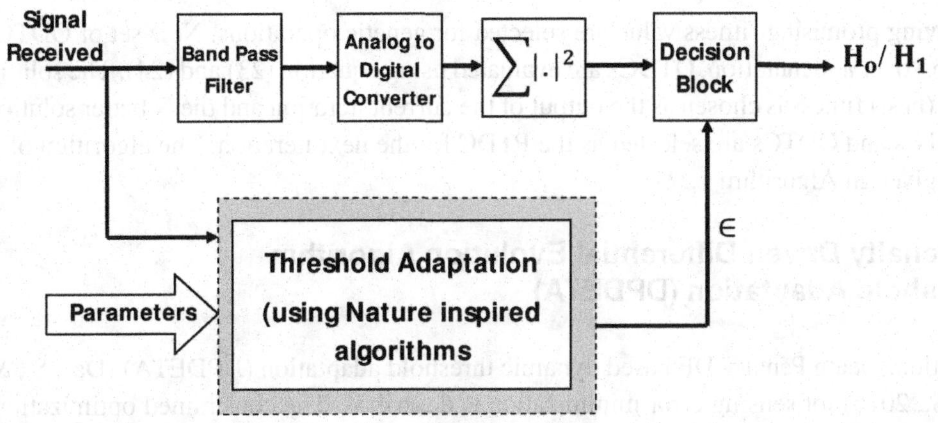

Based on above approach, five death penalty based nature inspired optimization algorithm is presented in this section and in the result section their merits and demerits will be evaluated. The algorithms are given as follows,

1. Death Penalty driven Genetic Algorithm for Threshold Adaptation (DPGATA)
2. Death Penalty driven Differential Evolution Algorithm for Threshold Adaptation (DPDETA) (Das & Mukhopadhyay, 2016)
3. Death Penalty driven Particle Swarm Optimization Algorithm for Threshold Adaptation (DPPSOTA)
4. Death Penalty driven Firefly Algorithm for Threshold Adaptation (DPFATA)
5. Death Penalty driven Bat Algorithm for Threshold Adaptation (DPBATA)

Out of these five algorithms, one has already been reported and in this chapter the other four algorithms along with the previously reported algorithm is discussed.

The performance of the above algorithms is compared to those of the previously reported GTA (Joshi, Popescu & Dobre, 2011) and DPDETA (Das & Mukhopadhyay, 2016).

Death Penalty Driven Genetic Algorithm for Threshold Adaptation (DPGATA)

Death Penalty GA based dynamic threshold adaptation (DPGATA) for sensing error minimization process is the modification of GA for constraint handling and its application on threshold adaptation. In the proposed algorithm, the chromosomes are essentially a set of N number of predicted detection thresholds $\varepsilon(n)$ encoded as m bit binary numbers and they are called as detection threshold chromosome (DTC).

These chromosomes may be in parent set or offspring set and they are termed as parent detection threshold chromosome (PDTC) and offspring detection threshold chromosome (ODTC), respectively. In the initialization step, the populations of chromosomes are randomly predicted in the search space that is in the range of possible values of operating threshold. In the fitness assessment step, the fitness of each individual PDTC is evaluated based on equation (17) and (18).

Lower the value of $eval\left(\varepsilon\left(n\right)\right)$ better is the solution and vice versa. In Parent Selection step, the PDTCs having promising fitness value are selected for genetic operations. New set of ODTC is generated by crossover and mutation. OTDCs are evaluated using equation (23) and (24). The solution having the lowest (best) fitness is chosen as the output of the current iteration and the N better solutions among all the PDTCs and ODTCs are selected as the PTDC for the next iteration. The algorithm of DPGATA scheme is given in Algorithm 1.

Death Penalty Driven Differential Evolution Algorithm for Threshold Adaptation (DPDETA)

In this section, Death Penalty DE based dynamic threshold adaptation (DPDETA) (Das, S., & Mukhopadhyay, S., 2016) for sensing error minimization is described. The constrained optimization problem is solved according to death penalty concept integrated with DE. Here, each individual in a population is actually a predicted detection threshold (ε) called as a detection threshold individual (DTI). In the initialization step, a population consisting of N number of initial DTI is randomly predicted with uniform probability in the range of possible values of operating threshold. The population is generated according to the guidelines of DE. Finally, the selection process is updated by integrating the death penalty concept and the new generation is selected.

To integrate the above death penalty technique into DE, the selection operator of the equation (12) is modified as

$$x_i^{G+1} = \begin{cases} trial_i^{G+1} & eval\left(trial_i^{G+1}\right) < eval\left(x_i^G\right) \\ x_i^G & eval\left(ttrial_i^{G+1}\right) \geq eval\left(x_i^G\right) \end{cases} \tag{25}$$

where $\epsilon\left(n\right) = x_i^G$.

Thus the selection operator rejects the infeasible solutions and handles the constraints. The algorithm of DPDETA scheme is given in Algorithm 2.

Death Penalty Driven Particle Swarm Optimization Algorithm for Threshold Adaptation (DPPSOTA)

In this section, sensing error minimisation using Death Penalty PSO based threshold adaptation is described. First death penalty constraint handling technique is integrated with PSO. In DPPSOTA, each particle position represents a predicted detection threshold ($\varepsilon\left(n\right)$). The algorithm is initialized by randomly predicting particle positions in the range of possible operating threshold values. The quality of an individual particle position is determined by its fitness evaluated using equations (23) and (24). Thus as per equations (23) and (24), the p_{best} $\left(\varepsilon pbest^i\right)$ of the ith particle and g_{best} $\left(\varepsilon gbest\right)$ are determined and the infeasible solutions are automatically rejected due to their large fitness values. Subsequently the particle positions are updated using equations (13) and (14). The algorithm of DPPSOTA scheme is given in Algorithm 3.

Algorithm 1. Death Penalty GA based threshold adaptation (DPGATA)

```
1. Input parameter: α,β,δ,N , max_gen;
```

2. Estimate the noise variance $\left(\sigma_u^2\right)$. (Paliwal,1988)

3. Measure the variance σ^2 of the received signal y(n)

4. Calculate primary user signal variance $\left(\sigma_s^2\right)$. using (7)

5. Initialize parent generation: Randomly predict N number of threshold values (PDTC) [$\in \left(n\right)_i$, i = 1,2, . ., N], in the search domain determined from error profile.

6. Fitness assessment of Parent Generation

For i = 1 to N do

Calculate P_m **and** P_{fa} **using (5), (6)**

Evaluate $\in \left(n\right)_i$ of initial parent generation using (23) and (24)

End for

7. Select the solution having best (minimum) fitness

8. Set t = 0

9. While (t≤ max_gen) do

  t = t + 1

  Mating Pool Generation by tournament selection:

For i = 1 to N do

  Select two parent solutions randomly

  Select the solution having the better fitness value to the

 mating pool

End For

  Genetic operations: formation of offspring from Mating pool solutions:

  Crossover

For (k = 1; k ≤ N; k = k + 2) do

 Select k^{th} and $(k+1)^{th}$ solutions from Parent generation

 Select a random bit position b_r

 Swap between the portions of the selected chromosomes after

  random bit (b_r) to form 2 new offspring

End For

  Mutation: Invert a randomly selected bit in each offspring solution

Fitness assessment of offspring: Calculate P_m and P_{fa} using (5), (6) for each offspring solution

  Evaluate each solution of offspring generation using (23) and (24)

Rearrange all solutions of Parent and Offspring Generation in descending order of fitness (ascending order of fitness value) in a single list

  Update Parent Generation with the best N solutions

  Output: the PDTC having the best (minimum) fitness as the optimal

threshold $\varepsilon^* = \varepsilon\left(t\right)$. **End while.**

Algorithm 2. Death Penalty driven Differential Evolution Algorithm for threshold adaptation (DPDETA)

1. Input parameter: α, β, δ, N , max_gen;
2. Estimate the noise variance $\left(\sigma_u^2\right)$. (Paliwal,1988)
3. Measure the variance σ^2 of the received signal y(n)
4. Calculate primary user signal variance $\left(\sigma_s^2\right)$ using (7)
5. Generate N number of random solutions DTI in the search domain determined from error profile
6. **Calculate** P_m **and** P_{fa} **using (5), (6)**

If $P_m \geq \alpha$ **or** $P_{fa} \geq \beta$

p $= +\infty$

else

 p = 0;

End If

7. Evaluate initial parent generation using equations (23) and (24)

While (number of iteration $\leq$ max_gen) do

Generate mutant vector using (10)

Generate trial vector using (11)

Calculate P_{fa} **and** P_m **using (5), (6) for trial vector**

If $P_m \geq \alpha$ **or** $P_{fa} \geq \beta$

p $= +\infty$;

else

p = 0;

End If

Evaluate trial vector using (23) and (24)

Select between trial vector or target vector using (25) to form

 new Generation

End while

Output the DTI having the minimum (best) fitness as the optimal threshold

$\varepsilon^* = \varepsilon\left(n\right)$

Death Penalty Driven Firefly Algorithm for Threshold Adaptation (DPFATA)

Here, sensing error minimization is done using death penalty driven Firefly Algorithm. The algorithm is initialized by predicting randomly firefly positions which are the threshold values (ε) for spectrum sensing. The random solutions are predicted in the range of the possible threshold values. The fitness is evaluated using equations (23) and (24) to incorporate the death penalty technique. Thus, the infeasible solutions (threshold (ε)) having large values are rejected. The firefly's positions are updated by equations (15), (16) and (17). The algorithm of DPFATA scheme is given in Algorithm 4.

Algorithm 3. Death Penalty driven Particle Swarm Optimization Algorithm for threshold adaptation (DPPSOTA)

1. Input parameter: α, β, δ, N , max_gen;
2. Estimate the noise variance (σ_u^2) (Paliwal,1988)
3. Measure the variance σ^2 of the received signal y(n)
4. Calculate primary user signal variance (σ_s^2) using (7)
5. Generate N number of particles in the search domain determined from error profile
6. Calculate P_m and P_{fa} using (5), (6)
If $P_m \geq \alpha$ or $P_{fa} \geq \beta$
p = $+\infty$;
else
 p = 0;
End If
7. Evaluate initial set of particles using equations (23) and (24)
While (t $\leq$ max_gen) do
For i=1 to N
 If $eval\left(\epsilon^i\left(t\right)\right) < eval(\epsilon pbest^i)$ **Then**
   $\epsilon pbest^i = \epsilon^i\left(t\right)$
End If
If $eval(\epsilon pbest^i) < eval\left(\epsilon gbest\right)$ **Then**
   $\epsilon gbest = \epsilon pbest^i$
  End If
  End For
For i=1 to N
 Update velocity and position $\left(\epsilon^i\left(t\right)\right)$. using equation (13) and (14)
End For
End while
Output the global best particle as the optimal threshold $\varepsilon^* = \varepsilon\left(t\right)$;

Death Penalty Driven Bat Algorithm for Threshold Adaptation (DPBATA)

In DPBATA, the death penalty technique is incorporated with Bat algorithm and error minimization is done which is described as follows. The position of a bat corresponds to a solution. Here, each solution is a detection threshold (ϵ). The optimal detection threshold for minimum error is obtained using Death Penalty driven Bat algorithm. At the beginning, N number of bats are randomly predicted, each corresponding to a solution, which are in turn detection thresholds (ε) in the range of possible threshold values. Each position is evaluated using equations (23) and (24) to incorporate the death penalty technique so that the infeasible solutions have a large fitness value and are treated as worse solutions to be rejected during selection. The positions of bats are updated using equations (18), (19) and (20).

Algorithm 4. Death Penalty driven Firefly Algorithm for threshold adaptation (DPFATA)

1. Input parameter: α, β, δ, N, max_gen;

2. Estimate the noise variance (σ_u^2) (Paliwal,1988)

3. Measure the variance σ^2 of the received signal y(n)

4. Calculate primary user signal variance $\left(\sigma_s^2\right)$ using (7)

5. Generate N number of fireflies in the search domain determined from error profile

6. Calculate P_m **and** P_{fa} **using (5), (6)**

If $P_m \geq \alpha$ **or** $P_{fa} \geq \beta$

p $= +\infty$;

else

 p = 0;

End If

7. Evaluate light intensity I of the fireflies using equations (23) and (24)

While (t $\leq$ max_gen) do

For i=1 to N

  For j=1 to N

  If $eval(\varepsilon^j\left(t\right)) < eval(\varepsilon^i)$ **Then**

The ith firefly will be attracted towards jth firefly. The attractiveness and movement of the firefly will be calculated as per equations (15), (16) and (17).

  End If

  End For

    End For

End While.

Rank the fireflies and find the best firefly as the optimal threshold $\varepsilon^* = \varepsilon\left(t\right)$.

The algorithm of DPFATA scheme is given in Algorithm 5.

In the experimental result section, of this chapter all the above-mentioned algorithms will be analyzed along with its comparative study.

EXPERIMENTAL RESULTS

The authors have performed extensive simulations to test the algorithms namely DPGATA, DPPSOTA, DPBATA and DPFATA and their performances are compared with that of GTA (Joshi, D. R., Popescu, D. C., & Dobre, O. A., 2011) and DPDETA (Das & Mukhopadhyay, 2016).

The algorithms were implemented in Matlab 8.1.0.604 (R2013a). To demonstrate the effectiveness of the algorithms in dynamic environment, the algorithms were simulated by changing the SNR$\left(\gamma\right)$ of

Algorithm 5. Death Penalty driven Bat Algorithm for threshold adaptation (DPBATA)

1. Input parameter: α, β, δ, N, max_gen;
2. Estimate the noise variance (σ_u^2) (Paliwal,1988)
3. Measure the variance σ^2 of the received signal y(n)
4. Calculate primary user signal variance (σ_s^2) using (7)
5. Initialize N number of Bats in the search domain determined from error profile and define pulse frequency f_i of all the bats using (18) where, i=1,2,…, N
6. **Calculate** P_m **and** P_{fa} **using (5), (6)**

If $P_m \geq \alpha$ **or** $P_{fa} \geq \beta$.

p = +∞;

else

p = 0;

End If

7. Initialize pulse rate r and loudness A.

While (t ≤ max_gen) do

Generate new solution by adjusting frequency and update the
 Velocity and threshold value using equations (19) and (20).

If(rand > r)

 Select a threshold among the best threshold

Generate a local threshold value around the selected best threshold

End if

Generate a new solution by flying randomly

If(rand < A & $eval\left(\varepsilon^i\right) < eval\left(\varepsilon^*\right)$

 Accept the new threshold

End If

End While

Rank the bats and find the best bat as the optimal threshold $\varepsilon^* = \varepsilon\left(t\right)$

the received PU signal as -3dB, -1dB, 0dB, and 3dB respectively at regular intervals for $\delta = 0.25, 0.5$ and 0.75 at $\alpha = 0.1$ and $\beta = 0.2$.

First, the lowest attainable sensing error (e^*) for $\gamma = -3dB, -1dB, 0dB, 3dB$ at $\delta = 0.25, 0.5$ and 0.75 are analytically calculated using equation (8) for a range of threshold values. Figure 8 (a), and (b) respectively shows the sensing error profile for $\gamma = -3dB, -1dB, 0dB, 3dB$ at $\delta = 0.5$ and the sensing error profile for $\delta = 0.25, 0.5$ and 0.75 at $\gamma = 0dB$, as a function of threshold. From these analytical plots, we can find the lowest achievable sensing error and the threshold at which the lowest error is achieved for each of the scenarios. Table 2 illustrates the lowest sensing error value (e^*) and the corresponding threshold value in each scenario. To compare the performance of the algorithms, the lowest sensing error and the corresponding optimal threshold obtained by experiment are compared to the values of Table 2.

Table 2. The lowest attainable sensing error ($e_{\min}$) value and the corresponding threshold value $\left(\varepsilon\right)$ for the dynamic scenarios

δ	δ = 0.25		δ = 0.5		δ = 0.75	
SNR(dB)	ϵ	$e*$	ϵ	$e*$	ϵ	$e*$
-3	149.45	0.0508	156.1	0.0531	162.25	0.0388
-1	162.1	0.0111	167.05	0.011	171.7	0.0078
0	169.1	0.0038	173.45	0.0036	177.6	0.0025
3	191.95	3.23E-05	195.2	2.82E-05	198.35	1.8E-05

We define deviation (η) as the difference of minimum error ($e_{\min}$) obtained by an algorithm from the achievable minimum error (e^*) in that particular environmental scenario. η gives a measure of its accuracy in that scenario. Again, η' is defined as the average η obtained by an algorithm over all the scenarios performing in the changing environment. η' is a metric which indicates the accuracy measure of the algorithm performing in the dynamic environment. These are given as

$$\eta = abs\left(e_{\min} - e^*\right) \tag{26}$$

$$\eta' = \frac{\sum_{i=1}^{E}\eta_i}{E} \tag{27}$$

where, abs(.) denotes the absolute difference, η_i denotes deviation η of the algorithm in the ith scenario and E is the total number of dynamic environmental scenarios.

For gradient descend based threshold adaptation algorithm (GTA) (Joshi, Popescu & Dobre, 2011) the algorithm tolerance was set at 10^{-5}. GTA was tested for gradiant step size $\mu = 0.1, 0.5 \, and \, 0.9$ at $\delta = 0.5$. γ was changed after every 6,00,000 iterations as $\gamma = -3dB, -1dB, 0dB, 3dB$, respectively. The iteration wise threshold and sensing error value obtained by GTA were plotted as shown in Figure 9. The threshold and error values obtained for the same γ are different for different values of μ. Again, the difference between the obtained optimal threshold or error values is not constant. Thus performance of GTA is not robust over all the scenarios with respect to the step size μ. This is a major drawback of GTA.

Now, GTA was tested for $\delta = 0.25, 0.5$ and 0.75 keeping $\mu = 0.5$ and changing SNR as $\gamma = -3dB, -1dB, 0dB, 3dB$. The threshold and error values obtained, at every iteration are plotted as shown in Figure 10. As γ changes, after a number of iterations, the threshold and error converge to new values.

In case of each nature inspired algorithm, to eliminate the effect of randomization, 25 independent test simulations were performed for $\delta = 0.25, 0.5$ and 0.75 changing γ as $-3dB, -1dB, 0dB, 3dB$ after a fixed number of maximum generations (max_gen). Now, with changing γ. the algorithms adjust

Figure 8. (a) Sensing error profile for $\gamma = -3dB, -1dB, 0dB$ and $3dB$ at $\delta = 0.5$, (b) Sensing error profile for $\delta = 0.25, 0.5$ and 0.75 at $\gamma = 0d$

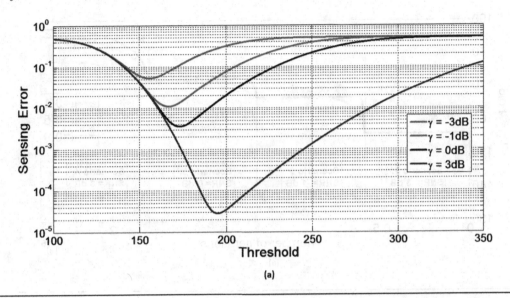

(a)

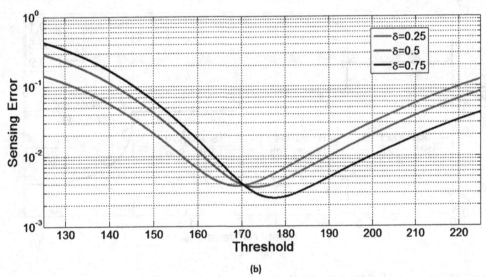

(b)

*For a more accurate representation see the electronic version.

the threshold value to minimize the sensing error. The test run for which the average deviation over all the scenarios (η') is minimum, is considered as the best run.

In DPGATA algorithm the fixed parameters are, solution width 16-bit, population size $N = 50$, and maximum generation max_gen = 200. The best threshold value and the minimum error obtained in each generation in the best of 25 runs is plotted against the generation number and shown in Figure 11. Similarly Figure 12, Figure 13, Figure 14 and Figure 15 illustrate the best threshold value and the minimum error obtained in each generation for DPDETA, DPPSOTA, DPFATA and DPBATA respec-

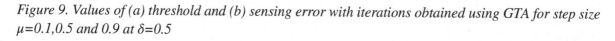

Figure 9. Values of (a) threshold and (b) sensing error with iterations obtained using GTA for step size $\mu=0.1, 0.5$ and 0.9 at $\delta=0.5$

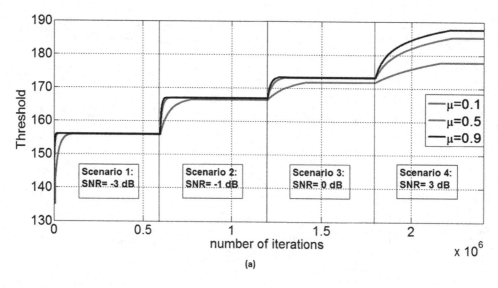

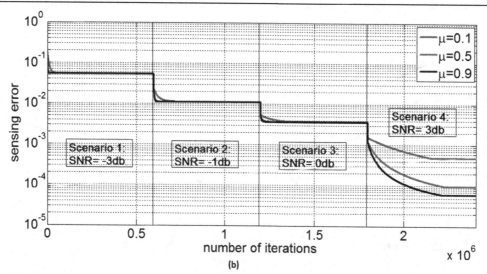

For a more accurate representation see the electronic version.

tively in the best run. The parameters fixed for DPDETA are, population size $N = 10$ and maximum generation max_gen = 200. For DPPSOTA $N = 20$ and max_gen = 200. For DPFATA $N = 50$ and max_gen = 200; and for DPBATA $N = 60$ and max_gen = 300. With the changing values of SNR, the algorithms adapt to a new threshold value with an aim to attain the minimum sensing error. The proposed algorithms are found to adapt to the new optimal threshold value very fast, which is well within the defined time constraint (Shellhammer, 2008) and can be applied in dynamic environments.

To find the average time required, for each iteration, of an algorithm, each was run for 50 times and the elapsed time is noted using Matlab. Then average time required for each run was calculated.

Figure 10. (a) Dynamic values of the threshold and (b) Dynamic values of the sensing error obtained using GTA. The SNR changes as $\gamma = -3dB, -1dB, 0dB$ and $3dB$ every 600000 iterations for different δ.

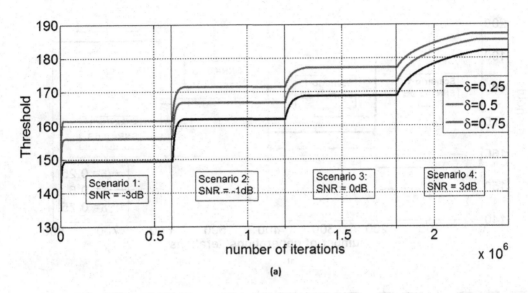

(a)

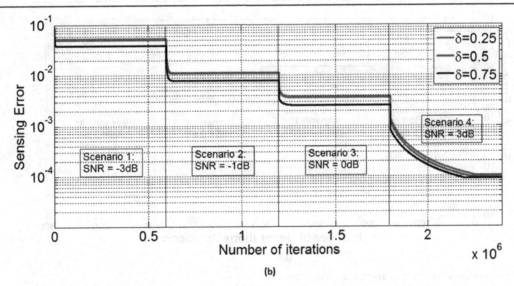

(b)

*For a more accurate representation see the electronic version.

Finally, period for each iteration/generation was calculated. This was found to be 17.773014 msec for each generation of DPGATA, 7.5374105 msec for each iteration of DPDETA; 10.31973 msec for each iteration of DPPSOTA; 7.362075833msec for each iteration of DPBATA; 21.7603093msec for each iteration of DPFATA.

Then, the convergence time (τ) is calculated by multiplying the number of generations required for convergence with average time required to execute each iteration/generation. Table 3 presents minimum sensing error (e_{min}), corresponding threshold value (ε), the threshold adaptation time (τ), deviation (

Figure 11. (a) Best threshold value obtained and (b) Minimum error obtained in each generation using DPGATA. The SNR changes as $\gamma = -3dB, -1dB, 0dB$ and $3dB$ at every 200 iterations for different δ in the best of 25 test runs

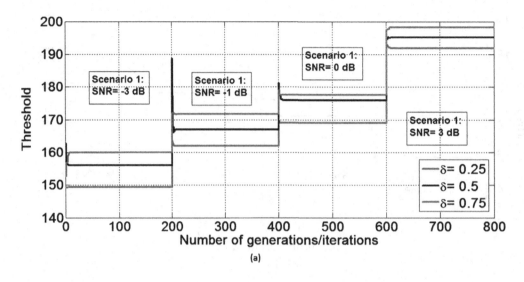

(a)

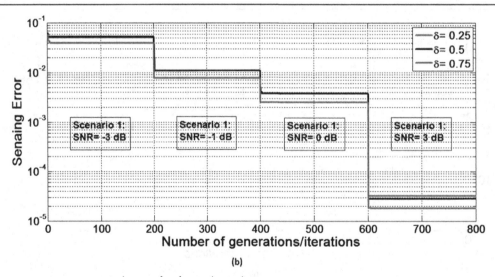

(b)

For a more accurate representation see the electronic version.

η) of $e_{\min}$ from e^*, P_{fa} and P_m obtained by GTA. Similarly, Table 4, Table 5, Table 6, Table 7 and Table 8 respectively presents the same values for DPGATA, DPDETA, DPPSOTA, DPFATA and DP-BATA in each of the scenarios in the best of the 25 test runs. P_m and P_{fa} are well within the limitations (α) and β).

In the bar graph of Figure 16, the time required by the algorithms to converge to the minimum error in each scenario is compared using bar chart. From the comparisons it can be concluded that, in most of the environmental scenarios, convergence time taken by GTA is the largest. Only for SNR=-3dB, $\delta = 0.25$ DPFATA takes more time than GTA to converge and for SNR=-3dB, $\delta = 0.75$ DPBATA

Figure 12. (a)Best threshold value obtained and (b) Minimum error obtained in each generation using DPDETA. The SNR changes as $\gamma = -3dB, -1dB, 0dB$ *and* $3dB$ *at every 200 iterations for different* δ *in the best of 25 test runs*

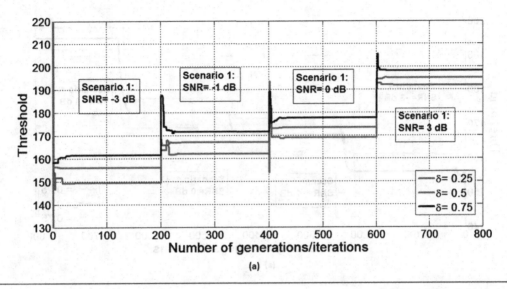

(a)

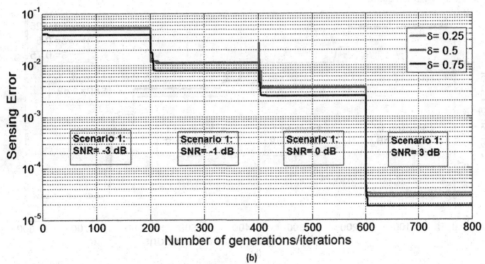

(b)

*For a more accurate representation see the electronic version.

takes greater time to converge than GTA. Again, only for SNR=-1dB, $\delta = 0.5$ and 0.75 DPBATA beats the evolutionary based algorithms in speed and is the fastest. Thus, on an average, deterministic algorithm GTA demonstrates the slowest performance.

In most of the scenarios, evolutionary algorithms namely DPGATA and DPDETA take least time to converge. The swarm-based algorithms DPPSOTA, DPFATA and DPBATA converges faster than GTA but slower than the evolutionary algorithms in most cases.

In each environmental scenario the deviation (η), of the minimum sensing error value obtained by the algorithms, from the minimum attainable sensing error is compared using bar chart in Figure 17. In

Figure 13. (a)Best threshold value obtained and (b) Minimum error obtained in each generation using DPPSOTA. The SNR changes as $\gamma = -3dB, -1dB, 0dB$ and $3dB$ at every 200 iterations for different δ in the best of 25 test runs

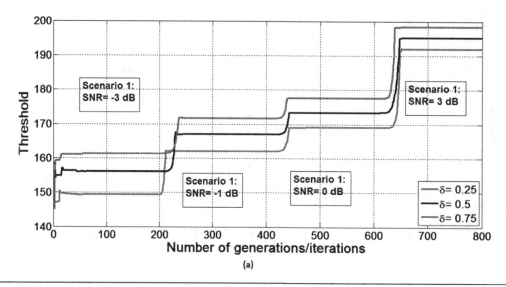

(a)

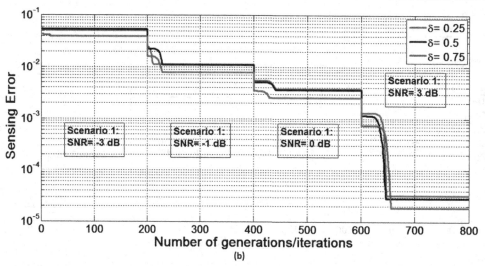

(b)

For a more accurate representation see the electronic version.

case of the GTA, η is greater in almost of the scenarios than the best run of the other algorithms. Only for SNR=-3dB, $\delta = 0.75$ most of the algorithms have higher deviation than DPFATA. For all other cases, deviation of the bio inspired algorithms is negligible compared to that of GTA. Thus, it can be concluded that the nature-inspired approaches for threshold adaptation are comparatively more promising approach than deterministic gradient descend based approaches (GTA) in most of the scenarios.

The above observations emphasizes on the fact that, for fast sensing applications in dynamic environment, nature inspired algorithms can be used very successfully.

Figure 14. (a)Best threshold value obtained and (b) Minimum error obtained in each generation using DPFATA. The SNR changes as $\gamma = -3dB, -1dB, 0dB$ and $3dB$ at every 200 iterations for different δ in the best of 25 test runs

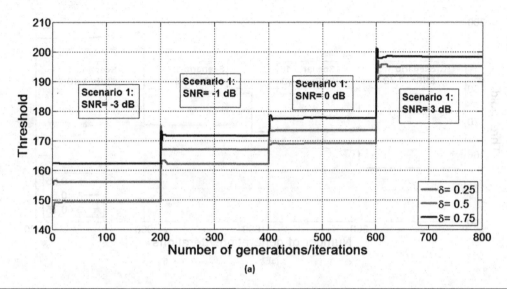

(a)

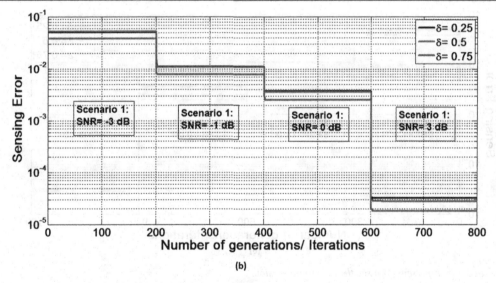

(b)

*For a more accurate representation see the electronic version.

Comparison Between Nature-Inspired Algorithms for Dynamic Threshold Adaptation Problem

Here, the performances of all the bio-inspired algorithms are compared to find the best algorithm in a given independent scenarios. Later, the scenarios are considered in a consecutive manner and the overall performance of an algorithm in dynamic environment has been reported individually. In order to compare the performance of the bio-inspired algorithms, they are ranked on the basis of the mean η obtained by them over the 25 independent test runs in each environmental scenario. Mean η over the

Figure 15. (a)Best threshold value obtained and (b) Minimum error obtained in each generation using DPBATA. The SNR changes as $\gamma = -3dB, -1dB, 0dB$ and $3dB$ at every 300 iterations for different δ in the best of 25 test runs

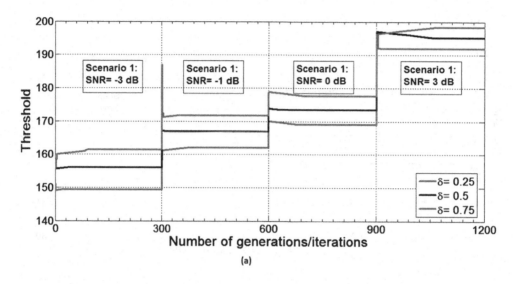

(a)

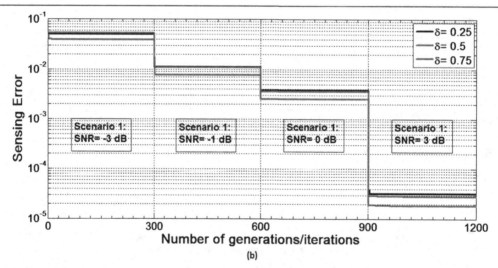

(b)

*For a more accurate representation see the electronic version.

25 runs of DPGATA, DPDETA, DPPSOTA, DPFATA and DPBATA in each scenario is shown in Table 9. In each case the algorithm that achieves the minimum average η value over all the 25 runs is marked by bold face and this indicates the best performer in that scenario. In Table 10 we have ranked the algorithms according to mean η of 25 runs obtained by them in different scenarios. Although DPFATA ranks 1 in 7 cases, it ranks 3 in remaining 5 cases. Whereas, DPDETA ranks 1 in 4 cases, 2 in 6 cases and 3 in the remaining 2 cases. The average rank of each algorithm over all the scenarios is also shown. It shows that, both DPFATA and DPDETA emerge as the better performers, followed by DPSOTA, DPGATA and DPBATA respectively.

Table 3. The minimum sensing error (e_{min}) obtained, the corresponding threshold value (ε), the time required for threshold adaptation(τ), number of generations or iterations required for convergence (ξ), deviation (η) of obtained minimum error value from the minimum attainable sensing error, P_{fa} and P_m obtained by GTA

δ	SNR (dB)	ε	e_{min}	η	P_{fa}	P_m	ξ	τ (msec)
0.25	-3	1.49E+02	0.050791	4.3608E-07	0.091	0.037	28624	585.357766
	-1	1.62E+02	0.011104	1.3993E-06	0.017	0.009	60669	1240.67462
	0	1.69E+02	0.0038	4.365E-05	0.0055	0.003	98100	2006.1346
	3	1.82E+02	1.02E-04	6.9679E-05	3.68E-04	1.32E-05	457700	9359.91648
0.5	-3	1.56E+02	0.053102	4.2662E-07	0.04005	0.0661528	25711	525.787225
	-1	1.67E+02	0.010956	1.3451E-06	0.007589	0.01432426	55250	1129.85664
	0	1.73E+02	0.003601	3.4118E-06	0.002433	0.00476955	93300	1907.97511
	3	1.85E+02	9.59E-05	6.7751E-05	1.74E-04	1.77E-05	427500	8742.32969
0.75	-3	1.61E+02	0.038879	0.00012073	0.018505	0.1	16048	328.179899
	-1	1.71E+02	0.007799	1.8022E-06	0.003285	· 0.02134026	65350	1336.40057
	0	1.77E+02	0.002516	4.6335E-06	1.08E-03	0.00683174	108700	2222.90348
	3	1.87E+02	8.85E-05	7.0302E-05	1.11E-04	2.10E-05	398700	8153.37274

Table 4. The minimum sensing error obtained (e_{min}), the corresponding threshold value (ε), the time required for threshold adaptation (τ), number of generations or iterations required for convergence (ξ), deviation (η) of obtained minimum error value from the minimum attainable sensing error, P_{fa} and P_m obtained by DPGATA

δ	SNR (db)	ε	e_{min}	η	P_{fa}	P_m	ξ	τ (msec)
0.25	-3	1.49E+02	0.050791	6.10065E-08	0.091104	0.03735301	9	159.957126
	-1	1.62E+02	0.011103	2.78095E-08	0.016916	0.00916577	6	106.638084
	0	1.69E+02	0.003756	1.23324E-08	0.005174	0.00328372	7	124.411098
	3	1.92E+02	3.23E-05	1.3109E-10	3.13E-05	3.27E-05	6	106.638084
0.5	-3	1.56E+02	0.053102	5.07455E-09	0.040186	0.06601865	7	124.411098
	-1	1.67E+02	0.010955		0.007395	0.0145157	10	177.73014
	0	1.73E+02	0.003598	3.23092E-10	0.002288	0.00490756	12	213.276168
	3	1.95E+02	2.82E-05	5.50827E-11	1.34E-05	4.29E-05	12	213.276168
0.75	-3	1.61E+02	0.03888	0.000121704	0.018514	0.09997664	5	88.86507
	-1	1.72E+02	0.007797	1.66388E-08	0.003176	0.02166053	13	231.049182
	0	1.78E+02	0.002511	6.43217E-10	9.74E-04	0.00712443	12	213.276168
	3	1.98E+02	1.82E-05	3.63767E-12	5.59E-06	5.61E-05	7	124.411098

Table 5. The minimum sensing error obtained (e_{min}), the corresponding threshold value (ε), the time required for threshold adaptation(τ), number of generations or iterations required for convergence (ξ), deviation (η) of obtained minimum error value from the minimum attainable sensing error, P_{fa} and P_m obtained by DPDETA

δ	SNR (db)	ε	e_{min}	η	P_{fa}	P_m	ξ	τ (msec)
0.25	-3	1.49E+02	0.050792	6.10169E-08	0.091558	0.03720336	19	143.2108
	-1	1.62E+02	0.011103	2.7919E-08	0.016637	0.0092583	34	256.271957
	0	1.69E+02	0.003756	1.24651E-08	0.00515	0.00329173	29	218.584905
	3	1.92E+02	3.23E-05	1.33333E-10	3.13E-05	3.26E-05	10	75.374105
0.5	-3	1.56E+02	0.053101	5.95604E-09	0.039812	0.0663904	20	150.74821
	-1	1.67E+02	0.010955	1.43309E-08	0.00743	0.01448053	30	226.122315
	0	1.73E+02	0.003598	5.51216E-10	0.002283	0.00491256	28	211.047494
	3	1.95E+02	2.82E-05	5.53533E-11	1.35E-05	4.29E-05	33	248.734547
0.75	-3	1.61E+02	0.038879	0.000120749	0.018506	0.09999741	33	248.734547
	-1	1.72E+02	0.007797	1.74429E-08	0.003176	0.02166195	35	263.809368
	0	1.78E+02	0.002511	6.61804E-10	9.76E-04	0.00711623	33	248.734547
	3	1.98E+02	1.82E-05	3.69627E-12	5.56E-06	5.62E-05	32	241.197136

Table 6. The minimum sensing error obtained (e_{min}), the corresponding threshold value (ε), the time required for threshold adaptation(τ), number of generations or iterations required for convergence (ξ), deviation (η) of obtained minimum error value from the minimum attainable sensing error, P_{fa} and P_m obtained by DPPSOTA

δ	SNR (db)	ε	e_{min}	η	P_{fa}	P_m	ξ	τ (msec)
0.25	-3	1.49E+02	0.050791	6.10169E-08	0.090659	0.03750122	46	474.70758
	-1	1.62E+02	0.011103	2.7919E-08	0.016719	0.00923083	13	134.15649
	0	1.69E+02	0.003756	1.24651E-08	0.005173	0.00328409	54	557.26542
	3	1.92E+02	3.23E-05	1.33333E-10	3.24E-05	3.23E-05	52	536.62596
0.5	-3	1.56E+02	0.053101	5.95604E-09	0.039829	0.06637359	45	464.38785
	-1	1.67E+02	0.010955	1.43309E-08	0.0074	0.0145	43	443.74839
	0	1.73E+02	0.003598	5.51216E-10	0.002278	0.00491727	42	433.42866
	3	1.95E+02	2.82E-05	5.53533E-11	1.35E-05	4.29E-05	51	526.30623
0.75	-3	1.61E+02	0.038883	0.000120749	0.0189	0.099	18	185.75514
	-1	1.72E+02	0.007797	1.74429E-08	0.0032	0.0217	45	464.38785
	0	1.78E+02	0.002511	6.61804E-10	9.76E-04	0.0071	38	392.14974
	3	1.98E+02	1.82E-05	3.69627E-12	5.56E-06	5.62E-05	112	1155.80976

Table 7. The minimum sensing error obtained (e_{min}), the corresponding threshold value (ε), the time required for threshold adaptation(τ), number of generations or iterations required for convergence (ξ), deviation (η) of obtained minimum error value from the minimum attainable sensing error, P_{fa} and P_m obtained by DPFATA

δ	SNR (db)	ε	e_min	η	P_fa	P_m	ξ	τ (msec)
0.25	-3	1.49E+02	0.050791	2.09936E-08	0.090614	0.03751617	33	718.090207
	-1	1.62E+02	0.011103	1.53883E-08	0.016667	0.00924808	13	282.884021
	0	1.69E+02	0.003756	9.72214E-09	0.005184	0.00328055	20	435.206186
	3	1.92E+02	3.23E-05	4.01591E-11	3.20E-05	3.24E-05	9	195.842784
0.5	-3	1.56E+02	0.053101	8.64608E-11	0.039856	0.06634596	10	217.603093
	-1	1.67E+02	0.010955	4.47235E-09	0.007385	0.01452568	8	174.082474
	0	1.73E+02	0.003598	4.6947E-11	0.00227	0.00492518	13	282.884021
	3	1.95E+02	2.82E-05	6.09598E-12	1.36E-05	4.28E-05	84	1827.86598
0.75	-3	1.62E+02	0.038758	0.000120795	0.016375	0.10590712	15	326.40464
	-1	1.72E+02	0.007797	2.53195E-09	0.003174	0.02166771	11	239.363402
	0	1.78E+02	0.002511	1.15315E-10	9.73E-04	0.00712506	8	174.082474
	3	1.98E+02	1.82E-05	3.7158E-13	5.56E-06	5.62E-05	87	1893.14691

Table 8. The minimum sensing error obtained (e_{min}), the corresponding threshold value (ε), the time required for threshold adaptation (τ), number of generations or iterations required for convergence (ξ), deviation (η) of obtained minimum error value from the minimum attainable sensing error, P_{fa} and P_m obtained by DPBATA

δ	SNR (db)	ε	e_min	η	P_fa	P_m	ξ	τ (msec)
0.25	-3	1.49E+02	0.050791	6.10169E-08	0.090708	0.03748481	24	176.68982
	-1	1.62E+02	0.011103	2.7919E-08	0.016715	0.00923212	76	559.517763
	0	1.69E+02	0.003756	1.24651E-08	0.005169	0.00328547	82	603.690218
	3	1.92E+02	3.23E-05	1.33333E-10	3.24E-05	3.23E-05	15	110.431137
0.5	-3	1.56E+02	0.053101	5.95604E-09	0.039817	0.06638527	43	316.569261
	-1	1.67E+02	0.010955	1.43309E-08	0.007412	0.01449778	9	66.2586825
	0	1.73E+02	0.003598	5.51216E-10	0.002275	0.00492021	36	265.03473
	3	1.95E+02	2.82E-05	5.53533E-11	1.35E-05	4.29E-05	160	1177.93213
0.75	-3	1.61E+02	0.038879	0.000120749	0.018506	0.09999818	97	714.121356
	-1	1.72E+02	0.007797	1.74429E-08	0.003174	0.0216675	6	44.172455
	0	1.78E+02	0.002511	6.61803E-10	9.78E-04	0.00711196	24	176.68982
	3	1.98E+02	1.82E-05	3.69625E-12	5.56E-06	5.62E-05	210	1546.03592

Figure 16. Comparison of convergence time taken by the algorithms in different environmental scenarios.

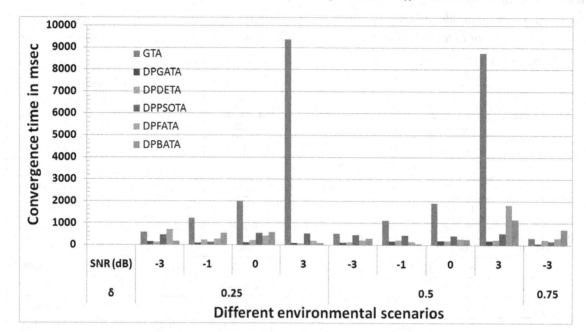

For a more accurate representation see the electronic version.

Figure 17. Comparison of deviation from minimum sensing error at different environmental scenarios of the algorithms

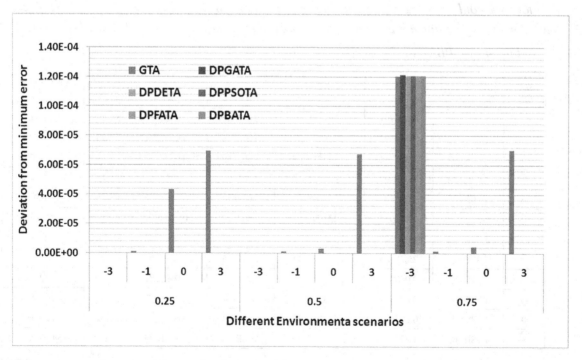

For a more accurate representation see the electronic version.

Table 9. Mean of deviation (η) from minimum error in each scenario (independent test-runs=25)

δ	SNR (db)	DPGATA	DPDETA	DPPSOTA	DPFATA	DPBATA
0.25	-3	3.12637E-06	6.10169E-08	6.101690E-08	**5.248198E-08**	1.562176E-04
	-1	4.76863E-05	2.79189807E-08	2.79189807E-08	**2.55164621E-08**	4.84656728E-06
	0	3.7763756E-06	1.246510510E-08	1.24651051E-08	**1.17630618E-08**	8.09219599E-06
	3	9.45630659E-10	1.333333574E-10	1.33333358E-10	**1.13545897E-10**	4.17121101E-08
0.5	-3	1.56634606E-07	**5.956040619E-09**	5.95604062E-09	1.26430283E-08	6.59779187E-04
	-1	1.35724515E-08	1.433086675E-08	1.43308668E-08	**1.30411699E-08**	7.44790405E-06
	0	7.27996694E-06	**5.512164836E-10**	5.51216484E-10	2.91088675E-09	1.26692215E-05
	3	8.99024490E-09	5.535325979E-11	5.53532598E-11	**4.55322201E-11**	7.90891596E-09
0.75	-3	6.86446328E-04	1.207493873E-04	**1.20749387E-04**	1.23343944E-04	4.28474913E-04
	-1	2.52741565E-07	1.744285173E-08	1.74428517E-08	**1.59113406E-08**	1.74428517E-08
	0	2.32402305E-06	**6.618035078E-10**	6.61803508E-10	2.64831261E-09	5.08218195E-07
	3	1.69555831E-09	**3.696272525E-12**	3.69627255E-12	7.00299726E-12	3.03581555E-08

Table 10. Result of ranking of different variants of death penalty based nature inspired algorithms.

δ	SNR (db)	DPGATA	DPDETA	DPPSOTA	DPFATA	DPBATA
0.25	-3	4	2	3	1	5
	-1	5	2	3	1	4
	0	4	2	3	1	5
	3	4	2	3	1	5
0.5	-3	4	1	2	3	5
	-1	2	3	4	1	5
	0	5	1	2	3	6
	3	5	2	3	1	4
0.75	-3	5	2	1	3	4
	-1	5	3	4	1	2
	0	5	1	2	3	4
	3	4	1	2	3	5
Average Rank		4.333333333	1.833333333	2.666666667	1.833333333	4.5

Again, average deviation (η') can be considered as the accuracy measure of the algorithm performing in a dynamic scenario. Now, η' in each of the 25 runs for the algorithms are calculated by equation (27). To find which algorithm performs best the mean value of η' over the 25 test runs is calculated and compared. This is shown in Table 11. The bar chart in Figure 18 illustrates a comparison between the mean η' obtained by the algorithms in the 25 independent test runs over the dynamic environmental scenario. It is evident that, of all the proposed algorithms, DPPSOTA performs best in changing environmental scenarios.

Table 11. Mean value of η' over the 25 independent test runs

DPGATA	DPDETA	DPPSOTA	DPFATA	DPBATA
6.258949299E-05	1.007416029E-05	**1.007416029E-05**	1.02900855E-05	1.065111058E-04

Figure 18. Comparison of mean η' for 25 runs in dynamic environment

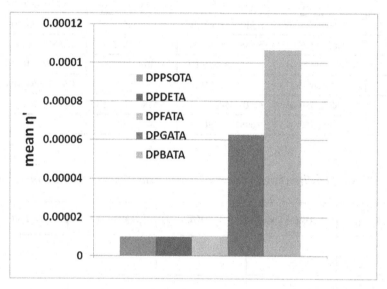

*For a more accurate representation see the electronic version.

Notably, when scenarios are separately considered, DPFATA performs best in 7 occasions, DPDETA in 4 occasions but DPPSOTA in only 1 occasion. But when average deviation over all scenarios in changing environment is considered, DPPSOTA performs best. This proves, DPPSOTA adapts threshold best in case of a changing environment, but for static environment, the respective algorithms perform well.

CONCLUSION

In this chapter spectrum sensing is investigated in the light of Big Data. Large spectrum samples are processed for sensing in real time. Also, huge volumes of historical spectrum occupancy data are stored for spectrum occupancy prediction. Such volumes of spectrum data can be characterized in terms Big Data. To minimize sensing error, large samples of signal are required to be processed in real time. This is done using nature inspired algorithms. Performance of two classes of nature inspired algorithms namely swarm-based algorithms (Firefly Algorithm, Particle swarm optimization, bat algorithm) and evolutionary algorithms (genetic algorithm and differential evolution) in sensing error minimization by threshold adaptation for dynamic environment is studied in this chapter. The authors reported four new algorithms for minimizing sensing error in energy detection by dynamic adaptation of threshold based on FA, BA, PSO and GA. The problem of sensing error minimization by threshold adaptation is formulated as a constrained optimization problem and death penalty constrained handing technique is integrated to the bio inspired algorithms for dealing with the constrains. Their performance is compared to two previously reported threshold adaptation algorithm namely gradient descend based threshold adaptation algorithm (GTA) (Joshi, Popescu & Dobre, 2011) and death penalty differential evolution based threshold adaptation DPDETA (Das & Mukhopadhyay, 2016). The algorithms are tested using Matlab in a simulated dynamic environment by changing the SNR of the input primary user signal at regular intervals. The algorithm dynamically adapts the threshold in order to minimize the sensing error depending on the SNR of the dynamic environment. The nature inspired algorithms are found to be faster to adapt the threshold and more accurate than deterministic gradient descent-based threshold adaptation algorithm (GTA) for the different dynamic environmental scenarios.

FUTURE RESEARCH DIRECTIONS

In this chapter, basic death penalty-based nature inspired algorithms are applied for sensing error minimization. But improved and hybrid versions of most of these algorithms are available with better performance metrics. This work shows the promising performance of nature inspired algorithms in sensing error minimization application. Further research can be done using improved versions of these basic algorithms. In most of practical sensing applications, speed is a very important factor. Again, system on chip implementations is required for compact portable applications. So, FPGA based hardware implementation of the above algorithms can be a very promising aspect for future research.

REFERENCES

Baykasoğlu, A., & Ozsoydan, F. B. (2015). Adaptive firefly algorithm with chaos for mechanical design optimization problems. *Applied Soft Computing*, *36*, 152–164. doi:10.1016/j.asoc.2015.06.056

Cabric, D., Mishra, S. M., & Brodersen, R. W. (2004, November). Implementation issues in spectrum sensing for cognitive radios. In *Conference record of the thirty-eighth Asilomar conference on Signals, systems and computers* (Vol. 1, pp. 772-776). IEEE. 10.1109/ACSSC.2004.1399240

Cabric, D., Mishra, S. M., & Brodersen, R. W. (2004, November). Implementation issues in spectrum sensing for cognitive radios. In *Conference record of the thirty-eighth Asilomar conference on Signals, systems and computers* (Vol. 1, pp. 772-776). IEEE. 10.1109/ACSSC.2004.1399240

Cruz, C., González, J. R., Pelta, D. A., Krasnogor, N., & Terrazas, G. (Eds.). (2010). *Nature Inspired Cooperative Strategies for Optimization (NICSO 2010)*. Springer.

Das, S., & Mukhopadhyay, S. (2016, December). Sensing error minimization for cognitive radio in dynamic environment using death penalty differential evolution based threshold adaptation. In *2016 IEEE Annual India Conference (INDICON)* (pp. 1-6). IEEE. 10.1109/INDICON.2016.7838865

Ding, G., Wu, Q., Wang, J., & Yao, Y. D. (2014). Big spectrum data: The new resource for cognitive wireless networking. arXiv:1404.6508

Dorigo, M., & Di Caro, G. (1999). Ant colony optimization: a new meta-heuristic. In *Proceedings of the 1999 Congress on Evolutionary Computation CEC 99 (Vol. 2,* pp. 1470-1477). IEEE.

Dorigo, M., & Gambardella, L. M. (1997). Ant colony system: A cooperative learning approach to the traveling salesman problem. *IEEE Transactions on Evolutionary Computation, 1*(1), 53–66. doi:10.1109/4235.585892

Eberhart, R., & Kennedy, J. (1995, October). A new optimizer using particle swarm theory. In *Proceedings of the Sixth International Symposium on Micro Machine and Human Science MHS'95* (pp. 39-43). IEEE. 10.1109/MHS.1995.494215

Farhang-Boroujeny, B. (2008). Filter bank spectrum sensing for cognitive radios. *IEEE Transactions on Signal Processing, 56*(5), 1801–1811. doi:10.1109/TSP.2007.911490

Fister, I., Yang, X. S., & Brest, J. (2013). A comprehensive review of firefly algorithms. *Swarm and Evolutionary Computation, 13,* 34–46. doi:10.1016/j.swevo.2013.06.001

Garey, M. R., Johnson, D. S., & Tarjan, R. E. (1976). The planar Hamiltonian circuit problem is NP-complete. *SIAM Journal on Computing, 5*(4), 704–714. doi:10.1137/0205049

Goldberg, D. E. (1989). *Genetic algorithms in search, optimization, and machine learning, 1989.* Reading: Addison-Wesley.

Hajeer, M. H., & Dasgupta, D. (2016, December). Distributed genetic algorithm to Big Data clustering. In *2016 IEEE Symposium Series on Computational Intelligence (SSCI)* (pp. 1-9). IEEE. 10.1109/SSCI.2016.7849864

Haykin, S., Thomson, D. J., & Reed, J. H. (2009). Spectrum sensing for cognitive radio. *Proceedings of the IEEE, 97*(5), 849–877. doi:10.1109/JPROC.2009.2015711

Holland, J. H. (1992). *Adaptation in natural and artificial systems: an introductory analysis with applications to biology, control, and artificial intelligence.* MIT press.

Joshi, D. R., Popescu, D. C., & Dobre, O. A. (2011). Gradient-based threshold adaptation for energy detector in cognitive radio systems. *IEEE Communications Letters, 15*(1), 19–21. doi:10.1109/LCOMM.2010.11.100654

Kennedy, J. (2011). Particle swarm optimization. In Encyclopedia of machine learning (pp. 760-766). Springer US.

Kuri-Morales, A., & Gutiérrez-García, J. (2002). Penalty function methods for constrained optimization with genetic algorithms: A statistical analysis. In *Advances in Artificial Intelligence* (pp. 187–200). MICAI.

Letaief, K. B., & Zhang, W. (2009). Cooperative communications for cognitive radio networks. *Proceedings of the IEEE, 97*(5), 878–893.

Li, M., Hei, Y., & Qiu, Z. (2017). Optimization of multiband cooperative spectrum sensing with modified artificial bee colony algorithm. *Applied Soft Computing*, *57*, 751–759. doi:10.1016/j.asoc.2017.03.027

Liang, Y. C., Zeng, Y., Peh, E. C., & Hoang, A. T. (2008). Sensing-throughput tradeoff for cognitive radio networks. *IEEE Transactions on Wireless Communications*, *7*(4), 1326–1337. doi:10.1109/TWC.2008.060869

Manikas, T. W., & Cain, J. T. (1996). Genetic algorithms vs. simulated annealing: A comparison of approaches for solving the circuit partitioning problem.

Mirjalili, S., Mirjalili, S. M., & Lewis, A. (2014). Grey wolf optimizer. *Advances in Engineering Software*, *69*, 46–61. doi:10.1016/j.advengsoft.2013.12.007

Neri, F., & Tirronen, V. (2010). Recent advances in differential evolution: A survey and experimental analysis. *Artificial Intelligence Review*, *33*(1-2), 61–106. doi:10.100710462-009-9137-2

Paliwal, K. (1987, April). Estimation of noise variance from the noisy AR signal and its application in speech enhancement. In IEEE International Conference on Acoustics, Speech, and Signal Processing ICASSP'87 (Vol. 12, pp. 297-300). IEEE. doi:10.1109/ICASSP.1987.1169682

Paliwal, K. K. (1988). Estimation of noise variance from the noisy AR signal and its application in speech enhancement. *IEEE Transactions on Acoustics, Speech, and Signal Processing*, *36*(2), 292–294.

Parpinelli, R. S., & Lopes, H. S. (2011). New inspirations in swarm intelligence: A survey. *International Journal of Bio-inspired Computation*, *3*(1), 1–16. doi:10.1504/IJBIC.2011.038700

Price, K., Storn, R. M., & Lampinen, J. A. (2006). *Differential evolution: a practical approach to global optimization*. Springer Science & Business Media.

Schroeck, M., Shockley, R., Smart, J., Romero-Morales, D., & Tufano, P. (2012). Analytics: The real-world use of Big Data. *IBM Global Business Services*, *12*, 1–20.

Shellhammer, S. J. (2008). Spectrum sensing in IEEE 802.22. *IAPR Wksp. Cognitive Info. Processing*, 9-10.

Shi, Y. (2001). Particle swarm optimization: developments, applications and resources. In *Proceedings of the 2001 Congress on evolutionary computation* (Vol. *1*, pp. 81-86). IEEE. 10.1109/CEC.2001.934374

Storn, R., & Price, K. (1997). Differential evolution–a simple and efficient heuristic for global optimization over continuous spaces. *Journal of Global Optimization*, *11*(4), 341–359. doi:10.1023/A:1008202821328

Wellens, M., & Mähönen, P. (2010). Lessons learned from an extensive spectrum occupancy measurement campaign and a stochastic duty cycle model. *Mobile Networks and Applications*, *15*(3), 461–474. doi:10.100711036-009-0199-9

Xue, H., Shao, Z., Pan, J., Zhao, Q., & Ma, F. (2016). A hybrid firefly algorithm for optimizing fractional proportional-integral-derivative controller in ship steering. *Journal of Shanghai Jiaotong University (Science)*, *21*(4), 419–423. doi:10.100712204-016-1741-0

Yang, X. S. (2009, October). Firefly algorithms for multimodal optimization. In *International symposium on stochastic algorithms* (pp. 169-178). Springer.

Yang, X. S. (2010). A new metaheuristic bat-inspired algorithm. In *Nature inspired cooperative strategies for optimization* (pp. 65–74). NICSO.

Yang, X. S. (2011). Bat algorithm for multi-objective optimisation. *International Journal of Bio-inspired Computation*, *3*(5), 267–274. doi:10.1504/IJBIC.2011.042259

Yang, X. S., & Deb, S. (2009, December). Cuckoo search via Lévy flights. In *World Congress on Nature & Biologically Inspired Computing NaBIC 2009* (pp. 210-214). IEEE.

Yang, X. S., & Hc, X. (2013). Bat algorithm: Literature review and applications. *International Journal of Bio-inspired Computation*, *5*(3), 141–149.

Yang, X. S., & He, X. (2013). Bat algorithm: Literature review and applications. *International Journal of Bio-inspired Computation*, *5*(3), 141–149. doi:10.1504/IJBIC.2013.055093

Yang, X. S., & Hossein Gandomi, A. (2012). Bat algorithm: A novel approach for global engineering optimization. *Engineering Computations*, *29*(5), 464–483. doi:10.1108/02644401211235834

Yeniay, Ö. (2005). Penalty function methods for constrained optimization with genetic algorithms. *Mathematical and Computational Applications*, *10*(1), 45–56. doi:10.3390/mca10010045

Yucek, T., & Arslan, H. (2009). A survey of spectrum sensing algorithms for cognitive radio applications. *IEEE Communications Surveys and Tutorials*, *11*(1), 116–130. doi:10.1109/SURV.2009.090109

Zhang, Q., Jia, J., & Zhang, J. (2009). Cooperative relay to improve diversity in cognitive radio networks. *IEEE Communications Magazine*, *47*(2), 111–117. doi:10.1109/MCOM.2009.4785388

Zhang, W., Mallik, R. K., & Letaief, K. B. (2008, May). Cooperative spectrum sensing optimization in cognitive radio networks. In *IEEE International conference on Communications ICC'08* (pp. 3411-3415). IEEE. 10.1109/ICC.2008.641

KEY TERMS AND DEFINITIONS

Evolutionary Algorithm: A set of meta-heuristic, population-based optimization techniques that uses nature inspired processes such as selection, reproduction, recombination, mutation, etc.

Heuristic Algorithms: Algorithms developed to find, in realistic time period, acceptable or near accurate solution to problems whose exact solution may require impractically long time

Primary Users: They are the users licensed to transmit in a particular radio frequency band and have the highest priority.

Secondary User: They are not licensed to use a particular frequency band for transmitting, and are allowed to opportunistically use the spectrum which is not in use by a primary user without causing any interference to the primary user transmission.

Spectrum Hole: The vacant spectrum band which is not in use by any user.

Swarm Based Algorithms: Optimization algorithms developed by mimicking the behaviour of animals moving in groups in search of shelter or food like a folk of birds or shoal of fish.

System on Chip (SoC): It is an electronic system fabricated inside a single integrated circuit (IC), and is capable of performing dedicated analog and/or digital applications.

Chapter 7
Wolf–Swarm Colony for Signature Gene Selection Using Weighted Objective Method

Prativa Agarwalla
Heritage Institute of Technology, Kolkata, India

Sumitra Mukhopadhyay
Institute of Radio Physics & Electronics, India

ABSTRACT

Microarray study has a huge impact on the proper detection and classification of cancer, as it analyzes the changes in expression level of genes which are strongly associated with cancer. In this chapter, a new weighted objective wolf-swarm colony optimization (WOWSC) technique is proposed for the selection of significant and informative genes from the cancer dataset. To extract the relevant genes from datasets, WOWSC utilizes four different objective functions in a weighted manner. Experimental analysis shows that the proposed methodology is very efficient in obtaining differential and biologically relevant genes which are effective for the classification of disease. The technique is able to generate a good subset of genes which offers more useful insight to the gene-disease association.

INTRODUCTION

Cancer is a heterogeneous disease which has different stages, classes and subtypes. Early prediction of subtypes and detection of advancement rate of disease can improve the mortality rate and also vital for the course of treatment. In biological terms, cancer can be defined as uncontrolled growth of certain cells due to changes in expression of genes in molecular level. For proper understanding of the disease and categorizing it into different classes, investigation of the changes in genetic expression level is necessary. Selection of relevant genes involved in tumor progression is very essential for the proper medical diagnosis as well as for drug target prediction. Gene expression data (Zhang, Kuljis & Liu, 2008) has a huge impact on the study of cancer classification and identification. It includes the expression levels of thousands of genes, collected from various samples. The expression of a gene in a carcinogenic cell is

DOI: 10.4018/978-1-5225-5852-1.ch007

compared with the expression in normal cell and then through proper analysis microarray gene expression dataset is formed. Proper analysis of the dataset is required as it contains the information regarding the abnormal behavior of a disease gene. But, the high dimensionality of gene microarray datasets makes it challenging to examine and extracting important feature genes from it. Again, the availability of larger number of genes compared to the small number of samples can cause the overfitting issue for classification of samples. Also, the presence of noise and the heterogeneous nature of dataset cause problem in the task of informative feature extraction. It motivates the researchers to apply various statistical and learning based techniques for realizing the useful information content of the dataset. The importance of classifying cancer and appropriate diagnosis of advancement of the disease using those feature genes has led to many research fields, from biomedical to the application of machine learning (ML) methods. The ability of machine learning approaches to detect key features from a huge complex dataset reveals their importance in the field of feature selection from datasets as well as the ability to examine big data framework. So, the modelling of cancer progression and classification of disease by investigating large microarray datasets can be studied by employing learning-based approaches.

Researchers have summarized the microarray data with various statistical approaches (Yang, Parrish & Brock, 2014; Pal, Ray, Cho & Pal, 2016; Arevalillo & Navarro, 2013; Peng, Long & Ding, C., 2005). Those provide fast and scalable output but overlook the feature dependencies of the datasets. Different classifier dependent stochastic bio-inspired algorithms-based learning methodologies are introduced to handle the problem. Recently, numerous hybrid approaches (Hsieh & Lu, 2011; Apolloni, Leguizamón & Alba, 2016) are proving to be very effective where both the statistical filters and the classifiers are implemented along with the optimization algorithms. The use of a particular statistical or classifier dependent objective functions are sometimes not enough for the job of finding out biologically relevant and cancer class identifier gene selection. So, multiple measurement metrics can be utilized for evaluation purpose. Different multi-objective methodologies are proposed in the literature (Mukhopadhyay & Mandal, 2014; Zheng, Yang, Chong & Xia, 2016; Mohamad, Omatu, Deris, Misman & Yoshioka, 2009) where nature inspired evolutionary and swarm algorithms are investigated to obtain a pareto-optimal solution for gene set. Generally, those approaches involve two objectives for the relevant gene selection from microarray dataset and in most of the cases the methodologies are based on a particular type of bio-inspired algorithm. So, it has the limit to produce more promising results compared to any hybrid swarm algorithm approaches. For extracting the most informative genes from the huge gene expression dataset, different measurement indices are to be optimized. Examining two or three objectives may not be sufficient for genuine selection of differentially expressed genes from the cancer data, as the choice of objective function plays an important role in this case. The optimization function should have the property to select the differentially expressed features for different subtype of a disease. Also, it needs to have the ability to detect the proper class of the disease. So, to produce more accurate results for the problem of gene selection from the huge microarray data, authors have involved multiple objectives at a time. As multiple objectives are to be optimized, a weighted fitness function is formed using weighted-objective optimization technique. Weighted factors are involved in mapping those multiple objectives into a one fitness objective to select the required features which are efficient in the classification purpose as well as having differential expressions from disease to disease.

Population based meta-heuristic searching algorithms work efficiently in the course of optimization. One of the popular tools is particle swarm optimization (PSO) (Kennedy, 2011), which is well known for its simplicity. Generally, it is observed that PSO suffers from two issues. It easily loses its diversity. Again, it sticks to local optima having a pre-matured and inaccurate convergence of the employed swarm.

Another recently established optimization approach Grey wolf optimizer (GWO) (Mirjalili, Mirjalili & Lewis, 2014) which provides promising results for different varieties of optimization problems. But, GWO suffers from low local search quality. In this chapter, motivated by both the drawbacks and advantages of the standalone approaches, a hybrid approach is proposed for the problem. This is a combination of particle swarm algorithm and grey wolf algorithm and the proposed algorithm is termed as wolf swarm colony algorithm. The key features of the wolf swarm colony algorithms are as follows.

- The exploration and exploitation part of PSO algorithm is improved by implementing the strategy of grey wolf optimization so that as a whole the proposed methodology can provide better optimization results.
- In PSO algorithm, a leader of the swarm is chosen based on its performance and other particles of the swarm follow the best one in the process of searching. At a certain point of time, if the leader of the swarm is stuck to any local optimum, the whole population which is following the leader is also stuck losing diversity in the searching process. To recover from the situation, the concept of more than one leader is introduced here. If one leader fails to guide the group towards betterment then other leader will try to cater the responsibility in an efficient manner.
- In GWO optimization, the total population of a wolf pack is divided into four hierarchical categories, generally known as alpha, beta, delta, and gamma. The whole population searches for the optimal being directed by alpha, beta, and delta wolf. The use of multiple leaders provides more diversity and exploration characteristics of the proposed hybrid algorithm will enhance.

The concept is implemented to provide more promising result in the field of optimization. In this chapter, a wolf-swarm hybrid algorithm is proposed by formulating the gene selection problem as a weighted-objective problem (Marler & Arora, 2010). The novel weighted objective wolf-swarm colony (WOWSC) works efficiently to find out the most relevant genes that are involved in the development of a particular type of cancer.

Experiments are performed using WOWSC based gene selection methodology for different types of cancer microarray datasets. The experimental dataset consists of microarray data of Prostate (Singh et al., 2002), Colon (Alon, 1999), Lymphoma-Leukemia (Golub et al., 1999) and DLBCL cancer (Shipp, 2002). The performance of the proposed gene selection technique is evaluated for those four real life cancers to establish its efficiency. The proposed method establishes good result indicating its ability to produce more robust gene selection activity. As a whole, it can be concluded that the proposed gene selection methodologies are more efficient in the detection of the relevant genes for all the different types of dataset. At the end of this chapter, the biological relevance of the resultant genes is also validated and demonstrated. It signifies the contribution of the selected genes in the field of bio-informatics. The gene selection scheme and the employed objective functions for WOWSC based technique are given briefly in the following section.

The remaining section of the chapter is organized as follows: First, an overview of microarray dataset is presented, followed by a brief review of the related work. The gene selection scheme and the employed objective functions for WOWSC based technique are given in the next section. After that, the result of the proposed technique is demonstrated. Next, the biological relevance of the result is also given. Finally, the work has been concluded.

BACKGROUND OF DATASETS

Cancer occurs due to malfunctioning of different genes. As the expressions of those genes related to the disease have been changed so, a study on the changes of the gene expressions is very fruitful to identify the cause behind it. Microarray technology (Zhang, Kuljis & Liu, 2008) is a recently developed advanced technology, which helps to confine the changes in gene at the molecular level. For visualization of the changes at the gene level, this technology is widely used for extracting the informative content and subsequently, a conclusion can be made by investigating the expression level. The formation of microarray dataset for a particular disease involves few steps. In a microarray database, thousands of gene expressions are arranged on a single microscope slide for different samples. The dataset is prepared by comparing the expression of genes of the cancerous cell with the genes of a normal cell. Samples from both the cancerous and normal tissue are taken and after that, the samples are dyed using fluorescent of different colour. Then the hybridization procedure is performed with on the microarray slide. Now, using scanner, the fluorescent intensity of the different area of microarray slide is analyzed. The information related to the intensity of the spot helps in parallel analysis of thousands of genes. The processing steps are demonstrated in Figure 1. For the experimental purpose, microarray datasets are collected from reliable sources such as National Centre for Biotechnology Information (NCBI). It is a data repository facility which includes data on gene expression from varied sources.

Description of Experimental Dataset

Here, four different types of cancer datasets are collected and each of the datasets is having two types of samples. For each dataset, samples are arranged row-wise whereas the expressions of genes are given in

Figure 1. Preparation steps of microarray database

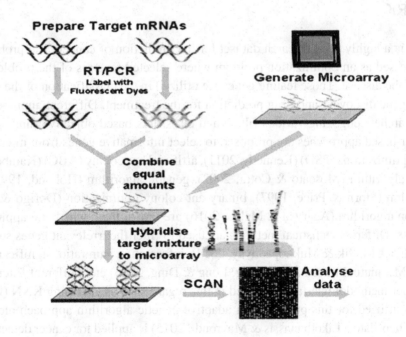

column. All of the experimental datasets are having thousands of gene expression data. One of them is having nearly 12000 columns. Analysing and extracting important features from those huge datasets is quite challenging. Second, due to the heterogeneity of expression of genes over the samples, appropriate optimization techniques are to be involved. Being motivated by this, WOWSC is applied to realize the useful information, contained in those high dimensional datasets. The successful application of WOWSC on the large microarray datasets establishes its ability in the field of examining big data framework. A brief description of the microarray dataset used for the experimental study is given below.

Prostate Cancer (Singh et al., 2002): The prostate cancer is related to the abnormal cell growth in the prostate. The dataset (Singh et al., 2002) is prepared using gene expression measurements for prostate tumors and for the adjacent normal tissue of the prostate. Total 102 samples are present. Among which 50 samples are of prostate tumors and 52 are of non-cancerous prostate tissues. Gene expression values are measured for 12533 genes.

Colon cancer (Alon, 1999): The Colon dataset contains expressions of 6,000 genes obtained from 62 cell samples, among which 40 biopsies are from tumors and 22 biopsy samples are from healthy parts of the colon of the same patients. The data are collected from a publicly available website: www. biconductor.com/datadet.

Lymphoma & Leukemia (GSE1577) (Golub et al., 1999): The Leukemia dataset consists of 72 microarray experiments with 5147 gene expression levels, including two types of Leukemia, namely AML (25 samples) and ALL (47 samples). Tissue samples were collected from bone marrow (62 cases) and peripheral blood (10 cases). The data are collected from a public website: www.biolab.si/supp/bi-cancer/projections/info/.

DLBCL (Shipp, 2002): Types of Diffuse Large B-cell Lymphoma dataset consists of two types. Total 7070 genes are there in the dataset. The number of samples of type DLBCL is 58 and type FL is 19. The data are collected from a public website: www.biolab.si/supp/bi-cancer/projections/info/.

REVIEW WORK

Microarray data is a highly used research dataset for the prediction of cancer. The problem of feature selection is addressed as an optimization problem where selected features of the problem are the significant genes of the disease. Those feature genes are utilized in the classification of the disease as well as helping it for gene discovery and drug prediction for the treatment. Different approaches are developed by the researchers engaging various filters and classifiers based objective functions. Numerous heuristic wrapper-based approaches are proposed to select informative genes from microarray dataset. Particle swarm optimizations (PSO) (Kennedy, 2011), artificial bee colony (ABC) (Karaboga & Basturk, 2007), memetic algorithm (Moscato & Cotta, 2002), genetic algorithm (Holland, 1992), differential evolution algorithm (Storn & Price, 1997), binary ant colony optimization (Dorigo & Blum, 2005), flower pollination algorithm (Agarwal & Mehta, 2016) are few of them which are applied in the field of bio-informatics. Different statistical methods are used to filter the irrelevant genes such as t-test, F-test (Bandyopadhyay, Mallik & Mukhopadhyay, 2014), information gain ratio, significance analysis of microarrays (SAM), mutual information (Peng, Long & Ding, 2005) etc. Different filter and classifier dependent wrapper methodologies are proposed in this regard such as GA using KNN (Lee, Lin, Chen & Kuo, 2011) is utilized for this purpose. An adaptive genetic algorithm approach along with SVM (Kleftogiannis, Theofilatos, Likothanassis & Mavroudi, 2015) is applied for cancer detection. PSO with decision tree (Chen et at., 2014) is developed. Also, a bacterial algorithm with SVM (Wang & Niu, 2017) is applied in this regard. Again, artificial bee colony (Amaratunga, Cabrera & Kovtun, 2008) is used for microarray learning. A pipelining based differential evolution algorithm (Dash & Misra, 2016) is also represented for microarray data classification. In a work, a modified binary coded ant colony algorithm (Wan, Wang, Ye & Lai, 2016) is introduced for the task of feature selection from datasets. Enhanced flower pollination algorithm (Agarwal & Mehta, 2016) is also applied for data clustering. Various multi-objective methodologies are proposed in the literatures (Mukhopadhyay & Mandal, 2014; Zheng, Yang, Chong & Xia, 2016; Mohamad, Omatu, Deris, Misman & Yoshioka, 2009) where nature inspired algorithms are investigated to find out the relevant genes of cancer.

Recently, some hybrid approaches are proving to be very effective where both the filters and the classifiers are implemented along with the randomized algorithms. For an example, a hybrid multi-filter embedded technique is proposed (Bonilla-Huerta, Hernández-Montiel, Morales-Caporal & Arjona-López, 2016) where GA along with the tabu-search algorithm is implemented using SVM on the dataset. In another approach CFS-tauchi-genetic algorithm with SVM classifier (Chauang et al., 2011) is proposed. Gene selection for cancer tumor detection is performed using memetic algorithm (Zibakhsh & Abadeh, 2013). In a work, simulated annealing based on fuzzy fitness function is introduced (Saha, Ekbal, Gupta & Bandyopadhyay, 2013) for cancer data classification. The Cuckoo optimization algorithm is implemented along with genetic algorithm (Elyasigomari, Mirjafari, Screen & Shaheed, 2015) for microarray studies. Two hybrid wrapper-filter feature selection algorithms (Apolloni, Leguizamón & Alba, 2016) are applied on the high-dimensional microarray experiments where a combination of binary differential evolution (BDE) algorithm with a rank-based filter method is applied for microarray dataset. Hybrid ant bee algorithm (GaneshKumar, Rani, Devaraj & Victoire, 2014) is also applied for microarray studies. The problem of feature selection is again solved using clustering approaches. In a very recent work in 2017 (Salem, Attiya & El-Fishawy, 2017), information gain is applied at the initial selection stage and then GA and Genetic Programming are used for the estimation of genes. In another recent work, a novel clustering approach (Luo, Huang, Ye, Zhou, Shao & Peng, 2011) is proposed for cancer marker identification. Very recently, a bi-stage hierarchical is proposed which is a combination of multi-fitness discrete particle swarm optimization (MFDPSO) and a blended laplacian artificial bee colony (BLABC) based automatic inter-class clustering technique (Agarwalla & Mukhopadhyay, 2018). The described methods use the filter output or the classifier output as the solution of the objective function that has to be gained. The main advantages using those stochastic methods are that they are less prone to local optima. However, the obtained gene feature set still lacks biological significance and the resulting top-ranked genes or features are often redundant.

In this work, for the selection of differentially expressed genes from two classes of cancer, the authors have implemented a new weighted objective wolf-swarm colony algorithm which is a combination of PSO and GWO. The hybrid algorithm provided good searching capability and secures good optimization results. The proposed WOWSC methodology identifies most significant genes for cancer progression when applied to the field of bio-informatics. A brief review work related to different bio-inspired algorithms, proposed for the microarray data studies is provided in Table 1. Here different wrapper filter, wrapper classifier and hybrid approaches, used for the gene identification from microarray dataset are given.

Table 1. Brief review of different methodologies used for feature gene identification

Category	Authors	Year	Used Methodology
Wrapper + filter	Dash et al.	2016	Differential Evolution
	Tan et al.	2006	Genetic algorithm
	Amaratunga et al.	2008	Artificial bee colony
	Wan et al.	2016	Binary ant colony optimization
Wrapper + classifiers	Lee et al.	2011	GA using KNN
	Chen et al.	2014	PSO with decision tree
	Kleftogiannis et al.	2015	Adaptive GA with SVM
	Wang et al.	2017	Novel bacterial algorithm with SVM
	Mukhopadhyay et al.	2016	Binary PSO
Hybrid approach	Chuang et. al	2011	CFS-taguchi-genetic algorithm with SVM
	Saha et al.	2013	Simulated annealing based on fuzzy fitness function
	Zibakhsh et al.	2013	Memetic algorithm having a fuzzy concept
	Ganesh Kumar et al.	2014	Hybrid ant bee algorithm
	Elyasigomari et al.	2015	Cuckoo optimization algorithm + Genetic algorithm
	Huerta et al.	2016	Multifilter + GA along with the tabu-search algorithm + SVM
	Apolloni et al.	2016	BDE with ML
	Agarwalla et al.	2018	Modified binary PSO + ABC algorithm

PROPOSED METHOD USING WEIGHTED OBJECTIVE WOLF-SWARM COLONY (WOWSC)

In this section, the proposed methodology will be described and the wolf-swarm colony algorithm will be represented along with its relevance in this context.

Pre-Processing Microarray Data

Noise in microarray data creates confusion. So, before applying any computational methodology, the noisy and irrelevant genes are to be eliminated. To analyze the noise amount, signal-to-noise ratio is calculated for each gene and based on the SNR value, the genes are arranged in descending order and then top 1000 genes are selected for computation. Next, the normalization procedure is employed on those 1000 genes using min-max normalization process (Bandyopadhyay et al., 2014). If the expression of a gene over the samples is represented by the variable x, then the min-max normalization formula for a data point xi is described by Equation (1). This generated data matrix is used for the next level of computation.

$$x_i(normalized) = \frac{x_i - \min(x)}{\max(x) - \min(x)} \tag{1}$$

Weighted Objectives

Now using weighted objective wolf-swarm colony (WOWSC) technique, authors are selecting marker genes for different types of cancer. For the reliable classification of a disease, multiple objectives play important roles. In the context of gene selection from the microarray dataset, four objectives are considered. Two of them allow selection of the most differentially expressed genes which help in identifying the separation between classes. These two objectives are basically filter based objectives. More considerations are given to the result of classification of the disease. For the selection of differentially expressed genes from heterogeneous gene expression dataset, authors employ t-score and p-value of Wilcoxon Ranksum test (Bandyopadhyay et al., 2014) as the filter-based metrics. Again, importance is given to the accuracy and F-score (Mukhopadhyay & Mandal, 2014) of classification result to obtain high performance of classification. Now a weighted objective problem is formulated where the weight values are set equal. The fitness objective function, used by WOWSC method for the estimation of selected gene subset, is given below.

Fitness= a. (t-score) + b. (1-(normalized p-value of WR test)) + c. (accuracy) + d. (F-score) (2)

a, b, c, d are the weight factor. Here, our aim is to maximize the fitness value by employing the proposed wolf-swarm colony optimization technique. Using WOWSC, if the proper combination of genes for the determination of disease can be identified, then it will be a significant contribution to the diagnosis of disease and the treatment will be more effective. The expressions of the individual objective are given as follows.

$$t - score = \frac{\mu_1 - \mu_2}{\sqrt{\frac{sd_1^2}{n_1} + \frac{sd_2^2}{n_2}}}$$ (3)

The first objective is the t-score where the mean expression of those selected genes over the samples for both the classes is calculated. Then the difference of the two mean expressions is computed. The expression is described in Eq. (3) where μ and sd represent the mean and the standard deviation value of the two classes respectively. Higher fitness function indicates the better selectivity of genes. The second one is the p-value of the Wilcoxon Ranksum test. It is a statistical hypothesis test. It is designed based on p-value of the selected genes where our aim is to minimize the p-value. The range of p-value is very small. So, before using it to calculate the ultimate fitness score, the value is normalized. For the third objective function, accuracy is estimated using the number of false positives (fp), true negatives (tn), false negatives (fn) and true positives (tp) samples, present during class prediction.

$$Accuracy = \frac{t_n + t_p}{t_n + t_p + f_p + f_n}$$ (4)

The fourth objective is the F-score which is expressed in terms of precision and sensitivity. Based on the classification results, precision and sensitivity are determined. The expression of F-score is given below.

$$Fscore = \frac{2 * precision * sensitivity}{precision + sensitivity} \tag{5}$$

where precision and sensitivity are termed as the following equations

$$precision = \frac{t_p}{t_p + f_p} \tag{6}$$

$$Sensitivity = \frac{t_p}{t_p + f_n} \tag{7}$$

The proposed methodology is discussed in brief in the following sections.

Proposed Methodology

In microarray data, the expressions of thousands of genes are arranged column-wise whereas the samples are arranged in row. Two classes of raw microarray data for different types of cancer are collected from the website: www.biolab.si/supp/bi-cancer/projections/info/ and have been pre-processed before computation using the techniques mentioned above. The format of the microarray dataset is given below. Here, G denotes the genes and $s_1, s_2, ... s_M$ are the M samples of different classes. The dimension of the data matrix is D_{Mx1000}. M is the total number of the samples present in the dataset.

The problem has been modeled as a feature selection problem from huge dataset where the features are selected based on different objectives and nature inspired swarm algorithm is employed for it. Authors have examined the extracted feature gene subset through cross validation technique. The steps of the proposed framework for the studying of gene expression data are stated below.

Figure 2. Presentation of the microarray data matrix

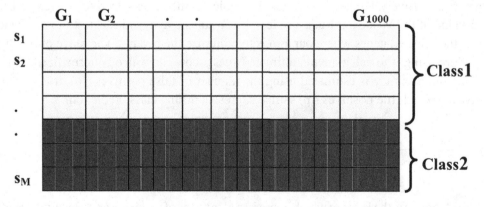

Processed Microarray Data Matrix (D_{Mx1000})

Step 1: First, the dataset is partitioned into training and test dataset. For the experimental purpose, the dataset is partitioned into ten partitions in a random fashion. Nine collectively form the training set and the remaining one is used for the testing purpose.

Step 2: The weighted objective function is defined using four objectives.

Step 3: Weighted objective wolf swarm colony (WOWSC) is applied to extract more relevant features. As mentioned, four objectives are used to obtain a weighted objective fitness function where the task is to maximize the fitness value using WOWSC technique.

Step 4: Through the WOWSC optimization algorithm, the optimized feature gene subset is selected.

Step 5: Next, supervised learning is involved. Classifier is trained with those extracted feature gene subsets.

Step 6: The results are 10 times 10-fold cross validated for the test dataset.

In this chapter, a new version of optimization algorithms, entitled as, weighted objective wolf swarm colony (WOWSC) is proposed. Authors have modified the particle swarm optimization algorithms integrating the concept of multiple leaders of GWO algorithm to provide better diversity in the PSO algorithm. In the course of searching for the optimization, the proposed methodology using WOWSC finds more accurate result compared to conventional optimization algorithms. The concept of WOWSC is described below.

Concept of Particle Swarm Optimization (PSO)

Eberhart and Kennedy developed Particle Swarm Optimization (PSO) in 1995 being inspired by the social behavior of a bird flock (Kennedy, J., 2011). Now-a-day PSO is one of the extensively used algorithms for solving the optimization problem. In the PSO algorithm, a swarm consists of many particles. They move in search of food where the location of a particle in the multi-dimensional problem space represents a possible solution for the optimization function, f(x). During movement, the velocity of a particle is influenced in the direction of its own past experience as well as the social behavior of the swarm has an impact on it. The particles feel attracted toward the swarm's best position g_{best}. The velocity and the position of each particle moving along each dimension of the problem space will be altered with each generation of movement. The mathematical formulas of velocity and position updation for i^{th} particle at t^{th} generation are given below.

$$v^i(t) = w \cdot v^i(t-1) + c_1.rand.\left(p_{best}^i - x^i\right) + c_2.rand.\left(g_{best}^i - x^i\right) \tag{8}$$

$$x^i(t) = x^i\left(t-1\right) + v^i(t) \tag{9}$$

where c_1, the cognitive learning factor, represents the attraction of a particle toward its own success p_{best} and c_2, social learning factor, and w is the inertia weight. At each iteration, the particles move towards the optimum solution searching the space. A particle updates its position if the fitness value is better than previous. At the end of searching g_{best} is found and it is the optimum solution of the problem.

Concept of Grey Wolf Optimizer (GWO)

The social behaviour of a wolf pack is modeled mathematically in Grey Wolf Optimizer (GWO) (Mirjalili, S., Mirjalili, S. M., & Lewis, A., 2014). A pack of wolf consists of different categories of wolves. The top of the hierarchical position is occupied by alpha wolf. The alpha wolf is called the most dominant wolf since other follow his/her orders for the hunting purpose. Alpha is the strongest candidate of the pack in terms of managing the pack. The second level in the hierarchy of grey wolf pack is beta that helps the alpha in decision-making and other pack activities. The omega(s) are the last wolves. They are the last candidates, allowed to eat. Delta wolves have to submit to alphas and betas, but they dominate the omega. Scouts, elders, hunters, and caretakers belong to this category. They have the responsibility for watching the boundaries of the territory, helping the alphas and betas for hunting etc. The best three solutions are termed as alpha, beta, and delta respectively. They involve in hunting and omegas follow them. The main three steps of hunting are 1) tracking and encircling the prey, 2) harassing the prey 3) attacking the prey.

1. **Encircling Prey:** The encircling of the prey during the hunt is modeled in GWO as follows

$$\vec{D} = \left| \vec{C}.\vec{X}_p(t-1) - \vec{X}(t-1) \right| \tag{10}$$

$$\vec{X}(t) = \vec{X}_p(t-1) - \vec{A}.\vec{D} \tag{11}$$

where t is the current iteration. $\vec{X}_p$ is the position of the prey and $\vec{X}$ is the position of grey wolf. $\vec{A}$ and $\vec{C}$ vectors are calculated as Eq. (12) and (13). Here, the component of vector $\vec{a}$ linearly decreases from 2 to 0 during iteration and r_1 and r_2 are two random vectors between 1 and 0.

$$\vec{A} = 2.\vec{a}.\vec{r}_1 - \vec{a} \tag{12}$$

$$\vec{C} = 2.\vec{r}_2 \tag{13}$$

2. **Hunting Stage:** Alpha, beta, and delta guide the whole pack to update their positions towards the prey. To update the position of a grey wolf obtains three direction vectors from alpha, beta, and delta. The average is the direction of movement of a grey wolf towards the prey. Basically, alpha, beta, and delta estimate the position of the prey, and other wolves update their positions randomly around the prey. The mathematical equations for guiding grey wolf in the direction of prey are given below.

$$\vec{D}_\alpha = \left| \vec{C}.\vec{X}_\alpha(t-1) - \vec{X}(t-1) \right|,$$

$$\vec{D}_\beta = \left| \vec{C}.\vec{X}_\beta(t-1) - \vec{X}(t-1) \right|,$$

$$\vec{D}_\delta = \left| \vec{C}.\vec{X}_\delta(t-1) - \vec{X}(t-1) \right|$$

$$\vec{X}_1 = \vec{X}_\alpha(t-1) - \vec{A}_1.\vec{D}_\alpha,$$

$$\vec{X}_2 = \vec{X}_\beta(t-1) - \vec{A}_2.\vec{D}_\beta,$$

$$\vec{X}_3 = \vec{X}_\delta(t-1) - \vec{A}_3.\vec{D}_\delta$$

$$\vec{X}(t) = \frac{\vec{X}_1 + \vec{X}_2 + \vec{X}_3}{3} \tag{14}$$

3. **Attacking Prey:** At the last stage, the wolves attack the prey. To move near to the prey, the value of the vector $\vec{a}$ is decreased to decrease the value of $\vec{A}$. $|A| < 1$ forces the wolves to attack towards the prey. In the first of the total iteration to provide divergence $|A|$ is kept greater than 1. It helps in exploration. In the last half $|A| < 1$ is used for exploitation purpose. At the end of the iteration, the wolves ultimately reach to the point of optimum.

Concept of Weighted-Objective Wolf-Swarm Colony Optimization Technique (WOWSC)

In basic PSO, the particles are following a particular g_{best} of the swarm. If during iteration, g_{best} loses its diversity and confines to a local point, the whole swarm, as following him, would converge to the point. As a result, the whole population loses its diversity in and premature convergence occurs. To recover the situation, multiple leader concept is implemented. The swarm is now directed towards more than one leader. It provides diversity and overcome the abovementioned stagnancy. In this chapter, the idea of multiple leaders of GWO algorithm is integrated with PSO and a new hybrid algorithm is established which is named as Wolf-Swarm Colony Optimization technique (WOWSC). It is found that hybrid algorithms perform better than any particular type of optimization algorithm. Being motivated by this a hybrid approach is established in this chapter. The development of the proposed algorithm is explained below.

In this work, a swarm or a group of particles, having a population 15-20, is considered. The particles move in the search space to get food for their living. During the movement, the positions of those particles indicated the probable solution of the problem. The whole swarm is divided into four categories which are stated here. The top most swarm is the alpha swarm that is the best swarm in terms of solution. Obviously, it is the strongest candidate of the swarm who can direct the whole swarm in the proper direction. As alpha is the best particle, others feel obliged to follow him and accordingly update themselves being influenced by alpha. The alpha interacts with others and guides them. Second category of the swarm is beta swarm. The fitness of beta particle is just after alpha. He is the second-best candidate. In absence or illness of alpha, beta gets the opportunity to conduct the whole swarm. And the third type of swarm is the delta swarm. They are the most aggressive swarm. Delta is very active and sporting particle. He looks after the whole swarm. The aggressive nature of delta helps the whole swarm during the hunting. Delta participates actively in searching along with alpha and beta. Delta is not the best solution but the energetic nature of delta gives him a dominant place in the swarm. Delta is selected among the particles considering the fitness values of previous few iterations. The fitness values of the particles are stored in an archive. The rate of change of fitness value with iteration is calculated for each particle. The particle having the highest number of rate change is termed as delta. The remaining particles except than alpha, beta, and delta belong to the fourth category of swarm.

Here, in the WOWSC algorithm, if somehow, alpha falls into local optimum, another solution beta is there to come out from the situation by guiding the whole swarm. Again, the delta solution is also dominating the swarm. So, there remains the scope of getting divergence and exploring a new area of searching space. There are different stages in WOWSC through which the swarm actively moves towards the food. The schematic diagram of the process of selection of bio-markers from gene expression profile is described in Figure 3. The total work is described by the following steps.

1. Initialization stage
2. Finding of food
   a. Exploration stage
   b. Exploitation stage
3. Termination

Initialization Stage

First, a weighted objective function is defined for the selection of relevant genes and the parameters of the algorithm are set. The velocity and the position of a particle are initialized randomly at this stage and the fitness values are assigned to the particles. The swarm is divided into the four categories and initially alpha, beta and, delta swarm are selected on the current fitness of the particles. The best two particles are alpha and beta respectively. Delta is selected randomly from the remaining particles of the swarm.

Finding of Food

The finding of food is a combination of two stages. First one is the exploration of food and second one is the exploitation of food. Generally, most of the conventional algorithms keep first half for the exploration of the food and the next half for exploitation. In the proposed WOWSC, the whole mechanism is the combination of the two stages. For example, for the first t_1 interval particles explore the food and then for the next t_2 interval, they search the nearby area of the solution. Again, for the next t_1 interval, particles use exploration equations and so on. If the maximum number of allowed iteration is T, then the combination of exploration and exploitation stage is described in the Figure 4. The descriptions of the two stages are given below.

Figure 3. Computational methods using WOWSC based approach

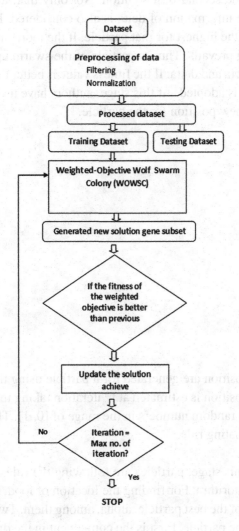

Figure 4. Combination of exploration and exploitation stage during food search

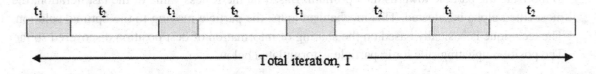

1. **Exploration Stage:** In the search space, particles are guided towards the food center by alpha, beta and delta swarm. Those particles help in exploration of new food center. The information about the probable food centre gathered by the alpha, beta and delta is conveyed to the other particles. The other particles set direction of the movement according to the knowledge acquired from alpha, beta and delta particle. Alpha being the best solution has an impact on the other particles. But its information about the solution may not be always correct as it may indicate a local optimum point. As the whole swarm is searching for a global solution, particles also consider the solution

obtained by beta that is the second-best solution. Not only that, as delta is the most active and energetic in nature, so the information of delta is also considered. Delta is selected as the rate of change in fitness value is the highest for that particle. It the more probable area of solution where a huge scope of searching prevails. Thus, a particle of the swarm updates their position based on the knowledge of alpha, beta and delta. If the fitness value is better than the previous iteration, then the new updated position is adopted. At this stage, authors have used the following mathematical equations to formulate a new position for the particle.

$$\vec{X}_1 = \vec{X}_\alpha(t-1) - \vec{X}(t-1),$$

$$\vec{X}_2 = \vec{X}_\beta(t-1) - \vec{X}(t-1),$$

$$\vec{X}_3 = \vec{X}_\delta(t-1) - \vec{X}(t-1)$$

$$\vec{X}(t) = \frac{C_1.\vec{X}_1 + C_2.\vec{X}_2 + C_3.\vec{X}_3}{3} \tag{15}$$

Three components of the position are generated for a particle using the position of alpha (X_α), beta (X_β), and delta (X_δ). The new position is estimated at t^{th} iteration taking the average of the three components. Here C_1, C_2, C_3 are three random numbers in the range of [0, 1]. The particles are diverged from its position using the above updating rule.

2. **Exploitation Stage:** At this stage, particles are following the rules for moving to the food using the conception of PSO algorithm. For finding the location of food, it utilizes its own past experience and the information of the best particle, alpha, among them. Two components are used for the updating the position of the particle. First is the component in the direction of its last position and second is directed towards the alpha. At this stage, only alpha plays the important role of leader to motivate the particle towards the optimum. Based on the fitness value of the last iteration, the most fitted alpha is selected. This mechanism helps the particle moving to the optimal solution. The technique is basically based on the sharing of information of best position discovered so far. The position updating rule for i^{th} particle is formulated below.

$$\vec{X}_1 = r_1.\left(\vec{X}_{best} - \vec{X}_i(t-1)\right),$$

$$\vec{X}_2 = r_1.\left(\vec{X}_\alpha - \vec{X}_i(t-1)\right)$$

$$\vec{X}_3 = \vec{X}_1 + \vec{X}_2$$

$$\vec{X}_i\left(t\right) = \vec{X}_i(t-1) + \vec{X}_3 \tag{16}$$

X_{best} is the best position of a particle discovered so far. r_1 and r_2 are two random numbers between 0 1nd 1. Now, if it found that the movements of the particles are stagnant for a number of iterations, then it indicates the improper guidance of the swarm. Generally, near the end of the searching, more emphasis should be given on the exploitation part. But in WOWSC, same emphasis is given on both the stages. As the solution used for exploration uses first two best solutions, alpha and beta which will not deviate the swarm from exploitation rather if there any stagnancy arrives, it will help to overcome the issue. This mechanism helps to come out the swarm from the problem of convergence to a local optimum point.

Termination

When the maximum allowed iteration is reached, the position of alpha is considered as the optimum result of the objective function.

Proposed WOWSC involves exploration stage and exploitation stage. A good balance between exploration and exploitation enhances the efficiency of an algorithm. That happens for proposed methodology. WOWSC maintains good diversity as well as extensive searching near about a possible solution is also considered. The concept of alpha, beta and delta of GWO algorithm is implemented to divergence the swarm. Those categories of wolves in a wolf pack are considered as leaders for the swarm. The multiple leader concept when integrated into PSO provides better possibility in searching. For the processing of microarray datasets, a weighted objective function is formulated using four objectives. The proposed weighted objective works effectively in the identification of informative and class predictive genes from a heterogeneous high dimensional dataset. The unique searching procedure of WOWSC provides better results for the optimization problem. So, here WOWSC is involved for the job of feature selection from the complex dataset. Experimental result shows that WOWSC outperforms in the analysis of gene expression data which validates the robustness of the proposed work. The values of parameters used in WOWSC algorithm are given in Table 2 and the algorithm of the proposed WOWSC is as follows.

EXPERIMENTAL RESULTS

The experimental data consist of microarray dataset of Prostate (Singh et al., 2002), Colon (Alon, 1999), Leukemia (Raetz et al., 2006) and DLBCL (Shipp, 2002) cancer dataset. The collected microarray dataset is first pre-processed and then the proposed methodology using WOWSC is applied to form an optimal subset of genes for supervised learning process in the field of cancer classification. The evaluation of the result is conducted in terms of classification results. To evaluate the performance of the proposed methodology 10 times 10-fold cross validation is performed and the average results are reported here. Different classifiers are involved for the classification such as support vector machine (SVM), C4.5 classifier, decision tree (DT), K-nearest neighbour (KNN) classifier and Naive Bayes (NB) classifier which are widely used in different literatures (Lee et. al., 2011), (Chen et. al., 2014). Again, the result is compared with other existing methods reported in different research articles. The proposed methodology establishes good result, indicating its ability to produce more robust gene selection activity.

Algorithm 1. WOWSC

1. **Initialization.**

    Total Number of particle=N

    (a) Randomly initialize the position of particles, X_i (1=1, 2,..., N)

    (b) Calculate the fitness value of the particles, $f(X_i)$

    (c) Initialize the own best of the particles $P_i=X_i$, $f(P_i)= f(X_i)$

    (d) alpha= *arg{max* $(f(X_i))$}, beta= *arg{second max*$(f(X_i))$}, delta= any of(X_i)

2. **Termination check.**

    (a) If the termination criterion holds go to step 8.

    (b) else go to step 3.

3. **Set** T=1(iteration counter)

    a) **If** the exploration criterion matches (for t_1 interval)

         For i= 1,2...N **Do**

        (a) Update the position according to Equation (15)

        (b) Evaluate the fitness of the ith particle $f(X_i)$

        (c) If $f(X_i)$ is better than $f(P_i)$ then $P_i = X_i$

      End For

        (e) Update alpha= *arg{max* $f(X_i)$}, beta= *arg{second max*$f(X_i)$}

        (f) Clear the archive

      End If

    b) **If** the exploitation criterion matches (for t_2 interval)

         For i= 1,2...N **Do**

        (a) Update the position according to Equation (16)

        (b) Evaluate the fitness of the ith particle $f(X_i)$

        (c) Store the fitness value of the particle in the archive.

        (d) If $f(X_i)$ is better than $f(P_i)$ then $P_i = X_i$

      End For

        (e) Update alpha= *arg{max* $f(X_i)$}, beta= *arg{second max*$f(X_i)$}, delta= max. rate of change $f(X_i)$;

      End If

    4. **Set** t=t+1.

    5. **Go to** step 2

    6. Solution is the *alpha*

Table 2. Parameters used in WOWSC algorithm

Algorithms	Parameters	Explanation	Value
WOWSC	N	Number of particle(s) in one swarm	10
	C_1, C_2, C_3	Random numbers	[0,1]
	r_1, r_2	Random numbers	[0,1]
	T	Total iteration	1000
	t_1	Exploration interval	10
	t_2	Exploitation interval	20

Analysis of the Result

Different analysis is carried out in this section. First, the performance of WOWSC with iteration is examined. Here the fitness function has four objectives and the problem is formulated as maximization problem. The number of maximum iteration is set to 1000 and the population size of WOWSC is kept to 20. For the fitness function, the value of t-score and p-value of WR test is normalized. As per Eq. (2) the fitness function is taken where the value of a, b, c, d are 0.5, 0.5, 1, 1 respectively. The choice of the values of a, b, c, d is done based on experiments. It is noticed that, the value of t-score and WR test are very changing with iterations which in turn affects the ultimate fitness function. So, the effect of those two scores is minimized compared to other two. Now the highest possible value of the fitness function is 3. The value of the fitness function is plotted with the number of iterations. Since, the problem is constructed as the maximization problem, the fitness value increases with the iteration number.

The average fitness value for 20 independent runs of the WOWSC is shown in Figure 5. Here plots are given for 300 iterations and from the graphs, it can be said that WOWSC is able to converge near to 300 iterations. Authors have run experiments for PSO and GWO algorithm also and the results are plotted in the same figure. The experimental results are shown for all the four cancer datasets. For Prostate data, PSO and GWO are performing similarly whereas the fitness value of WOWSC is less at the initial stage of iteration. But as the iteration progresses, WOWSC working better on the problem and approaching towards the good optimization value compared to other two. A similar pattern of performance is observed for Colon cancer. For DLBCL, WOWSC is able to obtain highest fitness value among the all algorithms. Though GWO is able to achieve the best fitness value for Leukemia cancer, the performance of WOWSC is also good. From the plots, it can be concluded that PSO is prone to faster convergence losing its further possibility of improvement. But WOWSC is moving towards the possible solution area at the later stages of iterations as it has the mechanism of getting out of the stagnancy. The experimental results establish the outperformance of WOWSC algorithm over PSO and GWO algorithm. It can be stated that a balanced approach between exploration and exploitation helps the proposed algorithm to reach to the optimum. As a whole, WOWSC is working efficiently to maximize the fitness value used for choosing the signature gene during cancer classification.

Classification Results

Using WOWSC, authors aim to identify top differentially expressed genes (DEGs) as well as those genes should perform well in the task of classification. The gene subset which is identified by WOWSC using some weighted objective is validated by analyzing the classification results. The result establishes that WOWSC is able to extract important features from microarray dataset and it is given in Table 3. Here, experiments are designed for 10 times 10-fold cross validation. The proposed methodology is implemented using four different well-known classifiers (SVM, DT, KNN, NB). Average results of classification are given in terms of sensitivity, specificity, accuracy, and F-score. For Prostate cancer, NB classifier shows better performance compared to others. Here, 97% accuracy is achieved and the value of sensitivity is 100%. For Colon dataset, SVM classifier is working efficiently in terms of providing a good sensitivity of the result. Highest accuracy is achieved by the KNN classifier which is equal to 87%. For Leukemia, most of the classifiers are providing 100% satisfying classification result. For DLBCL, both the SVM and NB are providing good sensitivity. Here, the maximum accuracy is 95% which is obtained by NB classifier.

Figure 5. Average fitness value Vs iteration plot for a) Prostate b) Colon c) DLBCL d) Leukemia cancer datasets.

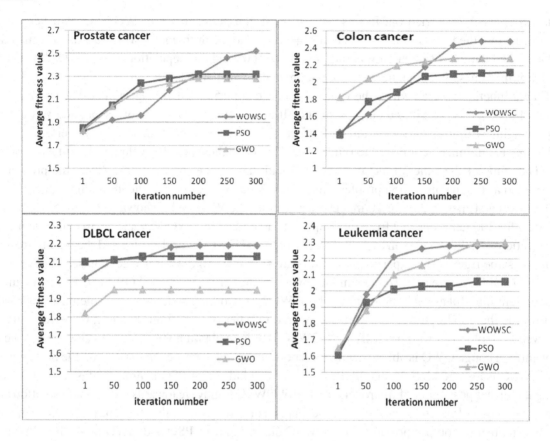

Statistical Wilcoxon rank sum test (Agarwal & Mehta, 2017) is performed on the classification results. For the statistical test, rank sum '*p*' is computed for two compared algorithms for 20 runs. The difference is considered if error is significant at 5% level of confidence. WOWSC algorithm with KNN, decision tree and NB classifier are compared with each other and with WOWSC-SVM on their accuracy of classification. Results are given in Table 4. For Prostate dataset, WOWSC -NB is better than all the other algorithms. WOWSC -KNN and WOWSC -tree are equally performing and better than SVM based methodology. The results are shown for all four datasets. From the statistical analysis, it can be concluded that WOWSC –NB is the best performing procedure for Prostate and DLBCL cancer. For Leukemia, all three mechanisms are providing equal and best accuracy. For Colon cancer, WOWSC-KNN is the best performer among all.

The accuracy of classification obtained using different classifier is also given in the form of bar chart in Figure 6 for better interpretability of the results. The comparative result shows that for Colon cancer KNN classifier is performing well whereas, for other three datasets, NB classifier can be selected for the task of classification as it is providing good results compared to other classifiers.

Table 3. Results of Classification for different cancer datasets

Dataset	Algorithms	Sensitivity	Specificity	Accuracy	F-score
Prostate	WOWSC -SVM	0.82	1.00	0.87	0.86
	WOWSC -KNN	1.00	0.87	0.92	0.92
	WOWSC -tree	0.93	0.89	0.92	0.91
	WOWSC -NB	1.00	0.94	0.97	0.97
Colon	WOWSC -SVM	1.00	0.58	0.81	0.84
	WOWSC -KNN	0.75	0.82	0.87	0.86
	WOWSC -tree	0.75	0.72	0.83	0.76
	WOWSC -NB	0.79	0.77	0.83	0.89
Leukemia	WOWSC -SVM	0.98	0.87	0.89	0.91
	WOWSC KNN	1.00	1.00	1.00	1.00
	WOWSC -tree	1.00	1.00	1.00	1.00
	WOWSC -NB	1.00	1.00	1.00	1.00
DLBCL	WOWSC SVM	0.96	0.67	0.78	0.83
	WOWSC -KNN	0.89	1.00	0.91	0.94
	WOWSC -tree	0.89	0.67	0.81	0.87
	WOWSC -NB	0.97	0.93	0.95	0.97

Table 4. Results of Wilcoxon rank sum test on accuracy for different cancer datasets.

Dataset	Algorithms	WOWSC -SVM	WOWSC -KNN	WOWSC -tree	WOWSC -NB	Better	Worse	Equal
Prostate	WOWSC -KNN	+		=	-	1	1	1
	WOWSC -tree	+	=		-	1	1	1
	WOWSC -NB	+	+	+		3	0	0
Colon	WOWSC -KNN	+		+	+	3	0	0
	WOWSC -tree	+	-		=	1	1	1
	WOWSC -NB	+	-	=		1	1	1
Leukemia	WOWSC KNN	+		=	=	1	0	2
	WOWSC -tree	+	=		=	1	0	2
	WOWSC -NB	+	=	=		1	0	2
DLBCL	WOWSC -KNN	+		+	-	2	1	0
	WOWSC -tree	+	-		-	1	2	0
	WOWSC -NB	+	+	+		3	0	0

Figure 6. Accuracy of classification using different classifiers for a) Prostate b) Leukemia c) Colon d) DLBCL cancer datasets.

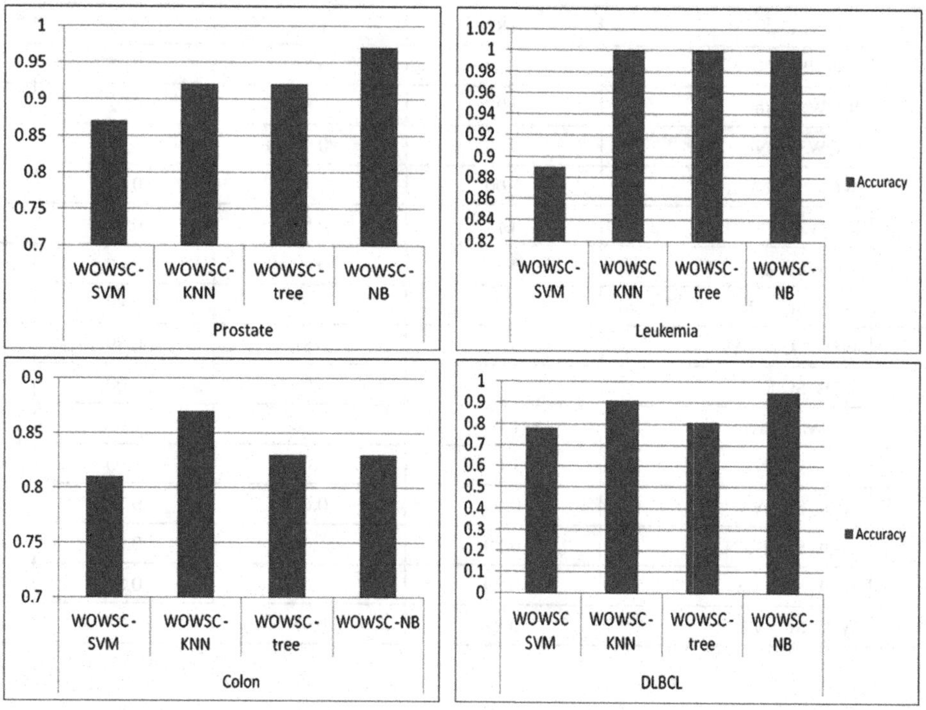

Comparative Results

To estimate the effectiveness of the proposed method, experimental results are compared with other approaches, reported in different kinds of literature for gene selection methodology. A comparative study is given in Table 5. From the result, it can be concluded that in the proposed work, WOWSC is able to perform more accurately for all the dataset except for the Colon dataset. But, the overall performance of the proposed is promising compared to others.

Table 5. Comparison of accuracy of classification with other results reported in the literature.

Reference	Year	Leukemia	Colon	DLBCL	Prostate
Luo et al.	2011	0.71	0.8	0.82	-
Bonilla-Huerta et al.	2016	0.99	0.9	0.93	-
Apolloni et al.	2016	0.82	0.75	0.93	-
Dash et al.	2016	0.95	0.68	-	-
Salem et al.	2017	0.97	0.85	0.94	-
Proposed	**2017**	**1.00**	**0.87**	**0.95**	**0.97**

Biological Relevance

To demonstrate the biological relevance of the selected gene markers by the proposed method, top 20% genes are selected for validation. Using disease-gene association database http://www.disgenet.org/, the information about those genes is collected. The number of Pubmed citations against the selected genes is also taken from the database. In Table 6, few disease information and the genes related to those diseases are given. The result validates the biological significance of the proposed work.

CONCLUSION AND FUTURE WORK

Relevant gene selection and then classification of disease is a very interesting topic in the study of bio-informatics. Microarray dataset is a huge dataset consisting of thousands of gene expressions for different samples. So, for the purpose of feature reduction and extraction from the huge dimension of the dataset, authors involve weighted objective wolf-swarm colony (WOWSC) optimization algorithm. The WOWSC is a new hybrid optimization technique which is proposed by integrating the idea of hunting of wolves with the particle swarm optimization. The proposed methodology is useful in the context of diagnosis of disease as it identifies significant genes related to the disease. The experimental result establishes that the proposed method shows promising result in comparison to other existing gene selection techniques. The proposed method is able to produce good classification accuracy, which reflects its efficiency and robustness. In the near future, the method can be applied for different feature reduction and feature selection problem from big datasets. Multi-objective pareto front technique can also be used to sum up different statistical and classification objectives.

Table 6. Biological significance of the proposed work

Dataset	Associated Diseases	Gene Symbol
Prostate	Prostatic Neoplasms	KLK3(75), IGF2(4), CCND2(2),
	Protate Carcinoma	KLK3(776), INS(30), IGF1(69), PTENP1(1)
	Malignant neoplasm of Prostate	KLK3(781), INS(31), IGF2(25), MAPK9(4)
LL	Leukemia	RAG1(3), IL7R(5), SPI1(7), ITGB2(3)
	Carcinogenesis	CCND3(6), MSH(6)
	Lymphoma	CCND3(7), MSH(5), ITGB2(6)
Colon	Colorectal Cancer	VCAM1(5), MAPK3(11)
	Colorectal Carcinoma	VCAM1(5), MAPK3(18), EGR1(14)
	Malignant tumor of Colon	VCAM1(1), MAPK3(5), EGR1(6)
DLBCL	T- cell Lymphoma	FASLG(2), AKT1(9)
	B- cell lymphoma	FASLG(1), TP53(54), MAPK3(2)

REFERENCES

Agarwal, P., & Mehta, S. (2016). Enhanced flower pollination algorithm on data clustering. *International Journal of Computers and Applications*, *38*(2-3), 144–155. doi:10.1080/1206212X.2016.1224401

Agarwal, P., & Mehta, S. (2017). Empirical analysis of five nature-inspired algorithms on real parameter optimization problems. *Artificial Intelligence Review*, 1–57.

Agarwalla, P., & Mukhopadhyay, S. (2018). Bi-stage hierarchical selection of pathway genes for cancer progression using a swarm based computational approach. *Applied Soft Computing*, *62*, 230–250. doi:10.1016/j.asoc.2017.10.024

Alon, U., Barkai, N., Notterman, D. A., Gish, K., Ybarra, S., Mack, D., & Levine, A. J. (1999). Broad patterns of gene expression revealed by clustering analysis of tumor and normal colon tissues probed by oligonucleotide arrays. In *Proceedings of the National Academy of Sciences of the United States of America*, *96*(12), 6745–6750. doi:10.1073/pnas.96.12.6745 PMID:10359783

Amaratunga, D., Cabrera, J., & Kovtun, V. (2008). Microarray learning with ABC. *Biostatistics (Oxford, England)*, *9*(1), 128–136. doi:10.1093/biostatistics/kxm017 PMID:17573363

Apolloni, J., Leguizamón, G., & Alba, E. (2016). Two hybrid wrapper-filter feature selection algorithms applied to high-dimensional microarray experiments. *Applied Soft Computing*, *38*, 922–932. doi:10.1016/j.asoc.2015.10.037

Arevalillo, J. M., & Navarro, H. (2013). Exploring correlations in gene expression microarray data for maximum predictive - minimum redundancy biomarker selection and classification. *Computers in Biology and Medicine*, *43*(10), 1437–1443. doi:10.1016/j.compbiomed.2013.07.005 PMID:24034735

Bandyopadhyay, S., Mallik, S., & Mukhopadhyay, A. (2014). A survey and comparative study of statistical tests for identifying differential expression from microarray data. *IEEE/ACM Transactions on Computational Biology and Bioinformatics*, *11*(1), 95–115. doi:10.1109/TCBB.2013.147 PMID:26355511

Bonilla-Huerta, E., Hernández-Montiel, A., Morales-Caporal, R., & Arjona-López, M. (2016). Hybrid framework using multiple-filters and an embedded approach for an efficient selection and classification of microarray data. *IEEE/ACM Transactions on Computational Biology and Bioinformatics*, *13*(1), 12–26. doi:10.1109/TCBB.2015.2474384 PMID:26336138

Chen, K. H., Wang, K. J., Tsai, M. L., Wang, K. M., Adrian, A. M., Cheng, W. C., & Chang, K. S. (2014). Gene selection for cancer identification: A decision tree model empowered by particle swarm optimization algorithm. *BMC Bioinformatics*, *15*(1), 1–12. doi:10.1186/1471-2105-15-49 PMID:24555567

Cheok, M. H., Yang, W., Pui, C. H., Downing, J. R., Cheng, C., Naeve, C. W., ... Evans, W. E. (2003). Treatment-specific changes in gene expression discriminate in vivo drug response in human leukemia cells. *Nature Genetics*, *34*(1), 85–90. doi:10.1038/ng1151 PMID:12704389

Chuang, L. Y., Yang, C. H., Wu, K. C., & Yang, C. H. (2011). A hybrid feature selection method for DNA microarray data. *Computers in Biology and Medicine, 41*(4), 228–237. doi:10.1016/j.comp-biomed.2011.02.004 PMID:21376310

Dash, R., & Misra, B. B. (2016). Pipelining the ranking techniques for microarray data classification: A case study. *Applied Soft Computing, 48*, 298–316. doi:10.1016/j.asoc.2016.07.006

Dorigo, M., & Blum, C. (2005). Ant colony optimization theory: A survey. *Theoretical Computer Science, 344*(2-3), 243–278. doi:10.1016/j.tcs.2005.05.020

Elyasigomari, V., Mirjafari, M. S., Screen, H. R. C., & Shaheed, M. H. (2015). Cancer classification using a novel gene selection approach by means of shuffling based on data clustering with optimization. *Applied Soft Computing, 35*, 43–51. doi:10.1016/j.asoc.2015.06.015

GaneshKumar, P., Rani, C., Devaraj, D., & Victoire, T. A. A. (2014). Hybrid ant bee algorithm for fuzzy expert system based sample classification. *IEEE/ACM Transactions on Computational Biology and Bioinformatics, 11*(2), 347–360. doi:10.1109/TCBB.2014.2307325 PMID:26355782

Golub, T. R., Slonim, D. K., Tamayo, P., Huard, C., Gaasenbeek, M., Mesirov, J. P., & Bloomfield, C. D. (1999). Molecular classification of cancer: class discovery and class prediction by gene expression monitoring. *science, 286*(5439), 531-537.

Hippo, Y., Taniguchi, H., Tsutsumi, S., Machida, N., Chong, J. M., Fukayama, M., ... Aburatani, H. (2002). Global gene expression analysis of gastric cancer by oligonucleotide microarrays. *Cancer Research, 62*(1), 233–240. PMID:11782383

Holland, J. H. (1992). Genetic algorithms. *Scientific American, 267*(1), 66–73. doi:10.1038cientificam erican0792-66

Hsu, H. H., Hsieh, C. W., & Lu, M. D. (2011). Hybrid feature selection by combining filters and wrappers. *Expert Systems with Applications, 38*(7), 8144–8150. doi:10.1016/j.eswa.2010.12.156

Karaboga, D., & Basturk, B. (2007). A powerful and efficient algorithm for numerical function optimization: Artificial bee colony (ABC) algorithm. *Journal of Global Optimization, 39*(3), 459–471. doi:10.100710898-007-9149-x

Kennedy, J. (2011). Particle swarm optimization. In Encyclopedia of machine learning (pp. 760-766). Springer US.

Kleftogiannis, D., Theofilatos, K., Likothanassis, S., & Mavroudi, S. (2015). YamiPred: A novel evolutionary method for predicting pre-miRNAs and selecting relevant features. *IEEE/ACM Transactions on Computational Biology and Bioinformatics, 12*(5), 1183–1192. doi:10.1109/TCBB.2014.2388227 PMID:26451829

Lee, C. P., Lin, W. S., Chen, Y. M., & Kuo, B. J. (2011). Gene selection and sample classification on microarray data based on adaptive genetic algorithm/k-nearest neighbor method. *Expert Systems with Applications, 38*(5), 4661–4667. doi:10.1016/j.eswa.2010.07.053

Luo, L. K., Huang, D. F., Ye, L. J., Zhou, Q. F., Shao, G. F., & Peng, H. (2011). Improving the computational efficiency of recursive cluster elimination for gene selection. *IEEE/ACM Transactions on Computational Biology and Bioinformatics, 8*(1), 122–129. doi:10.1109/TCBB.2010.44 PMID:20479497

Marler, R. T., & Arora, J. S. (2010). The weighted sum method for multi-objective optimization: New insights. *Structural and Multidisciplinary Optimization, 41*(6), 853–862. doi:10.100700158-009-0460-7

Mirjalili, S., Mirjalili, S. M., & Lewis, A. (2014). Grey wolf optimizer. *Advances in Engineering Software, 69*, 46–61. doi:10.1016/j.advengsoft.2013.12.007

Mohamad, M. S., Omatu, S., Deris, S., Misman, M. F., & Yoshioka, M. (2009). A multi-objective strategy in genetic algorithms for gene selection of gene expression data. *Artificial Life and Robotics, 13*(2), 410–413. doi:10.100710015-008-0533-5

Moscato, P., & Cotta, C. (2002). Memetic algorithms. Handbook of Applied Optimization, 157-167.

Mukhopadhyay, A., & Mandal, M. (2014). Identifying non-redundant gene markers from microarray data: A multiobjective variable length pso-based approach. *IEEE/ACM Transactions on Computational Biology and Bioinformatics, 11*(6), 1170–1183. doi:10.1109/TCBB.2014.2323065 PMID:26357053

Pal, J. K., Ray, S. S., Cho, S. B., & Pal, S. K. (2016). Fuzzy-Rough Entropy Measure and Histogram Based Patient Selection for miRNA Ranking in Cancer. *IEEE/ACM Transactions on Computational Biology and Bioinformatics*. PMID:27831888

Peng, H., Long, F., & Ding, C. (2005). Feature selection based on mutual information criteria of max-dependency, max-relevance, and min-redundancy. *IEEE Transactions on Pattern Analysis and Machine Intelligence, 27*(8), 1226–1238. doi:10.1109/TPAMI.2005.159 PMID:16119262

Saha, S., Ekbal, A., Gupta, K., & Bandyopadhyay, S. (2013). Gene expression data clustering using a multiobjective symmetry based clustering technique. *Computers in Biology and Medicine, 43*(11), 1965–1977. doi:10.1016/j.compbiomed.2013.07.021 PMID:24209942

Salem, H., Attiya, G., & El-Fishawy, N. (2017). Classification of human cancer diseases by gene expression profiles. *Applied Soft Computing, 50*, 124–134. doi:10.1016/j.asoc.2016.11.026

Shipp, M. A., Ross, K. N., Tamayo, P., Weng, A. P., Kutok, J. L., Aguiar, R. C., & Ray, T. S. (2002). Diffuse large B-cell lymphoma outcome prediction by gene-expression profiling and supervised machine learning. *Nature Medicine, 8*(1), 68–74. doi:10.1038/nm0102-68 PMID:11786909

Singh, D., Febbo, P. G., Ross, K., Jackson, D. G., Manola, J., Ladd, C., ... Lander, E. S. (2002). Gene expression correlates of clinical prostate cancer behavior. *Cancer Cell, 1*(2), 203–209. doi:10.1016/S1535-6108(02)00030-2 PMID:12086878

Storn, R., & Price, K. (1997). Differential evolution–a simple and efficient heuristic for global optimization over continuous spaces. *Journal of Global Optimization, 11*(4), 341–359. doi:10.1023/A:1008202821328

Tan, F., Fu, X., Zhang, Y., & Bourgeois, A. G. (2006, July). Improving feature subset selection using a genetic algorithm for microarray gene expression data. In *2006 IEEE International Conference on Evolutionary Computation* (pp. 2529-2534). IEEE.

Wan, Y., Wang, M., Ye, Z., & Lai, X. (2016). A feature selection method based on modified binary coded ant colony optimization algorithm. *Applied Soft Computing*, *49*, 248–258. doi:10.1016/j.asoc.2016.08.011

Wang, H., & Niu, B. (2017). A novel bacterial algorithm with randomness control for feature selection in classification. *Neurocomputing*, *228*, 176–186. doi:10.1016/j.neucom.2016.09.078

Yang, D., Parrish, R. S., & Brock, G. N. (2014). Empirical evaluation of consistency and accuracy of methods to detect differentially expressed genes based on microarray data. *Computers in Biology and Medicine*, *46*, 1–10. doi:10.1016/j.compbiomed.2013.12.002 PMID:24529200

Zhang, L., Kuljis, J., Li Zhang, L., Kuljis, J., & Liu, X. (2008). Information visualization for DNA microarray data analysis: A critical review. *IEEE Transactions on Systems, Man and Cybernetics. Part C, Applications and Reviews*, *38*(1), 42–54. doi:10.1109/TSMCC.2007.906065

Zheng, C. H., Yang, W., Chong, Y. W., & Xia, J. F. (2016). Identification of mutated driver pathways in cancer using a multi-objective optimization model. *Computers in Biology and Medicine*, *72*, 22–29. doi:10.1016/j.compbiomed.2016.03.002 PMID:26995027

Zibakhsh, A., & Abadeh, M. S. (2013). Gene selection for cancer tumor detection using a novel memetic algorithm with a multi-view fitness function. *Engineering Applications of Artificial Intelligence*, *26*(4), 1274–1281. doi:10.1016/j.engappai.2012.12.009

KEY TERMS AND DEFINITIONS

Cancer: It is a collection of disease due to abnormal proliferation of cell.

Classification: It is a process to categorize the objects so that they can be differentiated from others.

DNA Microarray: It is the gene expression level of thousand genes collected from different samples in a single microscopic chip.

Swarm Algorithm: A set of meta-heuristic, population-based optimization techniques that uses nature inspired processes.

Feature Selection: It is a machine learning technique which is used for selecting redundant subset of feature or attributes from a huge dataset.

p-Value: It is a statistical null hypothetical test that helps to determine the probability how the result differs from the observed values.

t-Test: It is a non-parametric statistical test that can be performed to differentiate two set of observations based on their mean and standard deviation.

Chapter 8
Scheduling Data Intensive Scientific Workflows in Cloud Environment Using Nature Inspired Algorithms

Shikha Mehta
Jaypee Institute of Information Technology, India

Parmeet Kaur
Jaypee Institute of Information Technology, India

ABSTRACT

Workflows are a commonly used model to describe applications consisting of computational tasks with data or control flow dependencies. They are used in domains of bioinformatics, astronomy, physics, etc., for data-driven scientific applications. Execution of data-intensive workflow applications in a reasonable amount of time demands a high-performance computing environment. Cloud computing is a way of purchasing computing resources on demand through virtualization technologies. It provides the infrastructure to build and run workflow applications, which is called 'Infrastructure as a Service.' However, it is necessary to schedule workflows on cloud in a way that reduces the cost of leasing resources. Scheduling tasks on resources is a NP hard problem and using meta-heuristic algorithms is an obvious choice for the same. This chapter presents application of nature-inspired algorithms: particle swarm optimization, shuffled frog leaping algorithm and grey wolf optimization algorithm to the workflow scheduling problem on the cloud. Simulation results prove the efficacy of the suggested algorithms.

INTRODUCTION

This chapter presents a study of scheduling data-intensive scientific workflows in IaaS clouds using nature inspired algorithms. Workflows are a commonly used computational model to perform scientific simulations (Juve et al., 2013). These models are mostly used to visualize and manage the computations as well as activities happening in scientific processes. They are employed to illustrate the applications

DOI: 10.4018/978-1-5225-5852-1.ch008

involving a series of computational tasks with data- or control-flow reliance among themselves. They are used to represent complex scientific problems prevailing in diverse fields such as Bioinformatics, Physics, weather data analysis and modelling, structural chemistry etc (Juve et al., 2013). However, scientific applications of this nature are, in general, data-driven, and use files to communicate data between tasks. The data and computing requirements of such these applications are ever-growing which are further featured by complex structures and entail heterogeneous services. Executing such data intensive workflow applications pose numerous challenges such as quality of service (QoS), scalability, data storage, computing resources along with heterogeneous and distributed data management (Juve & Deelman, 2011). Therefore, these demand a high-end computing environment in order to complete the task in a considerable duration. As the scientific data is growing at a pace faster than ever, it is no longer going to be feasible to transfer data from data centres to desktops for analysis. In contrast, processing will time and again take place on high-performance systems with local storage of data.

Cloud computing is basically a on demand method to purchase computing as well as storage resources via virtualization technologies (Buyya et al., 2009). Such services are available most prominently as per three models, namely, Infrastructure as a Service (IaaS), Software as a Service (SaaS) and Platform as a Service (PaaS). Internet is the backbone for all the cloud computing models. Software as a Service (SaaS) model of cloud computing allows users to access providers applications on a client's system without being bothered about the administration of the services which is being done by the vendor itself. SaaS is commonly used for providing cloud applications such as Web-based e-mail, social networking websites; online document editors etc. The second category of cloud model is the Platform as a Service (PaaS) that provides frameworks for use in development or customization of applications. This makes possible fast and cost-efficient application development, testing, and deployment. The last category of popular cloud model is Infrastructure as a Service (IaaS) that offers a heterogeneous collection of resources from which users can lease resources according to their requirements.

This chapter lays focus on task scheduling and resource provisioning particularly in Infrastructure as a Service (IaaS) clouds. Due to the availability of unlimited and diverse types of resources, IaaS cloud models are more appropriate for applications involving scientific workflows. IaaS provides a large shared pool of heterogeneous resources or virtual machines (VMs) to execute computationally expensive workflow applications. Cloud computing is a computing paradigm that is apt to deal with most of the challenges listed above. It provides a technique of acquiring compute and storage resources according to a user's requirement through virtualization technologies. Virtualization technology of clouds enables easy deployment, management and execution of workflow applications in clouds. This is the result of the benefits presented by virtualization such as migration of code and data, fault tolerance, process isolation and customization of services for users. This has made it possible for cloud computing platforms to allocate virtual machines dynamically as Internet services (for e.g. Amazon EC2/S3).

However, cloud services come at a pay-per-use basis and hence, it is necessary to schedule workflow applications in a way that reduces the total cost of leasing resources for execution, besides other possible criteria. Scheduling tasks on resources is a NP hard problem (Ullman, 1975; Lin &Lu, 2011). Therefore, using meta-heuristic algorithms is an obvious choice for the same. This chapter will present the application of nature-inspired algorithms, namely particle swarm optimization, shuffled frog leaping algorithm and bat algorithm to the scheduling problem for workflows on cloud (Zhan et al., 2015). The next section of the chapter will introduce the scheduling problem. Subsequently, the nature inspired algorithms and their application to the current problem will be explained in brief. Next, the metrics that can be used to evaluate computational performance of workflows in cloud environment will be discussed. This will be followed by a discussion of the mapping of considered algorithms to the scheduling problem. The results of simulation of nature inspired algorithms to scheduling are discussed next along with an analysis of results. Lastly, the concluding remarks are put forth.

INTRODUCTION TO SCHEDULING OF WORKFLOWS

Workflows help to combine multiple computational processes, linked by data or control flow dependencies, into a single well-structured unit. This enables the modelling of multiple scientific processes of varied complexities as workflows. Such workflows are present in wide application domains such as bioinformatics, astronomy, physics, image processing etc. Their size may vary from a small number of tasks to millions of tasks. Scientific workflows operate, in general, on large, complex and heterogeneous data and involve intensive computations. These workflows are usually dataflow-oriented and have a resemblance to data streaming and signal-processing applications. The result of their execution may be complex data products that may be reused in repeated executions with varying parameters or for different workflows

A workflow may be represented as a directed acyclic task graph, G(V, E), where V denotes the vertex or node set representing the set of tasks composing an application and E denotes the edges in the graph G where each edge corresponds to the dependencies between two tasks. Every task is associated with execution cost with respect to the given available. The R represents the various types of resources or Virtual Machines in IaaS clouds. The running time of a particular task on a specific VM can be computed if the processing capacity of a VM, in terms of floating point operations per second (FLOPS), is known. It may be available either from the VM provider or can be calculated to an approximation

Figure 1. A workflow with 9 tasks

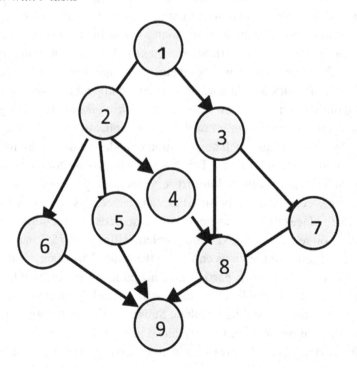

(Ostermann, 2010). A directed edge, E1,2 from node V1 to node V2 depicts that V1 precedes V2 in the task graph such that the task represented by N1 has to be finished before the task represented by N2 can start execution. The cost of communicating the output from node N1 to the node N2 is represented by the weight on edge E1,2. A node without any incoming edges is the entry task of the workflow while nodes with no outgoing edges represent the exit tasks. A workflow may also have a deadline, Δ associated with it indicates the time by which the workflow must finish execution. Fig. 1 illustrates an example of workflow with 9 tasks. Figure 2 illustrates an instance of a schedule related to the workflow of Fig. 1.

It may be assumed that IaaS providers make available varied types of VMs that users can hire based on the requirements. A workflow scheduling technique generates a mapping between tasks and resources and enlists the count of VMs that should be leased along with the time duration for which they should be leased. The goal of any scheduling algorithm is to generate a schedule which meets the users' specified requirements related to cost, deadlines, fault tolerance, priorities etc. The optimization criteria popularly used in workflow scheduling applications are minimization of application execution cost or time; maximization of resource utilization; meeting the deadline constraints, minimization of makespan which denotes the time at which the last task finishes, etc.

USE OF NATURE INSPIRED ALGORITHMS IN SCHEDULING WORKFLOWS IN CLOUDS

Scheduling of workflows in distributed systems is considered to be NP-hard problem. Therefore, finding an optimal solution in polynomial-time is difficult. Wide varieties of techniques have been developed to perform scheduling in multiprocessing systems. However, these techniques either provide sub-optimal solutions in low time or an optimum solution in an enormous amount of time. Techniques relying on heuristics as well as meta-heuristics techniques have been extensively applied for workflow scheduling in the domain of grid and cloud computing. The focus of scheduling schemes, however, differs in these two environments. The solutions for the grid computing environment assume the accessibility of only a restricted amount of computing resources most of the times and try to decrease an application's execution time without stressing on reduction in the cost of execution. In comparison, resource availability presents no restriction in the cloud computing environment and hence, workflow scheduling algorithms tend to minimize the execution cost or stick to execution deadlines in the cloud environment. In the last few years, researchers have explored the utility of nature inspired algorithms, for instance the genetic algorithm (GA), Particle Swarm Optimization (PSO) and Ant Colony Optimization (ACO) to generate efficient solutions of the problem. Nevertheless, there is still scope for improving efficiency of these

Figure 2. Schedule corresponding to a workflow

techniques. Hence, this chapter presents a Grey Wolf Algorithm based workflow scheduling technique optimized for cloud computing.

By introducing additional heuristics for decreasing the complexity of scheduling algorithms, two variants of genetic algorithms were developed in (Omara & Arafa, 2010) for improving the system performance. One out of these two GA variants employs two fitness functions. One of the fitness functions aims to minimize the total execution time and the objective of the second is to perform load balancing. The other variant of GA employs a technique for duplication of tasks for reducing the communication overhead between the processors. Results revealed that both the algorithms performed better than the conventional algorithms.

In literature researchers have explored Workflow scheduling for the grid computing environment. Three intelligent techniques have been introduced for task scheduling in grids by a recent study (Tripathy, Dash & Padhy, 2015). Authors firstly employed Directed Search Optimization (DSO) algorithm to formulate the task scheduling in the form of an optimization problem. Thereafter, the DSO was brought to use to train a three layered Artificial Neural Network (ANN) and a Radial Basis Function Neural Network (RBFNN). It was established that networks trained using DSO performed better than their counterparts.

Rahman, Venugopal & Buyya (2007) have proposed the idea of computing dynamic critical path (DCP) for workflow scheduling in grids. The workflow task graph was analyzed and a mapping established between resources and tasks while computing the critical path. In the critical path, tasks which were expected to complete earlier were allotted a higher priority as compared to others. The approach worked well as it was able to generate schedules for the majority of workflows for grids effectively.

For optimization, the algorithm given by (Chen & Zhang, 2009) have considered a number of QoS parameters such as the users' preferences, minimum thresholds for QoS and constraints due to QoS. An ant colony optimization (ACO) based algorithm was proposed for scheduling of large-sized workflows. The algorithm aimed to obtain a solution that was in agreement with the QoS constraints and optimized the QoS parameters as well. In the work presented by Yu & Buyya (2006), a genetic algorithm-based scheduling algorithm with budget constraint is presented. Authors considered the execution cost of application itself as the QoS parameter. The approach strives to optimize the execution time within the specified budget. The algorithm uses the utility grids over a common but secured network on a pay-per-use model. In case budget is very low, the genetic algorithm also employs Markov decision process for faster convergence. The authors of (Tao et al., 2013) have presented a PSO-variant, termed as a rotary chaotic particle swarm optimization (RCPSO) algorithm for trusted scheduling of workflows in grids. The factor of trust has been stressed upon since the issues of security, reliability and availability should also be taken care of besides handling of time and cost related limits. The performance of RCPSO algorithm is evaluated for scheduling with large number of resources in grid environment. The results depict that RCPSO outperforms Genetic Algorithm, ACO and PSO in grid workflow scheduling.

The various applications discussed above indicate the issues and some solutions for scheduling of workflows in grid computing. However, only a limited number of studies have explored algorithms utilizing meta-heuristics for scheduling of workflows in cloud computing.

A dynamic approach for minimizing the running cost of an application using a pricing-based model is proposed for cloud workflow scheduling by Mao, M. & Humphrey, M. (2011). Authors emphasized that a variety of VMs are available for lease-on demand at different costs in the Infrastructure as a Cloud service model. The presented approach is successful in reducing the cost only to a limited extent.

A number of static and dynamic algorithms for workflow scheduling on clouds have been presented by Malawski et al. (2012). The main focus of this work is successful execution of a maximum number of workflows while adhering to their respective cost and deadline constraints. These algorithms also assessed the overheads involved while renting the cloud based VMs and disparities in tasks' estimated execution time. Since the studies were performed considering all VMs of same type, performance of the approach considering the heterogeneity of IaaS clouds is still questionable.

Abrishami, Naghibzadeh & Epema (2013) have presented a static algorithm to schedule a particular instance of a workflow on an IaaS cloud. The algorithm endeavors to diminish the cost of execution while following the time deadline and the availability of resources. The approach takes into consideration the critical paths of a workflow, the cloud price models and the heterogeneity of VMs. However, the technique does not generate a global optimal solution as it optimizes at task level and hence is unable to utilize the complete configuration and characteristics of a workflow for generating an optimal solution. Another study (Pandey et al., 2010) has employed PSO algorithm to minimize the cost of execution and also perform balancing of load across VMs, with the assumption that there are fixed number of VMs.

A PSO variant, the Revised Discrete Particle Swarm Optimization (RDPSO) (Wu et al., 2010) is presented for application scheduling in cloud. The objective of the work is to minimize the make span which considers equally the cost of computation and the cost of data transmission based on the cloud model. Since the algorithm assumes initial set of VMs to be fixed, it does not make use of the elasticity of Infrastructure as a Service clouds.

In another study (Poola et al., 2014), authors presented an algorithm to minimize the makespan and cost for scheduling the workflow tasks on heterogeneous Cloud resources. Authors emphasized on the importance of robustness and introduced the same in workflow scheduling and execution in clouds by introducing redundancy in the system. However, as could be expected, increase in robustness of the schedule results in a relative increase in cost of execution.

In (Rodriguez & Buyya, 2014), authors designed an approach to leverage the resource diversity, high availability and elasticity in the cloud computing environment. Approach employs PSO algorithm for provisioning of resources and scientific workflow scheduling on IaaS clouds. The focus of the algorithm is to reduce the total execution cost while meeting the workflow deadline constraints. Through simulation experiments it was established that PSO based approach outperforms the other contemporary algorithms on well-established scientific workflows of wide-ranging sizes. A comprehensive survey of application of the evolutionary algorithms to the workflow scheduling problem in cloud computing is presented along with the related taxonomy in (Zhan et al., 2015). It has been reiterated that limited research has been performed in this domain and there exists scope for improvement in the state-of-art. Metaheuristic based scheduling techniques are surveyed in detail for the cloud computing environment and results are presented in (Kalra & Singh, 2015).

From the above studies, it can be inferred that the use of metaheuristic algorithms for finding near optimal solutions in the clouds is worth consideration. In (Kaur & Mehta, 2017), authors developed a variation of SFLA, Augmented Shuffled Frog Leaping Algorithm (ASFLA) for provisioning of resources and scheduling of workflows in clouds. Algorithm is evaluated for large size workflows (upto 1000) and it is established that ASFLA outperforms both PSO and SFLA in minimizing cost of execution and following the schedule deadlines. Other algorithms being explored in this area include Ant Colony Optimization (ACO), Genetic Algorithm (GA), BAT algorithm and League Championship Algorithm (LCA).

Workflow scheduling in clouds is a latest area of research and has an immense possibility for original and competent solutions. Recently, a metaheuristic algorithm, Grey Wolf Optimization (GWO) algorithm has been recognized to be effective in various applications such as economic emission dispatch problem (CEED) in power systems (Song, Sulaiman & Mohamed, 2014), PID controller parameters in DC motors (Madadi & Motlagh, 2014), selection of feature subsets (Emary et al., 2015), design of double later grids (Gholizadeh, 2015), forecasting of time (Yusof & Mustaffa, 2015), flow shop scheduling problem (Komaki & Kayvanfar, 2015), optimal power flow problem (El-Fergany & Hasanien, 2015), and optimization of cryptographic key values algorithms (Shankar & Eswaran, 2015). Therefore, the work presented in this chapter aims to evaluate the aptness of GWO algorithm in comparison to SFLA and PSO algorithms for provisioning of resources and scheduling of workflows in IaaS cloud computing.

OVERVIEW OF NATURE INSPIRED ALGORITHMS

Grey Wolf Optimization

In the last few years, nature-inspired algorithms have gained immense popularity among researchers from diverse fields; due to their simplicity and flexibility in providing solutions to complex optimization problems. Recently a novel swarm intelligent technique, known as Grey wolf optimization, was developed by Mirjalili et al. (2014) that mimics the leadership hierarchy and group hunting behavior of grey wolves in nature. Grey wolves belong to the Canidae family and are known as apex predators as they lie at the top of the food chain. The natural behavior of Grey wolves is to live in groups of size 5-12 approximately. The interesting part is that Grey wolves follow a strict hierarchy of dominance. In the hierarchy, there is a leader (male/female) commonly known as alpha (α) which is the most dominant member of the group and is responsible for decision making. Other members of the pack are supposed to follow the decisions (such as time for sleeping, waking up, hunting, etc.) taken by the leader. The second and third in hierarchy are beta and delta respectively. Beta gives advice to alpha and maintains discipline in the pack. Beta also selects the best candidate to be the new leader of the group in case alpha becomes old or passes away. On the other hand, delta wolves are subordinates to alpha and beta while they dominate the omega (lowest level in the social hierarchy of wolves). All other wolves in the pack are known as Omega and follow the top three wolves of the hierarchy. They are also known as scapegoats in the pack.

In order to perform optimization using GWO, the hunting techniques and the social behavior wolves are modeled mathematically. The best solution is considered as alpha (α) and the second and third fittest solutions are taken as beta (β) and delta (δ) respectively. All other solutions represent omega (ω) wolves. During hunting, grey wolves tend to encircle the prey. This behavior is modeled mathematically in the form of equation 1 and equation 2 given below

$$D= |C*X_p(t) - A*X(t)| \tag{1}$$

$$X(t+1) = X_p(t) - A*D \tag{2}$$

Where t refers to the current iteration, A and C stand for coefficient vectors, Xp and X represent the position vector of prey and grey wolf respectively. Vectors A and C are computed as follows:

A=2a*r1*a

C==2*r2

Where r1 and r2 are random vectors in [0,1]and both these components linearly decrease from 2 to 0 over the number of iterations.

The hunting operation is mainly guided by alpha. Though beta and delta wolves rarely participate in hunting, mathematical model is based on the assumption that all the three wolves that is alpha, beta and delta have better information about the prospective location of the prey. Therefore the position update equations are modeled as

$$D_\alpha = |C_1 * X_\alpha - X|, \tag{3}$$

$$D_\beta = |C_2 * X_\beta - X|, \tag{4}$$

$$D_\delta = |C_3 * X_\delta - X|, \tag{5}$$

$$X_1 = X_\alpha - A_1 * (D_\alpha) \tag{6}$$

$$X_2 = X_\beta - A_2 * (D_\beta) \tag{7}$$

$$X_3 = X_\delta - A_3 * (D_\delta) \tag{8}$$

$$X(t+1) = (X_1 + X_2 + X_3)/3 \tag{9}$$

Figure 3. Grey Wolf Optimization

Pseudocode: Grey Wolf Optimization Algorithm
Generate Initialize the population (P) of wolves (solutions) with random positions.
Initialize the vector's a, A and C
Calculate the fitness value of each solution
Assign the values of first, second and third best solutions to alpha(X_α), beta(X_β) and delta(X_δ)
do
Update all solutions using equations 6, 7 and 8.
Update a, A and C
Compute fitness of all solutions.
Update alpha(X_α), beta(X_β) and delta(X_δ)
While(stopping criteria)
Output X_α

Particle Swarm Optimization

Eberhart and Kennedy (1995) developed nature-inspired based stochastic optimization technique known as Particle swarm optimization (PSO). It is a population-based algorithm motivated by the cooperative behavior of a flock of migrating birds in search of food present at a destination unknown to the birds. Each bird, known as a particle, searches in a particular direction and communicates with other birds or particles in the flock as it flies. In this manner, the bird identifies the particle which is at the best location with respect to the food. Subsequently, each particle adjusts its speed towards the best particle according to its current position. The birds repeat this process till the flock reaches a desired destination. In the presented application, each particle represents a potential solution. A particle Ik in the swarm of size s is constituted of

- The x-vector that determines the particle's current position

$X: <x_{k0}, x_{k1}, \ldots, x_{kn-1}>$

- The v-vector that records the current velocity of the particle

$V: <v_{k0}, v_{k1}, \ldots, v_{kn-1}>$

- The p-vector that contains the particle's personal best location known so far.

$P: <p_{k0}, p_{k1}, \ldots, p_{kn-1}>$

PSO updates the positions of the particles using equations 10 and 11:

$$\text{New } V_{id} = w \times V_{id} + c_1 \times \text{rand()} \times (P_{id} - X_{id}) + c_2 \times \text{rand()} \times (P_{gd} - X_{id}) \tag{10}$$

$$\text{New position } X_{id} = \text{current position } X_{id} + \text{New } V_{id} \tag{11}$$

In equations 10 and 11, the constants c1 and c2 represent the learning factors governing the cognitive and social components respectively, g denotes the index of the particle which is recorded as the global best p-fitness, d represents the dth dimension and w is an inertia weight that controls the effect of the previous velocities on the current velocity. Therefore, evolution in PSO involves social interaction as well as intelligence in order that the particles learn from their own experience (i.e., local search) as well as from the experience of other birds in the flock (i.e., global search). The pseudo code for PSO is depicted in Fig. 3. As may be seen in the pseudo code, initialization of PSO is performed using a population of random solutions and a randomized velocity is given to each solution. The set of potential solutions, known as particles, then undergo the evolutionary process of PSO and explore the problem space. Each particle is required to maintain its best solution coordinates and its fitness value, pbest, achieved so far in the problem space. Another value that is recorded globally is the overall best value, gbest, and its location attained by any particle in the population after every iteration. At each time step, a particle adapts its velocity and moves according to its own pbest as well as the global gbest. The maximum and minimum change of particle's velocity is governed by the value of Vmax and Vmin. The pseudo-code makes use of a function, rand () for generation of random numbers in the range [0, 1].

Shuffled Frog Leaping Algorithm

Eusuff and Lansey (2003) developed a memetic meta-heuristic algorithm namely Shuffled Frog Leaping Algorithm (SFLA) for solving complex combinatorial optimization problems. It is a population-based algorithm inspired by natural memetics which provides high performance by integrating the potential benefits of both the Particle Swarm Optimization (PSO) and Memetic Algorithm (MA). SFLA is based on the evolution of memes that are carried by individuals and exchange of information due to interaction between the individuals globally within a population. The population in SFLA is composed of a set of frogs that are organized into diverse clusters, called the memeplexes. Each frog in the memeplex denotes a potential solution to a given optimization problem. Within every memeplex, each of the constituent frogs holds beliefs that are influenced by the beliefs of other frogs and cultivated through a process of memetic evolution, called the local search. Subsequent to a number of memetic evolutionary steps, the memeplexes are shuffled which leads to a global evolution. This process of exploitation and exploration continue till the pre-defined convergence criteria are not met.

The detailed steps of SFLA are listed in the pseudo code of Fig 5. SFLA firstly generates an initial, random population N of frogs Fi of size n. After calculating the fitness of the initial solutions, the entire population is sorted in the descending order of their fitness values. Thereafter, the solutions (Fi) are divided into m memeplexes M1, M2, M3...Mm as follows:

$$\left[M^d = \left\{ F_k^d \middle| F_k^d = F_{d-m(k-1)}, k = 1, 2, \ldots\ldots, n \right\} d = 1, 2, \ldots\ldots m \right] \tag{12}$$

Figure 4. Pseudo-code Particle Swarm Optimization algorithm

```
Start;
Create initial population of N random solutions (particles);
For each solution i in N: compute fitness (i);
  For every particle;
    Save Pl as the personal best position of particle i;
    If fitness (i) is better than pBest;
    Pl =fitness (i);
  End;
Save Pg as the global best fitness among all particles;
For every particle;
    Compute particle velocity
    New Vi =w  x current Vi+ c1 x  rand() x (Pi - Xi)+ c2 x  rand() x (Pg - Xi);
    Update particle position
    New_position Xi = current_position Xi+ New Vi          Vmax >= Vi>= Vmin
End;
Check if termination = true;
End;
```

In every memeplex, the fitness of weak particle is enhanced by adapting the fitness landscape as per the local and global best solutions using the equation 4 and equation 5 respectively. If the fitness of the solution is improved in this step, solution particle is replaced by the new improved particle otherwise a new randomly generated particle replaces this weak solution. In the pseudo-code, Dmax and Dmin represent the maximum and minimum allowed changes in a frog's position and rand() function is used to generate a random number between 0 and 1.

APPLICATION OF NATURE INSPIRED ALGORITHMS IN SCHEDULING WORKFLOWS IN CLOUDS

The size of scientific workflows, heterogeneity of resources and multiplicity of requirements or constraints require the application of efficient methods that guarantee optimal solutions to the scheduling problem. Nature inspired algorithms replicate the process of biological evolution in nature to yield good solutions for computationally hard problems. These algorithms traverse the search space of a given problem with the aim of maximizing or minimizing a specific goal. The central fields of nature-inspired computing are those of evolutionary computation and swarm intelligence. Evolutionary algorithms are driven by the concept of evolution using the technique of biological choice. Genetic algorithm (GA) and differential evolution (DE) are the dominant evolutionary algorithms (EAs). In contrast, Swarm Intelligence (SI) mimics the group mannerisms of social swarms, for instance honey bees, ant colonies and bird

Figure 5. Shuffled Frog Leaping Algorithm

```
Start;
Create initial population of P solutions randomly;
Calculate fitness for each individual i in P;
Sort all individuals in descending order of their fitness;
Save the fitness of global best solution( Xgb ) as fgb;
Divide all individuals into m memeplexes;
For each memeplex m
    Save the fitness of local best( Xlb )solution as flb;
    Determine the fitness of local worst( Xw ) solution as fw ;
  For each iteration k
   For each dimension d  in individual i
     // Local Search;
       Change in solution position (Dd) = rand () x (Xlb- Xw)   (3.4)      (Dmax >= Dd >= Dmin)
       New Position Xw = Xw + Dd ;
       Compute fitness of Xw ;
       If fitness improves
          New Position Xw = Xw + Dd ;
       Else
    //Local Search
       Change in solution position (Dd) = rand () x (Xgb - Xw)   (3.5)      (Dmax >= Dd >= Dmin)
       New Position Xw = Xw + Dd ;
       Compute fitness of Xw ;
       If fitness improves
          New Position Xw = Xw + Dd ;
       Else
          New Position Xw = rand() * Dmax  + rand() *(- Dmax );
     End;
   End;
  End;
Merge all the memeplexes and Sort all individuals in descending order of their fitness;
Test if terminating criteria is true;
End;
End;
```

flocks. SI utilizes the combined intelligence resulting from the communication and collaboration of a large number of homogenous agents in the nature. Swarm-based algorithms are known to produce fast and robust solutions with low costs for abundant complex problems. Examples of these algorithms are ant colony optimization (ACO) algorithm, particle swarm optimization (PSO), bat algorithm (BA), etc.

In this chapter, the workflow scheduling problem is modelled as a NIA problem. The tasks of a workflow are representative of an agent; namely a particle for PSO, a frog for SFLA and a wolf for GWO. The number of dimensions denotes the number of mobile services or tasks in the application workflow. In addition, the number of accessible resources, say n, establishes the search space for the agent where it has to look for the solution. Each dimension holds an integral value between 1 to n and gives the sequence number of the resource or VM on which it is scheduled.

For the grey wolf optimization, the solution to the scheduling problem is mathematically formulated as a n-dimensional position vector corresponding to a grey wolf's position. The value allocated to each dimension represents the resource assigned to a task in the workflow. GWO has been claimed to be superior to other swarm intelligence due to the use of hierarchical relationships between the agents, i.e., grey wolves. The alpha wolves exercise control over the entire period of space exploration. Apart from the use of societal hierarchy of grey wolves, pack hunting is the other attractive action used from the society grey wolves. This involves the actions of encircling, following and attacking the prey, i.e., exploring the search space and reaching the optimal solution.

Similarly, the scheduling problem is modeled for PSO and SFLA by representing a solution as a n-dimensional particle or frog respectively, if the workflow comprises of n tasks. The value of each dimension denotes the resource allocated to the task corresponding to the dimension.

Each agent (Particle, frog or grey wolf) is evaluated for its nearness to the optimal solution by means of a function called the fitness function. An agent is modified depending on its current fitness and the best available fitness values. This process is continued up to a pre defined number of iterations or until the desired solution is achieved.

For example, in GWO a ten dimensional agent's position is denoted by 10 coordinates (as depicted in Fig 6) and it corresponds to a workflow comprising ten tasks. A coordinate corresponding to the agent can assume an integer value between 0-3 if three VMs or resources are available to it. In this example,

Figure 6. A Ten Dimensional Agent's Position in GWO

Figure 7. Task to Resource mapping

the value 2.3 of the fifth coordinate denotes the fifth task and shows that the fifth task has been scheduled onto resource 2. The mapping is depicted by Fig 7.

Schedule Generation

Generation of an optimal solution for the scheduling problem using nature inspired algorithms involves initially design of a schedule from an agent and consequently evaluating its fitness value by means of a fitness function. The purpose or goal of the optimization problem derives the appropriate fitness function. In the current work, the focus of the presented algorithms is to reduce the workflow's overall execution cost while following the deadline requirements of the application. Therefore, the Entire Cost of Execution (ECE) for each schedule is evaluated and employed as the fitness function. The Entire Execution Time (EET) of a schedule is used for assessing if it adheres to the deadline limitations. In our algorithm, we have assumed that there are initially v number of VMs which are rented for the execution of the application. Here v represents the number of tasks that can be parallel executed for a particular workflow. This limits the size of search space and does not allow it to become too large. On the other hand, it also indicates availability of a sufficient number of resources for parallel execution of constituent tasks of a workflow.

It is assumed that the workflow tasks are represented by an array T. The time used to complete each task t_i using each resource, r_{M^i} existing in the set VMs_ Initial is computed, by means of an approximation method presented in [7]. These costs are stored in a n × v matrix, Task_RunTime, where n indicates the total number of workflow tasks and v is the number of VMs in VMs_ Initial. In addition, it is required to denote the inter-task dependencies for a workflow. These inter-task dependencies of the workflow are denoted by a n × n matrix, Depend, where Depend[i][j]=1 implies that task t_i depends on task t_j, and 0 implies otherwise. The time taken to move a task's output to its dependent task(s) is represented by the n × n matrix, Task_TransTime.

Next, we present an algorithm to transform an agent (a particle for PSO, a frog for SFLA or a wolf for GWO) into the required execution schedule which evaluates the agent's fitness by iterating through each dimension of the agent. The dimension M_k^i, represents a task t_i and its value represents a VM, given by VMs_ Initial[M^i]. The starting time of execution of a task is relies on the finish time of the tasks it is dependent on and also on the time when the requisite VM is accessible to it.

Data Structures for the algorithm:

ECE: Entire Cost of Execution

EET: Entire Execution Time

VMs_Initial: Group of Initial VMs

Task_RunTime: Matrix storing each task's execution time on every resource

Task_ TransTime: Matrix storing the time taken to move the output of each task to its dependent tasks

VMs_Leased: Group of VMs leased for execution of the workflow tasks

Depend: Matrix of the inter-task dependencies for the workflow; Depend[i][j] =1 if task t_i depends on task t_j; else 0

Beg_T_i: Time at which a task t_i begins execution

FinT_$_i$: Time at which a task t_i finishes execution

LBEG_VM: Time at which the lease begins for a VM

LFin_VM: Time at which the lease ends for a VM

Algorithm for Schedule Generation from an Agent:

```
Input:
T: Set of d workflow tasks
VMs_Initial: Initial set of VMs
A(k)=(Mₖ¹,Mₖ²,...,Mₖᵈ) //An agent
1. Initialize ECE=0, EET=0, VMs_Leased=Φ: marker =0
2. Compute Task_RunTime, Task_TransTime
3. Compute Depend
4. For i = 0 to (d-1)
i.        tᵢ =T[i]
ii.       VM(i)= VMs_ Initial[Mⁱ]
iii.      marker =0
iv.       for j=0 to (d-1)
If Depend[i][j]==1, { marker =1; BEG_ᵢ=max(BEG_ᵢ, FinTⱼ, LFIN_VM(VM(i)) }
If marker==0 BEG_ᵢ= LFIN_VM(VM(i))
v.        time_exe= Task_RunTime(tᵢ, VM(i))
vi.       for j=0 to (d-1)
If Depend[j][i]==1 and VM(j)<>VM(i)
time_trans+=time_trans+Task_Transtime[i][j]
vii.      Tot_time(i, VM(i))=time_exe+time_trans
viii.     FinT(i, VM(i))=BEG_i+ Tot_time(i, VM(i))
ix.       If VM(i) ∉ VMs_Leased, add it, LBEG__VM(VM(i))=BEG_ᵢ
x.        LFIN_VM(VM(i))= Tot_time(i, VM(i)) +BEG_ᵢ
5. For each VM c ∈ VMs_Leased
i.        ECE=ECE+((LFIN_VM[c]-LBEG__VM[c])*Cost[c])
ii.       if(LFIN_VM[c]>EET)
EET=LFIN_VM[c]
```

The above algorithm results in a group of VMs that should be acquired for a cost-optimal and deadline-constrained execution of the workflow. A VM, VM(i) is related to each task t_i and its lease start time and lease finish time are obtained as LBEG__VM(VM(i)) and LFIN_VM(VM(i)) respectively. Subsequently, the entire execution cost (ECE) and entire time for execution are calculated for the obtained solution. This mapping of virtual machines to tasks alongside the corresponding lease begin and finish times for these machines gives the required execution schedule for the workflow.

Lastly, each nature inspired algorithm, i.e., PSO, SFLA and GWO is combined with the schedule generation algorithm to obtain a near-optimal schedule as discussed subsequently. In SFLA, a frog's fitness is evaluated in terms of execution cost (ECE) which is computed by generating the schedule corresponding to the frog by the above algorithm. Similarly, the fitness of a particle or a wolf can be computed. In case the total execution time (EET) for the schedule obtained corresponding to an agent (frog/ particle or wolf) goes beyond the application's deadline, the NIA (SFLA/PSO or GWO) replaces the agent with a new agent that is randomly generated. Thus, the NIA keeps those schedules which adhere to the limit imposed by the application's time deadline.

METRICS FOR PERFORMANCE EVALUATION OF SCHEDULING ALGORITHMS

Any algorithm is required to be evaluated for overheads and costs before its implementation in real world scenarios. This is especially true while utilizing cloud computing resources since these are leased on pay-per-use basis. Here, there are obvious tradeoffs between cost and efficiency and users want to take full advantage of resources. Therefore, it is important to examine what types of applications have the potential to execute efficiently and cost effectively on this platform. Performance metrics provide a direction for evaluating application executions on varied resources and identifying the possible optimizations. if any. These include both multiple invocations of one application and executions of multiple applications. The selected metrics must allow for comparison of performance of heterogeneous applications in a way that is independent of the application (Cardoso et al., 2002; Cardoso et al., 2003; Chen & Deelman, 2012).

A scientific workflow application can comprise of jobs requiring high performance computing (HPC) as well as high-throughput computing (HTC). This has led to the definition of appropriate performance metrics since traditionally used HPC metrics or HTC metrics cannot assess a workflow application's execution completely. These specific metrics are used to evaluate both the degree as well as efficiency of the work performed by the application. On one hand, these measure the tangible computational performance in terms of number of operations, file accesses etc. On the other hand, these measure the workflow performance in terms of factors such as task and job scheduling etc. (Rimal & Maier, 2017).

Workflow execution metrics have been defined at three levels of granularity by Rimal & Maier (2017):

- Task level
- Workflow level
- Application level

Metrics at the task level evaluate the computational performance of individual executions. These are used to gauge the amount of work by conventionally used measures, such as:

- Number of Floating Point Operations (FLOPs) and rate of Number of Floating Point Operations (FLOPs/sec)
- Size of File that is input/output (I/O), file I/O/sec;
- Computation time of a task.

It is possible that a task may not be the basic unit of work for a workflow scheduler. In such cases, a job is defined as the unit of execution unit for the scheduler which schedules jobs, consisting of one or more tasks, to available resources. Some frequently used metrics in the context of jobs are:

- Delay per job
- Tardiness
- Laxity
- Mean scheduling execution time

- Resource utilization rate

Here, tardiness refers to a delay penalty which is charged in case a job does not finish by its due time. It denotes that the completion time of a job was later than the expected time and may be weighted corresponding to the delay. The laxity of a job indicates its urgency or importance. At a given time t, the difference between a job's deadline and the remaining computing time required gives the laxity of the job. A negative laxity is an indicator that the job's deadline cannot be met, while a laxity of zero implies that the job must be immediately scheduled and a job with positive laxity can be delayed.

Metrics at the level of the workflow indicate its performance in entirety, i.e., as an aggregate. These describe the usage of resources by a scientific workflow during execution and establish the computational work done on the whole. Some commonly used metrics at the workflow level are as follows:

- Number of Workflow FLOPs and Number of Workflow FLOPs/sec;
- Size of File that is input/output (I/O) to the Workflow, file I/O/sec;
- Computation time of a Workflow
- Makespan of a Workflow

The makespan of a workflow is the time taken from the submission of workflow till it finishes execution. In comparison, the workflow compute time is the time actually spent on execution and excluding the scheduling or waiting times. In addition to the workflow metrics above, the measure of Workflow parallel speedup has been defined to indicate the speedup achieved by executing workflow jobs in parallel. It is the fraction of the time spent in computation by the makespan of the workflow. Further, performance metrics are required at the application level since an application may consist of multiple workflows, or require multiple executions of a single workflow. These metrics represent an aggregation of results for execution of individual workflows comprising the entire application. Of these, the following metrics capture the computational aspects:

- Count of total FLOPs, and count of total FLOP/sec
- Total size of file I/O, file I/O/sec
- Count of number of tasks, tasks executed/sec
- Count of jobs, jobs executed/sec
- Count of failed jobs
- Computation time for an application, i.e., the total of the computation times taken by the component workflows

The above metrics are utilized at the application level apart from the task and workflow levels to explore the workflow execution for scalability bottlenecks. Further, an application parallel speedup metric is computed for measuring the parallelism at application-level. It is defined as the fraction of the time spent in computation by the application to its makespan. Other metrics have been defined in literature to capture essential aspects of performance with respect to specific applications Callaghan et al. (2011).

It is important that metrics be carefully selected for evaluation of an algorithm since considering any one in isolation can lead to incorrect interpretations. For instance, resource utilization of 100% is desirable since it indicates that all leased resources were always in use. However, a high resource utilization may be due to availability of fewer than required resources; thus, resulting in a high makespan or computation time. Similarly, differences in evaluation may occur due to heterogeneity of resources used in workflow executions. Upgrading of resources may result in decrease of makespan but will not change the value for workflow parallel speedup. On the other hand, an increase in parallelism even by using slower processors will cause an improvement in workflow parallel speedup.

SIMULATION RESULTS

This section illustrates the experiments that are executed to examine the efficacy of the nature-inspired approaches to the scheduling problem. The GWO algorithm was evaluated over random workflows for large number of tasks ranging from 150 to 500. A custom JAVA simulator was used to perform the experiments. The randomness aspect introduced in Section 4 for the GWO is also applied in the basic SFLA and PSO algorithms since the basic versions of PSO and SFLA may not be apt at addressing the specified constraints. Hence, for a reasonable comparison with GWO, proposed enhancement was done in the considered algorithms as it helps in generating the schedules which follow the requisite deadline limits. In the present study, all simulation experiments were carried out 25 times and the average results have been noted. Table 1 presents the various parameters being used to perform the simulations.

In our studies we assumed resources to be heterogeneous; as a result, there was variation in the time of execution of a task over different resources. The deadlines of various workflows were determined by taking the mean of lowest possible and highest possible execution time attained for each workflow execution. In order to find the maximum execution time; a single VM with the minimum cost is leased and each task in the workflow is executed on this VM. Similarly, the minimum execution time is calculated by considering one VM of the fastest type for every workflow task.

Effect of Size of Task Graph on the Entire Cost of Execution (ECE)

The objective of the study was to evaluate the efficacy of GWO algorithm in optimizing Entire Cost of Execution (ECE) for varied size of task graph. The algorithm has been compared with regard to PSO and SFLA algorithms. The study was performed by generating random workflows with varied number of tasks. As the resources were assumed to be heterogeneous, the cost of cloud resources was taken as 10, 20 and 30 units for the simulations. Figure 8 depicts the ECE obtained by GWO, PSO and SFLA over the varied number of tasks. It can be observed that for small as well as large number of tasks GWO performs better than both SFLA and PSO whereas PSO and SFLA show similar behaviour.

Table 1. Parameter values Used for the NI algorithms.

Algorithms_Used	Population_size	Number_of_generations	Control_parameters
Particle Swarm Optimization	100	50	$c1 = c2 = 2$.
Shuffled Frog Leaping Algorithm	100	50	No_of_Memeplex = 4, memetic_Iterations =5
Grey Wolf Optimization Algorithm	100	50	a diminishes from 2 to 0, r1 and r2 lies in the range [0-1]

Figure 8. ECE for GWO, PSO and SFLA

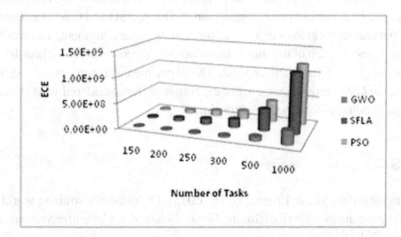

Table 2 depicts the values of ECE obtained due to PSO, SFLA and GWO. It can be inferred from the results of all random workflows that GWO reduces the overall cost of execution by 78% on the average in comparison to SFLA and reduces the ECE by approximately 79% on the average as compared to PSO.

CONCLUSION

This chapter investigates the appropriateness of nature inspired algorithms for obtaining a near-optimal resource technique for provisioning and scheduling of data intensive workflows on Infrastructure as a Service (IaaS) clouds. The focus of the work is to minimize the execution cost of an application while adhering to a given deadline. The chapter has presented the application of three nature inspired algorithms

Table 2. ECE for PSO, SFLA and GWO

WorkFlows	No of Tasks	OEC			Improvement of GWO vs PSO (%)	Improvement of GWO vs SFLA (%)
		Particle Swarm Optimization	**Shuffled Frog Leaping Algorithm**	**Grey Wolf Optimization Algorithm**		
Random Workflow1	150	3.37E+07	3.36E+07	7.77E+06	77	77
Random Workflow2	200	6.93E+07	6.88E+07	1.48E+07	79	78
Random Workflow3	250	1.16E+08	1.14E+08	2.34E+07	80	79
Random Workflow4	300	1.66E+08	1.65E+08	3.29E+07	80	80
Random Workflow5	500	4.3E+08	4.27E+08	8.23E+07	81	81
Random Workflow6	1000	1.21E+09	1.17E+09	2.69E+08	78	77

for the considered problem, namely the Particle Swarm Optimization, Shuffled Frog Leaping Algorithm and Grey Wolf Optimizer. A performance comparison of SFLA, PSO and GWO has been carried out for diverse randomly generated workflows in a heterogeneous cloud environment. The work has introduced an element of randomness in each of the three algorithms so that cost-optimal schedules may be derived such that they also meet the time deadline limit. The experimental results involving SFLA, PSO and GWO indicate that the GWO reduces the cost of execution of the considered workflows, in general, by 78% on an average, in comparison to other algorithms.

REFERENCES

Abrishami, S., Naghibzadeh, M., & Epema, D. H. (2013). Deadline-constrained workflow scheduling algorithms for Infrastructure as a Service Clouds. *Future Generation Computer Systems*, *29*(1), 158–169. doi:10.1016/j.future.2012.05.004

Amiri, B., Fathian, M., & Maroosi, A. (2009). Application of shuffled frog-leaping algorithm on clustering. *International Journal of Advanced Manufacturing Technology*, *45*(1-2), 199–209. doi:10.100700170-009-1958-2

Banati, H., & Mehta, S. (2013). Improved shuffled frog leaping algorithm for continuous optimisation adapted SEVO toolbox. *International Journal of Advanced Intelligence Paradigms*, *5*(1/2), 31. doi:10.1504/IJAIP.2013.054670

Buyya, R., Yeo, C. S., Venugopal, S., Broberg, J., & Brandic, I. (2009). Cloud computing and emerging IT platforms: Vision, hype, and reality for delivering computing as the 5th utility. *Future Generation Computer Systems*, *25*(6), 599–616. doi:10.1016/j.future.2008.12.001

Callaghan, S., Maechling, P., Small, P., Milner, K., Juve, G., Jordan, T. H., ... Brooks, C. (2011). Metrics for heterogeneous scientific workflows: A case study of an earthquake science application. *International Journal of High Performance Computing Applications*, *25*(3), 274–285. doi:10.1177/1094342011414743

Cardoso, J., Miller, J. A., Sheth, A. P., & Arnold, J. (2002). Modeling Quality of Service for Workflows and Web Service Processes. Retrieved from http://corescholar.libraries.wright.edu/knoesis/791

Cardoso, J., Sheth, A., & Miller, J. (2003). *Workflow Quality of Service*. (Vol. 108).

Chen, W., & Deelman, E. (2012). WorkflowSim: A toolkit for simulating scientific workflows in distributed environments. In *2012 IEEE 8th International Conference on E-Science, Chicago, IL* (pp. 1-8).

Chen, W., & Zhang, J. (2009). An ant colony optimization approach to a grid workflow scheduling problem with various QoS requirements. *IEEE Transactions on Systems, Man and Cybernetics. Part C, Applications and Reviews*, *39*(1), 29–43. doi:10.1109/TSMCC.2008.2001722

El-Fergany, A. A., & Hasanien, H. M. (2015). Single and multi-objective optimal power flow using grey wolf optimizer and differential evolution algorithms. *Electric Power Components and Systems*, *43*(13), 1548–1559. doi:10.1080/15325008.2015.1041625

Emary, E., Zawbaa, H. M., Grosan, C., & Hassenian, A. E. (2015). Feature subset selection approach by gray-wolf optimization. In Afro-European Conference for Industrial Advancement (Vol. 334).

Eusuff, M., Lansey, K., & Pasha, F. (2006). Shuffled frog-leaping algorithm: A memetic meta-heuristic for discrete optimization. *Engineering Optimization, 38*(2), 129–154. doi:10.1080/03052150500384759

Eusuff, M., Lansey, K., & Pasha, F. (2006). Shuffled frog-leaping algorithm: A memetic meta-heuristic for discrete optimization. *Engineering Optimization, 38*(2), 129–154. doi:10.1080/03052150500384759

Gholizadeh, S. (2015). Optimal design of double layer grids considering nonlinear behaviour by sequential grey wolf algorithm. *Journal of Optimization in Civil Engineering, 5*(4), 511–523.

Juve, G., Chervenak, A., Deelman, E., Bharathi, S., Mehta, G., & Vahi, K. (2013). Characterizing and profiling scientific workflows. *Future Generation Computer Systems, 29*(3), 682–692. doi:10.1016/j.future.2012.08.015

Juve, G., & Deelman, E. (2011). *Scientific Workflows in the Cloud* (pp. 71–91). Grids, Clouds and Virtualization; doi:10.1007/978-0-85729-049-6_4

Kalra, M., & Singh, S. (2015). A review of metaheuristic scheduling techniques in cloud computing. *Egyptian Informatics Journal, 16*(3), 275–295. doi:10.1016/j.eij.2015.07.001

Kaur, P., & Mehta, S. (2017). Resource provisioning and work flow scheduling in clouds using augmented Shuffled Frog Leaping Algorithm. *Journal of Parallel and Distributed Computing, 101*, 41–50. doi:10.1016/j.jpdc.2016.11.003

Kennedy, J., & Eberhart, R. (1995). Particle swarm optimization. In *Proceedings., IEEE International Conference on Neural Networks* (Vol. 4, pp. 1942-1948). 10.1109/ICNN.1995.488968

Komaki, G., & Kayvanfar, V. (2015). Grey Wolf Optimizer algorithm for the two-stage assembly flow shop scheduling problem with release time. *Journal of Computational Science, 8*, 109–120. doi:10.1016/j.jocs.2015.03.011

Lin, C., & Lu, S. (2011). Scheduling Scientific Workflows Elastically for Cloud Computing, In *International Conference on Cloud Computing* (pp. 746-747). 10.1109/CLOUD.2011.110

Madadi, A., & Motlagh, M. M. (2014). Optimum Control of DC motor using Grey Wolf optimizer algorithm. *TJEAS, 4*(4), 373–379.

Malawski, M., Juve, G., Deelman, E., & Nabrzyski, J. (2012). Cost-and deadline-constrained provisioning for scientific workflow ensembles in IaaS clouds. In *Proc. Int. Conf. High Perform. Comput., Netw., Storage Anal.* (Vol. 22, pp. 1–11).

Mao, M., & Humphrey, M. (2011) Auto-scaling to minimize cost and meet application deadlines in cloud workflows. In *Proc. Int. Conf. High Perform. Comput., Netw., Storage Anal.* (pp. 1–12).

Mehta, S., & Banati, H. (2012) Trust aware social context filtering using Shuffled Frog Leaping Algorithm. In *International conference on Hybrid Intelligent Systems* (pp. 342-347). 10.1109/HIS.2012.6421358

Mirjalili, S., Mirjalili, S. M., & Lewis, A. (2014). Grey wolf optimizer. *Advances in Engineering Software, 69*, 46–61. doi:10.1016/j.advengsoft.2013.12.007

Omara, F. A., & Arafa, M. M. (2010). Genetic algorithms for task scheduling problem. *Journal of Parallel and Distributed Computing*, *70*(1), 13–22. doi:10.1016/j.jpdc.2009.09.009

Ostermann, S., Iosup, A., Yigitbasi, N., Prodan, R., Fahringer, T., & Epema, D. (2010). A Performance Analysis of EC2 Cloud Computing Services for Scientific Computing. In International Conference on *Cloud Computing* (pp. 115-131). Springer. doi:10.1007/978-3-642-12636-9_9

Pandey, S., Wu, L., Guru, S. M., & Buyya, R. (2010). A particle swarm optimization-based heuristic for scheduling workflow applications in cloud computing environments. In *Proc. IEEE Int. Conf.Adv. Inform. Netw. Appl.* (pp. 400–407).

Poola, D., Garg, S. K., Buyya, R., Yun, Y., & Ramamohanarao, K. (2014). Robust Scheduling of Scientific Workflows with Deadline and Budget Constraints in Clouds. In *2014 IEEE 28th International Conference on Advanced Information Networking and Applications (AINA)* (pp. 858-865).

Rahman, M., Venugopal, S., & Buyya, R. (2007). A Dynamic Critical Path Algorithm for Scheduling Scientific Workflow Applications on Global Grids. In *IEEE International Conference on e-Science and Grid Computing* (pp. 35-42).

Rimal, B. P., & Maier, M. (2017). Workflow Scheduling in Multi-Tenant Cloud Computing Environments. *IEEE Transactions on Parallel and Distributed Systems*, *28*(1), 290–304. doi:10.1109/TPDS.2016.2556668

Rodriguez, M. A., & Buyya, R. (2014). Deadline Based Resource Provisioning and Scheduling Algorithm for Scientific Workflows on Clouds. *IEEE Transactions on Cloud Computing*, *2*(2), 222–235. doi:10.1109/TCC.2014.2314655

Shankar, K., & Eswaran, P. (2015). A secure visual secret share (VSS) creation scheme in visual cryptography using elliptic curve cryptography with optimization technique. *Australian Journal of Basic and Applied Sciences*, *9*(36), 150–163.

Song, H. M., Sulaiman, M. H., & Mohamed, M. R. (2014). An Application of Grey Wolf Optimizer for Solving Combined Economic Emission Dispatch Problems. *International Review on Modelling and Simulations*, *7*(5), 838. doi:10.15866/iremos.v7i5.2799

Tao, Q., Chang, H., Yi, Y., Gu, C., & Li, W. (2011). A rotary chaotic PSO algorithm for trustworthy scheduling of a grid workflow. *Computers & Operations Research*, *38*(5), 824–836. doi:10.1016/j.cor.2010.09.012

Tripathy, B., Dash, S., & Padhy, S. K. (2015). Dynamic task scheduling using a directed neural network. *Journal of Parallel and Distributed Computing*, *75*, 101–106. doi:10.1016/j.jpdc.2014.09.015

Ullman, J. (1975). NP-complete scheduling problems. *Journal of Computer and System Sciences*, *10*(3), 384–393. doi:10.1016/S0022-0000(75)80008-0

Wu, Z., Ni, Z., Gu, L., & Liu, X. (2010). A revised discrete particle swarm optimization for cloud workflow scheduling. In *Proc. IEEE Int. Conf. Comput. Intell. Security* (pp. 184–188).

Yu, J., & Buyya, R. (2006). A budget constrained scheduling of workflow applications on utility grids using genetic algorithms. In *Proc. 1st Workshop Workflows Support Large-Scale Sci.* (pp. 1–10).

Yusof, Y., & Mustaffa, Z. (2015). Time series forecasting of energy commodity using grey wolf optimizer. In *Proceedings of the International Multi Conference of Engineers and Computer Scientists (IMECS '15)*, Hong Kong (Vol. 1).

Zhan, Z., & Liu, X. Gong, Y-J. Zhang, J., Chung, H. & Li, Y. (2015). Cloud Computing Resource Scheduling and a Survey of Its Evolutionary Approaches. ACM Comput. Surv., 47(4).

Zhu, G., & Zhang, W. (2014). An improved Shuffled Frog-leaping Algorithm to optimize component pick-and-place sequencing optimization problem. *Expert Systems with Applications, 41*(15), 6818–6829. doi:10.1016/j.eswa.2014.04.038

Chapter 9
PSO–Based Antenna Pattern Synthesis:
A Paradigm for Secured Data Communications

Rathindra Nath Biswas
Acharya Jagadish Chandra Bose Polytechnic, India

Anurup Saha
Jadavpur University, India

Swarup Kumar Mitra
MCKV Institute of Engineering, India

Mrinal Kanti Naskar
Jadavpur University, India

ABSTRACT

An antenna pattern synthesis scheme based on particle swarm optimization (PSO) technique is proposed. Synthesized patterns always contain narrower beamwidth and minimum side-lobes level reducing coverage areas towards the attackers in wireless networks. On such patterns, deep nulls are also steered at various interfering directions as to provide a second layer of protection. Using selective patterns at each point-to-point link, data privacy is ensured throughout entire route from source to sink. This approach is simple enough to be commensurate with flexible design methods on a real-time platform. Thus, an FSM (finite state machine) rule-based digital system model is further developed and tested on Xilinx Virtex4 FPGA (field programmable gate array) board. Its performance under harsh radio environmental conditions is also verified with several fixed-point simulations in terms of pattern synthesis accuracy and computational overheads. These results corroborate such system integration onto wireless infrastructures for the secured data communication services.

DOI: 10.4018/978-1-5225-5852-1.ch009

INTRODUCTION

Wireless technologies usually provide numerous potential benefits like enormous bandwidth, less space, light weight, ease of installation and maintenance etc. Obviously, these are also essential requirements for the design of state-of-the-art communication systems. However, a continuous research growth during the last decade makes it possible simply to develop low power and low cost wireless devices and circuits on both of MMIC (monolithic microwave integrated circuits) as well as VLSI (very large scale of integration) architecture. Thus, wireless systems utilizing radio frequency (RF) signals or microwaves and millimeter waves are now extensively used in various sectors of communication services (Schafer et al, 2014; Schafer, 2003). For implementation of long-haul communication systems, multi-hop networks are generally constituted with several wireless transceivers (transmitter-receiver) to relay the broadcast messages at the receiving end in a cooperative manner. During transmission and reception of RF signals, the transceivers (also termed as nodes) inevitably share a common channel in free space. Consequently, data communications among the nodes become vulnerable to the attackers mostly at the physical and other outer layers (Zhou et al, 2014; Zhou et al, 2016). At most of the cases, attackers appear in pretention of the benevolent nodes within the networks and normally get access to the control systems of few nodes using malicious codes to compromise them. They mislead the entire system operation by transferring erroneous information through the multi-hop data links (Khan et al, 2014; Mahmoud et al, 2014). Therefore, preserving privacy and security of data along its route from source to destination has turned into a prime issue in modern wireless communication systems. Several popular cryptographic methods were proposed so far and these work well for protecting data at the application and other inner layers. Nonetheless, only few approaches were adopted to defend the physical layer attacks (Wong et al, 2007; Wong et al, 2011). Besides, the task of implementing a secured data communication network with simple structure that must ensure data privacy over its radio links still puts a great challenge to the system designers. Hence, much more research attention is required to enrich both of its algorithmic and architectural attributes.

Adversaries are supposed to sustain their activities via few compromised nodes in the network and thus a continuous evaluation of trust-worthiness of each node is always necessary prior to all data forwarding steps. Antenna pattern synthesis, however, could guarantee safe data transfer to some extent within a harsh radio propagation environment (Mailoux, 2005; Hong et al, 2014). Unlike omnidirectional pattern, it concentrates most of its radiated power in a particular direction and thus improves gain and directivity of the antenna significantly. This strategic approach also enhances the channel capacity of wireless medium. The nodes of wireless networks usually require patterns with narrower beamwidth and lower side-lobes level so that interferences from their neighborhood cannot hamper data privacy in a particular link. In fact, it also optimizes throughput and latency in the systems, selecting an optimal route for relaying data packets from source to sink (Bagchi et al, 1999; Mishra, 2008). On the contrary, advanced communication systems such as mobile ad-hoc networks (MANET) or internet of things (IoT) based wireless local area networks (WLAN) etc. now utilize smart devices that enable them to estimate interfering directions in a more convenient way (Yang et al, 2004; Jiang et al, 2007; Ilyas et al, 2005). Therefore, pattern synthesis methods would be much more effective to counteract the attacks, steering deep and wide nulls against the interferers. However, the scheme becomes trickier enough to put up this additional criterion. Antenna operation rather can be made more 'smart' considering any particular array configuration (i.e., linear, circular or planar etc.) and computing its weight vectors in terms of element excitation coefficients or phases iteratively on a digital signal processor (DSP) to obtain the desired pattern (Dikmese et al, 2011). This is commonly referred to as digital pattern synthesis (also known as digital beamforming) and it eliminates the requirement of analogue phase shifters in the system design. Incorporating several criteria such as prescribed side-lobes level, beamwidth and nulls etc. in the optimum pattern, the process would be a multi-objective design problem in nature. It is quite impossible to solve such a problem using the traditional approaches. In such cases, considering deviation of produced pattern from the desired one as the fitness function of optimization problems in any heuristic search method, the array weight vectors can be computed to find the optimum solution in a more convenient manner (Liu et al, 2014). In computational frameworks, particle swarm optimization (PSO) technique is found to possess higher convergence speed with simpler structure than other evolutionary algorithms and hence it is chosen for this work (Jin et al, 2007; Mandal et al, 2011). The modern communication systems usually operate at high frequency (order of few hundred MHz or few GHz) and they require higher sampling rate in their signal processing applications. Processors using traditional Von Neumann architecture with several Multiplier-Accumulator (MAC) stages are not suitable for computing such complex functions of desired patterns and hence there is a need of high speed parallel processor architectures. However, recent growth in microelectronics and digital technology makes the field programmable gate array (FPGA) families as flexible platforms suitably to develop digital signal processors for the antenna pattern synthesis algorithms (Wood et al, 2008; Dikmese et al, 2011). Thus design of an efficient PSO-based antenna pattern synthesis scheme and its subsequent implementation on scalable hardware architecture of Virtex4 FPGA chip is the main concern of this chapter.

The remaining portions of this chapter are organized as follows. In section 2, the research works at the domain of antenna pattern synthesis using both of traditional methods and evolutionary algorithms as well as their scope of implementation on FPGA platforms are briefly discussed. In section 3, a speculative design principle of robust wireless system for secured data communication services is briefly described. The proposed PSO-based pattern synthesis method and its practical implementation steps onto FPGA hardware are demonstrated in section 4 and section 5 respectively. In section 6, simulation results along with proper explanations are furnished. In section 7, the chapter is concluded with a track towards its future scope of extension.

BACKGROUND

During the past decades, antenna pattern synthesis schemes have been much enriched through various pioneering research works. Comprehensive surveys are made on recent progresses in the conventional and evolutionary algorithms based antenna synthesis methods. Both approaches apparently operate on the same principle to mitigate multipath fading in wireless channel, either placing deep nulls towards the interfering directions (null steering) or keeping main beam towards the desired direction (beam steering) (Mailoux, 2005). In this section, an effort is also made to explore the feasibility of FPGA based hardware implementation for such schemes producing several application specific patterns.

Conventional Design Methods

In conventional methods, pattern synthesis function is formulated as complex polynomial either with various electrical or physical parameters in any array geometry. Mautz and Harrington (1975) proposed some general numerical computation techniques for the discretized source and field both to synthesize antenna patterns with and without constraints. Balakrishnan et al. (1979) also presented a simple pattern optimization model reducing the spatial and excitation constraints of both linear and circular arrays with a nonlinear transformation technique called simplex algorithm. Steyskal (1982) described an extended version of least mean square pattern synthesis method including constraints like nulls and derivative nulls etc. at some prescribed angles. Prasad and Charan (1984) also developed a new method that optimizes linear and nonlinear constraints using Hooke and Jeeves algorithm to steer deep nulls in the beam patterns for circular and arc arrays. Er et al. (1990; 1993) presented two strategic ways to adjust beamwidth and side-lobes level in pattern minimizing the mean square error of the synthesis problem. Carlson and Willner (1992) presented an antenna pattern synthesis method using weighted least squares for both the cases of equal and unequal spaced linear and nonlinear arrays. Bucci et al. (1994) presented a more general pattern synthesis method that offers flexibility to find out the antenna excitations and geometry with constraints. It usually divides the problem into several segments to achieve a good trade-offs between speed and complexity in pattern design. Chang et al. (2000) presented another efficient pattern synthesis method in which current distributions of linear antenna arrays are obtained utilizing the spherical Bessel functions or Legendre polynomials of the first kind. Ismail et al. (2004) developed an analytical synthesis technique based on the Schelkunoff unit circle principle to steer nulls for suppressing the interferences by controlling phases of linear antenna arrays. Collin et al. (2010) presented variational method that optimizes characteristic parameters of a predefined mask function to get well matched patterns with optimum power waste. Yang et al. (2013) proposed a method using interpolation and iterative fast Fourier transform (FFT) to produce pencil shaped patterns for large non-uniform antenna arrays. Bruintjes et al. (2016) also developed scheme utilizing quasi-analytical modeling of collapsed distributions to realize an asymmetric shaped (null-free) pattern with very low ripple for planar antenna arrays. However, synthesis methods to obtain patterns with narrower beamwidth, lower side-lobes level and several deep nulls steered against the interferences are prime requirements for secured data communications through wireless channel. In most of these approaches, generation of such patterns is not ensured and hence they fail to perform well against various malicious attacks.

Evolutionary Algorithm Based Approaches

Evolutionary algorithms, on the other hand, have the potential capabilities of making proper balancing among the multi-objective design features in pattern generation. Hence, they are now mostly accepted for the complicated pattern synthesis issues. Farhat and Bai (1987) described a new procedure for optimum phased array synthesis using simulated annealing process. Lebret and Boyd (1997) also validated the efficiency of convex optimization methods to synthesize patterns in arrays with arbitrary geometry, element directivity and other constraints. Akdagli et al. (2003) also presented a flexible pattern synthesis technique based on optimization of the element excitations and/or positions using both tabu search and ant colony algorithm for linear antenna arrays. Using simulated annealing and genetic algorithm to optimize complex element excitations in a linear array, Trastoy et al. (2004) described pattern switching between narrow and wide beamwidths with constant side-lobes level. Using differential evolution algorithm, Guo and Li (2009) also proposed method to produce patterns with lower side-lobes for the conformal antenna arrays. Qubati et al. (2010) introduced a new evolutionary algorithm, named as central force optimization (CFO) that operates on the principle of gravitational kinematics, to synthesize antenna patterns in linear and circular arrays. Gunes and Tokan (2010) presented an efficient and derivative-free optimization tool namely Pattern search (PSearch) method that can be applied directly on the antenna array synthesis. El-

Kamchouchi (2010) proposed a new approach using an artificial neural network (ANN) to synthesize patterns with very low side-lobes level for circular ring arrays. Zheng et al. (2011) also presented an approach to generate patterns with prescribed null-width, synthesizing the time-modulated circular array with differential evolution algorithm. Similarly, Mandal et al. (Mandal et al, 2011) proposed a novel PSO (NPSO) method to steer deep nulls on the pattern by optimum perturbations of element current amplitudes in a symmetric linear array. Fuchs (2012) proposed a synthesis procedure for the sparse arrays using convex optimization algorithm. It works well minimizing the number of elements in arbitrary array geometry to produce a pattern with specific side-lobes level and main-lobe at a prescribed direction. Chaker et al. (2016) also described hybrid evolutionary optimization technique namely Genetical Swarm Optimization (GSO) to synthesize a pattern with low side-lobes level in dual-mode 1D and 2D unequally annular ring antenna arrays. These methods always converge towards the optimum synthesis goal evaluating a fitness function in an iterative manner. Hence, it is important to select suitable fitness function yielding higher convergence speed as well as maximum accuracy at minimum computational overheads in the optimization process. Li et al. (2017) proposed a biogeography-based optimization algorithm to determine optimal set of spacing and/or excitation current values for circular and linear antenna arrays respectively. It was observed to have better performance in reducing the maximum SLL compared with others like firefly algorithm. Mangaraj and Swain (2017) successfully demonstrated the design process of a linear antenna array using Gravitational search algorithm suitable for wireless communication system application at ultra-high frequency (UHF). A pattern of higher directivity, higher front-to-maximum-side-lobe level and low half-power beamwidth is realized with only 12 (twelve) number of dipole elements. Pappula and Ghosh (2014) proposed cat swarm optimization (CSO) to optimize the antenna element positions for both suppressing side lobes level and for achieving nulls in the desired directions. The results so obtained are compared with that of particle swarm optimization (PSO) and ant colony optimization (ACO) methods. Chatterjee et al. (2014) proposed a method for obtaining desired equal side lobes level (SLL) in non-uniformly excited linear arrays using Taylor distribution and classical particle swarm optimization (CPSO) algorithm. Elragal et al. (2011) introduced a new design method for reconfigurable phased arrays with prescribed null directions. Using hybrid differential evolution (DE) and enhanced particle swarm optimization (EPSO) technique, null steering is achieved by position perturbation of array elements in arbitrary directions with minimum side-lobes level change constraint.

Recioui (2012) proposed design based on element position perturbation of nonuniformly spaced linear array antennas using Particle Swarm Optimization method. Goudos et al. (2010) presented an unequally spaced linear array synthesis method for side-lobe suppression under constraints to beamwidth and null control using a Comprehensive Learning Particle Swarm Optimization (CLPSO) technique. Such algorithm outperforms the common PSO algorithms and a real-coded genetic algorithm (GA). Guney and Onay (2011) proposed a method based on harmony search algorithm (HSA) for the pattern synthesis of linear antenna arrays with the prescribed nulls. Pattern nulling is achieved with controlling individually the values of amplitude, the phase, and the position of the array. Ram et al. (2017) applied Cat swarm optimization (CSO) for the optimal radiation patterns by optimizing the current excitation weight of each element and the inter-element spacing. Dib and Sharaqa (2014) presented a biogeography-based optimization (BBO) method to design non-uniform concentric circular antenna arrays (CCAAs) of isotropic radiators with optimum side-lobe level (SLL) reduction.

From this perspective, a reference template of triangular function defining with pre-specified side-lobes level (SLL), beamwidth between first nulls (FNBW) and several deep nulls placed at certain directions is considered as the desired pattern for this work. Further, PSO algorithm is used to compute non-uniform amplitude excitation co-efficient within range of [0,1] for a linear array with uniform inter-element spacing. Pattern synthesis method is then realized as an FSMD (finite state machine with data path) modeling. Verilog hardware description language (HDL) code (Chu et al, 2008) is also used here for making a direct map onto Virtex4 FPGA board.

WIRELESS NETWORKS PRELIMINARIES

There are two categories of wireless network architectures present in practice such as: static and mobile according to the mobility features of nodes (Holt et al, 2010). Various microwave and satellite networks are example of the former one. Here data communication normally occurs through single hop fixed point-to-point link in most of the cases. The latter may be installed either with infrastructure (i.e., cellular networks) or without infrastructure (i.e., mobile sensor networks) support in an ad-hoc fashion. But data are usually relayed through multi-hop wireless links from source to sink node in both of the cases. Therefore, there is always a chance of being data fragility in presence of the adversary under both models (Khan et al, 2013).

In this section, an analysis on wireless network attributes (i.e., topologies, routing protocols, attack scenarios and radio environment etc.) was made. This discussion would be helpful unveiling necessary conditions to develop the robust and secure data communication systems under chaotic environments. It also includes a comprehensive description on the perspectives of antenna pattern synthesis towards the data security.

Security Challenges in Wireless Networks

Preserving confidentiality and integrity of the crucial data has now become the most challenging task in wireless networks. Although some security methods based on system authentication property were mentioned in the IEEE 802.11 standards, these are not alone so effective in hostile environments. Data communications between two mobile nodes is possible only sharing pair-wise key and MAC (medium access control) addresses via access points (AP). However, security level is questionable if MAC addresses are spoofed (Martellini et al, 2017).

Network Architectures and Protocols

Data security in static wireless networks can be made possible using several authentication and key management techniques. Since equipment are pre-installed and supported with proper infrastructure, security issues are trivial in them. In contrast, the rapid growth of handheld electronic gadgets like laptop, PDA (personal digital assistant), LTE (long term evolution) and sensor mote etc. introduces major security challenges in multi-hop ad hoc networks (Cayirci et al, 2009). Such network architectures could be deployed basically without any infrastructure support and hence they are now mostly accepted for deployment in various vital civilian and military services under hostile environments. However, these have been emerged as the tempting targets for different kinds of malicious attacks because mobile nodes usually remain unattended (Abdulameer et al, 2014). Therefore, precaution should be taken equally for both network topology and routing plus medium access control (MAC) protocols to form resilient data communication systems.

Radio Propagation Environments

Strength of signals emitted from a typical source usually decays as an exponential function with respect to their travelling distances in the physical layer. This phenomenon is known as path loss and governed by the Friis transmission formula. Path loss is caused due to variation in signal propagation characteristics such as reflection, diffraction, refraction and dispersion etc. around the obstacles or foliage over the network field. Signal to noise ratio (SNR) of the received signals at any sink node is affected greatly with a cumulative effect of such path loss components introduced in multi-hop radio links. Thus, the overall quality of data is quite dependent on the signal propagation characteristics over the free-space (Abdulameer et al, 2014).

Attack Scenarios

Adversarial attacks may occur in different forms but their goal remains the same as to tamper the data for misleading any decision making process in the network. Attackers usually corrupt data of few compromised nodes either directly capturing their control system or an indirect way to get access for the stored data. These data are then distributed over multi-hop network architecture. Several attacks namely sybil, replay and wormhole etc. are very common in wireless networks (Chen et al, 2010). In sybil attacks, the compromised nodes may lose control on their transmit power control (TPC) system and transmit signals with increased or reduced power. Consequently, they may appear as neighboring nodes to the new clusters of nodes in the network and deteriorate system performance malfunctioning the data routing among them. Likewise, compromised nodes receive data packets from benevolent neighboring nodes and may resend the same after tampering only to their contents (not to the source address) under replay type attacks. Hence, they may remain deceptive in the trust evaluation process whereas the original source nodes may be blocked due to their misbehaviors. This also really hampers the overall performance. The wormhole attacks, on the other hand, are very risky at the distributed networks. Here, data packets from compromised nodes at one side of the network are relayed via several benevolent nodes and may reach to the compromised nodes at the other side of the network like a 'wormwhole'. This causes massive loss of data integrity and may degrade quality of services significantly. However, attacks may also be in the form of compromised environments as discussed below.

Attack via Compromised Nodes

Attackers frequently use much more powerful and resourceful equipment to eavesdrop the data transfer protocols in certain portion of the networks. In contrast, wireless nodes are resource constrained in almost all of the cases and hence it is often unrealistic to incorporate computationally expensive security algorithms on them. It would be then much easier for the attackers to corrupt the vital data of nodes under their control with a malicious code.

Attack via Compromised Environments

Attackers may also use a strategic way to alter signal propagation characteristics through the wireless medium of any particular region in the network. For example, making smoke and spreading magnets over few specific areas, permittivity and permeability of free space medium can be changed. Thus, data estimation process in some nodes of those particular areas would be hampered to some extent.

Data Security Model Perspectives

For wireless networks, security mechanism should be much robust to maintain data privacy of the compromised nodes. In many cases, such privacy models need to be also simple enough for their realization on the resource constrained nodes making compatible with their processing capability as well as memory capacity (Myles et al, 2003). However, data security schemes can be primarily classified into two categories as: data encryption/decryption and the physical data security model. In the former case, cryptography is used to encrypt/decrypt data so that their exposure is prevented from the eavesdroppers during wireless communications. For example, wired equivalent privacy (WEP) and Wi-Fi protected access (WPA) are very common methods in wireless security. Instead, physical access of the intruders is restricted beyond the vicinity of wireless data links with the latter approaches. Antenna pattern synthesis methods are more alike to this one.

Weakness of Cryptographic Schemes

Cryptographic techniques mainly function through generation and distribution of secret keys only with the authorized nodes and utilization of a longer length key certainly improves its security level. Although such schemes would be very effective in case of external attackers, they could not work well with compromised nodes (Anjum et al, 2007). Attackers would be easily able to get access for stored keys and passwords in this case. Besides, complex computation of the cryptographic algorithms would limit their applications in resource constrained nodes. These methods also fail to protect the nodes from physical layer attacks.

Effectiveness of Pattern Synthesis Methods

Several affordable solutions like code obfuscation, data scrambling, trust management and intrusion detection mechanisms etc. are also adopted to counteract the attacks against compromised nodes. However, effectiveness of these methods relies on the degree of accuracy they obtained in some statistical measurements with their basis functions. Alternatively, directional transmission of signals over wireless channel, achieved through focusing of antenna pattern towards the desired receiving node, could enable formation of a direct data transfer link. This scheme is more effective in low power signal transmission environment of the ad hoc networks. This technique could be further modified for its better security aspects employing lobe switching principles of a phased array antenna. In this process, multiple beam focusing points are produced for multiplexing the signals through multiple radio links between source and sink node. Therefore, security is guaranteed because eavesdroppers can hardly get access to the entire signals from each link.

PSO BASED PATTERN SYNTHESIS METHODOLOGY

Antenna pattern synthesis (also termed as beam shaping or beamforming) is generally a technique to produce the prescribed beam patterns. Antenna patterns with higher directivity, narrower beamwidth and lower side-lobes level etc. are essential requirements for secured data transfer through long haul point-to-point wireless links. In such antenna patterns, main-lobe contains almost all of the radiated power particularly focused onto a desired node and nulls are steered at the direction of interferences. This improves channel capacity of the wireless links making them stable and secure to guarantee higher throughput in data transmission. However, patterns having all these criteria together cannot be met with single antenna element and hence, an array structure is used in most of the cases.

PSO Algorithm Outline

Particle swarm optimization (PSO) algorithm was modeled with the analogy of a social swarm behavior in collecting honey from the flowers over any unknown field (Jin et al, 2007). In the search space, each particle position (x) represents a possible solution to the optimization problem. Thus, each movement of any particle towards the optimization goal seems to be made on the basis of its own best position termed as personal best (pbest) and the best position achieved ever among the group known as global best (gbest). The particle best positions (pbest and gbest) are usually determined by evaluating a problem-specific objective function (also referred to as cost function or fitness function). These two components indicate local exploitation and global exploration abilities in respective search. Hence, an intelligent control on proper balancing between these two search abilities is essential to acquire higher convergence speed, avoiding the possibility of trapping at local optima. This is accomplished either by introducing an inertia weight (w) or a constriction factor in PSO algorithm. It is observed that an excellent result may be obtained if inertia weight value is decreased linearly in the range [0.9, 0.4]. Thus, the velocity and position update equations for i-th particle along the j-th dimension are now modified with inertia weight and they are expressed as

$$v_{ij}(t+1) = w.v_{ij}(t) + c_1.rand_1().\left\{pbest_{ij}(t) - x_{ij}(t)\right\} + c_2.rand_2().\left\{gbest_j(t) - x_{ij}(t)\right\} \tag{1}$$

$$x_{ij}(t+1) = x_{ij}(t) + v_{ij}(t+1) \tag{2}$$

where, c_1 and c_2 are called cognitive rate and social learning rate respectively. They are usually set to 2 for better performance. Similarly, $rand_1()$ and $rand_2()$ are two random function in the range [0, 1]. These help to mimic the nature-like swarm activities in the algorithm.

Antenna Pattern Synthesis Principles

In conventional methods, current and phase distribution of each array element was varied to get an optimal pattern. Thus, antenna array with uniform distributions (also known as uniform array) provides generally narrower beamwidths. Here, beamwidth varies as inversely proportional to the number of array elements. In this case, main-lobe to first side-lobe ratio is always independent to the number of array elements and remains constant at -13.5 dB. Hence, tapering of distributions was needed. Binomial, Chebyshev and Taylor distribution etc. were normally used in literature (Balanis, 2004). Binomial arrays usually produce wider beamwidths than the others. However, such patterns can be made without any side-lobe by choosing element spacing less than or equal to half of wavelengths. In contrast, for a specified beamwidths, equal amplitude and monotonically decreasing side-lobes can be obtained from the Chebyshev and Taylor arrays respectively. Besides, other approaches using Schelkunoff polynomial, Fourier series/transform and Woodward sampling etc. are available for antenna pattern synthesis.

Antenna Array Design Theory

Let us consider a linear array with uniform inter-element spacing (Δ) and non-uniform amplitude excitations (I_n). An array configuration having even number (2N) of antenna elements along the X-axis is also shown in Figure 1. Now, array factor (AF) or pattern synthesis function in such an array is typically expressed as

$$AF\left(\theta\right) = \sum_{n=0}^{2N-1} I_n e^{jn\psi} \tag{3}$$

where, $\psi = k\Delta\left(\sin\theta - \sin\theta_d\right)$ and $k = 2\pi/\lambda$

Normally, ψ is called progressive phase shift between the elements. Also, k is termed as the wave numbers and λ is wavelength of the transmitted signal. Magnitude of current for the nth element in array is denoted by I_n. Likewise, scanning angle θ is measured about the array axis in the range $[0^0, 180^0]$ and θ_d is a squinted angle at which the main-lobe orientation is to be done. Assuming symmetry in current distributions of the array elements about the origin, the expression of array factor (AF) in equation (3) is now modified and normalized as

$$AF_p\left(\theta\right) = \sum_{n=1}^{N} I_n \cos\left[\left(n - \frac{1}{2}\right)\psi\right] \tag{4}$$

Antenna Pattern Control Attributes

Antenna pattern features usually depend on the properties of array elements such as excitation co-efficient, phase and position of elements etc. in particular array geometry. Accordingly, patterns can be shaped in any desired form varying one or more of such array element properties. In this way, directivity can be enhanced increasing the number of incorporated elements in the array. Similarly, beamwidth can be made narrower by choosing suitable array polynomials such as Binomial, Chebyshev and Taylor etc. in evaluation of the element excitation co-efficient. Installation of more array elements also does the same task. Side-lobes can be managed by proper choice of inter-element spacing. However, amplitude of side-lobes can be controlled by tapering the current distributions as in the Chebyshev and Taylor functions.

Figure 1. A symmetrical configuration of linear array with 2N elements

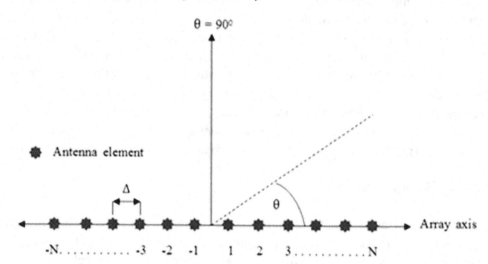

Proposed Pattern Synthesis Scheme

Most of the conventional methods described earlier are not suitable for using under the continuous changeable radio environments. Effects of interferences and multipath fading signals are to be cancelled out either placing deep and wide nulls or concentrating entire radiated power of the pattern towards the desired nodes. Data privacy is also to be maintained imposing certain side-lobes level limit in the pattern so that adjacent nodes are kept far away from the radio links. Otherwise, the intruders could even gain access to the stored data of mobile nodes by triangulation or trilateration method, getting coverage at two or more neighboring compromised nodes. Thus, antenna patterns with prescribed beamwidth, side-lobes level and desired plus null direction needs to be synthesized for secured data communications. Using PSO algorithm to optimize the array element excitation co-efficient, such patterns have been obtained in a more convenient way.

In this work, signals from all of the neighboring nodes (regardless of their trust-worthiness) are assumed as the interference to any point-to-point communication link between sources and sink node. Angle difference between two neighboring nodes with respect to the source node is also considered as beamwidth. Dimensions of the optimization variables in pattern synthesis problem are reduced to half of the total element numbers (2N) due to symmetrical array configuration. Boundary values of the optimization parameter (excitation co-efficient of array elements) in each dimension are also kept within the range [0, 1] so that a maximum dynamic shift of one in the optimization process is allowed. Fitness function (F) of the optimization algorithm is also formulated as

$$F = \min\left\{ \sum_{\theta=-90^0}^{\theta=90^0} D(\theta) \right\} \tag{5}$$

where,

$$D(\theta) = \begin{cases} 1 & if \; AF_d(\theta) - AF_p(\theta) < 0 \\ 0 & otherwise \end{cases}$$

Typically, $D(\theta)$ represents a deviation weight assigned for the difference between produced pattern $AF_p(\theta)$ and the desired one $AF_d(\theta)$ at any sample angle(θ) over the range $[-90^0, 90^0]$.

Primarily, desired pattern is considered as a triangular template as shown in Figure 2. Desired beam-width between the first nulls ($FNBW_d$) and desired side-lobes level (SLL_d) are denoted by corresponding length and base position of the triangle. Finally, imposing deep nulls (K) at the interfering directions, it takes the form as

$$AF_d(\theta) = \begin{cases} 1 - \dfrac{2}{FNBW_d}|\theta - \theta_d| & for \; |\theta - \theta_d| < \dfrac{FNBW_d}{2} \\ K & for \; \theta = null \, directions(\theta_i) \\ SLL_d & elsewhere \end{cases} \tag{6}$$

Now, considering M particles, each of them having N dimensions within the solution space, the PSO algorithm would produce two M X N dimensional matrix for its position (x) vectors and velocity (v) vectors. These vectors are randomly initialized for its faster convergence. In each iteration, fitness function is evaluated for each particle to find its pbest values as pbest = [pbest1 pbest2 .... pbestM] ^{T} and gbest value as gbest = min{pbest}. These values (pbest and gbest) along with respective positions are recorded and used to update velocity and position of each particle as per the equations (1) & (2). The termination condition for this algorithm is set to a maximum iteration number of 1000. Thus, fitness values are updated as to keep minimum number of deviations obtained for an angle interval of 1^0 over the range $[-90^0, 90^0]$ in every iteration. The global best position (gbest) achieved at the process termination (through random swarm movements over unknown search field) is defined as the optimum solution. Specifications of the desired parameters in an optimum pattern are listed in Table 1. Design and optimization parameters along with their boundary limits are also stipulated in Table 2. Convergence curve of the optimization method is illustrated in Figure 3. Thus, pattern obtained for 20 element linear arrays with desired node direction at 30^0 and four interferences at $-20^0, -5^0, 10^0$ and 60^0 is shown in Figure 4. In this optimized pattern, values of SLL_d, $FNBW_d$ and depth of nulls are set to -30 dB, 20^0 and -100 dB respectively.

Table 1. Specifications of the desired parameters for optimum pattern synthesis

Desired Parameters	Desired SLL (SLL_d)	Tolerance at SLL_d	Desired FNBW ($FNBW_d$)	Depth of Nulls (K)
Values	0.0316 (-30 dB)	Nil (0 dB)	20^0	0.0001 (-100 dB)

HARDWARE REALIZATION ON FPGA DEVICES

Two categories of processor architectures are available in the market for implementation of the proposed pattern synthesis method on digital platforms. These are commonly known as: general purpose processors and custom processors. Microprocessor unit (MPU) and digital signal processor (DSP) are example of the former type. Although more flexibility in computation of general purpose solutions is achieved with their fixed instructions set, but the sequential execution process makes them relatively slow, involving multiple clock cycles to complete any particular task. They also consume more power as these architectures are not optimized for particular application. In contrast, application specific integrated circuits (ASIC) are called custom processors. They normally enable computation with a customized architecture and always offer a specific solution in parallel mode. Hence, processing the entire task in a single clock cycle makes them both fast as well as power efficient. However, they are comparatively more expensive. Field programmable gate array (FPGA) family, on the other hand, integrates both the benefits of versatile design solutions and parallel processing capabilities on the same platform. On execution of the algorithms, they often develop reconfigurable distributed arithmetic structures with their internal logic blocks. This avoids the instruction fetch and data load/store bottlenecks of the conventional Von Neumann architecture (Wood et al, 2008).

ASMD Chart

The proposed pattern synthesis method basically operates on a fixed-point PSO processor that computes optimum values of the array element excitation co-efficient. Towards development of its system architecture on the Xilinx virtex4 FPGA board, a special flow chart known as algorithmic state machine with data path (ASMD) chart is used. It translates the sequence of steps in the algorithm more similar to an finite state machine with data path (FSMD) modeling. FSMD architectures normally include both the controller and data unit. Total process should be executed through finite logical operations called

Figure 2. A triangular template with the desired pattern specifications

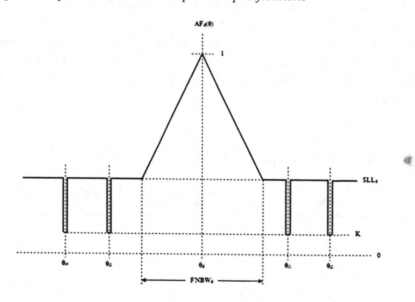

states $(S_0\text{-}S_{13})$ that imply sequential commands on the controller to actuate control signals for appropriate operations in the data unit. Here, FSM (finite state machine) acts as a controller. In the ASMD chart, each building block normally contains several RTL (register transfer level) notations that specify data manipulation and data transfer operations among several registers. Each RTL operation is synchronized with a master clock embedded in the system and thus executes clock by clock basis. The ASMD chart for the proposed pattern synthesis algorithm is illustrated in Figure 5. To synthesize a behavioral model of such FSMD design, Verilog code is used as hardware description languages (HDL), making direct map onto FPGA board.

Proposed Architecture

The RTL operations described in ASMD chart are normally performed by the data unit. It can be implemented well with registers, multiplexers and other combinational logic circuits that are required to design several data manipulation functions. To realize RTL operations on hardware, data from the source registers

Figure 3. Convergence curve in PSO-based pattern synthesis method

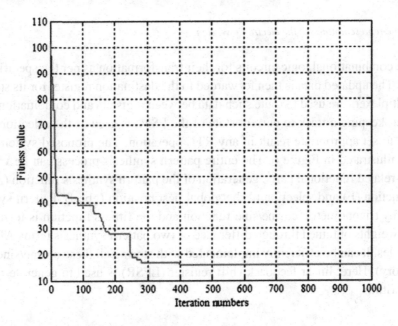

Table 2. Design parameters with boundary limits for pattern synthesis method

Design Parameters	Boundary Values	
	Lower Limit	**Upper limit**
Operating frequency (f)	2.4 GHz (fixed)	
Inter-element spacing (Δ)	0.5λ (fixed)	
elemental current distributions (I_n)	0	1
elemental phase shift (β)	0 (fixed)	

Figure 4. Optimal pattern obtained in PSO-based pattern synthesis method

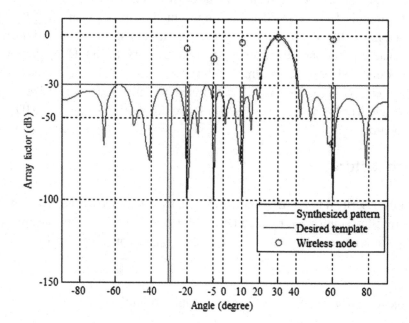

For a more accurate representation see the electronic version.

are passed to the combinational logic circuits for their transformation as per the specific function at the first clock cycle. The updated data is then forwarded to the destination register for its storage at the next clock cycle. Multiplexers are used to route such data between registers and combinational logic circuits. The state register, keeping a track to current state of the FSM, is used as the selection signal input for the multiplexers to set appropriate result in any RTL operation. The proposed system architecture on FPGA device is illustrated in Figure 6. The entire pattern synthesis process can be viewed as to have three basic inter-related functional parts: generation of the pattern synthesis function (AFp), evaluation of the fitness function (F) and selection of the global best position (gbest). Pattern synthesis function is characterized by trigonometric cosine/sine function and the fitness function is formulated as a sum of the deviation weights obtained through difference of two pattern synthesis terms AFd and AFp over finite sample angles. It can be efficiently implemented with storing all these cosine/sine values in ROM (read only memory). Here, linear feedback shift register (LFSR) is used to generate random numbers for the PSO algorithm.

PERFORMANCE ANALYSIS

Performance of the pattern synthesis scheme is verified with hardware level fixed-point simulations on its accuracy and computational overheads. In statistical measurement of signals arriving at multipath directions, both of AWGN (additive white Gaussian noise) and Rayleigh fading channel conditions are assumed. Some off-line PC (personal computer) generated data that closely relates with the real-time wireless radio propagation characteristics are considered here for both noise variance and fading co-efficient. The resulting data are obtained with 30 runs of the simulation program on the Xilinx Virtex4

Figure 5. ASMD chart for the proposed pattern synthesis method

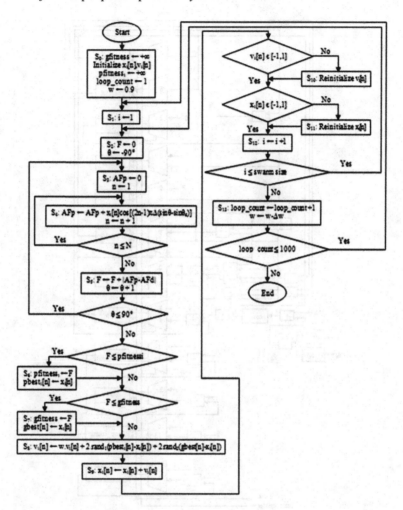

(device: XC4VLX60) FPGA environment. Moreover, analytical discussions on each of these results such as pattern synthesis accuracy, bit error rate (BER), FPGA resource utilization and computation time etc. is also made.

Simulation Results

Simulation results are presented in terms of accuracy in pattern synthesis method and average bit error rate assuming binary phase shift keying (BPSK) modulation technique in signal transmission over the wireless channel (Wang et al, 2007).

Pattern Synthesis Accuracy

Accuracy (A) in the synthesized pattern measures the degree of exactness towards its desired specifications. It is usually expressed (in percentage) as

Figure 6. System architecture for the proposed pattern synthesis method

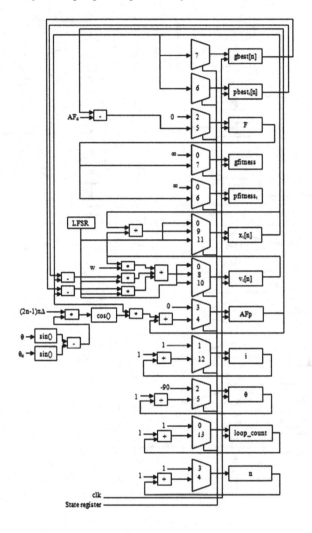

$$A = \left(1 - \epsilon\right) \times 100\% \tag{7}$$

where, ϵ represents error associated with the pattern synthesis method. It is defined as ratio of the aggregated value of deviation weights to the total number of sample points (P) and expressed by

$$\epsilon = \frac{\sum_{p=1}^{P} D\left(\theta_p\right)}{P}$$

Typically, θ_p is the p-th sample angle over the range $[-90^0, 90^0]$. The pattern features like beamwidths, SLL and nulls setting conditions etc. vary with number of multipath faded interfering signals and antenna elements in the array. Therefore, accuracy under various number of antenna elements and nulls at the direction of interferences are illustrated with their respective empirical cumulative distribution functions

(ECDF) in Figure 7(a) and Figure 7(b). In both cases, SLL and FNBW are kept constant (SLL= -30 dB and FNBW= 20^0). It is obvious that accuracy increases invariably with an increase in number of array elements or reducing the interferences. Another empirical cumulative distribution functions (ECDF) of accuracy under variable side-lobes level and beamwidths are also presented in Figure 7(c) and Figure 7(d). In this case, number of antenna elements and nulls at the interfering directions are set to a constant value (2N = 20 and Nulls = 4). It is also evident that an increase in magnitudes of SLL and FNBW can enhance the accuracy. The optimized values for element excitation coefficient in a linear and symmetrical array with different number of antenna elements are given in Table 3. Here, other parameters are also considered to have fixed values (SLL = -30 dB, FNBW = 20^0 and Nulls = 4).

Bit Error Rate

Bit error rate (BER) usually measures the probability of error in system performance due to various channel noise conditions. At particular signal-to-noise ratio (SNR) level, it usually depends on the number of antenna elements in the array with specific channel propagation conditions. Under AWGN channel, statistical measurement of bit error rate is governed by the formula (Rao et al, 2015) as

$$P_e = \frac{1}{2} erfc \left(\sqrt{2N \times SNR} \right) \approx \frac{1}{2} e^{\frac{-2N \times SNR}{2}} \qquad (8)$$

In contrast, average bit error rate estimation under Rayleigh fading channel due to random varying nature of the fading co-efficient, is described in (Hong et al, 2011) as

Figure 7a. ECDF of accuracy in proposed pattern synthesis method (Nulls = 4)

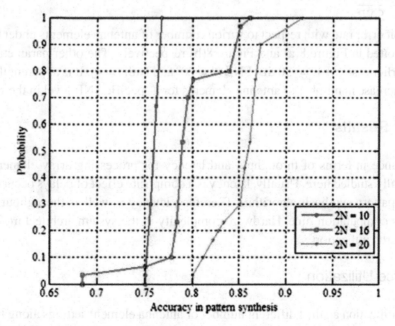

For a more accurate representation see the electronic version.

Figure 7b. ECDF of accuracy in proposed pattern synthesis method (2N = 20)

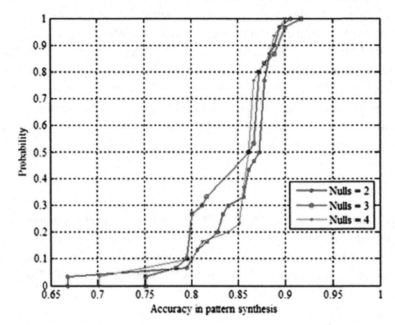

For a more accurate representation see the electronic version.

$$P_e = \frac{(1-\gamma)^{2N}}{2} \sum_{q=0}^{2N-1} \binom{2N+q-1}{q} \frac{(1+\gamma)^q}{2} \approx \binom{4N-1}{2N}\left(\frac{1}{2 \times SNR}\right)^{2N} \quad (9)$$

where, $\gamma = \sqrt{\dfrac{SNR}{2+SNR}}$

The average bit error rate with respect to various number of antenna elements under the both channel conditions are plotted in Figure 8(a) and Figure 8(b) respectively. The other parameter values remain same as in the earlier case (SLL = -30 dB, FNBW = 20⁰ and Nulls = 4). It is apparent that average BER decreases with increase in number of antenna elements for a specific SNR level in the wireless channel.

Experimental Results

System performance in terms of throughput and latency for processing array element excitation co-efficient is normally studied here. Usually, latency is a composite effect of delays occurred and mapping technique in the pattern synthesis algorithm. Therefore, latency as well as throughput of the system is validated with its computation time. Hardware complexity in the system architecture is also described with FPGA resource utilization.

FPGA Resource Utilization

FPGA resource utilization against different number of antenna element settings along the array is given in Table 4. Other parametric values are also kept constant (SLL = -30 dB, FNBW= 20⁰ and Nulls at the

Figure 7c. ECDF of accuracy in proposed pattern synthesis method (FNBW = 20⁰)

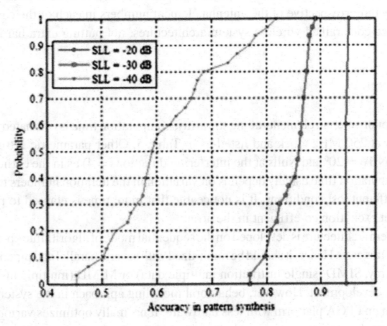

For a more accurate representation see the electronic version.

Figure 7d. ECDF of accuracy in proposed pattern synthesis method (SLL = - 30 dB)

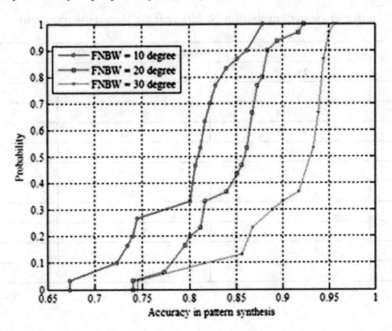

For a more accurate representation see the electronic version.

interfering directions = 4). It is obvious that only a fixed number of DSPs (multipliers) are occupied on the system architecture irrespective of the antenna element numbers in each of the cases. Thus, it suits best to the resource-constrained wireless system architectures, not putting extra hardware complexity on them.

Computation Time

For various number of antenna elements along the array, computation time is estimated with a maximum of 1000 iterations at 250 MHz clock and listed as in Table 5. Other parametric settings remain same (SLL = -30 dB, FNBW= 20^0 and Nulls at the interfering directions = 4) as in the earlier case. At FPGA environment, computation time usually depends on variation in the iteration numbers to execute Verilog program under different test conditions. It is noticeable that more time is elapsed to process the larger number of element excitation co-efficient in the array.

Since such system architecture is developed on the sequential mode of algorithmic operations, latency is more prominent in this case. Hence, it should be minimized with several parallel and pipelined architectures such as systolic array, SIMD (single instruction multiple data) or MIMD (multiple instruction multiple data) to its further development. However, behavioral modeling approach in the system design leads to its implementation on FPGA platform with less hardware. It normally optimizes various synthesis tools in CAD (computer aided design) flow to make system architecture on the re-configurable FPGA chip.

Table 3. Optimized antenna element excitation co-efficient for the symmetric array

Index (n)	Number of Array Elements (2N)		
	2N = 10	2N = 16	2N = 20
1	0.9483	0.8843	0.8666
2	0.8315	0.8949	0.8117
3	0.6233	0.7217	0.7585
4	0.3950	0.6675	0.6970
5	0.2118	0.4982	0.5454
6	--	0.3568	0.5201
7	--	0.2097	0.3670
8	--	0.1363	0.2389
9	--	--	0.1617
10	--	--	0.1274

Figure 8a. BER performance under AWGN channel

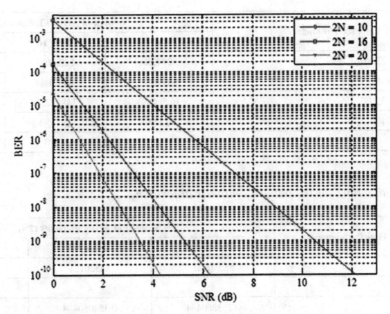

For a more accurate representation see the electronic version.

Figure 8b. BER performance under Rayleigh fading channel

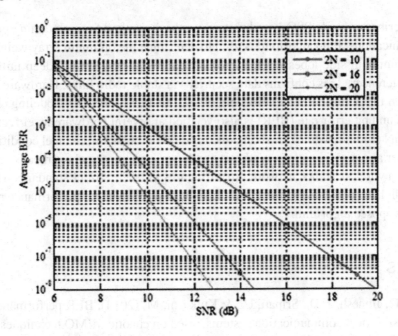

For a more accurate representation see the electronic version.

Table 4. FPGA resource utilization for the pattern synthesis algorithm

FPGA Resource Parameters	Number of Array Elements (2N)		
	2N = 10	2N = 16	2N = 20
No. of occupied Slices (26,624)	588 (2%)	822 (3%)	951 (3%)
No. of Slice Flip Flops (53,248)	483 (0%)	636 (1%)	731 (1%)
No. of 4 input LUTs (53,248)	1029 (1%)	1482 (2%)	1699 (3%)
No. of bonded IOBs (448)	13 (2%)	13 (2%)	13 (2%)
No. of DSPs 48s (64)	7 (10%)	7 (10%)	7 (10%)

Table 5. Computation time for the pattern synthesis algorithm

Computation Time Parameters	Number of Array Elements (2N)		
	2N = 10	2N = 16	2N = 20
No. of clock cycles	58340121	88520121	108640121
Clock time (ns)	4	4	4
Total time (s)	0.233360484	0.354080484	0.434560484

CONCLUSION

This chapter describes a simple PSO-based pattern synthesis method for maintaining privacy of data in wireless communications. PSO algorithm is used to determine the optimum array weights that produce a pattern with minimum side-lobes level, narrower beamwidth and several deep nulls steered at the direction of interferences. This confirms data security via stable radio links. Hardware implementation of such system on the Xilinx vitex4 FPGA chip is also made with FSMD modeling. The accuracy of pattern synthesis and bit error rate (BER) is also verified at several hardware level fixed-point simulations under AWGN (additive white Gaussian noise) and Rayleigh fading channel conditions. Simulation results with higher accuracy in pattern synthesis and lower computational overheads validate such system integration on wireless ad hoc network infrastructures in IEEE 802.11 standards. However, system design with parallel and pipelined architectures could also provide better performance reducing latency problem of the proposed algorithm.

REFERENCES

Abdulameer, L. F., Jignesh, J. D., Sripati, U., & Kulkarni, M. (2014). BER performance enhancement for secure wireless optical communication systems based on chaotic MIMO techniques. *Nonlinear Dynamics*, *75*(1-2), 7–16. doi:10.100711071-013-1044-z

Akdagli, A., & Guney, K. (2003). Shaped-beam pattern synthesis of equally and unequally spaced linear antenna arrays using a modified tabu search algorithm. *Microwave and Optical Technology Letters*, *36*(1), 16–20. doi:10.1002/mop.10657

Akdagli, A., Guney, K., & Karaboga, D. (2006). Touring ant colony optimization algorithm for shaped-beam pattern synthesis of linear antenna arrays. *Electromagnetics*, *26*(8), 615–628. doi:10.1080/02726340600978349

Anjum, F., & Mouchtaris, P. (2007). *Security for wireless ad hoc networks*. John Wiley & Sons, Inc. doi:10.1002/0470118474

Bagchi, S., & Mitra, S. K. (1999). The nonuniform discrete Fourier transform and its applications in signal processing. New York: Springer Science+Business Media, LLC. doi:10.1007/978-1-4615-4925-3

Balakrishnan, N., Murthy, P. K., & Ramakrishna, S. (1979). Synthesis of antenna arrays with spatial and excitation constraints. *IEEE Transactions on Antennas and Propagation*, *AP-27*(5), 690–696. doi:10.1109/TAP.1979.1142151

Balanis, C. A. (2004). *Antenna theory analysis and design* (2nd ed.). New York: John Wiley & Sons, Inc.

Bruintjes, T. M., Kokkeler, A. B. J., & Smit, G. J. M. (2016). Asymmetric shaped-pattern synthesis for planar antenna arrays. *International Journal of Antennas and Propagation*, *2016*, 1–13. doi:10.1155/2016/4746381

Bucci, O. M., D'elia, G., Mazzarella, G., & Panariello, G. (1994). Antenna pattern synthesis: A new general approach. *Proceedings of the IEEE*, *82*(3), 358–371. doi:10.1109/5.272140

Carlson, B. D., & Willner, D. (1992). Antenna pattern synthesis using weighted least squares. *IEE Proceedings-H*, *139*(1), 11-16.

Cayirci, E., & Rong, C. (2009). *Security in wireless ad hoc and sensor networks*. West Sussex, UK: John Wiley & Sons Ltd. doi:10.1002/9780470516782

Chaker, H., Abri, M., & Badaoui, H. A. (2016). Hybrid evolutionary algorithm genetical swarm optimization for 1D and 2D annular ring unequally spaced antennas arrays synthesis. *Electromagnetics*, *36*(8), 485–03. doi:10.1080/02726343.2016.1236008

Chang, H.-P., Sarkar, T. K., & Pereira-Filho, O. M. C. (2000). Antenna pattern synthesis utilizing spherical Bessel functions. *IEEE Transactions on Antennas and Propagation*, *48*(6), 853–859. doi:10.1109/8.865216

Chaouchi, H., & Laurent-Maknavicius, M. (Eds.). (2007). *Wireless and mobile network security*. Hoboken, NJ: John Wiley & Sons, Inc.

Chatterjee, S., Chatterjee, S., & Poddar, D. R. (2014). Synthesis of linear array using Taylor distribution and particle swarm optimisation. *International Journal of Electronics*, *102*(3), 514–528. doi:10.1080/00207217.2014.905993

Chen, Y., Yang, J., Trappe, W., & Martin, R. P. (2010). Detecting and localizing identity-based attacks in wireless and sensor networks. *IEEE Transactions on Vehicular Technology*, *59*(5), 2418–2434. doi:10.1109/TVT.2010.2044904

Chu, P. P. (2008). *FPGA prototyping by Verilog examples*. Hoboken, NJ: John Wiley & Sons, Inc. doi:10.1002/9780470374283

Collin, G., Geron, E., Lucas, J., & Ditchi, T. (2010). Fast antenna pattern synthesis using the variational method. *IET Microwaves, Antennas & Propagation*, *4*(11), 1689–1697. doi:10.1049/iet-map.2008.0399

Dib, N., & Sharaqa, A. (2015). Design of non-uniform concentric circular antenna arrays with optimal sidelobe level reduction using biogeography-based optimization. *International Journal of Microwave and Wireless Technologies*, 7(2), 161–166. doi:10.1017/S1759078714000610

Dikmese, S., Kavak, A., Kucuk, K., Sahin, S., & Tangel, A. (2011). FPGA based implementation and comparison of beamformers for CDMA2000. *Wireless Personal Communications*, 57(2), 233–253. doi:10.100711277-009-9855-4

EI-Kamchouchi, H. (2010). Ultra-low-sidelobe-level concentric-ring array pattern synthesis using Bessel neural networks. *IEEE Antennas & Propagation Magazine*, 52(4), 102–105. doi:10.1109/MAP.2010.5638242

Elragal, H. M., Mangoud, M. A., & Alsharaa, M. T. (2011). Hybrid differential evolution and enhanced particle swarm optimisation technique for design of reconfigurable phased antenna arrays. *IET Microwaves, Antennas & Propagation*, 5(11), 1280–1287. doi:10.1049/iet-map.2010.0525

Er, M. H. (1990). Linear antenna array pattern synthesis with prescribed broad nulls. *IEEE Transactions on Antennas and Propagation*, 38(9), 1496–1498. doi:10.1109/8.57004

Er, M. H., Sim, S. L., & Koh, S. N. (1993). Application of constrained optimization techniques to array pattern synthesis. *Signal Processing*, 34(3), 323–334. doi:10.1016/0165-1684(93)90139-2

Farhat, N. H., & Bai, B. (1987). Phased-array antenna pattern synthesis by simulated annealing. *Proceedings of the IEEE*, 75(6), 842–844. doi:10.1109/PROC.1987.13805

Fuchs, B. (2012). Synthesis of sparse arrays with focused or shaped beampattern via sequential convex optimizations. *IEEE Transactions on Antennas and Propagation*, 60(7), 3499–03. doi:10.1109/TAP.2012.2196951

Goudos, S. K., Moysiadou, V., Samaras, T., Siakavara, K., & Sahalos, J. N. (2010). Application of a comprehensive learning particle swarm optimizer to unequally spaced linear array synthesis with sidelobe level suppression and null control. *IEEE Antennas and Wireless Propagation Letters, 9*, 125-29.

Gunes, F., & Tokan, F. (2010). Pattern Search optimization with applications on synthesis of linear antenna arrays. *Expert Systems with Applications*, 37(6), 4698–05. doi:10.1016/j.eswa.2009.11.012

Guney, K., & Onay, M. (2011). Optimal synthesis of linear antenna arrays using a harmony search algorithm. *Expert Systems with Applications*, 38(12), 15455–15462. doi:10.1016/j.eswa.2011.06.015

Guo, J.-L., & Li, J.-Y. (2009). Pattern synthesis of conformal array antenna in the presence of platform using differential evolution algorithm. *IEEE Transactions on Antennas and Propagation*, 57(9), 2615–2621. doi:10.1109/TAP.2009.2027046

Holt, A., & Huang, C.-Y. (2010). *802.11 Wireless networks security and analysis*. London, UK: Springer-Verlag Ltd.

Hong, L., & Armada, A. G. (2011). Bit error rate performance of MIMO MMSE receivers in correlated Rayleigh flat-fading channels. *IEEE Transactions on Vehicular Technology*, 60(1), 313–317. doi:10.1109/TVT.2010.2090369

Ilyas, M., & Ahson, S. (2005). *Handbook of wireless local area networks applications, technology, security, and standards*. Boca Raton, FL: Taylor & Francis Group, LLC.

Ismail, T. H., Abu-Al-Nadi, D. I., & Mismar, M. J. (2004). Phase-only control for antenna pattern synthesis of linear arrays using the Levenberg-Marquardt algorithm. *Electromagnetics, 24*(7), 555–564. doi:10.1080/02726340490496707

Jiang, T., Wang, H. J., & Hu, Y.-C. (2007). Preserving location privacy in wireless LANs. In *Proceedings of the 5th international conference on Mobile systems, applications and services* (pp. 246–57). San Juan, Puerto Rico: ACM.

Jin, N., & Rahmat-Samii, Y. (2007). Advances in particle swarm optimization for antenna designs: Real-number, binary, single-objective and multiobjective implementations. *IEEE Transactions on Antennas and Propagation, 55*(3), 556–567. doi:10.1109/TAP.2007.891552

Khan, S., & Mauri, J. L. (2014). *Security for multihop wireless networks*. Boca Raton, FL: Taylor & Francis Group, LLC. doi:10.1201/b16754

Khan, S., & Pathan, A.-S. K. (Eds.). (2013). *Wireless networks and security issues, challenges and research trends*. Berlin: Springer-Verlag Ltd. doi:10.1007/978-3-642-36169-2

Lebret, H., & Boyd, S. (1997). Antenna array pattern synthesis via convex optimization. *IEEE Transactions on Signal Processing, 45*(3), 526–532. doi:10.1109/78.558465

Li, H., Liu, Y., Sun, G., Wang, A., & Liang, S. (2017). Beam pattern synthesis based on improved biogeography-based optimization for reducing sidelobe level. *Computers & Electrical Engineering, 60*(May), 161–174.

Liu, B., Aliakbarian, H., Ma, Z., Vandenbosch, G. A. E., Gielen, G., & Excell, P. (2014). An efficient method for antenna design optimization based on evolutionary computation and machine learning techniques. *IEEE Transactions on Antennas and Propagation, 62*(1), 7–18. doi:10.1109/TAP.2013.2283605

Mahmoud, M. M. E. A., & Shen, X. (2014). Security for multi-hop wireless networks. New York: Springer Science+Business Media, LLC.

Mailloux, R. J. (2005). *Phased array antenna handbook* (2nd ed.). Boston: Artech House.

Mandal, D., Ghoshal, S. P., & Bhattacharjee, A. K. (2011). Wide null control of symmetric linear antenna array using novel particle swarm optimization. *International Journal of RF and Microwave Computer-Aided Engineering, 21*(4), 376–382. doi:10.1002/mmce.20526

Mangaraj, B. B., & Swain, P. (2017). An optimal LAA subsystem designed using Gravitational search algorithm. *Engineering Science and Technology, an International Journal, 20*(2), 494-01.

Martellini, M., Gaycken, S. A. S., & Wilson, C. (2017). *Information security of highly critical wireless networks*. Cham, Switzerland: Springer International Publishing AG. doi:10.1007/978-3-319-52905-9

Mautz, J. R., & Harrington, R. F. (1975). Computational methods for antenna pattern synthesis. *IEEE Transactions on Antennas and Propagation, AP-32*(7), 507–512. doi:10.1109/TAP.1975.1141126

Mishra, A. (2008). *Security and quality of service in ad hoc wireless networks*. New York: Cambridge University Press. doi:10.1017/CBO9780511619755

Mismar, M. J., Ismail, T. H., & Abu-Al-Nadi, D. I. (2007). Analytical array polynomial method for linear antenna arrays with phase-only control. *International Journal of Electronics and Communications*, *61*(7), 485–492. doi:10.1016/j.aeue.2006.06.009

Myles, G., Friday, A., & Davies, N. (2003). Preserving privacy in environments with location-based applications. *IEEE Pervasive Computing*, *2*(1), 56–64. doi:10.1109/MPRV.2003.1186726

Pappula, L., & Ghosh, D. (2014). Linear antenna array synthesis using cat swarm optimization. *International Journal of Electronics and Communications*, *68*(6), 540–549. doi:10.1016/j.aeue.2013.12.012

Peter Hong, Y.-W., Lan, P.-C., & Jay Kuo, C.-C. (2014). Signal processing approaches to secure physical layer communications in multi-antenna wireless systems. New York: Springer Science+Business Media, LLC. doi:10.1007/978-981-4560-14-6

Prasad, S., & Charan, R. (1984). On the constrained synthesis of array patterns with applications to circular and arc arrays. *IEEE Transactions on Antennas and Propagation*, *AP-32*(7), 725–730. doi:10.1109/TAP.1984.1143404

Qubati, G. M., Formato, R. A., & Dib, N. I. (2010). Antenna benchmark performance and array synthesis using central force optimisation. *IET Microwaves, Antennas & Propagation*, *4*(5), 583–592. doi:10.1049/iet-map.2009.0147

Ram, G., Mandal, D., Ghoshal, S. P., & Kar, R. (2017). Optimal array factor radiation pattern synthesis for linear antenna array using cat swarm optimization: Validation by an electromagnetic simulator. *Frontiers of Information Technology & Electronic Engineering*, *18*(4), 570–577. doi:10.1631/FITEE.1500371

Rao, K. D. (2015). *Channel coding techniques for wireless communications*. Springer Pvt. Ltd.

Recioui, A. (2012). Sidelobe level reduction in linear array pattern synthesis using particle swarm optimization. *Journal of Optimization Theory and Applications*, *153*(2), 497–12. doi:10.100710957-011-9953-9

Schaefer, G., & Rossberg, M. (2014). *Security in fixed and wireless networks* (2nd ed.). Heidelberg, Germany: John Wiley & Sons Ltd.

Schafer, G. (2003). *Security in fixed and wireless networks: an introduction to securing data communications*. West Sussex, UK: John Wiley & Sons, Ltd. doi:10.1002/0470863722

Steyskal, H. (1982). Synthesis of antenna patterns with prescribed nulls. *IEEE Transactions on Antennas and Propagation*, *AP-30*(2), 273–279. doi:10.1109/TAP.1982.1142765

Trastoy, A., Rahmat–Samii, Y., Ares, F., & Moreno, E. (2004). Two-pattern linear array antenna: Synthesis and analysis of tolerance. *IEE Proceedings. Microwaves, Antennas and Propagation*, *151*(2), 127–130. doi:10.1049/ip-map:20040175

Wang, C., Au, E. K. S., Murch, R. D., Mow, W. H., Cheng, R. S., & Lau, V. (2007). On the performance of the MIMO zero-forcing receiver in the presence of channel estimation error. *IEEE Transactions on Wireless Communications*, *6*(3), 805–810. doi:10.1109/TWC.2007.05384

Wang, T., & Yang, Y. (2011). Location privacy protection from RSS localization system using antenna pattern synthesis. In *Proceedings of the IEEE INFOCOM* (pp. 2408-16). Shanghai, China: IEEE Explore. 10.1109/INFCOM.2011.5935061

Wong, F. L., Lin, M., Nagaraja, S., Wassell, I., & Stajano, F. (2007). Evaluation framework of location privacy of wireless mobile systems with arbitrary beam pattern. In *Proceedings of the fifth annual conference on communication networks and services research* (pp. 157-65). Frederlcton, NB, Canada: IEEE Explore. 10.1109/CNSR.2007.30

Yang, H., Luo, H., Ye, F., Lu, S., & Zhang, L. (2004). Security in mobile ad hoc networks: Challenges and solutions. *IEEE Wireless Communications*, *11*(1), 38–47. doi:10.1109/MWC.2004.1269716

Yang, K., Zhao, Z., & Liu, Q. H. (2013). Fast pencil beam pattern synthesis of large unequally spaced antenna arrays. *IEEE Transactions on Antennas and Propagation*, *61*(2), 627–634. doi:10.1109/TAP.2012.2220319

Zheng, L., Yang, S., & Nie, Z. (2011). Pattern synthesis with specified broad nulls in time-modulated circular antenna arrays. *Electromagnetics*, *31*(5), 355–367. doi:10.1080/02726343.2011.579770

Zhou, X., Song, L., & Zhang, Y. (2014). *Physical layer security in wireless communications*. Boca Raton, FL: Taylor & Francis Group, LLC.

Zou, Y., & Zhu, J. (2016). *Physical-layer security for cooperative relay networks*. Springer International Publishing AG. doi:10.1007/978-3-319-31174-6

Chapter 10
Nature–Inspired Algorithms in Wireless Sensor Networks

Ajay Kaushik
Delhi Technological University, India

S. Indu
Delhi Technological University, India

Daya Gupta
Delhi Technological University, India

ABSTRACT

Wireless sensor networks (WSNs) are becoming increasingly popular due to their applications in a wide variety of areas. Sensor nodes in a WSN are battery operated which outlines the need of some novel protocols that allows the limited sensor node battery to be used in an efficient way. The authors propose the use of nature-inspired algorithms to achieve energy efficient and long-lasting WSN. Multiple nature-inspired techniques like BBO, EBBO, and PSO are proposed in this chapter to minimize the energy consumption in a WSN. A large amount of data is generated from WSNs in the form of sensed information which encourage the use of big data tools in WSN domain. WSN and big data are closely connected since the large amount of data emerging from sensors can only be handled using big data tools. The authors describe how the big data can be framed as an optimization problem and the optimization problem can be effectively solved using nature-inspired algorithms.

NATURE INSPIRED ALGORITHMS

Real world problems are very challenging and difficult to solve and are sometimes NP hard problems as well. Optimization techniques are used to solve these problems but with no guarantee that optimization algorithms will provide the optimum solution. In fact there is no efficient algorithm for NP hard problems. They are solved usually by trial methods. New nature inspired algorithms are used to test their efficiency in solving these problems. Among these new algorithms many algorithms like particle swarm optimization, ant colony optimization, and biogeography based optimization have gained popularity due to their higher efficiency (Fister et al, 2013).

DOI: 10.4018/978-1-5225-5852-1.ch010

Inspiration From Nature

In most of nature inspired algorithms, the source of inspiration is nature. Nature has inspired much research in many ways based on some successful biological phenomenon. Among biology inspired algorithms, a popular class of algorithms is derived from swarm based intelligence. Thus some of the biology inspired algorithms are termed as swarm intelligence algorithms. Few examples are ant colony optimization, cuckoo search, bat algorithm, particle swarm optimization etc (Yang et al, 2009). However, not all the optimization algorithms are nature inspired. Some of them may be inspired from physics, chemistry or even music. (Fister et al, 2013)Hence the sources of inspiration for algorithm development are very diverse, and consequently, the algorithms are equally diverse.

Nature inspired algorithms have been used extensively for many applications such as data mining, wireless sensor networks, image processing etc. Earlier genetic algorithm was introduced as an optimization algorithm. But genetic algorithms had some basic flaws. Consequently, more diverse and better algorithms are introduced. In past 2 decades, almost 40 nature inspired optimization algorithms are proposed with relative advantages. For instance, in 2008, Biogeography based optimization was introduced by Dan Simon. In BBO entire population is not changed at the end of each generation which was the case in genetic algorithms. Wireless sensor networks are extensively used in the present age. There is a huge amount of sensed data generated that is generated by the sensors in WSN domain. To efficiently manage, handle and use this large amount of dataset emerging from WSNs, we need big data tools. Since big data and WSN data are closely connected, we first analyze the implementation of some of the famous nature inspired techniques in WSN domain. Later in the chapter, we describe how these nature inspired techniques can be applied to big data.

Wireless Sensor Networks

Wireless sensor networks are becoming increasingly popular with their utility being proved in many areas such as their deployment in battle fields, fighter jets, agriculture, weather and many more. (Akyidliz et al, 2002; Abood et al, 2016) Wireless sensor networks consist of many small size sensor nodes used to sense useful information. Each node is assigned to a cluster head or gateway. Node sense useful information and transmit this information to the gateway. A gateway receives information from sensor node, aggregate this information and forward it to the sink. This entire scenario forms a cluster in a wireless sensor network (Abood et al, 2016).

Clustering is important in WSN as it provides a hierarchal, organized and structured schema to collect useful information from various sources and transmit this information to sink through cluster heads. Also, clustering reduces energy consumption in a WSN as all sensor nodes need not to communicate with the sink rather only cluster head communicate with the sink as a representative of all sensor nodes contained in the cluster. Cluster heads bear extra load of receiving, aggregating and transferring the data from sensor nodes to the base station. Therefore cluster heads dissipate their energy at much faster pace. Once a cluster head dies, the entire network can go down (Kuila et al, 2013; Kuila et al, 2014; Morteza et al, 2015). Thus we aim to perform clustering in a wireless sensor network (Simon, 2008) in such a way that energy consumption of a cluster head can be minimized and lifetime of a WSN can be optimized. A WSN scenario is shown in figure 1.

Figure 1.

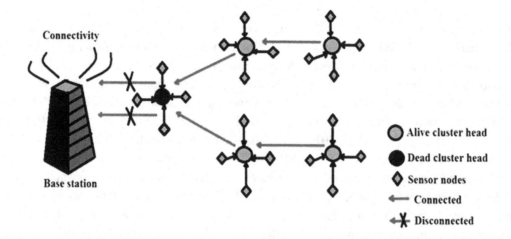

Nature inspired artificial techniques have become popular in recent years and used frequently to solve and optimize many problems including wireless sensor networks. In the past energy efficient wireless clustering are being implemented by using some traditional artificial intelligence technique like genetic algorithm, particle swarm optimization.

NATURE INSPIRED ALGORITHM IN WSN DOMAIN

When implemented for wireless sensor networks, nature inspired techniques have given very good results. Some of the applications of the nature inspired techniques on wireless sensor networks are explained below.

Related Work of Application of Nature Inspired Algorithms in WSN

Manny approaches have been used in which artificial intelligence techniques are used to improve lifetime of a wireless cluster. In (Low et al, 2008) a clustering algorithm is proposed in which a breadth first tree is used to find the gateway which is least loaded and then sensor node is assigned to that gateway. One big problem with this algorithm is it took a large amount of memory space to store and process BFS. Also execution time while calculating BFS is large. It has time complexity of the order $O(mn^2)$. In (Pratyay et al, 2014) a genetic algorithm based load balancing, clustering algorithm is proposed. Mutation step of genetic algorithm is used for load balancing. In (Ataul et al, 2009) genetic algorithm is used for routing of aggregated data between cluster head and sink. In this algorithm roulette wheel selection is used for selection of individuals and fitness of an individual is taken in terms of network lifetime. In (Gupta et al, 2013) another routing algorithm is proposed in which attempt is made to reduce communication distance between the sink and gateway using genetic algorithm. One thing to be noted in both (Ataul et al, 2009) and (Gupta et al, 2013), only the transmission of aggregated data from cluster head to the base station is focused upon, there is no emphasis on energy consumption in data transfer between individual node to cluster head. In (Pratyay et al, 2013) a particle swarm optimization based clustering is proposed to enhance lifetime of a wireless cluster.

Most of above algorithm focus on clustering only and do not take into account routing overhead involved in the clustering process. Also, some of the above algorithms focus only upon energy consumed in sending aggregated data from cluster head to sink while achieving energy efficient clustering, they do not take into account overhead involved in routing from an individual node to cluster head. The algorithms explained below uses nature inspire techniques to rectify these flaws by taking into account 1) Distance between gateway and sink 3) Residual energy of the gateway in HSI calculation. To our knowledge, there is no such algorithm existing presently, in which artificial intelligence techniques like BBO and Extended BBO are applied for energy efficient wireless clustering taking into account both individual nodes to gateway routing overhead and gateway to sink routing overhead. Later in the chapter we explain how the data coming from sensors in terms of sensed information is analogous to Big data and how the nature inspired algorithms like BBO and Extended BBO can be successfully applied to Big data domain in order to optimize the performance of big data tools.

We present an interconnected scenario where we show the significance of nature inspired techniques in WSN and propose the use of those nature inspired techniques in Big data domain.

Biogeography Based Optimization Based Wireless Sensor Networks

Introduction

Wireless sensor networks are constrained by limited battery lifetime. A wireless cluster goes down as soon as the battery of cluster heads is consumed. Therefore, extending the lifetime of the cluster heads is inevitable for long run operation of wireless sensor network. In this work we propose Biography based optimization algorithm for extending the lifetime of wireless cluster. The Biogeography based optimization algorithm uses migration of species to solve or to optimize the energy usage of cluster heads efficiently. BBO is a nature inspired technique to find optimum solution of the problem. BBO is implemented on a random set of sensor nodes. Fitness of entire population is depicted by Habitat suitability index value which is calculated in the paper such as to minimize energy consumption. HSI is calculated using 3 factors namely distance of the sensor node from the cluster head, distance of the sensor node from the sink and energy of the cluster head. A diverse, optimized population is obtained to give an efficient and a much better output in the paper. Unlike other algorithms proposed work is considering distance cluster head from the sink and this property makes the proposed BBO algorithm to perform much better than the existing algorithm. The proposed algorithm is simulated using Matlab simulation and shows better results than (i) particle swarm optimization in terms of network lifetime (tested for varying number of nodes, varying number of gateways and varying sink location) and number of packets received by the base station. (ii) BBO fuzzy technique in terms of alive sensor nodes, lifetime of the first dead node and average lifetime of the network. Its performance is compared with some existing algorithms like Fuzzy WSN (Abood et al, 2016), PSO based clustering (Akyildiz et al, 2002), GA based clustering (Yang et al, 2009), GLBCA (Low et al, 2008), LDC (Pratyay et al, 2013). Our algorithm outperforms PSO and BBO fuzzy algorithms which are the most recent work implemented to improve network performance in wireless sensor network and are considered to be best till date

BBO (Simon, 2008) is a evolutionary algorithm which depends upon migration of species. The goodness of a habitat is given by its Habitat suitability index (HSI/Fitness value). Habitats having high HSI value emigrate species to habitat having low HSI value. Similarly, habitat having low HSI value immigrate species from the habitat having high HSI value. Immigration and emigration form the migration step of BBO. Migration is used in BBO to maintain the diversity in the population. After migration, the species are modified with a mutation probability m_i. After migration and mutation HSI value of the resulting habitat is recalculated (Simon, 2008; Goel et al, 2013). A flowchart of the BBO algorithm is shown in figure 2. In the past BBO has been applied in many applications such as job scheduling, pattern recognition and remote sensing successfully. In this section a new evolutionary algorithm biogeography based optimization is used for clustering in WSN. BBO was introduced by Dan Simon in 2008 (Kuila et al, 2013). This is an algorithm similar to genetic algorithm with few changes. In BBO population consists of many habitats as a chromosome in GA. Goodness of a solution is given by habitat suitability index as fitness in GA. Each habitat have immigration and emigration rate based on its HSI value. Habitat with high HSI will emigrate species to habitat having low HSI. In this way migration is performed in BBO which is a main step to maintain diversity in the population. In BBO initial solution is never discarded, it is modified (Kuila et al, 2013). The proposed BBO based wireless clustering improves the lifetime of a gateway.

Problem Formulation

A WSN is constrained by limited battery lifetime. Cluster heads and sensor nodes are equipped with a limited battery. The working of the entire WSN may stop if one of the cluster heads stops working. Therefore it is important to have cluster heads with long working time (Kuila et al, 2013; Kuila et al,

Figure 2.

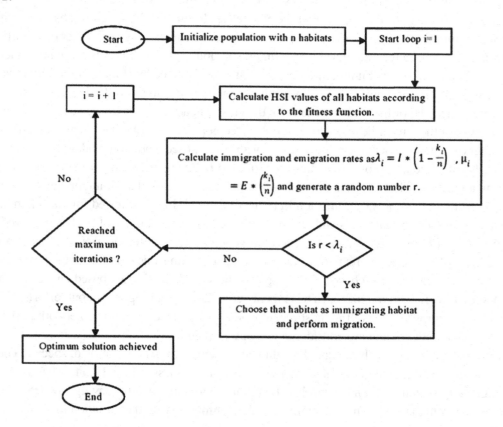

2014; Morteza et al, 2015). In WSN implemented in the past cluster heads were chosen out of ordinary sensor nodes that having same energy as any other sensor node. This resulted in the early death of cluster head and hence early death of the entire cluster. To deal with such problem a special node with some extra energy is proposed as a candidate to be cluster head. Gateways are similar to cluster heads and have same functionalities. They are also battery operated have limited lifetime.

Author's Contributions

As we studied above cluster heads in WSN are operated by battery which is a big hindrance in the efficient transmission of sensed information to the sink. Cluster dies as soon as battery of a gateway is consumed. Gateway with extra energy is introduced, but it is also constrained by battery life time. Hence an efficient clustering algorithm is required to achieve maximum cluster lifetime, even with the use of gateways.

BBO is applied to achieve energy efficient clustering in WSN. Sensor nodes and gateways are taken as habitats. Their HSI value is calculated taking into account 1) Distance of gateway from sink. 2) Residual energy of gateway. Based on HSI values immigration and emigration rates of habitats are calculated which further leads to migration operation between habitats. Migration operation is done using MPX crossover which increases the diversity in the population. HSI values of modified habitats are recalculated, which showed a improvement from HSI values before migration.

Network model is built with random deployment of sensor nodes and gateways. Each node is assigned with following parameters.

Sensor node (s_i) = (id, E, x, y, lambda, mue, HSI, CH, rank) where

Id = unique identification assigned to each node.
E = energy of node
x, y = x and y coordinated of the node
lambda = immigration rate of a node
mue = emigration rate of a node
HSI = high suitability index value of a node which gives goodness of a solution.
Rank = rank of a node/habitat assigned on the basis of HSI value.

Terminologies Used

1. The total number of sensor node is denoted by S_N = {s1, s2, s3, s4........sN}.
2. Total number of gateway or cluster head is denoted by G = {g1, g2, g3.....gN}.
3. Total number of habitats of the population are denoted by H = {h1, h2, h3, h4...... m}, m is pre-defined number of habitats.
4. HSI: habitat suitability index denoted goodness of a solution. Fitter or optimum solution will have high value of HSI.
5. Rank (i): denotes the rank of an individual habitat assigned according to its HSI value. It is denoted by k_i.
6. lambda (i): immigration rate of habitat i. Habitat with low HSI value will have high value of lambda.
7. mue (i): emigration rate of habitat i. Habitat with high HSI value will have high value of mue.
8. Energy (C.H): residual energy of a cluster head or gateway

9. Distance (Node, C.H): distance between a sensor node and its cluster head.
10. Distance (Sink, C.H): distance between cluster head and sink.

Implementation of BBO in WSN

Wireless clustering is performed using BBO and energy efficient clusters are made using the following technique.

Habitat Initialization

N sensor nodes are deployed randomly. S_N = {s1, s2, s3, s4....sN}. Gateways are chosen as G = {g1, g2, g3....gN}. Initialize habitats in the ecosystem with each habitat containing 2 vectors, one containing sensor nodes from s1 to sN and another containing corresponding gateways randomly assigned to sensor nodes. The length of both the vectors is same. Entire population contains many habitats like this. Calculate HSI value of every individual gateway in gateway vector.

Calculation of his

BBO is analogous to the genetic algorithm. In GA we use to calculate the fitness of every chromosome in the population. In BBO we calculate habitat suitability index value of each habitat of the population. The HSI value of a habitat is calculated using the following equation:

E = residual energy of cluster head
α = distance between sink and cluster head.

$$HSI = \sum_{1}^{S} \alpha + \sum_{1}^{G} E \qquad (1)$$

For every gateway vector of each habitat, take the sum of HSI of all individual gateways. This will give a total HSI value of entire habitat. Now we have all possible habitats and their HSI values. Sort HSI values in increasing order and assign a rank to each habitat such that worse habitat gets the first rank and best habitat gets the last rank. Subject to constraint that habitats are ranked in ascending order of sorting.

Above constraint make sure that habitat with higher HSI value does not have a higher immigration rate than habitat having low HSI value. If the best HSI habitat is assigned rank 1, it will end up with higher immigration rate than the low HSI habitat value according to the formula given in equation 6.3 and 6.4. This may disprove BBO.

Immigration and Emigration Rates

Emigration and immigration rates are calculated as follows:

Immigration rate $(\lambda) = I(1 - k_i/n)$

Emigration rate $(\mu) = E(k_i/n)$

I = maximum immigration rate.

E = maximum emigration rate.

K_i = rank of the habitat.

n = total number of habitats.

$$\lambda_i = I * \left(1 - \frac{k_i}{n}\right) \tag{2}$$

$$\mu_i = E * \left(\frac{k_i}{n}\right) \tag{3}$$

Habitats having high HSI value will have a low immigration rate and high emigration rate. SIV will migrate from high HSI value or high emigration rate habitat to the low HSI value of high immigration rate habitat.

Migration Operator

A random number r is generated. For habitat = i, If r < immigration rate (i), choose i as immigrating habitat. Choose habitat with highest HSI value as emigrating habitat. Make a crossover between these two habitats using MPX crossover. This will result in a modified gateway habitat/vector corresponding to sensor node vector to which gateways have been assigned now using this modified vector. In this way we will obtain many modified vector/habitat assigned to sensor nodes.

Mutation Operation

Habitat coming from the migration is modified according to mutation probability m_i as given in equation 4

$$m_i = m_{max} * \left(1 - p_i / p_{max}\right) \tag{4}$$

Calculate HSI values of all these resulting habitats again. Recalculated HSI values of habitats shows improvement in their HSI value which shows that a better network performance is obtained. Retain the habitat with best HSI value. The whole scenario is then simulated and optimum output is achieved.

After the migration and mutation operation, each sensor node is reassigned to its optimum cluster head.

Algorithm

- Consider a group of sensor nodes having 36 sensor nodes and 6 cluster heads. Each cluster has 6 sensor nodes.
- Consider habitats in the population, with each habitat containing 2 vectors

- A vector containing all sensor nodes.
- Vector containing cluster heads randomly assigned to each sensor node.
- Calculate HSI value for every individual cluster head in a habitat.

HSI=K*Energy (C .H)+(1/(Distance(Sink,CH)+Distance(node,CH))

- Take the sum of all these HSI values which will give overall HSI of the habitat.
- Similarly, many habitats are considered and their HSI value is calculated.
- Now calculate rank of every habitat based on HSI value and calculate immigration rate and emigration rate of each habitat based on the rank.
- Migration operation:
  ○ Migration is performed using MPX crossover as follows
- Generate a random number r [0,1]
- If r < lambda (i), choose I as immigrating habitat of gateways/cluster heads.
- Initially we have 2 vectors
- A vector of sensor nodes to which cluster heads are to be assigned.
- An empty vector of cluster heads whose bits are to be filled by migration – crossover operation.
- Crossover is performed between 2 following vectors:
- A vector having highest HSI value is taken as emigrating habitat.
- Vector obtained from step 9 is chosen as immigrating habitat.
- Crossover is performed between these 2 habitats as follows:
- Generate a random vector of 0's and 1's having size same as number of sensor nodes.
- If entry in random habitat is 1, choose a cluster head from immigrating habitat.
- If entry in random habitat is 0, choose a cluster head from emigrating habitat.
- A full vector of cluster heads corresponding to all the sensor nodes is formed.
- In this way every sensor node is assigned with a cluster head using migration step of BBO.
- This migration operation is performed many times (number of iterations) to obtain many modified habitats with sensor nodes assigned cluster heads through BBO.
- Calculate the HSI value of all habitats obtained from step 14. Compare HSI value and choose the habitat with best HSI value.
- IF (HSI_value_Migrated > HSI_Value_Before_Migrate)
- Better Efficiency of Network is achieved.
- Simulate the Whole Scenario and obtain the Graphical Results.

Illustration

Let us consider a scenario with number of sensor nodes = 24, and cluster heads = 4. A sink placed at a distant location. The size of both sensor node vector and gateway vector is same equal to 24 bits with each sensor node assigned a gateway randomly. This combination forms a habitat. There are many habitats like this in the population. The HSI value for each individual gateway in a habitat is calculated by equation 1. The HSI value of entire habitat is obtained by taking sum of HSI value of each individual gateway in the habitat. On the basis of HSI values rank habitats. Using rank of each habitat calculate immigration rate and emigration rate of habitats according to equation 2 and 3.

Select a random number r [0,1]. If $r < \lambda_i$, choose i as immigrating habitat. Choose the best HSI habitat in the population as emigrating habitat. Perform MPX crossover on these two habitats and obtain a new modified habitat of gateways assigned to corresponding sensor nodes. In the same way a number of such habitats are obtained. After maximum iterations recalculate HSI of each modified and choose habitat with a best HSI value among all modified habitats

In the tabular explanation below, selection procedure of a habitat as immigrating habitat is shown. in the first column different number of habitats are displayed. Its immigration rate value is calculated and tabulated according to formulas explained above in second column. Random number values are shown in column 3. Which habitat is chosen as immigrating habitat is shown in column 4. This selection is done on the basis of immigration rate of a habitat.

Above tabular explanation shows the habitat chosen as immigrating habitat, according to immigration rate (lambda). Among all habitats H_i (best) have highest HSI value, hence it is chosen as emigrating habitat. Also h2 and h6 are chosen as immigrating habitats from table 1. Now MPX crossover will be performed between habitat chosen on the basis of immigration rate and best habitat having highest HSI value.

MPX Crossover

MPX crossover is used in migration step. Generate a random vector of 0's and 1's having the same length as emigrating and immigrating habitat. If entry in random vector is 1, choose an SIV/cluster head from immigrating habitat. If entry in random vector is 0, choose a cluster head from emigrating habitat. The process is shown below.

Firstly, we have a vector of sensor nodes to which gateways are to be assigned. Now we will choose the gateways for these sensor nodes using crossover operation in migration step as shown in Tables 2-5.

From above tabular explanation we have a gateway vector of modified habitat. The sensor node vector along with the modified vector forms a new modified habitat. Many habitats like these are formed. Recalculate HSI values of these newly formed habitats. Newly calculated HSI values are drastically better than previously HSI value showing our solution has converged to optimum solution and existing solution is considerably improved. Choose habitat with highest recalculated HSI value (best case). Efficient network performance is obtained and the whole scenario is simulated to obtain results.

Table 1.

H_i	λ	r	Chosen ?
h1	.80	.86	No
h2	.34	.23	yes
h3	.24	.43	No
h4	.95	.97	No
h5	.42	.66	No
h6	.19	.12	Yes
h7	.76	.88	No
h24	.17	.32	No

Table 2. Random vector of 0's and 1's

Random Vector							
1	0	1	0	1	1	0	0

Table 3. Immigrating habitat

Gateway Vector of Immigrating Habitat							
g2	g1	g4	g2	g3	g4	g1	g3

Table 4. Gateway vector

Gateway Vector of Modified Habitat							
g2	g2	g4	g1	g3	g4	g4	g2

Table 5.

Gateway Vector of Emigrating Habitat							
g1	g2	g3	g1	g4	g3	g4	g2

We performed extensive simulations of proposed algorithm using Matlab. Results are compared with 2 previous works. Firstly, the results of the proposed algorithm are compared with BBO fuzzy algorithm (Akyildiz et al, 2002). Than results of the proposed algorithm are compared with PSO based clustering (Akyildiz et al, 2002). Parameters of both the existing algorithms are kept the same while comparing our algorithm with existing work.

Comparison of Proposed Algorithm With BBO Fuzzy Algorithm

Simulation Parameters are as follows Area (meters) is 100 * 100, Sink location (meters) is 90, Number of nodes are 100, Transmission distance is 30m, Initial energy of node is .5 J, Packet size is 2000 bit, E_{elec} is 50 nj/bit.

Firstly, we compare proposed algorithm with BBO fuzzy algorithm in terms of number of nodes still alive and the number of rounds as shown in figure 3 (Abood et al, 2016). Comparison is made in terms of number of packets in both existing and proposed work. It can be observed from the figure that the proposed algorithm performs much better than all three previous algorithms namely BBO, fuzzy and BBO fuzzy. In fact, our algorithm performs 10 times better than previous work which is considered to be best till date.

The proposed algorithm is compared with existing work in terms of number of rounds with the first dead node as shown in table 2. it is visible that the proposed algorithm performs better than previous algorithms in terms of number of rounds with the first node dead.

The proposed algorithm is compared with existing algorithms in terms of average network remaining energy and number of rounds in figure 4. Here the performance of the proposed BBO algorithm is steady in the beginning but outperforms the existing work as the number packets increases.

Comparison of Proposed Algorithm With PSO Algorithm

We have placed sensor nodes randomly. Cluster heads are also distributed randomly such that they are in transmission range of the sink.

Figure 3.

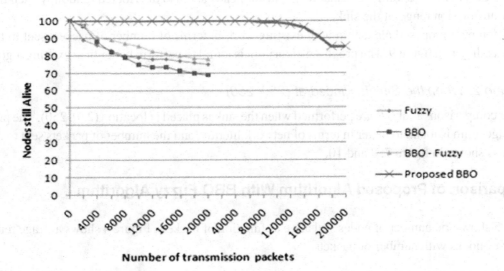

Figure 4.

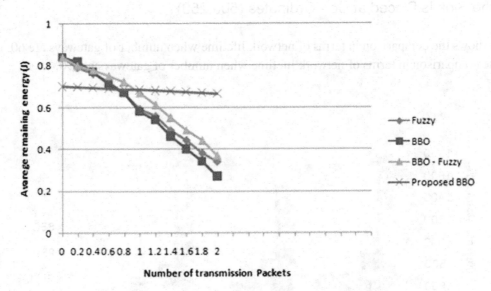

Simulation parameters are as follows Area (meters) is 500 * 500, Sink location (meters) is (500, 250), (250, 250), Number of nodes are 200 - 500, Gateways are 60 – 90, Transmission distance is 150 m, Initial energy of node is 2 J, Packet size is 4000 bit, E_{elec} is 50 nj/bit.

Scenario 1: When the Sink Is Placed at (500, 250)

We compare proposed algorithm with PSO, GLBCA, GA, LDC algorithm considering the first WSN scenario when the sink is placed at coordinates (500, 250) in terms of network lifetime of sensor nodes when number of gateways are 60 and 90 (Akyildiz et al, 2002) as shown in figure 5 and 6. As visible from the figure, network lifetime of sensor nodes is increased by implementing proposed BBO algorithm.

We have distributed sensor nodes randomly. Cluster heads are also distributed randomly such that they are in transmission range of the sink.

We compare proposed algorithm with existing work in terms of number of packets sent to the base station as shown in figure 9. The proposed algorithm is found to perform better than existing algorithms.

Scenario 2: When the Sink Is Placed at (250, 250)

Similar comparisons as above are performed when the sink is placed at location (250, 250). The proposed BBO algorithm is found to better in terms of network lifetime and the number of packets sent to the base station as shown in figure 7, 8 and 10.

Comparison of Proposed Algorithm With BBO Fuzzy Algorithm

Figure 3 shows the number of nodes still alive as function of packets. Figure 4 shows average remaining energy of nodes with number of packets.

Comparison of the Proposed Work With PSO

When the Sink Is Placed at Co - Ordinates (500,250)

Figure 5 shows the comparison in terms of network lifetime when number of gateways are 60. Figure 6 shows the comparison in terms of network lifetime when number of gateways are 90.

Figure 5.

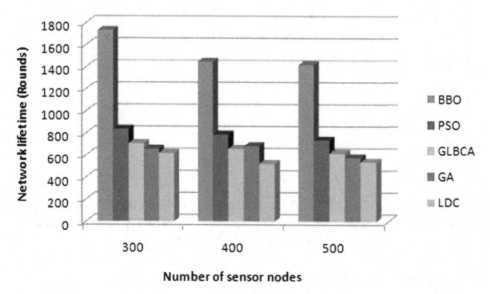

For a more accurate representation see the electronic version.

Figure 6.

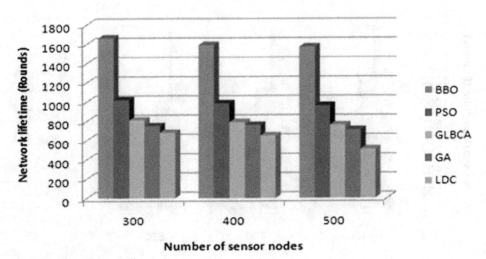

For a more accurate representation see the electronic version.

Figure 7.

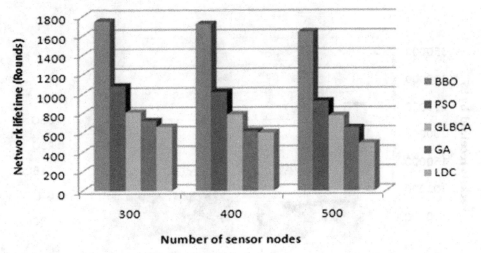

For a more accurate representation see the electronic version.

When Sink Is Placed at Co - Ordinates (250, 250)

Figure 7 shows the comparison in terms of network lifetime when number of gateways are 60. Figure 8 shows the comparison in terms of network lifetime when number of gateways are 90

Comparison in Terms of Packet Sent to the Base Station

When Sink Location Is (500, 250)

Figure 9 shows the comparison in terms of total packets sent to the base station.

Figure 8.

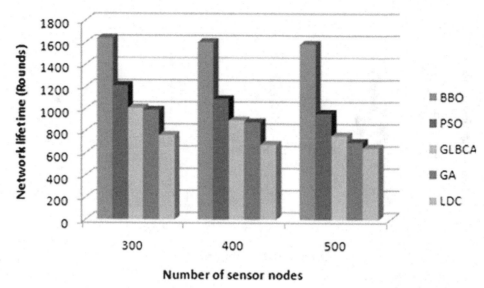

For a more accurate representation see the electronic version.

Figure 9.

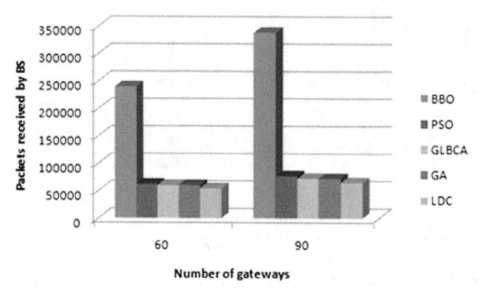

For a more accurate representation see the electronic version.

When Sink Location Is (250, 250)

Figure 10 shows the comparison in terms of total packets sent to the base station.

It can be seen from above results that BBO extends the network lifetime of the WSN in the most effectively.

Figure 10.

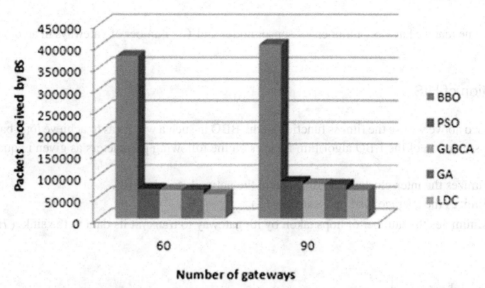

For a more accurate representation see the electronic version.

A Load Balancing Approach for Clustering in WSN Using BBO

Introduction

As explained above, BBO is an efficient technique to apply on wireless sensor networks. The lifetime of the cluster heads can be optimized using BBO. As a practical tool of BBO application in WSN, we can also use BBO for load balancing in WSN.

Significance

One of the main reasons why cluster heads die immature is the unbalanced load distribution among the cluster heads. The cluster head having more load will die quickly and the cluster head having less load will work for a long period of time. Hence it is very important to have an equal distribution of load among all the cluster heads. For this purpose of load balancing, we use BBO. Load balancing of the WSN not only achieves energy efficiency but also achieves stability of the entire network. Most of the past works aims to achieve energy efficient WSN which result in prolonging the network lifetime. The problem with energy efficient WSN is that the first cluster head dies very quickly thus resulting in reduced stability. Hence load balancing enhances the stability of the network. The fitness we use in load balancing of WSN using BBO caters for both stability as well as energy efficiency of WSN. As a result of load balancing of cluster heads, no cluster head is overloaded which make sure that the death of first cluster head is delayed.

Implementation

Let us assume that we have S_N numbers of sensor nodes and G_N number of gateways in an deployment area.

Calculation of HIS

As discussed above we use the fitness function of the BBO in such a way so as to achieve load balancing. The fitness function of the BBO algorithm focuses on the following parameters as given i equation 5.

1. Minimizes the inter-cluster head distance in the network scenario (β).
2. Minimizes the average load on a gateway (L)
3. 3. Minimizes the number of hops taken by ith gateway to transmit its data to the sink. ($H_{gat(i)}$)

$$HSI = \left(\frac{1}{L} + \frac{1}{\beta} + \frac{1}{H_{gat(i)}} \right) \tag{5}$$

We aim to maximize the HSI function which further minimizes the parameters L, β and $H_{gat(i)}$

Minimization of inter cluster head distance will minimize the distance through which a cluster head needs to transmit data which further minimizes the energy consumed by cluster head in sensing the data. Minimization of average load on a cluster head helps in the long run operation of the cluster head and it also ensures that load from all the cluster heads is reduced in the same proportion, which leads to equal load distribution in the entire network. Similarly $H_{gat(i)}$ is the number of hops taken by a cluster head to send data to the base station. More be the $H_{gat(i)}$, more will be energy consumed by the cluster head. (Kaushik et al, 2017) Hence we aim to minimize $H_{gat(i)}$ to achieve energy efficiency. The clustering is shown in figure 11 and figure 12.

Migration Operation

After the calculation of HSI, migration operation is performed using a standard crossover. We aim to maximize the HSI. For each individual habitat, immigration rates and emigration rates are calculated as per equation 6 and 7.

$$\lambda_i = I * \left(1 - \frac{k_i}{n} \right) \tag{6}$$

Figure 11.

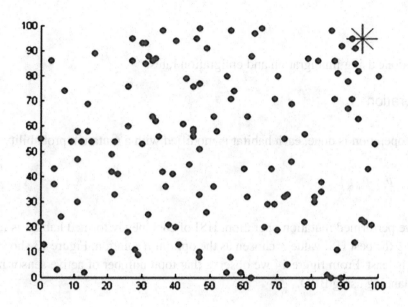

Figure 12.

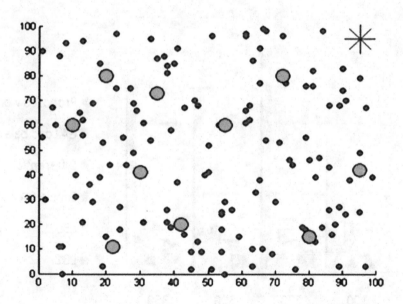

$$\mu_i = E * \left(\frac{k_i}{n} \right) \qquad (7)$$

Migration is done using immigration and emigration rates.

Mutation Operation

After migration operation is done, each habitat is modified with a mutation probability m_i

$$m_i = m_{max} * \left(1 - p_i / p_{max} \right) \qquad (8)$$

After we have performed mutation operation, HSI of each newly formed habitat is recalculated and the habitat having the best HSI value is chosen as the optimum solution. Figure 13 shows that deviation of load in BBO is least. From figure 14 we observe that total number of active sensor nodes are maximum in load balancing using BBO.

Figure 13.

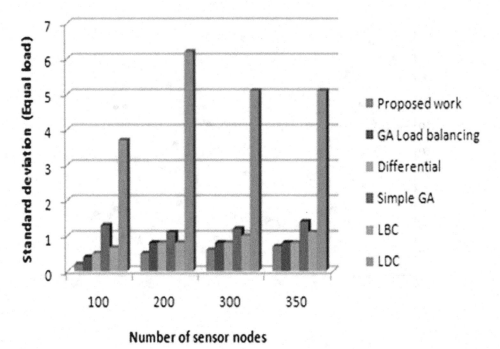

For a more accurate representation see the electronic version.

Figure 14.

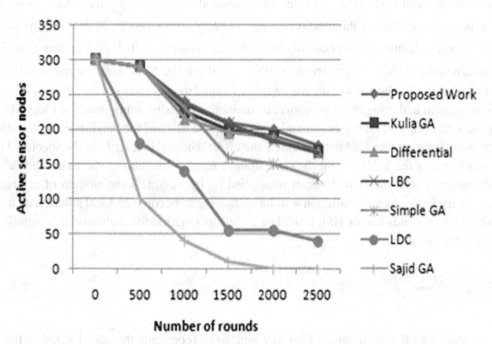

An Extended BBO Based Wireless Clustering Approach

Introduction

Above we have mentioned the application of BBO to wireless sensor networks. BBO algorithm has a few drawbacks which are improved in extended species abundance model or extended BBO. Extended BBO involves the concept of evolution and extinction of species (Goel et al, 2012; Kaushik et al, 2016) Also, in case of extended BBO the habitat suitability index (HSI) of a habitat does not depend only upon immigration and emigration rates. Instead, it is a function of different characteristics of SIVs.

$$HSI_i = func_i\left(SIV\right) \tag{9}$$

Above equation shows that HSI of ith habitat is a function of various combinations of its SIVs.
Let the set of SIVs ranges from m1 to mt .

The SIVs, which are not applicable for a particular habitat are removed in the HSI calculation by making their coefficient zero. w is the weight assigned to each sensor node. Weight is assigned to each sensor node based on distance of a sensor node to the gateway. Distance of gateway to the sink and number of hops taken by a gateway to reach the sink Adding this new factor w in the HSI calculation will help us reject those sensor nodes, which are far away from the gateways and the sink during cluster formation.

Initially the number of species is equal to number of candidate solutions and these solutions are put in a universal habitat. Define an isolated habitat with a zero solution as well as an ideal habitat with ideal characteristics. Ideal habitat is called feature habitat and consist of ideal SIV's. This feature habitat is used for its comparison with candidate solution. Calculate HSI of the feature habitat based on its

SIVs and calculate ideal HSI (HSI_{ideal}) value and threshold HSI (HSI_{th}) value. HSI_{th} is one third of HSI_{ideal}. Also calculate HSI of the candidate solution (HSI_{i}) based on its SIVs and compare its HSI with HSI_{th}. The candidate solution can only be made ideal solution if its HSI is greater than HSI_{th}. If HSI of the candidate solution is greater than HSI_{th}, find out the SIVs to be migrated and the effort required for migration of the SIVs using the weight assigned to those SIVs.

Use immigration and emigration operation to maintain diversity. Immigrate the ideal SIVs of the feature habitat that improves the solution and emigrate those SIVs of the candidate solution that deteriorates the solution to isolated habitat. Calculate the effort required in migrating the species. The effort required in migrating the SIVs during the computation for the selection of the best solution is given by the difference in ideal and actual values multiplied by its weight. If the amount of effort required is infinite or very large, then this solution will never be able to become an ideal solution as it does not satisfy the threshold condition for HSI. Calculate the effort required for each candidate solution by using the following equation.

$$Effort = \sum_i (HSI_{ideal} - HSI_i) * w, 1 < i < n \tag{10}$$

SIV_{ideal} represents the ideal value of ith SIV and SIV_i represents the actual value of the ith SIV. Above effort is calculated only for those candidate solutions whose HSI is greater than SIV_{th}. Now for these habitats, Calculate the selectivity factor. Selectivity factor is the factor which determines the selectivity of a particular habitat to be chosen as the best habitat. Selectivity factor is calculated as given in the following equation.

$$S_{fac} = (HSI_i - HSI_{th}) \frac{1}{Effort}, 1 < i < n \tag{11}$$

Author's contribution to this work are as follows:

- EBBO-CR extends the lifetime of the gateway by optimizing the location of the gateway related to sink and sensor node, along with minimizing the number of hops taken by a gateway to transmit data to the sink
- Improves network lifetime by non linear mapping of gateway identification. EBBO based routing and clustering algorithm minimizes the distance between a gateway and the sink and also minimizes the number of hops taken by a gateway to reach the sink using a single fitness function.
- Extended BBO introduces the concept of evolution and extinction of species. New species keep evolving and poor species keep getting extinct.
- Ensures 100% coverage of whole area covered by network.

Implementation of EBBO in Wireless Sensor Networks

For each sensor node, we have an importance vector. This importance vector contains the weights assigned to each sensor node for each cluster head based the distance of that sensor node from every cluster head in the network scenario. In this way, each sensor node has an importance vector. From these importance vectors, choose the best value from each and form a feature or ideal habitat. Calculate the HSI of this ideal habitat as per the following equation. A flowchart of the implementation of extended BBO in WSN is given in figure 15.

$$HSI_{ideal} = \frac{1}{\sum SIV_{ideal} \ of \ all \ importance \ vector} \tag{12}$$

From HSI_{ideal}, calculate HSI_{th} as one third of HSI_{ideal}. For each habitat, compare its HSI to the ideal habitat and chose only those habitats which has their HSI values greater than the threshold HSI. For those habitats, calculate the effort required to make them ideal habitats according to equation 11.

Based on the effort required, we calculate the selectivity factor for each individual. The habitat having highest selectivity factor is the optimum solution and is chosen as the best habitat. Selectivity factor is calculated according to equation 12.

Based on the selectivity factor optimum solution is chosen which gives better output than all the previous algorithms like BBO, PSO etc. EBBO extends the network lifetime in a more effective way. For the sake of comparison, PSO is also implemented to achieve energy efficiency in WSN. However, PSO is older than BBO and EBBO. The implementation of PSO on WSN is illustrated below. Figure 16 shows that EBBO prolongs the network lifetime more effectively. Figure 17 shows that number of hops used by the cluster heads to transfer information in EBBO are least which result in minimization of energy dissipated by the cluster heads.

Figure 15.

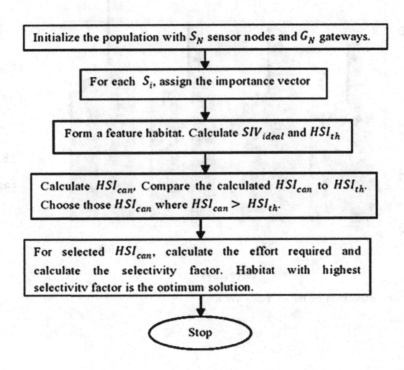

Figure 16.

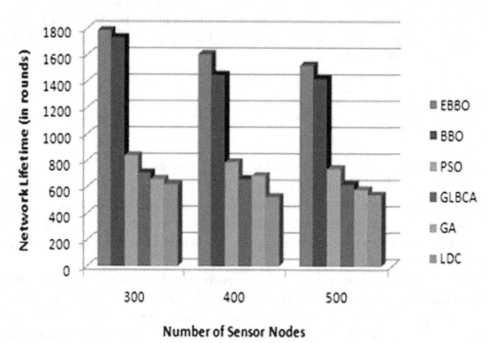

For a more accurate representation see the electronic version.

Figure 17.

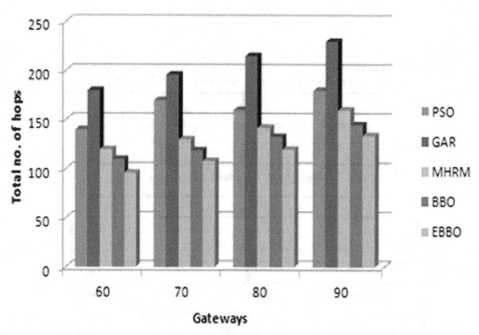

For a more accurate representation see the electronic version.

Particle Swarm Optimization

Introduction

\Particle swarm optimization (PSO) is inspired by natural life like bird flocking and fish schooling. It is a natural phenomenon that the animals move in a group without colliding with each other. This is due to the reason that particles adjust their position and velocity according to each other's position and velocity. Hence it reduces individual effort in searching for the food (Kuila et al, 2014).

PSO contains a population of particles with each particle P_i having velocity V_i and position X_i. The goodness of each particle is given by its fitness function. Each particle is assigned a fitness value and it approaches for its optimum fitness by following its personal best fitness and global best fitness. A flowchart of PSO is given in figure 18.

Figure 18.

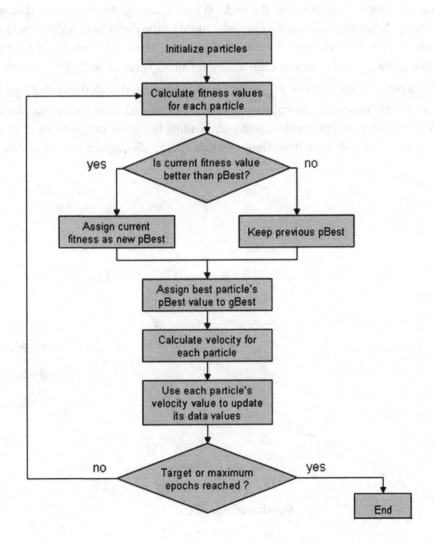

269

Implementation of PSO in WSNs

WSNs are constrained with limited battery lifetime. We implement PSO in WSNs to minimize the energy dissipation of the sensor nodes and cluster heads in the network and maximize the network lifetime. As mentioned above fitness of a particle define the goodness of an individual solution. In PSO implementation fitness of a particle is given by the following equation

$$Fitness\left(P_i\right) = \frac{1}{\sum_{i=1\,to}^{N} Dist_\alpha + \sum_{I=1\,to}^{N} Dist_\beta} \tag{13}$$

Here fitness is calculated for a particle P_i. $Dist_\alpha$ is the distance between a sensor node and a gateway while $Dist_\beta$ is the distance between a gateway and the sink. In our implementation we aim to maximize the fitness function which then leads to minimization of the distance between a sensor node and a gateway and distance between a gateway and the sink. While reducing the above two distances, we also minimize the energy dissipated by a gateway because more be the distance of a gateway from the sensor node or the sink, more will be the energy dissipated by the gateway to send data which may result in early death of the gateway. In this way in each iteration fitness value of particle P_i is calculated and is compared with its personal best fitness P_{best} which is then compared with the global best fitness G_{best}. The algorithm is stopped as soon as the optimum solution is achieved or maximum numbers of iterations are reached. A comparison of PSO with existing algorithms is shown in figure 10 in terms of energy dissipated by the nodes. It is evident from figure 19 that energy dissipation is least in case of PSO.

Figure 19.

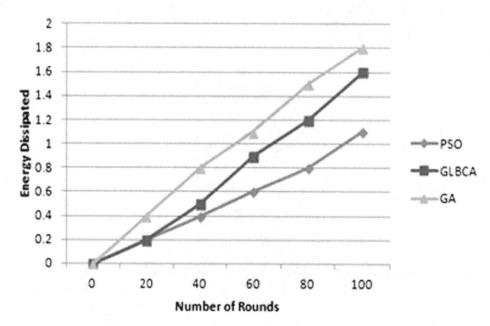

WIRELESS SENSOR NETWORK AND BIG DATA

Above we saw the utility of nature inspired techniques in wireless sensor networks. BBO, EBBO and PSO are successfully used to achieve an energy efficient WSN. The amount of data emerging from wireless sensor network is huge which encourage the use of big data tools in WSN data. A WSN scenario can operate effectively if it is merged with big data techniques. The three V's of big data namely variety, velocity and veracity are applicable to WSN as well. In the past nature inspired algorithms like Biogeography Based Optimization (BBO), Extended Biogeography Based Optimization (EBBO) and Particle Swarm Optimization (PSO) have proved its worth in the WSN domain. These algorithms are successfully implemented to achieve an energy efficient and stable WSN which encourages the use of such nature inspired techniques in big data domain as well. Since nature inspired techniques are used successively, in the next section we study how nature inspired techniques can play a crucial role in optimizing the performance of big data tools.

BIG DATA AND NATURE INSPIRED TECHNIQUES

Big Data

Big data is a novel field and an open area for research. We are now in the digital world. Amount of data being processed every day is increasing rapidly. The data being generated from different fields like retail, healthcare, social media and public domain etc. If we wish to store this amount of data onto DVDs, there will be a stack of DVDs from the earth all the way to Mars. According to an approximation, 30 million content is shared on Facebook every month. To handle such huge flow of data, Big data was introduced.

Big data handle large demands of data in an efficient manner. Like any other new innovation adoption of big data depend on its tangible benefits and business advantages.

Big data focus on 3 main factors as shown in figure 20. Velocity problem referring to huge handling huge amount of data rising at a rapid speed. Variety problem is also a big issue in the Big data. Data coming from various sources may be difficult to handle and use on a consistent single platform. Variety problem also refers with integration of the data coming from multiple sources and convert the data into meaningful datasets. Huge amount of data needs to be stored properly and efficiently. Volume refers to storing and processing large datasets for computing as well as achieving efficiency. Considering the needs of 3V's of Big data, the traditional data mining approach may not work properly and may fail in achieving analytical efficiency. The traditional data mining models involve loading the entire chunk of data and then dividing the data according to divide and conquer algorithm. Every time new and fresh data arrives which is typical of the process, the model needs to re run again and the model that is already built needs to rebuild again and again. Thus traditional data mining techniques are not efficient in case of 3V of Big data.

1. **Velocity:** Velocity of data processing is moving from the batch processing to streaming data.
2. **Volume:** Volume of data is growing from Terabytes to Zettabytes.
3. **Variety:** Both structured and unstructured data need to be processed in an efficient manner.

Figure 20.

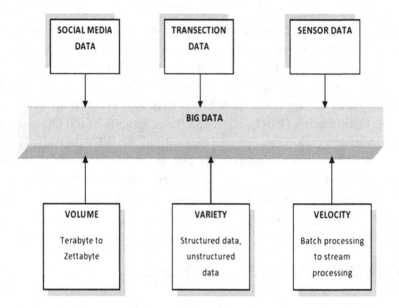

Big Data Parameters in WSN Domain

1. **Velocity:** Velocity in WSN is very crucial especially for real time applications like room surveillance, healthcare systems. Sensed data should be read and processed in a speedy manner in order to respond properly in real time applications. Velocity parameter of Big data is a feature of WSN as well.
2. **Volume:** Working of a WSN involves large volumes of data. There is a huge amount of information emerging from the sensors in the form of sensed data. This satisfies the big data parameter of volume to WSN as well.
3. **Variety:** There are many types of sensors sending a variety of information. The sensed data of light sensor will be different from the data of a temperature sensor or ultrasonic sensor or flex sensor. Different sensors deployed in different areas for different applications also generate a variety of data. Which map the big data parameter of variety to WSN.

Since nature inspired techniques are used successfully to optimize velocity, volume and variety in WSN. This encourages the use of nature inspired techniques to optimize velocity, volume and variety parameters of big data as well.

Role of Nature Inspired Techniques and Extension Required for Present Work

Nature inspired techniques can be usefully applied to data mining and big data. In the past swarm intelligence techniques are successfully used in big data domain. There are two kinds of approaches in which swarm intelligence can be used in data mining and big data (Cheng et al, 2013). In the first class individuals of a swarm moves through solution space and try to search for a solution for the big data task. This is called the search approach. The second class is called data organizing approach; in which the swarm intelligence is directly applied to the data samples. Since PSO is successfully implemented for data mining/big data tools, better techniques like BBO, EBBO can be implemented for the same purpose. Better nature inspired techniques like BBO and EBBO have shown very good results in WSN domain as demonstrated above. They are successfully used in WSN in achieving load balance, stable and energy efficient network which encourage the use of such techniques in Big data as well as WSN data and Big data are very similar.

Big data techniques involve mining a huge amount of data at a rapid speed i.e large datasets to be processed within a limited amount of time. This analytic problem can be referred as an optimization problem. The term optimization refers to finding the best possible solution in a limited amount of time out of a numerous number of available solutions. This problem can be solved as an optimization problem using nature inspired techniques such as BBO and EBBO. Although big data suffers from the curse of dimensionality problem, i.e. the performance of mining data degrade as the size of datasets increases (Bellman, 1961; Domingos, 2012; Indu et al, 2011). This problem can also be solved as an optimization problem using nature inspired techniques. Swarm intelligence and better nature inspired techniques like BBO and EBBO can be successfully used in handling dynamic changes in big data. In nature inspired techniques like BBO and EBBO, measures are taken so that they solve dynamic problems satisfactorily. Hence these nature inspired techniques can be used to cater for the dynamic requirements of big data.

A large amount of data will be generated from the WSN structure used in areas like surveillance of large space, security measures, engineering surveys etc (Indu et al, 2011; Kumar et al, 2014). Big data plays an important role here; it is used to convert this raw data into useful information as fast as possible. Nature inspired techniques can prove to be very effective in the process of obtaining useful information from such raw datasets (Kulkarni et al, 2011).

CONCLUSION

WSN and Big data are closely connected since a large amount of data emerging from sensors can be effectively handled using Big data tools. Nature inspired techniques like BBO and EBBO are widely implemented and have proved their worth in WSN domain. These techniques can be used to increase the efficiency of Big data tools. Searching for appropriate data in the limited amount of time can be framed as an optimization problem which can be effectively solved by nature inspired algorithms like BBO and EBBO. Furthermore, PSO is implemented in Big data. Successful implementation of PSO not only paves the path for nature inspired techniques in big data domain but also outline the need for better algorithms to be implemented in Big data in future.

REFERENCES

Abood, B. (2016). Energy efficient clustering in WSNs using fuzzy approach to improve LEACH protocol. *Int J Manag Inf Technol, 11*(2), 2641–2656.

Akyildiz. (2002). A survey on WSNs. *Computer Networks, 38*(4).

Ataul, B. (2009). A GA based approach for energy efficient routing in two-tiered WSNs. *Ad Hoc Networks, 7*, 665–676. doi:10.1016/j.adhoc.2008.04.003

Bellman, R. (1961). *Adaptive Control Processes: A guided Tour*. Princeton, NJ: Princeton University Press. doi:10.1515/9781400874668

Cheng, S. (2013). SI in big data analytics. In *Intelligent Data Engineering and Automated Learning–IDEAL* (pp. 417–426). Springer. doi:10.1007/978-3-642-41278-3_51

Chui, M. (2010). The IoT. *The McKinsey Quarterly, 2*, 1–9.

Domingos, P. (2012). A few useful things to know about machine learning. *Communications of the ACM, 55*(10), 78–87. doi:10.1145/2347736.2347755

Fister, Jr. (2013). A Brief Review of Nature-Inspired Algorithms for Optimization. *Elektrotehni˘ski vestnik, 80*(3), 1–7. (in Germany)

Goel. (2013). *Biogeography and geo-sciences based land cover feature extraction: a remote sensing perspective. In Applied Soft Computing* (pp. 4194–4208). Elsevier.

Goel, L. (2012). Extended species abundance models of BBO. *IEEE Conf. on Computational Intelligence Modelling and Simulation (Anaheim)*.

Gupta, S. K. (2013), GAR: an energy efficient GA-based routing for WSNs. LNCS, 7753, 267–277.

Indu, Prakasham, Chudhury, & Bhattacharyya. (2011). Self Organizing WSN to Enhance Event Coverage. *Int. J. on Smart Sensing and Intelligent Systems, 4*(1), 53–74. doi:10.21307/ijssis-2017-426

Kaushik, Indu, & Gupta. (2016). Energy efficient clustering and routing algorithm for WSNs: An Extended BBO approach. *IJCTA*.

Kaushik. (2017). *A Novel Load Balanced Energy Conservation Approach in WSN Using BBO*. Lyon, France: ICEESM.

Kuila. (2013). A novel evolutionary approach for load balanced clustering problem for WSNs. *Swarm and Evolutionary Computation*, 48–56. doi:10.1016/j.swevo.2013.04.002

Kuila, P. (2013). A novel evolutionary approach for load balanced clustering problem for WSNs. *Swarm and Evolutionary Computation*, 48–56. doi:10.1016/j.swevo.2013.04.002

Kuila, P. (2014). Energy efficient clustering and routing algorithms for WSNs: PSO approach. *Engineering Applications of Artificial Intelligence*, 127–140. doi:10.1016/j.engappai.2014.04.009

Kuila & Jana. (2014). *Energy efficient clustering and routing algorithms for WSNs: PSO approach* (pp. 127–140). Engineering Applications of AI.

Kulkarni. (2011). G.K.: PSO in WSN: A brief survey. *IEEE Transactions on Systems, Man, and Cybernetics, 41*(2), 262–267. doi:10.1109/TSMCC.2010.2054080

Kumar. (2014). Optimized Power Efficient Routing in WSN. *Int. J. of Next Generation Computing, 5*(2).

Low, C. P. (2008). Efficient load-balanced clustering algorithms for WSNs. *Computer Communications, 31*, 750–759. doi:10.1016/j.comcom.2007.10.020

Martens, D. (2011). Editorial survey: SI for data mining. *Machine Learning, 82*(1), 1–42. doi:10.100710994-010-5216-5

Morteza. (2015). *A survey on centralized and distributed clustering routing algorithm for WSNs*. IEEE.

Simon. (2008). BBO. *IEEE Transactions on Evolutionary Computation, 12*(6).

Yang, X.-S., & Deb, S. (2009). Cuckoo search via l'evy flights. In *Nature & Biologically Inspired Computing, 2009. NaBIC 2009. World Congress on* (pp. 210–214). IEEE.

Chapter 11
Aircraft Aerodynamic Parameter Estimation Using Intelligent Estimation Algorithms

Abhishek Ghosh Roy
IIT Kharagpur, India

Naba Kumar Peyada
IIT Kharagpur, India

ABSTRACT

Application of adaptive neuro fuzzy inference system (ANFIS)-based particle swarm optimization (PSO) algorithm to the problem of aerodynamic modeling and optimal parameter estimation for aircraft has been addressed in this chapter. The ANFIS-based PSO optimizer constitutes the aircraft model in restricted sense capable of predicting generalized force and moment coefficients employing measured motion and control variables only, without formal requirement of conventional variables or their time derivatives. It has been shown that such an approximate model can be used to extract equivalent stability and control derivatives of a rigid aircraft.

INTRODUCTION

Parameter estimation methods for extracting aircraft parameters (stability and control derivatives) from recorded time history in the linear flight regime of aircraft have seen good amount of success in the past (Maine et al, 1986). With the introduction of highly maneuverable aircrafts opened fresh research opportunities to look for appropriate models and parameter estimation algorithms exclusively for these aircrafts operating in unstable flight envelopes (Zerweckh et al, 1990). The fundamental problems encountered while performing estimation of parameters of an aircraft is: a full order model of an aircraft has a very large number of parameters to be taken into consideration, and thus, too many of them give satisfactory estimates by any of the conventional parameter estimation methods. To relief some of the effort involved in dynamic analysis and control synthesis and to minimize computational burden during simulation, lower order models of vehicle with simplified dynamics have been proposed by Waszak &

DOI: 10.4018/978-1-5225-5852-1.ch011

Schmidt (1988). The model reduction processes mostly depends on numerical techniques and/or transformations, and thereby, in the resulting models, the physics of the system is sometimes not so straight forward (Waszak et al, 1988). Ghosh & Raisinghani (1993) gave a solution to this problem by proposing a reduced order model of an aircraft containing important parameters of aircraft dynamics, and also facilitates physical interpretation of the parameters involved in the reduced order model. The availability of a sound mathematical model is also another issue because the conventional model falls short when describing higher order dynamics of the systems.

This chapter deals with a novel approach to estimate the parameters of any stable aircraft (rigid) from pre recorded time history of the aircraft's motion variables in the absence of an accurate mathematical model. Conventional parameter estimation approaches viz. Maximum Likelihood (ML) method (Peyada et al, 2008), the Filter Error Method (FEM) (Jategaonkar et al, 1988), etc. require a priori postulation of aircraft model. On the other hand, a class of Adaptive Neuro-Fuzzy Inference System (ANFIS) uses neural architecture based fuzzy set theory to map inputs (features in the case of fuzzy classification) to outputs (classes in the case of fuzzy classification), and can efficiently approximate a function (piecewise continuous) to a desired degree of accuracy (Jategaonkar et al, 1988). Currently, FIS architecture is being used for navigation (Ta, however, there are very few literatures on aircraft parameter estimation using ANFIS model proposed by Sugeno. This work addresses this issue by proposing a novel method of estimating the aircraft parameters from the flight data, and the validation is carried out using simulated and real flight data (stable aircraft).

Computer simulations envisage the efficacy of the proposed method to optimally estimate the aerodynamic parameters by using renowned Particle Swarm Optimization (PSO) (Hui et al, 2006). The selection of PSO is justified because of its simplicity in coding, fewer control parameters, good accuracy (Eberhart et al, 1995) and fast speed of convergence (Zhenya et al, 1998). The essence of the present work is to estimate and validate the model utilizing the measured data without being provided with the mathematical input-output relationship of the model. The design philosophy adopted here is to realize the model input-output relationship using ANFIS platform. It is worth mentioning that our proposed technique does not require either a priori postulation or solution of equation of motion.

NEURO-FUZZY SYSTEM BASED ON TAKAGI AND SUGENO'S APPROACH

The neuro fuzzy system developed based on Takagi and Sugeno's approach of FLC is also known as Adaptive Neuro Fuzzy Inference System (ANFIS). Let us suppose that an ANFIS is to be developed to model a process involving two inputs (I_1, I_2) and one output (O). The input I_1 is represented using three linguistic terms viz. LW: Low; M: Medium; H: High. Similarly three other linguistic terms, such as SM: Small, LR: Large; VL: Very Large are utilized to indicate another input I_2. The membership function distributions of the first and second input are considered to be triangular and symmetric in nature .The symbols d_1 and d_2 indicate the base width of the isosceles triangles representing the membership functions of the first and second inputs. We have considered two inputs and each have been represented by three linguistic terms, there is a maximum of $3^2 = 9$ possible combinations of them. According to Takagi and Sugeno's model of FLC, the output of each rule can be expressed as follows:

According to first-order Takagi and Sugeno's model of FLC

Figure 1. Membership function distributions of input variables

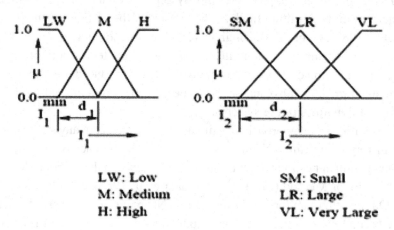

LW: Low
M: Medium
H: High

SM: Small
LR: Large
VL: Very Large

$y_i = a_i I_1 + b_i I_2 + c_i$

where $i = 1, 2, \ldots, 9$

a_i, b_i, c_i are coefficients

Let us assume that the following 4 rules are fired, corresponding to a set of inputs: I_1^* and I_2^*

If I_1 is LW and I_2 is SM then $y_1 = a_1 I_1 + b_1 I_2 + c_1$

If I_1 is LW and I_2 is LR then $y_2 = a_2 I_1 + b_2 I_2 + c_2$

If I_1 is M and I_2 is SM then $y_4 = a_4 I_1 + b_4 I_2 + c_4$

If I_1 is M and I_2 is LR then $y_5 = a_5 I_1 + b_5 I_2 + c_5$

Layer 1: Linear TF (output = input)

$^1O_1 = {}^1I_1 = I_1^*$

$^1O_2 = {}^1I_2 = I_2^*$

Layer 2: Fuzzification
Layer 3: Firing strengths of the rules are calculated considering the products of μ values

$w_1 = \mu_{LW}(I_1^*) * \mu_{SM}(I_2^*)$

Similarly, we get w_2, w_4 and w_5

Figure 2. ANFIS architecture

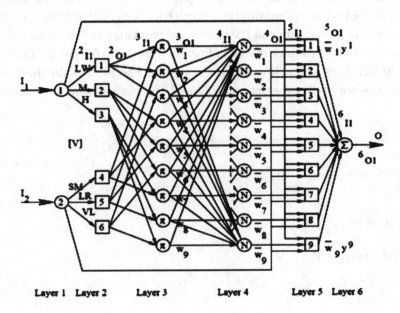

Layer 4: Calculate normalized firing strength of each rule

Similarly, we calculate

$$5_{O_1} = \overline{w_1} * y^1$$
$$5_{O_2} = \overline{w_2} * y^2$$
$$5_{O_4} = \overline{w_4} * y^4$$
$$5_{O_5} = \overline{w_5} * y^5$$

Layer 5: Output is calculated as the product of normalized firing strength and output of the corresponding fired rule y

Layer 6: Overall output

Performance depends on membership function distributions of input variables; a_i, b_i, c_i

THE PARTICLE SWARM OPTIMIZATION

The PSO is a stochastic swarm intelligence algorithm proposed by Kenedy and Eberhart. The PSO is in many ways resembles evolutionary computing based procedures in producing a random population to start with and goes on producing next populations based on present cost function value, but instead of mutation or crossover based heuristicsPSO relies on social behavioral strategies while producing next generation .

In our paper, we have made use of one of the many popular variants of PSO algorithm viz. Dynamic spread factor (SFPSO), the reason for choosing this variant have been motivated by certain improvements that this variant has which the conventional PSO lacks viz. premature convergence and preservation of diversity. The Strategy is to vary the inertia weight linearly from 0.9 to 0.3 during a run. Prudent choice of the inertia weight facilitates an equilibrium between global and local explorations which results in less number of iterations for finding the optimal solution. The mathematical representation of SFPSO is given by

$$
\begin{aligned}
x_{id_{present}} &= x_{id} + v_{id} \\
v_{id_{present}} &= (w * v_{id}) + c_1(r_1(p_{id} - x_{id})) + c_2(r_2(p_{gd} - x_{gd}))
\end{aligned}
$$

(2)

where w, c_1, c_2 are given by

$$
\begin{aligned}
w &= \exp(-iter / (sf * maxiter)) \\
sf &= 0.5(s + \Delta) \\
c_1 &= 2(1 - iter / maxiter) \\
c_2 &= 2
\end{aligned}
$$

(3)

where x_{id} and v_{id} represent the position vector and velocity vector respectively corresponding to the i_{th} particle in the search space. The velocity vector is subdivided into three components first the previous velocity to provide motion to the particle the second and third components are the local (cognitive) and global (social) explorations undertaken by PSO. It is imperative that an optimization algorithm's solution population must know their relative distances from each other, the spread factor (sf) denotes the distribution of particles in the search space along with the accuracy with respect to the global optimum. The flowchart in Figure 3 represents the process of SFPSO in vivid details.

THE ANFIS-PSO METHOD

Longitudinal flight data are obtained at a trim flight condition corresponding to straight and level cruise at an altitude of 2000 m and at an Indicated Air Speed (IAS) of 50 m/s. The elevator deflection to achieve trim was around 5 degrees. The simulated flight data has been procured with an elevator deflection following a multi-step (3−2−1−1 type) control input (Jategaonkar, 2006). The control surfaces is deflected in steps of 3, 2, 1 and 1 second in the +ve, -ve, +ve and -ve direction respectively, maximum amplitude being about 7 degrees. Typically, initiating from trim flight conditions, the control input is applied in an attempt to excite the chosen aerodynamic modes (short period mode). Inertial Measurement Unit (IMU) installed on the test aircraft provides measurements using dedicated sensors to find aircraft motion variables, atmospheric conditions, control surface deflection etc. Measurements are made in flight recorded on board at a sampling rate of 50Hz using appropriate interface with standard Laptop (separately installed DAQ) (Basappa et al, 1995).

Figure 3. The flowchart of SFPSO algorithm

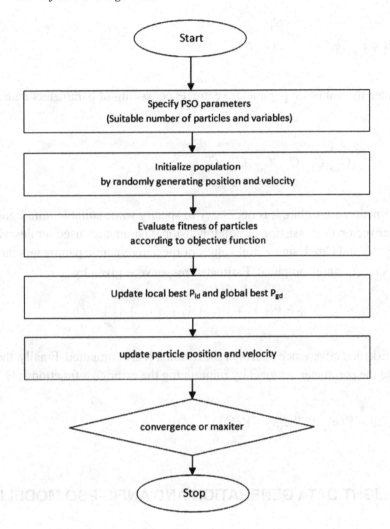

It is noteworthy that the performance of Neuro-Fuzzy System introduced by Takagi and Sugeno's approach of Fuzzy Inference System also known as ANFIS, used to model the system, is dependent on membership function distributions of the input variables decided by d values (i.e. d1 and d2); coefficients: a_i, b_i, c_i and the optimal values of them has been determined by a batch mode of training carried out with the help of Particle Swarm Optimization (PSO).

For illustration, flight data pertaining to longitudinal case is considered. In the first step neural model is developed using input vector U(k) and output vector Z(k+1) for longitudinal parameter estimation.

The input vector is reconstructed by keeping the same initial conditions $(\alpha(k), \theta(k), q(k), v(k))$ used for training however $C_D(k), C_L(k)$ and $C_M(k)$ corresponding to identical control input used for generating flight data are modified as per the chosen aerodynamic model in the estimating algorithm. The chosen aerodynamic model for longitudinal parameter estimation is given by

$$C_D = C_{D_0} + C_{D\alpha}\alpha + C_{D\delta_e}\delta_e$$
$$C_L = C_{L_0} + C_{L\alpha}\alpha + C_{L_q}(q\bar{c}/2V) + C_{D\delta_e}\delta_e$$
$$C_m = C_{m_0} + C_{m\alpha}\alpha + C_{m_q}(q\bar{c}/2V) + C_{m\delta_e}\delta_e$$

Aim is to estimate the unknown parameter vector Θ consisting of parameters namely, $C_{D0,}C_{D\alpha}...C_{mq}$ and $C_{m\,\delta e}$.

$$\Theta = \left[C_{D_0}, C_{D\alpha}, C_{D\delta_e}, C_{L_0}, C_{L\alpha}, C_{Lq}, C_{L_{\delta_e}}, C_{m_0}, C_{m_\alpha}, C_{m_{\delta_e}} \right]^T$$

To start the estimation algorithm, it is necessary to specify some suitable initial guess values of the unknown parameter vector Θ consisting of nondimensional parameters used for description of aerodynamic model of C_D, C_L and Cm. Using initial values of the aerodynamic parameters the estimated coefficients $C_{D_{\delta e}}$, $C_{L_{\delta e}}$ and $C_{M_{\delta e}}$ are computed. Estimated response is given by

$$Y(k+1) = [\alpha(k+1) + \theta(k+1) + q(k+1) + V(k+1) + a_x(k+1) + a_z(k+1)]^T \tag{5}$$

Residual error E(k) and covariance matrix of the residual R are computed. Finally, the PSO algorithm is applied to update the parameter vector Θ by minimizing the error cost function J(Θ,R)

$$J(\Theta, R) = \frac{1}{2} \sum_{k=1}^{N} [z(k) - Y(k)]^T R^{-1}[Z(k) - Y(k)] \tag{6}$$

SIMULATED FLIGHT DATA GENERATION AND ANFIS-PSO MODELING

As a first step towards validation of the proposed method, flight data for the longitudinal short period mode of a rigid stable aircraft are analyzed, in most cases, longitudinal stability and control maneuvers predominantly excite the short period mode and not the phugoid mode. Furthermore, an appropriate selection of control (elevator) input form can ensure excitation of short period dynamics. This means that the flight velocity is essentially constant during the maneuver. The longitudinal state equations for this simplified case are given by equations.

$$\dot{V} = -(\bar{q}S/m)C_D + g\sin(\alpha - \theta) + (F_{eng}/m)\cos\alpha \tag{7}$$

$$\dot{\alpha} = -(\bar{q}S/mV)C_L + q + (g/V)\cos(\alpha - \theta) - (F_{eng}/mV)\sin\alpha \tag{8}$$

$$\dot{\theta} = q \tag{9}$$

$$\dot{q} = (qS\bar{c} / I_y)C_m + (F_{eng} / I_y)l_{tz} \tag{10}$$

The example aircraft selected for generating simulated data is Hansa-3 aircraft (Peyada et al, 2009). The aircraft mass, moment of inertia, geometric characteristics, flight conditions etc are summarized in Tables 1 and 2.

The trim flight corresponds to straight and level cruise at altitude 2000 m and at a Indicated Airspeed (IAS) of 50 m/s. The elevator deflection to achieve trim was about 5 degrees. The simulated flight data has been generated by deflecting elevator following a multi-step 3-2-1-1 type control input. The control surface is deflected in the steps of 3,2,1 and 1 second along +ve, -ve, +ve, -ve directions respectively. The maximum amplitude is around 7 degrees, unless specifically stated otherwise. The flight data showing the validation and estimation cycle time histories of $\alpha, \theta, q, V, a_x, a_z$ and δ_e is presented in Figure 5.

Table 1. Flight conditions, geometric, mass and inertia characteristics of example aircraft

Physical Quantities	Values
True Air Speed	V=52m/s
Mean Aerodynamic Chord	C=1.211m
Wing Span	B=10.47m
Aspect Ratio	AR=8.8m
Wing Area	S=12.47m²
Span Efficiency Factor	e=0.9
Mass	M=758kg
Moment of Inertia	I_y=925kg-m²
Engine Thrust	F_{eng}=1136N

Table 2. Aerodynamic characteristics of example aircraft

S. No	1	2	3	4	5	6
Parameters	C_{D_0}	C_{D_α}	$C_{D_{\delta e}}$	C_{L_0}	C_{L_α}	C_{L_q}
True Value	0.036	0.061	0.152	0.23	4.886	37.259
S.No	7	8	9	10	11	12
Parameters	$C_{L_{\delta e}}$	C_{m_0}	C_{M_α}	C_{m_α}	C_{m_q}	$C_{m_{\delta e}}$
True Value	0.376	0.091	-0.412	-3	-8.792	-0.735

As a first step of validation of the proposed method, the input vector U(k) and output vector Z(k+1) were constructed as per Figures (1) and (5) respectively. Flight dynamic model was created using ANFIS-PSO as per the scheme presented in Figure 4. It was ensured that the network has been tuned using a suitable optimizer (Genetic Algorithm in our case) and had acceptable prediction capability.

PARAMETER ESTIMATION VIA THE ANFIS-PSO METHOD

The ANFIS-PSO method possesses some features that could be used advantageously when estimating parameters of an aircraft. Because the network is trained separately for each of the force or moment coefficients, it can be subsequently used for estimating parameters, one at a time, corresponding to that force or moment coefficient. Thus, rather than estimating the whole set of parameters in one go, the estimation is carried out in separate steps equal to the number of force or moment coefficients involved. For example, the stability and control derivatives corresponding to each of the six degrees-of-freedom are obtained separately. This property is of special significance for an aircraft since the number of unknown parameters is very large. Conventional methods like the maximum likelihood (ML) method would require

Figure 4.

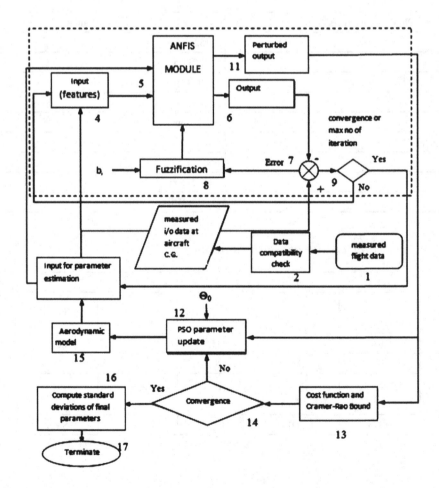

Figure 5.

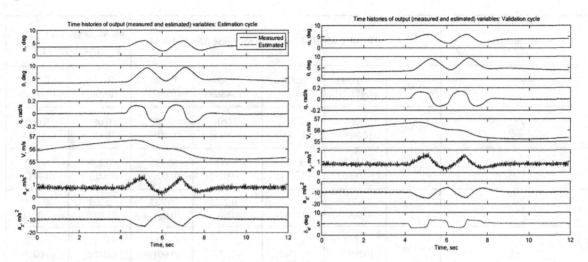

solution of these coupled equations to generate the model response which is compared with the measured response to form the cost function to be minimized by the ML algorithm. Also, the ML method needs a reasonable estimate for initial values of parameters to begin the algorithm. In contrast, the ANFIS-PSO methods require neither the solution of such coupled equations nor any guess values of the parameters.

A study was undertaken to assess the effect of number of iterations on the accuracy of the estimated parameters. The architecture of the network was kept fixed while number of iterations was varies from 50 to 50,000. The ANFIS network could be tunes approximately within 80 iterations. However, parameter estimation via proposed method showed that increase in the number of iterations up to about 1000 did lead to better estimates. Beyond 1000, improvement was only marginal. Once the training was accomplished, the system output Y(k+1), Residual error R and error cost function J(Θ,R) were computed . ANFIS-PSO method was used to estimate aerodynamic parameters by minimizing the cost function J(Θ,R). The estimates obtained after applying ANFIS-PSO method on simulated flight data (without noise) are presented in column 3 of Table 3. For the sake of comparison, estimates obtained after applying LS method on the same flight data are given in column 4 of Table 3

In order to investigate the effect of measurement noise on parameter estimates, simulated pseudo noise of varying intensity was added to the motion variables (α, q, a_x, a_y, a_z etc) and the flight estimated aerodynamic coefficients ($C_D, C_L, C_Y, C_l, C_m, C_n$). The reasons for adding noise to motion variables are as follows. in the case of real flight data, we would have access to noisy raw data of $\alpha, \theta, q, a_x, a_y, a_z$ and q along with the control input δ which is generally assumed to be noise free. Values of aerodynamic coefficients are computed using the motion variables. It is thus appropriate to add noise to simulate $C_D, C_L, C_Y, C_l, C_m, C_n$.

The noise was simulated by generating successive uncorrelated pseudo random numbers having normal distribution with zero mean and assigned standard deviation, the standard deviation approximately correspond to designated percentage (1%.5%) of the maximum amplitude of the corresponding variables. The results from proposed method when applied to 5% noisy data, are compared in column 5 of Table 3. The results obtained using LS method on these data are presented in column 6 of Table 3

Table 3. Parameter estimates for simulated flight data

Parameter	True Values	0% Noise ANFIS-PSO LS		5% Noise ANFIS-PSO LS		5% Noise Without $C_{m\dot{\alpha}}$ ANFIS-PSO LS	
C_{D_0}	0.036	0.0359 (2.45e-5)*	0.036 (3e-5)*	0.0364 (0.0002)	0.0367 (0.0005)	0.0368 (0.0003)	0.037 (0.0007)
C_{D_α}	0.061	0.061 (2.5e-4)	0.061 (0.0003)	0.061 (0.0012)	0.063 (0.0014)	0.062 (0.0012)	0.063 (0.0018)
$C_{D_{\delta e}}$	0.152	0.152 (0.0002)	0.152 (2.5e-4)	0.152 (0.0016)	0.150 (0.0019)	0.150 (0.0016)	0.150 (0.0017)
C_{Lo}	0.23	0.23 (0.0001)	0.23 (0.0004)	0.23 (0.0007)	0.233 (0.0012)	0.234 (0.0069)	0.233 (0.0007)
C_{L_α}	4.886	4.887 (0.0012)	4.889 (0.0042)	4. 885 (0.0012)	4.938 (0.0017)	4.937 (0.0038)	4.939 (0.0069)
C_{L_q}	37.259	37.236 (0.1256)	37.211 (0.1472)	36.234 (0.2754)	37.931 (0.5449)	35.83 (0.2671)	35.031 (0.2695)
$C_{L_{\delta e}}$	0.376	0.375 (0.0014)	0.374 (0.0043)	0.375 (0.0076)	0.323 (0.174)	0.321 (0.0082)	0.326 (0.0086)
C_{m_0}	0.091	0.091 (0.0001)	0.091 (0.0002)	0.091 (0.0015)	0.089 (0.0012)	0.089 (0.0014)	0.088 (0.0015)
C_{m_α}	-0.412	-0.41 (0.0019)	-0.411 (0.0039)	-0.41 (0.0012)	-0.439 (0.0031)	-0.418 (0.0483)	-0.422 (0.0493)
$C_{m_{\dot{\alpha}}}$	-3	-2.928 (0.0530)	-2.937 (0.0039)	-2.931 (0.0494)	-3.072 (0.5824)	Not modeled	Not modeled
C_{m_q}	-8.792	-8.846 (0.0469)	-8.719 (0.1240)	-7.814 (0.6774)	-6.943 (2.0744)	-11.993 (0.6357)	-10.777 (0.7106)
$C_{m_{\delta e}}$	-0.735	-0.734 (0.0013)	-0.73 (0.0008)	-0.734 (0.01167)	-0.632 (0.0136)	-0.712 (0.0108)	-0.707 (0.0121)

*Values in parenthesis represent sample standard deviation

We reiterate: it is only for the sole purpose of generating simulated flight data that the coupled equations of motion (7) to (10) are required, and not for estimating parameters via the ANFIS-PSO method. The flight data so generated always contain the generalized force and moment coefficients in the output file of the network always contain all the effects. However, the variables used in the network input file can be varied. In the present work, the results for the following two cases are presented.

CONCLUSION

Validation for any parameter estimation method must come from its successful demonstration on real aircraft data. Flight database for identification studies is gathered from flight maneuvers carried out using the test aircraft (Hansa-3). The experiments performed with the test aircraft Hansa-3 also indicate that PSO based ANFIS model outperforms other realizations in real environment, thereby justifying the efficacy of the proposed method.

REFERENCES

Basappa, K., & Jategaonkar, R. V. (1995). *Aspects of feed forward neural network modeling and its application to lateral-directional flight data.* DLR IB-111-95a30.

Eberhart, R., & Kennedy, J. (1995, October). A new optimizer using particle swarm theory. In *Micro Machine and Human Science, 1995. MHS'95., Proceedings of the Sixth International Symposium on* (pp. 39-43). IEEE. 10.1109/MHS.1995.494215

Ghosh, A. K., & Raisinghani, S. C. (1993). Parameter estimates of an aircraft as affected by model simplifications. *J. Aarcraft, 31*, S52–S5S.

Hui, N. B., Mahendar, V., & Pratihar, D. K. (2006). Time-optimal, collision-free navigation of a car-like mobile robot using neuro-fuzzy approaches. *Fuzzy Sets and Systems, 157*(16), 2171–2204. doi:10.1016/j.fss.2006.04.004

Jategaonkar, R. (2006). *Flight vehicle system identification: a time domain methodology* (Vol. 216). Reston, VA: AIAA. doi:10.2514/4.866852

Jategaonkar, R., & Plaetschke, E. (1988). *Estimation of aircraft parameters using filter error methods and Extended Kalman Filter.* Forschungsbericht- Deutsche Forschungs- und Versuchsanstalt fur Luft- und Raumfahrt.

Jategaonkar, R. V., Fischenberg, D., & Gruenhagen, W. (2004). Aerodynamic modeling and system identification from flight data-recent applications at dlr. *Journal of Aircraft, 41*(4), 681–691. doi:10.2514/1.3165

Maine, R. E., & Iliff, K. W. (1986). *Identification of dynamic system-application to aircraft. Part I.* Agard AG-300.

Ozger, E. (2013). Parameter Estimation of Highly Unstable Aircraft Assuming Nonlinear Errors. In AIAA Atmospheric Flight Mechanics (AFM) Conference (p. 4751). AIAA. doi:10.2514/6.2013-4751

Peyada, N. K., & Ghosh, A. K. (2009). Aircraft parameter estimation using a new filtering technique based upon a neural network and Gauss-Newton method. *Aeronautical Journal, 113*(1142), 243–252. doi:10.1017/S0001924000002918

Peyada, N. K., Sen, A., & Ghosh, A. K. (2008, March). Aerodynamic characterization of hansa-3 aircraft using equation error, maximum likelihood and filter error methods. *Proceedings of the International MultiConference of Engineers and Computer Scientists, 2.*

Sinha, M., Kuttieri, R. A., & Chatterjee, S. (2013). Nonlinear and linear unstable aircraft parameter estimations using neural partial differentiation. *Journal of Guidance, Control, and Dynamics*, *36*(4), 1162–1176. doi:10.2514/1.57029

Suresh, S., Omkar, S. N., Mani, V., & Sundararajan, N. (2005). Nonlinear adaptive neural controller for unstable aircraft. *Journal of Guidance, Control, and Dynamics*, *28*(6), 1103–1111. doi:10.2514/1.12974

Takagi, H., Suzuki, N., Koda, T., & Kojima, Y. (1992). Neural networks designed on approximate reasoning architecture and their applications. *IEEE Transactions on Neural Networks*, *3*(5), 752–760. doi:10.1109/72.159063 PMID:18276473

Waszak, M. R., & Schmidt, D. K. (1988). Flight dynamics of aeroelastic vehicles. *Journal of Aircraft*, *25*(6), 563–571. doi:10.2514/3.45623

Zerweckh, S. H., Von Flotow, A. H., & Murray, J. E. (1990). Flight testing a highly flexible aircraft-Case study on the MIT Light Eagle. *Journal of Aircraft*, *27*(4), 342–349. doi:10.2514/3.25278

Zhenya, H., Chengjian, W., Luxi, Y., Xiqi, G., Susu, Y., Eberhart, R. C., & Shi, Y. (1998, May). Extracting rules from fuzzy neural network by particle swarm optimisation. In *Evolutionary Computation Proceedings, 1998. IEEE World Congress on Computational Intelligence., The 1998 IEEE International Conference on* (pp. 74-77). IEEE. 10.1109/ICEC.1998.699325

Section 3
Nature–Inspired Solutions for Web Analytics

Chapter 12
Analysis of Multiplex Social Networks Using Nature-Inspired Algorithms

Ruchi Mittal
Netaji Subhas Institute of Technology, India

M. P. S. Bhatia
Netaji Subhas Institute of Technology, India

ABSTRACT

Many real-life social networks are having multiple types of interaction among entities; thus, this organization in networks builds a new scenario called multiplex networks. Community detection, centrality measurements are the trendy area of research in multiplex networks. Community detection means identifying the highly connected groups of nodes in the network. Centrality measures indicate evaluating the importance of a node in a given network. Here, the authors propose their methodologies to compute the eigenvector centrality of nodes to find out the most influential nodes in the network and present their study on finding communities from multiplex networks. They combine a few popular nature-inspired algorithms with multiplex social networks to do the above tasks. The authors' experiments provide a deep insight into the various properties of the multiplex network. They compare the proposed methodologies with several alternative methods and get encouraging and comparable results.

INTRODUCTION

The online social network is one of the prominent and active areas of research. Due to advancement in technologies, it is growing at an exponential rate. For example, there are millions of users on Twitter and Facebook, and this count keeps increasing. A social network is defined as the graph formed by entities or users, which are connected with each other via some relationship. Analysis of social network reveals various information about users behavior. Community detection, centrality measures, and structural holes are the few popular methods used for the social network analysis. The term community means the subset of users from a network, which is highly connected. Community detection implies the identifica-

DOI: 10.4018/978-1-5225-5852-1.ch012

tion of such highly correlated subset of users from a given network. The community detection provides a macro level description of the network. Centrality measures mean identification of most influential users of the network, using centrality one can find the status of a node in the network. Centralities find the influential power of nodes in the network. There are various types of centralities defined in network theory such as degree, closeness, eigenvector, Katz, page rank and so on. (Cardillo, Gómez-Gardenes, and Boccaletti, 2013). The basic description of each of these centrality are given as follow:

- Degree centrality is measured as the total count of the connections made by a node with other nodes of the network. In case of directed graphs, compute the in-degree (total incoming connections with other nodes), out-degree (total outgoing connections with other nodes) and total degree (sum of incoming and outgoing connections with other nodes) of a node (L. Leydesdorff, 2009).
- Closeness centrality is given by reciprocal of the sum of the shortest distances made by a node to every other node of the network (Bavelas, A., 1950).
- The relative score of the neighboring nodes gives Eigenvector centrality of a node. This is widely used to find the powerful nodes of the network (Newman, 2014).
- Katz centrality computes the relative degree of impact for a node. The total number of walks between two nodes computes the relative degree of impact (Katz, 1953).
- Page rank centrality was introduced by Google to measure the appearance of web pages according to search made at Google search engine (Jiang, 2016).

Depending on the application, selection of centrality measure is done and applied to find out the importance of the nodes in the network. For example, Page rank (Newman, 2003) centrality measure uses the hyperlink structure of the WWW, and it is used to rank the web pages by their importance.

The concept of structural hole is also performs a significant role for analyzing the behavior of the nodes in social networks. Holes are the nodes, which plays a vital role to setup the communication between two different groups. In a general social network, there exist some closely knitted subgroups or communities of nodes. To such network, some nodes might not be part of any of the subgroup but act as a communicator or bridge between two or more subgroups (Burt, 1992).

Due to progression in technologies, users connected with each other via multiple relationships. For example, one user is connected to other via facebook, twitter, and WhatsApp. These multiple types of connections emerges a new form of the network called multiplex or multilayer network (Kivela, Arenas, Barthelemy, Gleeson, Moreno, and M. Porter, 2014). Analysis of multiplex networks provides authors more considerable results. Such networks provide lots of information about users so as to analyze the users' behavior rigorously and also find much concrete outcomes (Cozzo et al, 2015).

In this book chapter, authors' propose methodologies for finding out the closeness centrality and structural hole nodes from a given multiplexed networks. Authors' work emphases on to find such nodes, which connects two different subgroups of a network and are act as a bridge between two different sub network. Authors' propose the methodology to compute structural holes and centralities by incorporating concepts of nature-inspired algorithms with multiplex social network. There are numerals of approaches exist to find centralities and structural holes in the simplex network, whereas finding these measures in the multiplex network along with nature-inspired algorithms is still untouched (Mittal & Bhatia, 2018) (Noh, 2004) (Boldi and Vigna, 2014) (Lazer et al, 2009).

Nature Inspired Algorithms are defined as the algorithms which are modeled by analyzing the behavior and various activities done by multiple species such as ants, bees, lion and so on. These multiple activities include their style of living, their approach to searching for food, etc. The area of the nature-inspired algorithm is trendy among researchers. The scope of these algorithms is extensive, and these can easily incorporate with multiple domains such as social network, cloud computing, computer network and so on. Some of the popular nature-inspired algorithms are Artificial Bee Colony Algorithm, Genetic Algorithm, Firefly Algorithm, Ant Colony, Social Spider Algorithm, Simulated Annealing, Tabu search, Spider Monkey Optimization (SMO) algorithm, Bat Algorithm, Plant Propagation Algorithm, Strawberry Algorithm, Cultural Algorithms, Spiral Dynamic Algorithm and many others (X. S. Yang and S. Deb, 2010)(X. S. Yang and S. Deb, 2009) (S. Walton et al., 2011). As, in this book chapter, authors' are solving some problems for the multiplex social network using nature-inspired algorithms. The multi-layer architecture of multiplex social network increases the complexity of the problem and also increases the computation overhead. From authors study, authors' found that nature-inspired algorithms easily optimize the complex issues and find optimal solutions to such issues.

Collaborating nature-inspired algorithm with multiplex networks headed to the new area of research and find out few exciting results. From study, authors' discuss one of the popular nature-inspired algorithms for multiplex social networks, i.e., ant colony algorithm and bees algorithm. The ant colony algorithm is inspired by the trail made by ants for food. This algorithm is best suited to find the centrality of a node in the network. Authors collaborate ant colony algorithm with the multiplex network to find out the closeness centrality of a node. For the experiments, authors' incorporate few popular multiplex social networks such as airline multiplex network dataset, star war multiplex network dataset and authors' collaboration multiplex network dataset. Authors experiments provide a deep keenness about the theory of structural holes and closeness centrality of nodes along with the nature-inspired algorithms using the multiplex network. Authors' compare the proposed methods with the aggregated simple network. The experiments on these methods suggest that the selection of nature-inspired algorithms and other techniques (which authors' discuss in later sections) is essential.

BACKGROUND

Due to burst in Internet usages and technologies, the social interaction among users form a network type of structure, in which set of nodes are joined together by interaction or edges called the social network (Newman, 2003). The area of social network attracts many researchers to analyze various properties of network and behavior of interaction among users (Newman, 2004). (M. E. J. Newman, 2001) proposed many theories for the analysis of the various social network such as a proposed algorithm for finding communities in social networks, how the social networks are diverse from other networks and so on. The analysis of social networks leads to many interesting findings such as sentiment analysis done on Twitter. The analysis of social network could be done by analyzing various features of the network such as community structure, degree distributions, centrality measures, structural holes and so on (V. L. F. Battison and V. Nicosia, 2014). Communities are the highly connected subset of nodes and are the subpart of the whole network. Analysis of communities may use to analyze various features of the network such as users behavior in a group, or how deep connected nodes act in the whole network and so on.

Identifying essential communities is a prominent field of research and is widely used for understanding the behavior of entities in an extensive network (Girvan and Newman, 2002). For example, in mobile phone network, authors' use community analysis to uncover the success or failure of a mobile plan among users. In a collaboration network (Girvan and Newman, 2002), one can find out the latest collaborative research area using communities. Network organization plays a vital role in community detection. Depending on the network organization one can discover communities accordingly. Majorly vast network is organized in multiple ways like hierarchical organization, evolutionary organization and modular organization (Fortunato, 2010).

When authors' want to find the prominence of nodes individually in the network, then concept of centrality measures are used. The importance of a node could reveal the individual behavior and reachability in the network(Girvan and Newman, 2002). There exist many centrality measures proposed by several researchers few of them are as follow: Eigenvector centrality, Katz centrality, degree centrality, closeness centrality and so on. Depending on the type of application and usage these measures applied to the network.

There are substantial numbers of scientific methods exist to analyze the structural properties of multiplex social networks and nature inspired algorithms (Gardenes et al., 2012). Here, authors' first discuss some of the important findings done by many researchers in multiplex networks. (Boccaletti et al., 2014) offer a extensive details about the dynamic nature of multiplex networks, encounter various issues while working on the multiplex networks, benefits of multiplex networks, applications where multiplex architecture provides considerable results and redefine the structural properties of network. (Battison and Nicosia, 2014) They propose some methods to identify the various properties in multiplex networks such as the degree of nodes in the network, overlapping of edges, transitive property, clustering coefficient and navigation across multiple layers of the network. They perform their experiments on the terrorist dataset and apply their proposed methodologies to get some interesting findings.

Centrality measures are generally used to understand the prominence of nodes in a given network. (Xiangnan, Kong and Zhang, 2013) proposes some methodologies for centrality measures in multiplex network. They reformulate some of the centrality measures according to multiplex network architecture. (Sola et al., 2013) define a new formulation for eigenvector centrality for the multiplex network. (Chakraborty and Narayanam, 2016) presents algorithm for computing the betweenness centrality for the multiplex network. They reformulate the betweenness centrality formula and also define a methodology for community detection using betweenness centrality in multi-layer network. (Arda, Pietro, and Halu, 2013) define page rank centrality measure for multiplex by using the idea of the biased random walk. Identifying essential communities is an active area of research and is widely used for understanding the behavior of entities in an extensive network (Boccaletti et al., 2014). For example, in mobile phone network, authors' use community analysis to uncover the success or failure of a mobile plan among users. In a collaboration network (Nicosia, Bianconi, Latora, and Barthelemy, 2014), one can find out the latest collaborative research area using communities. Many algorithms for community detection in simple social network or simplex network proposed lots of authors. In case of multiplex network, the complixity of algorithms increases due to increase in number of layers. (Kuncheva and Montana, 2015) propose a algorithm called LART for community detection in the multiplex network. In this algorithm, a community may include a group of nodes either from some layers or all layers of the multiplex network and complexity of the algorithm is high. (Domnico et al., 2015) propose a community detection algorithm called Infomap, which is based on the flow of the information done in network as well as between small groups of nodes of the network. This method mainly works well with edge-colored multiplex networks having interconnection of layers. (Domenico and Porter, 2014) design a software called MuxViz, which is widely used by number of researcher for their work in the area of multiplex network. This tool cover many algorithms to analyze the structural properties of multiplex network such as node overlapping across layers, edge overlapping across layers, correlation between nodes, centrality measures, community detection and so on. This tool also includes the visualization part of the network. (Jiang and Li, 2014) present the cascading of information in the multiplex network. (Valdez, Macri,Stanley, & Braunstein,2013) Proposed a methodology to find the inter-layer degree and intra-layer degree of nodes in the multiplex social network. (Zhou, Stanley, D'Agostino, G. & Scala, 2012) includes the concept of degree correlations in multi layer networks. (Watanabe & Kabashima, 2014) examined interdependent networks with both within layer and across layer degree correlations

(Huang, Shao, Wang, Buldyrev, Stanley & Havlin,2013)(Shao, Wang, Buldyrev, Stanley & Havlin,2014) studied percolation cascades in interdependent networks in which multiplex networks are produced using some random-graph models with clustering (Newman,2009).

Optimizing problems are highly significant in solving many real-world problems. Nature was a source of motivation for developing many real-world optimization problems such as the behavior of bees for searching for food, the territory of a lion, etc. inspire many researchers to solve complex problems or optimize complex problems (Gao, Lan, Zhang and Deng, 2013). The algorithms, which are inspired by nature, are called nature-inspired algorithms. These algorithms got the inspiration from the behavior of social insect colonies and other animal societies interacting locally with one another.

(Rivero, Cuadra, Calle, and Isasi, 2012) proposed methodology inspired by the ant colony algorithm and finds the path search problem in the social network. (Bojic, Lipic, and Podobnik, 2012) have demonstrated the synchronization of Firefly can be optimized for community detection in networks and data diffusion in machine networks. (Gao, Lan, Zhang, and Deng Y, 2013) proposed a methodology for biological weighted networks. Their methodology combines the centrality measures with K-shell index, to find the leading node in a weighted network.

(Zhang B, Zhong S, Wen K, Li R, Gu X, 2013) proposed an improved Particle Swarm Optimization (PSO) algorithm to find the most influential users of Sina Weibo for the famous microblogging service in China. Authors utilize the structure of social interactions among user to find an optimal solution.

Particle Swarm Optimization (PSO) is a population-based optimization technique motivated by the social behavior of bird congregating or fish discipline (Kennedy & Eberhart, 1995). Particle Swarm Optimization algorithm is quite similar to Genetic algorithms, which means these algorithms hold the evolutionary behavior (Castillo & Melin, 2002). This algorithm starts with a group of random answers and explorations for optima by renewing the generations. However, unlike the genetic algorithms, Particle Swarm Optimization algorithm does not have any evolving operators such as crossover and deviation. In PSO, the potential solutions, called particles, fly through the problem space by following the current optimum particles (Angeline, 1998). Due to the evolutionary behavior of the genetic algorithm, these are used in modern material science because modern material science requires strong support of computation and are quickly fulfilled by genetic algorithms (Ohno, Esfarjani, Kawazoe, 1999). (Yun et al., 2011) proposed novel methods to determine optimal feature subsets by using nature-inspired algorithms. (M. B. Imani. et al., 2012) Make use of Ant Colony Optimization (ACO) and Genetic Algorithm for feature selection in their proposed work. The selection of these two nature-inspired algorithm speed up the feature selection process. (Yang et al., 2014) suggested a novel approach using a Binary Cuckoo Search (BCS) inspired by the breeding behavior of cuckoo birds for feature selection

MAIN FOCUS OF THE CHAPTER

Research Contribution

The explosive rate at which social interaction is growing open the wide is of research to analyze the user's behavior in many ways. There exists lots of work done in the simple network and to investigate the users' interaction in multiple networks; it is good to focus on the area of multi-layer or multiplex social networks. Also, nature-inspired algorithms provide authors methodologies to analyze extensive data in many ways. So, Analysis of multiplex social network along with nature-inspired algorithms brings authors more centered results. So in this book chapter, authors' propose the following:

- The ant colony algorithm is inspired by the trail made by ants for food. Here, authors' collaborate ant colony algorithm with the multiplex network to find out the closeness centrality of a node. The closeness centrality measure provides the most central nodes of a network. Here, authors' offer a new methodology for measuring the closeness centrality in the multiplex network.
- The bees' algorithm is inspired by the forging behavior of the honeybees. Here, authors' use the bees' algorithm to find the top-k structural holes of the multiplex network. The structural holes are the nodes, which connects two subgroups of a network.

Multiplex Social Network

The Multiplex social network is formally defined as the network having multiple layers of the network over the same set of entities and those entities are connected with one another via numerous interactions (Pujari and KAnawati, 2015) (Hminida and Kanawati, 2015). It can be given as follow:

Consider a graph $G = (N_m, C_m, L_m)$, where Nm is the set of nodes, C_m is the set of connection between nodes and L_m is the set of layers. Niα is a node from the set and $N_i \varepsilon N_m$ and $\alpha \varepsilon L_m$. Assume all nodes belongs to V_m exist in all the layers such as $|N_m| = N \times L$.

In Figure 1, authors' show a sample two-layer multiplex network having five nodes, which authors' generate using E-R random graph algorithm. From the figure authors' can see, all five nodes exist in both the layers but the interaction among nodes varies in each layer. The straight line in the figure shows the connection between two nodes belongs to the same layer. Whereas, the dotted line connects the same node exist in multiple layers.

Ant Colony Algorithm for Shortest Path

The ant colony algorithm is one of the popular optimization techniques of nature-inspired algorithm. This algorithm is based on the trail made by and followed by ants for searching the food source. This algorithm is widely used for optimizing routing protocols and other np-hard problems. Ant colony algorithm is also called as pheromone model, which means while searching for food ants release pheromone to guide other ants for the route (Dorigo, Birattari and Stützle, 2006) (Dorigo, 2002). The fundamental component of this algorithm is positive response given by ants, which is used for the interpretations for fast encounter of new outcomes. Disseminated computations are made to avoid hasty confluence. The

Figure 1. Multilex Network

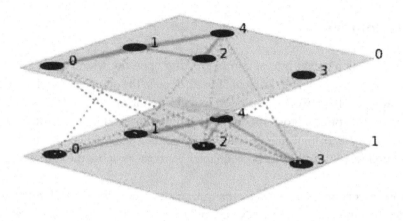

use of efficient greedy experiment helps to find the satisfactory outcomes in the early stage of the hunt activity(Dorigo and Socha, 2007).

The basic steps followed by ACO algorithm is given as below:

- InitializePheromoneValue ()
- While conclusive situation is not met do
- FindSolution ()
- EvaluateSolution ()
- UpdatePheromoneValue ()
- Return best solution

Bees' Algorithm

The problem of identifying influential users during an exceptional event in micro-blogging sites or co-authorship network is robust. The proposed approach converges on finding the optimal solution of finding influential users using fundamental properties of swarm intelligence. The user's information is dig out by analyzing the activities and the knowledge of the other neighboring users. Investigating such several features of users can approach the problem of identifying influential users (Karaboga and Basturk, 2008) (Seeley, 2009) (Haddad, Afshar and Marino, 2006).

In this book chapter, authors' make use of ABC algorithm inspired by foraging behavior of honey-bees on seeking huge amount flowers for collecting the honey. The core part of the bees' algorithm is a combination of the global-local search feature and waggle dance process. The whole process includes exchanging and learning information and the whole community would always spot approximately best food source. The bees' algorithm is best suited for the analysis of collaboration network and Twitter network (Pham, Soroka, Koc, Ghanbarzadeh and Otri 2007). Authors in collaboration network consider as waggle dancers, who attract other authors by their weight (count of publication). The influencer authors play a vital role in spreading new areas of research and invite more authors for collaboration work.

Authors approach starts with selecting top-k maximum weight nodes across all layers of the network. The steps defined for the bees' algorithm are given as follow.

```
Data: Multiplex collaboration network
Result: Top-k influential nodes
1.          Find the degree centrality of nodes of the network.
2.          Consider the degree value for each node as weight of the node.
3.          Prepare a set E from the node set having top-k degree across all
layers
4.          Compute the local fitness value of each node  in set E (Employer
Bees);
5.          Prepare a set S (scout bees) having the nearest neighbor nodes in
set E;
6.          Initialize empty set O (onlooker bees);
7.          while set S is not null do
8.          for each i in S          ▷ starting with the highest Weight;
9.          Compute local fitness value of i;
10.          if local fitness value of i > local fitness value of any j ∈ E then
11.          add  i to set E;
12.          add j to set O;
13.          update the status of nodes in set O;
14.          Update set S;
15.          Compute global fitness value;
16.          Return the set  K (employer bees);
```

The proposed algorithm aims to find the subset of nodes E such that E ⊂ V has top-k influential nodes. In this algorithm, authors' first evaluate the local fitness value of each node in set E. Next initialize the set S by analyzing the nearest neighbor for nodes in set E. Store these influenced nodes in set O ⊂ V of onlooker bees. Next, authors' start an iterative process by selecting scout bee with the highest weight and compare it with the scout bees. If the scout bee weight is high then authors', update the status of scout bees and onlooker bees. This process is being repeated until the set of scout bees become null. This whole process results in authors to give the employer bees, which are having maximum influence in the network.

Closeness Centrality

In this section, authors' discuss the concept of closeness centrality in details. The closeness centrality of a node is given by reciprocal of the sum of the shortest distance to other node of the network (Bonacich, P., 1987)(Bonacich, P., 1991) (Borgatti, S.P., 1995). It can be formulated as follow:

$$C(i) = \frac{1}{\sum d^*(p_i \to j)} \tag{1}$$

Here, $C(i)$ is the closeness centrality of node i. The function $d^*(p_i \to j)$ provides the path length between the vertex i to vertex j and $\sum d^*(p_i \to j)$ is the total path between the vertex i and vertex j of the network. In figure 2 below, authors' find the closeness centrality of each node and show the highest centrality node. Here, node 1 and node 36 has the highest closeness centrality.

Structural Holes

The concept of structural holes suggests that find those nodes in a network, which makes communication between two different groups the network. Ronald S Brut first proposed the theory of structural holes. The structural holes node satisfies a gap between two different society and communities. The link or the bridge, which fills the gaps, plays a vital role in identifying structural holes in a network (Hargadon, and Andrew, 2002) (Mitchell and Lawrence, 2003). For example, in a collaboration network, an author working in multiple domains may act as a structural hole for people working in one area only. Figure 3 shows a network containing structural hole node. Node A is the structural hole node, which connects 3 different subgroups of the network. Example of Structural hole node.

Figure 2. Closeness centrality of nodes

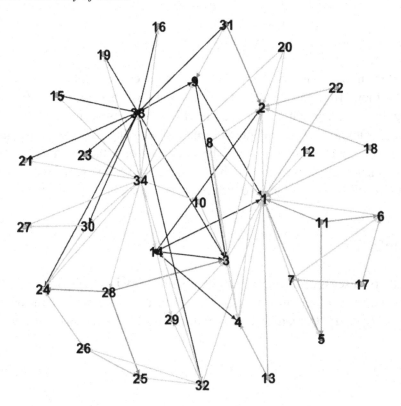

Figure 3. Structural hole node

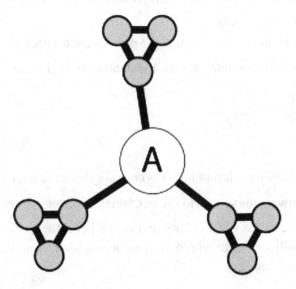

APPROACH

There are various algorithms exists for measuring the closeness centrality of vertices in simple networks, but from authors extensive literature survey, authors' were unable to find the algorithm for finding closeness centrality of nodes in multi-layer social networks or multiplex networks. In this book chapter, authors' propose a methodology for detecting the closeness centrality of nodes in the multiplex network using ant colony algorithm, which authors' discuss in the previous section. Similarly, there are numerous of methods exists for finding structural holes in simplex networks and multiplex network. Here, authors' try an attempt to find out the structural holes by combining the bees' algorithm with some fundamental properties of the multiplex social network. In this section, authors' elaborate authors two proposed methods for finding multi-layer closeness centrality using ant colony algorithm and multi-layer structural holes using bees' algorithm.

Multi-Layer Closeness Centrality Using Ant Colony Algorithm

The ant-colony algorithm is inspired by the trail made by the ants for food and uses the shortest path to reach their destination. This nature-inspired algorithm is best utilized to find out the closeness centrality measure in the multiplex network. Here, authors' incorporate the zest of the ant colony algorithm in the multiplex network to find out the most central nodes of the network (Falih and KAnawati, 2015) (Csardi and Nepusz, 2006).

Authors proposed algorithm starts with finding shortest path length using the method proposed by Rivero et. al [21], to get the distance between entities within the layer or across layers. Authors' create a path length list for each node of the network, which contains the list of path length to all other nodes. Finally, authors' compute the closeness centrality using path length list by applying authors proposed formula. Authors' describe authors proposed algorithm in following steps.

- Find the shortest path $p_{i^\alpha \to j^\beta}$ from node i (layer α) to node j (layer β) in graph G using the ant colony algorithm for shortest path.
- Define a distance function $d(p_{i^\alpha \to j^\beta})$ to find the path length for each $p_{i^\alpha \to j^\beta}$
- The Mutli- layer closeness centrality for multiplex network is given as

$$C(i) = \gamma \frac{1}{\sum d^*(p_{i^\alpha \to j^\alpha})} + (1 - \gamma) \frac{1}{\sum d^*(p_{i^\alpha \to j^\beta})} \qquad (2)$$

Here, $C(i)$ gives the multi-layer layer closeness centrality value of node i. The function $d^*(p_{i^\alpha \to j^\alpha})$ provides the path length between the vertex i to vertex j, which are belongs to same layer and $\sum d^*(p_{i^\alpha \to j^\beta})$ is the total path between the vertex i of one layer and vertex j of different layer. γ is the tuning factor, which balance the reachability of edge within layer or across layer. Note that, to find the cross layer closeness centrality, authors' can keep $\gamma < 0.5$.

Structural Holes Using Bees' Algorithm

The foraging behavior of the honeybees inspires the bees' algorithm. A cluster of honeybees repeatedly searches the territory for new flower patches. Here, authors' find the structural holes nodes using the collective intelligence of honeybees. Authors first compute the set of working bees from the network, which gave positive feedback for the food and provides the maximum coverage. Next, authors' find the betweenness centrality for each node of the network. It is computed as the sum of numbers of shortest paths between any two nodes of the network is passing through the given node. Authors found that nodes with highest betweenness centrality value are found at the borders of the closely knitted sub-network of a system. Next, authors' take the intersection of above two computations and pick the top-k values nodes called the structural holes in the network. Authors' describe authors proposed algorithm in following steps.

- Create the aggregated network of the multiplex network.
- Find the node set using bees algorithm discussed earlier as V_{EB}.
- Evaluate the betweenness centrality for nodes using the cross-layer betweenness centrality algorithm given by Tanmoy et. al [15] for the multiplex network.
- Create a node set V_{BN} and include all the highest valued betweenness centrality nodes of the network.
- Intersect the above two set as follow to get the structural holes in the network.

$$SHoles = V_{EB} \cap V_{BN} \qquad (3)$$

Here, 'Sholes' is the set of top-k structural holes of the network.

DATASET DESCRIPTION

In this section, authors' discuss the various dataset and the properties of the dataset used for the experiments on different proposed approaches. Authors' pick up a verity of the dataset to show the versatility in authors investigations for the multiplex social network using nature-inspired algorithms. For Example, Authors' picked up the arXiv dataset as collaboration dataset to find out the most central nodes and structural holes nodes from the network. Collaboration network datasets are best suited for authors both the proposed scenario because there are authors, which are working in multi-disciplinary areas and act as a bridge between different research groups and provide the shortest trail. Also, The most prominent authors are acting as employer bees for the network because they get the most favorable output, i.e., they connect maximum nodes. Authors' also use airline network multiplex dataset and star-war movie dataset to show the versatility in their work and validate the proposed approaches. These are the standard multiplex datasets, and many researchers used them for their experiments. Below authors' discuss the basic description and essential features of these datasets.

Airline Network Dataset

Cardillo et al. [6] compiled the airlines' network dataset by analyzing the services operated by four major airline companies at many airports of Europe. The four airlines denote the four layer of the multiplex network, each airport denotes the vertex and flight service between two airports denotes the link between two vertexes. Table 1 shows the primary metrics of each layer of the dataset such as the number of vertex in each layer, number of edges in each layer, the average density of each layer and the average diameter length of each layer.

The computations of above metrics to the dataset are essential for the analysis. From these measurements, authors' get to know about the average reachability of a node, density of the network and so on. In general, airports are not restricted to one airline only; multiple airlines may operate from the same airport. So, intersection of nodes exists in the network and this intersection of nodes may increase the computation overhead and complexity of the system but provides authors more concrete results. Figure 4 shows the amount of intersection of nodes exists across various layers, which authors' normalize from 0 to 1.

Table 1. Airline Dataset Statistics

Layers	# Nodes	# Edges	#Density	#Diameter
Vueling	36	66	1.3	6
British Airways	65	63	1.0	5
Lufthansa	106	244	2.3	4
Ryanair	128	601	4.7	4

Figure 4. Intersection of nodes across layers

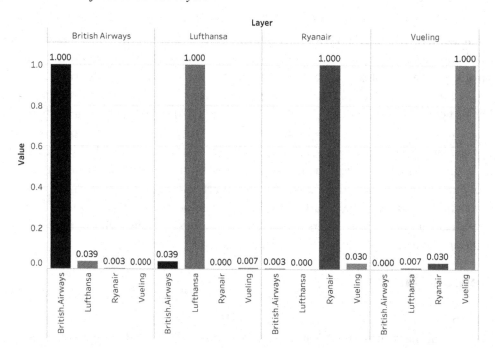

Star War Network Dataset

The Star-Wars dataset was compiled by Eveliang [7] by analyzing the interaction among various characters of the famous television series Star-Wars. In this book chapter, authors' pick the dataset of 6 episodes of the show, in which each episode denotes the layer of the network, the character of the show denotes the vertices or nodes of the network and interaction between characters represents an edge. Tables 2 show the underlying metrics of the dataset like count of nodes, count of edges, count of connected components and mean path length. As discussed in airline dataset, observation of overlapping of nodes is essential; figure 5 shows the observation for overlapping nodes between layers of the network.

The computations of above metrics to the dataset are essential for the analysis. From these measurements, authors' get to know about the average reachability of a node, density of the network and so on.

Table 2. Dataset Statistics

Layers	# Nodes	# edges	#Mean Path Distance	#Components
Episode 1	38	148	2.1	55
Episode 2	33	103	2.1	60
Episode 3	24	67	2.0	69
Episode 4	21	61	1.9	72
Episode 5	21	59	2.0	72
Episode 6	20	60	2.0	72

Figure 5. Intersection of nodes across layers in star war dataset

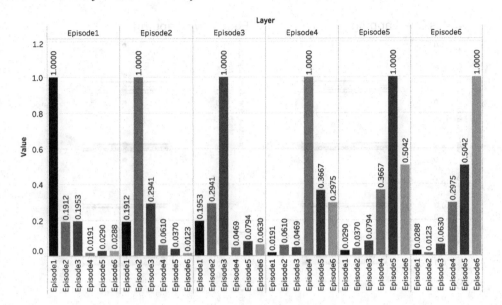

Collaboration Network Dataset

(Malino et al., 2015) complied the collaboration network dataset from the popular arXiv repository. The author picked the word "network" exist in title and abstract of papers belongs to different subcategories of the arXiv repository. This dataset is composed of 13 layers, where each layer represent different category mentioned at arXiv, each author denotes a node, and an edge represents paper done by two authors. In table 1, authors' show the basic statistics of the dataset.

Table 3. Collaboration Network Dataset Statistics

Layers	No. of Nodes	No. of Edges	Diameter
physics.soc-ph	1594	3019	20
physics.bio-ph	2956	6097	17
physics.data-an	5465	14485	19
cond-mat.stat-mech	1451	2582	13
q-bio.MN	1905	4423	26
math.OC	1605	4427	14
cond-mat.dis-nn	3506	7341	23
q-bio	660	868	5
math-ph	361	592	4
q-bio.BM	700	1145	9
cs.SI	4946	11600	19
nlin.AO	1270	1953	18
cs.CV	377	494	5

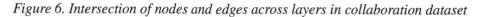

Figure 6. Intersection of nodes and edges across layers in collaboration dataset

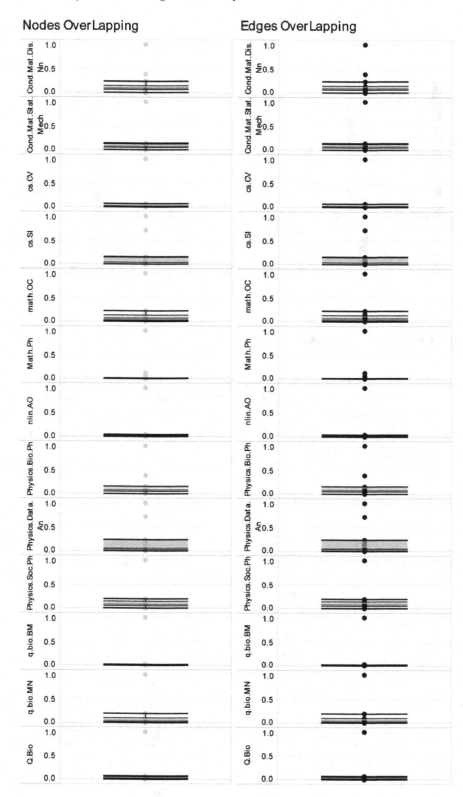

The computations of above metrics to the dataset are essential for the analysis. From these measurements, authors' get to know about the average reachability of a node, density of the network and so on.

EXPERIMENTAL RESULTS

Authors' applied the proposed approaches for finding closeness centrality using ant-colony algorithm and mining structural holes using bees' algorithm to discussed datasets. Authors' compare the results for multiplex networks with aggregated network results and get likely outcomes.

Performance Metrics

Authors' run the Pearson correlation and linear trend line to measure the performance of proposed methodologies. They also compare the results with other similar algorithms to validate the outcomes. Pearson correlation finds the correlation between the previous results with proposed relations and finds the similarity score between two. Linear trend line find the error rate, t-value, p-value and so on to measure the accuracy of the proposed algorithm results.

- Pearson correlation finds the linear correlation between two variables. It is very popular technique and widely used in many areas of science and engineering. The value of pearson correlation varies from +1 to -1, where +1 means a positive correlation, -1 means negative correlation and 0 means no correlation.
- A linear trend line is a best-fit straight line, which is used with linear datasets. This performance evaluation technique is used when your output or data points the linear path in the graph plot. A linear trend line normally provides the performance evaluation statistics when something is growing or declining at a uniform rate.

Cross Layer Closeness Centrality Results

Authors' run the cross-layer closeness centrality methodology to airline network dataset and star-war network dataset. From the dataset description, authors' saw that there is only 0.0% to 2% intersecting of nodes exist between layers of airline network dataset, whereas start-war dataset comparably holds large intersection of nodes between layers, which is ranges from 2% to 50%. This variation of node overlapping in two dataset heads authors to check the methodology more broadly, which means lesser the overlapping of nodes lesser the closeness centrality nodes and vice versa. Authors' compare the results of these multiplex networks results with the aggregated networks and with other similar centrality measures to see the difference in the performance of the proposed approach with the existing ones.

Airline Dataset Results

In this dataset, the average diameter of the nodes is less, which means reachability between nodes is also less. Also, there is less intersection of nodes exists between layers so, the average cross-layer closeness centrality of nodes is even less. Only 9.6% of nodes of the whole networks have higher closeness centrality, and these nodes control the 37% of other nodes of the network.

Authors' start the experiments by applying the ant colony optimization algorithm to find the shortest path between two nodes across layer layers and within layers. Authors' initialize the pheromone value and check until the route provides the nodes is the most concise or not. If it shortest then jump to next node else update the pheromone value. This procedure continues till authors' get the shortest path set for all the nodes. From this set, authors' compute the distance function discussed in the earlier section and calculate the closeness centrality using equation 2.

The results show that more than 70% of the nodes have same closeness centrality, which concludes that the network is sparse network and there is less interaction exist in the network. Authors' also compute the closeness centrality for the aggregated network, and 60% of nodes hold same closeness centrality. There is least difference found in the values of low ranked and high ranked nodes using closeness centrality algorithm for both types of network. Figure 7 shows the comparative analysis of closeness centrality values utilizing the multiplex network and aggregated network.

Authors' also apply the linear trend line model to see the output of the proposed methodology for the multiplex network with the aggregated network. From the analysis, authors' found that this model is significant at $p <= 0.05$. The equation for the same is given as:

Equation: Aggregated = 1.40474*Multiplex + -0.456422

Figure 7. Closeness centrality results using the proposed algorithm vs aggregated network results

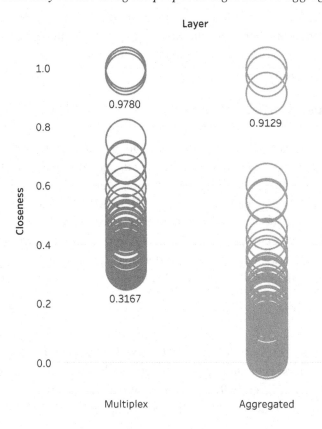

The table 4 shows the other metrics for performance evaluation such as standard error, mean squared error, standard error and so on.

Star War Dataset Results

In this In this dataset, the intersection of nodes among the layers of the network is high and the number of connected components in each layer is low, which results in getting the optimal percentage of nodes having high closeness centrality. The results of the network show that more than 23% of the nodes have closeness centrality, which concludes that the network is a firmly connected network and there is high interaction exist in the network. When authors' compute the closeness centrality for the aggregated network, authors' get 14% of nodes have high closeness centrality. There is comparable difference found in the values of low ranked and high ranked nodes using closeness centrality algorithm and aggregated network. Figure 8 shows the comparative analysis two networks.

Collaboration Dataset Results

The initial step of authors proposed algorithm is to pick the top-k ranked nodes of the network. This ranking is measured collectively using the weight and the degree of the nodes, and authors' performed the experiments on different values of k. Using Local search or exploration process analyses, authors' compute the local fitness value for each top-k nodes. Next, authors' consider the neighbor nodes of a

Table 4. Performance Metrics Statistics

Model Formula	(Multiplex + Intercept)
Number of modeled observations:	449
Residual degrees of freedom (DF):	447
Model degrees of freedom:	2
R-Squared:	0.781108
Standard error:	0.0501937
p-value (significance):	< 0.0001
Number of filtered observations:	0
Model degrees of freedom:	2
SSE (sum squared error):	1.12618
Number of filtered observations:	0
MSE (mean squared error):	0.0025194

Table 5. Individual Trend Lines

Panes		Line		Coefficients				
Row	Column	p-Value	DF	Term	Value	StdErr	t-Value	p-Value
Aggregated	Multiplex	< 0.0001	447	Multiplex	1.40474	0.0351723	39.9388	< 0.0001
				intercept	-0.456422	0.0130917	-34.8635	< 0.0001

Figure 8. Closeness centrality results using authors proposed algorithm vs aggregated network results

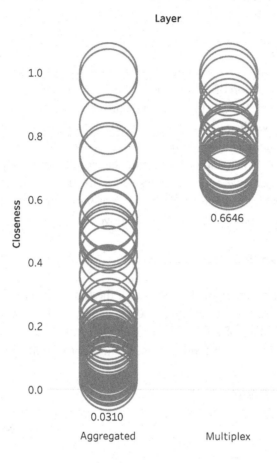

Table 6. Performance Metrics Statistics

Model Formula	(Multiplex + Intercept)
Number of modeled observations:	92
Number of filtered observations:	0
Residual degrees of freedom (DF):	90
Model degrees of freedom:	2
MSE (mean squared error):	0.0023063
p-value (significance):	< 0.0001
SSE (sum squared error):	0.207565
Standard error:	0.0480237
R-Squared:	0.943647

Table 7. Individual Trend Lines

Panes		Line		Coefficients				
Row	**Column**	**p-Value**	**DF**	**Term**	**Value**	**StdErr**	**t-Value**	**p-Value**
Aggregated	Multiplex	< 0.0001	90	Multiplex	0.957872	0.024674	38.8211	< 0.0001
				intercept	-0.0010645	0.0064014	-0.166288	0.868304

Figure 9. Linear Trend Results of Star-war dataset

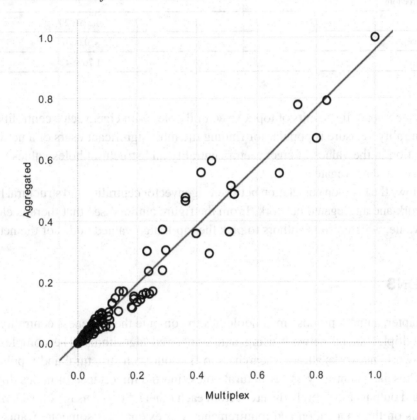

top-k ranked as the scout node and calculate the local fitness function for the same. If the scout nodes have higher fitness value then its top-k listed node then, revise the current set of top-k ranked nodes with scout nodes. This process is repeated until it covers all nodes of the network. Next, authors' find the multiplexed betweenness centrality of the nodes, because nodes with maximum betweenness centrality are found at the borders of the tightly knitted sub-network of a network. This feature of betweenness centrality is close to the definition of structural holes. At last, authors' take the intersection of above two measures and compute the top-k structural holes. Authors' compare the results with their earlier proposed methodology for top-k structural holes (Mittal & Bhatia, 2017) as well as with the aggregated network. From the results, authors' found that if k is 10, then 82.5% nodes are similar if k is 50 then 92.23% nodes are similar if k is 100 then 94% nodes are identical between the proposed methodology and the methodology proposed by (Mittal & Bhatia, 2017). In the table below, authors' show linear trend line results of top-k structural hole nodes from the proposed algorithm vs. aggregated network.

Table 8. Performance Metrics Statistics

Model Formula	(Strength and Intercept)
Number of modeled observations:	14488
Number of filtered observations:	0
MSE (mean squared error):	2.919e-24
Residual degrees of freedom (DF):	14486
R-Squared:	1
Model degrees of freedom:	2
SSE (sum squared error):	4.229e-20
p-value (significance):	< 0.0001
Standard error:	1.709e-12

Authors' also compare the results of top-k structural holes with eigenvector centrality measure. The eigenvector centrality measure is popular for finding the most significant users of a network. Figure 10 shows the variation in the values of eigenvector centrality and structural holes values of the nodes for multiplex network and aggregated network.

Figure 11 shows the Pearson correlation between eigenvector centrality and structural holes values for multiplex network and aggregated network. From the figure authors' see that there is close correlation exist between value, which results authors to pick the top-k high valued nodes of the network.

APPLICATIONS

In this book chapter, authors propose methodologies to compute the closeness centrality and structural holes in the multiplex social network using nature-inspired algorithms. The complex and dynamic natures of real-world networks attract researchers to find out such structural and topological issues of the networks. Closeness centrality and structural holes find the importance of nodes differently (Their methodology and outputs are entirely different from each other). So, the usage of each of the technique entirely depends on the application and requirements. For example, if someone wants a node, which is easily reachable, then closeness centrality is used and if someone needs to find nodes, which set up the links between two different groups then structural holes, are the need to identify. In this section, authors present some real-life applications of multiplex networks, in which mining closeness centrality or structural holes are impactful.

Table 9. Individual Trend Lines

Line		Panes		Coefficients				
p-Value	p-Value	Row	Column	Term	Value	StdErr	t-Value	p-Value
< 0.0001	< 0.0001	F15	Strength	Strength	1	1.385e-16	7.21777e+15	< 0.0001
				intercept	-312	4.44e-14	-7.02766e+15	< 0.0001

Figure 10. The average eigenvector centrality and structural holes measures in multiplex network versus aggregated network

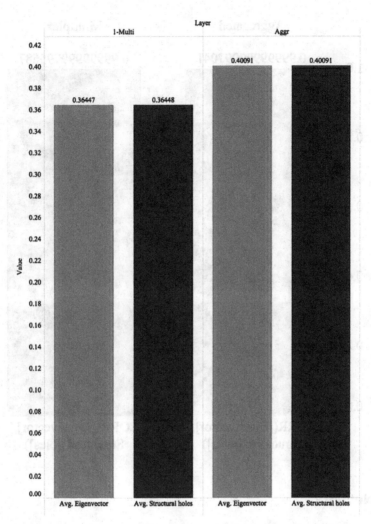

Telecommunication Multiplex Network

In Telecommunication multiplex network, authors consider regions as layers of the network and call data of caller and callee made the nodes and edges of the network. This network is regarded as the weighted network, in which the total number of calls made between caller and callee is the weight assigned to the link between caller and callee. Closeness centrality is measured to find the callees or callers who spend more time over the call and are central in the network. The cellular company made such analysis is to uncover the success or failure of a calling mobile plan among users of a region or multiple regions. Also, they provide some beneficial plans to the high valued closeness centrality users to set up proper customer relationship.

Figure 11. The correlation values of eigenvector centrality measure and structural hole measure in multiplex network versus aggregated network

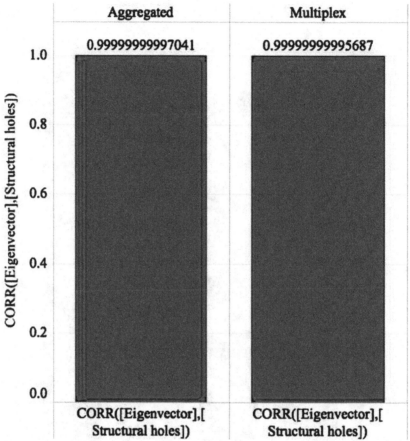

Collaboration Network

Collaboration network are formed by the research papers published by many researcher. Closeness centraltiy finds the most prominent authors in the colloboration network. From authors earlier findings, high valued closeness centrality aurthors publishes many colloborative papers. Structural holes finds the authors who connects the multiple groups of authors working are in different domains.

Biological Network

Biological network such as neural network are formed with the set of neurons. Identifying closeness centrality and structural holes in neural network helps to analyze the behavior of neurons as individual.

Recommender System Network

A Recommender system network is formed using the data of similar items or users shares similar interest. Identifying structural holes and closeness centrality improve the collaborative filtering process of recommender system. Authors create a matrix of items and users similarity structure. To this matrix, they apply swarm optimization algorithm to find the community. Based on the discovered communities, items are recommended to users.

CONCLUSION

In this book chapter, authors' present an empirical analysis of multiplex network along with nature-inspired algorithms. Authors' propose a methodology to find out the closeness centrality measure to get the most central nodes in the multiplex network by applying ant colony algorithm. Authors' also collaborate the bees algorithm with the multiplex social network to find out the most influential nodes or the authors from the collaboration network. This attempt of the collaboration of nature-inspired algorithms with multiplex social network offers a path to get information from the multiplex network and further investigate the behavior of entities extensively.

With the growth in technologies and social interaction via multiple modes, the domain of the multiplex social network is expanding day by day, and it is fascinating to analyze such networks. So, Authors' can further extend the proposed methodologies for more types of network such as directed networks, weighted networks and so on. Similarly, authors' are planning to collaborate other nature-inspired algorithms with the multiplex social networks to get different exciting outcomes.

ACKNOWLEDGMENT

Authors' like to thank all the colleagues, fellow research scholars and my family members for their support, encouragement and help for fulfillment of the work.

REFERENCES

Arda, M. R. J., Pietro, P., & Halu, B. G. (2013). Multiplex pagerank. *PLoS One*, *8*(10), e78293. doi:10.1371/journal.pone.0078293 PMID:24205186

Battiston, V. L. F., Nicosia, V., & Latora, V. (2014). Structural measures for multiplex networks. *Physical Review. E*, *89*(3), 032804. doi:10.1103/PhysRevE.89.032804 PMID:24730896

Bavelas, A. (1950). Communication Patterns in Task-Oriented Groups. *The Journal of the Acoustical Society of America*, *22*(6), 725–730. doi:10.1121/1.1906679

Boccalettia, S., Bianconic, G., Criadod, R., & del Geniof, C. (2014). The structure and dynamics of multilayer networks. *Physics Reports*, *544*(1), 1–122. PMID:25484487

Bojic, I., Lipic, T., & Podobnik, V. (2012). Bio-inspired clustering and data diffusion in machine social networks. In *Computational Social Networks* (pp. 51–79). Springer. doi:10.1007/978-1-4471-4054-2_3

Boldi, P., & Vigna, S. (2014). Axioms for Centrality. *Internet Mathematics*, *10*(3-4), 222–262. doi:10.1080/15427951.2013.865686

Bonacich, P. (1987). Power and centrality: A family of measures. *American Journal of Sociology*, *92*(5), 1170–1182. doi:10.1086/228631

Bonacich, P. (1991). Simultaneous group and individual centralities. *Social Networks*, *13*(2), 155–168. doi:10.1016/0378-8733(91)90018-O

Borgatti, S. P. (1995). Centrality and AIDS. *Connections*, *18*(1), 112–114.

Burt, R. S. (1992). *Structural Holes: The Social Structure of Competition*. Harvard University Press.

C. Y. (2011). Feature subset selection based on bio-inspired algorithms. *Journal of Information Science and Engineering*, *27*, 1667–1686.

Cardillo, G.-G., & Zanin, R. Papo, del Pozo, & Boccaletti. (2013). Emergence of network features from multiplexity. *Scientific Reports, 3*, 1344. Retrieved from https://github.com/evelinag/StarWars-social-network/blob/master/networks/,2015

Castillo, O., Valdez, F., & Melin, P. (2007). Hierarchical genetic algorithms for topology optimization in fuzzy control systems. *International Journal of General Systems*, *36*(5), 575–591. doi:10.1080/03081070701321860

Chakraborty, T., & Narayanam, R. (2016). *Cross-layer Betweenness Centrality in Multiplex Networks with Applications*. ICDE. doi:10.1109/ICDE.2016.7498257

Coleman, J. S., Katz, E., & Menzel, H. (1966). Medical Innovation: A Diffusion Study. Bobbs-Merrill.

Cozzo, Kivel, Domenico, Sol, Arenas, Gmez, … Moreno. (2015). *Clustering coefficients in multiplex networks*. Academic Press.

Csardi, G., & Nepusz, T. (2006). The igraph software package for complex network research. *Inter. Journal of Complex Systems*, 1695.

De Domenico, M., Lancichinetti, A., Arenas, A., & Rosvall, M. (2015). Identifying modular flows on multilayer networks reveals highly overlapping organization in interconnected systems. *Physical Review X*, *5*(1), 011027. doi:10.1103/PhysRevX.5.011027

De Domenico, M., Lancichinetti, A., Arenas, A., & Rosvall, M. (2015). - "Identifying Modular Flows on Multilayer Networks Reveals Highly Overlapping Organization in Interconnected Systems" -. *Physical Review X*, *5*(1), 011027. doi:10.1103/PhysRevX.5.011027

De Domenico, M., & Porter, M. A. (2014). Muxviz: A tool for multilayer analysis and visualization of networks. *Journal of Complex Networks*, 1–18.

Dorigo, M., Birattari, M., & Stützle, T. (2006). Ant Colony Optimization – Artificial Ants as a Computational Intelligence Technique. *IEEE Computational Intelligence Magazine.*

Dorigo, M., & Socha, K. (2007). *An Introduction to Ant Colony Optimization. In T. F. Gonzalez (Ed.), Approximation Algorithms and Metaheuristics.* CRC Press.

Dorigo, M., & Stützle, T. (2002). The Ant Colony Optimization Metaheuristic: Algorithms, Applications, and Advances. In Handbook of Metaheuristics. Academic Press.

Falih, I., & Kanawati, R. (2015). Muna: A multiplex network analysis library. *The 2015 IEEE/ACM International Conference on Advances in Social Networks Analysis and Mining*, 757–760.

Fortunato, S. (2010). Community detection in graphs. *Physics Reports*, *486*(3-5), 75–174. doi:10.1016/j.physrep.2009.11.002

Freeman, L. (1979). Centrality in Social Networks: Conceptual Clarification. *Social Networks*, *1*(3), 215–239. doi:10.1016/0378-8733(78)90021-7

Gao, C., Lan, X., Zhang, X., & Deng, Y. (2013). A bio-inspired methodology of identifying influential nodes in complex networks. *PLoS One*, *8*(6), e66732. doi:10.1371/journal.pone.0066732 PMID:23799129

Girvan, M., & Newman, M. E. J. (2002). Community structure in social and biological networks. *Proceedings of the National Academy of Sciences of the United States of America*, *99*(12), 7821–7826. doi:10.1073/pnas.122653799 PMID:12060727

Gomez-Gardenes, Reinares, Arenas, & Mario Floria. (2012). Evolution of cooperation in multiplex networks. *Nature Scientific Reports, 2*, Article N. 620.

Haddad, O. B., Afshar, A., & Marino, M. A. (2006). Honey-Bees mating optimization (HBMO) algorithm: A new heuristic approach for water resources optimization. *Water Resources Management*, *20*(5), 661–680. doi:10.100711269-005-9001-3

Hargadon, A. B. (2002). Brokering Knowledge: Linking Learning and Innovation. In Research in Organizational Behavior (vol. 24). Greenwich, CT: JAI Press. doi:10.1016/S0191-3085(02)24003-4

Hmimida, M., & Kanawati, R. (2015). Community detection in multiplex networks: A seed-centric approach. *Networks and Heterogeneous Media*, *10*(1), 71–85. doi:10.3934/nhm.2015.10.71

Huang, X., Shao, S., Wang, H., Buldyrev, S. V., Stanley, H. E., & Havlin, S. (2013). The robustness of interdependent clustered networks. *Europhysics Letters*, *101*(1), 18002. doi:10.1209/0295-5075/101/18002

Imani, M. B. (2012). A new feature selection method based on ant colony and genetic algorithm on Persian font recognition. *International Journal of Machine Learning and Computing*, *2*(3), 1–5.

Jiang, B. (2006). Ranking spaces for predicting human movement in an urban environment. *International Journal of Geographical Information Science*, *23*(7), 823–837. doi:10.1080/13658810802022822

Karaboga, D., & Basturk, B. (2008). On the performance of artificial bee colony (ABC) algorithm. *Appl. Soft Comput. J.*, 687–697.

Katz, L. (1953). A New Status Index Derived from Sociometric Analysis. *Psychometrika*, *18*(1), 39–43. doi:10.1007/BF02289026

Kennedy, J., & Eberhart, R. C. (1995). Particle swarm optimization. *Proceedings of IEEE international conference on neural networks*, 1942–1948. 10.1109/ICNN.1995.488968

Kivela, M., Arenas, A., Barthelemy, M., Gleeson, J., Moreno, Y., & Porter, M. (2014). Multilayer networks. *Journal of Complex Networks*, *2*(3), 203–271. doi:10.1093/comnet/cnu016

Kuncheva, Z., & Montana, G. (2015). *Community detection in multiplex networks using locally adaptive random walks*. Retrieved from http://arxiv.org/abs/1507.01890

Lazer, D., Pentland, A., Adamic, L., Aral, S., Barabasi, A.-L., Brewer, D., ... Alstyne, M. V. (2009). Computational social science. *Science*, *323*(5915), 721–723. doi:10.1126cience.1167742 PMID:19197046

Leydesdorff, L. (2009). Betweenness centrality as an indicator of the interdis- ciplinarity of scientific journals. *Journal of the American Society for Information Science and Technology*, (9): 1303–1319.

Li, Z., & Jiang, Y. (2014). Cross-layers cascade in multiplex networks. *Proceedings of the International Conference on Autonomous Agents and Multi-agent Systems, ser. AAMAS '14*, 269–276.

Martin, T., Zhang, X., & Newman, M. E. J. (2014). Localization and centrality in networks. *Phys. Rev. E*, *90*(5), 052808. doi:10.1103/PhysRevE.90.052808 PMID:25493835

Mitchell, L. E. (2003). *Structural Holes, CEOs, and Informational Monopolies: The Missing Link in Corporate Governance*. Working paper. Law School, George Washington University.

Mittal, R., & Bhatia, M. P. S. (2017). Mining top-k structural holes in multiplex networks. *8th International Conference on Computing, Communication and Networking Technologies (ICCCNT)*, 1-6. 10.1109/ICCCNT.2017.8204129

Mittal, R., & Bhatia, M. P. S. (2018). Anomaly Detection in Multiplex Networks. *Procedia Computer Science, 125*, 609-616.

Newman, M. E. J. (2001). The Structure of Scientific Collaboration Networks. *Proceedings of the National Academy of Sciences of the United States of America*, *98*(2), 404–409. doi:10.1073/pnas.98.2.404 PMID:11149952

Newman, M. E. J. (2003). The structure and function of complex networks. *SIAM Review*, *45*(2), 167–256. doi:10.1137/S003614450342480

Newman, M. E. J. (2003). Fast algorithm for detecting community structure in networks. *Phys. Rev. E*, *69*(6), 066133. doi:10.1103/PhysRevE.69.066133 PMID:15244693

Newman, M. E. J. (2009). Random graphs with clustering. *Physical Review Letters*, *103*(5), 058701. doi:10.1103/PhysRevLett.103.058701 PMID:19792540

Nicosia, V., Bianconi, G., Latora, V., & Barthelemy, M. (2014). *Non- linear growth and condensation in multiplex networks*. Retrieved from http://arxiv.org/abs/1312.3683

Noh, J. D., & Rieger, H. (2004). Random Walks on Complex Networks. *Physical Review Letters, 92*(11), 118701. doi:10.1103/PhysRevLett.92.118701 PMID:15089179

Ohno, K., Esfarjani, K., & Kawazoe, Y. (1999). *Computational Materials Science: From Ab Initio to Monte Carlo Methods*. Berlin: Springer Verlag. doi:10.1007/978-3-642-59859-3

Pham, D. T., Soroka, A. J., Koc, E., Ghanbarzadeh, A., & Otri, S. (2007). Some Applications of the Bees Algorithm in Engineering Design and Manufacture. *Proceedings of International Conference On Manufacturing Automation (ICMA 2007)*.

Pujari, M., & Kanawati, R. (2015). Link prediction in multiplex networks. *Networks and Heterogeneous Media, 10*(1), 17–35. doi:10.3934/nhm.2015.10.17

Rivero, J., Cuadra, D., Calle, J., & Isasi, P. (2012). Using the ACO algorithm for path searches in social networks. *Applied Intelligence, 36*(4), 899–917. doi:10.100710489-011-0304-1

Seeley, T. D. (2009). *The Wisdom of Hive: The Social Physiology of Honey Bee Colonies*. Cambridge, MA: Harvard University Press.

Shao, S., Huang, X., Stanley, H. E., & Havlin, S. (2014). Robustness of a partially interdependent network formed of clustered networks. *Phys. Rev. E, 89*(3), 032812. doi:10.1103/PhysRevE.89.032812 PMID:24730904

Sola, L., Romance, M., Criado, R., Flores, J., del Amo, A. G., & Boccaletti, S. (2013). Eigenvector centrality of nodes in multiplex networks. *Chaos (Woodbury, N.Y.), 3*(033131). PMID:24089967

Valdez, L. D., Macri, P. A., Stanley, H. E., & Braunstein, L. A. (2013). Triple point in correlated interdependent networks. *Phys. Rev. E, 88*(5), 050803. doi:10.1103/PhysRevE.88.050803 PMID:24329204

Walton, S., Hassan, O., Morgan, K., & Brown, M. R. (2011). Modified cuckoo search: A new gradient-free optimization algorithm. *Chaos, Solitons, and Fractals, 44*(9), 710–718. doi:10.1016/j.chaos.2011.06.004

Watanabe, S., & Kabashima, Y. (2014, January). influences of intranetwork and internetwork degree-degree correlations. *Phys. Rev. E, 89*(1), 012808. doi:10.1103/PhysRevE.89.012808

Xiangnan Kong, P. Y., & Zhang, J. (2013). Inferring anchor links across multiple heterogeneous social networks. In CIKM, Burlingame, CA.

Yang. (2014). A Binary Cuckoo Search Algorithm for Feature Selection. *Studies in Computational Intelligence, 516*, 141–154.

Yang, X. S., & Deb, S. (2009). Cuckoo search via Lévy flights. In *World Congress on Nature Biologically Inspired Computing*. IEEE Publications. 10.1109/NABIC.2009.5393690

Yang, X. S., & Deb, S. (2010). Engineering optimization by cuckoo search. *International Journal of Mathematical Modeling and Numerical Optimization, 1*(4), 330–343. doi:10.1504/IJMMNO.2010.035430

Zhang, B., Zhong, S., Wen, K., Li, R., & Gu, X. (2013). Finding high–influence microblog users with an improved PSO algorithm. International Journal of Modelling. *Identification and Control, 18*(4), 349–356. doi:10.1504/IJMIC.2013.053540

Zhou, D., Stanley, H. E., D'Agostino, G., & Scala, A. (2012). Assortativity decreases the robustness of interdependent networks. *Phys. Rev. E, 86*(6), 066103. doi:10.1103/PhysRevE.86.066103 PMID:23368000

Chapter 13
Pedagogical Software Agents for Personalized E-Learning Using Soft Computing Techniques

Mukta Goyal
Jaypee Institute of Information Technology, India

Rajalakshmi Krishnamurthi
Jaypee Institute of Information Technology, India

ABSTRACT

Due to the emerging e-learning scenario, there is a need for software agents to teach individual users according to their skill. This chapter introduces software agents for intelligent tutors for personalized learning of English. Software agents teach a user English on the aspects of reading, translation, and writing. Software agents help user to learn English through recognition and synthesis of human voice and helps users to improve on handwriting. Its main objective is to understand what aspect of the language users wants to learn. It deals with the intuitive nature of users' learning styles. To enable this feature, intelligent soft computing techniques have been used.

INTRODUCTION

Agent is a computer programs that simulate a human relationship by doing something that another user can do for other user. Agent can be human, robot, software, pedagogical. A human agent has eyes, ears, and other organs for sensors; hands, legs, mouth, and other body parts for actuators (Russell & Norvig, 2003). A robotic agent has cameras and infrared range finders for sensors and various motors for actuators. The sensors for software agent are keystrokes, file contents, received network packages whereas displays on the screen, files, sent network packets act as actuators for software agent. Two common types of notions are also associated with the agent namely weak notion and strong notion. In generally,

DOI: 10.4018/978-1-5225-5852-1.ch013

the characteristic such as autonomy, social ability, reactivity and pro-activeness are considered to be as weak notion of the agent. Whereas belief, desire, intention are known as strong notion of the agent.

(Dincer, S., & Doganay, 2015) Pedagogical software agent along with computer-assisted instruction programs would enhance motivations among the learners. In order to increase the motivation level to the highest, these programs should be personalized. In this regard, Intelligent tutoring system (ITS) have been implemented with the use of artificial intelligence techniques. Here, the primary objective is to integrate the notion of co-operation to the teaching-learning process using multi-agents. Particularly, the focus is on techniques and methods that would allow users to work in a co-operative way taking into account external human agents and internal agents modelled in the machine (computer). Thus, intelligent software agent technology can be extended to intelligent tutoring systems in such way that the need for social context for learning can be fulfilled (Giraffa & Viccari, 1998).

Pedagogical agent software need to model, the knowledge and human pedagogical behaviour, correctly. In addition it has to model non-instructional behaviour as well. For example, the societal norms and values for acceptable behaviours also have to be considered. (Sun, & Zhang, 2009) Pedagogical agent system also can be regarded as information delivery or as a social event. It is observed that, pedagogical agents have the potential to broaden the bandwidth of social communication between computers and students and increase student engagement and motivation.

This chapter introduces a pedagogical agent that teaches English Language to users, based on the aspects of reading, translation and writing. This requires a mixture of three domain areas like artificial intelligence, image processing and speech processing. According to John McCarthy (2004) artificial intelligence is the science and engineering of making intelligent machines, especially intelligent computer programs. It is related to the similar task of using computers to understand human intelligence, but Artificial Intelligence does not have to confine itself to methods that are biologically observable. Therefore, Artificial Intelligence is an important part of pedagogical agent as it deals with teaching a human and making it an automated task, which was earlier done by human tutors.

Similarly, Speech Processing is a branch of Artificial Intelligence. It mainly comprises of speech recognition and speech synthesis by the machines. Further, Machine Translation (MT) is also integrated with speech processing to devise Speech-to-Speech Translation Systems (S2ST).

Speech processing mechanism consists of the following categories within it:

- Speech recognition which deals with analysis of the linguistic content of a speech signal.
- Recognition that aims to recognize the identity of the speaker.
- Speech coding is a specialized form of data compression.
- Voice analysis for medical purposes.
- Speech synthesis is an artificial synthesis of speech, usually computer-generated speech.

Another aspect of pedagogical agent is Image Processing. Basic definition of Image processing is that, it is a form of signal processing for which the input is an image, such as a photograph or video frame; the output of image processing may be either an image or, a set of characteristics or parameters related to the image. This chapter focus on character recognition from images in order to improve one's handwriting. The input image is captured from the webcam and then image is processed. Based on image processing techniques, handwriting of user is analysed and then guidance is provided to improve the handwriting. With the current state-of-art, the large number and variety of languages and the increasingly global nature of life, the human interests in learning natural languages is drastically increasing. Interestingly, the common reasons that motivate people to learn a new language include: befriending with a location and people around; getting well-versed in one's mother tongue, understanding culture of a particular area etc.

Hence, in this fast moving world there is more and more demand of educational systems which enable just-in-time learning, on demand learning, any time learning and lifelong learning. The traditional classroom learning does not adequately meet these demands and also faces challenges such as location, time constraints etc. In this chapter, pedagogical agent is represented as an automated and intelligent system for language learning. The agent teaches English Language to the user along with support for handwriting, translation, reading assistance and phonetics.

This chapter introduces the following modules:

Handwriting Improver and Helper

This module implements the optical character recognition to help the user, develop skills in handwriting and improve it. Image processing is used for this purpose. The user is asked to write on a white paper and then image will be captured by the camera. Each sentence is broken into words and each word is broken into alphabets. Each alphabet is being analysed using pre-structured alphabets. Based on the image processing analysis, the improvements will be suggested to the intended learner.

Speech Translation From Hindi to English

This module translates the speech inputs from one language and it gives the translated audio outputs in another language. The grammar is used for Speech to Speech Translation (S2ST) and Machine Translation. For instance, when the user gives command to the system, to translate the sentence into English and then system would response with the synthesized speech output for the translated sentence. For example:

If user speaks in Hindi: "Main ghar ja raha hu."

Then system will respond as: "I am going home."

Reading Assistance

This module assist the user to read via taking his speech inputs and tell him whether he is going right or wrong or will interrupt him in between of his speech. In this case, the system requires timer to know when and where the user is getting trouble.

Phonetics Learning

This module helps the user to develop proper pronunciation and phonetics, through listening and speaking the same. It would be a user interactive module as it depends which set of sentence the user would like to listen to in order to be more fluent and proficient in speaking English.

Next section describes the related work on pedagogical agent systems.

RELATED WORK

Window 7 has a tool which takes speech as input and the break it down into commands that are used by the system (Gu et.al., 2006). There are other medium also which provide learning for different languages. Marathi Mitra is a website which teaches spoken "Marathi" language. English is used as the supporting language of instruction. It is mainly for those who know English and desire to learn Marathi. It introduces a separate pronunciation key for Marathi. The course content covers vocabulary in various categories (general and advanced), basic grammar for Marathi language, day to day expressions, few conversations. Almost all the language constructs are associated with audio files (Hashimoto et.al., 2011). CHAMELEON is a speech recognizing and synthesizing tool used to ask questions to the chameleon and it replies to user back again(Nakamura, 2009). LAURENBOT is an online chat bot that uses speech synthesis to reply to whatever user type. It takes input from typed information processes it using AI and then synthesise the speech to reply to user (Rane, 2005).

Windows Vista and Windows 7 include personalization features that learn a user's writing patterns and/or vocabulary for English, Japanese, Chinese Traditional, Chinese Simplified and Korean. The features include a "personalization wizard" that prompts for samples of a user's handwriting and uses them to retrain the system for higher accuracy recognition (Sakti, et.al., 2009). A Tablet PC is a special notebook computer that is outfitted with a digitizer tablet, and allows a user to handwrite text on the unit's screen (Rahman et.al., 2010). The operating system recognizes the handwriting and converts it into typewritten text. It is an Open Source handwriting recognition program written for Linux. It was developed by Michael Levin. Cell Writer is designed to be writer-dependent, so input training is required prior to use. It includes an English word-recognition engine to aid recognition accuracy, an on-screen keyboard and the ability to fine tune or correct mistakes through a context menu(Xiang, B., Deng, Y., & Gao, Y. (2008).

A create text message application in HTC phone outfitted with a stylus allows a user to handwrite text on its screen and recognizes the text to generate the characters and hence the message(Kavallieratos et.al.,1997). Siri is a personal assistant application for iOS. The application uses natural language processing to answer questions, make recommendations, and perform actions by delegating requests to an expanding set of web services. Siri claims that the software adapts to the user's individual preferences over time and personalizes results, as well as accomplishing tasks such as making dinner reservations and reserving a cab(Begel and Graham, 2005). Siri was originally introduced as an iOS application available in the Application Store. Siri was acquired by Apple Inc. on April 28, 2010. Siri had announced that their software would be available for BlackBerry and for Android-powered phones, but all development efforts for non-Apple platforms were cancelled after Apple's purchase. Siri is now an integrated part of iOS 5, and available only on the iPhone 4S, launched in October 2011.

Speech to Speech translation System (S2ST) comprises of speech recognition, machine translation & speech synthesis. The impact of speech recognition errors on machine translation is alleviated by using N-best list or word lattice output from the speech recognition component as input to the machine translation component. Consequently, these approaches can improve the performance of S2ST significantly. Weighted finite state transducers and Re-Rank sentence from N- best output is used for quality of synthesized speech. This system is *HiFST*: a hierarchical phrase-based system implemented with weighted finite-state transducers. Evaluators listened to speech & assigned score for following categories based on naturalness WER- Word Error Rate. Five Point Mean Opinion Score-TTS, S2ST-Adequacy,S2ST-Fluency,MT-Adequacy,MT-Fluency.There is an important phenomenon on Llewelyn reaction. It is that evaluators perceive lower speech quality when the sentences are less fluent or the content of the sentences is less natural, even if the actual quality of synthesized speech is same the naturalness and intelligibility of the synthesized speech are strongly affected by the fluency of sentences. It is well known in the field of machine translation that the fluency of translated sentences can be improved by using long-span word-level N-Gram (Hashimoto et.al., 2011). Noise Suppression technique notably improves speech recognition performance. The corpus based approach followed in this paper is that it gives wide coverage, robustness & portability to new languages and domains. Minimum Mean Square Error (MMSE) and a particle filter are introduced for suppression interference and noise. MDL-SSS is an algorithm that automatically determines the appropriate number of parameters according to the size of the training data based on the Maximum Description Length criterion. A phase based statistical machine translations (SMT) and Expectation & Maximum Algorithm (EM) are explained. EM matches a given source sentence against the source language parts of translation examples. If an exact match is achieved, the corresponding target language sentence will be output. To realize connections between internal and external speech-to-speech translation resources (e.g. speech recognition, machine translation, speech synthesis servers of other language / language pairs), it defines a first draft of Machine Translation Markup Language(STML) and implemented web services using STML(Nakamura, 2009). The authors has discussed about two classes of users: Foreign Visitors and Indian new to language. Authors have also discussed two types of models such as traditional models where primary sources are books, magazine etc. to create courses by a native expert. They start with script of the language and pronunciations of syllabus. Secondly, the web based educational System: these systems exploit various advantages of internet such as unlimited temporal and special access to learning. Unlike paper-based, online content can also incorporate multimedia such as audio, video flash.

A hybrid data drivenMT system is developed with the combination of statistical machine translation (SMT), example based MT (EBMT and rule based (RBMT) to increase the fluency, accuracy and grammatical precision which improve the quality of a machine translation system(Dhariya, Malviya, & Tiwary, 2017).

Intelligent Tutoring System (ITS), is customized according to learner's requirement of how and what to learn. In general, E-learning for language learning has three main important points. Firstly, the Pedagogical Principles which is based on Technology-Pedagogy co-operation of a web based computer assisted language learning (CALL) including practice, learner orientation and motivation, changing role of teacher, situation based learning and written vs. spoken. Secondly, Technological Advances such as internet adaptation. It helps in tracking user's behaviour. Thirdly, Computer Aided Language Learning or (CALL). In India not much works/literatures are available on use of CALL. For example, Devanagiri Script Tutor (DST) teaches recognizing and writing Devanagiri script. Similar, Intelligent Tutoring System (ITS) teaches Marathi and addressing most of the pedagogical principles of language learning with the target audience for those who want to learn conversational or spoken Marathi. Architecture of an intelligent tutoring system has an expert model (EM), student model (SM), and instruction model (IM). The EM represents the domain knowledge. The SM represents updation and reasoning with student module. The IM modules control the representation of instructional knowledge. Finally, the implementation Modules comprises of authentication module, introduction and pronunciation module, basic vocabulary module, expression module, conversational module, examination module and instructional module. Intelligent CALL (ICALL) is based on traditional CALL model, along with the additional, intelligence component. Such a system delivers instruction to a student based on his knowledge level in the language. Learn Indian language (LILA) through AI, says that by using the tracer board provided in the software the user will be able to trace each alphabet of Hindi and simultaneously listen to pronunciation of alphabet that is being traced (Rane, 2005) . English is used as support language. The courseware is represented in form of different lessons. A pronunciation key is converted into basic vocabulary. Then this basic vocabulary is converted into an expression and then expression is converted into a conversation. In many dimensions improvement can be done for richer & more comprehensive learning experience. Mechanisms for continuous monitoring should be implemented. There should be inclusion of more extensive vocabulary. Asian Speech Translation Advanced Research (A – STAR) includes Spoken language technology servers, Speech Translation Mark-up Language (STML) servlet, Client application, Communication server. This machine translation system acts as an engine for all combinations of language pair. As for the TTS engine, the English, Japanese and Chinese Speech synthesis engines are developed. Deals with root word Bangla sentences. The root word is to be translated from Bangla to English sentence. To be noted that, the Machine Translation is one classified area of natural language processing (NLP).English sentences have fixed structure. If structure changes meaning also changes. However, in Bangla most of the time, this is not true. The Paper uses fixed database instead of morphological analysis. Structural Differences can include placement of subject, object and verb or english fixed position for the words have certain meaning or modifiers position differ in Bangla and English. Six test cases has been analysed the work of our proposed architecture for machine translation of Bangla to English. The machine translation system for Bangla is capable of translating Bangla sentences into English. Particularly, where the affirmative sentences are in indefinite and present continuous tenses are considered. The Product is based on strong dictionary (Rahman et. al.,2010). Some of the authors focus on domain source language data available example audio transcripts. They have translated the source language with current baseline system. Then select the translation hypothesis and add to original corpus. They utilize the untranslated source data. Instead of retraining the system from scratch, phrase table is built with selected data entry only. The amount of source language data is relatively large, we may also incrementally select them to improve translation model (Xiang et.al.,2008). It involves a reading system that is capable of extracting the handwritten part of the text from common application forms and recognizing the alpha numeric upper-case characters. The feature extraction algorithm has been applied which leads to a very fast recognition. The system recognizes 60 alphanumeric characters (26 English upper-case letters, 24 Greek upper-case letters and 10 digits). Firstly the application form is scanned and the handwritten parts are found, separated and transformed into matrices with binary values (0s for the black and 1s for the white ones). Then area of each character is finding in the matrix through character segmentation part. Then comes the feature extraction part in which each character is divided vertically so that their primitive features are visible. Then a left-to-right hidden Markov model is applied for the recognition procedure (Kavallieratos,et.al.,1997). Authors have discussed the verbalization of the programming language. It can be very helpful for the programmers who suffer from repetitive stress injuries and find difficult to spend long amounts of time typing the code. Spoken programs contain lexical, syntactic and ambiguities that do not appear in written programs. Other than that it would be very difficult for a programmer to edit the program text. So spell each word or describe the text may be very tedious. Programming languages are also structured differently from natural languages to be much more precise and mathematical. Surveys were done on people who knew java and who do not. Spoken programs are hard to write down. Similarly written codes are hard to speak. Various voice code commands are designed which can be interpreted as the java code lines. A speech based program can be made that can use the program analysis to disambiguate what the programmer said and enable programming by voice(Begel and Graham, 2005). A novel learning OCR model has been proposed which is capable to learn from input samples constantly and optimize the reference patterns set. The concept behind the learning algorithm is based on taking a short and long-term memory and a ranking mechanism which manages the transition of reference patterns between two memories (Ahmadi et.al., 2006). Later an optimization algorithm is also applied for optimizing the reference vector's magnitude and their distribution. A reading device is used to capture the text data and input it to the system via an I/O port. Pipelining architecture is used to pre-process the data parallel. Then a searching process on the reference patterns memory is applied to classify it to the correct class. A learning unit is designed to learn the new unknown patterns and optimize the present reference patterns. Simultaneously data registering through pipelines is being done with some intermediate memory. A handwritten character recognition system without feature extraction using an off-line neural network has been introduced for classifying/recognizing 26 English alphabets. The accuracy of the same has also been calculated and is found to be better than a recognition system with feature extraction. Firstly, image acquisition is done through any scanner or digital camera. Then image pre-processing is done. It is a series of algorithms for linearization, edge detection, dilation and filling. The final pre-processed image at this segmented stage is a sequence of characters. It is decomposed into sub-image of individual characters and each individual character is uniformly resized into 30*20 pixels. The neural classifier with two hidden layers and one output and input layer then classifies the resized characters of 600 pixels (Pradeep et.al.,2011). A set of algorithms have been introduced by author that can test the readability of OCR algorithms by impairing characters using different types of damage. It also introduces several methods of studying the effects of damages on OCR algorithms and determining the damages in percentage. There are several types of damages that can occur to a character on a silicon wafer. There can be a black damage in a silicon wafer which occurs when there is a large variation if intensity on the character or the white damage which comes when either the actual wafer is damaged if the light reflected is at an unfavourable angle. The algorithm starts from the leftmost point; starts increasing the damage till the characters are not recognizable and calculate the position and width of the damage. This also tells the most damage possible starting at that location in which the network can still read a character successfully. Once the character is so much damaged that it is not recognizable, it then restores the last line of bits. A random damage can occur in cases when the background is too much bright and the network becomes confused for what's white and what's black. Minimum character damage can be found by an algorithm which takes each character and counts different pixels with every other character. It then moves on to the next character and finds the difference of each other character. The one with the least difference in pixels is the one closest resembling to the character (Desrochers and Saengdeejing, 2001). The system for mobile can be very useful in quick translation of foreign words, store notes space efficiently from lecture slides or notice boards or as a tool for visually challenged people. The system was implemented in Symbianc++ and tested on a NOKIA phone. The work shows the feasibility of an OCR system on a portable camera mobile phone without relying on external resources such as a server computer or specialized image processing hardware. Prior to this work there were mobile OCR systems which were not published and marketed only in South Korea and were poorly documented and focused on feature extraction and classification only. Either they were used previously captured images for processing or they captures images and sends them to an external server for the actual OCR processing. The data undergoes four preparative stages before the actual recognition of characters. In image capturing and pre-processing stage, colored images are converted to grey scale image by simple addition of the tristimulus (RGB) values and division by three. Then global linearization was used as a pre-processing operation. The next stage, segmentation can be completed using skew angle detection and X-Y Tree decomposing. In skew angle detection, fast algorithms are used to find approximation of the skew angle and then a slow algorithm is used to test the few approximate angles found by the fast algorithm. The X-Y tree decomposition is another segmentation algorithm which uses projections to separate text lines and individual characters. The gaps between lines of text as well as individual characters can easily be found from horizontal and vertical projections. The whole image is projected in the direction of the skew angle, and then the baselines are found along with their x-height, ascent and descent measures. There are three types of locations/classes. Type G are gap locations which are between the text lines, type N are near the actual body which is the thickest part, and type B belongs to the actual body of characters from baseline to the top of x-height. Each character is extracted into a small rectangular raster whose width and height is ascent descent. At each starting location, the algorithm starts to record pixels into the raster, until all pixels of a connected component are recorded. After the termination of this process, the rest of the raster is filled with zeroes. In the next stage, feature extraction, the centroid-to-boundary distance features are used to quickly obtain a great simplified feature vector from a character image. The system then classifies it by comparing it to the stored feature vectors representing all the used characters. It allows location and size invariant recognition to be performed very easily (Laine and Nevalainen, 2006). Arabic language is written with 28 different characters, most of the characters take different shape. Unlike English there are sub-words in Arabic. Each word can have 1 or more sub-words. Pre-processing is required before the actual text recognition because of the factors like quality and uniformity of the text. Features like loops, dots, branches are more important than the statistical features in latin characters which include characteristics like pixel densities, invariant moments etc. Recognition algorithms like Hidden Markov Models (HMMs) and Neural Networks (NNs) may be applied on individual characters or on complete words. HMMs usually model single-dimensional sequences of data and are composed of states and transition probabilities. Neural Networks are composed of different layers of interconnected, computing nodes. Different sets of input values when passed through the layers produce different outputs. The efficiency and speed of hardware based OCR is much greater than the traditional software only methods (Beg, et.al., 2010). In the algorithm mentioned in the paper, the scanned grey scale image is read into an image matrix which is converted into a monochromatic image matrix. Pixel values are assigned 0 for black points and 255 for white points. The searching is done from top and the topmost point is found, then all the characters linked to that point are given the same value. Then a search from bottom to top is used to find the lowest point of that first word through its assigned value. Similarly using a left and right search method neural network the leftmost and rightmost point of the first word can be found out. The word can then be extracted and stored in a different matrix. There are four artificial neural networks used. Each neural network consists of an input layer, three hidden layers and an output layer. The output layer consists of 26 neurons since there are 26 alphabets that are to be identified. The outputs of these four artificial neural networks are fed into the genetic algorithm which chooses the best solution for the recognized alphabet. A "1" is set at the index of the characters that has been recognized. The number of 1s at the output of each neural network is calculated. The one with the minimum number of 1s is selected and the characters corresponding to the index of those 1s are shortlisted. The values are then sent to the fitness function for the computation of correlation coefficient of the selected indexes. If the correlation coefficient is less than a defined threshold value 0.50, the step is repeated for a different training set. And if the value is very low for example less than 0.3, then discard the indexes. The index which has the maximum correlation coefficient is selected with the input matrix and the selected character is given as the output (Kala, et.al., 2010). In this paper the need of computer grammar have been demonstrated. Computer grammar has been designed for the structural representations (SRs) of the sentences.

It presents the design of one of the versatile computer grammar to understand efficiently most of the possible syntactical constructs of compound-complex, multiple compound, and multiple-complex English sentences. Two major problems were faced – to discover simple and revealing computer grammar for natural languages and to create versatile structures based on the study of syntactical constructs of the language under consideration. There are two basic motivations for the properly formulated grammar that is able to identify and understand correct sentences of the language. Cognitive science or linguistic motivation has a better understanding of communication using a natural language and technical motivation to design and create intelligent computer systems that is capable of automatic machine translation, text analysis, providing natural language interface to a database, computer aided instruction etc. There is natural language required for the communication either by listening or by writing. Authors has discussed the category of mathematical logic and formal languages to specify a method of language comprehension to such a level of details that an efficient system programmer could convert the developed grammar into a computer program which can understand and produce the details of English language sentences. Compound-complex, multiple-compound and multiple-compound and multiple-complex English sentences are analysed as available in various literature of English language. Then, the design of the structural representations of all kinds of compound sentences has been framed as per the syntactic construction of these sentences. According to the structural design, the computer grammar is designed to understand the English sentences using the Context Free Grammar (CFG) or Backus Naur Form (BNF) notations. This may be used to increase the level of automation in already existing automated industries. This grammar may be used in further empowering the existingtext processing software packages with capability of checking and correcting all kinds of English sentences available in the literature of English language and may also be used in the design of speech recognition and synthesis system to make the system more powerful and robust(Jaiswal et.al., 2009).The author focuses on the improvement of listening comprehension as it can do good to the other three basic skills of speaking, reading and writing as well as lay a good foundation for the development of student's English communication skills. The most important step in it is to improve the pronunciation. Chinese students have a very prominent and long-term-existed problem in English learning due to their inaccurate pronunciation, which is a basis for learning a language. The inaccurate pronunciation can be classified into several types. Some are caused by carelessness which can be avoided. They are generally caused due to the similarity of one or more words in pronunciation yet having different meanings. The other types are difficult to be corrected. They are caused by the different accents of the students or by the wrong gasping of the International Phonetic Alphabet. At present, multi-media teaching is a definite trend in modern education and has both pros and cons. From the advantage point of view, it allows teachers to control the entire class by using a small mouse and allows students to hear more Standard English. Meanwhile students can see immediately what they have just heard when needed, all this can be done only by clicking on the mouse. From the disadvantages point of view, students listen to the dialogues and passages in class. Improvement of English listening comprehension means not just the improvement of listening, but it actually represents the improvement of comprehensive English ability, that is, improvement in pronunciation, vocabulary, phrases, idioms, and translation (Rubin, 1994). English is one of the most widely spoken languages in the world these days. A phrase reordering approach is incorporated in machine translation system for making translation easier. The objective of natural language processing is to design and build computer based systems that have ability to read, analyse, understand and generate required results and inferences from given language scenario into text form. Three phases can be seen for the machine translation - analysis of source language to choose appropriate target language lexical item for each source language, reordering phrase where the chosen target language string, and disambiguation of word sense where the correct meaning of words is chosen for translation. A lexical analyser is required in the first step which is breaking input text into individual syllabic words or token and define the limit of word boundary. A rule-based algorithm is designed to read the input text. The aim of proposed reordering model that can be incorporated into the statistical machine translation system (SMTS) and working steps of reordering model and how source language reordering model can assist machine translation system. Chunking divides text into segments which correspond to a certain syntactic units such as noun phrases, verb phrases etc. The approach is a rule base one and context free grammar (CFG) rules as the base for chunking and heuristics rules were used to identify subject, object and indirect object for each verb which is not an auxiliary. Scanning and tokenization are the first step of natural language processing (NLP) applications and to identify a word boundary of Myanmar text. Deterministic Finite Automaton (DFA) which may be implemented as a lexical analyser generator in JAVACC and Visible Markov Chain (VMC) algorithm, which was used to perform the checking of a word which is already in the language or not. Statistical Natural Language processing methods are popular because one does not have to spend a long time learning and discovering all the rule of a language. In this system, the input Myanmar sentence is tokenized, segmented and tagged with POS and then this sentence is translated to English sentence generation. The system produces proper English sentences as output. Machine translation engine can be classified according to the architecture of machine translation system: Transformer architecture i.e. direct and Linguistic Knowledge i.e. indirect architecture are the main idea that input sentences can be transformed into output sentences by carrying out the simplest possible parse, replacing source word with their target language equivalents as specified in a bilingual dictionary. They roughly re-arrange their order to suit the rules of the target language. The linguistic knowledge architecture is translation from source language to target language based on linguistic knowledge base. The three steps in the Linguistic knowledge architecture: the first, analysis step involves using the parser and the source grammar to analyse the source input text. The second, transfer step involves changing the underlying representation of a target sentence. The third, synthesis step and final major step involves changing the underlying target representation into a target sentence, using a generator and the target language grammar. The proposed algorithm is created reordering algorithm. The raw English sentence from translation process will be reordered by using English grammar rules. The translated sentence is entered as input sentence in the system that is not ordering. The systems are reordered and add appropriate article word and then produced the correct English sentence by using English grammar rule (SVO) for simple sentence (Win, 2011). Authors have attempt to illustrate a central role that knowledge representation can play to automate intelligent tutoring system design and implementation. A Diagnosis, Interaction and Treatment (DIT) model has been proposed. The system relies upon a knowledge representation system whose structured encoding of English lexical information makes it possible to initiate the relevant dialogue with learners when the system is not sure about learner's intentions, trigger the appropriate lexical knowledge based on their responses, and automatically generate practice and test exercises based on this knowledge. DIT is responsible for sentence parsing, lexical errors checking, triggering of clarification dialogue in case of ambiguity, grammar aids and automatic generation of exercises from the dictionary's structured knowledge. InfoMap is ontology with tree-like structure. Nodes in Infomap are either concept nodes or function nodes. Concept nodes represent entities, attributes, states, events etc. and function nodes show how the concepts are interconnected. The DIT model for lexical errors provides an open writing environment. The input window has no length limitation. Algorithms for identifying specific error types and accessing the relevant information are stored as scripts. The information on the dialogue window is extracted and the semantic dialogue guides the student to choose what he intended to write. DIT can be extended to address grammatical, syntactic and semantic errors (Hsieh,et.al., 2002).

Direct Machine Translation System provides direct translation without using any intermediate representation. It uses a bilingual dictionary for the word by word translation. Firstly identification of root words is done by removing suffixes from source language words. Then, dictionary look up is done to get the target language words/morphemes. Finally word order is changed to match with the target language. Transfer based machine translation method has three modules, the first analysis module produces source language structure. The second transfer module transfers the source language structure representation to the target language representation. The final generation module generates target language using target language structure. The major approach in Interlingua based machine translation is defining a universal interlingua which preserves the meaning of a sentence (Nair and David 2012).This is an effective way of handling differences between source and target languages in statistical machine translation systems. Initially the parse tree of the sentence of the source language is made and a probabilistic model is set up which assigns probabilities to trees such that the word order in trees which are assigned higher probability match the order of words in the target language. The model involves two assumptions: Firstly the children of a node are ordered independently of all other nodes and secondly the reordering at a particular node is dependent only on the label of its children. For each sentence with a parse tree we find the tree that makes the given alignment for that sentence pair most monotone. The average position of words in the target sentence that are aligned to the set of words that are descendants to each node in the tree of the source language is thus calculated. If a word is not aligned to any target word, it's left from the mean position. For each node in the tree, the tree is transformed by sorting the list of children of each node according to the average position of words of the target language (Visweswariah et.al., 2010). Authors has described two different approaches for describing syntactic structure, Dependency Structure (DS) and phrase structure (PS) have been explained. In a phrase structure all and only the leaf nodes are labelled with words from the sentence, while interior nodes are labelled with non-terminal labels, i.e. it groups consecutive words hierarchically into phrases. In a dependency structure all nodes are labelled with words from the sentence, i.e. it represents syntactic dependency as a syntactic relation.

In Hindi language there are at the most two arguments which are called subject and object in English. The realization of case of these two arguments is not lexically dependent. In Prop Bank the arguments of the verb in the transitive structure receive semantic role labels. In Phase structure, the two arguments are structurally distinguished using node labels and thus no functional tags are used to identify the two arguments (Palmeret.al., 2009).

For Speech to Speech translation we need Automated Speech Recognition (ASR), Machine Translation (MT), Natural Language Understanding (NLU), Natural Language Generation (NLG) and Text To Speech (TTS) as shown in Figure 1.

A particle filter is to be introduced for suppressing interference and noise.To realize connection between internal and external speech to speech translation resources, a draft of Markup language is used as shown in Figure 2.

Each Asian Speech Translation Advanced Research(A-STAR) module: automatic speechrecognition (ASR), machine translation (MT), and text-tospeech(TTS) through Web servers are shown in Figure 3.

Structural differences can be shown due to the placement of subject, object, noun and verbs. Figure 4 shows root word detection technique.

Figure 1. Speech to speech translation process

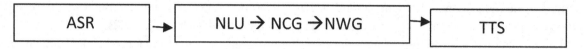

Figure 2. System Architecture

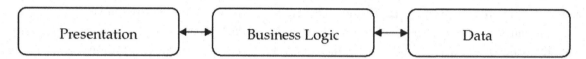

Figure 3. Text to speech translation

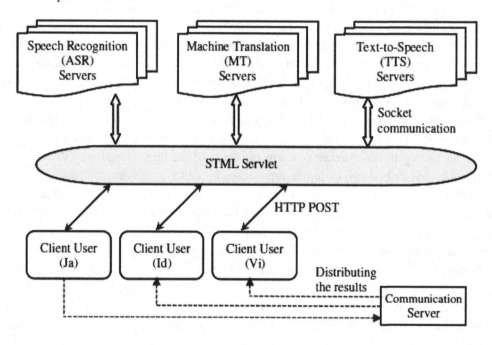

The two major issues in a Machine Translation System are accuracy of translation and speed. Accuracy-wise, smart tools for handling transfer grammar and translation standards including equivalent words, expressions, phrases and styles in the target language are to be developed. The grammar should be optimized with a view to obtaining a single correct parse and hence a single translated output. Speed-wise, innovative use of corpus analysis, efficient parsing algorithm, design of efficient Data Structure and run-time frequency-based rearrangement of the grammar which substantially reduces the parsing and generation. A fully automatic Machine translation system should have different modules such as Morphological analyzer, Part of speech tagger, Chunker, Named entity recognizer, Word sense disambiguator, Syntactic transfer module and Target word generator. A comparison between different translations schemes are given below.

Figure 4. Root Word Detection

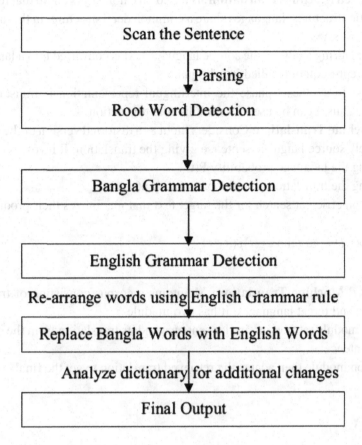

1. **Direct Machine Translation Systems:** Provide direct translation, without using any intermediate representation. This is done on a word by word translation using a bilingual dictionary followed by some syntactic arrangement. Steps:
   a. Identification of root words by removing suffixes from source language words.
   b. dictionary look up to get the target language words/morphemes.
   c. word order is changed to match with the target language.
2. **Transfer Based Machine Translation:** Involves parsing of input text to get the structure of the input sentence. It has three modules:
   a. Analysis module produces source language structure.
   b. Transfer module transfers the source language structure representation to a target language representation.
   c. Generation module: generates target language text using target language structure.

English structure Hindi structure
VP->V NP VP->NP
V PP-> P NP PP-> NP P
VG->ADV V VG->V ADV

3. **Interlingua Based Machine Translation:** Is based on Chomsky''s claim that regardless of varying surface syntactic structures, languages share a common deep structure. In this approach translation is a two step process:
    a. **Analysis:** During analysis, the source language text is converted into a language independent meaning representation called interlingua.
    b. **Synthesis:** In synthesis phase the interlingual representation is translated into any target language. Thus it can be used for multilingual translation.
4. **Statistical Machine Translation:** Considers input as a distorted version of the target language and finds most likely source language sentence giving the translation. It involves three steps:
    a. Estimating the language probability P(t) .
    b. Estimating the translational model probability p(s/t) .
    c. Devising an efficient search for the target text that maximizes their product.

$$P(s,t) = \arg\max_t p(s,t) = \arg\max_t p(t)p(s\,/\,t)$$

5. **Example Based Machine Translation:** Maintains a corpus consisting of translation examples between source and target languages. It has two modules:
    a. Retrieval module retrieves a similar sentence and its translation from the corpus for the given source sentence.
    b. Adaptation module then adapts the retrieved translation to get the final corrected translation.

METHODOLOGY

This section explains the method to teach English to the user in each and every aspect of it. The motive is to improve user's knowledge in English in terms of speaking, understanding, writing, reading and listening. There are four modules namely Phonetic Learning, Speech Translation to English, Reading Assistance and Handwriting Improver.

The main page consist a click button to proceed to Phonetic Learning. After accessing that page user access a new window frame where user ask to enter the text which he/she wants to hear phonetically correct. Any text entered by the user is speech synthesized by the system. The user has to speak something in Hindi whenever he/she proceed from Speech Translation to English. The corresponding speech is synthesized by the system using spoken words into English text. A help is provided by the reading assistance, after writing the text in text area, if needed. If user finds any difficulty in reading any words, the system identifies those words with the help of a timer. The speech is synthesized where the user faced the problem.

Handwriting skills are improved by writing few sentences on the white sheet. Image of written text is captured by the camera. The characters are recognized by the system. System is provided specialized tips to improve that word/alphabet. The intuitive nature of user speech and writing style is recorded. Accuracy is taken into prime consideration while the task of recognition is been established on the text written by any user. Further the accuracy is enhanced by using the training data sets of various users and then training the system via those stored database entries and then précising the recognition process through it. The time is depending on the total time to speak, and write or upload a handwritten image.

These four modules are independent of each other. A validity check is applied to all four modules to smooth function of all modules. The exact sequences of the operations are: *speech to speech translation* where Hindi spoken words, Hindi Text, Hindi Text to English Text, English Text to English Speech are synthesized. In a module called *Phonetic learning, when* a user inputs the text, it translates the text in to English Speech synthesis. Figure 5. shows the different module where user can enter into different part of the system.

A code written in java *For Reading Assistance:* user pastes text to read, timer on, user reads, English Speech synthesis. The effects of different parameters are analyzed on the basis of speech to speech. Performance requirements involves, the analysis for the performance of the various modules i.e. how successfully the operation takes place, performance of the response time of the system in interpreting and recognizing a particular context based sketch. This specifies the logical requirements for any information that is to be placed into a database.

IMPLEMENTATION AND RESULT

To implement this application Net Beans IDE and Netbeans Platform has been used. The Jar files formed can be used in Androids and other mobile devices supporting Java to make the application reliable at the time of delivery. For security purposes specific data related to the objects and information should be stored and communications between some areas of the program is restricted such as restricting the database access from the user and allow him to perform only certain functions. To ease the maintenance of the software, modularity is taken into consideration and separate modules like phonetic learning,

Figure 5. Proposed pedagogical software agent based e-learning tool

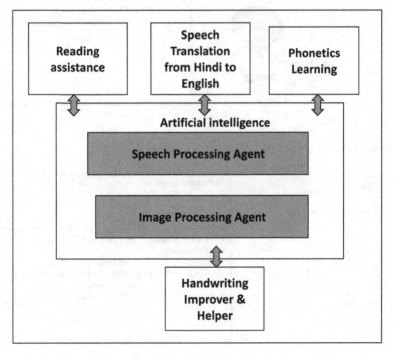

speech recognition, speech synthesis and handwriting improver is involved. The user interfaces for the input via mouse events is maintained. The application can easily be portable to PDAs and other hand held devices in classrooms, seminars, meetings, etc, as JAVA has been used as a language for development of the application. Figure 6. shows the graphical interface code for handwriting recognition software agent. This is the main class which calls the constructor of the main GUI via which whole project is operated. Figure 7. shows the module to enter the text and to perform speech recognition.

The project uses application programmable interface with which we parse our translations using JSON object. The json object is like XML format which stores data in form of cookies as given in Figure 8. The handwritten is processed into speech as shown in Figure 9.

Java language provides try and catch block for handling exceptions generate by run time environment. Various file handling, input output I/O exception, null Pointer exception error, FileNotFoundException, IOException, InterruptedException etc.Various errors occur in dealing with recognition and synthesis in Java and sometimes the code gets hanged up.

FUTURE ISSUES

Stability is one of the main issues. With the continuous advancement of technology, it would be difficult to keep up with the changing requirements of the user in terms of new voices to recognize and synthesize. It requires regular feedback and suggestions by the user. The software is generally for high performance

Figure 6. Graphical interface code

Figure 7. Different modules to enter text

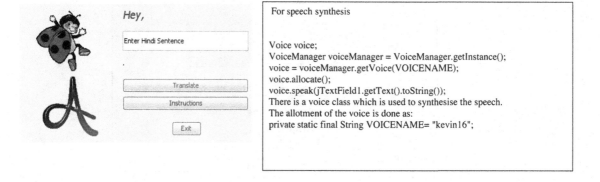

Figure 8. Translation of speech

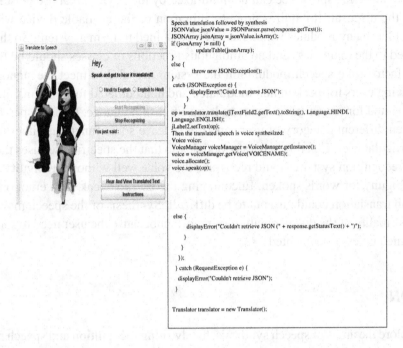

```
Speech translation followed by synthesis
JSONValue jsonValue = JSONParser.parse(response.getText());
JSONArray jsonArray = jsonValue.isArray();
if (jsonArray != null) {
          updateTable(jsonArray);
}
else {
          throw new JSONException();
}
catch (JSONException e) {
       displayError("Could not parse JSON");
    }
op = translator.translate(jTextField2.getText().toString(), Language.HINDI,
Language.ENGLISH);
jLabel2.setText(op);
Then the translated speech is voice synthesized:
Voice voice;
VoiceManager voiceManager = VoiceManager.getInstance();
voice = voiceManager.getVoice(VOICENAME);
voice.allocate();
voice.speak(op);



else {
        displayError("Couldn't retrieve JSON (" + response.getStatusText() + ")");
    }
  }
});
} catch (RequestException e) {
   displayError("Couldn't retrieve JSON");
}


Translator translator = new Translator();
```

Figure 9. Agent for Handwriting

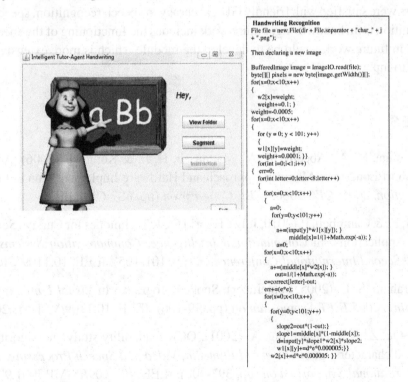

```
Handwriting Recognition
File file = new File(dir + File.separator + "char_" + j
+ ".png");

Then declaring a new image

BufferedImage image = ImageIO.read(file);
byte[][] pixels = new byte[image.getWidth()][];
for(x=0;x<10;x++)
{
   w2[x]=weight;
   weight+=0.1; }
weight=-0.0005;
for(x=0;x<10;x++)
{
   for (y = 0; y < 101; y++)
   {
   w1[x][y]=weight;
   weight+=0.0001; }}
  err=0;
   for(int letter=0;letter<8;letter++)
   {
     for(x=0;x<10;x++)
       {
         a=0;
          for(y=0;y<101;y++)
          {
            a+=(input[y]*w1[x][y]); }
                middle[x]=1/(1+Math.exp(-a)); }
         a=0;
       for(x=0;x<10;x++)
       {
         a+=(middle[x]*w2[x]); }
            out=1/(1+Math.exp(-a));
       e=correct[letter]-out;
       err+=(e*e);
       for(x=0;x<10;x++)
       {
            for(y=0;y<101;y++)
            {
              slope2=out*(1-out);}
              slope1=middle[x]*(1-middle[x]);
              d=input[y]*slope1*w2[x]*slope2;
              w1[x][y]+=d*e*0.000005;}}
              w2[x]+=d*e*0.000005; }}
```

microphones. The noise in input voice can be minimized by the devices that use least Minimum Mean Square Error at the disposal. It requires proper calibration of the available device with the software. Since the tutorial has many modules which has to be combined to form a system. So the proper classes should be mapped to the main class and no ambiguous functions or classes should be there. With some pre-determined factors like speech modulation the system may fail to meet the standards in terms of units. Only allowing users to speak in non modulated and demodulated form i.e. maintains single tone. The software is suited for anyone who wants to learn English language. But the specific requirements may vary between different category of users and it will leave some functions either useless or inefficient for that particular user. Creating separate modules so that the specific user uses the module of his/her choice. The recognition system should recognize the voice well without ambiguity. But sometimes, it may yield ambiguity for words spoken. Encouraging the user to speak with emotions and expecting the same result in translation could turn out to be difficult. Synthesis of the speech may not give human like voice. The formality of the documentation is important because the user need to follow steps which cannot be explained unless documented.

CONCLUSION

This chapter explore the areas of speech synthesis, handwriting recognition and speech recognition. The procedures to implement these modules have been found. Neural network is used to train the image that receives by the user and gives the result of the character. The software is used for bet testing in which many naive users were satisfied with friendly GUI, accuracy in speech recognition, speech synthesis and character recognition from handwriting. Future work includes the functioning of the speech recognition. The main focus in future work would be to develop the module which is more extensive to user inputs and is sensitive to inputs

REFERENCES

Ahmadi, A., Ritonga, M. A., Abedin, M. A., Mattausch, H. J., & Koide, T. (2006). A Learning OCR System Using Short/Long-term Memory Approach and Hardware Implementation in FPGA. In *Evolutionary Computation, 2006. CEC 2006. IEEE Congress on* (pp. 687-693). IEEE.

Beg, A., Ahmed, F., & Campbell, P. (2010, July). Hybrid OCR Techniques for Cursive Script Languages-A Review and Applications. In *Computational Intelligence, Communication Systems and Networks (CICSyN), 2010 Second International Conference on* (pp. 101-105). IEEE. 10.1109/CICSyN.2010.36

Begel, A., & Graham, S. L. (2005, September). Spoken programs. In *Visual Languages and Human-Centric Computing, 2005 IEEE Symposium on* (pp. 99-106). IEEE. 10.1109/VLHCC.2005.58

Desrochers, D., Qu, Z., & Saengdeejing, A. (2001). OCR readability study and algorithms for testing partially damaged characters. In *Intelligent Multimedia, Video and Speech Processing, 2001. Proceedings of 2001 International Symposium on* (pp. 397-400). IEEE. 10.1109/ISIMP.2001.925417

Dhariya, O., Malviya, S., & Tiwary, U. S. (2017, January). A hybrid approach for Hindi-English machine translation. In *Information Networking (ICOIN), 2017 International Conference on* (pp. 389-394). IEEE. 10.1109/ICOIN.2017.7899465

Dincer, S., & Doganay, A. (2015). The Impact of Pedagogical Agent on Learners' Motivation and Academic Success1. *Practice and Theory in Systems of Education, 10*(4), 329–348. doi:10.1515/ptse-2015-0032

Giraffa, L. M. M., & Viccari, R. M. (1998, November). The use of agent's techniques on intelligent tutoring systems. In *Computer Science, 1998. SCCC'98. XVIII International Conference of the Chilean Society of* (pp. 76-83). IEEE

Gu, L., Gao, Y., Liu, F. H., & Picheny, M. (2006). Concept-based speech-to-speech translation using maximum entropy models for statistical natural concept generation. *IEEE Transactions on Audio, Speech, and Language Processing, 14*(2), 377–392. doi:10.1109/TSA.2005.860769

Hashimoto, K., Yamagishi, J., Byrne, W., King, S., & Tokuda, K. (2011, May). An analysis of machine translation and speech synthesis in speech-to-speech translation system. In *Acoustics, Speech and Signal Processing (ICASSP), 2011 IEEE International Conference on* (pp. 5108-5111). IEEE. 10.1109/ICASSP.2011.5947506

Hsieh, C. C., Tsai, T. H., Wible, D., & Hsu, W. L. (2002, December). Exploiting knowledge representation in an intelligent tutoring system for English lexical errors. In *Computers in Education, 2002. Proceedings. International Conference on* (pp. 115-116). IEEE.

Jaiswal, U. C., Kumar, R., & Chandra, S. (2009, December). A Structure Based Computer Grammar to Understand Compound-Complex, Multiple-Compound and Multiple-Complex English Sentences. In *Advances in Computing, Control, & Telecommunication Technologies, 2009. ACT'09. International Conference on* (pp. 746-751). IEEE.

Kala, R., Vazirani, H., Shukla, A., & Tiwari, R. (2010). *Offline handwriting recognition using genetic algorithm.* arXiv preprint arXiv:1004.3257

Kavallieratos, E., Antoniades, N., Fakotakis, N., & Kokkinakis, G. (1997, July). Extraction and recognition of handwritten alphanumeric characters from application forms. In *Digital Signal Processing Proceedings, 1997. DSP 97., 1997 13th International Conference on* (Vol. 2, pp. 695-698). IEEE. 10.1109/ICDSP.1997.628447

Laine, M., & Nevalainen, O. S. (2006, September). A standalone OCR system for mobile cameraphones. In *Personal, Indoor and Mobile Radio Communications, 2006 IEEE 17th International Symposium on* (pp. 1-5). IEEE. 10.1109/PIMRC.2006.254074

McCarthy, J. (2004). The Web - Early Visions, Present Reality, the Grander Future. *IEEE/WIC/ACM International Conference on Web Intelligence.* 10.1109/WI.2004.10003

Nair, L. R., & David Peter, S. (2012). Machine translation systems for Indian languages. *International Journal of Computer Applications, 39*(1).

Nakamura, S. (2009, August). Development and application of multilingual speech translation. In *Speech Database and Assessments, 2009 Oriental COCOSDA International Conference on* (pp. 9-12). IEEE. 10.1109/ICSDA.2009.5278383

Palmer, M., Bhatt, R., Narasimhan, B., Rambow, O., Sharma, D. M., & Xia, F. (2009, December). Hindi syntax: Annotating dependency, lexical predicate-argument structure, and phrase structure. In *The 7th International Conference on Natural Language Processing* (pp. 14-17). Academic Press.

Pradeep, J., Srinivasan, E., & Himavathi, S. (2011, March). Neural network based handwritten character recognition system without feature extraction. In *Computer, Communication and Electrical Technology (ICCCET), 2011 International Conference on* (pp. 40-44). IEEE. 10.1109/ICCCET.2011.5762513

Rahman, M. S., Mridha, M. F., Poddar, S. R., & Huda, M. N. (2010, October). Open morphological machine translation: Bangla to English. In *Computer Information Systems and Industrial Management Applications (CISIM), 2010 International Conference on* (pp. 460-465). IEEE.

Rane, A. K. (2005). *Intelligent Tutoring System For Marathi*. Karnataka State Open University Mysore.

Rubin, J. (1994). A review of second language listening comprehension research. *Modern Language Journal*, 78(2), 199–221. doi:10.1111/j.1540-4781.1994.tb02034.x

Russell, S. J., Norvig, P., Canny, J. F., Malik, J. M., & Edwards, D. D. (2003). Artificial intelligence: a modern approach: Vol. 2. *No. 9*. Upper Saddle River, NJ: Prentice hall.

Sakti, S., Kimura, N., Paul, M., Hori, C., Sumita, E., Nakamura, S., . . . Arora, K. (2009, November). The Asian network-based speech-to-speech translation system. In *Automatic Speech Recognition & Understanding, 2009. ASRU 2009. IEEE Workshop on* (pp. 507-512). IEEE. 10.1109/ASRU.2009.5373353

Sun, X., & Zhang, L. (2009, August). Basic Factors Design of Pedagogical Agent System in an Ecology View. In *Hybrid Intelligent Systems, 2009. HIS'09. Ninth International Conference on* (Vol. 3, pp. 183-186). IEEE. 10.1109/HIS.2009.250

Visweswariah, K., Navratil, J., Sorensen, J., Chenthamarakshan, V., & Kambhatla, N. (2010, August). Syntax based reordering with automatically derived rules for improved statistical machine translation. In *Proceedings of the 23rd international conference on computational linguistics* (pp. 1119-1127). Association for Computational Linguistics.

Win, A. T. (2011, March). Words to phrase reordering machine translation system in Myanmar-English using English grammar rules. In *Computer Research and Development (ICCRD), 2011 3rd International Conference on* (Vol. 3, pp. 50-53). IEEE.

Xiang, B., Deng, Y., & Gao, Y. (2008, March). Unsupervised training for farsi-english speech-to-speech translation. In *Acoustics, Speech and Signal Processing, 2008. ICASSP 2008. IEEE International Conference on* (pp. 4977-4980). IEEE. 10.1109/ICASSP.2008.4518775

Chapter 14
Graph and Neural Network–Based Intelligent Conversation System

Anuja Arora
Jaypee Institute of Information Technology, India

Aman Srivastava
Haptik Inc., India

Shivam Bansal
Exzeo Software Private Limited, India

ABSTRACT

The conventional approach to build a chatbot system uses the sequence of complex algorithms and productivity of these systems depends on order and coherence of algorithms. This research work introduces and showcases a deep learning-based conversation system approach. The proposed approach is an intelligent conversation model approach which conceptually uses graph model and neural conversational model. The proposed deep learning-based conversation system uses neural conversational model over knowledge graph model in a hybrid manner. Graph-based model answers questions written in natural language using its intent in the knowledge graph and neural conversational model converses answer based on conversation content and conversation sequence order. NLP is used in graph model and neural conversational model uses natural language understanding and machine intelligence. The neural conversational model uses seq2seq framework as it requires less feature engineering and lacks domain knowledge. The results achieved through the authors' approach are competitive with solely used graph model results.

DOI: 10.4018/978-1-5225-5852-1.ch014

INTRODUCTION

Chatbots are artificial intelligent systems and usually interact in text or voice interface form. In past, these interactions were straight forward, for example:

- Customer care inquiry systems which provide fix number of option according to users' problems;
- Weather report system;
- Bot troubleshoots a problem with Internet Service;
- etc.

In recent years, Chatbots have gained popularity and has become hot computational research topic. Many companies are developing bots which may have natural conversations indistinguishable from human ones. Efficiency of chatbot systems depend on the suitability and coherence of system generated outcome from the knowledge base corresponding to user query. For example: User asked query from the search engine chatbot system is "Which other American singer was born in the same year as Elvis Presley?". Google search has generated an outcome which is shown in figure 1(a) whereas based on knowledge understanding outcome should looks like as presented in figure 1(b). The outcome as shown in figure 1(b) is possible using DBpedia knowledge base but depends on how system has been built.

As shown in figure 1, outcome/ response are basically dependent on the natural conversation instead of terms used/ asked in the system. In this research paper, we are hoping to develop chatbot system to have natural conversation indistinguishable from human ones. Researchers are generally using linguistic rule based approaches, natural language processing, and deep learning techniques to achieve it.

Figure 1. Chatbot and Search Engine result comparison

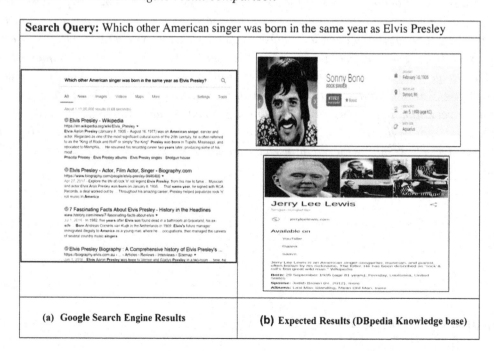

- **Chatbot System- Framework:** Chatbot conversation system framework[1] (See Figure 2) is basically classified in two categories - Retrieval Based systems and generative based systems.
- **Retrieval Based Systems:** Natural Language processing and information retrieval techniques are used in heuristic manner to determine the appropriate response from a set of predefined response archive. Under heuristic, developers' have applied wide spectrum of approaches which starts from rule based approaches to ensemble learning classifiers. Retrieval based approaches (Montet et al, 2003) does not generate any kind of new response, response of asked input generates from fixed response set. It is impossible to generate a retrieval based system for open domain, usually rule based retrieval system has been implemented by developers.
- **Generative Based Systems:** Generative models based systems are not dependent on pre-defined response set/ archive. Response corresponding to input is typically formed using machine translation techniques. Generative model based chatbot systems are considered as wisest systems but these are problematic and hard to implement.

Definitely, both retrieval based system and generative based systems have their own advantages and disadvantages, these pros and cons are detailed in Table 1.

Chatbot System: Issues and Challenges

- **Open Domain vs. Closed Domain:** Open domain chatbot systems (Quarteroni et al, 2009) are hard to implement. In these kind of chatbot systems user's posted input does not have any well framed intent corresponding to specific entity. Users can post anything of their own choice and

Figure 2. Chatbot Conversation Framework

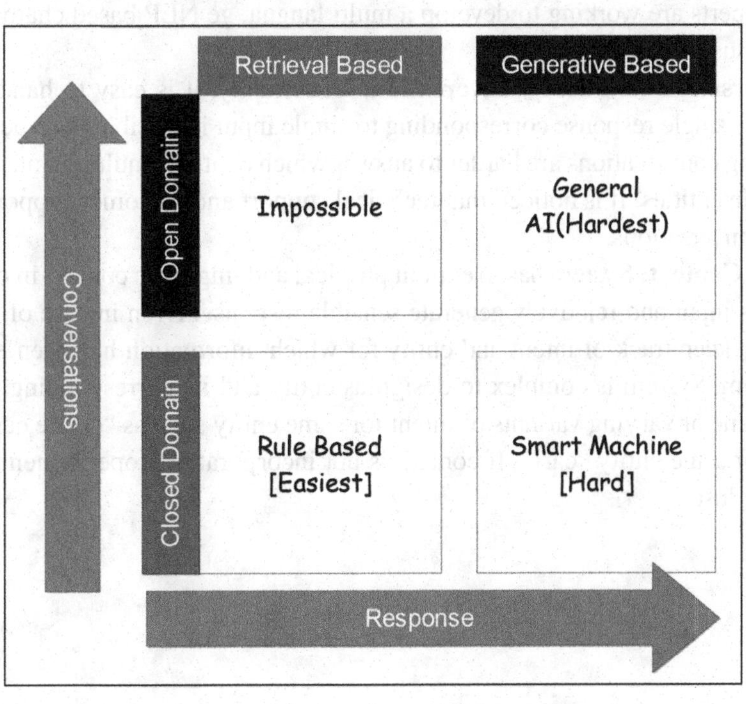

341

Table 1. Pros and Cons of Retrieval and Generative Model based Chatbot systems

Features	Retrieval Based Chatbot Systems	Generative Model Based Chatbot Systems
Response Archive	Depends on response repository	Generate response from scratch
Grammatical Mistakes	Don't make grammatical mistakes	Can make grammatical mistakes
New Cases	Can't handle unseen and new cases if pre-defined response do not exist	Smart systems, designed to handle unseen and new cases
Contextual Information	Can't handle contextual entity information	handle contextual entity information up to an extent.
complexity	Easy to handle	Hard to train

system has to relatively respond to the users. These systems are required in case of social media sites such as twitter, facebook, Instagram (Rodrigo et al, 2012; Wang et al, 2010; Wazur et al, 2011) etc. On these open domain sites, users' post can reach to number of directions/ topics/ themes and system has to generate appropriate response by understanding the user context from world knowledge base.

Whereas, closed domain chatbot systems (Radhouani et al, 2009) are designed for a limited, distinctive, and specific domain. Even, these systems generate outcome/ response for a limited set of user query and for a specific topic. Technical support system (Shawar et al, 2007; Radhouni et al, 2009), Law section retrieval (Opijnen et al, 2017; Koniaris et al, 2017), Insurance policy assistants, etc are examples of closed domain systems.

- **Multilingual:** Still, language specific chatbot/ conversation systems are part of researchers study and existence of language specific systems is presumable (Sahin et al, 2013; Liddy et al, 1999) Global AI experts are working to develop a multi langua. ge NLP based chatbot system which is regarded as elusive challenge.
- **Long Conversation vs. Short Conversation:** Uncertainly, it is easy to handle short conversation. Generate single response corresponding to single input is feasible in an accurate manner. On other end, long conversations are harder to answer which contains multiple intent those harmonize along multiple entities. It is noticed that technical support and customer support systems are generally long conversations.
- **Incorporate Context:** System has to exploit physical and linguistic context in order to understand the searcher's input and relatively generate sensible response. Even in case of long conversation, system has to keep track of intent and entity for which information has been exchanged in users and bot system. System is complex to design as entity and its corresponding intent keep on expanding by time or varying variants of intent for same entity such as "create cart", "remove cart", "edit cart" for same entity "cart". If context is not incorporated properly then whole response of question may lost.

Brief About Proposed Approach

To address the above issues, an intelligent conversation model approach is developed which is fundamentally a generative model. So, a generative model based chatbot system has been investigated to overcome the obstacle and provide an effective conversation system. The easiest method is to respond for a specific user input according to the available response list. On the other end, recently used deep learning based chatbot systems are implemented to train a generative model based chatbot systems subject to extremely promising and exciting results. The intelligent conversation model which is implemented in this research work is a composite approach to provide advancement to conventional generative model. This composite approach is basically integration in two steps/ process-

- The first step has been made to generate response for a specific user input using graph model based technique. Graph model based technique is used to learn the system and the intent of the user input. Graph model based techniques helps in building and modifying the chat flow according to states and corresponding actions of users.
- The second step is used to improvise graph model based generated results and to cover responses those are not handled by graph model based approach. For this purpose, sequence to sequence (seq2seq) model is adopted which was introduced by Kyunghyun cho et. al. in 2014.Neural conversation model is adapted from the original seq2seq model.

ORGANIZATION OF BOOK CHAPTER

The remainder of the Chapter is ais organized as follows: Section 2 comprises of the related literature and background related to research done in this direction. Section 3 is most important section which contains the detailed description about intelligent conversation system. Intelligent conversation system is a composite framework of graph Based and Neural network-based conversation model. Intelligent conversation model Framework is also described in this same section3. Interpretations and findings from the validated model have been highlighted in section 4, which is followed by conclusion in last section.

RELATED WORK

Conversation System/ chatbot systems have shown an explosive growth due to its ubiquitous existence in technical support systems, but this area is still in early stage. Researchers try to design chatbot systems which can address the high expectations of users towards chatbot. The IT industry giants Google, LinkedIn, Facebook, Amazon, etc. plays key role and giving their own patented chatbots which proves its requirement and importance in market.

Chatbot Systems Fundamentals

Existing conversation systems are basically modeled with the help of specification language AIML-Artificial Intelligence Markup Language. Few AIML based existing chatbot systems are Mitsuku and A.L.I.C.E. Details of these systems are as follows:

- **Mitsuku[2]:** It is written in AIML (Artificial Intelligence Markup Language); an XML based "language" that lets developers write rules for the bot to follow. Basically, you write a PATTERN and a TEMPLATE, such that when the bot encounters that pattern in a sentence from user, it replies with one of the templates. Let us call this model of bots, Rule based model.
- **A.L.I.C.E. Chatbot[3]:** A.L.I.C.E. (Artificial Linguistic Internet Computer Entity) is a free software chatbot created in AIML (Artificial Intelligence Markup Language), an open, minimalist, stimulus-response language for creating bot personalities like A.L.I.C.E.

Few programming interface, API, utilities etc. are available to support developers while implementing chatbot systems are as follows:

- **Telegram Bot API [4]:** The Bot API is an HTTP-based interface created for developers keen on building bots for Telegram. Telegram released its bot API, providing an easy way for developers, to create bots by interacting with a bot, the Bot Father - 2015
- **Myshkin[5]:** Nodejs that answers any query with a quote. The program uses the linux utility fortune, a pseudorandom message generator.
- **hodor-Bot[6]:** This program implements a funny little chatbot which says, under certain conditions, "Hodor." It serves as a simple example of an IRC bot in python. It joins channels when invited and replies to private messages. One existing feature is that it (intermittently) speaks in channels when others are speaking and conveniently presents protocol information on stdout.

However, conversation systems exist but then also existing chatbot systems are difficult to scale for manually built patterns and information retrieval is unsusceptible. Still promising and favorable chatbot building model/ process is mandatorily required for task oriented conversation systems. To build successful chatbot systems, various online resources (blogs, tools and communities) are available.

- Well-Known chatbot blogs are- Chatbots Life[7], ChatbotMagazine[8] and ChatbotWeekly[9].
- Popular chatbot communities are- ChatBots Public Group | Facebook[10], Chatbot's Life (@ ChatbotsLife) | Twitter[11], and Chatbot Mastermind Group | Facebook[12].

State-of-Art Approaches

Efficiency of any conversation system depends on the suitability and coherence of system generated response from the knowledge base corresponding to the conversation held in between Bot and User. Varying conversation systems have been investigated for varying domains obtaining varying paradigm and solution approaches. In broader spectrum, Chatbot specific approaches and paradigm are classified in two categories: Retrieval Systems and Generative Models.

Retrieval based chatbot system uses responses repository and apply some heuristic based approach which is required to extract the most relevant response based on user query and its context. Various researchers have contributed in this direction and published their work. Based on the literatures, the current state of art for information retrieval in conversational system direction has been put forth in three major classes - Knowledge Engineering based Retrieval System, Natural Language based Retrieval System, and Information Retrieval System.

Rather than a generic conversation system as used to handle any domain inquiry, domain specific information retrieval systems are gaining importance due to their specific structure, keywords, and context (Radhouni et al, 2009; Verma et al, 2017). This lead to dimension-based information retrieval systems as shown by Radhouani et al., wherein the authors are created an interface for retrieval of relevant information pertaining to human anatomy. Such usage has been shown to avoid complex hierarchical frameworks.

On the other end, Generative model based conversation systems are useful for personal assistant and designed in goal-oriented and transactional manner. The workhorse approach under this direction is slot-filling (Wang et al, 2013; Lemon et al, 2006), this approach fills slots in a conversation according to pre-defined structure. The Graph based approach used in this work is extension of same slot filling approach introduced by Lemon et. al. in 2006. Consider an example of reminder system, Date, time, location and description can be various pre-defined slots for reminder system. This approach used to be well-defined and well-accepted approach in conversation industry but it contains few drawbacks as well. This is not a effective and reliable source for any new domain conversation system. It is quite impossible to satisfy, fill and encode all features solely using slot filling approach (ordes et al, 2016). Slot filling and Graph based conversation systems have their own dependencies and unsolved domain/ past conversation problems. Henceforth, novel neural network based approach has been emerged to resolve slot filling issue of conversation systems (Sutskever et al, 2014; Shang et al, 2015; Sordoni et al, 2015; Serban et al, 2016; Vinyals et al, 2015).

Neural network based conversation system trains itself based on historical conversation content and even domain dependency is also not a hurdle for neural network based conversation systems. According to literature studied, Neural Network is perfect and gives rich performance in case of light informal/ social conversation (i.e. socially not having any informative conversation) (Ritter et al, 2011; Wang et al, 2013). The reason is that neural network trains to predict the next conversation based on persistent knowledge base. Whereas, domain specific product assistant conversation system requires querying knowledge base then persistent knowledge base. Product assistant conversation system interprets response from queries (or fixed set) to display appropriate response to users.

It is doubtful and hard to relay on individual neural network based or graph model based conversation system. In particular Graph model/ slot filling conversation system techniques are useful in case of domain specific and menu driven conversation system and for chit-chat sort of conversation (social conversation) neural network based conversation system is applicable. But, it is unclear to compare performance of one over other (Liu et al, 2016). This research work introduces an intelligent conversation system which is basically a hybrid approach and is combination of graph based and neural network based conversation system applied on Food ordering assistant application. System validity and performance has been measured by comparing results of graph model based and neural network based conversation system.

INTELLIGENT CONVERSATION MODEL

Conversation systems are basically generated to handle two variety of queries- Factoid Query System and Non-Factoid Query System.

Definition 1: *Factoid Query: Queries are concise and objective facts, Such as- Who is Prime Minister of India?*

Definition 2: *Non-Factoid Query: Non-Factoid is an umbrella term which covers all queries beyond factoid QA and might have some overlap with factoid one. Such as: Can you update the task 'ABC' with a new Date of Completion?*

This paper focuses on building the conversation system for non-factoid QA system using generative model. As a result, we propose a two- way intelligent conversation Model approach. In this Two-way approach, graph model based response generation has been used as primary approach which uses heuristics to fill the free chat state slot. Later, as second approach Seq-2-Seq model based neural conversation model is used as generative model which refines graph model generated results. Hence, to develop Bot which can respond as natural conversation indistinguishable from humans, an intelligent Conversation model Framework is developed as shown in Figure 3. Before deep detailing of our conversation model, starting off by detailing the following:

- **Where We Are Right Now:** Entities collected so far.

Definition 3: *Entity: Represent concepts that are often specific to a Domain Such as- Cart, Catalogue, Reminder etc.*

- **What Is Possible as Response:** Intent/ state

Definition 4: *Intent: Represent mapping between user mentioned actions which should be performed on Entity by chatbot system. Such as- Create, Remove, Edit, etc.*

- **What Is the Intention of User Handling Chatbot:** Context i.e. messages exchanged so far.

Definition 5: *Context: Set of strings (Contain action) that represent the current context of the User.*

Intelligent Conversation System is generally revolves around these three above discussed parameters – Entity, Intent, Context. Usually, most of the chatbot APIs are using these parameters for a conversation system.

According to all performed analysis, Generative model is a smart and well-defined model. Generative model don't rely on the response repository/ pre-defined responses, this model generates new response from scratch. But, on other end it contains some issues which degrade its performance as detailed in Table 1. It is factual that generative model suffers from some inevitable issues such as misspelling, ideal chat-flow deviation, code-mixed queries, and domain shift. To Avoid all these issue, we introduce intelligent conversation model which is combination of Graph Based Model and Neural Conversation model.

Model Framework

Model Framework has been visualized in Figure 4, System is starting off from two Global parameters- Entities in collection and context of conversations which have been held. For any new domain initial impetus has made to process and update content corresponding to these two parameters (Entity and Context). For example: A conversation System for Food Ordering site "Swiggy". Entity List contains all dish names, restaurant names, cities, Ingredients, many more. 'Context' contains message exchanged so far. Later state / Intent has been identified in graph model which stores current state of the conversation such as- Order, find, refund, edit, complaints, etc. and every state is followed by an action.

In our deep learning driven conversation model, initially new query will be handled by Graph Model which is used to identify the probable next state (discussed in detail in section 3.2). It computes a similarity score in current state and probable next states. System selects next state as current state whichever is having high computed similarity score. Further, we have to identify that all entities are collected or not. In case of all entities are collected then system will perform corresponding action, whereas if not collected then system has to send data collection as response to user as user has to collect remaining associated entities (Example shown in Figure 3)

In case graph Model is not able to identify entity and state/ intent of user query then to refine results sequence to sequence (Seq-2-Seq) model has been used. Seq-2-Seq model used neural network architecture which is known as Recurrent Neural Network (RNN), this RNN acts as encoder and decoder combination (discussed in detail in section 3.3). Neural conversation model result will be either in form of text or state/ intent. Henceforth, if response is text then send it as bot reply otherwise state will return back to graph model and compute score with consecutive states.

If response generated through Graph or neural conversation model is more than a mapping threshold value then send it as final response otherwise manual response is activated.

Graph Model

Solution Approach has deep impact on the correct and consistent response of conversation system. Graph Model produces fundamental advancement in response (as outcome) generation. It is used to identify state which is hidden in input query based on its corresponding states. Hence, the main objective of using graph model is to use heuristic to extract state and mapping of adjacent states. Graph based model helps in building conversation flow for users. State is intent of user corresponding to an entity and further system performs action according to user state/ Intent if all entities are collected otherwise system asks for some more linked entities from user and send response to collect some more data.

Consider a scenario of food ordering conversation system as shown in Figure 5 which show conversation flow of order pizza in 5(a) and its graph model is shown in Figure 5(b) which depicts entity, states and intent in whole conversation.

Graph Model can be described as states and action mapping in sequential order. It is used as slot filling terminology where heuristics have been used to fill state as slot and navigation between states. Although, graph model has its disadvantages as well, statefulness nature creates a "menu maze" effect to conversation system and it forces users to follow conversation menu but natural conversation experience is hidden. Solely, this approach may eliminate challenges and conversation may reach towards waste,

Figure 3. Sample example for associated entity collection in Graph Model

User	:	I want to order Food (Entity: Food; Intent: Order)
Bot Reply (Graph Model)	:	Sure, What Food item you like to have? (All associated entities are not collected, bot sent message to collect remaining entities)

Figure 4. Overall Intelligent Conversation System Framework

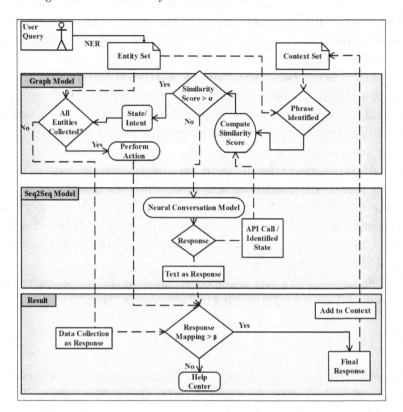

useless and unnecessary direction. Henceforth, in order to serve more important, natural and challenging discussion, Neural network based approach has been used to flesh out and deal with natural (not menu based) conversations.

Sequence to Sequence Model

As per our observation, graph model is able to attempt queries containing states and having relevant context perfectly but in few cases graph model does not response appropriately and randomly generate response sentence. It is noticed that graph model collapses due to some reasons such as- Diversion in conversion flow, Domain-Shift, and code-mixed queries. Therefore, to improve efficiency of intelligent conversation system, Seq-2-Seq Model has been used.

In 2014, Sequence to sequence was first introduced by Cho et. al. (2014) and the solution approach is similar and relevant to approach given by Kalchbrenner and Blunsom in 2013. Kalchbrenner and Blunsom (2013) first time mapped the input sentences to vector. In sequence to sequence model, two recurrent neural network (RNN) has been used. First RNN model works as encoder and takes conversation word sequence as input and second RNN model works as decoder and provides corresponding output sequence as shown in Figure 6. Both model trains together to attain maximum conditional probability and model stops process after finding "End of Statement" token (EOS).

Figure 5. Graph Model of Food Ordering System: (a) Conversation Flow "Order Pizza"; (b) Graph Model of "Order Pizza" Conversation held in 5(a)

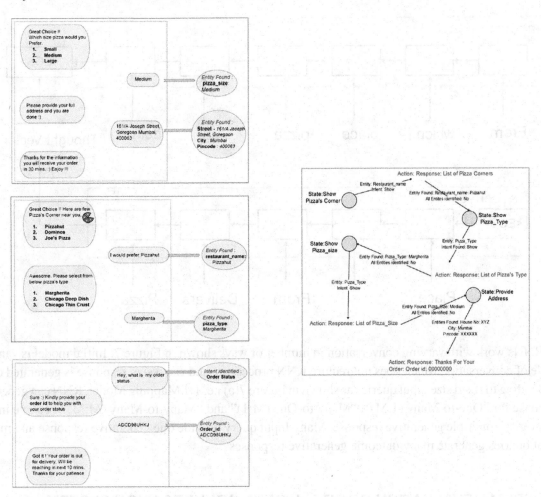

To achieve reasonably accurate response, context has been incorporated i.e. system keeps track of past exchanged conversations. System may consider long conversation sequence to generate response. Conversation vector length is to be decided in order to generate sensible response as outcome. Hence, RNN output not only depends on immediate input whereas it is based on series of input posted in past. Context of response depends on series of input instead of just recently inputted query and we can choose length of context and response vector. While training model, conversation up to a level encodes the information and produces a thought vector. Further though vector is responsible to generate response by feeding to decoder. Similarity of predicted response and actual response is measured using dot product of both the vectors.

High value of computed dot product shows similarity maximization and response receives high score. At end, sigmoid function has been applied to find out probability with the help of computed score.

Figure 6. Seq-2-Seq reads an input sentence "From which place pizza will deliver" and produces "Pizza delivers from Place X" as the output sentence.

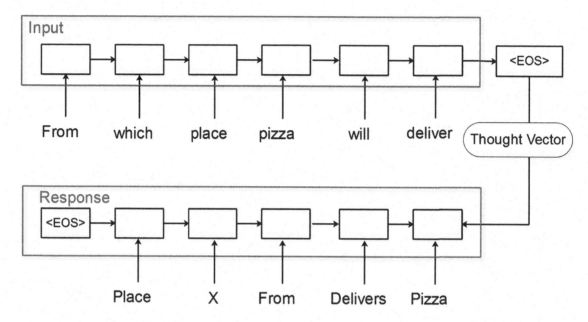

RNNs work with varying conversation in number of ways shown in Figure 7. Initial model is vanilla mode of conversation which does not require RNN processing and fixed size response is generated corresponding to fixed size input queries as shown in Figure 7(a) i.e. 1:1 Mapping Model. RNN can generate response for "One-to-Many (1:M)", "Many-to-One (M:1)" and "Many-to-Many (M:M)" i.e. One input query gives multiple generative response. Many Input query provide one generative response and many input queries generate many outcome generative responses.

EMPIRICAL EVALUATION OF INTELLIGENT CONVERSATION SYSTEM

The goal of proposed intelligent conversation system is to predict bot utterances and its preciseness. These bot results can be sentences or API calls and even model is able to generate entirely new sentences those do not exist in the training set. These are the prime reasons to refer this as a generative model. In this context, following section discusses the dataset and performance evaluation measures have been used for tuning and evaluation of the system.

Description Analysis of Dataset

We have performed experiments on existing as well as self generated datasets. Existing dataset is a 'Personalized dialog dataset13' which shows conversation while booking a table in a restaurant, this dataset is provided by Joshi et. al. in 2017. They have artificially generated bAPI dialog tasks to achieve goal which is "To Book a table in a Restaurant". Dataset details are listed in Table 1, which shows coverage of restaurant parameters such as cuisine, locations, price range, party size, and rating. Restaurants

Figure 7. RNN deals in variety of processes (a) Vanilla mode (1:1) (b) One-to-Many (c) Many-to-One (d) Many-to-Many

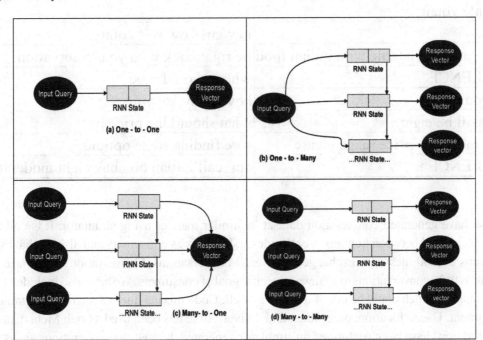

address, menu, and phone number is also part of dataset on which experiments have been performed. Joshi et. al. provided API calls also corresponding to dialogs. API calls are associated with five prime parameters (cuisine, location, price, people, and rating) to book a table.

Dataset is kept in a specific format/ template as shown in Figure 8. For each and every conversation first line contains user profile attribute including number 1 and conversation of user and bot starts from second line which also include one id attribute which starts from 2 and goes up to count of conversation end.

Table 2. Descriptive details about 'Personalized Dialog dataset'

User profiles	6 Numbers (female_elderly, female_middle-aged, female_young, male_elderly, male_middle-aged, male_young)
Data set Variants	2 (Full Dialogs, small dialogs)
Full Dialogs	6000/ 12000 (Training set, Test set, Development set- Each)
Small Dialogs	1000 (Training set, Test set, Development st- Each)
Cuisine	10 (Italian, Indian, etc.)
Locations	10 (London, Tokya, etc.)
Price Range	3(cheap, moderate, or expensive)
Party Size	4 options (2,6,4, or 8 people)
Rating	1-8

Figure 8. Conversation sample

1 female young	
2 hi	hey girl how is it going
3 can you book a table with italian food	be right back with your reservation
4 <SILENCE>	where should it be
5 in bombay	how many are you
6 we will be eight	what should the price be
7 in a moderate price range please	sure finding some options
8 <SILENCE>	api_call italian bombay eight moderate

We also have generated conversation dataset in similar manner using simulator. It is collection of messages exchanged between humans at both side i.e. Humans as consumers and also as chat assistants. This contains 20,000 messages exchanged in overall conversations. Conversations size varies from 2 conversations to 20 conversations to achieve a specific goal of consumers. We have also included informal/ irrelevant queries which could be out of domain as well. Code mixing queries are not entertained under this experiment. Users' location, order time, and delivery time has been used as rich Meta data content.

Few operations have been performed on simulator generated dataset, these operations are as follows-Replace message and Structure message to informal conversation.

In Replace message, user texted message has been used to extract entities: _location_, _cuisine_, _price-range_, etc. Information about these entities helps in reducing vocabulary and provides accurate and precise response correspondingly to user query.

For example:

```
                USER: I would like to book a table for dinner near my
home for tomorrow.
Transformed query: I would like to book a table for dinner near _location for
_date.
```

Before sending response to user, system structuralize message in an informal conversation to present it like personal chit-chat assistance.

For example:

Table 3. Simulator generated Data set details

Conversations	20,000
Users	800
Conversation per user	7-8 Average
Messages per Conversation	5-6 Average

```
System Generated Answer: "Booked table"
Cuisine: italian
Location: bombay
Person: eight
Price range: moderate
Restaurant: resto_x
Bot response: awesome, you are done. Here you go to resto_x at bombay which is
having 2 star rating and restaurant address is XXXXX. Your table is booked for
Italian cuisine for eight persons with moderate price.
User reply: thanks
Bot response: Do you need something else?
```

Performance Evaluation Measures and Results

First evaluation is applied to compute the importance of used approaches i.e. graph model approach and neural network approach. This is used to find out how much query is successfully handled by Graph model and by neural network model. As these two approaches are applied in a incremental manner and after computation, we get to know that graph model was able to handle/ respond 65% queries and to achieve more accuracy and preciseness neural model is applied. Usually, informal/ casual conversations are not managed by graph model, for that neural is applicable. Some Chat flow including response is coming using which approach is shown in Figure 9.

Researchers usually use machine translation performance metrics such as BLEU and METEOR for evaluating conversation systems. ROUGE has also been used to validate summarization score of conversation system. Liu et. al. (2018) mentioned and depicted in his work that these metrics decrepit easily corresponding to human response. Therefore, particularly in our proposed conversation system evaluation, we focus on comparing the system generated response to the actual response using two conversation system specific metrics- End2End Conversation metric and Agent occupancy rate metric.

Figure 9. Conversation sample

Sender	Message
User	Hllo foodbot (Spelling Mistake Handle)
Neural	Hi Prince, How can I help you?
User	I want to Book a table
Graph	Please tell be your location.
User	I want to Book a table at chanakya puri, NewDelhi.
Graph	This is your location restaurant list.
User	Suggest me some North Indian restaurant.
Graph	………….. is best North Indian Restaurant in chanakyapuri . Shoul
User	Can you give me some option which can serve me at 3:00 at night
Neural	Sorry, we can provide you phone numbers of chankyapuri North Indian restaurants, you have to confirm yourself about closing time.

- **End2End Conversation Metric (E2E):** E2E evaluation metric measures all the chats those are handled by conversation system without any human assistant intervention. Even, consumer satisfaction has been validated while evaluating this metric i.e. consumers' conversation reaches to a satisfaction level. This is measured based on dialogues received at end of conversation from consumer side. Higher value of E2E metric reflects the performance of system.
- **Min_Response:** Min_response metric is measured to compute number of messages where atleast one response is sent by the conversation system. This Min_response metric computes the conversations which are able to receive atleast one message for a specific conversation using our proposed conversation system. This metric is used to measures users' query where system initially tried to respond and handle user inquiry but later it is not able to understand user's intent in conversations. We observed that usually these chats contain chit-chat/ informal conversations.

Figure 10 shows result proposed intelligent conversation system evaluation results in form of E2E and Min_response metric. E2E metric shows, system is able respond 66% end-to-end conversations using graph model solely and performance has been increased by 12.5% if we integrated graph model with neural network model. Finally, system achieves 78% overall accuracy in giving appropriate response of users' query. This E2E conversation signifies that user query is appropriately handled and user's intentions/ intent is correctly understood. Secondly, we measure Min_Response metric which shows system performance with respect to count of response automatically handled by system. System is able to respond 87 percentage response using graph model and 94% response are able to handle by combination of graph and neural model. This shows that system tries to answer even causal/ chit-chat conversations of users. Min_response shows the overall message catered by the system in overall system testing. One

Figure 10. Performance Evaluation of proposed Conversation system.

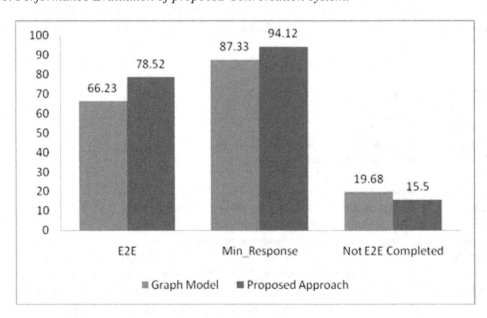

For a more accurate representation see the electronic version.

last computation is a combination metric 'Not E2E Completed' which is used to compute system not responded end-to end combination but tried to respond i.e. user query is not completely answered but system tried to respond. 19.68% and 15.5% conversations not E2E handled by graph model and combined model respectively otherwise having minimum response at-least one. Therefore, Graph model is able to give 66% accurate results and combined model (graph model and neural network combined) reached up to 78.52% appropriate responses.

CONCLUSION

This paper proposed and discussed an intelligent conversation system that is developed using two advance level approaches- Graph model based conversation and Neural network Based conversation. For neural network, seq2seq model is used to train recurrent neural network. Initially Graph model is applied on user query/conversation which detects state and intent from the user conversations by taking end2end conversation in consideration. According to experiments, graph model is able to handle 70% user queries. For casual/ chit-chat conversation neural network has been used. Result shows that proposed conversation model is able to generate users' conversations effectively. Even chit-chat / casual conversation is also addressed perfectly. Combined model results are evaluated with the help of two most appropriate and suitable metrics- end2end metric and min_response metric. With the help of proposed approach system achieved 78.5% accuracy to cover end2end conversations with users. Even though the model has obvious limitations and because of that 15.5% conversations not reached to end and satisfactory user outcome. However, the model further may require substantial modifications to be able to deliver realistic conversations.

REFERENCES

Bordes, A., & Weston, J. (2016). *Learning end-to-end goal-oriented dialog.* arXiv preprint arXiv:1605.07683

Cho, K., Van Merriënboer, B., Gulcehre, C., Bahdanau, D., Bougares, F., Schwenk, H., & Bengio, Y. (2014). *Learning phrase representations using RNN encoder-decoder for statistical machine translation.* arXiv preprint arXiv:1406.1078

Joshi, C. K., Mi, F., & Faltings, B. (2017). *Personalization in Goal-Oriented Dialog.* arXiv preprint arXiv:1706.07503

Kalchbrenner, N., & Blunsom, P. (2013). Recurrent continuous translation models. EMNLP.

Kerly, A., Hall, P., & Bull, S. (2007). Bringing chatbots into education: Towards natural language negotiation of open learner models. *Knowledge-Based Systems, 20*(2), 177–185. doi:10.1016/j.knosys.2006.11.014

Koniaris, M., Anagnostopoulos, I., & Vassiliou, Y. (2017). Evaluation of Diversification Techniques for Legal Information Retrieval. *Algorithms, 10*(1), 22. doi:10.3390/a10010022

Lemon, O., Georgila, K., Henderson, J., & Stuttle, M. (2006, April). An ISU dialogue system exhibiting reinforcement learning of dialogue policies: generic slot-filling in the TALK in-car system. In *Proceedings of the Eleventh Conference of the European Chapter of the Association for Computational Linguistics: Posters & Demonstrations* (pp. 119-122). Association for Computational Linguistics. 10.3115/1608974.1608986

Liddy, E. D., Paik, W., Edmund, S. Y., & Li, M. (1999). *U.S. Patent No. 6,006,221*. Washington, DC: U.S. Patent and Trademark Office.

Liu, C.-W., Lowe, R., Serban, I. V., Noseworthy, M., Charlin, L., & Pineau, J. (2016). *How not to evaluate your dialogue system: An empirical study of unsupervised evaluation metrics for dialogue response generation.* arXiv preprint arXiv:1603.08023

Mazur, M., Rzepka, R., & Araki, K. (2011). Proposal for a conversational English tutoring system that encourages user engagement. In *Proceedings of the 19th International Conference on Computers in Education* (pp. 10-12). Academic Press.

Montet, I., Dalmasso, E., & Siegel, A. (2003). *U.S. Patent Application No. 10/441,754*. Washington, DC: US Patent Office.

Quarteroni, S., & Manandhar, S. (2009). Designing an interactive open-domain question answering system. *Natural Language Engineering, 15*(1), 73–95. doi:10.1017/S1351324908004919

Radhouani, S., Mottaz Jiang, C. L., & Falquet, G. (2009). Flexir: A domain-specific information retrieval system. *Polibits, 39*, 27–31. doi:10.17562/PB-39-4

Radhouani, S., Mottaz Jiang, C. L., & Falquet, G. (2009, June). Flexir: A domain-specific information retrieval system. *Polibits, 39*, 27–31. doi:10.17562/PB-39-4

Ritter, A., Cherry, C., & Dolan, W. B. (2011). Data-driven response generation in social media. *Proceedings of the Conference on Empirical Methods in Natural Language Processing.*

Rodrigo, S. M., & Abraham, J. G. F. (2012, April). Development and implementation of a chat bot in a social network. In *Information Technology: New Generations (ITNG), 2012 Ninth International Conference on* (pp. 751-755). IEEE. 10.1109/ITNG.2012.147

Şahin, M., & Duman, D. (2013). Multilingual Chat through Machine Translation: A Case of English-Russian. Meta: Journal des traducteurs/Meta: Translators'. *Journal, 58*(2), 397–410.

Serban, I. V., Sordoni, A., Bengio, Y., Courville, A. C., & Pineau, J. (2016, February). Building End-To-End Dialogue Systems Using Generative Hierarchical Neural Network Models. In AAAI (pp. 3776-3784). Academic Press.

Shang, L., Lu, Z., & Li, H. (2015). *Neural responding machine for short-text conversation.* arXiv preprint arXiv:1503.02364

Shawar, B. A., & Atwell, E. (2007). Chatbots: are they really useful? In *LDV Forum* (Vol. 22, No. 1, pp. 29-49). Academic Press.

Sordoni, A., Galley, M., Auli, M., Brockett, C., Ji, Y., Mitchell, M., . . . Dolan, B. (2015). *A neural network approach to context-sensitive generation of conversational responses*. arXiv preprint arXiv:1506.06714

Sutskever, I., Vinyals, O., & Le, Q. V. (2014). Sequence to sequence learning with neural networks. In Advances in neural information processing systems (pp. 3104-3112). Academic Press.

Van Opijnen, M., & Santos, C. (2017). On the concept of relevance in legal information retrieval. *Artificial Intelligence and Law, 25*(1), 65–87. doi:10.100710506-017-9195-8

Verma, A., & Arora, A. (2017, January). Reflexive hybrid approach to provide precise answer of user desired frequently asked question. In *Cloud Computing, Data Science & Engineering-Confluence, 2017 7th International Conference on* (pp. 159-163). IEEE. 10.1109/CONFLUENCE.2017.7943142

Vinyals, O., & Le, Q. (2015). *A neural conversational model*. arXiv preprint arXiv:1506.05869

Wang, B., Wang, X., Sun, C., Liu, B., & Sun, L. (2010, July). Modeling semantic relevance for question-answer pairs in web social communities. In *Proceedings of the 48th Annual Meeting of the Association for Computational Linguistics* (pp. 1230-1238). Association for Computational Linguistics.

Wang, H., Lu, Z., Li, H., & Chen, E. (2013). A dataset for research on short-text conversations. EMNLP.

Wang, Z., & Lemon, O. (2013, August). A Simple and Generic Belief Tracking Mechanism for the Dialog State Tracking Challenge: On the believability of observed information. In *SIGDIAL Conference* (pp. 423-432). Academic Press.

ENDNOTES

1. http://info.contactsolutions.com/digital-engagement-blog/a-chatbot-framework
2. http://www.mitsuku.com/
3. https://www.chatbots.org/chatbot/a.l.i.c.e/
4. https://core.telegram.org/bots/api
5. https://github.com/suriyadeepan/myshkin
6. https://github.com/clintonc/hodor-bot
7. https://chatbotslife.com/
8. https://chatbotsmagazine.com/
9. http://www.chatbotsweekly.com/
10. https://www.facebook.com/groups/aichatbots/
11. http://twitter.com/ChatbotsLife
12. https://www.facebook.com/groups/ChatbotMastermindGroup/
13. https://github.com/chaitjo/personalized-dialog

Chapter 15
Big Data Analytics Using Apache Hive to Analyze Health Data

Pavani Konagala
Vaagdevi College of Engineering, India

ABSTRACT

A large volume of data is stored electronically. It is very difficult to measure the total volume of that data. This large amount of data is coming from various sources such as stock exchange, which may generate terabytes of data every day, Facebook, which may take about one petabyte of storage, and internet archives, which may store up to two petabytes of data, etc. So, it is very difficult to manage that data using relational database management systems. With the massive data, reading and writing from and into the drive takes more time. So, the storage and analysis of this massive data has become a big problem. Big data gives the solution for these problems. It specifies the methods to store and analyze the large data sets. This chapter specifies a brief study of big data techniques to analyze these types of data. It includes a wide study of Hadoop characteristics, Hadoop architecture, advantages of big data and big data eco system. Further, this chapter includes a comprehensive study of Apache Hive for executing health-related data and deaths data of U.S. government.

INTRODUCTION

In today's life, web is playing an important role. A large amount of data is available online. These data are getting generated from various sources such as twitter, face book, cell phone GPS data, healthcare etc. Big data analytics (Chen et al, 2014) is the process of collecting and analysing large complex data sets containing a variety of data types to find customer preferences and other useful information. The processing of such data is difficult using traditional data processing applications. Therefore, to manage and process these types of data requires a new set of frameworks. Hadoop is an open software project for structuring Big Data and for making this data useful for analytics purposes. The creator of this software is Doug Cutting. He is an employee at Yahoo for the Nutch search engine project. He named it after seeing his son's toy elephant. The symbol for Hadoop is a yellow elephant. Hadoop serves as a core platform to enable the processing of large data sets over cluster of servers. These servers are designed to be scalable with high degree of fault tolerance.

DOI: 10.4018/978-1-5225-5852-1.ch015

- **Seven V's of Big Data Analytics:** The Big Data (Sagiroglu et al, 2013) is broken into seven dimensions: Volume, Variety, Velocity, Veracity, Visualisation, Variability and Value.
  - **Volume:** Volume is the amount of data. The volume of data stored in an organisation has grown from megabytes to petabytes. The big volume represents Big Data.
  - **Variety:** Variety refers to the many sources and types of data such as structural, semi structural and un structural.
  - **Velocity:** It deals with the speed at which data flows from different sources such as social media sites, mobile device, business process, networks and human interaction etc. This velocity of data should be handled to make valuable business decisions.
  - **Veracity:** It is virtually worthless, if the data set being analysed is incomplete and inaccurate. This may happen due to the collection of data set from various sources with different formats, with noise and errors. Large amount of time may be involved to clean up this noisy data rather than analysing it.
  - **Visualisation:** Once the data set is processed it should be presented in readable format. Visualisation may contain many parameters and variables which cannot be represented using normal graphical formats or spread sheets. Even three-dimensional visualisations also may not help. So, the visualisation has become a new challenge of Big Data Analytics. AT & T has announced a new package called Nanocubes for visualisation.
  - **Variability:** Variability refers to the data set whose meaning and interpretations changes constantly. These changes occur depending on the context. Particularly this is true with Natural Language Processing. A single word may have different meanings. Over time new meanings may be created in place of old one. Interpreting them is essential in the applications like social media analytics. Therefore, the boundless variability of Big Data presents a unique challenge for Data scientists.
  - **Value:** There is a high potential value for Big Data Analytics. In the applications such as US health care system, Big Data Analytics have reduced the spending to 12-17 percent. The Big Data offers not only new and effective methods of selling but also new products to meet previously undetected market demands. Many industries use Big Data for reducing the cost of their organisations and their customers.

Although the popular 3 V's (Volume, Velocity, and Variety) of Big Data Analytics are intrinsic but the other V's (Variability, Veracity, Value and Visualisation) are also important attributes. All of them are useful to analyse and benefit from Big Data Analytics.

- **Hadoop Advantages:** The characteristics or advantages of Hadoop which makes it best solution to handle the data is as listed below.
- **Scalability:** Depending on amount of client data more systems are added to store any amount of data. i.e. Hadoop can scale up incrementally.
- **Flexibility:** Hadoop can store any variety of data i.e. structured and un structured data or semi structured data.
- **Cost Effective:** Hadoop is an open source and can be downloaded freely.
- **Fault Tolerance:** By using the facility of Replication factor the data can replicated or duplicated on two, three or more systems. If one system crashes also the data is available on other system.
- **High Performance:** Hadoop provides high performance in presence of failures also.

COMPONENTS OF HADOOP

HDFS (Hadoop File System) (Patnaik, 2013) and MAP REDUCE are the two core components of Hadoop (Dhawan et al, 2013). Hadoop provides reliable shared storage by Hadoop File System and analysis by Map Reduce.

- **HDFS:** Hadoop Distributed File System is a file system which is used for storing large data sets in a default block of size of 64 MB in distributed manner. Hadoop creates a cluster of computer machines. Each cluster can be built within expensive computer machines. Hadoop coordinates work among the cluster of machines. In case of failure, Hadoop operates continually by shifting the work to remaining machines in the cluster. HDFS stores the data on the cluster in form of 64 MB (by default) or 128 MB blocks each. And each block is replicated 3 times by default. This replication factor may be incremented depending on the requirement.

Components of HDFS

As shown in the figure 1, the main components of HDFS are Name Node, Data Node and Secondary Name Node. Name Node works as a master of the system. It manages and maintains the blocks which are present on Data Node. However Data Nodes serve as slaves which are deployed on each machine and provide actual storage. It also processes the read and write requests of the clients. Secondary Name Node works as a backup for Name Node metadata. It connects to Name Node every hour. If Name Node fails, Secondary Name Node sends metadata back to Name Node so that it can be built again. Name Nodes meta data contains list of files, list of blocks for each file, list of Data Node for each block and file attributes such as access time, replication factor etc.

Figure 1. Components of Hadoop File System.

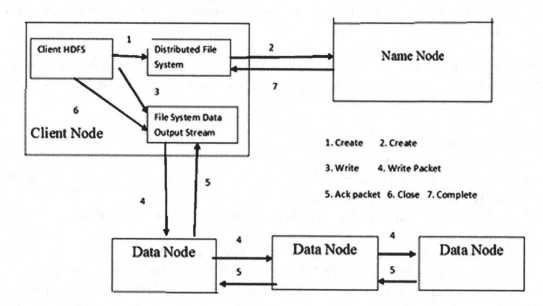

- **MapReduce:** MapReduce (Pandey, 2016) is created by Google and works as a programming framework for distributed computing. It is based on divide and conquer method to solve complicated Big Data problems into small units of work and process them parallel. In other words, we can say that the data set is reduced into smaller subset where analytics can be applied. Basically, there are two main functions of Map Reduce. They are listed below.
- **Map:** This function splits up the input data into multiple jobs and executes them in parallel. It takes key/value pairs as input and generates an intermediate set of key/value pairs.
- **Reduce:** This function receives the mapped intermediate values and key then produces the final result.
- **Job Tracker and Task Tracker:** A Job Tracker node is assigned to each Map Reduce. It distributes mapper and reducer functions to available Task Trackers and monitors the result. i.e. it schedules and manages jobs. However, a Task Tracker executes map and reduce functions on each cluster node and then result is communicated back to the Job Tracker. The high-level architecture of Map Reduce is shown in the Figure 2.

HADOOP ECO SYSTEM

Many technologies are built on the top of Hadoop to increase its efficiency and performance. These sets of technologies along with the Hadoop are known as Hadoop Eco System (Bhradwaj et al, 2015; Garg et al, 2016; Urmila et al, 2016) This Hadoop Eco System is represented in the figure 3 which consists of following technologies.

Figure 2. High level architecture of MapReduce

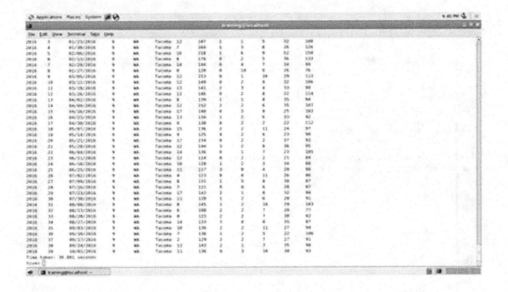

- **Apache Pig:** It was developed by Yahoo for creating and executing MapReduce (Harshawardhan et al, 2014; Dhyani et al, 2014) jobs on very large data sets. Then it was moved to Apache Software Foundation and known as Apache pig. The language used for this platform is known as pig Latin. It is an alternative to java for writing MapReduce programs. Pig scripts take 5% of the time compared to writing MapReduce programs. Similar to actual pig that can digest almost any type of food, Apache pig can handle any type of data. Using pig, overall development and testing time is reduced as we have to write only fewer lines of codes.

- **Sqoop:** It is similar to an ETL (Extract, Transfer and Load) tool which is used to transfer bulk data between Apache Hadoop and structured data stores such as Relational Database servers and vice versa. It facilitates bidirectional exchange of data between relational databases and HDFS. With Sqoop the contents of table are imported to HDFS which further may be used as MapReduce jobs and can be exported from HDFS to Relational databases.

- **Hbase:** In Hadoop, the data is accessed in a sequential manner only. That is, even for a simplest job, entire data set has to be searched. So, a new solution is needed to access data in random manner. Applications such as Hbase, MongoDB, Dynamo and couchDB are some of databases that store large amount of data and allows data access in random manner. Hbase is an open source, horizontally scalable which built on top of Hadoop. It is a column-oriented database. It provides quick and fast random access of large amount of structured data set.

- **Zookeeper:** Apache Zookeeper is an open source project to provide centralized infrastructure. This centralised infrastructure helps to synchronize across the Hadoop cluster. The architecture of Zookeeper has hierarchical name space architecture. Each node in the Zookeeper architecture is called as Znode. These Znodes can be updated by any node in the cluster. These changes are informed to Znode by any node in the cluster. Zookeeper was designed to store Metadata such as status information, configuration, location information etc.

Figure 3. Hadoop Eco System.

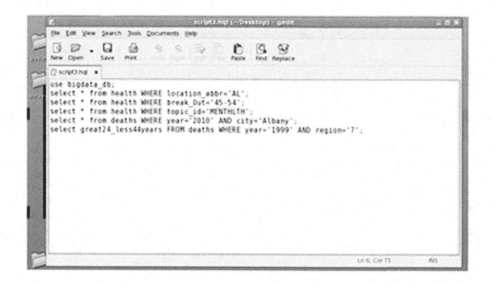

- **Flume:** Flume is used in social media analytics. It is a reliable, distributed and available service to collect, aggregate large amounts of data sets efficiently. It is used for moving large amount of streaming data sets into Hadoop Distributed File System. This application is built on the top of Hadoop. The stream data may be generated from various sources such as sensor, machine data, logs, face book, twitter or any other social media. The data model for flume consists of source, sink, channel and agent. Through source the stream data enters into the Flume. Sink is used to deliver the data to the destination. However, channel will act as a medium between source and sink. Agent is the Java Virtual Machine which creates an environment to run Flume.

- **Solr:** Like Flume, Solr is also used in social media analytics. Flume is used to stream web data where as Solr is used to store this web data. This can be done by indexing via XML, JSON, CSV, python, Ruby or binary. Queries are executed and results are received inform of XML, JSON, CSV, python, Ruby or binary. It is reliable, scalable and fault tolerant.

- **Hue:** Hadoop User Experience (HUE) is an open source project which provides a web user interface or Graphical User Interface (GUI) for the users. As it provides web GUI, users can easily interact with Apache Hadoop to increase productivity.

- **Oozie:** It is a scheduling tool which is a part of Hue. Oozie is a java web application used to schedule Hadoop jobs. There are two basic types of Oozie Jobs. They are Oozie Workflow and Oozie scheduler. After creating the job it is submitted to work flow with all the inputs. After submitting the job through work flow it comes to scheduler. The Scheduler will schedule the jobs. Oozie can be accessed through hue.

- **Impala:** Impala is a flavour of Cloudera and it is 20 to 100 times faster than Hive for retrieval of the data. It is a distributed SQL engine. Clients can connect to Impala through JDBC or ODBC and authentication is done using Kerberos. Once job is submitted to Job Tracker, job is executed by Impala server. There are three key components of Cloudera Impala. They are Impala shell, Impalad, Impala-state-store. Impala shell is used to start the shell script and queries are executed here. On each Hadoop data node, Impalad runs which plans and executes the queries sent from Impala shell. The location information about all the running Impalad instances is stored by Impala-state-store.

- **Tableau:** Tableau transforms the data into interactive visualisations called dashboards. It is fast and easy tool for analysing the data. It is also used for Visualisation and information sharing. Hadoop is one of the data sources for Tableau. That is, it can connect to any flavours of Hadoop, corporate Data Warehouse, Microsoft Excel or web-based data.

- **Yarn:** Apache Hadoop Yarn is a cluster management tool which is redesigned as resource manager. Two separate daemons are created for the functionalities of resource management and job scheduling/monitoring. Yarn has two basic components: a global Resource Manager (RM) and a per-application Application Master (AM). Scheduler and Applications Manager are the two components of Resource Manager. Scheduler allocates the resources to various running applications. However, Application Manager accepts job submissions and executes the application specific application Master and provides the service for restarting the Application Master container on failure.

- **Spark:** Apache spark is an open source cluster computing framework. It provides up to 100 times faster performance compared to Map reduce. Map Reduce is suitable for batch processing whereas spark is suitable for batch processing and real time processing. Spark provides machine learning algorithms which allow programs to load and query data repeatedly. The core components of spark are: Spark Core and Resilient Distributed Datasets, Spark SQL, Spark Streaming, MLib and GraphX.

- **Apache HIVE:** It is developed by Face book initially then it was taken by Apache software and named as Apache Hive (Singh et al, 2015). Hive provides a platform to develop scripts similar to SQL. The developers can write the queries in Hive using Hive Query Language. It is an open source and scalable query language. It analyses large datasets stored in Hadoop's HDFS. The architecture of Hive is represented in the figure 4. The main components of Hive architecture are Meta store, Driver, Compiler, Optimizer, Executer and command line interface and user interface. Meta data about each table is stored in Meta store. This Meta data may store information such as schema and location of table etc. It helps the driver to keep track of the data sets distributed over network. Driver receives the HIVE query statements and executes them by creating sessions. It also monitors the life cycle and progress of the execution and stores the necessary meta data generated during the execution of query statement. The driver contains three parts compiler, optimizer and executor. Compiler converts the Hive query to an Abstract Syntax Tree (AST). Then this AST is converted into Directed Acyclic Graph (DAG). However, an Optimizer performs various transformations such as converting a pipeline of joins by a single join etc to get an optimized DAG. After compilation and optimization, the executer executes the tasks according to the DAG by interacting with the job tracker.

Command Line Interface (CLI) and User Interface (UI) are used to allow an external user to interact with HIVE by submitting queries. The process status is also monitored here. Like JDBC and ODBC servers, a Thrift server also allows the external clients to interact with HIVE (Lakavath et al, 2014).

Figure 4. Hive Architecture or components of Hive.

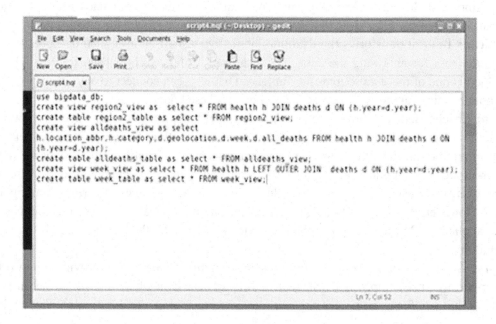

HIVE provides a query language called Hive Query Language (HQL) which is similar to Structured Query Language (SQL). HIVE Query Language supports commands such as select, project, join, aggregate, union all and sub queries. HIVE supports Data Definition Language (DDL) statements to create tables. Then the data can be loaded from external sources into Hive tables using load command. Two different types of tables can be created by using HIVE. They are Managed tables and External tables. The data in managed tables are managed by HIVE whereas the data in External tables are managed outside HIVE. That means when a file is loaded into a managed table, the file is moved to data warehouse by HIVE. So, when the table is dropped, both the data and metadata are deleted. However, when a file is loaded into external table, no files are moved. So, when the table is dropped only metadata is deleted and the data is left alone. External tables are useful when more than one schema is used on the same data and to share the data between HIVE and other Hadoop applications.

While creating the table the data can be partitioned based on the value of column (Frank et al, 2013). This partitioned data is used effectively for applying filters than unpartitioned data. In addition to primitive data types such as integer, float, double and string HIVE also supports associative arrays, lists and structures. To speed up the queries HIVE provides the concept of bucketing. Bucketing splits the data by a particular column. The benefit of bucketing is that, it imposes extra structure on table which can be used to speed up the queries. It improves performance when sampling the data. Number of buckets used can be specified using CLUSTERED BY clause. If the bucket to be sorted, then the command SORTED BY is used.

Hive also supports SQL join statements but supports only equi-joins. It supports inner joins, left outer joins, right outer joins, full outer joins, left semi joins, Map-side joins and Cartesian product joins. Currently Hive is not supporting update and delete of rows in existing tables.

EXPERIMENTAL RESULTS

This section highlights a case study which is based on Health & Human Services. The goal was a big data solution for predictive analysis of Health & Human Services. The challenge was to design a data warehouse to consolidate Health & Human Service data. In this work pre-configured Cloudera Hadoop 4.3.0 ("Index of Documents, n.d.; Rathbone, 2013) with virtual machine10 is used. The data set used for the experiments is collected from U.S. Department of Health & Human Services. This data set gives the Health Related Quality of Life (HRQOL) of people. This data set is collected from Behavioural Risk Factor Surveillance System (BRFSS). This data can be used to evaluate the public health programs introduced by U.S. government. This data is collected from non-institutionalized adults, 18 years old or older. The other data set used for the experiments is on Deaths in 122 U.S. cities. This data set contains the cause of death by age group. Also, the place and week of the death was included in the data set. The size of the data set "Behavioural Risk Factor Data: Health-Related Quality of Life (HRQOL)" is 32,228 KB with 1,26,466 rows whereas the size of the data set "Deaths in 122 U.S. cities - 1962-2016. 122 Cities Mortality Reporting System" is 17,146 KB with 3,46,344 rows. Figure 5 shows the organisation of this section to describe the implementation of Health data case study.

Figure 5. Flowchart to implement Health data case study

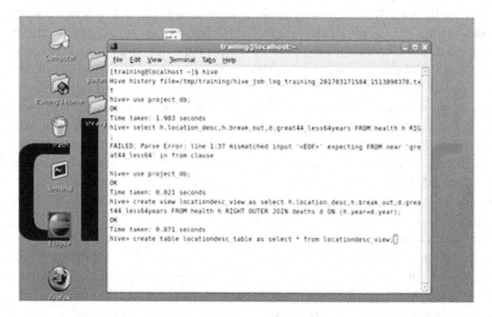

Hive scripts are executed to create tables for two data sets and to load them to Hive. Then two more scripts have written to join these two data sets and to create views. Figures 6 to 14 shows the screen shots of experiments conducted on the data sets using Hive Query Language (hql).

The above case study provides an overview of the utilisation of Big Data Technologies as an emerging discipline in health & human services. It explores the health condition of US citizens. It also calculates death rates per year.

Figure 6. Creation of health database

Figure 7. Description of health database.

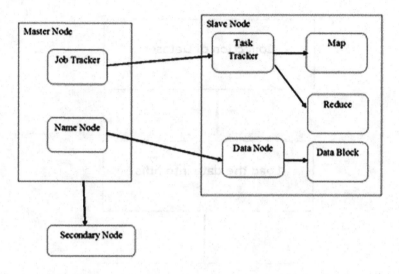

Figure 8. Contents of health database table.

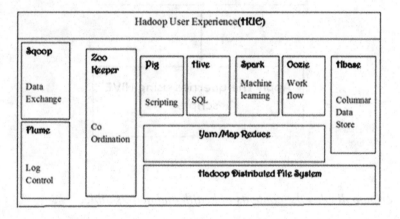

Figure 9. Creation of deaths database

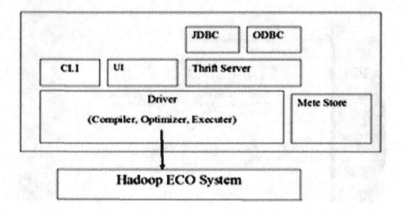

Figure 10. Contents of deaths database table.

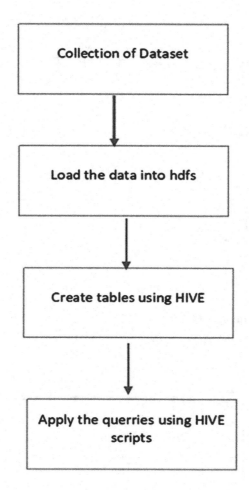

Figure 11. Hive script to display the contents of health and deaths table.

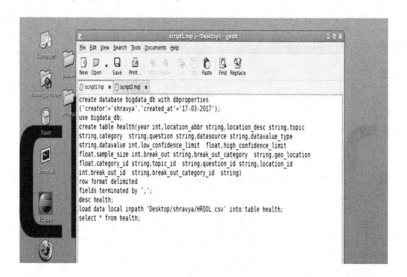

Figure 12. Hive script to create the view and join.

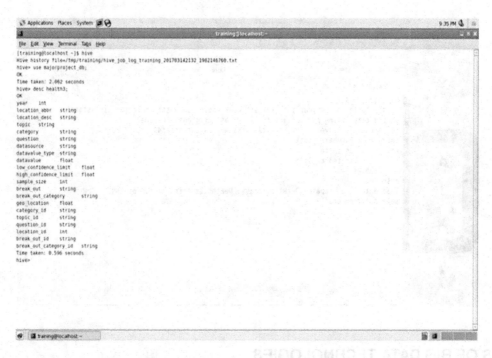

Figure 13. Hive script on right outer join.

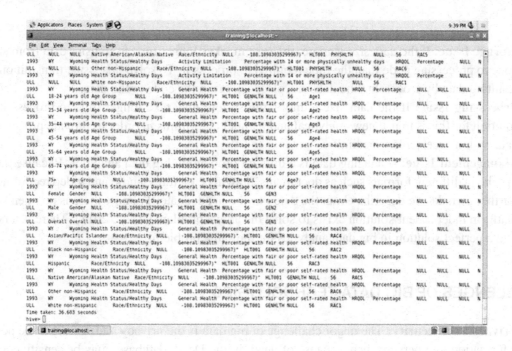

Figure 14. Hive script on full outer join.

ISSUES OF BIG DATA TECHNOLOGIES

Storage, Processing and Management are the three issues which are to be addressed in dealing with big data.

- **Storage Issue:** If the data size is more, the system takes longer time to transfer data from storage node to processing node than the time required to process it. To solve this issue, transmit only the resulting data by processing the data in a place i.e. bring the code to the data.
- **Processing Issue:** If the data size is more, the system may take longer time to process it. One solution for this is to use new analytical and parallel algorithms in order to provide processing of data within acceptable time limits.
- **Management Issue:** Managing data is a difficult problem in big data analytics. Because the data may be in different formats such as documents, drawings, pictures, audio and video recordings etc. Further metadata to describe about the data may be in adequate. Till now there is no open source, platform independent solution exists to solve the above problem (Jason, 2018). There is a need to find a perfect solution in big data analytics for the same problem.

CHALLENGES OF BIG DATA TECHNOLOGIES

- **Privacy and Security:** The major challenge of big data is the privacy and security. The personal information of a person, such as cause of death in the Death database, may be sensitive and the person might not want any other person to know about them.

- **Fault Tolerance:** Fault Tolerance is another challenge of big data. In case of failure the damage should be in the acceptable limits. It is very difficult to achieve 100 percent fault tolerant system. However, a method should be employed to reduce the failure to an acceptable limit. One method is to divide the task into sub tasks and compute these sub tasks on different nodes.

CONCLUSION

Big Data analytics has become most promising research area over the globe. Also, it is generating new opportunities and new challenges for business across each industry. The challenge is to integrate data from social media and other unstructured data into traditional Business Environment. Apache Hadoop provides a cost-effective solution for this challenge.

This paper describes characteristics of Big Data along with 7Vs, Volume, Variety, Velocity, Veracity, Visualisation, Variability and Value of it. Also, this paper described the Hadoop Eco system which can be used to process structured, semi structured and un structured data sets. Hive is used to load the dataset of about 1 lakh thirty thousand rows within 36 seconds. The concepts such as Join and Views are also applied to integrate the two data sets. From the results we can conclude that HIVE can be used effectively on large data sets for analysis. Also, for the developers who are good in SQL language, Hive provides an easy platform for analysis. Further this work may be extended by implementing a new and emerging Big Data tools to improve the performance of Hadoop.

REFERENCES

Bhradwaj, A. (2015). Big Data emerging Technologies: A case Study with Analyzing Twitter Data using Apache Hive. In *RAECS UIET Punjab University Chandigarh*. IEEE.

Chen, M., Mao, S., & Liu, Y. (2014). Big data: A survey. Mobile Networks and Applications, 9(2), 171-209. doi:10.100711036-013-0489-0

Dhawan & Rathee. (2013). Big Data Analytics using Hadoop Components like Pig and Hive. In *American International Journal of Research in Science* (pp. 88–93). Technology, Engineering & Mathematics.

Dhyani, B., & Barthwal, A. (2014). Big Data Analytics using Hadoop. *International Journal of Computers and Applications*, 108(12), 1–59. doi:10.5120/18960-0288

(2016). Dr. Urmila R. Pol: Big Data Analysis: Comparison of Hadoop MapReduce, pig and Hive, International Journal of Innovative Research in Science. *Engineering and Technology*, 5(6), 9687–9693.

Garg, R., & Agarwal, H. (2016). Big Data Analytics Recommendation Solutions for Crop Disease using Hive and Hadoop Platform. *Indian Journal of Science and Technology*, 9(32), ●●●. doi:10.17485/ijst/2016/v9i32/100728

Harshawardhan, Bhosale, Devendra, & Gadekar. (2014). A Review Paper on Big Data and Hadoop. *International Journal of Scientific and Research Publications, 4.*

Index of Documents. (n.d.). Apache Hadoop. Retrieved from https://hadoop.apache.org/docs/

JASON. (2008). Data Analysis Challenges. The Mitre Corporation, JSR-08-142.

Lakavath, S. (2014). *A Big Data Hadoop Architecture for Online Analysis*. Academic Press.

Matthew Rathbone Blog. (2013). *A Beginners Guide to Hadoops*. Accessed May 3rd 2018: http://blog.mattherwrathbone.com/2013/04/17/what-is-hadoop.html

Pandey, P., Kumar, M., & Srivastav, P. (2016). Classification Techniques for Big Data: A Survey. *IEEE International Conference on Computing for Sustainable Global Development*, 3625-3629.

Patnaik, L. M. (2014). Bid Data Analytics: An Approach using Hadoop Distributed File System. International Journal of Engineering and Innovative Technology, 3, 239-243.

Sagiroglu, S., & Sinanc, D. (2013). Big data: A review. *IEEE International Conference on Collaboration Technologies and System (CTS)*, 42-47.

Singh, J., & Singhla, V. (2015). Big Data:Tools and Technologies in Big Data. *International Journal of Computers and Applications*.

Stephen, K., & Frank, A. J. (2013). Big data: Issues and challenges moving forward. *IEEE International Conference on System Science*.

Compilation of References

Abdulameer, L. F., Jignesh, J. D., Sripati, U., & Kulkarni, M. (2014). BER performance enhancement for secure wireless optical communication systems based on chaotic MIMO techniques. *Nonlinear Dynamics*, *75*(1-2), 7–16. doi:10.100711071-013-1044-z

Abood, B. (2016). Energy efficient clustering in WSNs using fuzzy approach to improve LEACH protocol. *Int J Manag Inf Technol*, *11*(2), 2641–2656.

Abrishami, S., Naghibzadeh, M., & Epema, D. H. (2013). Deadline-constrained workflow scheduling algorithms for Infrastructure as a Service Clouds. *Future Generation Computer Systems*, *29*(1), 158–169. doi:10.1016/j.future.2012.05.004

Acharya, U. R., & Dua, P. (2014). *Machine Learning in Healthcare Informatics* (Vol. 56). Springer Berlin Heidelberg. doi:10.1007/978-3-642-40017-9

Agarwalla, P., & Mukhopadhyay, S. (2018). Bi-stage hierarchical selection of pathway genes for cancer progression using a swarm based computational approach. *Applied Soft Computing*, *62*, 230–250. doi:10.1016/j.asoc.2017.10.024

Agarwal, P., & Mehta, S. (2014). Nature-Inspired Algorithms: State-of-Art, Problems and Prospects. *International Journal of Computers and Applications*, *100*(14), 14–21. doi:10.5120/17593-8331

Agarwal, P., & Mehta, S. (2015). Comparative Analysis of Nature Inspired Algorithms on Data Clustering. In *IEEE International Conference on Research in Computational Intelligence and Communication Networks (ICRCICN)* (pp. 119–124). 10.1109/ICRCICN.2015.7434221

Agarwal, P., & Mehta, S. (2016). Enhanced flower pollination algorithm on data clustering. *International Journals of Computers and Applications, Taylor and Francis*, *7074*(August), 1–12. doi:10.1080/1206212X.2016.1224401

Agarwal, P., & Mehta, S. (2017). Empirical analysis of five nature-inspired algorithms on real parameter optimization problems. *Artificial Intelligence Review*, 1–57. doi:10.100710462-017-9547-5

Aggarwal, C., Wolf, J., Yu, P., C. Procopiuc, & Park., J. (1999). Fast Algorithm for Projected Clustering. *CM SIGMoD Record*, *28*(2), 61-72.

Agrawal, R., Gehrke, J., Gunopulos, D., & Raghavan, P. (1998). *Automatic subspace clustering of high dimensional data for data mining applications. In 1998 ACM SIGMOD international conference on Management of data* (pp. 94–105).

Ahmadi, A., Ritonga, M. A., Abedin, M. A., Mattausch, H. J., & Koide, T. (2006). A Learning OCR System Using Short/Long-term Memory Approach and Hardware Implementation in FPGA. In *Evolutionary Computation, 2006. CEC 2006. IEEE Congress on* (pp. 687-693). IEEE.

Akdagli, A., & Guney, K. (2003). Shaped-beam pattern synthesis of equally and unequally spaced linear antenna arrays using a modified tabu search algorithm. *Microwave and Optical Technology Letters*, *36*(1), 16–20. doi:10.1002/mop.10657

Akdagli, A., Guney, K., & Karaboga, D. (2006). Touring ant colony optimization algorithm for shaped-beam pattern synthesis of linear antenna arrays. *Electromagnetics*, *26*(8), 615–628. doi:10.1080/02726340600978349

Akyildiz. (2002). A survey on WSNs. *Computer Networks, 38*(4).

Alon, U., Barkai, N., Notterman, D. A., Gish, K., Ybarra, S., Mack, D., & Levine, A. J. (1999). Broad patterns of gene expression revealed by clustering analysis of tumor and normal colon tissues probed by oligonucleotide arrays. In *Proceedings of the National Academy of Sciences of the United States of America*, *96*(12), 6745–6750. doi:10.1073/pnas.96.12.6745 PMID:10359783

Amaratunga, D., Cabrera, J., & Kovtun, V. (2008). Microarray learning with ABC. *Biostatistics (Oxford, England)*, *9*(1), 128–136. doi:10.1093/biostatistics/kxm017 PMID:17573363

Amiri, B., Fathian, M., & Maroosi, A. (2009). Application of shuffled frog-leaping algorithm on clustering. *International Journal of Advanced Manufacturing Technology*, *45*(1-2), 199–209. doi:10.100700170-009-1958-2

Anh Tuan, T., Tal, H., Iacopo, M., & Gerard, M. (2017). Regressing robust and discriminative 3D morphable models with a very deep neural network. In *IEEE Conference on Computer Vision and Pattern Recognition*. Honolulu, HI.

Anjum, F., & Mouchtaris, P. (2007). *Security for wireless ad hoc networks*. John Wiley & Sons, Inc. doi:10.1002/0470118474

Apolloni, J., Leguizamón, G., & Alba, E. (2016). Two hybrid wrapper-filter feature selection algorithms applied to high-dimensional microarray experiments. *Applied Soft Computing*, *38*, 922–932. doi:10.1016/j.asoc.2015.10.037

Arbor, A. (1992). On the Handling of Continuous-Valued Attributes in Decision Tree Generation. *Machine Learning*, *8*(1), 87–102. doi:10.1007/BF00994007

Arda, M. R. J., Pietro, P., & Halu, B. G. (2013). Multiplex pagerank. *PLoS One*, *8*(10), e78293. doi:10.1371/journal.pone.0078293 PMID:24205186

Arel, I., Rose, D., & Coop, R. (2009). DeSTIN: A scalable deep learning architecture with application to high-dimensional robust pattern recognition. In *AAAI Fall Symposium* (pp. 11-15).

Arevalillo, J. M., & Navarro, H. (2013). Exploring correlations in gene expression microarray data for maximum predictive - minimum redundancy biomarker selection and classification. *Computers in Biology and Medicine*, *43*(10), 1437–1443. doi:10.1016/j.compbiomed.2013.07.005 PMID:24034735

Ash, T. (1989). Dynamic node creation in backpropagation neural networks. *Connection Science*, *1*(4), 365–375. doi:10.1080/09540098908915647

Assent, I. (2012). Clustering high dimensional data. *Wiley Interdisciplinary Reviews. Data Mining and Knowledge Discovery*, *2*(4), 340–350. doi:10.1002/widm.1062

Assent, I., Krieger, R., Müller, E., & Seidl, T. (2008). INSCY: Indexing subspace clusters with in-process-removal of redundancy. In *Eighth IEEE International Conference on Data Mining ICDM'08. (pp. 719-724). IEEE.*

Ataul, B. (2009). A GA based approach for energy efficient routing in two-tiered WSNs. *Ad Hoc Networks*, *7*, 665–676. doi:10.1016/j.adhoc.2008.04.003

Audebert, N., Saux, B., & Lefevre, S. (2016). Semantic segmentation of earth observation data using multimodal and multi-scale deep networks. In *Asian Conference on Computer Vision*, Taipei, Taiwan.

Bache, K., & Lichman, M. (2006). UCI machine learning repository. Retrieved from http://archive.ics.uci.edu/ml

Bagchi, S., & Mitra, S. K. (1999). The nonuniform discrete Fourier transform and its applications in signal processing. New York: Springer Science+Business Media, LLC. doi:10.1007/978-1-4615-4925-3

Balakrishnan, N., Murthy, P. K., & Ramakrishna, S. (1979). Synthesis of antenna arrays with spatial and excitation constraints. *IEEE Transactions on Antennas and Propagation, AP-27*(5), 690–696. doi:10.1109/TAP.1979.1142151

Balanis, C. A. (2004). *Antenna theory analysis and design* (2nd ed.). New York: John Wiley & Sons, Inc.

Banati, H., & Mehta, S. (2013). Improved shuffled frog leaping algorithm for continuous optimisation adapted SEVO toolbox. *International Journal of Advanced Intelligence Paradigms, 5*(1/2), 31. doi:10.1504/IJAIP.2013.054670

Bandyopadhyay, S., Mallik, S., & Mukhopadhyay, A. (2014). A survey and comparative study of statistical tests for identifying differential expression from microarray data. *IEEE/ACM Transactions on Computational Biology and Bioinformatics, 11*(1), 95–115. doi:10.1109/TCBB.2013.147 PMID:26355511

Basappa, K., & Jategaonkar, R. V. (1995). *Aspects of feed forward neural network modeling and its application to lateral-directional flight data*. DLR IB-111-95a30.

Battiston, V. L. F., Nicosia, V., & Latora, V. (2014). Structural measures for multiplex networks. *Physical Review. E, 89*(3), 032804. doi:10.1103/PhysRevE.89.032804 PMID:24730896

Bavelas, A. (1950). Communication Patterns in Task-Oriented Groups. *The Journal of the Acoustical Society of America, 22*(6), 725–730. doi:10.1121/1.1906679

Baykasoğlu, A., & Ozsoydan, F. B. (2015). Adaptive firefly algorithm with chaos for mechanical design optimization problems. *Applied Soft Computing, 36*, 152–164. doi:10.1016/j.asoc.2015.06.056

Beg, A., Ahmed, F., & Campbell, P. (2010, July). Hybrid OCR Techniques for Cursive Script Languages-A Review and Applications. In *Computational Intelligence, Communication Systems and Networks (CICSyN), 2010 Second International Conference on* (pp. 101-105). IEEE. 10.1109/CICSyN.2010.36

Begel, A., & Graham, S. L. (2005, September). Spoken programs. In *Visual Languages and Human-Centric Computing, 2005 IEEE Symposium on* (pp. 99-106). IEEE. 10.1109/VLHCC.2005.58

Bellman, R. (1961). *Adaptive Control Processes: A guided Tour*. Princeton, NJ: Princeton University Press. doi:10.1515/9781400874668

Benavoli, A., Corani, G., & Mangili, F. (2016). Should we really use post-hoc tests based on mean-ranks? *Journal of Machine Learning Research, 17*, 1–10.

Bengio, Y., Courville, A., & Vincent, P. (2013). Representation learning: A review and new perspectives. *IEEE Transactions on Pattern Analysis and Machine Intelligence, 35*(8), 1798–1828. doi:10.1109/TPAMI.2013.50 PMID:23787338

Bergen, M. (2015, July 15). Deep learning AI is taking over tech what is it? *Recode.net*. Retrieved from http://recode.net/2015/07/15/deep-learning-ai-is-taking-over-tech-what-is-it/

Bertsekas, D., & Tsitsiklis, J. (1996). *Neuro-dynamic programming*. Belmont, MA: Athena Scientific.

Bhradwaj, A. (2015). Big Data emerging Technologies: A case Study with Analyzing Twitter Data using Apache Hive. In *RAECS UIET Punjab University Chandigarh*. IEEE.

Boccalettia, S., Bianconic, G., Criadod, R., & del Geniof, C. (2014). The structure and dynamics of multilayer networks. *Physics Reports, 544*(1), 1–122. PMID:25484487

Bojic, I., Lipic, T., & Podobnik, V. (2012). Bio-inspired clustering and data diffusion in machine social networks. In *Computational Social Networks* (pp. 51–79). Springer. doi:10.1007/978-1-4471-4054-2_3

Boldi, P., & Vigna, S. (2014). Axioms for Centrality. *Internet Mathematics*, *10*(3-4), 222–262. doi:10.1080/15427951 .2013.865686

Bonacich, P. (1987). Power and centrality: A family of measures. *American Journal of Sociology*, *92*(5), 1170–1182. doi:10.1086/228631

Bonacich, P. (1991). Simultaneous group and individual centralities. *Social Networks*, *13*(2), 155–168. doi:10.1016/0378-8733(91)90018-O

Bonilla-Huerta, E., Hernández-Montiel, A., Morales-Caporal, R., & Arjona-López, M. (2016). Hybrid framework using multiple-filters and an embedded approach for an efficient selection and classification of microarray data. *IEEE/ACM Transactions on Computational Biology and Bioinformatics*, *13*(1), 12–26. doi:10.1109/TCBB.2015.2474384 PMID:26336138

Bordes, A., & Weston, J. (2016). *Learning end-to-end goal-oriented dialog.* arXiv preprint arXiv:1605.07683

Borgatti, S. P. (1995). Centrality and AIDS. *Connections*, *18*(1), 112–114.

Boulle, M. (2004). Khiops: A Statistical Discretization Method of Continuous Attributes. *Machine Learning*, *55*(1), 53–69. doi:10.1023/B:MACH.0000019804.29836.05

Boullé, M. (2006). MODL: A Bayes optimal discretization method for continuous attributes. *Machine Learning*, *65*(1), 131–165. doi:10.100710994-006-8364-x

Bradley, P. S., Fayyad, U., & Reina, C. (1998). Scaling Clustering Algorithms to Large Databases. In KDD-98 (pp. 1–7).

Brazdil, P., & Soares, C. (2000). A Comparison of Ranking Methods for Classification Algorithm Selection. *Machine Learning: ECML*, *1810*, 63–75. doi:10.1007/3-540-45164-1_8

Bruintjes, T. M., Kokkeler, A. B. J., & Smit, G. J. M. (2016). Asymmetric shaped-pattern synthesis for planar antenna arrays. *International Journal of Antennas and Propagation*, *2016*, 1–13. doi:10.1155/2016/4746381

Bucci, O. M., D'elia, G., Mazzarella, G., & Panariello, G. (1994). Antenna pattern synthesis: A new general approach. *Proceedings of the IEEE*, *82*(3), 358–371. doi:10.1109/5.272140

Burt, R. S. (1992). *Structural Holes: The Social Structure of Competition.* Harvard University Press.

Buyya, R., Yeo, C. S., Venugopal, S., Broberg, J., & Brandic, I. (2009). Cloud computing and emerging IT platforms: Vision, hype, and reality for delivering computing as the 5th utility. *Future Generation Computer Systems*, *25*(6), 599–616. doi:10.1016/j.future.2008.12.001

C. Y. (2011). Feature subset selection based on bio-inspired algorithms. *Journal of Information Science and Engineering*, *27*, 1667–1686.

Cabric, D., Mishra, S. M., & Brodersen, R. W. (2004, November). Implementation issues in spectrum sensing for cognitive radios. In *Conference record of the thirty-eighth Asilomar conference on Signals, systems and computers* (Vol. 1, pp. 772-776). IEEE. 10.1109/ACSSC.2004.1399240

Callaghan, S., Maechling, P., Small, P., Milner, K., Juve, G., Jordan, T. H., ... Brooks, C. (2011). Metrics for heterogeneous scientific workflows: A case study of an earthquake science application. *International Journal of High Performance Computing Applications*, *25*(3), 274–285. doi:10.1177/1094342011414743

Cardillo, G.-G., & Zanin, R. Papo, del Pozo, & Boccaletti. (2013). Emergence of network features from multiplexity. *Scientific Reports, 3*, 1344. Retrieved from https://github.com/evelinag/StarWars-social-network/blob/master/networks/,2015

Cardoso, J., Miller, J. A., Sheth, A. P., & Arnold, J. (2002). Modeling Quality of Service for Workflows and Web Service Processes. Retrieved from http://corescholar.libraries.wright.edu/knoesis/791

Cardoso, J., Sheth, A., & Miller, J. (2003). *Workflow Quality of Service.* (Vol. 108).

Carlson, B. D., & Willner, D. (1992). Antenna pattern synthesis using weighted least squares. *IEE Proceedings-H, 139*(1), 11-16.

Carneiro, G., & Nascimento, J. C. (2013). Combining multiple dynamic models and deep learning architectures for tracking the left ventricle endocardium in ultrasound data. *IEEE Transactions on Pattern Analysis and Machine Intelligence, 35*(11), 2592–2607. doi:10.1109/TPAMI.2013.96 PMID:24051722

Castillo, O., Valdez, F., & Melin, P. (2007). Hierarchical genetic algorithms for topology optimization in fuzzy control systems. *International Journal of General Systems, 36*(5), 575–591. doi:10.1080/03081070701321860

Cayirci, E., & Rong, C. (2009). *Security in wireless ad hoc and sensor networks.* West Sussex, UK: John Wiley & Sons Ltd. doi:10.1002/9780470516782

Chaker, H., Abri, M., & Badaoui, H. A. (2016). Hybrid evolutionary algorithm genetical swarm optimization for 1D and 2D annular ring unequally spaced antennas arrays synthesis. *Electromagnetics, 36*(8), 485–03. doi:10.1080/02726343.2016.1236008

Chakraborty, J., Konar, A., Jain, L. C., & Chakraborty, U. K. (2009). Cooperative multi-robot path planning using differential evolution. *Journal of Intelligent & Fuzzy Systems, 20*(1, 2), 13-27.

Chakraborty, T., & Narayanam, R. (2016). *Cross-layer Betweenness Centrality in Multiplex Networks with Applications.* ICDE. doi:10.1109/ICDE.2016.7498257

Chan, C. (1991). Determination of quantization intervals in rule based. In *Decision Aiding for Complex Systems* (pp. 1719–1723). Conference.

Chang, H.-P., Sarkar, T. K., & Pereira-Filho, O. M. C. (2000). Antenna pattern synthesis utilizing spherical Bessel functions. *IEEE Transactions on Antennas and Propagation, 48*(6), 853–859. doi:10.1109/8.865216

Chan, K. C. C., & Ching, J. Y. (1995). Class-Dependent Discretization for Inductive Learning from Continuous and Mixed-Mode Data. *IEEE Transactions on Pattern Analysis and Machine Intelligence.* doi:10.1109/34.391407

Chaouchi, H., & Laurent-Maknavicius, M. (Eds.). (2007). *Wireless and mobile network security.* Hoboken, NJ: John Wiley & Sons, Inc.

Chatterjee, S., Chatterjee, S., & Poddar, D. R. (2014). Synthesis of linear array using Taylor distribution and particle swarm optimisation. *International Journal of Electronics, 102*(3), 514–528. doi:10.1080/00207217.2014.905993

Chen, M., Mao, S., & Liu, Y. (2014). Big data: A survey. Mobile Networks and Applications, 9(2), 171-209. doi:10.100711036-013-0489-0

Chen, W., & Deelman, E. (2012). WorkflowSim: A toolkit for simulating scientific workflows in distributed environments. In *2012 IEEE 8th International Conference on E-Science, Chicago, IL* (pp. 1-8).

Cheng, Q., Zhou, H., & Cheng, J. (2011). The Fisher-Markov Selector. *Fast Selecting Maximally Separable Feature Subset for Multiclass Classification with Applications to High-Dimensional Data, 33*(6), 1217–1233. PMID:21493968

Cheng, S. (2013). SI in big data analytics. In *Intelligent Data Engineering and Automated Learning–IDEAL* (pp. 417–426). Springer. doi:10.1007/978-3-642-41278-3_51

Chen, K. H., Wang, K. J., Tsai, M. L., Wang, K. M., Adrian, A. M., Cheng, W. C., & Chang, K. S. (2014). Gene selection for cancer identification: A decision tree model empowered by particle swarm optimization algorithm. *BMC Bioinformatics*, *15*(1), 1–12. doi:10.1186/1471-2105-15-49 PMID:24555567

Chen, S., Caojin, Z., Ming, D., Jialiang, L., & Mike, R. (2017). *Using ranking-CNN for age estimation*. doi:10.1109/CVPR.2017.86

Chen, W., & Zhang, J. (2009). An ant colony optimization approach to a grid workflow scheduling problem with various QoS requirements. *IEEE Transactions on Systems, Man and Cybernetics. Part C, Applications and Reviews*, *39*(1), 29–43. doi:10.1109/TSMCC.2008.2001722

Chen, Y., Yang, J., Trappe, W., & Martin, R. P. (2010). Detecting and localizing identity-based attacks in wireless and sensor networks. *IEEE Transactions on Vehicular Technology*, *59*(5), 2418–2434. doi:10.1109/TVT.2010.2044904

Cheok, M. H., Yang, W., Pui, C. H., Downing, J. R., Cheng, C., Naeve, C. W., ... Evans, W. E. (2003). Treatment-specific changes in gene expression discriminate in vivo drug response in human leukemia cells. *Nature Genetics*, *34*(1), 85–90. doi:10.1038/ng1151 PMID:12704389

Chmielewski, M. R., & Grzymala-Busse, J. W. (1996). Global discretization of continuous attributes as preprocessing for machine learning. *International Journal of Approximate Reasoning*, *15*(4), 319–331. doi:10.1016/S0888-613X(96)00074-6

Cho, K., Van Merriënboer, B., Gulcehre, C., Bahdanau, D., Bougares, F., Schwenk, H., & Bengio, Y. (2014). *Learning phrase representations using RNN encoder-decoder for statistical machine translation*. arXiv preprint arXiv:1406.1078

Chollet, F. (2017). *Deep Learning with Python*. New York, USA: Manning Publications.

Chowdhury, A., Rakshit, P., Konar, A., & Nagar, A. K. (2014, July). A modified bat algorithm to predict Protein-Protein Interaction network. In *2014 IEEE Congress on Evolutionary Computation (CEC)* (pp. 1046-1053). IEEE. 10.1109/CEC.2014.6900518

Chuang, L. Y., Yang, C. H., Wu, K. C., & Yang, C. H. (2011). A hybrid feature selection method for DNA microarray data. *Computers in Biology and Medicine*, *41*(4), 228–237. doi:10.1016/j.compbiomed.2011.02.004 PMID:21376310

Chu, C. T., Kim, S. K., Lin, Y. A., Yu, Y., Bradski, G., Ng, A. Y., & Olukotun, K. (2007). *Map reduce for machine learning on multicore* (pp. 281–288). Advances in Neural Information Processing Systems Vancouver.

Chui, M. (2010). The IoT. *The McKinsey Quarterly*, *2*, 1–9.

Chu, P. P. (2008). *FPGA prototyping by Verilog examples*. Hoboken, NJ: John Wiley & Sons, Inc. doi:10.1002/9780470374283

Coleman, J. S., Katz, E., & Menzel, H. (1966). Medical Innovation: A Diffusion Study. Bobbs-Merrill.

Collin, G., Geron, E., Lucas, J., & Ditchi, T. (2010). Fast antenna pattern synthesis using the variational method. *IET Microwaves, Antennas & Propagation*, *4*(11), 1689–1697. doi:10.1049/iet-map.2008.0399

Cozzo, Kivel, Domenico, Sol, Arenas, Gmez, ... Moreno. (2015). *Clustering coefficients in multiplex networks*. Academic Press.

Crego, E., Muñoz, G., & Islam, F. (2013, May 26). Big Data and Deep Learning: Big Deals or Big Delusions? *Huffington Post*. Retrieved from https://www.huffingtonpost.com/george-munoz-frank-islam-and-ed-crego/big-data-and-deep-learnin_b_3325352.html

Cruz, C., González, J. R., Pelta, D. A., Krasnogor, N., & Terrazas, G. (Eds.). (2010). *Nature Inspired Cooperative Strategies for Optimization (NICSO 2010).* Springer.

Csardi, G., & Nepusz, T. (2006). The igraph software package for complex network research. *Inter. Journal of Complex Systems,* 1695.

Dahl, G. E., Yu, D., Deng, L., & Acero, A. (2012). Context-dependent pre-trained deep neural networks for large-vocabulary speech recognition. *IEEE Transactions on Audio, Speech, and Language Processing, 20*(1), 30–42. doi:10.1109/TASL.2011.2134090

Das, S., & Mukhopadhyay, S. (2016, December). Sensing error minimization for cognitive radio in dynamic environment using death penalty differential evolution based threshold adaptation. In *2016 IEEE Annual India Conference (INDICON)* (pp. 1-6). IEEE. 10.1109/INDICON.2016.7838865

Dash, R., & Misra, B. B. (2016). Pipelining the ranking techniques for microarray data classification: A case study. *Applied Soft Computing, 48,* 298–316. doi:10.1016/j.asoc.2016.07.006

Das, S., Abraham, A., & Konar, A. (2008). Automatic Clustering Using an Improved Differential Evolution Algorithm. *IEEE Transactions on Systems, Man, and Cybernetics. Part A, Systems and Humans, 38*(1), 218–237.

Das, S., & Suganthan, P. N. (2011). Differential Evolution: A Survey of the. *IEEE Transactions on Evolutionary Computation, 15*(1), 4–31. doi:10.1109/TEVC.2010.2059031

Daszykowski, M., Walczak, B., & Massart, D. L. (2001). Looking for natural patterns in data: Part 1. density-based approach. *Chemometrics and Intelligent Laboratory Systems, 56*(2), 83–92. doi:10.1016/S0169-7439(01)00111-3

Dauphin, Y., Pascanu, R., Gulcehre, C., Cho, K., Ganguly, S., & Bengio, Y. (2014). Identifying and attacking the saddle point problem in high-dimensional non-convex optimization. In *27th International Conference on Neural Information Processing Systems,* Montreal, Canada (pp. 2933-2941).

Davison, A. J., Reid, I. D., Molton, N. D., & Stasse, O. (2007). MonoSLAM: Real-time single camera SLAM. *IEEE Transactions on Pattern Analysis and Machine Intelligence, 29*(6), 1052–1067. doi:10.1109/TPAMI.2007.1049 PMID:17431302

Daxwanger, W. A., & Schmidt, G. (1996). Neural and fuzzy approaches to vision-based parking control. *Control Engineering Practice, 4*(11), 1607–1614. doi:10.1016/0967-0661(96)00176-1

De Domenico, M., Lancichinetti, A., Arenas, A., & Rosvall, M. (2015). Identifying modular flows on multilayer networks reveals highly overlapping organization in interconnected systems. *Physical Review X, 5*(1), 011027. doi:10.1103/PhysRevX.5.011027

De Domenico, M., & Porter, M. A. (2014). Muxviz: A tool for multilayer analysis and visualization of networks. *Journal of Complex Networks,* 1–18.

De Luca, A., Oriolo, G., & Samson, C. (1998). Feedback control of a nonholonomic car-like robot. In *Robot motion planning and control* (pp. 171–253). Berlin: Springer. doi:10.1007/BFb0036073

Dean, J., Corrado, G. S., Monga, R., Chen, K., Devin, M., Le, Q. V., ... Ng, A. Y. (2012). Large scale distributed deep networks. In *Conference on Neural Information Processing Systems,* Lake Tahoe, NV.

Dean, J., & Ghemawat, S. (2008). Mapreduce: Simplified data processing on large clusters. *Communications of the ACM, 51*(1), 107–113. doi:10.1145/1327452.1327492

Demšar, J. (2006). Statistical Comparisons of Classifiers over Multiple Data Sets. *Journal of Machine Learning Research, 7,* 1–30. doi:10.1016/j.jecp.2010.03.005

Deng, L., Seltzer, M., Yu, D., Acero, A., Mohamed, A., & Hinton, G. (2010). Binary coding of speech spectrograms using a deep auto-encoder. In INTERSPEECH 2010,Makuhari, Chiba.

Deng, L. (2014). *A tutorial survey of architectures, algorithms, and applications for deep learning*. In *APSIPA Transactions on Signal and Information Processing*.

Deng, L., Hinton, G., & Kingsbury, B. (2013). New types of deep neural network learning for speech recognition and related applications: An overview. *International Conference on Acoustics, Speech and Signal Processing*. Vancouver, Canada. 10.1109/ICASSP.2013.6639344

Desrochers, D., Qu, Z., & Saengdeejing, A. (2001). OCR readability study and algorithms for testing partially damaged characters. In *Intelligent Multimedia, Video and Speech Processing, 2001. Proceedings of 2001 International Symposium on* (pp. 397-400). IEEE. 10.1109/ISIMP.2001.925417

Dhariya, O., Malviya, S., & Tiwary, U. S. (2017, January). A hybrid approach for Hindi-English machine translation. In *Information Networking (ICOIN), 2017 International Conference on* (pp. 389-394). IEEE. 10.1109/ICOIN.2017.7899465

Dhawan & Rathee. (2013). Big Data Analytics using Hadoop Components like Pig and Hive. In *American International Journal of Research in Science* (pp. 88–93). Technology, Engineering & Mathematics.

Dhyani, B., & Barthwal, A. (2014). Big Data Analytics using Hadoop. *International Journal of Computers and Applications*, *108*(12), 1–59. doi:10.5120/18960-0288

Diao, R., & Shen, Q. (2015). Nature inspired feature selection meta-heuristics. *Artificial Intelligence Review*, *44*(3), 311–340. doi:10.100710462-015-9428-8

Dib, N., & Sharaqa, A. (2015). Design of non-uniform concentric circular antenna arrays with optimal sidelobe level reduction using biogeography-based optimization. *International Journal of Microwave and Wireless Technologies*, *7*(2), 161–166. doi:10.1017/S1759078714000610

Dikmese, S., Kavak, A., Kucuk, K., Sahin, S., & Tangel, A. (2011). FPGA based implementation and comparison of beamformers for CDMA2000. *Wireless Personal Communications*, *57*(2), 233–253. doi:10.100711277-009-9855-4

Dincer, S., & Doganay, A. (2015). The Impact of Pedagogical Agent on Learners' Motivation and Academic Success1. *Practice and Theory in Systems of Education*, *10*(4), 329–348. doi:10.1515/ptse-2015-0032

Ding, G., Wu, Q., Wang, J., & Yao, Y. D. (2014). Big spectrum data: The new resource for cognitive wireless networking. arXiv:1404.6508

Dolgov, D., Thrun, S., Montemerlo, M., & Diebel, J. (2010). Path planning for autonomous vehicles in unknown semi-structured environments. *The International Journal of Robotics Research*, *29*(5), 485–501. doi:10.1177/0278364909359210

Domingos, P. (2012). A few useful things to know about machine learning. *Communications of the ACM*, *55*(10), 78–87. doi:10.1145/2347736.2347755

Dorigo, M., & Di Caro, G. (1999). Ant colony optimization: a new meta-heuristic. In *Proceedings of the 1999 Congress on Evolutionary Computation CEC 99* (*Vol. 2*, pp. 1470-1477). IEEE.

Dorigo, M., & Stützle, T. (2002). The Ant Colony Optimization Metaheuristic: Algorithms, Applications, and Advances. In Handbook of Metaheuristics. Academic Press.

Dorigo, M., & Birattari, M. (2011). Ant colony optimization. In *Encyclopedia of machine learning* (pp. 36–39). Boston, MA: Springer.

Dorigo, M., Birattari, M., & Stützle, T. (2006). Ant Colony Optimization – Artificial Ants as a Computational Intelligence Technique. *IEEE Computational Intelligence Magazine.*

Dorigo, M., & Blum, C. (2005). Ant colony optimization theory: A survey. *Theoretical Computer Science, 344*(2-3), 243–278. doi:10.1016/j.tcs.2005.05.020

Dorigo, M., & Gambardella, L. M. (1997). Ant colony system: A cooperative learning approach to the traveling salesman problem. *IEEE Transactions on Evolutionary Computation, 1*(1), 53–66. doi:10.1109/4235.585892

Dorigo, M., & Socha, K. (2007). *An Introduction to Ant Colony Optimization. In T. F. Gonzalez (Ed.), Approximation Algorithms and Metaheuristics.* CRC Press.

Dubins, L. E. (1957). On curves of minimal length with a constraint on average curvature, and with prescribed initial and terminal positions and tangents. *American Journal of Mathematics, 79*(3), 497–516. doi:10.2307/2372560

Eberhart, R., & Kennedy, J. (1995, October). A new optimizer using particle swarm theory. In *Proceedings of the Sixth International Symposium on Micro Machine and Human Science MHS'95* (pp. 39-43). IEEE. 10.1109/MHS.1995.494215

EI-Kamchouchi, H. (2010). Ultra-low-sidelobe-level concentric-ring array pattern synthesis using Bessel neural networks. *IEEE Antennas & Propagation Magazine, 52*(4), 102–105. doi:10.1109/MAP.2010.5638242

El-Fergany, A. A., & Hasanien, H. M. (2015). Single and multi-objective optimal power flow using grey wolf optimizer and differential evolution algorithms. *Electric Power Components and Systems, 43*(13), 1548–1559. doi:10.1080/1532 5008.2015.1041625

Elragal, H. M., Mangoud, M. A., & Alsharaa, M. T. (2011). Hybrid differential evolution and enhanced particle swarm optimisation technique for design of reconfigurable phased antenna arrays. *IET Microwaves, Antennas & Propagation, 5*(11), 1280–1287. doi:10.1049/iet-map.2010.0525

Elyasigomari, V., Mirjafari, M. S., Screen, H. R. C., & Shaheed, M. H. (2015). Cancer classification using a novel gene selection approach by means of shuffling based on data clustering with optimization. *Applied Soft Computing, 35*, 43–51. doi:10.1016/j.asoc.2015.06.015

Emary, E., Zawbaa, H. M., Grosan, C., & Hassenian, A. E. (2015). Feature subset selection approach by gray-wolf optimization. In Afro-European Conference for Industrial Advancement (Vol. 334).

Er, M. H. (1990). Linear antenna array pattern synthesis with prescribed broad nulls. *IEEE Transactions on Antennas and Propagation, 38*(9), 1496–1498. doi:10.1109/8.57004

Er, M. H., Sim, S. L., & Koh, S. N. (1993). Application of constrained optimization techniques to array pattern synthesis. *Signal Processing, 34*(3), 323–334. doi:10.1016/0165-1684(93)90139-2

Eusuff, M., Lansey, K., & Pasha, F. (2006). Shuffled frog-leaping algorithm: A memetic meta-heuristic for discrete optimization. *Engineering Optimization, 38*(2), 129–154. doi:10.1080/03052150500384759

Fahad, A., Alshatri, N., Tari, Z., Alamri, A., Khalil, I., Zomaya, A. Y., ... Bouras, A. (2014). A survey of clustering algorithms for big data: Taxonomy and empirical analysis. *IEEE Transactions on Emerging Topics in Computing, 2*(3), 267–279. doi:10.1109/TETC.2014.2330519

Falih, I., & Kanawati, R. (2015). Muna: A multiplex network analysis library. *The 2015 IEEE/ACM International Conference on Advances in Social Networks Analysis and Mining*, 757–760.

Farhang-Boroujeny, B. (2008). Filter bank spectrum sensing for cognitive radios. *IEEE Transactions on Signal Processing, 56*(5), 1801–1811. doi:10.1109/TSP.2007.911490

Farhat, N. H., & Bai, B. (1987). Phased-array antenna pattern synthesis by simulated annealing. *Proceedings of the IEEE, 75*(6), 842–844. doi:10.1109/PROC.1987.13805

Fayyad, U., & Irani, K. (1993). Multi-interval discretization of continuous-valued attributes for classification learning. In Machine Learning (pp. 1022-1027).

Fister, Jr. (2013). A Brief Review of Nature-Inspired Algorithms for Optimization. *Elektrotehniˇski vestnik, 80*(3), 1–7. (in Germany)

Fister, I., Yang, X. S., & Brest, J. (2013). A comprehensive review of firefly algorithms. *Swarm and Evolutionary Computation, 13*, 34–46. doi:10.1016/j.swevo.2013.06.001

Fortunato, S. (2010). Community detection in graphs. *Physics Reports, 486*(3-5), 75–174. doi:10.1016/j.physrep.2009.11.002

Freeman, L. (1979). Centrality in Social Networks: Conceptual Clarification. *Social Networks, 1*(3), 215–239. doi:10.1016/0378-8733(78)90021-7

Fuchs, B. (2012). Synthesis of sparse arrays with focused or shaped beampattern via sequential convex optimizations. *IEEE Transactions on Antennas and Propagation, 60*(7), 3499–03. doi:10.1109/TAP.2012.2196951

Gajawada, S., & Toshniwal, D. (2012). Projected Clustering Using Particle Swarm Optimization. *Procedia Technology, 4*, 360–364. doi:10.1016/j.protcy.2012.05.055

GaneshKumar, P., Rani, C., Devaraj, D., & Victoire, T. A. A. (2014). Hybrid ant bee algorithm for fuzzy expert system based sample classification. *IEEE/ACM Transactions on Computational Biology and Bioinformatics, 11*(2), 347–360. doi:10.1109/TCBB.2014.2307325 PMID:26355782

Gao, C., Lan, X., Zhang, X., & Deng, Y. (2013). A bio-inspired methodology of identifying influential nodes in complex networks. *PLoS One, 8*(6), e66732. doi:10.1371/journal.pone.0066732 PMID:23799129

Garcia, S., Fernandez, A., Luengo, J., & Herrera, F. (2009). A study of statistical techniques and performance measures for genetics-based machine learning: Accuracy and interpretability. *Soft Computing, 13*(10), 959–977. doi:10.100700500-008-0392-y

García, S., Luengo, J., & Herrera, F. (2015). *Data Preprocessing in Data Mining* (Vol. 72). Intelligent Systems Reference Library; doi:10.1007/978-3-319-10247-4

Garcia, S., Luengo, J., Sáez, J. A., Lopez, V., & Herrera, F. (2013). A Survey of Discretization Techniques: Taxonomy and Empirical Analysis in Supervised Learning. *IEEE Transactions on Knowledge and Data Engineering, 25*(4), 734–750. doi:10.1109/TKDE.2012.35

García, S., Molina, D., Lozano, M., & Herrera, F. (2009). A study on the use of non-parametric tests for analyzing the evolutionary algorithms' behaviour: A case study on the CEC'2005 special session on real parameter optimization. *Journal of Heuristics, 15*(6), 617.

Garey, M. R., Johnson, D. S., & Tarjan, R. E. (1976). The planar Hamiltonian circuit problem is NP-complete. *SIAM Journal on Computing, 5*(4), 704–714. doi:10.1137/0205049

Garg, R., & Agarwal, H. (2016). Big Data Analytics Recommendation Solutions for Crop Disease using Hive and Hadoop Platform. *Indian Journal of Science and Technology, 9*(32), ●●●. doi:10.17485/ijst/2016/v9i32/100728

Gholizadeh, S. (2015). Optimal design of double layer grids considering nonlinear behaviour by sequential grey wolf algorithm. *Journal of Optimization in Civil Engineering, 5*(4), 511–523.

Ghosh, A. K., & Raisinghani, S. C. (1993). Parameter estimates of an aircraft as affected by model simplifications. *J. Aarcraft, 31*, S52–S5S.

Giraffa, L. M. M., & Viccari, R. M. (1998, November). The use of agent's techniques on intelligent tutoring systems. In *Computer Science, 1998. SCCC'98. XVIII International Conference of the Chilean Society of* (pp. 76-83). IEEE

Giráldez, R., Aguilar-Ruiz, J. S., Riquelme, J. C., Ferrer-Troyano, F., & Rodr'iguez, D. (2002). Discretization Oriented to Decision Rules Generation. *Frontiers in Artificial Intelligence and Applications, 82*, 275–279.

Girvan, M., & Newman, M. E. J. (2002). Community structure in social and biological networks. *Proceedings of the National Academy of Sciences of the United States of America, 99*(12), 7821–7826. doi:10.1073/pnas.122653799 PMID:12060727

Goebl, S., Xiao, H., Plant, C., & Bohm, C. (2014). Finding the Optimal Subspace for Clustering. In *2014 IEEE International Conference on Data Mining* (pp. 130–139). 10.1109/ICDM.2014.34

Goel. (2013). *Biogeography and geo-sciences based land cover feature extraction: a remote sensing perspective. In Applied Soft Computing* (pp. 4194–4208). Elsevier.

Goel, L. (2012). Extended species abundance models of BBO. *IEEE Conf. on Computational Intelligence Modelling and Simulation (Anaheim).*

Goldberg, D. (1991). Real-coded genetic algorithms, virtual alphabets, and blocking. *Complex Systems, 5(2)*, 139–167.

Goldberg, D. E. (1989). *Genetic algorithms in search, optimization, and machine learning, 1989.* Reading: Addison-Wesley.

Goldberg, D. E., & Holland, J. H. (1988). Genetic Algorithms and Machine Learning. *Machine Learning, 3*(2), 95–99. doi:10.1023/A:1022602019183

Golub, T. R., Slonim, D. K., Tamayo, P., Huard, C., Gaasenbeek, M., Mesirov, J. P, & Bloomfield, C. D. (1999). Molecular classification of cancer: class discovery and class prediction by gene expression monitoring. *science, 286*(5439), 531-537.

Gomez-Gardenes, Reinares, Arenas, & Mario Floria. (2012). Evolution of cooperation in multiplex networks. *Nature Scientific Reports, 2*, Article N. 620.

Gonzalez-Abril, L., Cuberos, F. J., Velasco, F., & Ortega, J. A. (2009). Ameva: An autonomous discretization algorithm. *Expert Systems with Applications, 36*(3 PART 1), 5327–5332. doi:10.1016/j.eswa.2008.06.063

Goudos, S. K., Moysiadou, V., Samaras, T., Siakavara, K., & Sahalos, J. N. (2010). Application of a comprehensive learning particle swarm optimizer to unequally spaced linear array synthesis with sidelobe level suppression and null control. *IEEE Antennas and Wireless Propagation Letters, 9*, 125-29.

Graves, A., & Jaitly, N. (2014). Towards end-to-end speech recognition with recurrent neural networks. In *31st International Conference on Machine Learning*. Beijing, China.

Gu, L., Gao, Y., Liu, F. H., & Picheny, M. (2006). Concept-based speech-to-speech translation using maximum entropy models for statistical natural concept generation. *IEEE Transactions on Audio, Speech, and Language Processing, 14*(2), 377–392. doi:10.1109/TSA.2005.860769

Gunes, F., & Tokan, F. (2010). Pattern Search optimization with applications on synthesis of linear antenna arrays. *Expert Systems with Applications, 37*(6), 4698–05. doi:10.1016/j.eswa.2009.11.012

Guney, K., & Onay, M. (2011). Optimal synthesis of linear antenna arrays using a harmony search algorithm. *Expert Systems with Applications, 38*(12), 15455–15462. doi:10.1016/j.eswa.2011.06.015

Guo, J.-L., & Li, J.-Y. (2009). Pattern synthesis of conformal array antenna in the presence of platform using differential evolution algorithm. *IEEE Transactions on Antennas and Propagation, 57*(9), 2615–2621. doi:10.1109/TAP.2009.2027046

Gupta, S. K. (2013), GAR: an energy efficient GA-based routing for WSNs. LNCS, 7753, 267–277.

Haddad, O. B., Afshar, A., & Marino, M. A. (2006). Honey-Bees mating optimization (HBMO) algorithm: A new heuristic approach for water resources optimization. *Water Resources Management, 20*(5), 661–680. doi:10.100711269-005-9001-3

Haehnel, D., Thrun, S., & Burgard, W. (2003, August). An extension of the ICP algorithm for modeling nonrigid objects with mobile robots. In *IJCAI'03 Proceedings of the 18th international joint conference on Artificial intelligence* (pp. 915–920).

Hajeer, M. H., & Dasgupta, D. (2016, December). Distributed genetic algorithm to Big Data clustering. In *2016 IEEE Symposium Series on Computational Intelligence (SSCI)* (pp. 1-9). IEEE. 10.1109/SSCI.2016.7849864

Hargadon, A. B. (2002). Brokering Knowledge: Linking Learning and Innovation. In Research in Organizational Behavior (vol. 24). Greenwich, CT: JAI Press. doi:10.1016/S0191-3085(02)24003-4

Harshawardhan, Bhosale, Devendra, & Gadekar. (2014). A Review Paper on Big Data and Hadoop. *International Journal of Scientific and Research Publications, 4.*

Hasanpour, S. H. (2018). Model Zoo. Retrieved from https://github.com/BVLC/caffe/wiki/Model-Zoo

Hashimoto, K., Yamagishi, J., Byrne, W., King, S., & Tokuda, K. (2011, May). An analysis of machine translation and speech synthesis in speech-to-speech translation system. In *Acoustics, Speech and Signal Processing (ICASSP), 2011 IEEE International Conference on* (pp. 5108-5111). IEEE. 10.1109/ICASSP.2011.5947506

Havaei, M., Davy, A., Farley, D., Biard, A., Courville, A., Bengio, Y., . . . Larochelle, H. (2015). *Brain tumor segmentation with deep neural networks.* Retrieved from http://arxiv.org/abs/1505.03540

Haykin, S., Thomson, D. J., & Reed, J. H. (2009). Spectrum sensing for cognitive radio. *Proceedings of the IEEE, 97*(5), 849–877. doi:10.1109/JPROC.2009.2015711

He, K., Zhang, X., Ren, S., & Sun, J. (2016). Deep residual learning for image recognition. In *IEEE Conference on Computer Vision and Pattern Recognition*, Las Vegas, NV (pp. 770-778).

Hihi, S. E., & Bengio, Y. (1996). Hierarchical recurrent neural networks for long-term dependencies. In D. S. Touretzky, M. C. Mozer, & M. E. Hasselmo (Eds.), (pp. 493–499). Advances in Neural Information Processing Systems. MIT Press.

Hinton, G., Deng, L., Yu, D., Dahl, G., Mohamed, A., Jaitly, N., ... Kingsbury, B. (2012). Deep neural networks for acoustic modeling in speech recognition. *IEEE Signal Processing Magazine, 29*(6), 82–97. doi:10.1109/MSP.2012.2205597

Hinton, G., Osidero, S., & Teh, Y. (2006). A fast learning algorithm for deep belief nets. *Neural Computation, 18*(7), 1527–1554. doi:10.1162/neco.2006.18.7.1527 PMID:16764513

Hippo, Y., Taniguchi, H., Tsutsumi, S., Machida, N., Chong, J. M., Fukayama, M., ... Aburatani, H. (2002). Global gene expression analysis of gastric cancer by oligonucleotide microarrays. *Cancer Research, 62*(1), 233–240. PMID:11782383

Hmimida, M., & Kanawati, R. (2015). Community detection in multiplex networks: A seed-centric approach. *Networks and Heterogeneous Media, 10*(1), 71–85. doi:10.3934/nhm.2015.10.71

Ho, K., & Scott, P. (1997). Zeta: A global method for discretization of continuous variables. In Proceedings of the 3rd International Conference on Knowledge Discovery and Data Mining (pp. 191-194). Retrieved from http://www.aaai.org/Papers/KDD/1997/KDD97-037.pdf

Holland, J. H. (1962). Outline for a Logical Theory of Adaptive Systems. *Journal of the Association for Computing Machinery, 9*(3), 297–314. doi:10.1145/321127.321128

Holland, J. H. (1973). Genetic algorithms and the optimal allocation of trials. *SIAM Journal on Computing, 2*(2), 88–105. doi:10.1137/0202009

Holland, J. H. (1992). *Adaptation in natural and artificial systems: an introductory analysis with applications to biology, control, and artificial intelligence.* MIT press.

Holland, J. H. (1992). Genetic algorithms. *Scientific American, 267*(1), 66–73. doi:10.1038cientificamerican0792-66

Holm, S. (1979). A Simple Sequentially Rejective Multiple Test Procedure. *Scandinavian Journal of Statistics, 6*(2), 65–70.

Holt, A., & Huang, C.-Y. (2010). *802.11 Wireless networks security and analysis.* London, UK: Springer-Verlag Ltd.

Hong, L., & Armada, A. G. (2011). Bit error rate performance of MIMO MMSE receivers in correlated Rayleigh flat-fading channels. *IEEE Transactions on Vehicular Technology, 60*(1), 313–317. doi:10.1109/TVT.2010.2090369

Horvitz, E., & Mitchell, T. (2010). *From data to knowledge to action: A global enabler for the 21st century* (White Paper). A Computing Community Consortium.

Houari, R., Bounceur, A., Kechadi, M., Tari, A., & Euler, R. (2016). Dimensionality reduction in data mining: A Copula approach. *Expert Systems with Applications, 64*, 247–260. doi:10.1016/j.eswa.2016.07.041

Hsieh, C. C., Tsai, T. H., Wible, D., & Hsu, W. L. (2002, December). Exploiting knowledge representation in an intelligent tutoring system for English lexical errors. In *Computers in Education, 2002. Proceedings. International Conference on* (pp. 115-116). IEEE.

Hsu, H. H., Hsieh, C. W., & Lu, M. D. (2011). Hybrid feature selection by combining filters and wrappers. *Expert Systems with Applications, 38*(7), 8144–8150. doi:10.1016/j.eswa.2010.12.156

Huang, J., Cai, Y., & Xu, X. (2007). A hybrid genetic algorithm for feature selection wrapper based on mutual information. *Pattern Recognition Letters, 28*(13), 1825–1844. doi:10.1016/j.patrec.2007.05.011

Huang, J., & Kingsbury, B. (2013). Audio-visual deep learning for noise robust speech recognition. In *IEEE International Conference on Acoustics, Speech and Signal Processing*, Vancouver, Canada. 10.1109/ICASSP.2013.6639140

Huang, X., Shao, S., Wang, H., Buldyrev, S. V., Stanley, H. E., & Havlin, S. (2013). The robustness of interdependent clustered networks. *Europhysics Letters, 101*(1), 18002. doi:10.1209/0295-5075/101/18002

Hubel, D., & Wiesel, T. (1968). Receptive fields and functional architecture of monkey striate cortex. *The Journal of Physiology, 195*(1), 215–243. doi:10.1113/jphysiol.1968.sp008455 PMID:4966457

Huei-Fang, Y., Kevin, L., & Chu-Song, C. (2018). Supervised Learning of Semantics-Preserving Hash via Deep Convolutional Neural Networks. *IEEE Transactions on Pattern Analysis and Machine Intelligence*, 437–451. PMID:28207384

Hui, N. B., Mahendar, V., & Pratihar, D. K. (2006). Time-optimal, collision-free navigation of a car-like mobile robot using neuro-fuzzy approaches. *Fuzzy Sets and Systems, 157*(16), 2171–2204. doi:10.1016/j.fss.2006.04.004

Ilyas, M., & Ahson, S. (2005). *Handbook of wireless local area networks applications, technology, security, and standards.* Boca Raton, FL: Taylor & Francis Group, LLC.

Imani, M. B. (2012). A new feature selection method based on ant colony and genetic algorithm on Persian font recognition. *International Journal of Machine Learning and Computing, 2*(3), 1–5.

Index of Documents. (n.d.). Apache Hadoop. Retrieved from https://hadoop.apache.org/docs/

Indu, Prakasham, Chudhury, & Bhattacharyya. (2011). Self Organizing WSN to Enhance Event Coverage. *Int. J. on Smart Sensing and Intelligent Systems, 4*(1), 53–74. doi:10.21307/ijssis-2017-426

Ismail, T. H., Abu-Al-Nadi, D. I., & Mismar, M. J. (2004). Phase-only control for antenna pattern synthesis of linear arrays using the Levenberg-Marquardt algorithm. *Electromagnetics, 24*(7), 555–564. doi:10.1080/02726340490496707

Jaiswal, U. C., Kumar, R., & Chandra, S. (2009, December). A Structure Based Computer Grammar to Understand Compound-Complex, Multiple-Compound and Multiple-Complex English Sentences. In *Advances in Computing, Control, & Telecommunication Technologies, 2009. ACT'09. International Conference on* (pp. 746-751). IEEE.

JASON. (2008). Data Analysis Challenges. The Mitre Corporation, JSR-08-142.

Jategaonkar, R. (2006). *Flight vehicle system identification: a time domain methodology* (Vol. 216). Reston, VA: AIAA. doi:10.2514/4.866852

Jategaonkar, R. V., Fischenberg, D., & Gruenhagen, W. (2004). Aerodynamic modeling and system identification from flight data-recent applications at dlr. *Journal of Aircraft, 41*(4), 681–691. doi:10.2514/1.3165

Jategaonkar, R., & Plaetschke, E. (1988). *Estimation of aircraft parameters using filter error methods and Extended Kalman Filter.* Forschungsbericht- Deutsche Forschungs- und Versuchsanstalt fur Luft- und Raumfahrt.

Jiang, B. (2006). Ranking spaces for predicting human movement in an urban environment. *International Journal of Geographical Information Science, 23*(7), 823–837. doi:10.1080/13658810802022822

Jiang, T., Wang, H. J., & Hu, Y.-C. (2007). Preserving location privacy in wireless LANs. In *Proceedings of the 5th international conference on Mobile systems, applications and services* (pp. 246–57). San Juan, Puerto Rico: ACM.

Jin, N., & Rahmat-Samii, Y. (2007). Advances in particle swarm optimization for antenna designs: Real-number, binary, single-objective and multiobjective implementations. *IEEE Transactions on Antennas and Propagation, 55*(3), 556–567. doi:10.1109/TAP.2007.891552

Joshi, C. K., Mi, F., & Faltings, B. (2017). *Personalization in Goal-Oriented Dialog.* arXiv preprint arXiv:1706.07503

Joshi, D. R., Popescu, D. C., & Dobre, O. A. (2011). Gradient-based threshold adaptation for energy detector in cognitive radio systems. *IEEE Communications Letters, 15*(1), 19–21. doi:10.1109/LCOMM.2010.11.100654

Juve, G., Chervenak, A., Deelman, E., Bharathi, S., Mehta, G., & Vahi, K. (2013). Characterizing and profiling scientific workflows. *Future Generation Computer Systems, 29*(3), 682–692. doi:10.1016/j.future.2012.08.015

Juve, G., & Deelman, E. (2011). *Scientific Workflows in the Cloud* (pp. 71–91). Grids, Clouds and Virtualization; doi:10.1007/978-0-85729-049-6_4

Kailing, K., Kriegel, H.-P., & Oger, P. K. (2004). Density-connected subspace clustering for high-dimensional data. In *Proceedings of the 2004 SIAM International Conference on Data Mining* (pp. 246-256). Society for Industrial and Applied Mathematics.

Kala, R., Vazirani, H., Shukla, A., & Tiwari, R. (2010). *Offline handwriting recognition using genetic algorithm.* arXiv preprint arXiv:1004.3257

Kalchbrenner, N., & Blunsom, P. (2013). Recurrent continuous translation models. EMNLP.

Kalra, M., & Singh, S. (2015). A review of metaheuristic scheduling techniques in cloud computing. *Egyptian Informatics Journal, 16*(3), 275–295. doi:10.1016/j.eij.2015.07.001

Karaboga, D., & Basturk, B. (2008). On the performance of artificial bee colony (ABC) algorithm. *Appl. Soft Comput. J.*, 687–697.

Karaboga, D., & Basturk, B. (2007). A powerful and efficient algorithm for numerical function optimization: Artificial bee colony (ABC) algorithm. *Journal of Global Optimization, 39*(3), 459–471. doi:10.100710898-007-9149-x

Karaboga, D., & Basturk, B. (2008). On the performance of artificial bee colony (ABC) algorithm. *Applied Soft Computing, 8*(1), 687–697. doi:10.1016/j.asoc.2007.05.007

Karami, A., & Johansson, R. (2014). Choosing DBSCAN Parameters Automatically using Differential Evolution. *International Journal of Computers and Applications, 91*(7), 1–11. doi:10.5120/15890-5059

Katz, L. (1953). A New Status Index Derived from Sociometric Analysis. *Psychometrika, 18*(1), 39–43. doi:10.1007/BF02289026

Kaur, A., & Datta, A. (2014). {SUBSCALE:} Fast and Scalable Subspace Clustering for High Dimensional Data. In *2014 IEEE International Conference on Data Mining Workshops, ICDM Workshops 2014, Shenzhen, China, December 14* (pp. 621-628). doi:10.1109/ICDMW.2014.100

Kaur, A., & Datta, A. (2015). A novel algorithm for fast and scalable subspace clustering of high-dimensional data. *Journal of Big Data, 2*(1), 17. doi:10.118640537-015-0027-y

Kaur, P., & Mehta, S. (2017). Resource provisioning and work flow scheduling in clouds using augmented Shuffled Frog Leaping Algorithm. *Journal of Parallel and Distributed Computing, 101*, 41–50. doi:10.1016/j.jpdc.2016.11.003

Kaushik, Indu, & Gupta. (2016). Energy efficient clustering and routing algorithm for WSNs: An Extended BBO approach. *IJCTA*.

Kaushik. (2017). *A Novel Load Balanced Energy Conservation Approach in WSN Using BBO.* Lyon, France: ICEESM.

Kavallieratos, E., Antoniades, N., Fakotakis, N., & Kokkinakis, G. (1997, July). Extraction and recognition of handwritten alphanumeric characters from application forms. In *Digital Signal Processing Proceedings, 1997. DSP 97., 1997 13th International Conference on* (Vol. 2, pp. 695-698). IEEE. 10.1109/ICDSP.1997.628447

Kennedy, J. (2011). Particle swarm optimization. In Encyclopedia of machine learning (pp. 760-766). Springer US.

Kennedy, J., & Eberhart, R. (1995). Particle swarm optimization. In *Proceedings., IEEE International Conference on Neural Networks* (Vol. 4, pp. 1942-1948). 10.1109/ICNN.1995.488968

Kerber, R. (1992). Chimerge: Discretization of numeric attributes. In *Proceedings of the Tenth National Conference on Artificial Intelligence* (pp. 123–128). Retrieved from http://dl.acm.org/citation.cfm?id=1867154%5Cnpapers2://publication/uuid/F1C11C06-12F0-4A83-82D3-CC62A52FBE75

Kerly, A., Hall, P., & Bull, S. (2007). Bringing chatbots into education: Towards natural language negotiation of open learner models. *Knowledge-Based Systems, 20*(2), 177–185. doi:10.1016/j.knosys.2006.11.014

Khan, S., & Mauri, J. L. (2014). *Security for multihop wireless networks.* Boca Raton, FL: Taylor & Francis Group, LLC. doi:10.1201/b16754

Khan, S., & Pathan, A.-S. K. (Eds.). (2013). *Wireless networks and security issues, challenges and research trends.* Berlin: Springer-Verlag Ltd. doi:10.1007/978-3-642-36169-2

Khokhar, S., Zina, A. A. M., Memon, A. P., & Mokhtar, A. S. (2016). A new optimal feature selection algorithm for classification of power quality disturbances using discrete wavelet transform and probabilistic neural network. *Measurement, 95*, 246–259. doi:10.1016/j.measurement.2016.10.013

Kim, Y., Lee, H., & Provost, E. (2013). Deep learning for robust feature generation in audiovisual emotion recognition. In *IEEE International Conference on Acoustics, Speech and Signal Processing*. Vancouver, Canada. 10.1109/ICASSP.2013.6638346

Kira, K., & Rendell, L. (1994). A practical approach to feature selection. In *Proceedings of the Ninth International Conference on Machine Learning*.

Kivela, M., Arenas, A., Barthelemy, M., Gleeson, J., Moreno, Y., & Porter, M. (2014). Multilayer networks. *Journal of Complex Networks*, 2(3), 203–271. doi:10.1093/comnet/cnu016

Kleftogiannis, D., Theofilatos, K., Likothanassis, S., & Mavroudi, S. (2015). YamiPred: A novel evolutionary method for predicting pre-miRNAs and selecting relevant features. *IEEE/ACM Transactions on Computational Biology and Bioinformatics*, 12(5), 1183–1192. doi:10.1109/TCBB.2014.2388227 PMID:26451829

Koller, O., Ney, H., & Bowden, R. (2016). Deep hand: how to train a CNN on 1 million hand images. *IEEE International Conference on Computer Vision and Pattern Recognition*, Las Vegas, NV.

Komaki, G., & Kayvanfar, V. (2015). Grey Wolf Optimizer algorithm for the two-stage assembly flow shop scheduling problem with release time. *Journal of Computational Science*, 8, 109–120. doi:10.1016/j.jocs.2015.03.011

Kong, S. G., & Kosko, B. (1990). Comparison of fuzzy and neural truck backer-upper control systems. In *1990 IJCNN International Joint Conference on Neural Networks* (pp. 349-358). IEEE.

Koniaris, M., Anagnostopoulos, I., & Vassiliou, Y. (2017). Evaluation of Diversification Techniques for Legal Information Retrieval. *Algorithms*, 10(1), 22. doi:10.3390/a10010022

Kothari, D., Narayanan, S. T., & Devi, K. K. (2014). Extended Fuzzy C-Means with Random Sampling Techniques for Clustering Large Data. *International Journal of Innovative Research in Advanced Engineering*, 1(1), 1–4.

Kriegel, H.-P., Kroger, P., & Renz, M., & Wurst., S. (2005). A generic framework for efficient subspace clustering of high-dimensional data. In *Proceedings of the Fifth IEEE International Conference on Data Mining* (pp. 250-257). 10.1109/ICDM.2005.5

Kriegel, H.-P., Kröger, P., & Zimek, A. (2009). Clustering high-dimensional data: a survey on subspace clustering, pattern-based clustering, and correlation clustering. *ACM Transactions on Knowledge Discovery from Data*, 3(1), 1–58. doi:10.1145/1497577.1497578

Krizhevsky, A., Sutskever, I., & Hinton, G. (2012). Imagenet classification with deep convolutional neural networks. *Advances in Neural Information Processing Systems*, 25, 1106–1114.

Kuila & Jana. (2014). *Energy efficient clustering and routing algorithms for WSNs: PSO approach* (pp. 127–140). Engineering Applications of AI.

Kuila. (2013). A novel evolutionary approach for load balanced clustering problem for WSNs. *Swarm and Evolutionary Computation*, 48–56. doi:10.1016/j.swevo.2013.04.002

Kuila, P. (2014). Energy efficient clustering and routing algorithms for WSNs: PSO approach. *Engineering Applications of Artificial Intelligence*, 127–140. doi:10.1016/j.engappai.2014.04.009

Kulkarni. (2011). G.K.: PSO in WSN: A brief survey. *IEEE Transactions on Systems, Man, and Cybernetics*, 41(2), 262–267. doi:10.1109/TSMCC.2010.2054080

Kumar. (2014). Optimized Power Efficient Routing in WSN. *Int. J. of Next Generation Computing, 5*(2).

Kumar, D., Bezdek, J. C., Palaniswami, M., Rajasegarar, S., Leckie, C., & Havens, T. C. (2016). A Hybrid Approach to Clustering in Big Data. *IEEE Transactions on Cybernetics, 46*(10), 2372–2385. doi:10.1109/TCYB.2015.2477416 PMID:26441434

Kuncheva, Z., & Montana, G. (2015). *Community detection in multiplex networks using locally adaptive random walks.* Retrieved from http://arxiv.org/abs/1507.01890

Kurgan, L. A., & Cios, K. J. (2004). CAIM Discretization Algorithm. *IEEE Transactions on Knowledge and Data Engineering, 16*(2), 145–153. doi:10.1109/TKDE.2004.1269594

Kuri-Morales, A., & Gutiérrez-García, J. (2002). Penalty function methods for constrained optimization with genetic algorithms: A statistical analysis. In *Advances in Artificial Intelligence* (pp. 187–200). MICAI.

Kurzweil, R. (2012). *How to create a mind: The secret of human thought revealed.* Audio Book.

Lai, K., Bo, L., Ren, X., & Fox, D. (2013). RGB-D object recognition: Features, algorithms, and a large scale benchmark. In A. Fossati, J. Gall, H. Grabner, X. Ren, & K. Konolige (Eds.), *Consumer depth cameras for computer vision* (pp. 167–192). London: Springer-Verlag. doi:10.1007/978-1-4471-4640-7_9

Laine, M., & Nevalainen, O. S. (2006, September). A standalone OCR system for mobile cameraphones. In *Personal, Indoor and Mobile Radio Communications, 2006 IEEE 17th International Symposium on* (pp. 1-5). IEEE. 10.1109/PIMRC.2006.254074

Lakavath, S. (2014). *A Big Data Hadoop Architecture for Online Analysis.* Academic Press.

Laugier, C., Fraichard, T. H., Garnier, P., Paromtchik, I. E., & Scheuer, A. (1999). Sensor-based control architecture for a car-like vehicle. *Autonomous Robots, 6*(2), 165–185. doi:10.1023/A:1008835527875

Laumond, J. P., Sekhavat, S., & Lamiraux, F. (1998). Guidelines in nonholonomic motion planning for mobile robots. In *Robot motion planning and control* (pp. 1–53). Berlin, Heidelberg: Springer. doi:10.1007/BFb0036070

Lazar, C., Taminau, J., Meganck, S., Steenhoff, D., Coletta, A., Molter, C., ... Nowe, A. (2012). A Survey on Filter Techniques for Feature Selection in Gene Expression Microarray Analysis. *IEEE/ACM Transactions on Computational Biology and Bioinformatics, 9*(4), 1106–1119. doi:10.1109/TCBB.2012.33 PMID:22350210

Lazer, D., Pentland, A., Adamic, L., Aral, S., Barabasi, A.-L., Brewer, D., ... Alstyne, M. V. (2009). Computational social science. *Science, 323*(5915), 721–723. doi:10.1126cience.1167742 PMID:19197046

Lebret, H., & Boyd, S. (1997). Antenna array pattern synthesis via convex optimization. *IEEE Transactions on Signal Processing, 45*(3), 526–532. doi:10.1109/78.558465

LeCun, Y., Bengio, Y., & Hinton, G. (2015). Deep Learning. *Nature, 521*(7553), 436–444. doi:10.1038/nature14539 PMID:26017442

Lee, C. H. (2007). A Hellinger-based discretization method for numeric attributes in classification learning. *Knowledge-Based Systems, 20*(4), 419–425. doi:10.1016/j.knosys.2006.06.005

Lee, C. P., Lin, W. S., Chen, Y. M., & Kuo, B. J. (2011). Gene selection and sample classification on microarray data based on adaptive genetic algorithm/k-nearest neighbor method. *Expert Systems with Applications, 38*(5), 4661–4667. doi:10.1016/j.eswa.2010.07.053

Lemon, O., Georgila, K., Henderson, J., & Stuttle, M. (2006, April). An ISU dialogue system exhibiting reinforcement learning of dialogue policies: generic slot-filling in the TALK in-car system. In *Proceedings of the Eleventh Conference of the European Chapter of the Association for Computational Linguistics: Posters & Demonstrations* (pp. 119-122). Association for Computational Linguistics. 10.3115/1608974.1608986

Lenz, I., Lee, H., & Saxena, A. (2013). Deep learning for detecting robotic grasps. *International Conference on Learning Representations*. Scottsdale, Arizona.

Le, T. M., Paul, J. S., & Ong, S. H. (2010). Computational Biology. *Applied Bioinformatics*, *673*(1), 243–271. doi:10.1007/978-1-4419-0811-7

Letaief, K. B., & Zhang, W. (2009). Cooperative communications for cognitive radio networks. *Proceedings of the IEEE*, *97*(5), 878–893.

Leydesdorff, L. (2009). Betweenness centrality as an indicator of the interdis- ciplinarity of scientific journals. *Journal of the American Society for Information Science and Technology*, (9): 1303–1319.

Li, J., Li, X., & Zhang, W. (2016). A Filter Feature Selection Method Based LLRFC and Redundancy Analysis for Tumor Classification Using Gene Expression Data. In *2016 12th World Congress on Intelligent Control and Automation (WCICA)* (pp. 2861-2867). IEEE.

Liang, J. J., Qu, B. Y., Suganthan, P. N., & Hernández-Díaz, A. G. (2013). Problem definitions and evaluation criteria for the CEC 2013 special session on real-parameter optimization (Technical Report). Computational Intelligence Laboratory, Zhengzhou University, Zhengzhou, China and Nanyang Technological University, Singapore.

Liang, Y. C., Zeng, Y., Peh, E. C., & Hoang, A. T. (2008). Sensing-throughput tradeoff for cognitive radio networks. *IEEE Transactions on Wireless Communications*, *7*(4), 1326–1337. doi:10.1109/TWC.2008.060869

Liddy, E. D., Paik, W., Edmund, S. Y., & Li, M. (1999). *U.S. Patent No. 6,006,221*. Washington, DC: U.S. Patent and Trademark Office.

Li, H., Liu, Y., Sun, G., Wang, A., & Liang, S. (2017). Beam pattern synthesis based on improved biogeography-based optimization for reducing sidelobe level. *Computers & Electrical Engineering*, *60*(May), 161–174.

Li, M., Hei, Y., & Qiu, Z. (2017). Optimization of multiband cooperative spectrum sensing with modified artificial bee colony algorithm. *Applied Soft Computing*, *57*, 751–759. doi:10.1016/j.asoc.2017.03.027

Lin, C., & Lu, S. (2011). Scheduling Scientific Workflows Elastically for Cloud Computing, In *International Conference on Cloud Computing* (pp. 746-747). 10.1109/CLOUD.2011.110

Lin, L., Gen, M., & Liang, Y. (2014). A hybrid EA for high-dimensional subspace clustering problem. In *Proceedings of the 2014 IEEE Congress on Evolutionary Computation, CEC 2014* (pp. 2855–2860). 10.1109/CEC.2014.6900313

Lin, W., Tsai, C., Chen, Z., & Ke, S. (2016). Keypoint selection for efficient bag-of-words feature generation and effective image classification. *Information Sciences*, *329*, 33–51. doi:10.1016/j.ins.2015.08.021

Liu, C.-W., Lowe, R., Serban, I. V., Noseworthy, M., Charlin, L., & Pineau, J. (2016). *How not to evaluate your dialogue system: An empirical study of unsupervised evaluation metrics for dialogue response generation*. arXiv preprint arXiv:1603.08023

Liu, B., Aliakbarian, H., Ma, Z., Vandenbosch, G. A. E., Gielen, G., & Excell, P. (2014). An efficient method for antenna design optimization based on evolutionary computation and machine learning techniques. *IEEE Transactions on Antennas and Propagation*, *62*(1), 7–18. doi:10.1109/TAP.2013.2283605

Liu, H., Hussain, F., Tan, C. L., & Dash, M. (2002). Discretization: An enabling technique. *Data Mining and Knowledge Discovery*, *6*(4), 393–423. doi:10.1023/A:1016304305535

Liu, H., Motoda, H., Setiono, R., & Zhao, Z. (2010). Feature Selection: An Ever Evolving Frontier in Data Mining. In *The Fourth Workshop on Feature Selection in Data Mining* (pp. 4–13).

Liu, H., & Setiono, R. (1997). Feature selection via discretization. *IEEE Transactions on Knowledge and Data Engineering*, *9*(4), 642–645. doi:10.1109/69.617056

Li, X., & Yin, M. (2013). Multiobjective binary biogeography based optimization for feature selection using gene expression data. *IEEE Transactions on Nanobioscience*, *12*(4), 343–353. Retrieved from http://www.ncbi.nlm.nih.gov/pubmed/25003163 doi:10.1109/TNB.2013.2294716 PMID:25003163

Li, Z., & Jiang, Y. (2014). Cross-layers cascade in multiplex networks. *Proceedings of the International Conference on Autonomous Agents and Multi-agent Systems, ser. AAMAS '14*, 269–276.

Low, C. P. (2008). Efficient load-balanced clustering algorithms for WSNs. *Computer Communications*, *31*, 750–759. doi:10.1016/j.comcom.2007.10.020

Luo, J., Feng, Z., Zhang, J., & Lu, N. (2016, August). approach for classification of motor imageries. *Computers in Biology and Medicine*, *75*, 45–53. doi:10.1016/j.compbiomed.2016.03.004 PMID:27253616

Luo, L. K., Huang, D. F., Ye, L. J., Zhou, Q. F., Shao, G. F., & Peng, H. (2011). Improving the computational efficiency of recursive cluster elimination for gene selection. *IEEE/ACM Transactions on Computational Biology and Bioinformatics*, *8*(1), 122–129. doi:10.1109/TCBB.2010.44 PMID:20479497

Lu, Y., Wang, S., Li, S., & Zhou, C. (2011). Particle swarm optimizer for variable weighting in clustering high-dimensional data. *Machine Learning*, *82*(1), 43–70. doi:10.100710994-009-5154-2

Madadi, A., & Motlagh, M. M. (2014). Optimum Control of DC motor using Grey Wolf optimizer algorithm. *TJEAS*, *4*(4), 373–379.

Mahmoud, M. M. E. A., & Shen, X. (2014). Security for multi-hop wireless networks. New York: Springer Science+Business Media, LLC.

Mailloux, R. J. (2005). *Phased array antenna handbook* (2nd ed.). Boston: Artech House.

Maimon, O., & Rokach, L. E. (2002). Handbook of Data Mining and Knowledge Discovery. Oxford University Press.

Maine, R. E., & Iliff, K. W. (1986). *Identification of dynamic system-application to aircraft. Part I*. Agard AG-300.

Malawski, M., Juve, G., Deelman, E., & Nabrzyski, J. (2012). Cost-and deadline-constrained provisioning for scientific workflow ensembles in IaaS clouds. In *Proc. Int. Conf. High Perform. Comput., Netw., Storage Anal.* (Vol. 22, pp. 1–11).

Mandal, D., Ghoshal, S. P., & Bhattacharjee, A. K. (2011). Wide null control of symmetric linear antenna array using novel particle swarm optimization. *International Journal of RF and Microwave Computer-Aided Engineering*, *21*(4), 376–382. doi:10.1002/mmce.20526

Mangaraj, B. B., & Swain, P. (2017). An optimal LAA subsystem designed using Gravitational search algorithm. *Engineering Science and Technology, an International Journal*, *20*(2), 494-01.

Manikas, T. W., & Cain, J. T. (1996). Genetic algorithms vs. simulated annealing: A comparison of approaches for solving the circuit partitioning problem.

Mann, G., McDonald, R., Mohri, M., Silberman, N., & Walker, D. D. (2009). *Efficient large-scale distributed training of conditional maximum entropy models.* In Advances in Neural Information Processing Systems.

Manyika, J., Chui, M., Brad, B., Bughin, J., Dobbs, R., Roxburgh, C., & Hung Byers, A. (2011, May). Big data: The next frontier for innovation, competition, and productivity. *McKinsey.* Retrieved March 4, 2015, from http://www.mckinsey.com/insights/business_technology/big_data_the_next_frontier_for_innovation

Mao, M., & Humphrey, M. (2011) Auto-scaling to minimize cost and meet application deadlines in cloud workflows. In *Proc. Int. Conf. High Perform. Comput., Netw., Storage Anal.* (pp. 1–12).

Marler, R. T., & Arora, J. S. (2010). The weighted sum method for multi-objective optimization: New insights. *Structural and Multidisciplinary Optimization, 41*(6), 853–862. doi:10.100700158-009-0460-7

Martellini, M., Gaycken, S. A. S., & Wilson, C. (2017). *Information security of highly critical wireless networks.* Cham, Switzerland: Springer International Publishing AG. doi:10.1007/978-3-319-52905-9

Martens, D. (2011). Editorial survey: SI for data mining. *Machine Learning, 82*(1), 1–42. doi:10.100710994-010-5216-5

Martinez-Cantin, R., Castellanos, J. A., & de Freitas, N. (2007). Multi-robot marginal-slam. In Workshop On Multirobotic Systems For Societal (p. 52).

Martin, T., Zhang, X., & Newman, M. E. J. (2014). Localization and centrality in networks. *Phys. Rev. E, 90*(5), 052808. doi:10.1103/PhysRevE.90.052808 PMID:25493835

Matthew Rathbone Blog. (2013). *A Beginners Guide to Hadoops.* Accessed May 3rd 2018: http://blog.mattherwrathbone.com/2013/04/17/what-is-hadoop.html

Mautz, J. R., & Harrington, R. F. (1975). Computational methods for antenna pattern synthesis. *IEEE Transactions on Antennas and Propagation, AP-32*(7), 507–512. doi:10.1109/TAP.1975.1141126

Mazur, M., Rzepka, R., & Araki, K. (2011). Proposal for a conversational English tutoring system that encourages user engagement. In *Proceedings of the 19th International Conference on Computers in Education* (pp. 10-12). Academic Press.

McCarthy, J. (2004). The Web - Early Visions, Present Reality, the Grander Future. *IEEE/WIC/ACM International Conference on Web Intelligence.* 10.1109/WI.2004.10003

Mehta, S., & Banati, H. (2012) Trust aware social context filtering using Shuffled Frog Leaping Algorithm. In *International conference on Hybrid Intelligent Systems* (pp. 342-347). 10.1109/HIS.2012.6421358

Mehta, S., & Banati, H. (2014). Context aware filtering using social behavior of frogs. *Swarm and Evolutionary Computation, 17*, 25–36. doi:10.1016/j.swevo.2014.02.003

Mehta, S., Parthasarathy, S., & Yang, H. (2005). Toward Unsupervised Correlation Preserving Discretization. *IEEE Transactions on Knowledge and Data Engineering, 17*(9), 1174–1185. doi:10.1109/TKDE.2005.153

Method, D. D., Cerquides, J., & De Mantaras, R. L. (1992). Proposal and Empirical Comparison of a Parallelizable. In *KDD: Proceedings / International Conference on Knowledge Discovery & Data Mining. International Conference on Knowledge Discovery & Data Mining* (pp. 139–142). Retrieved from http://citeseerx.ist.psu.edu/viewdoc/summary?doi=10.1.1.109.7428

Mikolov, T., Karafiat, M., Burget, L., Cernocky, J., & Khudanpur, S. (2010). Recurrent neural network based language model. In *11th Annual Conference of the International Speech Communication Association*, Chiba, Japan (pp. 1045-1048).

Mikolov, T., Kombrink, S., Burget, L., Cernocky, J., & Khudanpur, S. (2011). Extensions of recurrent neural network language model. In *36th International Conference on Acoustics, Speech and Signal Processing*, Prague, Czech Republic (pp. 5528-5531). 10.1109/ICASSP.2011.5947611

Mirjalili, S., Mirjalili, S. M., & Lewis, A. (2014). Grey wolf optimizer. *Advances in Engineering Software, 69*, 46–61. doi:10.1016/j.advengsoft.2013.12.007

Mishra, A. (2008). *Security and quality of service in ad hoc wireless networks*. New York: Cambridge University Press. doi:10.1017/CBO9780511619755

Mismar, M. J., Ismail, T. H., & Abu-Al-Nadi, D. I. (2007). Analytical array polynomial method for linear antenna arrays with phase-only control. *International Journal of Electronics and Communications, 61*(7), 485–492. doi:10.1016/j. aeue.2006.06.009

Misra, S., & Ray, S. S. (2017). Finding optimum width of discretization for gene expressions using functional annotations. *Computers in Biology and Medicine, 90*, 59–67. doi:10.1016/j.compbiomed.2017.09.010 PMID:28941844

Mitchell, L. E. (2003). *Structural Holes, CEOs, and Informational Monopolies: The Missing Link in Corporate Governance*. Working paper. Law School, George Washington University.

Mittal, R., & Bhatia, M. P. S. (2018). Anomaly Detection in Multiplex Networks. *Procedia Computer Science, 125*, 609-616.

Mittal, R., & Bhatia, M. P. S. (2017). Mining top-k structural holes in multiplex networks. *8th International Conference on Computing, Communication and Networking Technologies (ICCCNT)*, 1-6. 10.1109/ICCCNT.2017.8204129

Miyata, H., Ohki, M., Yokouchi, Y., & Ohkita, M. (1996). Control of the autonomous mobile robot DREAM-1 for a parallel parking. *Mathematics and Computers in Simulation, 41*(1-2), 129–138. doi:10.1016/0378-4754(95)00065-8

Mohamad, M. S., Omatu, S., Deris, S., Misman, M. F., & Yoshioka, M. (2009). A multi-objective strategy in genetic algorithms for gene selection of gene expression data. *Artificial Life and Robotics, 13*(2), 410–413. doi:10.100710015-008-0533-5

Mohamed, A., Dahl, G., & Hinton, G. (2009). Deep belief networks for phone recognition. In *NIPS Workshop*. Vancouver, Canada.

Mohamed, A., Dahl, G., & Hinton, G. (2012). Acoustic Modeling using Deep Belief Networks. *IEEE Transactions on Audio, Speech, and Language Processing, 20*(1), 14–22. doi:10.1109/TASL.2011.2109382

Mohamed, A., Yu, D., & Deng, L. (2010). *Investigation of full-sequence training of deep belief networks for speech recognition*. Makuhari, Japan: Interspeech.

Mohsenzadeha, Y., Sheikhzadehb, H., & Nazari, S. (2016). Incremental relevancesample-feature machine: a fast marginal likelihood maximization approach for jointfeature selection and classification. *Pattern Recognition, 60*, 835–848. doi:10.1016/j.patcog.2016.06.028

Moise, G., Sander, J., & Ester, M. (2006). P3C: A robust projected clustering algorithm. In *Proceedings of the Sixth International Conference on Data Mining* (pp. 414–425).

Moise, G., & Sander, J. (2008). Finding non-redundant, statistically significant regions in high dimensional data: a novel approach to projected and subspace clustering. In *Proceedings of the 14th ACM SIGKDD international conference on Knowledge discovery and data mining* (pp. 533–541). 10.1145/1401890.1401956

Molano, V., Cobos, C., Mendoza, M., & Herrera-viedma, E. (2014). Feature Selection Based on Sampling and C4. 5 Algorithm to Improve the Quality of Text Classification Using Naïve Bayes. In *Mexican International Conference on Artificial Intelligence* (pp. 80–91). Springer.

Montet, I., Dalmasso, E., & Siegel, A. (2003). *U.S. Patent Application No. 10/441,754.* Washington, DC: US Patent Office.

Moran, A., & Nagai, M. (1995). Autonomous parking of vehicles with intelligent fuzzy-neural networks. *JSAE Review*, *2*(16), 216.

Morgan, N. (2012). Deep and wide: Multiple layers in automatic speech recognition. *IEEE Transactions on Audio, Speech, and Language Processing*, *20*(1), 7–13. doi:10.1109/TASL.2011.2116010

Morteza. (2015). *A survey on centralized and distributed clustering routing algorithm for WSNs.* IEEE.

Moscato, P., & Cotta, C. (2002). Memetic algorithms. Handbook of Applied Optimization, 157-167.

Motoji, Y., & Akira, M. (1995). Automatic Parking Motion Control for a Car-Like Robot Using a Fuzzy Neural Network. *JSAE Review*, *1*(16), 98. doi:10.1016/0389-4304(95)94722-Y

Mozer, M. C. (1989). A focused back-propagation algorithm for temporal sequence recognition. *Complex Systems*, *3*, 349–381.

Mukhopadhyay, A., & Mandal, M. (2014). Identifying non-redundant gene markers from microarray data: A multiobjective variable length pso-based approach. *IEEE/ACM Transactions on Computational Biology and Bioinformatics*, *11*(6), 1170–1183. doi:10.1109/TCBB.2014.2323065 PMID:26357053

Müller, E., Günnemann, S., Assent, I., Seidl, T., & Färber, I. (2009). Evaluating Clustering in Subspace Projections of High Dimensional Data. Retrieved from http://dme.rwth-aachen.de/en/OpenSubspace/evaluation

Müller, E., Günnemann, S., Assent, I., & Seidl, T. (2009). Evaluating clustering in subspace projections of high dimensional data. *Proceedings of the VLDB Endowment International Conference on Very Large Data Bases*, *2*(1), 1270–1281. doi:10.14778/1687627.1687770

Myles, G., Friday, A., & Davies, N. (2003). Preserving privacy in environments with location-based applications. *IEEE Pervasive Computing*, *2*(1), 56–64. doi:10.1109/MPRV.2003.1186726

Nair, L. R., & David Peter, S. (2012). Machine translation systems for Indian languages. *International Journal of Computer Applications, 39*(1).

Najafabadi, M., Villanustre, F., Khoshgoftaar, T., Seliya, N., Wald, R., & Muharemagic, E. (2015). Deep learning applications and challenges in big data analytics. *Journal of Big Data, 2*.

Nakamura, S. (2009, August). Development and application of multilingual speech translation. In *Speech Database and Assessments, 2009 Oriental COCOSDA International Conference on* (pp. 9-12). IEEE. 10.1109/ICSDA.2009.5278383

Neri, F., & Tirronen, V. (2010). Recent advances in differential evolution: A survey and experimental analysis. *Artificial Intelligence Review*, *33*(1-2), 61–106. doi:10.100710462-009-9137-2

Newman, M. E. J. (2001). The Structure of Scientific Collaboration Networks. *Proceedings of the National Academy of Sciences of the United States of America*, *98*(2), 404–409. doi:10.1073/pnas.98.2.404 PMID:11149952

Newman, M. E. J. (2003). Fast algorithm for detecting community structure in networks. *Phys. Rev. E*, *69*(6), 066133. doi:10.1103/PhysRevE.69.066133 PMID:15244693

Newman, M. E. J. (2003). The structure and function of complex networks. *SIAM Review*, *45*(2), 167–256. doi:10.1137/S003614450342480

Newman, M. E. J. (2009). Random graphs with clustering. *Physical Review Letters*, *103*(5), 058701. doi:10.1103/PhysRevLett.103.058701 PMID:19792540

Ngiam, J., Khosla, A., Kim, M., Nam, J., Lee, H., & Ng, A. (2011). Multimodal deep learning. In *28th International Conference on Machine Learning*, Bellevue.

Nguyen, V., Gächter, S., Martinelli, A., Tomatis, N., & Siegwart, R. (2007). A comparison of line extraction algorithms using 2D range data for indoor mobile robotics. *Autonomous Robots*, *23*(2), 97–111. doi:10.100710514-007-9034-y

Nicosia, V., Bianconi, G., Latora, V., & Barthelemy, M. (2014). *Non- linear growth and condensation in multiplex networks*. Retrieved from http://arxiv.org/abs/1312.3683

Noh, J. D., & Rieger, H. (2004). Random Walks on Complex Networks. *Physical Review Letters*, *92*(11), 118701. doi:10.1103/PhysRevLett.92.118701 PMID:15089179

Nourashrafeddin, S., Arnold, D., & Milios, E. (2012). An evolutionary subspace clustering algorithm for high-dimensional data. In *Proceedings of the Fourteenth International Conference on Genetic and Evolutionary Computation Conference Companion* (pp. 1497–1498). 10.1145/2330784.2331011

Ohno, K., Esfarjani, K., & Kawazoe, Y. (1999). *Computational Materials Science: From Ab Initio to Monte Carlo Methods*. Berlin: Springer Verlag. doi:10.1007/978-3-642-59859-3

Oliveira, L. S., Morita, M., & Sabourin, R. (2006). (n.d.). *Feature Selection for Ensembles Using the Multi-Objective Optimization Approach*, *74*, 49–74.

Omara, F. A., & Arafa, M. M. (2010). Genetic algorithms for task scheduling problem. *Journal of Parallel and Distributed Computing*, *70*(1), 13–22. doi:10.1016/j.jpdc.2009.09.009

On Circulation. (n.d.). Deep Dreaming with Google. Retrieved from https://oncirculation.com/2015/07/14/deep-dreaming-with-google/

Ostermann, S., Iosup, A., Yigitbasi, N., Prodan, R., Fahringer, T., & Epema, D. (2010). A Performance Analysis of EC2 Cloud Computing Services for Scientific Computing. In International Conference on *Cloud Computing* (pp. 115-131). Springer. doi:10.1007/978-3-642-12636-9_9

Ozger, E. (2013). Parameter Estimation of Highly Unstable Aircraft Assuming Nonlinear Errors. In AIAA Atmospheric Flight Mechanics (AFM) Conference (p. 4751). AIAA. doi:10.2514/6.2013-4751

Paliwal, K. (1987, April). Estimation of noise variance from the noisy AR signal and its application in speech enhancement. In IEEE International Conference on Acoustics, Speech, and Signal Processing ICASSP'87 (Vol. 12, pp. 297-300). IEEE. doi:10.1109/ICASSP.1987.1169682

Paliwal, K. K. (1988). Estimation of noise variance from the noisy AR signal and its application in speech enhancement. *IEEE Transactions on Acoustics, Speech, and Signal Processing*, *36*(2), 292–294.

Pal, J. K., Ray, S. S., Cho, S. B., & Pal, S. K. (2016). Fuzzy-Rough Entropy Measure and Histogram Based Patient Selection for miRNA Ranking in Cancer. *IEEE/ACM Transactions on Computational Biology and Bioinformatics*. PMID:27831888

Palmer, M., Bhatt, R., Narasimhan, B., Rambow, O., Sharma, D. M., & Xia, F. (2009, December). Hindi syntax: Annotating dependency, lexical predicate-argument structure, and phrase structure. In *The 7th International Conference on Natural Language Processing* (pp. 14-17). Academic Press.

Pandey, S., Wu, L., Guru, S. M., & Buyya, R. (2010). A particle swarm optimization-based heuristic for scheduling workflow applications in cloud computing environments. In *Proc. IEEE Int. Conf.Adv. Inform. Netw. Appl.* (pp. 400–407).

Pandey, P., Kumar, M., & Srivastav, P. (2016). Classification Techniques for Big Data: A Survey. *IEEE International Conference on Computing for Sustainable Global Development*, 3625-3629.

Pappula, L., & Ghosh, D. (2014). Linear antenna array synthesis using cat swarm optimization. *International Journal of Electronics and Communications, 68*(6), 540–549. doi:10.1016/j.aeue.2013.12.012

Parpinelli, R. S., & Lopes, H. S. (2011). New inspirations in swarm intelligence: A survey. *International Journal of Bio-inspired Computation, 3*(1), 1–16. doi:10.1504/IJBIC.2011.038700

Parsons, L., Parsons, L., Haque, E., Haque, E., Liu, H., & Liu, H. (2004). Subspace Clustering for High Dimensional Data: A Review. *ACM SIGKDD Explorations Newsletter, 6*(1), 90–105. doi:10.1145/1007730.1007731

Patnaik, L. M. (2014). Bid Data Analytics: An Approach using Hadoop Distributed File System. International Journal of Engineering and Innovative Technology, 3, 239-243.

Peng, H., Long, F., & Ding, C. (2005). Feature selection based on mutual information criteria of max-dependency, max-relevance, and min-redundancy. *IEEE Transactions on Pattern Analysis and Machine Intelligence, 27*(8), 1226–1238. doi:10.1109/TPAMI.2005.159 PMID:16119262

Peter Hong, Y.-W., Lan, P.-C., & Jay Kuo, C.-C. (2014). Signal processing approaches to secure physical layer communications in multi-antenna wireless systems. New York: Springer Science+Business Media, LLC. doi:10.1007/978-981-4560-14-6

Peyada, N. K., & Ghosh, A. K. (2009). Aircraft parameter estimation using a new filtering technique based upon a neural network and Gauss-Newton method. *Aeronautical Journal, 113*(1142), 243–252. doi:10.1017/S0001924000002918

Peyada, N. K., Sen, A., & Ghosh, A. K. (2008, March). Aerodynamic characterization of hansa-3 aircraft using equation error, maximum likelihood and filter error methods. *Proceedings of the International MultiConference of Engineers and Computer Scientists, 2*.

Pfaff, P., Triebel, R., & Burgard, W. (2007). An efficient extension to elevation maps for outdoor terrain mapping and loop closing. *The International Journal of Robotics Research, 26*(2), 217–230. doi:10.1177/0278364906075165

Pham, D. T., Soroka, A. J., Koc, E., Ghanbarzadeh, A., & Otri, S. (2007). Some Applications of the Bees Algorithm in Engineering Design and Manufacture. *Proceedings of International Conference On Manufacturing Automation (ICMA 2007)*.

Pol, U. R. (2016). Big Data Analysis: Comparison of Hadoop MapReduce, pig and Hive. *International Journal of Innovative Research in Science. Engineering and Technology, 5*(6), 9687–9693.

Poola, D., Garg, S. K., Buyya, R., Yun, Y., & Ramamohanarao, K. (2014). Robust Scheduling of Scientific Workflows with Deadline and Budget Constraints in Clouds. In *2014 IEEE 28th International Conference on Advanced Information Networking and Applications (AINA)* (pp. 858-865).

Potamianos, G., Neti, C., Luettin, J., & Matthews, I. (2004). Audio-visual automatic speech recognition: An overview. In G. Potamianos, C. Neti, J. Luettin, & I. Matthews (Eds.), *Issues in visual and audio-visual speech processing* (pp. 356–396). Cambridge: MIT Press.

Pradeep, J., Srinivasan, E., & Himavathi, S. (2011, March). Neural network based handwritten character recognition system without feature extraction. In *Computer, Communication and Electrical Technology (ICCCET), 2011 International Conference on* (pp. 40-44). IEEE. 10.1109/ICCCET.2011.5762513

Prasad, S., & Charan, R. (1984). On the constrained synthesis of array patterns with applications to circular and arc arrays. *IEEE Transactions on Antennas and Propagation, AP-32*(7), 725–730. doi:10.1109/TAP.1984.1143404

Price, K., Storn, R. M., & Lampinen, J. A. (2006). *Differential evolution: a practical approach to global optimization.* Springer Science & Business Media.

Procopiuc, C. M., Jones, M., Agarwal, P. K., & Murali, T. M. (2002, June). A Monte Carlo algorithm for fast projective clustering. In *Proceedings of the 2002 ACM SIGMOD international conference on Management of data* (pp. 418-427). ACM.

Pujari, M., & Kanawati, R. (2015). Link prediction in multiplex networks. *Networks and Heterogeneous Media, 10*(1), 17–35. doi:10.3934/nhm.2015.10.17

Qi, C., Zhou, Z., Sun, Y., Song, H., Hu, L., & Wang, Q. (2016). Feature selection and multiple kernel boosting framework based on PSO with mutation mechanism for hyperspectral classification. *Neurocomputing, 220*, 181–190. doi:10.1016/j.neucom.2016.05.103

Quarteroni, S., & Manandhar, S. (2009). Designing an interactive open-domain question answering system. *Natural Language Engineering, 15*(1), 73–95. doi:10.1017/S1351324908004919

Qubati, G. M., Formato, R. A., & Dib, N. I. (2010). Antenna benchmark performance and array synthesis using central force optimisation. *IET Microwaves, Antennas & Propagation, 4*(5), 583–592. doi:10.1049/iet-map.2009.0147

Quinlan, J. R. (2014). *C4. 5: programs for machine learning.* Elsevier.

Radhouani, S., Mottaz Jiang, C. L., & Falquet, G. (2009). Flexir: A domain-specific information retrieval system. *Polibits, 39*, 27–31. doi:10.17562/PB-39-4

Rahman, M. S., Mridha, M. F., Poddar, S. R., & Huda, M. N. (2010, October). Open morphological machine translation: Bangla to English. In *Computer Information Systems and Industrial Management Applications (CISIM), 2010 International Conference on* (pp. 460-465). IEEE.

Rahman, M., Venugopal, S., & Buyya, R. (2007). A Dynamic Critical Path Algorithm for Scheduling Scientific Workflow Applications on Global Grids. In *IEEE International Conference on e-Science and Grid Computing* (pp. 35-42).

Ram, G., Mandal, D., Ghoshal, S. P., & Kar, R. (2017). Optimal array factor radiation pattern synthesis for linear antenna array using cat swarm optimization: Validation by an electromagnetic simulator. *Frontiers of Information Technology & Electronic Engineering, 18*(4), 570–577. doi:10.1631/FITEE.1500371

Ramírez-Gallego, S., García, S., Benítez, J. M., & Herrera, F. (2016). Multivariate Discretization Based on Evolutionary Cut Points Selection for Classification. *IEEE Transactions on Cybernetics, 46*(3), 595–608. doi:10.1109/TCYB.2015.2410143 PMID:25794409

Rane, A. K. (2005). *Intelligent Tutoring System For Marathi.* Karnataka State Open University Mysore.

Rao, K. D. (2015). *Channel coding techniques for wireless communications.* Springer Pvt. Ltd.

Rebelo, C., Sá, D., Soares, C., & Knobbe, A. (2016). Entropy-based discretization methods for ranking data. *Information Sciences, 329*, 921–936. doi:10.1016/j.ins.2015.04.022

Recioui, A. (2012). Sidelobe level reduction in linear array pattern synthesis using particle swarm optimization. *Journal of Optimization Theory and Applications, 153*(2), 497–12. doi:10.100710957-011-9953-9

Rimal, B. P., & Maier, M. (2017). Workflow Scheduling in Multi-Tenant Cloud Computing Environments. *IEEE Transactions on Parallel and Distributed Systems, 28*(1), 290–304. doi:10.1109/TPDS.2016.2556668

Ritter, A., Cherry, C., & Dolan, W. B. (2011). Data-driven response generation in social media. *Proceedings of the Conference on Empirical Methods in Natural Language Processing.*

Rivero, J., Cuadra, D., Calle, J., & Isasi, P. (2012). Using the ACO algorithm for path searches in social networks. *Applied Intelligence*, *36*(4), 899–917. doi:10.100710489-011-0304-1

Road, H., & Jose, S. (1998). Automatic Subspace Clustering Mining of High Dimensional Applications for Data. In *Proceedings of the 1998 ACM SIGMOD International Conference on Management of Data* (pp. 94-105). doi:10.1145/276305.276314

Rodrigo, S. M., & Abraham, J. G. F. (2012, April). Development and implementation of a chat bot in a social network. In *Information Technology: New Generations (ITNG), 2012 Ninth International Conference on* (pp. 751-755). IEEE. 10.1109/ITNG.2012.147

Rodriguez, M. A., & Buyya, R. (2014). Deadline Based Resource Provisioning and Scheduling Algorithm for Scientific Workflows on Clouds. *IEEE Transactions on Cloud Computing*, *2*(2), 222–235. doi:10.1109/TCC.2014.2314655

Ropero, R. F., Renooij, S., & van der Gaag, L. C. (2018). Discretizing environmental data for learning Bayesian-network classifiers. *Ecological Modelling*, *368*, 391–403. doi:10.1016/j.ecolmodel.2017.12.015

Roy, A. G., Rakshit, P., Konar, A., Bhattacharya, S., Kim, E., & Nagar, A. K. (2013, June). Adaptive firefly algorithm for nonholonomic motion planning of car-like system. In *2013 IEEE Congress on Evolutionary Computation (CEC)* (pp. 2162-2169). IEEE. 10.1109/CEC.2013.6557825

Rubin, J. (1994). A review of second language listening comprehension research. *Modern Language Journal*, *78*(2), 199–221. doi:10.1111/j.1540-4781.1994.tb02034.x

Ruiz, F. J., Angulo, C., & Agell, N. (2008). IDD: A supervised interval distance-based method for discretization. *IEEE Transactions on Knowledge and Data Engineering*, *20*(9), 1230–1238. doi:10.1109/TKDE.2008.66

Russell, S. J., Norvig, P., Canny, J. F., Malik, J. M., & Edwards, D. D. (2003). Artificial intelligence: a modern approach: Vol. 2. *No. 9*. Upper Saddle River, NJ: Prentice hall.

Sagiroglu, S., & Sinanc, D. (2013). Big data: A review. *IEEE International Conference on Collaboration Technologies and System (CTS)*, 42-47.

Saha, S., Ekbal, A., Gupta, K., & Bandyopadhyay, S. (2013). Gene expression data clustering using a multiobjective symmetry based clustering technique. *Computers in Biology and Medicine*, *43*(11), 1965–1977. doi:10.1016/j.comp-biomed.2013.07.021 PMID:24209942

Şahin, M., & Duman, D. (2013). Multilingual Chat through Machine Translation: A Case of English-Russian. Meta: Journal des traducteurs/Meta: Translators'. *Journal*, *58*(2), 397–410.

Sainath, T., Mohamed, A., Kingsbury, B., & Ramabhadran, B. (2013). Deep convolutional neural networks for LVCSR. In *IEEE International Conference on Acoustics, Speech and Signal Processing*. Vancouver, Canada.

Sakti, S., Kimura, N., Paul, M., Hori, C., Sumita, E., Nakamura, S., . . . Arora, K. (2009, November). The Asian network-based speech-to-speech translation system. In *Automatic Speech Recognition & Understanding, 2009. ASRU 2009. IEEE Workshop on* (pp. 507-512). IEEE. 10.1109/ASRU.2009.5373353

Salem, H., Attiya, G., & El-Fishawy, N. (2017). Classification of human cancer diseases by gene expression profiles. *Applied Soft Computing*, *50*, 124–134. doi:10.1016/j.asoc.2016.11.026

Schaefer, G., & Rossberg, M. (2014). *Security in fixed and wireless networks* (2nd ed.). Heidelberg, Germany: John Wiley & Sons Ltd.

Schafer, G. (2003). *Security in fixed and wireless networks: an introduction to securing data communications*. West Sussex, UK: John Wiley & Sons, Ltd. doi:10.1002/0470863722

Schroeck, M., Shockley, R., Smart, J., Romero-Morales, D., & Tufano, P. (2012). Analytics: The real-world use of Big Data. *IBM Global Business Services*, *12*, 1–20.

Seeley, T. D. (2009). *The Wisdom of Hive: The Social Physiology of Honey Bee Colonies*. Cambridge, MA: Harvard University Press.

Sequeira, K., & Zaki, M. (2004). SCHISM: A new approach for interesting subspace mining. In *Proceedings of the Fourth IEEE International Conference on Data Mining* (pp. 186–193).

Serban, I. V., Sordoni, A., Bengio, Y., Courville, A. C., & Pineau, J. (2016, February). Building End-To-End Dialogue Systems Using Generative Hierarchical Neural Network Models. In *AAAI* (pp. 3776-3784). Academic Press.

Shang, L., Lu, Z., & Li, H. (2015). *Neural responding machine for short-text conversation*. arXiv preprint arXiv:1503.02364

Shankar, K., & Eswaran, P. (2015). A secure visual secret share (VSS) creation scheme in visual cryptography using elliptic curve cryptography with optimization technique. *Australian Journal of Basic and Applied Sciences*, *9*(36), 150–163.

Shao, S., Huang, X., Stanley, H. E., & Havlin, S. (2014). Robustness of a partially interdependent network formed of clustered networks. *Phys. Rev. E*, *89*(3), 032812. doi:10.1103/PhysRevE.89.032812 PMID:24730904

Shawar, B. A., & Atwell, E. (2007). Chatbots: are they really useful? In *LDV Forum* (Vol. 22, No. 1, pp. 29-49). Academic Press.

Shellhammer, S. J. (2008). Spectrum sensing in IEEE 802.22. *IAPR Wksp. Cognitive Info. Processing*, 9-10.

Shi, Y. (2001). Particle swarm optimization: developments, applications and resources. In *Proceedings of the 2001 Congress on evolutionary computation* (Vol. *1*, pp. 81-86). IEEE. 10.1109/CEC.2001.934374

Shin, H., Orton, M., Collins, D., Doran, S., & Leach, M. (2013). Stacked autoencoders for unsupervised feature learning and multiple organ detection in a pilot study using 4D patient data. *IEEE Transactions on Pattern Analysis and Machine Intelligence*, *35*(8), 1930–1943. doi:10.1109/TPAMI.2012.277 PMID:23787345

Shipp, M. A., Ross, K. N., Tamayo, P., Weng, A. P., Kutok, J. L., Aguiar, R. C., & Ray, T. S. (2002). Diffuse large B-cell lymphoma outcome prediction by gene-expression profiling and supervised machine learning. *Nature Medicine*, *8*(1), 68–74. doi:10.1038/nm0102-68 PMID:11786909

Simon. (2008). BBO. *IEEE Transactions on Evolutionary Computation*, *12*(6).

Singh, D., Febbo, P. G., Ross, K., Jackson, D. G., Manola, J., Ladd, C., ... Lander, E. S. (2002). Gene expression correlates of clinical prostate cancer behavior. *Cancer Cell*, *1*(2), 203–209. doi:10.1016/S1535-6108(02)00030-2 PMID:12086878

Singh, J., & Singhla, V. (2015). Big Data:Tools and Technologies in Big Data. *International Journal of Computers and Applications*.

Sinha, M., Kuttieri, R. A., & Chatterjee, S. (2013). Nonlinear and linear unstable aircraft parameter estimations using neural partial differentiation. *Journal of Guidance, Control, and Dynamics*, *36*(4), 1162–1176. doi:10.2514/1.57029

Siniscalchi, S. M., Yu, D., Deng, L., & Lee, C. (2013). Exploiting deep neural networks for detection-based speech recognition. *Neurocomputing*, *106*, 148–157. doi:10.1016/j.neucom.2012.11.008

Socher, R., Lin, C., Ng, A., & Manning, C. (2011). Learning continuous phrase representations and syntactic parsing with recursive neural networks. In *International Conference on Machine Learning*. Bellevue, Washington, USA.

Sola, L., Romance, M., Criado, R., Flores, J., del Amo, A. G., & Boccaletti, S. (2013). Eigenvector centrality of nodes in multiplex networks. *Chaos (Woodbury, N.Y.)*, *3*(033131). PMID:24089967

Song, H. M., Sulaiman, M. H., & Mohamed, M. R. (2014). An Application of Grey Wolf Optimizer for Solving Combined Economic Emission Dispatch Problems. *International Review on Modelling and Simulations*, *7*(5), 838. doi:10.15866/iremos.v7i5.2799

Sordoni, A., Galley, M., Auli, M., Brockett, C., Ji, Y., Mitchell, M., . . . Dolan, B. (2015). *A neural network approach to context-sensitive generation of conversational responses*. arXiv preprint arXiv:1506.06714

Srivastava, N., Hinton, G., Krizhevsky, A., Sutskever, I., & Salakhtdinov, R. (2014). Dropout: A simple way to prevent neural networks from overfitting. *Journal of Machine Learning Research*, *15*, 1929–1958.

Statnikov, A., Tsamardinos, I., Dosbayev, Y., & Aliferis, C. F. (2005). GEMS: A system for automated cancer diagnosis and biomarker discovery from microarray gene expression data. *International Journal of Medical Informatics*, *74*(7–8), 491–503. doi:10.1016/j.ijmedinf.2005.05.002 PMID:15967710

Stephen, K., & Frank, A. J. (2013). Big data: Issues and challenges moving forward. *IEEE International Conference on System Science*.

Steyskal, H. (1982). Synthesis of antenna patterns with prescribed nulls. *IEEE Transactions on Antennas and Propagation*, *AP-30*(2), 273–279. doi:10.1109/TAP.1982.1142765

Storn, R., & Price, K. (1997). Differential evolution – a simple and efficient heuristic for global optimization over continuous spaces. *Journal of Global Optimization*, *11*(4), 341–359. doi:10.1023/A:1008202821328

Stoyanov, V., Ropson, A., & Eisner, J. (2011). Empirical risk minimization of graphical model parameters given approximate inference, decoding, and model structure. In 14th International Conference on Artificial Intelligence and Statistics, Fort Lauderdale, FL (pp. 725-733). .

Su, C. T., & Hsu, J. H. (2005). An Extended Chi2 algorithm for discretization of real value attributes. *IEEE Transactions on Knowledge and Data Engineering*, *17*(3), 437–441. doi:10.1109/TKDE.2005.39

Sun, X., & Zhang, L. (2009, August). Basic Factors Design of Pedagogical Agent System in an Ecology View. In *Hybrid Intelligent Systems, 2009. HIS'09. Ninth International Conference on* (Vol. 3, pp. 183-186). IEEE. 10.1109/HIS.2009.250

Sun, H., & Xiong, L. (2009). Genetic Algorithm-Based High-dimensional Data Clustering Technique. In *2009 Sixth International Conference on Fuzzy Systems and Knowledge Discovery* (pp. 485–489). 10.1109/FSKD.2009.215

Suresh, S., Omkar, S. N., Mani, V., & Sundararajan, N. (2005). Nonlinear adaptive neural controller for unstable aircraft. *Journal of Guidance, Control, and Dynamics*, *28*(6), 1103–1111. doi:10.2514/1.12974

Sutskever, I., Vinyals, O., & Le, Q. V. (2014). Sequence to sequence learning with neural networks. In Advances in neural information processing systems (pp. 3104-3112). Academic Press.

Sutskever, I., Martens, J., & Hinton, G. (2011). Generating text with recurrent neural networks. In *28th International Conference on Machine Learning*. Bellevue, USA.

Sutton, R., & Barto, A. (1998). *Reinforcement learning: An introduction (Adaptive computation and machine learning)*. Cambridge, MA: MIT Press.

Tahan, M. H., & Asadi, S. (2017). MEMOD: A novel multivariate evolutionary multi-objective discretization. *Soft Computing*. doi:10.100700500-016-2475-5

Tahan, M. H., & Asadi, S. (2018). EMDID: Evolutionary multi-objective discretization for imbalanced datasets. *Information Sciences*, *432*, 442–461. doi:10.1016/j.ins.2017.12.023

Takagi, H., Suzuki, N., Koda, T., & Kojima, Y. (1992). Neural networks designed on approximate reasoning architecture and their applications. *IEEE Transactions on Neural Networks*, *3*(5), 752–760. doi:10.1109/72.159063 PMID:18276473

Tan, F., Fu, X., Zhang, Y., & Bourgeois, A. G. (2006, July). Improving feature subset selection using a genetic algorithm for microarray gene expression data. In *2006 IEEE International Conference on Evolutionary Computation* (pp. 2529-2534). IEEE.

Tao, Q., Chang, H., Yi, Y., Gu, C., & Li, W. (2011). A rotary chaotic PSO algorithm for trustworthy scheduling of a grid workflow. *Computers & Operations Research*, *38*(5), 824–836. doi:10.1016/j.cor.2010.09.012

Taylor, G., Hinton, G., & Roweis, S. (2006). Modeling human motion using binary latent variables. In *Annual Conference on Neural Information Processing Systems*, Vancouver, Canada (pp. 1345-1352).

Teo, C. H., Le, Q., Smola, A., & Vishwanathan, S. V. (2007). A scalabe modular convex solver for regularized risk minimization. In *Conference on Knowledge Discovery and Data Mining*, San Francisco, CA.

Timmerman, M. E., Ceulemans, E., De Roover, K., & Van Leeuwen, K. (2013). Subspace K-means clustering. *Behavior Research Methods*, *45*(4), 1011–1023. doi:10.375813428-013-0329-y PMID:23526258

Tran, B., Xue, B., & Zhang, M. (2016). A New Representation in PSO for Discretisation-Based Feature Selection. Retrieved from http://homepages.ecs.vuw.ac.nz/~xuebing/Papers/tran_Cybernetics2017.pdf

Trastoy, A., Rahmat–Samii, Y., Ares, F., & Moreno, E. (2004). Two-pattern linear array antenna: Synthesis and analysis of tolerance. *IEE Proceedings. Microwaves, Antennas and Propagation*, *151*(2), 127–130. doi:10.1049/ip-map:20040175

Tripathy, B., Dash, S., & Padhy, S. K. (2015). Dynamic task scheduling using a directed neural network. *Journal of Parallel and Distributed Computing*, *75*, 101–106. doi:10.1016/j.jpdc.2014.09.015

Tsai, C. J., Lee, C. I., & Yang, W. P. (2008). A discretization algorithm based on Class-Attribute Contingency Coefficient. *Information Sciences*, *178*(3), 714–731. doi:10.1016/j.ins.2007.09.004

Tsai, C. W., Chiang, M. C., Ksentini, A., & Chen, M. (2016). Metaheuristic Algorithms for Healthcare: Open Issues and Challenges. *Computers & Electrical Engineering*, *53*, 421–434. doi:10.1016/j.compeleceng.2016.03.005

Ullman, J. (1975). NP-complete scheduling problems. *Journal of Computer and System Sciences*, *10*(3), 384–393. doi:10.1016/S0022-0000(75)80008-0

Valdez, L. D., Macri, P. A., Stanley, H. E., & Braunstein, L. A. (2013). Triple point in correlated interdependent networks. *Phys. Rev. E*, *88*(5), 050803. doi:10.1103/PhysRevE.88.050803 PMID:24329204

Van Opijnen, M., & Santos, C. (2017). On the concept of relevance in legal information retrieval. *Artificial Intelligence and Law*, *25*(1), 65–87. doi:10.100710506-017-9195-8

Verma, A., & Arora, A. (2017, January). Reflexive hybrid approach to provide precise answer of user desired frequently asked question. In *Cloud Computing, Data Science & Engineering-Confluence, 2017 7th International Conference on* (pp. 159-163). IEEE. 10.1109/CONFLUENCE.2017.7943142

Vijendra, S., & Laxman, S. (2013). Subspace Clustering of High-Dimensional Data: An Evolutionary Approach. *Applied Computational Intelligence and Soft Computing*, *2013*(1), 1–13. doi:10.1155/2013/863146

Vinyals, O., & Le, Q. (2015). *A neural conversational model*. arXiv preprint arXiv:1506.05869

Visweswariah, K., Navratil, J., Sorensen, J., Chenthamarakshan, V., & Kambhatla, N. (2010, August). Syntax based reordering with automatically derived rules for improved statistical machine translation. In *Proceedings of the 23rd international conference on computational linguistics* (pp. 1119-1127). Association for Computational Linguistics.

Wade, B. S. C., Joshi, S. H., Gutman, B. A., & Thompson, P. M. (2015). Machine Learning on High Dimensional Shape Data from Subcortical Brain Surfaces: A Comparison of Feature Selection and Classification Methods. *Pattern Recognition, 63*, 731–739. doi:10.1016/j.patcog.2016.09.034

Walton, S., Hassan, O., Morgan, K., & Brown, M. R. (2011). Modified cuckoo search: A new gradient-free optimization algorithm. *Chaos, Solitons, and Fractals, 44*(9), 710–718. doi:10.1016/j.chaos.2011.06.004

Wang, T., & Yang, Y. (2011). Location privacy protection from RSS localization system using antenna pattern synthesis. In *Proceedings of the IEEE INFOCOM* (pp. 2408-16). Shanghai, China: IEEE Explore. 10.1109/INFCOM.2011.5935061

Wang, Z., & Lemon, O. (2013, August). A Simple and Generic Belief Tracking Mechanism for the Dialog State Tracking Challenge: On the believability of observed information. In *SIGDIAL Conference* (pp. 423-432). Academic Press.

Wang, B., Wang, X., Sun, C., Liu, B., & Sun, L. (2010, July). Modeling semantic relevance for question-answer pairs in web social communities. In *Proceedings of the 48th Annual Meeting of the Association for Computational Linguistics* (pp. 1230-1238). Association for Computational Linguistics.

Wang, C., Au, E. K. S., Murch, R. D., Mow, W. H., Cheng, R. S., & Lau, V. (2007). On the performance of the MIMO zero-forcing receiver in the presence of channel estimation error. *IEEE Transactions on Wireless Communications, 6*(3), 805–810. doi:10.1109/TWC.2007.05384

Wang, H., Lu, Z., Li, H., & Chen, E. (2013). A dataset for research on short-text conversations. EMNLP.

Wang, H., & Niu, B. (2017). A novel bacterial algorithm with randomness control for feature selection in classification. *Neurocomputing, 228*, 176–186. doi:10.1016/j.neucom.2016.09.078

Wan, Y., Wang, M., Ye, Z., & Lai, X. (2016). A feature selection method based on modified binary coded ant colony optimization algorithm. *Applied Soft Computing, 49*, 248–258. doi:10.1016/j.asoc.2016.08.011

Waszak, M. R., & Schmidt, D. K. (1988). Flight dynamics of aeroelastic vehicles. *Journal of Aircraft, 25*(6), 563–571. doi:10.2514/3.45623

Watanabe, S., & Kabashima, Y. (2014, January). influences of intranetwork and internetwork degree-degree correlations. *Phys. Rev. E, 89*(1), 012808. doi:10.1103/PhysRevE.89.012808

Wellens, M., & Mähönen, P. (2010). Lessons learned from an extensive spectrum occupancy measurement campaign and a stochastic duty cycle model. *Mobile Networks and Applications, 15*(3), 461–474. doi:10.100711036-009-0199-9

Win, A. T. (2011, March). Words to phrase reordering machine translation system in Myanmar-English using English grammar rules. In *Computer Research and Development (ICCRD), 2011 3rd International Conference on* (Vol. 3, pp. 50-53). IEEE.

Wong, F. L., Lin, M., Nagaraja, S., Wassell, I., & Stajano, F. (2007). Evaluation framework of location privacy of wireless mobile systems with arbitrary beam pattern. In *Proceedings of the fifth annual conference on communication networks and services research* (pp. 157-65). Frederlcton, NB, Canada: IEEE Explore. 10.1109/CNSR.2007.30

Wu, Z., Ni, Z., Gu, L., & Liu, X. (2010). A revised discrete particle swarm optimization for cloud workflow scheduling. In *Proc. IEEE Int. Conf. Comput. Intell. Security* (pp. 184–188).

Wu, Q., Bell, D. A., Prasad, G., & Mcginnity, T. M. (2007). A distribution-index-based discretizer for decision-making with symbolic Al approaches. *IEEE Transactions on Knowledge and Data Engineering*, *19*(1), 17–28. doi:10.1109/TKDE.2007.250582

Wu, Q., Bell, D., McGinnity, M., Prasad, G., Qi, G., & Huang, X. (2006). Improvement of decision accuracy using discretization of continuous attributes. In *International Conference on Fuzzy Systems and Knowledge Discovery* (pp. 674–683).

Wu, X. (1996). A Bayesian Discretizer for real-valued attributes. *The Computer Journal*, *39*(8), 688–691. doi:10.1093/comjnl/39.8.688

Xiang, B., Deng, Y., & Gao, Y. (2008, March). Unsupervised training for farsi-english speech-to-speech translation. In *Acoustics, Speech and Signal Processing, 2008. ICASSP 2008. IEEE International Conference on* (pp. 4977-4980). IEEE. 10.1109/ICASSP.2008.4518775

Xiangnan Kong, P. Y., & Zhang, J. (2013). Inferring anchor links across multiple heterogeneous social networks. In CIKM, Burlingame, CA.

Xue, H., Shao, Z., Pan, J., Zhao, Q., & Ma, F. (2016). A hybrid firefly algorithm for optimizing fractional proportional-integral-derivative controller in ship steering. *Journal of Shanghai Jiaotong University (Science)*, *21*(4), 419–423. doi:10.100712204-016-1741-0

Yang, X. S., & Deb, S. (2009, December). Cuckoo search via Lévy flights. In *World Congress on Nature & Biologically Inspired Computing NaBIC '09* (pp. 210-214). IEEE.

Yang, X. S., & Deb, S. (2009, December). Cuckoo search via Lévy flights. In *World Congress on Nature & Biologically Inspired Computing NaBIC 2009* (pp. 210-214). IEEE.

Yang, X.-S., & Deb, S. (2009). Cuckoo search via l'evy flights. In *Nature & Biologically Inspired Computing, 2009. NaBIC 2009. World Congress on* (pp. 210–214). IEEE.

Yang. (2014). A Binary Cuckoo Search Algorithm for Feature Selection. *Studies in Computational Intelligence*, *516*, 141–154.

Yang, D., Parrish, R. S., & Brock, G. N. (2014). Empirical evaluation of consistency and accuracy of methods to detect differentially expressed genes based on microarray data. *Computers in Biology and Medicine*, *46*, 1–10. doi:10.1016/j.compbiomed.2013.12.002 PMID:24529200

Yang, H., Luo, H., Ye, F., Lu, S., & Zhang, L. (2004). Security in mobile ad hoc networks: Challenges and solutions. *IEEE Wireless Communications*, *11*(1), 38–47. doi:10.1109/MWC.2004.1269716

Yang, K., Zhao, Z., & Liu, Q. H. (2013). Fast pencil beam pattern synthesis of large unequally spaced antenna arrays. *IEEE Transactions on Antennas and Propagation*, *61*(2), 627–634. doi:10.1109/TAP.2012.2220319

Yang, P., Li, J.-S., & Huang, Y.-X. (2011). HDD: A hypercube division-based algorithm for discretisation. *International Journal of Systems Science*, *42*(4), 557–566. doi:10.1080/00207720903572455

Yang, P., & Yang, Hwa, Y., Zhou, B.B., & Zomaya, A.Y. (2010). A review of ensemble methods in bioinformatics. *Current Bioinformatics*, *5*(4), 296–308. doi:10.2174/157489310794072508

Yang, X. S. (2009, October). Firefly algorithms for multimodal optimization. In *International symposium on stochastic algorithms* (pp. 169-178). Springer.

Yang, X. S. (2010). A new metaheuristic bat-inspired algorithm. In *Nature inspired cooperative strategies for optimization (NICSO 2010)* (pp. 65–74). Berlin: Springer. doi:10.1007/978-3-642-12538-6_6

Yang, X. S. (2010). A new metaheuristic bat-inspired algorithm. In *Nature inspired cooperative strategies for optimization* (pp. 65–74). NICSO.

Yang, X. S. (2011). Bat algorithm for multi-objective optimisation. *International Journal of Bio-inspired Computation*, *3*(5), 267–274. doi:10.1504/IJBIC.2011.042259

Yang, X. S., & Deb, S. (2009). Cuckoo search via Lévy flights. In *World Congress on Nature Biologically Inspired Computing*. IEEE Publications. 10.1109/NABIC.2009.5393690

Yang, X. S., & Deb, S. (2010). Engineering optimization by cuckoo search. *International Journal of Mathematical Modeling and Numerical Optimization*, *1*(4), 330–343. doi:10.1504/IJMMNO.2010.035430

Yang, X. S., & He, X. (2013). Bat algorithm: Literature review and applications. *International Journal of Bio-inspired Computation*, *5*(3), 141–149. doi:10.1504/IJBIC.2013.055093

Yang, X. S., & Hossein Gandomi, A. (2012). Bat algorithm: A novel approach for global engineering optimization. *Engineering Computations*, *29*(5), 464–483. doi:10.1108/02644401211235834

Yang, Y., & Webb, G. I. (2009). Discretization for naive-Bayes learning: Managing discretization bias and variance. *Machine Learning*, *74*(1), 39–74. doi:10.100710994-008-5083-5

Yeniay, Ö. (2005). Penalty function methods for constrained optimization with genetic algorithms. *Mathematical and Computational Applications*, *10*(1), 45–56. doi:10.3390/mca10010045

Yihui, H., Xiangyu, Z., & Sun, J. (2017). Channel Pruning for Accelerating Very Deep Neural. In *IEEE International Conference on Computer Vision*, Venice, Italy (pp. 1389-1397).

Yiu, M. L., & Mamoulis, N. (2003). Frequent-pattern based iterative projected clustering. In *Proceedings of the Third IEEE International Conference on Data Mining* (pp. 689–692).

Yu, D., & Deng, L. (2010). Deep-structured hidden conditional random fields for phonetic recognition. In Eleventh Annual Conference of the International Speech Communication Association. Makuhari, Japan: Interspeech.

Yucek, T., & Arslan, H. (2009). A survey of spectrum sensing algorithms for cognitive radio applications. *IEEE Communications Surveys and Tutorials*, *11*(1), 116–130. doi:10.1109/SURV.2009.090109

Yu, D., Wang, S., & Deng, L. (2010). Sequential labeling using deep structured conditional random fields. *IEEE Journal of Selected Topics in Signal Processing*, *4*(6), 965–973. doi:10.1109/JSTSP.2010.2075990

Yu, D., Wang, S., Karam, Z., & Deng, L. (2010). Language recognition using deep-structured conditional random fields. In *IEEE International Conference on Acoustics Speech and Signal Processing*, Dallas, TX (pp. 5030-5033). 10.1109/ICASSP.2010.5495072

Yu, J., & Buyya, R. (2006). A budget constrained scheduling of workflow applications on utility grids using genetic algorithms. In *Proc. 1st Workshop Workflows Support Large-Scale Sci.* (pp. 1–10).

Yusof, Y., & Mustaffa, Z. (2015). Time series forecasting of energy commodity using grey wolf optimizer. In *Proceedings of the International Multi Conference of Engineers and Computer Scientists (IMECS '15)*, Hong Kong (Vol. 1).

Zerweckh, S. H., Von Flotow, A. H., & Murray, J. E. (1990). Flight testing a highly flexible aircraft-Case study on the MIT Light Eagle. *Journal of Aircraft*, *27*(4), 342–349. doi:10.2514/3.25278

Zhan, Z., & Liu, X. Gong,Y-J. Zhang, J., Chung, H. & Li, Y. (2015). Cloud Computing Resource Scheduling and a Survey of Its Evolutionary Approaches. ACM Comput. Surv., 47(4).

Zhang, W., Mallik, R. K., & Letaief, K. B. (2008, May). Cooperative spectrum sensing optimization in cognitive radio networks. In *IEEE International conference on Communications ICC'08* (pp. 3411-3415). IEEE. 10.1109/ICC.2008.641

Zhang, B., Zhong, S., Wen, K., Li, R., & Gu, X. (2013). Finding high–influence microblog users with an improved PSO algorithm. International Journal of Modelling. *Identification and Control, 18*(4), 349–356. doi:10.1504/IJMIC.2013.053540

Zhang, C., & Zhang, Z. (2014). Improving multiview face detection with multi-task deep convolutional neural networks. In *IEEE Winter Conference on Applications of Computer Vision*, Steamboat Springs, CO (pp. 1036-1041). 10.1109/WACV.2014.6835990

Zhang, L., Kuljis, J., Li Zhang, L., Kuljis, J., & Liu, X. (2008). Information visualization for DNA microarray data analysis: A critical review. *IEEE Transactions on Systems, Man and Cybernetics. Part C, Applications and Reviews, 38*(1), 42–54. doi:10.1109/TSMCC.2007.906065

Zhang, Q., Jia, J., & Zhang, J. (2009). Cooperative relay to improve diversity in cognitive radio networks. *IEEE Communications Magazine, 47*(2), 111–117. doi:10.1109/MCOM.2009.4785388

Zheng, C. H., Yang, W., Chong, Y. W., & Xia, J. F. (2016). Identification of mutated driver pathways in cancer using a multi-objective optimization model. *Computers in Biology and Medicine, 72*, 22–29. doi:10.1016/j.compbiomed.2016.03.002 PMID:26995027

Zheng, L., Yang, S., & Nie, Z. (2011). Pattern synthesis with specified broad nulls in time-modulated circular antenna arrays. *Electromagnetics, 31*(5), 355–367. doi:10.1080/02726343.2011.579770

Zhenya, H., Chengjian, W., Luxi, Y., Xiqi, G., Susu, Y., Eberhart, R. C., & Shi, Y. (1998, May). Extracting rules from fuzzy neural network by particle swarm optimisation. In *Evolutionary Computation Proceedings, 1998. IEEE World Congress on Computational Intelligence., The 1998 IEEE International Conference on* (pp. 74-77). IEEE. 10.1109/ICEC.1998.699325

Zhoua, X., Gaob, X., Wanga, J., Yua, H., Wangc, Z., & Chid, Z. (2016). Eye Tracking Data Guided Feature Selection for Image Classification. *Pattern Recognition, 63*, 56–70. doi:10.1016/j.patcog.2016.09.007

Zhou, D., Stanley, H. E., D'Agostino, G., & Scala, A. (2012). Assortativity decreases the robustness of interdependent networks. *Phys. Rev. E, 86*(6), 066103. doi:10.1103/PhysRevE.86.066103 PMID:23368000

Zhou, X., Song, L., & Zhang, Y. (2014). *Physical layer security in wireless communications*. Boca Raton, FL: Taylor & Francis Group, LLC.

Zhu, G., & Zhang, W. (2014). An improved Shuffled Frog-leaping Algorithm to optimize component pick-and-place sequencing optimization problem. *Expert Systems with Applications, 41*(15), 6818–6829. doi:10.1016/j.eswa.2014.04.038

Zibakhsh, A., & Abadeh, M. S. (2013). Gene selection for cancer tumor detection using a novel memetic algorithm with a multi-view fitness function. *Engineering Applications of Artificial Intelligence, 26*(4), 1274–1281. doi:10.1016/j.engappai.2012.12.009

Zighed, D. A., Rabaséda, S., & Rakotomalala, R. (1998). Fusinter: A method for discretization of continuous attributes. *International Journal of Uncertainty, Fuzziness and Knowledge-based Systems.* doi:10.1142/S0218488598000264

Zinkevich, M., Weimer, M., Smola, A., & Li, L. (2010). Parallelized stocastic gradient descent. In *Conference on Neural Information Processing Systems*, Vancouver, Canada.

Zou, Y., & Zhu, J. (2016). *Physical-layer security for cooperative relay networks*. Springer International Publishing AG. doi:10.1007/978-3-319-31174-6

About the Contributors

Hema Banati completed her Ph.D (2006) after her Masters in Computer Applications(M.C.A) (1993) both from Department of Computer Science, University of Delhi, India. At present she is an Associate Professor in the Department of Computer Science, Dyal Singh College, University of Delhi. She has over 20 years of teaching experience to both undergraduate and postgraduate classes. Her research publications span across various reputed national, international journals, conferences and books. The progress of her research journey is marked with the collaboration of the work of students; she has supervised for Ph.D in diverse areas such as Elearning, e-commerce, soft computing and semantic web.At present she is actively working in area of Soft computing, social networks, big data.

Shikha Mehta is working as Associate Professor in Jaypee Institute of Information Technology, NOIDA, India. She completed her Doctor of Philosophy from Delhi University, Delhi in 2013. Her research interests are large scale optimization, Nature Inspired Algorithms, Soft Computing, Big data analysis, Social Network Analysis etc.

Parmeet Kaur received Ph.D. in Computer Engineering from NIT, Kurukshetra in 2016, M.Tech. in Computer Science from Kurukshetra University, India in 2008 and B.E. in Computer Science and Engineering from P.E.C., Chandigarh, India in 1998. She is currently working in Jaypee Institute of Information Technology, NOIDA, India. Her research interests include fault tolerance in mobile systems, scheduling in cloud computing etc.

* * *

Parul Agarwal received her B.Tech and M.Tech degree in computer science and engineering. Presently, she is an assistant professor at JIIT and pursuing Ph.D. under supervision of Dr. Shikha Mehta. She is working on nature inspired algorithms, data mining and machine learning.

Prativa Agarwalla received the Bachelor and Master Degree, both from Calcutta University in Radio Physics and Electronics in 2010 and 2012 respectively. She is currently an Assistant Professor with the Heritage Institute of Technology. Her main research interests include optimization, soft computing, evolutionary computation and computational biology.

Rajendra Akerkar is a professor of Information Technology at Vestlansforsking, Norway. He leads big data research group at the institute. His research and teaching experience includes over 24 years in the Academia spanning universities in Asia, Europe and North America. His recent research focuses on application of big data methods to real-world challenges, and social media analysis in a wide set of semantic dimensions. He has extensive experience in managing research and innovation projects funded by both industry and funding agencies, including the EU Framework Programs and the Research Council of Norway. He is actively involved in several international ICT initiatives for more than 20 years.

Anuja Arora has completed her Masters from Birla Institute of Information Technology and Doctor of Philosophy from Banasthali University in Year 2013. Currently, she is Associate Professor in Computer Science and Engineering Department of Jaypee Institute of Information Technology. Over 14 years of accomplished career demonstrates her success with excellent academic record, extensive background of involvement in team building activities, effective communicator with excellent planning, organizational and negotiation strengths as well as the ability to lead, reach consensus, establish goals, and attain results. Her prime research interests are Web Intelligence, Social Network Analysis, Social Media Analysis and Mining, Evolutionary Computing, Web Testing, Information Retrieval and Data Mining. She has published various book chapters and around 40 research papers in reputed international journals and conferences. She has also organized, coordinated and attended FDPs, Trainings, Seminars and Workshops.

Shivam Bansal had pursued BTech in computer science from JIIT, Noida. He is currently working as Lead Data Scientist at one of the leading company Exzeo software private limited in India. His prime interest and expertise areas are Machine Learning, Data Science, Natural Language processing, neural network, social media analytics. He is actively working in the field of Data science from past six years and handled various complex data mining problems.

Mohinder Pal Singh Bhatia received his Ph.D. in Computer Engineering from the University of Delhi, Delhi. He has been working as a Professor in the Computer Engineering Department of Netaji Subhas Institute of Technology, New Delhi, India. He has guided many M.Tech and Ph.D. students. He has authored several papers in refereed journals, book chapters, and conferences. His research interests include Software Engineering, Cyber Security and Privacy, Social Network Analysis, Data Mining, Machine Learning, Pattern Recognition, Semantic Web, Big Data and Analytics.

Rathindra Nath Biswas received his M.E degree in Electronics and Tele-Communication Engineering from Jadavpur University, West Bengal, India in 2008.Currently, he is associated as lecturer in Electronics and Tele-Communication Engineering at Acharya Jagadish Chandra Bose Polytechnic, West Bengal, India since 2008.

Soumyadip Das did his B.Sc. degree in Electronics in 2008 from Dinabandhu Andrew's College (University of Calcutta, India), M. Sc. in Electronics in 2010 from Acharya Prafulla Chandra College (West Bengal State University, India) and M. Tech. in Microelectronics and VLSI Tech. in 2012 from West Bengal University of Technology. He is currently doing research for his Ph.D in the Institute of Radio Physics and Electronics in University of Calcutta. His current research interests include design, FPGA based hardware prototype development and application of bio-Inspired optimization algorithm.

Abhishek Ghosh Roy received his Bachelor's Degree in Electronics and Instrumentation Engineering. He did his Master's Degree in Control System Engineering from the Department of Electrical Engineering, Jadavpur University. Currently, he is a Research Scholar in the Department of Aerospace Engineering, IIT Kharagpur. Area of research: Aircraft Parameter Estimation, Flight Mechanics, Control & Path planning.

Mukta Goyal is Ph.D. (CSE) from Jaypee Institute of Information Technology, Noida. She received her Graduation (CSE) from Govt. college of engineering, Trivandrum, Kerala University and Masters (CSE) from Banasthali University. She has more than 17 years of teaching experience.

Daya Gupta is a Professor in the Department of Computer Engineering, Delhi Technological University, Delhi. She has done Ph.D. in Computer Engineering from University of Delhi and M.Sc. (Maths), Post M.Sc. Diploma (Computers Sc.) from IIT, Delhi. She is a senior member of IEEE and a life member of CSI. Her research interests are in the field of requirement engineering, network security, ad hoc networks and image classification in remote sensing. She has published several research papers in international journals and conferences and has chaired sessions and delivered invited talks at many national and international conferences.

S. Indu is a Professor in the Department of Electronics and communication Engineering, Delhi Technological University, Delhi, and is currently the head of the department there. She has done Ph.D. in Computer Engineering from University of Delhi and M.Tech, Post B.Tech. from University of Kerala, Kerala. She was awarded the Best Branch Counselor award 2013 IEEE USA. Her research interests are in the field of Computer Vision, Image Processing, and wireless sensor network. She has 3 completed sponsored research projects. She published several research papers in international journals and conferences.

Ajay Kaushik is a senior research fellow (PhD scholar) in the Department of Computer Engineering at Delhi Technological University (DTU), Delhi, India. His areas of interest are Wireless sensor networks and Nature Inspired Intelligence. He did his M.Tech. (Master of Technology), Post B.Tech. in Computer Science & Engineering from Kurukshetra University, Kurukshetra. He qualified UGC NET-JRF with a percentage of 70.8% in year 2013. He has always been among the top rank-holders of the university in these courses.

Pavani Konagala working as Professor at Vaagdevi College of Engineering, Warangal, India. She has Completed her Ph.D, M.Tech from JNTU, Hyderabad and B.Tech from KITS, Warangal. She has 13 Publications and two books to her credit. She was a session chair and reviewer at various conferences.

Rajalakshmi Krishnamurthi obtained her Ph. D in Computer Science and Engineering from Jaypee Institute of Information Technology Noida, India. She did her M. E (CSE), and B. E. (EEE) from Bharathiar University, Coimbatore, India. She is currently an Assistant Professor (Senior Grade) with the Department of Computer Science and Engineering, Jaypee Institute of Information Technology, Noida. Her current research interests include Mobile computing, Wireless networks, Cloud Computing, Pervasive Computing.

Swarup Kumar Mitra is attached as Associate Professor in Department of ECE MCKV Institute of Engineering, Liluah, Howrah India and awarded with Ph.D.(Engg.) in the year 2012. His present area of research is FPGA, Wireless Sensor Network and its architecture, etc.

Ruchi Mittal is a research scholar and is presently pursuing a Ph.D. in the Department of Computer Engineering at Netaji Subhas Institute of Technology, University of Delhi. Her areas of interest include Social network analysis, graph analysis, and data mining.

Sumitra Mukhopadhyay received the Master Degree and Ph.D degree, both from Jadavpur University in Electronics and Communication Engineering in 2004 and 2009 respectively. She is currently an Assistant Professor with the University of Calcutta. Her main research interests include embedded system, field-programmable gate array-based prototype design, optimization, soft computing, evolutionary computation, Bio-informatics.

Mrinal Kanti Naskar holds a Ph.D.(Engg.) degree in Electronics and Telecommunications Engineering (E.T.C.E) from Jadavpur University, Kolkata, India, and an MTech degree and B.Tech degree in Electronics and Electrical Communications Engineering, I.I.T, Kharagpur. His research interests include wireless sensor networks, computer architecture, and digital design. At present, he is a professor in the Department of E.T.C.E, Jadavpur University, Kolkata, India.

Naba Kumar Peyada is an Assistant Professor, Aerospace Engineering Department, IIT Kharagpur. His research interests are among System Identification/Parameter Estimation - Neural Networks, Flight Dynamics, Control.

Pratyusha Rakshit received her Bachelor's Degree in Electrical Engineering from The West Bengal University of Technology (WBUT), West Bengal and completed the Master's Degree in Electronics and Telecommunication Engineering Department with specialization in control systems from Jadavpur University. Currently, she is an assistant professor in the Department of Electronics and Telecommunication Engineering, Jadavpur University.

Anurup Saha is currently pursuing his B.E in Electronics and Telecommunications Engineering from Jadavpur University, Kolkata, India. His research area includes FPGA based digital system design.

Priti Srinivas Sajja (b.1970) has been working at the Post Graduate Department of Computer Science, Sardar Patel University, India since 1994 and presently holds the post of Professor. She received her M.S. (1993) and Ph.D (2000) in Computer Science from the Sardar Patel University. Her research interests include knowledge-based systems, soft computing, multiagent systems, and software engineering. She has produced 186 publications in books, book chapters, journals, and in the proceedings of national and international conferences out of which five publications have won best research paper awards. She is author of Essence of Systems Analysis and Design (Springer, 2017) published at Singapore and co-author of Intelligent Techniques for Data Science (Springer, 2016); Intelligent Technologies for Web Applications (CRC, 2012) and Knowledge-Based Systems (J&B, 2009) published at Switzerland and

USA, and four books published in India. She is supervising work of a few doctoral research scholars while seven candidates have completed their Ph.D research under her guidance. She has served as Principal Investigator of a major research project funded by University Grants Commission, India.

Deepak Singh is pursuing the Ph.D. degree at Department of Computer Science and Engineering National Institute of Technology Raipur. His research interests include Evolutionary Computation, Machine Learning, and Data Mining.

Pradeep Singh has received the PhD degree in Computer Science & Engineering from the National Institute of Technology, Raipur. Currently, working as Assistant Professor at National Institute of Technology, Raipur. His research focus is on software engineering, machine learning and evolutionary computing (in software defect prediction and other applications). He has published papers in prestigious journals including, e.g., IEEE Transactions on Systems, Man, and Cybernetics: Systems, IEEE/ACM Transactions on Computational Biology and Bioinformatics and J Electr Eng Technology. In 2012 he was a summer research fellow under Prof. Nikhil R. Pal (Fellow IEEE) at Indian Statistical Institute, Kolkata. He is also Principle investigator of one research project funded by Chhattisgarh Council of Science & Technology(CGCOST), Raipur.

Dilip Singh Sisodia received the Bachelor of Engineering and Master of Technology degrees respectively in computer science & engineering and information technology (with specialization in artificial intelligence) from the Rajiv Gandhi Technological University, Bhopal, India. He received the Ph.D. degree in computer science and engineering from the National Institute of Technology Raipur, India. Dr. Sisodia is an assistant professor with the department of computer science engineering, National Institute of Technology Raipur. He has over thirteen years of experience of various reputed institutes in the field of academics & research. He has published over 20 referred articles in SCI/Scopus journals and conferences and also served as a reviewer for several international journals, and conferences. His current research interests include web usage mining, Machine learning, and computational intelligence. Dr. Sisodia is actively associated with various professional societies including IEEE, ACM, CSI, IETE, IE (India), etc.

Aman Srivastava had pursued BTech in Information Technology from JIIT, Noida. He is currently working as Machine Learning Engineer at one of the leading AI chatbot firm Haptik Inc. in India. He has expertise in the field of Machine Learning, NLP, Neural Networks, Social Media Analysis. He has worked with companies to derive their business problem to data science problem and build full stack solution using machine learning. Actively in the field of Data Science since last 2 years working different analytics startups in FNB, Finance, Social Media and chatbot domain.

Balamurugan Subramanian is working as a Professor and Head of Information Technology Department with K.L.N. College of Information Technology, Sivagangai, Taminadu, India. He has published more than 200 Journal and Conference papers in the area of Data mining and Big Data Analytics with Elsevier Science Direct, Springer and IEEE publishers. He has published seven International Scientific books in KDD and DM.

Index

A

Accuracy 4, 22-23, 25-26, 35-39, 47, 49, 51, 53, 58-59, 61-67, 70-71, 76, 78, 87-89, 91, 103, 106, 111, 126, 128, 134, 140, 150, 163, 177, 187-188, 190-191, 218, 222, 225, 232-237, 240, 277, 280, 285, 305, 322-323, 325, 330, 332, 336, 353-355

Agents 207, 319-320

aircraft 276-277, 280, 282-284, 287

ANFIS 276-277, 279, 281, 285, 287

Antenna Arrays 221-222

artificial neural network 1-5, 8, 14, 200, 222

B

BBO 222, 246-247, 250-252, 256-258, 260-262, 264-265, 267, 271, 273

big data 1-3, 5-7, 11-12, 14-16, 50-51, 75, 124-126, 128-129, 164, 171, 174, 246-247, 249, 271-273, 358-359, 365-366, 370-371

Big Data Analytics 1-2, 6, 358-359, 371

Binary discretization 22, 29, 31, 33, 37, 41

C

Cancer 11, 22-23, 25, 87-88, 91, 170-175, 177-178, 185, 187-188, 190, 195

chatbot 339-344, 346

Classification 1, 22-28, 31, 37-39, 41-42, 51, 59, 75-78, 83, 87-91, 130, 170-171, 174-175, 177, 185, 187-188, 190-191, 195, 277, 325

closeness centrality 291-293, 297-300, 305-308, 310-313

Cloud Computing 196-197, 199-202, 210, 292

Cluster Head 247-249, 251, 253, 255, 261-262, 267

Cognitive Radio 124-126, 128-129, 142

community detection 290-291, 293-294

Conversation system 339, 343-348, 350, 353-355

D

Data Security 223, 225, 240

Deep learning 1-2, 4-12, 14-16, 340, 343, 347

deep models 1-2, 8

Differential Evolution 47, 49, 51, 53, 56-57, 71, 126-127, 135-137, 144, 164-165, 174-175, 206, 221-222

DNA Microarray 23, 195

E

edges 198-199, 292-293, 301-302, 304, 311

eigenvector centrality 290, 293, 310-312

E-learning 319, 323, 333

Energy Detection 125-126, 128, 132, 165

Evolutionary Algorithm 24-26, 42, 49-51, 56, 126-127, 168, 221, 249-250

Extended BBO 249, 265, 267

F

F1_Measure 47, 49, 51, 53, 58-59, 61-68, 70-71

Feature Selection 22-28, 31, 75-79, 87, 89-91, 171, 174-175, 178, 185, 191, 195, 294

Field Programmable Gate Array 218, 220, 230

Finite State Machine With Data Path 223, 230

Fisher Markov Feature Selection 22, 24

fruit fly optimization 75, 78-79, 82

G

generative model 343, 345-346, 350

Graph Model 339, 345-349, 353-355

Grey Wolf Optimizer 172, 180, 214

H

Heuristic Algorithms 168

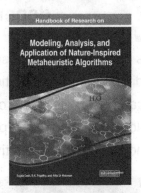

Ensure Quality Research is Introduced to the Academic Community

Become an IGI Global Reviewer for Authored Book Projects

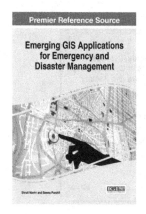

Premier Reference Source

Emerging GIS Applications for Emergency and Disaster Management

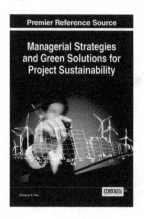

Premier Reference Source

Managerial Strategies and Green Solutions for Project Sustainability

Premier Reference Source

Comparative Approaches to Using R and Python for Statistical Data Analysis

Premier Reference Source

Solutions for High-Touch Communications in a High-Tech World

The overall success of an authored book project is dependent on quality and timely reviews.

In this competitive age of scholarly publishing, constructive and timely feedback significantly expedites the turnaround time of manuscripts from submission to acceptance, allowing the publication and discovery of forward-thinking research at a much more expeditious rate. Several IGI Global authored book projects are currently seeking highly qualified experts in the field to fill vacancies on their respective editorial review boards:

Applications may be sent to:
development@igi-global.com

Applicants must have a doctorate (or an equivalent degree) as well as publishing and reviewing experience. Reviewers are asked to write reviews in a timely, collegial, and constructive manner. All reviewers will begin their role on an ad-hoc basis for a period of one year, and upon successful completion of this term can be considered for full editorial review board status, with the potential for a subsequent promotion to Associate Editor.

If you have a colleague that may be interested in this opportunity, we encourage you to share this information with them.

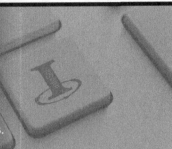

Printed in the United States
By Bookmasters